THE INTERNET OF THINGS

Legal Issues, Policy, and Practical Strategies

AF694541

EDITORS

Cynthia H. Cwik,
Christopher A. Suarez,
and Lucy L. Thomson

ABA Section of Science & Technology Law

Cover design by Cory Ottenwess/ABA Design

The materials contained herein represent the opinions of the authors and/or the editors, and should not be construed to be the views or opinions of the law firms or companies with whom such persons are in partnership with, associated with, or employed by, nor of the American Bar Association or the Section of Science & Technology unless adopted pursuant to the bylaws of the Association.

Nothing contained in this book is to be considered as the rendering of legal advice for specific cases, and readers are responsible for obtaining such advice from their own legal counsel. This book is intended for educational and informational purposes only.

© 2019 American Bar Association. All rights reserved.

No part of this publication may be reproduced, stored in a retrieval system, or transmitted in any form or by any means, electronic, mechanical, photocopying, recording, or otherwise, without the prior written permission of the publisher. For permission contact the ABA Copyrights & Contracts Department, copyright@americanbar.org, or complete the online form at http://www.americanbar.org/utility/reprint.html.

Printed in the United States of America.

23 22 21 20 19   5 4 3 2 1

Library of Congress Cataloging-in-Publication Data

Names: Cwik, Cynthia H., editor. | Suarez, Christopher, editor. | Thomson, Lucy L., editor.
Title: The internet of things / Edited by Cynthia Cwik, Christopher Suarez, and Lucy Thomson.
Description: Chicago : American Bar Association, 2019. | Includes index.
Identifiers: LCCN 2019001945 | ISBN 9781641053631 (print)
Subjects: LCSH: Electronic commerce—Law and legislation. | Internet—Law and legislation. | Internet of things.
Classification: LCC K1005 .I697 2019 | DDC 343.7309/944—dc23
LC record available at https://lccn.loc.gov/2019001945

Discounts are available for books ordered in bulk. Special consideration is given to state bars, CLE programs, and other bar-related organizations. Inquire at Book Publishing, ABA Publishing, American Bar Association, 321 N. Clark Street, Chicago, Illinois 60654-7598.

www.ShopABA.org

Contents

Foreword

Michael Chertoff

The so-called Internet of Things encompasses the ability to connect and direct almost any kind of mechanical system, whether it's automotive, medical, residential, or critical infrastructure. Increasingly, utilities are deploying smart grid technologies, wirelessly connecting thermostats to the utility to measure usage patterns and allow energy supplies to be adjusted, with precision based on need. Companies are working on clocks, kitchen appliances, and other household products that monitor consumer behavior to turn on your coffee machine moments before you wake up; warn you when you are low on supplies; order groceries for the week; and allow you to remotely operate your locks and lights so you need not be home to admit a visitor, or to check that your residence is secure. Regulating these various systems via network connectivity can add convenience and save money, but doing so can also arm malicious actors with an unprecedented ability to create chaos.

Despite the proliferation of these devices, they remain among the most vulnerable hacker targets in the cyber ecosystem. Each of these Internet-connected devices is enabled by a miniature, embedded, very capable computer processor and software intended to perform a small number of functions. The software may contain errors; the devices are often not supported to allow for corrections in flawed software code; and they may also contain hard-coded passwords or be otherwise difficult to maintain.

At conferences over the past several years, researchers have demonstrated the ability to use wireless connections to interfere with or halt operation of automobiles or medical devices, such as pacemakers and insulin pumps. Not only can many of these new "smart" connected devices be easily hacked, but they can also be turned into a massive network of remotely controlled zombie machines—a botnet. In a 2016 incident, printers, cameras, baby monitors, and similar devices were infected with Mirai malware. They were then remotely directed to generate a massive volume of traffic, and one of the largest Internet routing providers, Dyn, was overwhelmed.[1] Internet users were shut out of numerous websites across much of the United States for many hours. In this case, innocent Internet users—and many brand-named businesses—suffered the consequences of inadequate security manufactured into hundreds of thousands of cameras and other IoT devices.

Not only does this phenomenon open a larger surface area for interfering with physical systems, but it also generates enormous data about personal behavior. Individuals and most commercial enterprises produce increasing volumes of data about themselves—both deliberately and as an incident to their daily activities—but few understand the full scope of what is online. Even though you are totally unaware, your car and fridge could be generating information about your daily routine and interests. Thus, risks from these networked devices also include scenarios whereby unwanted visitors can hack into your home, determine when you are away, and what your pattern of life is.

To combat this threat, key stakeholders—manufacturers of IoT devices, owners of networks, and consumers themselves—must assume new responsibilities and roles, consider new architectures, and revise best practices. Today, for the most part, liability for cybersecurity software and firmware development weaknesses—meaning those responsible for writing code that can be manipulated to perform in a way contrary to that anticipated by its writers—is almost nonexistent. The standard shrink-wrap contract that comes with any software package disclaims liability, and for the most part courts have upheld those contracts. Responsibility (and liability) lies with the end user. We will likely face a set of circumstances soon where a safety "disaster" will occur, and a company will be

1. https://www.us-cert.gov/ncas/alerts/TA16-288A.

held liable for poor code in consumer products. I don't know what Internet of Things sector such a disaster will occur in. But imagine if an autonomous bus were to drive off the road killing 30 school children. Or imagine if ransomware akin to WannaCry exploited a vulnerability in a line of cars, making tens of thousands of them inert. There would certainly be a public uproar and changes to law. Where life and death are at issue, responsibility and liability cannot be far behind. This will impact the insurance industry and may result in regulatory intervention if the industry is not proactive in its approach to securing IoT devices. In addition to best practices for cybersecurity and standards of software development, this will also require the development of, as yet nonexistent, audit and grading mechanisms to validate effectiveness (and potentially support insurance risk rating).

The consumer IoT industry should work hard to support the development of a liability standard and a functioning insurance market. Some companies may hope they can forestall software security liability for the foreseeable future. I think that is highly unlikely, and if industry groups don't proactively set the goal of helping in the development of cybersecurity liability standards, then Washington, D.C., policy makers—who consider this a national security issue—will intervene and set the standards for them. For example, in the wake of the aforementioned Mirai botnet attacks, the Federal Trade Commission began considering the need for security regulations.

The consumer IoT industry should have a voluntary set of standards and a self-assessment model for the cybersecurity of its products that asks, broadly speaking, the following questions:[2]

2. Paul Rosenzweig, *The Evolving Landscape of Cybersecurity Liability*, THE CHERTOFF GROUP, https://www.chertoffgroup.com/blog/the-evolving-landscape-of-cybersecurity-liability.

- Can you explain to policy makers and insurers how it is that you securely design and develop your devices and software products? Do you employ adversarial testing programs for your products and for critical components of your supply chain? If not, why not?
- Are you open to learning about third-party research that finds flaws in your systems? Too often developers are resistant to outside scrutiny. If you receive a good-faith report of a problem, how do you respond to it?
- What are the forensics of your systems? Do they provide tamper evident, forensically sound logging and evidence capture to facilitate safety investigations?
- Are your systems capable of being securely updated in a prompt and agile way?
- Finally, how are your cyber systems incorporated in the physical vehicles you are building? Is there, for example, a physical and logical isolation that separates critical systems from noncritical systems?

IoT technologies hold tremendous promise for our communities by making them safer and more efficient. As with any other technology, they also entail security risk, and the risks associated with IoT technologies must be aggressively managed. We can do so, with industry's help, by working to leverage standards and liability and insurance mechanisms to ensure that IoT's foundational building blocks are secure and effective.

Preface

It is our great pleasure to introduce this book on the Internet of Things (IoT), which features chapters on IoT legal and policy issues by some of the leading authorities and thinkers from government, academia, and private practice, and includes insights from U.S. Senator Mark Warner, the current vice-chair of the Senate Select Committee on Intelligence, and Secretary Michael Chertoff, who served as Secretary of the Department of Homeland Security under President George W. Bush. The IoT, along with related technological developments, is transforming our world. We are in the relatively early stages of a new technological revolution, where everyday objects, such as our appliances, cars, medical devices, and wearables, as well as industrial control systems, are communicating with us and with each other. Today, it is estimated that the global number of devices connected to the Internet is over 17 billion, or more than two devices per every human on the planet, and it is projected that this number of connected devices could more than double by 2025. The IoT has been described as a game-changer for businesses, policy makers, and attorneys, and it has recently been projected that applications of IoT technologies will produce over a trillion dollars of value for industrial companies.

This book contains chapters by more than 30 experts from a variety of backgrounds and points of view addressing a wide range of topics relating to the IoT with a multidisciplinary approach. The issues that the book addresses include the use of IoT technology in connected cars, health tech, and unmanned aerial vehicles (aka drones); IoT and technological developments such as 5G and blockchain; the current state of laws and regulations relating to the IoT both in the United States and globally; risks associated with IoT devices, including security and privacy issues; how state attorneys general protect consumers in the IoT era; the impact of the

IoT on intellectual property and insurance; guidelines for employers, including corporate counsel, regarding the IoT in the workplace; and the future of the IoT from the perspective of an MIT research scientist.

The promise of the IoT, as well as the potential challenges and risks associated with it, was becoming increasingly evident when Cynthia served as chair of the American Bar Association Section of Science & Technology Law (SciTech) from 2015 to 2016. In 2015, it was the 50th anniversary of Moore's Law. In 1965, Gordon Moore, the research director of Fairchild Semiconductor Company, observed that the number of transistors per silicon chip doubles about every two years, which led to the prediction that computing would dramatically increase in power and speed, and decrease in relative cost, at an exponential pace. Moore's Law helped to predict the potential for the digital transformation we are now experiencing with the IoT. In addition, advances in cloud computing, big data and deep learning analytics, connectivity and networks, edge computing, and artificial intelligence algorithms also are playing a critical role in the explosive growth of the IoT. The Section wanted to harness the knowledge and expertise of its members to focus its energy on these cutting-edge, rapidly developing issues. The Section, under Cynthia's leadership, formed for the first time a separate committee that focused on IoT issues and also organized the first National Institute on the Internet of Things, a two-day conference in Washington, D.C., that featured more than 40 leading experts on IoT. The Institute included government leaders, academics, lawyers, judges, and experts from the private sector who came together to explore the legal challenges and concerns surrounding the use of "smart" devices. We are proud that SciTech has continued to sponsor highly successful IoT National Institutes every year since the inaugural Institute in 2016, and several of the speakers from these Institutes are authors of chapters in this book.

Many members of the Section have worked hard to organize these Institutes, and Lucy Thomson in particular has played a critical role each year. The Section began its focus on how mobile devices are transforming our economy, our culture, and our legal systems during Lucy's term as SciTech chair from 2012 to 2013. Under her leadership, the Section created a new Privacy, Security, and Information Law division and conducted a year-long exploration into the opportunities, challenges, risks, and legal implications of the explosion of mobile technologies and their uses around the world. Cynthia and Lucy are pleased that Chris, an attorney with deep technology expertise and a background in RFID technology (one of the precursors to the IoT), has joined the Section's IoT efforts.

This book reflects the hard work and dedication of many people, and we want to thank the ABA SciTech Section director, Caryn Cross Hawk, and her staff; the Section's Book Publishing Committee under the leadership of Bonnie Fought and Michael Hawes; and the ABA Publishing staff, especially Marisa L'Heureux and Sarah Orwig, for working with us to ensure the timely publication of this book. We also want to thank our families for their support and understanding as we have each spent countless hours working on this book.

SciTech's mission is to provide leadership on emerging issues at the intersection of law, science, and technology and to promote sound policy and public understanding of these issues. We created this book to further the mission of the Section by focusing on this important emerging area of IoT.

Cynthia Cwik
Christopher Suarez
Lucy Thomson

Reflections on the Internet of Things

Senator Mark Warner

I've long thought of myself as *the Tech Guy* in Congress. As someone who was in the tech business longer than I've been in the Senate, I'm a big believer in the power of technology to improve people's lives.

I was living out of my car when I founded my first cell phone company. I later founded and had success with Nextel, and in the years since, I've had a front-row seat to the ways the phones in our pockets have changed the world. Tech, telecommunications, and IT have long been interests of mine and topics I've pursued not only in my time as senator, but also when I was governor of Virginia.

Since January 2017, I've served as the vice chairman of the Senate Select Committee on Intelligence. Out of all the issues that come across our plate—all of the problems and challenges facing us in the world—what most keeps me up at night are issues related to cybersecurity.

The cyber threat is growing as we as a society and as a world become increasingly networked and dependent on connected devices. At the same time, our adversaries are aggressively exploiting our openness and these networks to steal sensitive personal data and IP, disrupt operations of our critical infrastructure, and spread disinformation. Many of our foreign adversaries amplify their efforts using non-state surrogates to expand their reach, and they are constantly scoping and probing our networks—across all sectors—to see where they can hit us.

We saw the most successful attack to date during 2016, when Russia flooded our social media platforms with disinformation and hacked and leaked—and, in some cases, doctored—e-mails to discredit and undermine Hillary Clinton's presidential campaign.

But these attacks extend far beyond our and our allies' elections and have hit all sectors of society in the United States and around the world. This is an active battlefield. Almost every government agency—at the federal, state, and local levels—and every sector of society are vulnerable. Drill down on a more micro level: Not only is it companies and governments that are vulnerable to these attacks—bad actors are also targeting the data of individuals.

Despite this clear, far-reaching, and urgent threat, our country lacks a coherent and developed cyber-doctrine. Even as vice chair of the Intelligence Committee, at this moment in time I have no idea how the government would react if our power grid went down in a major metropolitan area due to a foreign attack. I don't know what the federal government's game plan would be if we discovered a significant disruption of future elections.

We, as a nation, have not mapped out a strategy that effectively brings together the resources and talent in the private sector and across all levels of government to improve our defenses.

This isn't a challenge that Congress alone can overcome. We need an approach that includes the innovation and expertise in the private sector and draws upon the best and the brightest in our society to adequately prepare for these sorts of incidents and attacks.

Magnifying the challenges we face is the fact that this isn't a static problem. These threats are dynamic and evolve and grow every hour of every day. With each day that passes without serious and deliberate action, we fall farther behind, with the acceleration of the degree to which technologies across the globe are connected and as more and more of the functioning of everyday systems and appliances is turned over to complex software. It is fact that the explosion of a wide range of new devices with expanded capability and connectivity not only makes us more intertwined but more vulnerable as well.

Today, we exist in a cyber domain with exponentially more intrusion points. The National Institute of Standards and Technology (NIST) estimates that the average piece of software has 25 errors for every 1,000 lines of code. Now consider that a new Mercedes-Benz, for example, has over 20 million lines of code—that's potentially 500,000 individual vulnerabilities in one car. While not every one of those bugs is something that a hacker can exploit, or that would cause some sort of error, we're still living with an unacceptably low level of security in commercial software and in Internet-connected devices.

This is an understanding that is thankfully spreading and gaining traction within government. Serving on one of the committees charged with addressing this national security threat, I've seen this firsthand. Each year, our nation's military and intelligence leaders come before our committees to discuss the range of global threats that are targeting the United States.

One of these such hearings in March 2018 featured the director of the Defense Intelligence Agency (DIA), Lieutenant General Robert P. Ashley. Now, the DIA, being responsible for providing intelligence to the military and to defense policy makers, has a pretty good insight into the threats that we as a nation must confront. According to Lt. Gen. Ashley, "[t]he most important emerging cyberthreats to our national security will come from exploitation of our weakest technology components: mobile devices and the Internet of Things (IoT)."

Much of the necessity for our acting on this threat is informed by its massive scale. Look at the number of Internet-connected devices in existence—by 2020, it is expected that 20 billion IoT devices will be online. There are estimates that, by that point, machine-generated data will exceed Internet traffic generated by humans, as growing numbers of sensors, servers, and computers are collecting and sharing information back and forth. This makes it pretty clear to me that the challenge of securing our home and business networks will be made even more difficult in the years to come.

There exists an element of market failure in at least a portion of this fast-growing IoT market. On both the enterprise and consumer sides, I'm concerned that manufacturers don't have appropriate market incentives to build effective security into their products, particularly those that are below a certain price point or have shorter anticipated life cycles.

For too long, industry has treated security and innovation as a trade-off, with innovation always seeming to win out. As manufacturers add "smart" functionality to everyday products, quality assurance and security are often afterthoughts. IoT devices are constantly shipped with default and unchangeable passwords, with remotely accessible ports—akin to open doors—and with well-known vulnerabilities that could easily have been patched before shipment.

This is a classic case of market failure. And, unfortunately, consumers lack any real and easy means of comparing one product's security to another's. At the very least, we should be prodding industry to immediately adopt minimum device standards or trustworthy third-party ratings. We should also drive the market toward fixing the no-brainer problems—like hard-coded, fixed passwords and software that can't be updated. In the infamous Mirai botnet attack, the vulnerabilities that were exploited were well-known and could have easily been remedied. Securing IoT devices often doesn't require new research or innovations. It simply requires secure development.

Congress should look closely at having federal agencies work with vendors to develop effective minimum standards for IoT products and to develop a mechanism for remediating or recalling insecure products already in the stream of commerce—just as we do with conventional consumer products that pose harm.

In the meantime, we should be ensuring that minimum standards exist for IoT devices that the government buys, and I've introduced legislation that would accomplish that. The *Internet of Things Cybersecurity Improvement Act*, which I crafted with Senator Cory Gardner (R-CO), would set basic security hygiene standards to address some low-hanging problems, like ensuring that devices are patchable, don't have hard-coded passwords, and are free of known vulnerabilities (or, if they are unavoidable, are at least disclosed to government purchasers).

The United States has to take a leading role in crafting solutions to the challenges associated with IoT security. The EU is moving forward, not just with minimum security standards, but with a certification regime. The U.S. voice in policy discussions such as this one is incredibly important, and it's my view that a light-touch approach like the one that Senator Gardner and I have proposed would be a very worthwhile path forward.

The scale of this challenge highlights a common theme when thinking about our nation's challenges in cyberspace. These challenges are bigger—are more complex—than would allow us to simply legislate or regulate our way out of. In order for us to make meaningful progress, we need to think through a whole-of-society strategy for addressing these challenges.

About the Editors

Cynthia H. Cwik is currently a Distinguished Careers Institute Fellow at Stanford University. She is focusing on cutting-edge technology issues at Stanford, including cybersecurity, data protection and privacy, the digital economy, and artificial intelligence. She has practiced law at two global law firms, including serving five years as a partner with Jones Day and 15 years as a partner with Latham & Watkins. She has successfully represented major companies in complex, high-stakes, high-profile matters. She has experience with companies in various industries, including technology, energy, and manufacturing. She has been selected seven times as a California "Top Female Litigator," and she has repeatedly been listed in Best Lawyers in America.

Ms. Cwik has been a leader with the American Bar Association (ABA) Section of Science & Technology Law, including serving as chair from 2015 to 2016. In 2016, under her leadership, the Section organized the first ABA National Institute on the Internet of Things.

She has served as a leader of several other organizations, including serving as president and chair of the Executive Committee of the Yale Law School Association. She has served on the board of directors for various organizations.

Ms. Cwik is a frequent lecturer and author about topics relating to science and technology. She has been a presenter at ABA Presidential Showcase programs regarding technology issues and at programs for the Association of General Counsel and the National Judicial College. While at Latham & Watkins, she served on the firm's Equal Employment Opportunity Committee and Pro Bono Committee, and at Jones Day she served on the firm's Recruiting Committee.

She received her BA from Yale College summa cum laude, Phi Beta Kappa, and her JD from Yale Law School. She was a judicial clerk for the Honorable Thomas Meskill on the Second Circuit Court of Appeals.

Christopher A. Suarez is a trial and appellate litigator at Williams & Connolly in Washington, D.C. He focuses generally on complex litigation, with an emphasis on technology, antitrust, and education matters.

Mr. Suarez's technology practice spans both electronics and the life sciences, and comprises intellectual property litigation, licensing, the Internet of Things (IoT), cybersecurity and privacy, and other technology issues. He has represented a wide range of clients in high technology industries, including leading manufacturers of smartphones, tablets, IoT devices, and semiconductors, as well as clients in the oil and gas sector. Mr. Suarez has handled IP and technology cases before several U.S. District Courts, the U.S. Court of Appeals for the Federal Circuit, and the Patent Trial and Appeal Board. He has participated in international arbitrations of patent disputes and is a registered practitioner before the U.S. Patent and Trademark Office (PTO).

Mr. Suarez is a member of the American Bar Association (ABA), the Federal Circuit Bar Association (FCBA), the American Intellectual Property Law Association, the Giles Rich American Inn of Court, and the PTAB Bar Association. Mr. Suarez was nationally recognized in the "ABA On the Rise—Top 40 Young Lawyer List" by the Young Lawyers Division. He is a Young Lawyer Fellow of the ABA Intellectual Property Law Section and serves as a committee leader in the FCBA.

Mr. Suarez is a 2011 graduate of Yale Law School, where he was active in the Information Society Project. After law school, he clerked for Judge Timothy Dyk of the U.S. Court of Appeals for the Federal Circuit and Judge Joan Gottschall of the U.S. District Court for the Northern District of Illinois. He earned dual SB degrees in electrical engineering with computer science (EECS) and political science from the Massachusetts Institute of Technology (MIT).

Lucy L. Thomson is the founding principal of Livingston PLLC in Washington, D.C. She focuses her practice on cybersecurity, global data privacy, compliance, and risk management. Ms. Thomson assists companies and government clients nationally and internationally address complex challenges arising from new technologies and their implementations—the convergence of cyber and physical systems, industrial control systems, the Internet of Things (IoT), big data analytics and cloud computing, third-party vendor outsourcing, supply chain risk, vulnerable election systems, and digital crime.

Appointed Consumer Privacy Ombudsman in 25 federal bankruptcy cases, she evaluated the sale of "assets" consisting of sensitive personal information and has overseen the disposition of more than 250 million electronic consumer records. Her work on privacy risks in bankruptcy cases is featured in the *Norton Annual Survey of Bankruptcy Law*, 2017 edition.

Previously a senior engineer at CSC, a Fortune 200 technology company, she gained extensive hands-on experience conducting privacy and risk assessments and developing FISMA security plans on two of the government's largest technology modernization projects. While at CSC, she was appointed an Information System Security Officer (ISSO). A career attorney at the U.S. Department of Justice, she managed and conducted complex litigation in the Criminal and Civil Rights Divisions. She is a member of the American Law Institute (ALI).

Ms. Thomson served as chair of the ABA Section of Science & Technology Law and is a member of the House of Delegates and the Cybersecurity Legal Task Force. She is editor of the *Data Breach and Encryption Handbook*, and a contributing author to the

ABA Cybersecurity Handbook (2d ed.) and *Homeland Security and Emergency Management* (3d ed.).

Ms. Thomson received a master's degree from Rensselaer Polytechnic Institute (RPI) in 2001, earned the CISSP and CIPP/US certifications, and holds a JD degree from Georgetown University Law Center.

About the Authors

Aida Joaquin Acosta is a senior public official and an affiliate at Harvard University's Berkman Klein Center. She has more than ten years of experience advising on European regulatory and policy issues at the intersection of law, emerging technologies, and public policy. She has worked at the European Commission and the Ministries of Public Administration, Presidency, and Transport and Infrastructure of the Spanish Government.

She has been a Fulbright scholar at the University of Washington and a fellow at the Berkman Klein Center. As a Fulbright scholar, she obtained an LLM focused on robotics law and developed a methodology to help reduce uncertainty on emerging technologies, receiving an Academic Excellence Award. Her educational background includes a degree in computer engineering focused on artificial intelligence (AI) and robotics, and a law degree focused on international law.

At Harvard, Ms. Acosta researches the ethics and governance of AI and the impact of emerging technologies such as AI, autonomous vehicles (AV), and the Internet of Things in law, public policy, and society. She has developed a series of policy papers for regulators and policy makers to help them govern AV, and written for the American Bar Association and the China Computer Federation (CCF). She is part of the Ethics and Governance of AI Initiative of the Berkman Klein Center and MIT Media Lab. Ms. Acosta is interested in developing practical tools for regulators and policy makers to help them govern emerging technologies such as AI and promote innovations for the benefit of society.

Michael Aisenberg is principal cyber policy counsel at The MITRE Corp. His work involves support on legal and policy issues in a wide range of technology matters at agencies of the federal national security and intelligence communities. In 2015, he was appointed Senior Fellow at the George Washington University Center for Cyber & Homeland Security, and in 2018, he was named a fellow of the Institute for Critical Infrastructure Technology (ICIT).

Since 2015, Mr. Aisenberg has been serving his second term as chair of the ABA Section of Science & Technology Law (SciTech) Information Security Committee. He is a past chair of the U.S. IT Sector Coordinating Council (IT SCC), a member of the Industry Executive Subcommittee of the President's National Security Telecommunications Advisory Committee (NSTAC), the State Department Advisory Committee on International Telecom Policy, and board member of the IT-ISAC on behalf of both Digital Equipment Corp. and VeriSign, Inc. He serves on the ABA SciTech Editorial Board and is assistant editor of *The Sci/Tech Lawyer*. From 2000 to 2007, Mr. Aisenberg was director of Corporate Government and International Relations for VeriSign. From 1981 to 1997, he served as Digital Equipment Corporation's director of Corporate Government Relations. His work in technology policy began as an attorney in the Office of Legislative Counsel, Federal Communications Commission (1976–81). He holds a JD from the University of Maine School of Law (1976); his undergraduate degree is from the University of Pennsylvania (BA 1973).

Ruth Hill Bro (Chicago) has focused her legal career on advising businesses on privacy and information management strategy, cybersecurity, global compliance, e-workplace, and e-business issues. She has been featured as a speaker over 170 times and has over 95 published works on these topics (including two chapters in the 2018 *ABA Cybersecurity Handbook*, ambar.org/cybersecurity).

In the American Bar Association (ABA), Ms. Bro co-chairs the Cybersecurity Legal Task Force (ambar.org/cyber) and serves on the

E-Mail Stakeholder Committee. In the Section of Science & Technology Law (SciTech), she was SciTech's 2008–09 Section chair, and currently serves as senior advisor for the Privacy, Security, and Emerging Technology Division, liaison to the Commission on Women in the Profession, and on the planning committee for the ABA Internet of Things (IoT) National Institutes (2015–19). She was Membership and Diversity Committee chair (2009–16), and E-Privacy Law Committee founder/chair (2000–05). Ms. Bro served on the Standing Committees on Technology and Information Systems (2009–12; 2012–15 as chair), Continuing Legal Education (2012–15, as liaison), Disaster Response and Preparedness (2016–17), and the Commission on the Future of Legal Services (2014–16) and the Board of Governors Communications Task Force (2017).

After earning a BA degree (and seven years as a major-gifts fundraiser) at Northwestern and a JD degree at the University of Chicago, Ms. Bro started her legal career at McBride Baker & Coles (now Holland & Knight) and spent nearly a decade at Baker & McKenzie (Chicago office partner; founding North American member of the Global Privacy Steering Committee).

John Buchanan of Covington & Burling LLP in Washington, D.C., has represented insurance policyholders for over three decades. He contributed to one of the earliest publications on cyber insurance in 2001. Starting with the TJX network intrusion in 2006, he has represented multiple policyholders seeking coverage for historically major data breaches. He also advises policyholders in purchasing coverage for cyber- and IoT-related risks.

Mr. Buchanan teaches a graduate course on Insurance Litigation at the University of Connecticut Law School's Insurance Law Center. He speaks and writes frequently on topics related to insurance, litigation and alternative dispute resolution, including insurance issues arising from the Internet of Things, artificial intelligence, autonomous vehicles, blockchain, drones, and spoofing fraud.

He has been an advisor to the American Law Institute's *Restatement of the Law of Liability Insurance* and serves on the members' consultative group for ALI's Compliance, Enforcement, and Risk Management Principles project. Among other bar activities, he co-chairs the Cyber Risks and Data Privacy Subcommittee of the ABA Litigation Section's Insurance Coverage Litigation Committee, as well as the Cyber & Computer Crime Committee of the American College of Coverage Counsel, of which he is an elected fellow.

Mr. Buchanan is a graduate of Princeton, Oxford, and Harvard Law School; he clerked on the Third Circuit before joining Covington. *Chambers USA* ranks him Band 1, both in D.C. and nationally; Best Lawyers has named him DC Lawyer of the Year for Insurance; and he appears in *Best of the Best USA* and other peer-reviewed lawyer listings.

Katherine Campbell is a Senior Assistant Attorney General at the Oregon Department of Justice, where she enforces Oregon's consumer protection laws. As part of her consumer protection work, Ms. Campbell handles data privacy matters on various subjects. Ms. Campbell also regularly informs businesses and organizations about their duty to provide reasonable security for Oregonians' data. Prior to joining the Oregon Department of Justice, she worked at the Federal Trade Commission in the Bureau of Consumer Protection. Ms. Campbell holds a JD degree from Northeastern University School of Law, an MPH from Tufts University School of Medicine, and a BA from Lewis and Clark College.

Michael Chertoff was Secretary of the U.S. Department of Homeland Security (DHS) from 2005 to 2009, where he led the country in blocking would-be terrorists from crossing our borders or implementing their plans if they were already in the country. He also transformed FEMA into an effective organization following

Hurricane Katrina. His greatest successes have earned few headlines—because the important news is what didn't happen.

At Chertoff Group, Mr. Chertoff provides high-level strategic counsel to corporate and government leaders on a broad range of security issues, from risk identification and prevention to preparedness, response, and recovery. "Risk management has become the CEO's concern," he says. "We help our clients develop comprehensive strategies to manage risk without building barriers that get in the way of carrying on their business."

Before heading DHS, Mr. Chertoff served as a federal judge on the U.S. Court of Appeals for the Third Circuit. Earlier, during more than a decade as a federal prosecutor, he investigated and prosecuted cases of political corruption, organized crime, corporate fraud and terrorism—including the investigation of the 9/11 terrorist attacks.

Mr. Chertoff is a magna cum laude graduate of Harvard College (1975) and Harvard Law School (1978). From 1979 to 1980 he served as a clerk to Supreme Court Justice William Brennan, Jr. In addition to his role at Chertoff Group, Mr. Chertoff is also senior of counsel at Covington & Burling LLP and a member of the firm's White Collar Defense and Investigations practice group.

Dustin Cho of Covington & Burling LLP in Washington, D.C., is a litigator who focuses on representing policyholders in coverage disputes with their insurers. He has helped policyholders recover more than $100 million in insurance for a wide variety of claims, including data security breaches. He frequently advises on disputes that intersect with technology, from spectrum interference disputes to property rights in video games.

Mr. Cho received a BA and MA from Yale University in 2008 and a JD from Harvard Law School in 2011. At Harvard, he chaired the articles committee of the *Harvard Law Review* and was a finalist in the Ames Moot Court Competition. He served as a law clerk for Judge Debra Ann Livingston of the U.S. Court of Appeals for the Second Circuit from 2011 to 2012.

Jodi Daniel is a partner in Crowell & Moring's Health Care Group and a director at C&M International (CMI), an international policy consulting affiliate. She leads the firm's Digital Health Practice and provides strategic, legal, and policy advice to health care and technology clients navigating the dynamic regulatory environment to help them achieve their business goals.

Prior to joining Crowell & Moring, Ms. Daniel was the founding director of the Office of Policy in the Office of the National Coordinator for Health Information Technology (ONC), U.S. Department of Health and Human Services (HHS), where she led the agency's federal advisory committees, building consensus on health IT standards and policy, and established national health IT policy on privacy, security, consumer e-health, and health IT safety and oversight. Ms. Daniel established ONC's regulatory capacity, led the development of health IT standards and certification regulations, and advised CMS on health IT incentive programs.

At HHS's Office of General Counsel, Ms. Daniel was a key drafter of the original HIPAA Privacy and Enforcement Rules. She served as the first senior counsel for health IT at HHS, where she developed the foundational legal strategies, established and chaired the health IT practice group within OGC, and worked closely with CMS in the development of e-prescribing regulations and related Stark and anti-kickback rules.

Ms. Daniel received her BA in economics and community health from Tufts University, her master's degree in Public Health from Johns Hopkins School of Public Health, and her JD from Georgetown University Law Center.

Peter Gillespie is a partner with Laner Muchin, Ltd. in Chicago, one of the oldest and most highly regarded law firms in the country dedicated exclusively to the practice of labor and employment law. He represents and counsels management on a wide array of employment law-related issues, including workplace safety and health, wage and hour laws, covenants not to compete, discrimination and harassment, wrongful discharge, whistleblower claims, class actions, hiring, discipline, promotion and dismissal decision making, workplace privacy, and statutory compliance.

Mr. Gillespie handles litigation in both federal and state courts, as well as claims pending with state and federal agencies, including the Occupational Safety and Health Administration (OSHA), the Equal Employment Opportunity Commission (EEOC), the U.S. Department of Labor (DOL), the Illinois Department of Human Rights (IDHR), and the Illinois Department of Labor (IDOL). He is the author of the *Illinois Human Resources Manual* and has served in a number of leadership capacities within the ABA Section of Science & Technology Law. Mr. Gillespie received a BA from Northwestern University, where he attended as a Chick Evans Scholar, and received his JD from Georgetown University Law Center.

Melissa Goldman is an associate at Baker Donelson in the Fort Lauderdale office, advising clients on health care regulatory compliance with particular attention to telehealth, digital health, and health care technology. Ms. Goldman anticipates potential issues, providing practical and strategic counsel to health care providers and technology companies on innovative relationships, business models, and reimbursement opportunities that address regulatory requirements while effectively and efficiently meeting clients' business objectives. She is also a member of the Government Enforcement and Investigations Practice.

As former associate general counsel and interim Chief Compliance Officer at one of the United States' largest telehealth companies, Ms. Goldman has a depth of experience advising on a broad range of health care technology issues, including federal and state fraud and abuse issues, federal and state privacy and security issues, Medicare, Medicaid and third-party billing and compliance requirements, state licensure, credentialing and accreditation matters, and structuring arrangements with third parties (such arrangements include billing, management, consulting, vendor, and provider services; managed care contracts; credentialing delegations; and technology licensing).

Cheryl Hiemstra is the Deputy Legislative Director and an Assistant Attorney General at the Oregon Department of Justice. She develops policy at the state level on consumer protection, data security, and privacy. She also works on consumer protection cases, enforcing the Oregon Unlawful Trade Practices Act. Ms. Hiemstra earned a BA from Dordt College and a JD from Willamette University College of Law.

Matthew Henshon is a founding partner of Henshon Klein. His practice encompasses a wide range of issues affecting corporations, including governance, intellectual property and technology licensing, and mergers and acquisitions. His experience includes representation of all sides of the privately held, emerging company: founders, investors, and employees.

During 1999–2000, he served as special assistant and senior advisor to Senator Bill Bradley. During Senator Bradley's presidential campaign, Mr. Henshon served as "traveling chief-of-staff." He has written multiple law- and business-related articles in legal and business publications, and his political analysis has appeared on the *New York Times* op-ed page.

Mr. Henshon is a leader with the ABA Section of Science & Technology Law, and since 2007 he has served as chair of the Artificial Intelligence and Robotics Committee.

For the four years preceding the Bradley Campaign, Mr. Henshon worked at the Boston law firm of Hill & Barlow, P.C.

Mr. Henshon graduated from Princeton University in 1991 with an AB cum laude from its Wilson School of Public and International Affairs. He graduated from Harvard Law School cum laude in 1995. While at Princeton, he was a starter at forward for Princeton's Ivy League champion basketball team (ranked Top 25 in the country). In 1990, he played in the then-most-watched men's college basketball game in the history of ESPN (Princeton vs. Arkansas, NCAA First Round), a record that lasted for 16 years. He was recently featured in an ESPN 30-for-30 Short entitled "The Billion Dollar Game," about the 1989 Princeton–Georgetown tournament game.

Adam Isles is a principal at the Chertoff Group, where he helps clients build programs to manage security risk. Mr. Isles works with Fortune 500 clients in financial services, technology, electric utilities, retail, consumer packaged goods, transportation, and other sectors. He led the process for obtaining DHS SAFETY Act approval for the Chertoff Group's Security Risk Management Methodology. Prior to joining the Chertoff Group, Mr. Isles worked at Raytheon Company where he was the director of Strategy and Policy Consulting for Homeland Security. He is a certified Raytheon Six Sigma specialist.

Previously, Mr. Isles served as deputy chief of staff at the U.S. Department of Homeland Security (DHS) (2007–09). Before joining DHS, Mr. Isles served at the U.S. Department of Justice, where he began his legal career as a trial attorney in the Criminal Division in 1997. Among other roles, he served as counsel to the Assistant Attorney General, Criminal Division, from 2004–2005. He was detailed to the National Security Council staff from 2002 to 2003 to help manage multilateral security policy and served as secretary of the G-8 High Tech Crime Experts Group from 1998 to 2001.

Mr. Isles holds a JD from Harvard Law School and a BA in history from Yale University. He is a Certified Information Systems Security Professional (CISSP).

Thomas Jarvis is chair of the ITC practice at Winston & Strawn LLP in Washington, D.C. He litigates patent and other unfair competition cases at the U.S. International Trade Commission (ITC). Mr. Jarvis has a top-tier rating for his ITC representation of an "array of technology sector clients" (Chambers USA), including designers and manufacturers of telecommunications equipment, smartphones, microprocessors, digital signal processors, memory devices, networking equipment, semiconductor fabrication processes and packaging, and various operating systems and application software. His cases extend to diverse technologies such as medical devices, industrial equipment, design automation tools, alkaline batteries, and a variety of consumer products.

At Winston, Mr. Jarvis has led two Ericsson ITC cases against Apple that included a trial resulting in a settlement, two Taiwanese semiconductor company cases against Spansion that settled favorably after trial in the ITC, and defended Ericsson in the ITC against Adaptix/Acacia. Previously, Mr. Jarvis led the defense of Research In Motion (BlackBerry) that invalidated a Kodak patent. He also led multiple HTC, S3 Graphics, and VIA Technologies cases through trial against Apple.

Mr. Jarvis was a senior investigative attorney at the ITC where he litigated patent cases for ten years in the Office of Unfair Import Investigations. He is former president of the ITC Trial Lawyers Association and former chairman of ABA Subcommittee on ITC Practice. Mr. Jarvis received his BA in chemistry and communications from the University of North Carolina, Chapel Hill (1978) and his JD from the University of North Carolina Law School (1985).

Richard Johnson is a partner at Jones Day and a former federal prosecutor with over 15 years of government and law firm experience in litigation, investigations, and regulatory compliance. Having previously tried a number of cases to juries in federal court, Mr. Johnson represents companies facing complex litigation and advises on regulatory compliance measures, with an emphasis on data privacy, cybersecurity, and white collar issues. He also co-founded and serves as lead partner editor of Jones Day's *Global Privacy & Cybersecurity Update*, a regular publication produced by a 30-attorney team.

Prior to joining Jones Day, Mr. Johnson was an Assistant U.S. Attorney in the Eastern District of Texas and the district-wide coordinator for computer hacking and intellectual property issues. In that capacity, he guided the district's preparation for and response to cyber and IP crime and counseled prosecutors on collecting electronic evidence. He also led numerous trial and investigations teams involving fraud, identity theft, and other federal crimes. He received the Justice Department Director's Award for Superior Performance as lead trial counsel in the prosecution of a large-scale mortgage fraud scheme.

Mr. Johnson is an adjunct faculty member of the SMU Dedman School of Law where he teaches data privacy and cybersecurity. He also serves on the Leadership Council of the ABA Section of Science & Technology Law and is vice chair of the board of directors for the Boys & Girls Clubs of Greater Dallas.

Laura Kim of Covington & Burling LLP in Washington, D.C., is vice chair of the firm's Advertising and Consumer Protection Practice Group and a member of the Internet of Things (IoT) Initiative. Ms. Kim rejoined Covington after a 12-year tenure at the FTC, where she served as assistant director in two divisions of the Bureau of Consumer Protection (BCP), as well as BCP chief of staff.

Jennifer Johnson, co-chair of Covington's IoT initiative, represents and advises content distributors, broadcast companies, trade associations, and other media and technology entities on a wide range of issues. On IoT issues, she collaborates with Covington's global, multidisciplinary team to assist companies navigating the complex legal and regulatory constructs surrounding this evolving area.

Covington builds strong cross-disciplinary teams that create comprehensive legal solutions for the firm's clients' IoT issues such as product safety, including autonomous vehicles; privacy and cybersecurity; procurement; connectivity and spectrum; banking; the electricity grid; Federal Aviation Administration regulation and drones; and state regulation of the IoT.

Laura Kim and **Jennifer Johnson** led the effort to prepare Chapter 6, which includes contributions from **Sarah Wilson** and **Brandon Johnson** (product safety); **Wade Ackerman**, **Elizabeth Guo**, **Christopher Hanson**, and **Christina Kuhn** (medical device regulation); **Laura Kim** and **Lindsay Brewer** (privacy and cybersecurity); **Susan Cassidy** (procurement); **Matthew DelNero** and **Thom Parisi** (connectivity and spectrum); **Michael Nonaka** (financial services regulation); **Jack Schenendorf** (drones); **Mark Perlis** (energy); and **Jake Levine** (state regulatory trends).

Richard Martinez is a partner with Jones Day and a member of the firm's Cybersecurity, Privacy, and Data Protection practice. He focuses on all aspects of technology-related licensing, compliance, and litigation. Mr. Martinez has extensive U.S. and global experience in cybersecurity, data privacy, information law, and intellectual property. He represents clients in complex privacy and cybersecurity matters, including disputes relating to the ownership of data. Mr. Martinez also represents clients in ensuing investigations, enforcement actions, and litigation by state attorney generals, federal regulators, and private litigants. He provides practical, seasoned advice to in-house counsel, executives, and directors.

Rob Maier is an intellectual property and patent trial lawyer at Baker Botts. Recognized for his depth of skills and experience in all phases of litigation, Mr. Maier regularly handles Markman hearings and complex patent trial work in high profile disputes.

His practice also extends beyond litigation into patent preparation and prosecution, counseling on IP and big data issues, licensing, IP asset evaluation, and due diligence in connection with mergers and acquisitions. Multinational clients involved in patent disputes and other matters across a broad spectrum of technologies, from smartphones and display technologies to drink packaging and stem cells, rely on Mr. Maier's extensive experience. He has been recognized as a New York Super Lawyer—Rising Star by Thomas Reuters, as a Rising Star by the *New York Law Journal*, recommended in *The Legal 500 U.S.*, and recognized by Intellectual Asset Management's IAM Patent 1000 as one of The World's Leading Patent Practitioners.

Mr. Maier is also the bi-monthly patent and trademark columnist for the *New York Law Journal*, where he writes on current hot topics in IP law. From 2012 to 2017, Mr. Maier taught patent litigation as an adjunct associate professor of law at Brooklyn Law School.

Mr. Maier received his BS degree from George Washington University in computer engineering, and his JD from Fordham University School of Law. After earning his undergraduate degree, Mr. Maier worked as a software engineer at a mobile telecom company, where he was responsible for the design and implementation of test systems.

Joseph Masullo of Winston & Strawn LLP in Washington, D.C., focuses his practice on patent litigation in federal district courts as well as in section 337 proceedings before the U.S. International Trade Commission (ITC). He uses his technical background to provide technical analysis on patent litigations, and he also works closely with technical expert witnesses to develop infringement and invalidity positions.

Mr. Masullo's patent experience involves a range of technologies, including semiconductor devices, medical devices, electronics, telematics devices, processors and memory devices, mobile devices, authentication systems, computer software and algorithms, and computer systems generally. He has worked for a variety of companies on complex litigation matters in the automotive, cable, telecommunications, semiconductor, and medical device industries. He has also worked on matters before the PTO, including challenges and defenses to patent validity based on inter parties review petitions.

Mr. Masullo received his BA in economics from New York University in 2003 and an MS in computer science in 2009 from the George Washington University School of Engineering and Applied Science. He received his JD from George Washington University Law School in 2009. During law school, he interned at the U.S. Department of Justice, Civil Rights Division and the New York City Law Department Summer Honors Program.

Mauricio Paez is a partner with Jones Day and a member of the firm's Cybersecurity, Privacy, and Data Protection practice. He has over 20 years of experience advising companies on legal issues with digital transformations, space-based data services, global e-commerce, digital marketing, data protection and privacy, cybersecurity, cyber governance, and global technology sourcing transactions.

His clients are in a variety of industries such as Internet, technology, retail, financial services, health care, utilities, automotive, aviation, satellite, manufacturing, communications, and marketing. He is a leading attorney in emerging technology legal issues, and advises clients on industrial internet applications, consumer and industrial IoT, cloud services, big data, artificial intelligence and cognitive, autonomous machines, space-based data services, global privacy, cybersecurity breach response and investigations, and related global compliance.

Mr. Paez has represented some of the world's leading companies to develop and implement worldwide digital strategies, compliance programs to address new legal risks, safeguarding digital assets, cross-border transfers of data, and cybersecurity oversight and management. He also supports technology commercial and corporate transactions, such as mergers and acquisitions.

His clients have included Abbott Laboratories, Adobe, Aireon, Apple, Bunge, Cardinal Health, Chevron, Citgo, Cooper Tire, Experian, General Electric, General Motors, Goldman Sachs, Google, Groupon, Iridium Satellite, Nokia, SAP, The Internet Corporation of Assigned Names and Numbers, and other leading institutions.

Mr. Paez is an author and a frequent speaker and was recognized as a leading cybersecurity and privacy lawyer by Legal500. He was also named a Cybersecurity & Data Privacy Trailblazer by the *National Law Journal*.

Jill Rhodes is vice president and chief information security officer (CISO) for Option Care Enterprises, Ltd, a national health care company based in Chicago.

Prior to joining the private sector, Ms. Rhodes spent more than 20 years working in and with the federal government, including the Office of the Director of National Intelligence, Central Intelligence Agency, Department of Homeland Security, and the Department of Defense. She was a foreign service officer with the State Department, stationed in Bolivia and Russia.

Ms. Rhodes has written, published, and spoken on information security and national security law topics. Most recently, she was co-editor of *The ABA Cybersecurity Handbook: A Resource for Attorneys, Law Firms, and Business Professionals* (2018, 2d ed). She also co-edited the first edition (2013) and edited the book *National Security Law, Fifty Years of Transformation: An Anthology* (2012), sponsored by the ABA Standing Committee on Law and National Security.

Ms. Rhodes is a graduate of the University of Illinois at Urbana-Champaign, the University of Cincinnati College of Law (JD), and the George Washington University College of Law (LLM). She is a certified information security manager (CISM), certified information privacy professional/IT (CIPP/IT), and a certified project management professional (PMP).

Ellen Rosenblum A former federal prosecutor and state trial and appellate judge, Ellen Rosenblum was first elected to a four-year term as Oregon's 17th Attorney General in 2012 and was re-elected to a second term in November 2016. She is the first woman to serve as Oregon Attorney General.

Attorney General Rosenblum has been active in local and national organizations of lawyers, judges, and attorneys in general. She has served on the Executive Committee of the National Association of Attorneys General (NAAG) and she is a past chair of the Conference of Western Attorneys General. She served as secretary of the American Bar Association and as chair of the ABA Section of State & Local Government Law.

Ashley Southerland is counsel in the Washington, D.C., office of Crowell & Moring where she practices in the firm's Health Care group and is a member of the Digital Health Practice. Ms. Southerland advises health care clients on matters involving digital health and health information technology (health IT), health care regulatory compliance investigations, and litigation risk management.

In her digital health practice, Ms. Southerland provides strategic, policy, and regulatory advice to a range of organizations, including hospital systems, plans, health care consortiums, start-up companies, and large technology companies. Her digital health practice spans several areas, including interoperability and information blocking compliance, telehealth, health IT reimbursement, health IT vendor contracting, e-prescribing and prescription drug monitoring program (PDMP) compliance, FDA safety (software as a medical device and IoT), HIPAA compliance, and emerging technologies in health care (artificial intelligence, blockchain, and 3-D printing). Ms. Southerland's work on blockchain and health care has been published in Bloomberg BNA's Health IT Law & Industry Report and spotlighted in FierceHealthcare.

Before joining Crowell & Moring, Ms. Southerland served as a law clerk to the Honorable Charles Wilson of the U.S. Court of Appeals for the Eleventh Circuit. Immediately prior, she served as a law clerk to the Honorable Jillyn Schulze, Magistrate Judge of the U.S. District Court for the District of Maryland.

Ms. Southerland received her JD from Cornell Law School and her AB in sociology, with distinction in the major, from Duke University.

Brian Subirana is director of the MIT Auto-ID lab and also teaches at Harvard University. His Harvard class on artificial intelligence (AI) is the first MIT-run nonresidential online class to offer academic credit. His MIT Sloan class was the first course to offer a recorded lecture on MIT open courseware. Before becoming an academic, he worked at The Boston Consulting Group.

His research centers on the Internet of Things and AI (blockchain, electric vehicles, supply chain) and on developing a Mathematical Theory for Deep Learning with Forgetting (Conversational Commerce and Digital Learning).

Professor Subirana obtained his PhD in computer science at the MIT Artificial Intelligence Laboratory (now CSAIL) and his MBA at the MIT Sloan School of Management. He has founded three start-ups and has been affiliated with MIT for over 20 years in various capacities, including visiting professor at the MIT Sloan School.

Kerianne Tobitsch is an attorney at Jones Day and focuses her practice on data privacy, cybersecurity, and complex commercial litigation and transactions for institutional clients in the financial services, technology, consumer reporting, and health care sectors. She advises clients on U.S. and international data privacy and cybersecurity compliance and governance issues, data use, management of digital assets, technology transactions, cross-border data transfer arrangements, and cybersecurity incident response. Ms. Tobitsch helps clients develop and implement strategies and compliance programs to address legal and operational issues for emerging technologies, including the consumer and industrial Internet of Things, connected vehicles, drones, and big data.

Ms. Tobitsch is editor in chief of Jones Day's *Global Privacy & Cybersecurity Update*, a bimonthly publication produced by a global 30-attorney team. She received her JD from Columbia Law School and a bachelor's degree from Northwestern University.

Maya Uppaluru, an associate in the Crowell & Moring Washington, D.C., office, provides strategic product counseling and policy advice to a range of organizations at the forefront of health innovation, including health systems, large tech companies, start-ups, plans, and venture capital firms. Ms. Uppaluru joined the White House in 2015 in the Office of Science and Technology Policy, launching President Obama's Precision Medicine Initiative and serving as a policy advisor to the U.S. chief technology officer, where she helped to shape national policies around health data interoperability and led public–private collaborations to facilitate better access to health data for medical research.

Ms. Uppaluru has a track record of helping technologists successfully navigate complex regulations to achieve their design and product goals. She worked directly with engineers, data scientists, designers, and product managers on the launch of the All of Us Research Program at the National Institutes of Health. She also worked with the Centers for Medicare and Medicaid Services (CMS) to improve data sharing with physicians participating in the Quality Payment Program, and transition Medicare from fee-for-service to value-based care under the Medicare Access and CHIP Reauthorization Act.

Ms. Uppaluru received her JD from the University of Maryland School of Law and a BA in political science from the University of California at Irvine.

Joe Whitley leads Baker Donelson's Government Enforcement and Investigations practice. He represents clients nationally and internationally in white-collar criminal matters and regulatory enforcement, corporate internal investigations, Foreign Corrupt Practices Act (FCPA) and U.S. export controls and compliance. He also advises clients on corporate compliance, health care fraud, and FDA-related matters.

In 2003, Mr. Whitley was appointed by President George W. Bush as the first General Counsel of the U.S. Department of Homeland Security (DHS), the highest-ranking legal official at DHS. He held that position for two years, working for DHS Secretaries Tom Ridge and Michael Chertoff, before returning to private practice.

Mr. Whitley has had a wide-ranging career in the Department of Justice (DOJ). During the Ronald Reagan and George H.W. Bush administrations, he served as acting Associate Attorney General, the third-ranking position at Main Justice. He was appointed by Presidents Reagan and Bush, respectively, to serve as the U.S. Attorney in the Middle and Northern Districts of Georgia. Throughout his career, Mr. Whitley has served under five U.S. attorneys general and four presidents in a number of key operational and policy positions. Earlier in his career, Mr. Whitley served as an assistant district attorney in the Chattahoochee Judicial Circuit in Columbus, Georgia. Mr. Whitley maintains strong professional relationships with the state and federal law enforcement community.

Stephen Wu is a shareholder with Silicon Valley Law Group in San Jose, California. He advises clients on compliance, liability, audit, governance, security, and privacy matters regarding the latest technologies in areas such as robotics, artificial intelligence, the Internet of Things, and big data. Mr. Wu acts as outside general counsel to Silicon Valley start-ups and technology clients, drafting and negotiating managed service agreements, software as a service subscription agreements, licenses, marketing agreements, and other technology contracts. His litigation practice includes resolving information technology and intellectual property disputes.

Mr. Wu served as the 2010–11 chair of the ABA Section of Science & Technology Law (SciTech). In 2007, he helped found the Section's Artificial Intelligence and Robotics Committee. He later helped create section committees on the Internet of Things and big data. From 2001 to 2004, he was co-chair of the section's Information Security Committee.

Mr. Wu graduated from Harvard Law School in 1988 and was VeriSign's second in-house attorney. Before VeriSign, he practiced with two international law firms in the areas of product liability, intellectual property, commercial and general litigation, as well as technology licensing and transactions. Mr. Wu has written books and made frequent presentations on artificial intelligence, robotics, Internet of Things, big data, and information security at numerous continuing legal education programs and AI, robotics, and information security industry conferences.

The ABA Section of Science & Technology Law published his seventh book, *A Guide to HIPAA Security and the Law*, second edition, in 2016.

PART I

NEW AND EMERGING IOT TECHNOLOGIES

Chapter 1

Connected Cars

Impact on Cars and Other Intelligent Transportation Systems

Stephen S. Wu

I. Introduction

The Internet of Things (IoT) connects machines to other machines in a wide variety of fields and industries. In our digital lives, we are connecting devices to our networks at work and at home. In addition to work and home, however, we spend much of our waking time in transit from one place to another, often in our private automobiles. The Internet of Things is extending our digital lives to our cars, trucks, and other road vehicles. With this new integration comes privacy, security, and other legal issues.

A 2015 episode of the CBS television show *60 Minutes* vividly illustrates what can happen when we connect cars with information technology networks. In the show, reporter Lesley Stahl sat behind the wheel of a nondescript dark gray sedan while driving through a tree-lined suburban parking lot. She appeared on a *60 Minutes* segment that aired on February 8, 2015.[1] In the driver's seat next to her was Kathleen Fisher, a veteran of the Defense Advanced Research Projects Agency or DARPA for short. As Stahl navigated

1. A preview of the segment is available on YouTube. *60 Minutes, Preview: DARPA Dan* (Feb. 6, 2016), https://www.youtube.com/watch?v=7E1WsdODxu0.

one end of the cleared parking lot, two men stood at the other end—Karl Koscher, a University of Washington Ph.D. student, and Dan Kaufman, who was then director of DARPA's Information Innovation Office. Koscher used a laptop sitting on black boxes of what appeared to be equipment, while Kaufman provided instructions.

Kaufman told Koscher, "You wanna hit the fluids?" Koscher typed something on the laptop and suddenly the windshield wiper fluid sprayed onto the windshield of Stahl's car and the wipers started moving back and forth. Stahl said "I did nothing" to turn on the spray. And yet, without Stahl doing anything, Koscher had taken control of the wipers and fluid. In a cut-away scene, Stahl explained that hackers had contacted the car's emergency communications system, flooded it with sound data, and inserted a piece of code that reprogrammed the car's software so the researchers could take complete remote control of the car. Further demonstrating this control, Koscher caused the horn to sound, again without Stahl's knowledge or action.

Fisher then instructed Stahl to drive up to a set of cones in the lot and stop in front of them. As Stahl drove forward, at Kaufman's direction, Koscher disabled the brakes remotely. A close-up showed Stahl's black pump shoe pressing down on the brake pedal. Nonetheless, the brakes would not work and Stahl called out "Oh, no. No. No. No. No. No. No!" Notwithstanding Stahl's vigorous attempt to apply the brakes, the car wouldn't stop and instead bowled over the cones Stahl was trying to avoid.

This television segment showed the vulnerability of contemporary cars to hacking. Cars are increasingly connected to various kinds of communications systems. While connected cars have the promise of making our lives easier, safer, more comfortable, and more entertaining, connecting information technology to cars also has a dark side. In the future, with even tighter integration of cars with external information technology systems, security risks will only increase. Moreover, security vulnerabilities give rise to legal issues, and data security raises just one set of issues. This chapter covers various issues attorneys are likely to face in coming years and decades with the sale and deployment of connected car technologies and other intelligent transportation systems.

II. Overview

Welcome to the future of intelligent transportation. The era of connected transportation is already underway. Within the next ten years, we will increasingly connect our on-road motor vehicles—cars, trucks, and other vehicles—to networks, both public and private.

Connecting cars, trucks, and other vehicles to the Internet of Things is part of the picture of the future of intelligent transportation systems. In the narrowest sense, the IoT involves connecting electronic devices to the public Internet.[2] Accordingly, vehicles can become part of the IoT if manufacturers and owners connect them to the public Internet. For example, connections may involve pushing new software to vehicles through the Internet or manufacturers collecting data via the public Internet from the vehicles they sell to understand how purchasers use them and the vehicles' performance.[3] Connectivity may be embedded, requiring the car to have one or more antennas and communications chips, or an operator may be able to connect a device already connected to the Internet, like a smartphone, to the vehicle by tethering.[4]

---

2. *See* Jacob Morgan, *A Simple Explanation of "The Internet of Things,"* FORBES (May 13, 2014, 12:05 AM) ("Simply put, this is the concept of basically connecting any device with an on and off switch to the Internet (and/or to each other)."), https://www.forbes.com/sites/jacomorgan/2014/05/13/simple-explanation-internet-things-that-anyone-can-understand/#230c65351d09.

3. *See* Andrew Meola, *Automotive Industry Trends: IoT Connected Smart Cars & Vehicles*, BUSINESS INSIDER (Dec. 20, 2016, 12:12 PM), https://www.businessinsider.com/internet-of-things-connected-smart-cars-2016-10.

4. *See id.*

Nonetheless, direct and indirect networking and connectivity beyond the public Internet are also possible. Other examples of connectivity include:

- Connecting vehicles by closed information technology networks (e.g., "walled gardens," so that they are separated from the public Internet).
- Unconnected sensors and systems that collect data aboard the vehicle, which are accessed sometime after data gathering for the purpose of downloading or transferring the data to other systems for analysis.
- Connected sensors aboard the vehicle that communicate only with special purpose communications devices, such as devices to read information from event data recorders (black boxes), which are in turn connected to the public Internet or closed networks.

Machine-to-machine communications covered by this chapter may include communications that occur over the public Internet, private wired networks, cellular wireless networks, Wi-Fi, radio, or satellite systems.

Regardless of the type of connectivity, we are connecting our vehicles for a number of reasons. Some of the connections will assist in the task of driving, such as providing navigation assistance, warnings, traffic information, and eventually coordinated automated driving systems of all aspects of the dynamic driving task for autonomous driving. We already have systems to connect cars to roadside assistance services to obtain help after an accident or other event. Other connections will facilitate occupant communications, including text, voice, and video communications. Fleet owners are already capable of using communications to track the location of fleet vehicles. Additional applications will focus on entertainment systems, integrating onboard systems with offboard media and preferences. Some cars already serve as Wi-Fi hotspots, which manufacturers market to families to enable entertainment, social media, and other personal uses. Manufacturers will work together with technology companies to expand these capabilities for personal and business productivity, such as integrating navigation and communication systems with personal calendars. Yet other connections will integrate vehicles with other smart systems, including smart home and smart city systems. In short, our digital lives will extend to our cars and other vehicles, integrating them with numerous information technology systems, and making them, in essence, another mobile computing platform.

While connected transportation systems have the potential to increase road safety, improve traffic, save energy, entertain us, promote efficient fleet operations, and increase our personal and business productivity, advanced systems also pose risks. Recent crashes of partially automated vehicles show risks associated with automation. For instance, on March 18, 2018, an Uber test car driving in autonomous mode, with a safety driver in the vehicle, struck and killed a woman walking a bicycle across a street in Tempe, Arizona. Volvo and Uber worked together on the autonomous driving system controlling the car, although unfortunately, Volvo's default advanced collision avoidance technology was not enabled in the car. While the Uber vehicle was not centrally controlled, it was a "connected car" in the sense that it communicated with the satellite-based GPS system to monitor its location.

Failures in connected transportation systems will inevitably cause accidents. Moreover, information technology systems in ground vehicles may distract human drivers and cause other accidents. Accidents will, in turn, generate legal issues and litigation. Aside from accidents, various kinds of legal issues involved with connected transportation systems will arise in connection with the manufacture, distribution, sale, and operation of connected transportation systems.

This chapter discusses the legal issues arising for lawyers counseling sellers and operators of connected transportation systems.

Section III provides an overview of technologies for connecting on-road motor vehicles. Section IV covers the regulation and governance of connected transportation and the compliance issues raised by such regulation. It explains the key laws that place requirements on sellers and operators. Section V focuses on liability arising from the sale and operation of connected transportation systems. This section describes the various types of claims that can create liability, possible defenses, and techniques for managing risk. Section VI discusses data protection, including privacy and security risks. Finally, Section VII concentrates on transactional issues relating to connected transportation technology.[5]

III. Overview of Connected Transportation Technology

"Connected" motor vehicles make use of a number of different IoT and other technologies. The communications technologies that are and will connect motor vehicles in the future include:

- Wired Internet and private network connections to the vehicle
- Wi-Fi connecting the vehicle to the Internet or private networks

5. This chapter covers on-road motor vehicles: cars, trucks, motorcycles, buses, shuttles, and recreational vehicles. The focus of this chapter, "connected transportation systems," includes the on-road motor vehicles themselves as well as supporting information technology systems to facilitate communications, computing, and intelligence on the vehicle or in supporting communications infrastructure. This chapter does not cover connected bicycles and scooters, although sharing services for bicycles and scooters are becoming increasingly common. Farm equipment and off-road vehicles, such as racing motorcycles, trail bikes, mini bikes, dune buggies, all-terrain vehicles, jeeps, and snowmobiles, are outside the scope of this chapter. This chapter focuses on ground vehicles, rather than airborne or maritime vehicles, which have different regulators and laws than ground vehicles. Nonetheless, some of the general principles in this chapter may be helpful to manage legal issues of vehicles and transportation systems beyond the scope of this chapter.

- Cellular communications, including allowing the vehicle to create its own local Wi-Fi hotspot.
- Bluetooth, such as keyless entry systems or allowing consumer mobile devices to connect with the vehicle.
- Dedicated short-range radio communications (DSRC), which facilitates high bandwidth data transmission for safety applications.[6]
- Satellite communications, including receivers on vehicles that can receive data from global positioning system (GPS) satellites.[7]

The main applications for connecting motor vehicles include:

- **Driving automation.** Partially automated and autonomous vehicles will, as a practical matter, need connectivity to receive GPS location data and updated maps. In the future, they will also coordinate with other vehicles and coordinate with traffic management supervision systems to allow traffic to flow more efficiently.
- **Vehicle operation.** Examples include keyless entry systems and smartphone-operated remote unlocking and starting.

6. DSRC can enable vehicle-to-vehicle (V2V) communications, for instance to signal location and speed to alert other vehicles. DSRC can also enable vehicle-to-infrastructure (V2I) to communicate alerts and traffic information to operators. Other communications are possible, such as vehicle-to-pedestrian (V2P) and vehicle-to-network (V2N). Collectively, these forms of communication are referred to as "vehicle-to-everything" (V2X). Siam Ahmed, *Get to Know Connected Vehicle Technology: V2V, V2X, V2I* (Feb. 9, 2018), https://www.geotab.com/blog/connected-vehicle-technology/. Likewise, information from cars can feed back to traffic management supervision systems to adjust traffic light timing and set variable speed limits.

7. GPS systems allow motor vehicles to locate themselves with a high degree of accuracy. Satellite radio receivers in vehicles can utilize sideband channels to receive data such as firmware updates and more in bulk.

- **Operation safety.** Examples include coordination with a central traffic management facility, other vehicles, and pedestrians.
- **Updates and maintenance.** Motor vehicles are already making use of connections to update their software.
- **Entertainment.** Connections allow operators to integrate their sources of entertainment media with the motor vehicle to enjoy during travel and facilitate Internet connections.
- **Personal productivity.** Manufacturers are working on the integration of personal productivity applications (such as calendar apps) with motor vehicle systems.
- **Smart home integration.** Operators will be able to monitor events in their homes and control home automation devices using integration with smart home systems.
- **Smart city integration.** Communications can allow municipal systems to monitor traffic and drivers can use apps to use city services, such as automatic parking payments.

IV. Regulation and Governance of Connected Transportation Systems

A. Backdrop of Regulating and Governing Driving Practices and Motor Vehicle Safety

Regulation of operating motor vehicles in the United States consists of a mixture of state, federal, and international law. The states have vehicle codes that govern the rules of the road and the safe operation of motor vehicles on highways. They have requirements for drivers to act safely, and state vehicle codes prohibit driving unsafe vehicles on state highways.[8] Federal law, principally

8. State vehicle codes may contain specific incompatible requirements regarding certain aspects of vehicle operation, such as emissions requirements, use of certain types of lighting and equipment, and traffic laws (e.g., permitting right turns on red lights).

through Federal Motor Vehicle Safety Standards, governs the safety of motor vehicles themselves. The United States is also a signatory to the Geneva Convention on Road Traffic.[9] The Geneva Convention harmonizes traffic laws among the signatory nations and establishes certain minimum standards for operating motor vehicles.[10] Manufacturers need to make sure that any connected vehicle systems they install in their vehicles will comply with these laws.

In addition to applicable law, manufacturers may work among themselves and industry groups to establish technical standards to facilitate safety, interoperation, and efficiency. Technical standards may establish protocols and methods of implementing certain technologies. Organizations such as the International Organization for Standardization (ISO), Institute of Electrical and Electronics Engineers (IEEE), SAE International, and Underwriters Laboratories (UL LLC) establish these standards. Manufacturers may need to adhere to these standards in order to sell their connected car products.

B. Regulating Communications with and among Vehicles

The federal government has established a program overseen by the Federal Communications Commission (FCC) and the Department of Transportation (DOT) to regulate dedicated short-range radio communications (DSRC) used for vehicle-to-vehicle communications and vehicle-to-infrastructure communications. The FCC sets aside and allocates radio frequency spectrum based on

---

9. Convention on Road Traffic, Geneva, Sept. 19, 1949, 3 U.S.T. 3008, 125 U.N.T.S. 3, https://treaties.un.org/doc/publication/UNTS/Volume%20125/v125.pdf.

10. For an overview of the different sources of law governing vehicles in the context of automated vehicles, see Bryant Walker Smith, *Automated Vehicles Are Probably Legal in the United States*, 1 TEX. A&M L. REV. 411, 417 (2014).

its rulemaking authority under the Communications Act of 1934, as revised under the Telecommunications Act of 1996. The Federal Communications Commission reserved 75 MHz of spectrum around the 5.9 GHz band in 1999 for DSRC communications. Manufacturers seeking to sell connected vehicle systems and infrastructural base station systems will need to comply with FCC rules.

C. Truck Platooning Legislation

Connecting freight trucks with connected systems permits trucks to coordinate the driving function. Platooning allows two or more trucks to form ad hoc groups traveling down a highway in which the acceleration and braking is coordinated. A cloud-hosted network operations center communicates with trucks to coordinate creating or dissolving platoons. Drivers continue to be responsible for the steering function. But the lead truck sets the pace for speed. And if the lead truck driver applies its brakes, the following trucks automatically brake. With this coordination using vehicle-to-vehicle communications, trucks can follow each other much more closely. Closely coordinated travel reduces air resistance and thus saves fuel. It also improves safety.

Currently, 16 states have laws that exempt platooning trucks from laws against following too closely or otherwise allow platooning.[11] One other state allows testing and pilots for platooning.[12]

---

11. Ala. Code §§ 32-1-1.1(79), 32-5A-89(d); Ark. Code Ann. §§ 27-51-305(c)-(d), 27-51-1408; Ga. Code Ann. § 40-6-49(c); Ind. Code §§ 9-21-8-14(a), 9-21-8-15(a), 9-21-8-16(a)(2); Ky. Rev. Stat. Ann. §§ 189.340(9)(c), 281.010(39); La. Rev. Stat. Ann. §§ 32:1(95), 32:81(D)-(F); Mich. Comp. Laws §§ 257.40c, 257.643(4), 643a(2), 257.665(9), (10); Miss. Code Ann. §§ 63-3-103(k), 63-3-619(3); Nev. Rev. Stat. §§ 482A.032, 482A.075, 484B.127(4); N.C. Gen. Stat. § 20-152(c); Or. Rev. Stat. § 811.485(3); S.C. Code Ann. § 56-5-1930(D); Tenn. Code Ann. §§ 55-4-108(c), 55-8-101(51), 55-8-124(d), 55-8-201, 55-12-102(10); Tex. Transp. Code § 545.062(d); Utah Code Ann. 41-6a-711; Wis. Stat. § 346.14(1b), (2)(c).

12. Fla. Stat. §§ 316.003(19), 316.303(3); H.B. 7061, 2016 Fla. Sess. § 54 (2016).

Operators of trucks considering testing or deploying platooning systems should consult the platooning laws in the states where they operate and ensure that they comply with the requirements in those laws.

D. Marketing Oversight

Consumer protection laws prohibit unfair and deceptive trade practices of various kinds, as well as misleading advertising practices. At the federal level, the Federal Trade Commission Act prohibits such conduct, and the Federal Trade Commission enforces the act. At the state level, state laws prohibit such conduct and attorneys general and district attorneys have the authority to enforce such state laws. Consumers and businesses may have private rights of action to assert claims based on such conduct as well.

A manufacturer's claims concerning what features, capabilities, and characteristics a system has will trigger scrutiny. As discussed in more detail in Section V(A), Tesla is already facing a suit against it relating to its advertising claims. If a manufacturer's advertisements exaggerate what a system can do, the discrepancy between what the manufacturer advertised and what it can actually do may trigger liability for unfair or deceptive trade practices. Accordingly, manufacturers should create internal policies and procedures to review and manage marketing messages to make sure they can deliver what they are promising.

V. Liability Issues

Product liability suits frequently follow accidents involving the product in question. For instance, accidents on the roads and highways of the country played a prominent role in the development of American tort law. "Products liability, like America, grew up with the automobile. Prior to the entry of motorcars onto the nation's highways, 'there simply were not large numbers of product-related lawsuits.' Once America embraced the automobile, it inevitably embraced automotive products suits as well."[13] In other words, once manufacturers began selling automobiles, and the public began using them on mass scale, accidents occurred, and product liability suits inevitably followed. Two key cases in product liability arose for car accidents: *MacPherson v. Buick Motor Co.*[14] and *Henningsen v. Bloomfield Motors, Inc.*,[15] both of which rejected privity as a defense to a case involving a defective product. These cases would permit pedestrians injured by autonomous or other connected cars to sue manufacturers even though they had no contractual relationship with the manufacturers.

Once connected transportation systems are widely deployed and used, we can expect a similar growth and perhaps explosion of product liability suits for IoT-connected cars. Accidents and other mishaps are bound to occur, and litigation will inevitably follow. In fact, the litigation has already begun. Section V(A) discusses the class action against Tesla alleging the ineffectiveness of its advanced driver assistance system. As with the conventional automobile and other products, product liability suits will occur because of accidents and the resulting damage.

Not only is litigation inevitable but manufacturers of connected cars face a risk of enormous verdicts against them, especially in cases involving catastrophic injuries. If connected vehicle systems cause accidents, and manufacturers decide to try these cases, we can expect that some cases may involve shockingly disfigured plaintiffs injured by what attorneys for plaintiffs argue were out-of-control systems after tragic, frightful accidents. In assessing its risk in front of the jury, any defendant manufacturer in such a case

13. 1 LOUIS R. FRUMER & MELVIN I. FRIEDMAN, PRODUCTS LIABILITY § 1.02 (2018) [hereinafter, FRUMER] (footnote omitted).

14. 217 N.Y. 382, 111 N.E. 1050 (1916). The court reasoned that a manufacturer putting a defective product on the market should be liable for negligence, regardless of the presence or absence of a contract between the plaintiff and the manufacturer defendant. *See id.* at 389–91.

15. 32 N.J. 358, 161 A.2d 69 (1960).

would need to consider the catastrophic nature of the plaintiff's injuries and the risk that a jury, even one trying to be impartial, cannot help but feel at least some unconscious sympathy for the plaintiff. In this fraught setting, the trial would place the defendant manufacturer's engineering and business practices under exacting scrutiny. It would be up to the jury to determine whether the manufacturer's design decisions could have avoided the accident.

During the design phase of any automated or other connected system, the manufacturer's design team may have opportunities to implement different safety features, but adding additional safety features will likely increase the cost of the product and reduce its profitability. When making these kinds of decisions, manufacturers can think more clearly and assess risk more effectively by imagining themselves in a courtroom setting, defending their practices in litigation arising from a catastrophic accident.

Manufacturers should also keep in mind that "[a]ngry jurors mean high damages."[16] Juries award very large verdicts when they become angry at a manufacturer based on what the manufacturer did or didn't do in designing the product. Jurors see a punitive damages award as a way of sending a message to the manufacturer to say that its conduct is unacceptable.

For instance, in the famous Ford Pinto case[17] arising from a catastrophic rear-end collision rupturing the gas tank and causing an explosion, the jury heard testimony that Ford was aware of the problems with the fuel system during the design of the car. A part costing $11 could have prevented the damage to the fuel system. Nonetheless, Ford decided that the cost of using the part surpassed the overall value of the human lives that would have been saved. The jury evidently concluded that Ford was more interested in

16. Robert D. Minick & Dorothy K. Kagehiro, *Understanding Juror Emotions: Anger Management in the Courtroom*, FOR THE DEFENSE, July 2004, at 3 (emphasis added).

17. Grimshaw v. Ford Motor Co., 119 Cal. App. 3d 757 (1981).

maximizing its profits than in protecting human life. The apparent callous disregard for safety led to the jury anger,[18] resulting in a jury award of over $2.5 million in compensatory damages and punitive damages in the amount of $125 million.[19]

The lesson from the Ford case is that accidents and resulting product liability can lead to large financial consequences for manufacturers. More recent cases underscore the human and financial impact of alleged product defects leading to numerous accidents. For instance, starting in the 2000s, there were media reports about a phenomenon in which Toyota and Lexus drivers said that their cars would suddenly speed up without warning and would not stop. According to some reports, the Toyota sudden acceleration phenomenon may have caused accidents that claimed the lives of 89 people.[20] According to news reports, Toyota may be responsible for over $4 billion to settle financial loss cases, potential criminal charges, shareholder claims, and fines for violating federal vehicle safety laws in addition to product defect cases.[21] Likewise, General Motors had to pay over $4 billion to resolve claims arising from the use of ignition switches that unexpectedly caused engines to stall while being driven, shutting off the power steering and disabling the air bags at the same time.[22] "GM says the problem has caused at least 13 deaths, but some members of Congress put the death toll near 100."[23] In short, the human toll and the financial costs from product defects can both be considerable.

18. *Id.* at 813.

19. *See id.* at 771–72.

20. CBS News and Associated Press, *Toyota "Unintended Acceleration" Has Killed 89*, CBS NEWS (May 25, 2010), http://www.cbsnews.com/news/toyota-unintended-acceleration-has-killed-89/.

21. *Id.*

22. Tom Krisher, *GM's Ignition Switch: What Went Wrong*, COLUMBUS DISPATCH (July 8, 2014, 6:09 AM), http://www.dispatch.com/content/stories/business/2014/07/08/gms-ignition-switch-what-went-wrong.html.

23. *Id.*

A. Types of Claims

In liability cases arising out of accidents, plaintiffs most commonly assert claims for strict product liability, negligence, and breach of warranty. State law typically governs the liability of product manufacturers for allegedly defective products, and laws vary by state.[24]

We already have a real-life example of a product liability case involving connected cars—*Sheikh v. Tesla, Inc.*[25] As of the date of this chapter, *Sheikh* is pending in the U.S. District Court for the Northern District of California. The suit followed a May 2016 accident in which a Canton, Ohio, Tesla driver named Joshua Brown died in a crash in his Tesla, which was under control of the driver assistance system, when the Tesla failed to brake for a truck turning left in front of his car. Brown also failed to intervene to stop the car. The National Transportation Safety Board (NTSB) identified three causes of the accident: the truck driver's failure to yield the right of way when making its turn, Brown's inattention and overreliance on the Tesla's driver assistance systems, and Tesla's reliance on a forward collision warning system that was not designed to detect lateral movement such as that of the truck.[26] In other words, the NTSB concluded that there was plenty of blame to go around.

In *Sheikh*, the plaintiff purchasers contend that Tesla oversold the capabilities of the Tesla enhanced Autopilot advanced driver assistance system. They allege Tesla's advertising implied that

---

24. For a survey of case law bearing on autonomous vehicle product liability, see Stephen S. Wu, *Unmanned Vehicles and US Product Liability Law*, J.L., Info. & Sci., 2011/2012, at 234. Product liability issues concerning IoT devices are addressed in Chapter 14.

25. No. 5:17-cv-02193 BLF (N.D. Cal. Complaint filed Apr. 19, 2017).

26. Nat'l Transportation Safety Board, Collision Between a Car Operating with Automated Vehicle Control Systems and a Tractor-Semitrailer Truck Near Williston, Florida, May 7, 2016, ¶¶ 3.1(3), 3.2, at 41, 42 (2017) [hereinafter NTSB Report].

Tesla's system was fully autonomous, as shown in a sales video,[27] when in fact it is not. According to the purchasers who later filed suit against Tesla, they paid $5,000 for the enhanced Autopilot system of the kind depicted in the video, but Tesla failed to deliver the Autopilot features in the time frame Tesla promised. Moreover, they say the Autopilot system that these owners received was unusable and dangerous.[28]

The *Sheikh* plaintiffs allege violations of California consumer protection laws, as well as fraud by concealment. They also allege similar violations of consumer protection laws under Colorado, Florida, and New Jersey laws. The plaintiffs' theory of recovery is that they paid many thousands of dollars for a product they didn't receive; they say they didn't receive the benefit of their bargain.[29] To bolster their claims, the plaintiffs quote a sentence that allegedly appeared on the Tesla website saying, "All Tesla vehicles produced in our factory, including Model 3, have the hardware needed for full self-driving capability at a safety level substantially greater than that of a human driver."[30] In addition, they quote the language appearing in the video mentioned above: Consumers "first would be invited to see a video lasting over two minutes, in which the initial frames shouted: 'THE PERSON IN THE DRIVER'S SEAT IS ONLY THERE FOR LEGAL REASONS. HE IS NOT DOING ANYTHING. THE CAR IS DRIVING ITSELF.'"[31]

Plaintiffs contend that Tesla's statements imply that Autopilot is a fully automated system, while in fact Autopilot is merely a

---

27. Tesla, *Tesla Autopilot 2.0*, YouTube (Oct. 20, 2016), https://www.youtube.com/watch?v=C3DbrYx-SN4. (reposted by Daniel as *Tesla Autopilot 2.0 – Level 5 Autonomy. Full Self-Driving Hardware*").

28. Second Am. Class Action Compl. ¶ 1, at 1, *Sheikh v. Tesla, Inc.*, No. 5:17-cv-02193 BLF (N.D. Cal. Complaint filed Apr. 19, 2017).

29. *Id.* ¶ 4, at 2.

30. *Id.* ¶ 38, at 10–11.

31. *Id.* ¶ 38, at 11.

driver assistance system, requiring the driver to monitor all driving tasks at all times.[32] The plaintiffs used Tesla's own words against it to show that the company allegedly exaggerated the capabilities of the Autopilot system.

B. Potential Defenses

While plaintiffs may be able to assert a number of claims against defendants for alleged defects in connected systems, defendants may have a number of available defenses. Some of the defenses relate to the plaintiff's own conduct. A plaintiff may have caused or contributed in some way to an accident. A plaintiff's failure to exercise reasonable care may constitute contributory or comparative negligence. Also, a plaintiff's misuse or modification of the product may be a cause of an accident. Further, a defendant may be able to allege that the plaintiff assumed the risk of an open, obvious hazard. Finally, a plaintiff's failure in some way to mitigate the alleged damages may reduce any award against the defendant.

Unlike with conventional products, some kinds of connected transportation systems may operate autonomously. One issue that may arise with any attempt to use the plaintiff's own conduct as a defense is whether the plaintiff was in control of the product at the time of the accident. If the product was acting in autonomous mode, there may have been no way for the plaintiff to have contributed to the accident. For instance, with regard to autonomous vehicles, if the vehicle was driving itself and in control of all driving tasks at the time of the accident, then a plaintiff's carelessness at that moment could not have contributed to the accident.

32. The National Transportation Safety Board called Tesla's Autopilot system an SAE International "Level 2 automated vehicle system." NTSB REPORT, *supra* note 26, § 1.3.3, at 9. SAE Level 2 means that the human driver is responsible for continuously monitoring the driving environment and is prepared to take over driving at any time.

Nonetheless, events preceding the accident could bear on the plaintiff's conduct. For example, if the plaintiff modified the vehicle to drive faster than the speed limit and safety limits set by the manufacturer, the plaintiff's conduct could have contributed to the accident even though the vehicle was in autonomous mode right before the accident occurred. It is foreseeable that some people will modify their automated vehicles or try to exceed their limits in some way. Likewise, pedestrian and bystander accident victims might contribute to accidents by abusing automated vehicles by darting in front of them to see how they try to avoid a collision.

Given the fast-moving nature of artificial intelligence technology, manufacturers may also want to assert a "state of the art" defense to product liability cases involving automated vehicles and other connected transportation systems. Defendant manufacturers could claim that at the time the product in question left their hands, a safer design was not technologically feasible. Some states recognize a state of the art defense, while others do not.[33]

A defendant may also assert the economic loss defense. This defense precludes tort claims for product liability where the alleged damages are financial and not for bodily injury or damage to property other than damage to the product itself. Another available defense in some cases is preemption. Under this defense, federal law under the U.S. Constitution's Supremacy Clause[34] preempts inconsistent state law. Also, a manufacturer may be able to shift responsibility to a "sophisticated user" or a "sophisticated" or "learned intermediary." Some products may be appropriate for use by engineers, technicians, and other sophisticated users. In that case, a manufacturer's duty to provide warnings and instructions would only require the level of information needed by the class of likely users and purchasers, rather than the greater level of

33. FRUMER, *supra* note 13, § 8.04.
34. U.S. CONST. art. VI, cl. 2.

warnings or instructions needed if a member of the general public were to start using it. Certain transportation systems and components could fall within this category of product. Finally, a manufacturer may be able to assert a "government contractor" defense. If the manufacturer made a product in accordance with government specifications, in certain cases, it may have a defense to an action based on issues inherent with the government specifications, rather than any fault of the manufacturer.

In warranty cases, depending on state law, defendants have a number of defenses, including privity, a requirement that the plaintiff provide the seller notice of the alleged breach, and the ability for a seller to disclaim warranties.[35] In most U.S. jurisdictions, privity will not preclude purchasers of a product or their family members from suing companies in the chain of distribution under a warranty theory.[36]

C. Risk Management and Insurance

Given the large human and financial consequences of defective products, manufacturers seek to manage the risk of product liability litigation and costly recalls. If manufacturers can proactively prevent defects and resulting accidents from occurring in the first place, they can prevent the need to defend product liability claims and can place themselves in the best position possible to prevail in product liability cases that do arise. A proactive approach to design safety means that the manufacturer takes the steps today to implement a commitment to safety, which will minimize its risk from future suits. As one commentator stated, "The most effective way for [counsel for] a corporate defendant to reduce anger toward his or her client is to show all the ways that the client went *beyond*

35. *See* Robert Shields & Carolyn Callaway, *Breach of Warranty*, *in* 1 Products Liability Practice Guide § 6.02[4] (John Vargo ed., 2018).

36. *Id.*

what was required by the law or industry practice."[37] "A successful defense can also be supported by walking jurors through the relevant manufacturing or decision-making process, showing all of the testing, checking, and follow-up actions that were included."[38] The most important thing to a jury is that the manufacturer tried hard to do the right thing.[39]

In addition to adhering to international standards, insurance will play an important role in managing connected transportation system product liability risk. The insurance industry is in the early stages of understanding automated driving risk and creating coverage that effectively manages risk.[40] In the short run, manufacturers may need to tailor-make insurance coverage with bespoke policies that fit their risk profiles. Over time, carriers will enter the market and create standard policies, reducing premium costs over the longer run.

VI. Data Protection

One key barrier to the adoption, deployment, and acceptance of connected transportation systems is widespread concern about data protection, including issues of privacy and security. With regard to privacy, connected transportation systems (including connected cars) will gather large volumes of data about their operators, including sensitive geolocation data, driving patterns, and even shopping and purchase habits. Personal data from mobile devices may be shared with connected vehicles as well. As a result, privacy advocates fear that connected transportation systems will allow manufacturers or operators to intrude into private spheres for marketing purposes, charge consumers more for products or services,

---

37. Minick & Kagehiro, *supra* note 16, at 2 (emphasis added).
38. *Id.*
39. *See id.*
40. *See generally Autonomous Vehicles Handing Over Control: Opportunities and Risks for Insurance*, Lloyd's 8 (2014), https://www.lloyds.com/news-and-risk-insight/risk-reports/library/technology/autonomous-vehicles.

and exploit or sell personal data. Moreover, this data will be at risk of exposure to malicious third parties or data breaches.

While manufacturers and operators gain increased access to personal data of owners and passengers of connected vehicles, they face increasing compliance challenges from existing and emerging data protection requirements and data breach notification laws. As a general matter, laws imposing privacy requirements in the United States focus on specific markets, such as health care[41] and financial services,[42] or apply to specific types of data, such as video rental information[43] and social security numbers.[44] General laws, such as the consumer protection laws against unfair and deceptive trade practices or false advertising, help the Federal Trade Commission and state attorneys general take action against companies that violate the privacy and security of consumers' personal data.

One particular privacy law applicable to vehicle technology is the Driver Privacy Act of 2015 relating to event data recorders (EDR). EDRs capture information about a "vehicle's dynamic time-series data during the time period just prior to a crash event."[45] EDRs must meet certain standards, and owners' manuals must contain a disclosure of information about them.[46] Congress passed the Driver Privacy Act to establish that EDR data belongs to the

41. *See, e.g.*, Health Insurance Portability and Accountability Act of 1996, Pub. L. No. 104-191, 110 Stat. 1936 (1996) (HIPAA statute); Health Insurance Reform: Security Standards; Final Rule, 68 Fed. Reg. 8334 (2003) (codified at 45 C.F.R. pts. 160, 162, 164) (requirements for securing protected health information under HIPAA).

42. *See, e.g.*, Gramm-Leach-Bliley Act, Pub. L. No. 106-102, 113 Stat. 1338 (1999) (imposing data protection requirements on financial institutions).

43. Video Privacy Protection Act of 1988, Pub. L. No. 100-618, 102 Stat. 3195 (1988).

44. *See, e.g.*, Cal. Civil Code § 1798.85 (limiting disclosure and collection of social security numbers).

45. 45 C.F.R. § 563.5(b) (definition of "event data recorder").

46. *Id.* §§ 563.1–563.12.

vehicle's owner or lessee.[47] Someone other than the owner or lessee may not access EDR data, except in instances of a court order in a proceeding (subject to admissibility standards), consent of the owner or lessee, or other special exceptions.[48] While EDRs are not connected to a network such as the Internet of Things in real time, the act does protect electronic data generated by vehicles having them.[49]

Other compliance issues will arise from new and emerging privacy regimes internationally and at the state level. On May 25, 2018, the European Union's General Data Protection Regulation (GDPR)[50] came into effect. GDPR established a comprehensive set of privacy and security requirements to protect the personal data of individuals located in the European Union (EU). GDPR is now in force in the EU and the broader European Economic Area (EEA). GDPR's territorial scope reaches beyond the EU and EEA to foreign businesses, including those located in the United States.[51] Connected vehicle technology vendors will fall within GDPR if any of the following conditions are true:

- They have operations in the EEA in which they are collecting or processing personal data in EEA countries.[52]

---

47. Driver Privacy Act of 2015, within the Fixing America's Surface Transportation Act, Pub. L. No. 114-94, § 24302(a), 129. Stat. 1312 (2015) (codified at 49 U.S.C. § 30101 note).

48. *Id.* § 24302(b), (c).

49. At least one court has held that a search of an EDR requires a warrant based on the Driver Privacy Act and a reasonable expectation of privacy in EDR data. State v. Worsham, 227 So. 3d 602, 607–08 (Fla. Ct. App. 2017).

50. Regulation (EU) 2016/679 of the European Parliament and of the Council of 27 April 2016 on the protection of natural persons with regard to the processing of personal data and on the free movement of such data, and repealing Directive 95/46/EC (General Data Protection Regulation), Council Regulation No. 2016/679, 2016 O.J. (L 119) 1.

51. *See id.* art. 3.

52. *See id.* art. 3(1).

- They are marketing, selling, or otherwise offering goods or services to individuals located in the EEA, even if they have no operations or activity there.[53]
- They are monitoring the behavior of individuals located in the EEA.[54]
- They are vendors providing services to businesses that are covered by GDPR because of one of the preceding conditions and will receive access to personal data of individuals located in the EEA.

Connected vehicle technology vendors covered by GDPR will need to comply with a comprehensive set of privacy and security requirements. For instance, they will need a lawful basis to collect, use, and disclose personal data of individuals located in the EEA, such as obtaining the consent of the individual whose personal data they are using. They will need to accommodate a number of individual rights, chief among them the right to have personal data erased when it is no longer needed and the right to opt out of further usage or sharing. Personal data may not be exported from the EEA unless there is an adequate level of protection provided either by applicable law in the country where the personal data are transferred or the data importer agrees to a set of terms by contract or approved "binding corporate rules" within a conglomerate to provide the needed level of protection. A full recitation of GDPR's requirements is beyond the scope of this publication. Nonetheless, it is sufficient to note GDPR's data protection requirements are considered the most stringent in the world.

In addition to GDPR, the new California Consumer Privacy Act (CCPA)[55] will give California residents some of the protections reminiscent of those appearing in GDPR. CCPA covers a broad

53. *See id.* art. 3(2)(a).
54. *See id.* art. 3(2)(b).
55. A.B. 375, 2017–2018 Reg. Sess. (Cal. 2018).

range of "personal information,"[56] including "geolocation data" that connected vehicles will likely collect.[57] CCPA covers larger businesses (with $25 million or more in gross revenues or access to personal information of 50,000 or more California residents) or those making most of their revenues from the "sale" of personal information.[58] Businesses covered by the law will need to disclose the categories and items of personal information the business collected or sold, provide California residents with the right to opt out of sales of personal information, and delete personal information about a resident upon request.[59] At the time of this writing, California's legislature is considering postponing implementation of CCPA from its current January 1, 2020, effective date and amendments that may change the requirements, and the attorney general is directed to issue regulations to clarify CCPA and add additional guidance.[60] Nonetheless, if CCPA becomes effective in its current form, connected vehicle technology companies will likely need to expand their privacy programs to cover new CCPA rights. Other states may follow California's example, moving CCPA closer to becoming a de facto national standard.

Finally, California's connected device security law enacted in September 2018[61] will require manufacturers to consider security features of vehicles. The law requires manufacturers of connected devices to equip them with a reasonable security feature or features.[62] It covers devices connected directly or indirectly to the Internet,[63] which would include many connected motor vehicles.

56. Cal. Civil Code § 1798.140(o)(1) (definition of "personal information").
57. *Id.* § 1798.140(o)(1)(G).
58. *See id.* § 1798.140(c).
59. *See id.* §§ 1798.100(a), 1798.105(a), 1798.110(a), 1798.115(a), 1798.135(a).
60. *See id.* § 1798.185.
61. *See id.* §§ 1798.91.04–1798.91.05.
62. *Id.* § 1798.91.04(a).
63. *Id.* § 1798.91.05(b).

Nonetheless, the law does not specify specific security controls manufacturers must implement.

To address compliance with these emerging data protection frameworks, and more effectively govern data protection as a general matter, manufacturers and operators of connected motor vehicles should establish privacy and security policies and procedures. Privacy policies and procedures should cover:

- How the organization will notify individuals of its privacy practices.
- What kinds of personal data the organization will collect, create, receive, maintain, or transmit.
- How the organization will use personal data.
- With whom the organization will share personal data, and under what circumstances and conditions.
- How individuals can obtain access to stored personal data about them, including to amend or update it.
- How individuals consent to and/or have the right to opt out of the collection, use, and sharing of personal data.

With regard to security risks, as the Lesley Stahl *60 Minutes* segment in Section I demonstrates, it is clear that current vehicles are vulnerable to cyberattack. In addition to the *60 Minutes* show, a well-publicized research project showed that Jeep vehicles are hackable. As described in a 2015 *Wired* magazine article, the researchers were able to take control of the brakes, acceleration, and dashboard functions of the hacked vehicles.[64] Government

64. Andy Greenberg, *Hackers Remotely Kill a Jeep on the Highway—with Me in It*, Wired, (July 21, 2015, 6:00 AM), https://www.wired.com/2015/07/hackers-remotely-kill-jeep-highway/.

reports concur that current vehicles have numerous vulnerabilities.[65] Of particular concern is the Controller Area Network (CAN) Bus, which is a hardware device facilitating communications among various vehicle components forming an internal data network in a vehicle. Attackers can exploit vulnerabilities in CAN Bus systems, compromise communications, and thereby manipulate the vehicle's operational systems. Another common vulnerability relates to the cloning of electronic control unit keys to gain unauthorized access via keyless entry systems.[66] Given the vulnerability of current vehicles with their limited connectivity, it is likely that with increased connectivity of future intelligent transportation systems, the degree of vulnerability will almost certainly increase commensurately.

One conclusion is obvious. Hacks and data breaches will lead to litigation. In fact, the *Wired* story prompted the filing of a class action against Chrysler (FCA), captioned *Flynn v. FCA US LLC*.[67] Plaintiffs in that case alleged that the researchers told FCA about the hacking vulnerability in 2011, but FCA did nothing about it, until the *Wired* story forced FCA to come clean.[68] The plaintiffs even attached a copy of the *Wired* story to their complaint.[69] In July 2018, the district court granted a motion for class certification in the case. As of the date of this publication, the case remains

---

65. *See, e.g.*, United States Government Accountability Office, Vehicle Cybersecurity: DOT and Industry Have Efforts Under Way, but DOT Needs to Define Its Role in Responding to a Real-world Attack 12–19 (2016); National Highway Traffic Safety Administration, Cybersecurity Best Practices for Modern Vehicles 5 (2016).

66. Flavio D. Garcia, et al., *Lock It and Still Lose It—On the (In)Security of Automotive Remote Keyless Entry Systems*, Proceedings of the 25th USENIX Security Symposium (Aug. 10–12, 2016), *available at* https://www.usenix.org/system/files/conference/usenixsecurity16/sec16_paper_garcia.pdf.

67. No. 3:15-cv-00855-MJR-DGW (S.D. Ill. Complaint Filed Aug. 4, 2015).

68. Second Am. Class Action Compl. ¶ 2, at 2, Flynn v. FCA US LLC, 3:15-cv-00855-MJR-DGW (S.D. Ill. Filed Sept. 21, 2017).

69. *Id.* ex. A.

pending. If this case is resolved, as many product cases are after a court certifies a class, FCA will need to pay something to settle this case.

How can manufacturers make their connected vehicle systems more secure? As a general matter, security policies and procedures should include administrative, physical, and technical safeguards to protect vehicles and supporting infrastructure. Administrative safeguards are the nontechnical, "soft" measures that management establishes regarding acceptable employee conduct, personnel procedures, and correct technology usage within an organization. Physical safeguards consist of the business policies, procedures, and recordkeeping required to protect an organization's physical facilities and equipment that contain systems vulnerable to tampering or data against specified hazards. Technical safeguards are security controls protecting data that are carried out via technology or are managed by technology. Security hardware and software enable the organization to implement such controls. Among other things, technical safeguards prevent unauthorized access to security-sensitive data, protect against malicious software, provide audit trails for investigation or assessments, and prevent corruption or tampering with systems.

In addition, the federal government has published a series of guides to enhance vehicle cybersecurity. Although a comprehensive listing of security controls would be beyond the scope of this chapter, examples of government ideas to improve vehicle security include:

- Limiting developer access to code in production devices.
- Controlling access to cryptographic keys.
- Limiting maintenance diagnostic access to security sensitive systems.
- Controlling access to firmware.
- Limiting the ability to modify firmware.

- Hardening vehicle systems by limiting network ports, protocols, and services.
- Segmenting and isolating portions of vehicle networks to limit the ability for attackers to use one area of the network to access another.
- Controlling internal vehicle communications.
- Logging events to create an audit trail.
- Controlling communications between vehicles and back-end servers.
- Controlling wireless interfaces.[70]

It may also be possible to harden the CAN Bus system to secure network communications,[71] as well as other types of components that may be currently vulnerable.

VII. Transactions Involving Connected Transportation Technology

Many of the legal issues from connected transportation systems will arise from the procurement process. Manufacturers will need to obtain components and supplies from companies in their supply chain. They will need to license certain software. In turn, they may make money by selling their products and licensing their software. They may work together with business partners to develop and market products and services. And they may have a network of distributors and resellers to market and sell their products and services. Agreements are important to memorialize the business terms of these transactions.

Agreements set the expectations of the parties and performance requirements. They establish, memorialize, and evidence what the

70. *See* Nat'l Highway Traffic Safety Administration, *Cybersecurity Best Practices for Modern Vehicles* 17–20 (Oct. 2016), *available at* https://www.nhtsa.gov/sites/nhtsa.dot.gov/files/documents/812333_cybersecurityformodernvehicles.pdf.

71. *See, e.g.*, Ali Shuja Siddiqui, et al., *Secure Communications over CAN-Bus*, in IEEE, 2017 IEEE 60th International Midwest Symposium on Circuits and Systems (MWSCAS) 1264 (Aug. 2017).

parties agreed to. Also, contracts facilitate compliance with a set of standards or obligations. Moreover, they establish the scope and limits of the parties' relationships. Finally, contracts allocate risk and establish or limit remedies.

Some connected transportation contracts will involve the sale of hardware, equipment, and mechanical or electrical components. Critical deal points will include:

- What is the seller selling and what are its specifications and features?
- How will the seller ship the hardware to the buyer and when does the risk of loss pass to the buyer, in case the shipment is lost or damaged?
- Are there specific environmental conditions necessary for the buyer to establish in order for the hardware to operate properly?
- What warranties does the seller offer and what are the buyer's remedies? Are there any exclusive remedies for breaches of some of the warranties?
- Does the seller limit damages, such as:
  - By limiting the elements of recoverable damages, such as consequential and incidental damages?
  - By placing a cap on the total damages recoverable by the buyer?
- Are there any carveouts from the limitations of liability?
- What happens if the seller's product infringes on the intellectual property rights of third parties? Will the seller defend and indemnify the buyer from third party claims? What are the buyer's remedies in case of infringement?
- What other indemnities are the parties seeking?
- What support, training, and maintenance services does the seller offer?
- Will the seller offer professional services to install and configure the hardware? Under what terms?

Some transactions will involve software. Connected vehicle systems may require different types of software, including enterprise software, to be licensed and installed on servers at the buyer's premises, software and firmware embedded or installed in hardware sold to the buyer, and software provided to the buyer as a managed service. Key deal points will include:

- Does the software satisfy the buyer's needs? Are there requirements or specifications the software must meet?
- How is the vendor providing the software? Is it software as a service (SaaS), is the software delivered electronically, will a vendor technician install the software, or is the vendor shipping the software on physical media?
- The scope of the license or usage rights.
- Possible restrictions on what the procuring company can do with the software.
- Are there compatibility, hardware, or other environmental requirements to obtaining or using the software?
- What warranties does the vendor offer and on what terms? Are there any exclusive remedies?
- Limitations of liability that limit the elements of recoverable damages, liability caps, and carveouts from these limitations.
- Intellectual property infringement indemnities and remedies.
- Other indemnities sought by the parties.
- Support, training, and maintenance services provided by the vendor.
- Terms for professional services to install or configure the software.

Contracting issues especially important in the connected transportation sector include:

- Covenants and warranties concerning technical specifications, such as requirements for the supplier to meet certain industry-specific specifications.
  - A buyer may want to undertake acceptance testing to determine the quality and characteristics of the product or service.
  - Alternatively, it may require proof of a third certification, audit and attestation report, or assessment to show that the product or service meets the specifications required by the buyer.
- Requirements regarding the collection, use, disclosure, and disposal of personal information.
- Information security requirements, which may flow from specific industry benchmarks or may be customized for certain types of products or services.
- Insurance requirements. The procuring party may seek assurance that the vendor has certain types of coverage. The vendor may want the procuring party to have certain coverage to mitigate the vendor's own risk arising from the procuring party's use or incorporation of the vendor's products into its own products or services.
- Warranties regarding compliance with applicable law, which may be important in certain contexts in the highly regulated transportation sector.
- Service level agreements, especially for cloud-hosted platforms and software, to set minimum requirements for service availability. These agreements are especially important for infrastructure supporting connected transportation systems.
- Special liability allocations, such as disclaimers of certain obligations, warranties, or liabilities specific to connected transportation. Are there certain risks for which a vendor does not want to be responsible?

From a procuring party's perspective, conducting thorough due diligence of prospective vendors is crucial. Procuring parties also need to monitor the performance of vendors over time. Procuring parties should also be aware of the supply chain supporting a vendor as issues and vulnerabilities may arise not only from a vendor but also its component and materials suppliers.

VIII. Conclusion

Connected vehicles are here already, and their integration into the Internet of Things and private networks will only increase over time. Vehicles will become more tightly tied to our personal and work digital lives. As with all technology advances, accidents and other mishaps will occur. The technology may not work as advertised. As a result, legal issues will arise from connected vehicle systems and the underlying technology. Lawyers will play a key role in mitigating and managing the risks to clients that provide connected vehicle products and services.

Chapter 2

Health IoT

Trends and Legal Issues

Jodi G. Daniel
Ashley N. Southerland
Maya Uppaluru

I. Introduction and Scope

With rapid advances in digital health technology and innovation, the health care industry is in the midst of a considerable transformation. Policy makers and the health care industry as a whole are focused on improving health outcomes and lowering health care costs, while also enhancing the experiences and satisfaction of patients and providers. These key goals are guiding the industry's transition from volume-based care to value-based care. They have also caused major shifts in the way that relationships are forged between traditional and nontraditional industry players to improve health care delivery overall.

Health information technology (health IT)—including the Internet of Things (IoT)—has the potential to be a significant catalyst for change. Health IT has been considered one of the most important opportunities for improving health care delivery and health outcomes.[1] Over the past 15 years, the primary focus of health IT has been on (1) electronically capturing health information in electronic health records (EHRs); (2) sharing information through health information exchanges (HIEs); and (3) transferring information electronically or through application programming interfaces (APIs). Today, as connected health care devices, applications, and cloud services proliferate in the marketplace, they have caused an explosion in the types of health-related information and decision support tools available to better understand and monitor patients outside the health care setting.

Health IoT (sometimes referred to as the Internet of Medical Things (IoMT)[2] or medical IoT (mIoT)) are internet-connected tools, sensors, and devices that collect health or health-related information to be used by health care providers, patients, caregivers, and researchers for the purpose of health management, diagnosis, decision making, and health improvement. Some of these tools can support changes in care delivery (both the type of services and location), the type and quantity of data available for health care

1. Neil Calman, Kwame Kitson & Diane Hauser, *Using Information Technology to Improve Health Quality and Safety in Community Health Centers*, U.S. Nat'l Library of Medicine, Nat'l Institutes of Health (Dec. 2009), *available at* https://www.ncbi.nlm.nih.gov/pmc/articles/PMC2788767/#R1 ("[Health IT] considered fundamental to improving the quality of health care.").

2. The "Internet of Medical Things" (IoMT) is commonly understood to mean the network of medical devices and applications connected to health care information technology (IT) systems. Colloquially, IoMT is understood to be the health care application of IoT technologies. *See Medtech and the Internet of Medical Things: How Connected Medical Devices Are Transforming Healthcare*, Deloitte Centre for Health Solutions, 02 (July 2018), *available at* https://www2.deloitte.com/content/dam/Deloitte/global/Documents/Life-Sciences-Health-Care/gx-lshc-medtech-iomt-brochure.pdf ("The rise in the number of connected medical devices, together with advances in the systems and software that support the capture and transmission of medical grade data, connectivity technologies and services, have created the Internet of Medical Things (IoMT).").

decision making, and behavior change that may greatly improve health care outcomes. As an emerging technology in health care, there is a significant value proposition for integrating connected devices into the health care context.

Information about an individual's daily life—what they eat, where they live, and what their stressors are—can have an even greater impact on their health than what happens at the point of care. All of this information is relevant to crystalize the full picture of well-being for a patient. Health IoT gives providers an in-depth window into the daily routines of their patients, affording increased opportunities for patient engagement, more informed clinical decision making, and preemptive health care interventions that ultimately result in better patient health outcomes. Integrating health IoT into the care continuum also gives clinicians the ability to personalize the services provided to patients. By bringing in new sources of information about individuals, health IoT can support the goal of a person-centered care approach.[3] Patient-generated health data (PGHD) available from health IoT devices provides invaluable information to support better patient outcomes and value-based care efforts. Ultimately, the integration of health IoT devices will spawn "P4 Medicine"—care that is participatory, personalized, predictive, and preventative.[4]

A. Types of Connected Health Devices

There are many types of health IoT tools, which implicate different legal frameworks, risks, and opportunities:

---

3. Jodi Daniel, MaryJo Deering & Michelle Murray, *Issue Brief: Using Health IT to Put the Person at the Center of Their Health and Care by 2020* (Jan. 10, 2014), *available at* https://www.healthit.gov/sites/default/files/person_at_thecenterissuebrief.pdf.

4. Dimiter V. Dimitrov, *Medical Internet of Things and Big Data in Healthcare*, 22 HEALTHCARE INFORM. RES. 157 (July 2016).

1. **Patient-facing health IoT devices.** Patient-facing connected health devices enable remote patient monitoring and support behavior change that may be critical for health outcomes. These tools can provide information solely for use by individuals, by patients and caregivers, or for sharing with clinicians. For example, the U.S. Food and Drug Administration (FDA) has approved smart pills that record when a medication is taken;[5] implantable continuous glucose monitors that can notify patients in advance of an adverse insulin event;[6] and small, heart-sensing electrodes embedded in stretchable fabrics.[7] Health IoT devices are increasingly used by researchers to track activity and health outcomes. Some of these tools are simply consumer devices with limited claims for use (such as fitness trackers that track exercise or smart mattresses that track sleep patterns), while others may meet greater standards for safety

5. *See* Press Release, U.S. Food & Drug Administration, FDA Approves Pill with Sensor That Digitally Tracks If Patients Have Ingested Their Medication (Nov. 13, 2017), *available at* https://www.fda.gov/newsevents/newsroom/press announcements/ucm584933.htm.

6. *See* Press Release, U.S. Food & Drug Administration, FDA Approves First Continuous Glucose Monitoring System with a Fully Implantable Glucose Sensor and Compatible Mobile App for Adults with Diabetes (June 21, 2018), *available at* https://www.fda.gov/newsevents/newsroom/pressannouncements/ucm611454.htm.

7. *Textronics, Inc. Receives FDA Clearance on Textile Electrode*, Business Wire (Feb. 18, 2008, 10:26 AM), https://www.businesswire.com/news/home/20080218005310/en/Textronics-Receives-FDA-Clearance-Textile-Electrode.

and effectiveness in health care delivery (such as those that monitor cardiac activity).[8]

2. **Health IoT devices supporting virtual care.** As patients seek care remotely through telehealth or other types of virtual care, there may be more IoT devices that enable a provider to examine a patient remotely. Current examples include devices that allow physicians to examine a patient's ears, throat, heart, lungs, abdomen, and skin, and capture a patient's heart rate and temperature data remotely.[9]
3. **Clinical health IoT devices.** This category of health IoT devices includes those used for administrative or clinical functions. Administrative examples can include (1) asset management (allowing clinicians to track medical equipment); (2) personnel management solutions (that measure staff efficiency and productivity); (3) patient flow management (to track patients across the continuum of care); (4) inventory management (which allows clinicians to reorder medication, supplies, and medical devices); and (5) environment and energy monitoring (controls for everything from electricity usage to optimizing environmental conditions in patient and storage areas). Clinical examples include digital devices ranging from stethoscopes to imaging machines to connected pacemakers that can be adjusted remotely.

---

8. *See* Letter from U.S. Food & Drug Administration to Apple Inc. c/o Donna-Bea Tillman (Sept. 11, 2018), *available at* https://www.accessdata.fda.gov/cdrh_docs/pdf18/DEN180044.pdf; *see* Statement from FDA Commissioner Scott Gottlieb, M.D. and Center for Devices and Radiological Health Director Jeff Shuren, M.D., J.D., on Agency Efforts to Work with Tech Industry to Spur Innovation in Digital Health, U.S. Food & Drug Administration (Sept. 12, 2018), *available at* https://www.fda.gov/NewsEvents/Newsroom/PressAnnouncements/ucm620246.htm?utm_campaign=09122018_Statement_FDA%20Statement.

9. *See TytoHome: A Comprehensive Exam and Telehealth Visit, Anytime and Anywhere*, TYTOCARE, https://www.tytocare.com/tytohome/ (last visited Oct. 5, 2018).

Today, 3.7 million medical devices are connected to and monitor various parts of the body.[10] By 2020, the average person will generate 1.5 GB of data per day,[11] and 40 percent of IoT technology will be health-related—making up $117 billion[12] of an approximately $1.7 trillion global IoT marketplace.[13] By 2019, it is estimated that 87 percent of health care organizations will have adopted some form of IoT medical devices.[14] The industry has also seen new approaches to oversight from agencies like FDA, as well as new players in the health care marketplace.

While health IoT shows great promise for transforming health and health care, it also raises new questions, challenges, and risks. Existing regulations and policies may not have contemplated the use of health and medical data in connected devices—or the accompanying risks. Moreover, the regulations and policies governing the health IoT landscape are changing rapidly, leaving many questions and significant uncertainty about how best to effectively implement health IoT tools.

In this chapter, we explore the integration of connected devices into the health care ecosystem; strategies to capitalize on the rapid growth in connected health care; real-world challenges and risks, as well as how to mitigate them; and strategies for navigating the health IoT landscape of the future.

---

10. Bernard Marr, *Why the Internet of Medical Things (IoMT) Will Start to Transform Healthcare in 2018*, Forbes (Jan. 25, 2018), https://www.forbes.com/sites/bernardmarr/2018/01/25/why-the-internet-of-medical-things-iomt-will-start-to-transform-healthcare-in-2018/#11b9bcb4a3ca.

11. *What Is Edge Computing?*, CB Insights, ii (Aug. 8, 2018), https://www.cbinsights.com/research/what-is-edge-computing/.

12. Dimitrov, *supra* note 4, at 156.

13. *What Is Edge Computing?*, *supra* note 11, at 1.

14. Juliet Van Wagenen, *Why Healthcare IoT Is on the Rise*, HealthTech (Aug. 27, 2018), https://healthtechmagazine.net/article/2018/08/why-healthcare-iot-rise-infographic.

II. Real-World Operational Challenges

While privacy, security, and liability are top-of-mind when it comes to addressing the risks inherent in connected health devices, a number of on-the-ground, real-world challenges exist in the operationalization of health IoT devices:

1. **Trust, transparency, and data reliability.** The need for clinicians to rely on the data available to them naturally begs the question of whether the data is reliable in the first place. There must be mechanisms in place to verify the accuracy of the data and to provide context for the data. These data "chain of custody" and data provenance considerations are both critical and relevant to the use of health IoT data to provide patient care. These considerations are also relevant to ensure data derivatives (like artificial intelligence algorithms, for example), do not build biases into health IoT tools or tools using IoT data.
2. **Network connectivity and bandwidth issues.** The sheer ability to transmit data collected by health IoT devices can be impacted by network and bandwidth issues. The Federal Communications Commission (FCC) has programs in place to encourage and financially support connected health initiatives, as well as the transmission of data for telehealth. However, the FCC is not authorized to support the hardware (e.g., broadband lines) necessary to take advantage of connected health initiatives.
3. **Discriminatory use of data.** There may also be "collateral consequences" in the collection of data by connected health devices. Although connected health information is most likely intended for use at the point of care to facilitate better health outcomes, data collection in some circumstances can have an impact on credit, insurance, and employment decisions.

4. **Data overload at the point of care.** While the goal is to provide clinicians with information to make more informed treatment decisions, it is possible for there to be too much information at the point of care. With the realities of physician burnout and the increased administrative burdens that come along with the advancements in digital health, streamlined insights, easy-to-use interfaces, and analytics that are able to sort relevant from irrelevant data will also become increasingly necessary as the sheer volume of data increases. Developers facilitating the use of health IoT data will need to consider the end users of such tools and integrate data into the clinician workflow.
5. **Security risks that pose risks to patient safety.** While all IoT devices raise security risks, the consequences of security risks in health IoT are not just about issues of data loss or inefficiencies from systems that must be taken off-line. Health IoT security risks can lead to significant patient harm. If the data is inaccurate, clinicians may make treatment decisions that can adversely impact patients. If a health IoT device is controlling the dose of a medication (as is the case with an automated insulin pump) or is maintaining bodily functioning (as is the case with a pacemaker), a security breach can have severe health consequences.

III. Integration and Interoperability: Increasing the Flow of Patient Information

A key priority for health IoT is ensuring that these devices function within the larger health care system, and that data flows from the health IoT devices to other technologies that can make use of the information. In order to unlock the vast potential of health IoT, the industry must ensure that data from various sources are machine readable and interoperable across multiple systems and technologies. Interoperability is not just a technical problem with a technical solution. Instead, significant business, human, and cultural factors can impact interoperability.

Streamlined standards and policies for health information exchange promote efficiency of data transfer; foster communication; allow users to optimize data for health and medical applications; and promote innovation that can improve health disparities, reduce costs, and increase patient engagement. This is why, in general, the federal government is trying to promote open access to and availability of data to support health care improvements, as well as practices that enhance interoperability.

A. Interoperability

Data created by health IoT devices is not valuable if it is kept in the "silos" in which it is captured. For example, individuals visit various health care providers, each of which has a separate record of the patient's visit and any resulting treatments. With the advent of health IoT, there is the potential for even more sources of data that can provide insights to improve health and patient care. However, if this information cannot be connected and made available when needed, then there is limited value to the health IoT tools.

Interoperability—the ability for systems to electronically exchange and process information—involves technical challenges. However, legal, business, and cultural limitations are often the most difficult to address. First, health care is regional, and there are often different practices and laws in different states and geographies that govern the interoperability landscape. There is also no single, nationwide network for sharing electronic health information, even for treatment purposes. Second, there are business disincentives for sharing information. Many health care entities (and technology companies that capture that information for health care providers) see health information as an asset that provides them with a business advantage. EHR vendors see easy access to information on their systems to be a competitive advantage, and often do not want competitors to have access to that data. The solution to the interoperability challenge must address all of these competing (and often complicated) factors.

1. EHR Incentive Programs

In an effort to address the interoperability problem, Congress established the Medicare and Medicaid EHR Incentive Programs under the American Recovery and Reinvestment Act of 2009,[15] aimed at encouraging health care providers to adopt and demonstrate their "meaningful use" of EHR technology (Meaningful Use Program). Under these programs, the Department of Health and Human Services (HHS) provided incentive payments to health care providers to (1) adopt certified EHR technology (CEHRT) and (2) use CEHRT to meet certain requirements intended to improve health care delivery. This means that much of the nation's health information is now digital—representing a huge opportunity for EHRs to be augmented by health IoT data (including physiologic, wellness, behavioral, and social determinants data) to bring a fuller picture of a patient's health to her care team. One of the key goals of the program was to support the exchange and availability of electronic health information, no matter where the patient is located. With an increase in EHR adoption by physicians from 20.8 to 86.9 percent (2004–2015)[16] and by acute care hospitals from 9.4 to 83.8 percent (2008–2015),[17] improved interoperability can bring health IoT data to the point of care to impact clinical decision making and

15. Pub. L. 111–5.

16. *Office-Based Physician Electronic Health Record Adoption*, ONC Health IT Dashboard, https://dashboard.healthit.gov/quickstats/pages/physician-ehr-adoption-trends.php (last visited Sept. 28, 2018).

17. *Adoption of Electronic Health Record Systems among U.S. Non-Federal Acute Care Hospitals: 2008–2015*, ONC Health IT Dashboard, https://dashboard.healthit.gov/evaluations/data-briefs/non-federal-acute-care-hospital-ehr-adoption-2008-2015.php (last visited Sept. 28, 2018).

ultimately patient health outcomes. Standards and certification are, therefore, critical components of these efforts.

B. Standards and Certification

To enable health IoT devices to connect the data from these tools with other health data, it is important to understand the standards that are used for clinical care and the process and regulations for adopting standards that can enable the sharing of health data. While there may not be specific standards for all health IoT needs, where standards have been identified or adopted, it may be beneficial to incorporate these into emerging health IoT tools.

The HHS Office of the National Coordinator for Health Information Technology (ONC) has authority under the Health Information Technology for Economic and Clinical Health Act (HITECH Act) to adopt standards and certification criteria for health IT. ONC oversees a voluntary certification program for health IT developers to encourage the adoption of industry standards and implementation specifications. The certification program is intended to provide assurance to purchasers and other users that an EHR system meets certain baseline technical standards, as well as functionality and security requirements adopted by HHS. This includes standards for health information exchange,[18] for the content of the data,[19] and for data vocabulary.[20] The requirements for certified health IT are updated periodically through notice-and-comment rulemaking. While provider participation in the certification program is voluntary, use of certified health IT is required for participation in certain federal programs, including incentive programs (such as the EHR incentive program, now called "Promoting Interoperability")[21] and

18. 45 C.F.R. § 170.202.
19. *Id.* § 170.205.
20. *Id.* § 170.207.
21. *See* 83 Fed. Reg. 41144.

for reimbursement (such as for chronic care management).[22] Therefore, EHR vendors must meet these certification requirements to sell their products in many inpatient and ambulatory care markets.

In addition to regulatory standards, ONC has a more agile and evolving list of standards. The Interoperability Standards Advisory (ISA) provides the health care industry with a federally curated list of standards and implementation specifications that can address specific clinical needs.[23] The ISA is updated annually and reflects industry recommendations, subject matter expert feedback, and public comments on proposed interoperability standards. There are not yet standards for PGHD, and therefore there are no federally identified standards to which technology developers can look in developing consumer-facing health IoT systems that seek to connect data. As the health IoT proliferates, standardization will become increasingly relevant.

There is also a growing effort to enable the exchange of information through software APIs, which can enable health IoT devices and other tools that need access to clinical data to support or enhance their value to patients or clinicians. The Fast Healthcare Interoperability Resources (FHIR) standard, for example, is an interoperability standards framework for exchanging health care information through an API,[24] and which is getting traction among regulators. Although regulators have not yet required the use of FHIR for EHR vendors (as of the date of this publication), most vendors and health IoT companies are voluntarily adopting FHIR to enable greater interoperability—which means that FHIR is essentially the de facto industry standard for health data APIs

22. CPT code 99490 calls for recording of patient information using certified EHR technology.

23. *Introduction to the ISA*, HEALTHIT.GOV, https://www.healthit.gov/isa/ (last visited Aug. 22, 2018).

24. *FHIR Overview*, FHIR, https://www.hl7.org/fhir/overview.html (last visited Aug. 22, 2018).

for the near future. The Consumer Technology Association (CTA) has also developed some industry-led standards and performance criteria through its Health and Fitness work group, covering areas such as physical activity monitors.[25]

While health IoT devices may not need to undergo certification or meet technical or functional standards, and there is no mandate to follow standards from the ISA, incorporating these standards can be important for the commercialization strategies of device manufacturers, particularly if their customers—such as hospitals or provider practices—need these devices to integrate with certified EHR systems in order to meet CMS requirements or simply to create a more streamlined workflow for clinicians.

C. Information Blocking

Despite efforts to promote information exchange, business, policy, and cultural obstacles continue to stand in the way of achieving interoperability, as described previously. Because of this, the government was concerned about eliminating policies and practices that limit health information exchange. As a result, in December 2016, Congress passed the 21st Century Cures Act (Cures Act),[26] which established a new legal prohibition against "information blocking." The prohibition penalizes organizations (including providers, health IT developers, exchanges, and networks) that "know or should know" that a particular business practice is unreasonable and likely to interfere with, prevent, or materially discourage the access, exchange, or use of electronic health information.[27] The Cures Act bestows the HHS Office of the Inspector General (OIG) with authority to levy up to $1 million in penalties per

25. https://www.cta.tech/Research-Standards/Standards.aspx?cat=Health Fitness_Wellness.

26. Pub. L. No. 114–255.

27. Pub. L. No. 114–255, div. A, tit. IV, § 4004 (adding § 3022); 42 U.S.C. § 300jj-52(a).

violation. Rulemaking is required to identify reasonable and necessary activities that do not constitute information blocking. The federal government's efforts to encourage interoperability, combined with the significant information-blocking penalties, evince the critical importance of breaking down the barriers to information exchange—and support the integration of EHR data and data from health IoT devices.

IV. Privacy and Security and Data Use: Protecting Patients' Health Data to Engender Patient Trust

There is a delicate balance between the importance of having access to health data and the need to protect sensitive patient information. As the health care industry transitions to value-based care and reimbursement models that are based on patient health outcomes, data generated by health IoT devices can be uniquely leveraged to meet these goals. However, health IoT devices and data management processes must also be balanced against the ever-present need for patient safety and security, as well as potential liability risks.

A. Health Insurance Portability and Accountability Act of 1996 (HIPAA)

The privacy[28] and security rules[29] promulgated under HIPAA[30] set forth the framework for protecting health information in the United States. The HIPAA rules limit uses and disclosures of protected health information (PHI), which is information created or received by a covered entity regarding a patient's health status, treatment, payment, or demographic characteristics. However, the HIPAA rules do not apply to de-identified data, which requires either

28. 45 C.F.R. pt. 160; 45 C.F.R pt. 164, subpts. A and E.

29. 45 C.F.R. pt. 160; 45 C.F.R. pt. 164, subpts. A and C.

30. Pub. L. No. 104-191, 110 Stat. 1936 (1996); 42 U.S.C. § 300gg and 29 U.S.C § 1181 *et seq.* and 42 U.S.C. 1320d *et seq.*

stripping a list of certain identifiers (including device identifiers), or ensuring that the data are statistically de-identified.[31]

1. HIPAA Coverage and Gaps

HIPAA only protects PHI disclosed by covered entities and business associates. Covered entities are health plans, health care providers that engage in standard electronic transactions under HIPAA, and health care clearinghouses.[32] Entities that create, receive, maintain, or transmit PHI on behalf of a covered entity are business associates,[33] and business associates likewise have obligations to comply with certain provisions under HIPAA. However, if the exact same data is held by the consumer, by a product, or by a company that only has a relationship with the consumer (e.g., non-covered entities), then that data may not covered by HIPAA. For this reason, numerous health IoT devices—including wellness devices and wearables that track exercise or nutrition and devices that capture medical information (such as home blood glucose monitors for patient use)—may not be covered by HIPAA at all.

Increasingly, consumer technology companies are partnering with health systems and plans to exchange data. This often includes giving patients access to their own PHI through a mobile application, or transmitting PGHD from a wearable device to the patient's doctor. Depending on these data flow arrangements, the consumer technology company that manufactures a health IoT device may be a business associate of the health care system or plan. In light of these partnerships, the lines are often blurred between consumer-facing health technologies and technologies used by covered entities to support their treatment, payment, and health care operations functions.

31. 45 C.F.R. §§ 164.502(d)(2), 164.514(a), (b).
32. *Id.* § 160.103.
33. *Id.*

HHS's Office of Civil Rights (OCR) issued guidance to help entities understand whether certain companies are business associates or whether they are outside the scope of HIPAA entirely.[34] This guidance clarifies, for example, that a technology company that is collecting health data through a remote patient monitoring device must comply with HIPAA as a business associate if it is providing the remote patient monitoring service on behalf of a doctor or hospital—but not if the technology is collecting remote patient monitoring data only for the patient's own use. The lines become even more blurred if the consumer-facing remote patient monitoring service allows the data to be shared with a doctor or nurse. In that case, whether HIPAA applies will depend on the arrangement and the relationship between the technology company and the health care provider. Given these complexities, consumers of health IoT cannot assume that HIPAA rights apply, or that developers of health IoT tools are required to protect information in accordance with HIPAA.

2. *HIPAA Privacy Rule*

When an entity that offers a health IoT product is covered under HIPAA, data uses and disclosures must be limited to what is permitted by the Privacy Rule (and by a business associate agreement). There are many permitted uses and disclosures of PHI, including for treatment, payment, and health care operations;[35] research;[36] public health;[37] and as required by law.[38] However, these permissible disclosures are limited to only the minimum amount of

34. *See* "Health App Use Scenarios & HIPAA," https://hipaaqsportal.hhs.gov/community-library/accounts/92/925889/Public/OCR-health-app-developer-scenarios-2-2016.pdf (last visited Oct. 8, 2018).

35. 45 C.F.R. §§ 164.502(a)(1)(ii), 164.506(a).

36. *Id.* § 164.512(i).

37. *Id.* § 164.512(b).

38. *Id.* § 164.512(a).

information necessary for a particular purpose,[39] and the disclosing entity must verify the identity and authority of the recipient prior to disclosure.[40] Disclosures are always permissible with the individual's authorization.[41] There are also restrictions on certain commercial uses of PHI—most importantly limits on the sale[42] and marketing[43] of PHI.

In addition, the HIPAA rules include individual rights. Particularly relevant in the health IoT context is the HIPAA individual right of access,[44] which dictates that an individual has a right to access and obtain a copy of his or her own health information. If that information is maintained electronically, the individual has a right to an electronic copy. Furthermore, patients may compel providers and health plans to send their health information to the application or entity of the patient's choosing. This may enable patients to combine data from health IoT devices with data from other non-health sources, which further complicates the HIPAA analysis. OCR released guidance on the right of access to clarify these requirements.[45]

3. HIPAA Security Rule

All health IoT entities that are subject to HIPAA must also comply with the security rule. Amassing various sources of data and increasing connection between devices inherently involves increased security risk. Health data is one of the most frequently

39. *Id.* §§ 164.502(b), 164.514(d).
40. *Id.* § 164.514.
41. *Id.* § 164.508.
42. *Id.* § 164.502(a)(5)(ii)(A).
43. *See id.* §§ 164.508(a)(3); 164.501(2)(ii), (3).
44. *Id.* § 164.524.
45. Individuals have a right under HIPAA to access their own health information. *See* 45 C.F.R. § 164.524; *see also* "Individuals' Right under HIPAA to Access Their Health Information 45 CFR § 164.524," HHS.gov, https://www.hhs.gov/hipaa/for-professionals/privacy/guidance/access/index.html (last visited Sept. 28, 2018).

targeted types of data for cyber-attacks, and attacks can range "from malware that compromises the integrity of systems and privacy of patients to distributed denial of service (DDoS) attacks that disrupt facilities' ability to provide patient care."[46]

Under HIPAA, covered entities and business associates must conduct a security risk assessment,[47] which includes an assessment of any health IoT devices and any data sharing facilitated by such tools. Data encryption must be addressed under HIPAA and can reduce the risks of security breach and the costs of notification in the event of a security incident.[48] As a best practice, health IoT developers may wish to preemptively comply with HIPAA due to requirements or expectations of providers who may wish to access data using these tools. The HIPAA Security Rule also requires adoption of "reasonable" practices for specific categories of confidentiality, integrity, and availability, but does not set specific requirements. Health IoT developers should implement reasonable data security practices in order to prevent unauthorized access to and misuse of personal information; attacks on the entire network via unsecured connected devices; and (especially relevant in the connected health space) risks to personal safety. Health systems that are leveraging health IoT tools should update their security risk assessment regularly and mitigate any risks before incorporating health IoT tools into their systems.

---

46. *Cyber Attacks: In the Healthcare Sector*, CENTER FOR INTERNET SECURITY, https://www.cisecurity.org/cyber-attacks-in-the-healthcare-sector/ (last visited Aug. 24, 2018).

47. 45 C.F.R. § 164.308(a)(1)(ii)(A).

48. "Guidance to Render Unsecured Protected Health Information Unusable, Unreadable, or Indecipherable to Unauthorized Individuals," HHS.gov, https://www.hhs.gov/hipaa/for-professionals/breach-notification/guidance/index.html (last visited Sept. 28, 2018).

B. Other Laws Affecting the Privacy of Health Data

If an entity is not a covered entity or a business associate, the data held by these entities is not PHI and these entities are not subject to HIPAA. However, the Federal Trade Commission (FTC) does enforce laws pertaining to consumer protection generally, including enforcement against unfair or deceptive acts or practices.[49] FTC has used this authority when a company has a stated privacy or security policy and fails to act in accordance with this policy. For example, FTC has enforcement authority if a non-covered entity states that it does not sell consumer data in its public privacy policy, but in practice does in fact sell individuals' data behind the scenes. This could be considered a violation of the FTC Act.

State laws may also apply to privacy and security analyses. The recently passed California Consumer Privacy Act is an example of sweeping state-level legislation that encompasses a broad definition of personal information, including health and biometric data held by non-covered entities. Many of these laws contain exceptions for covered entities under HIPAA.

C. Other Privacy and Security Resources

For health IoT companies operating outside of HIPAA, there are other policy frameworks to draw upon as entities construct their privacy policies. The federal government promulgated a Precision Medicine Policy and Trust Framework, as well as Security Principles and Framework, that may be instructive for companies working with sensitive health data within a research context or otherwise.[50] The Future of Privacy Forum has also led an effort with

---

49. 15 U.S.C. §§ 41–58. *See* Federal Trade Commission Act, https://www.ftc.gov/enforcement/statutes/federal-trade-commission-act.

50. https://allofus.nih.gov/about/program-overview/precision-medicine-initiative-privacy-and-trust-principles and https://allofus.nih.gov/about/program-overview/precision-medicine-initiative-data-security-policy-principles-and-framework-overview.

consumer genetic testing companies to develop best practices to protect individuals' data.[51] App stores, such as those curated by Apple and Google, have also set guidelines for app developers as to what they can and cannot do with individuals' health data.[52] The vast—and varied—privacy and security landscape means that health IoT developers must be vigilant in their analyses of these issues.

V. Safety: Ensuring Appropriate, Responsible, and Quality-Based Use of Health IoT

A. FDA and Connected Health Devices

Today, FDA is working to achieve a delicate balance between innovation and patient safety. While safety is at the forefront of FDA's mission and responsibilities, recent changes in agency policy—driven largely by the Cures Act—have also amplified the importance of fostering innovation. FDA recognized this relative tension in its Digital Health Innovation Action Plan, which outlined FDA's "vision for fostering digital health innovation while continuing to protect and promote the public health."[53]

Consistent with this vision for boosting innovation in connected health and clinical-grade medical devices, FDA recently released several guidance documents and instituted agency-wide programs relevant to health IoT that are designed to implement statutory

---

51. https://fpf.org/2018/07/31/future-of-privacy-forum-and-leading-genetic-testing-companies-announce-best-practices-to-protect-privacy-of-consumer-genetic-data.

52. Apple HealthKit Guidelines: https://developer.apple.com/documentation/healthkit/protecting_user_privacy?changes=_6; Google Fit guidelines: https://developers.google.com/fit/overview#responsible_use_of_google_fit.

53. "Digital Health Innovation Action Plan," U.S. Food & Drug Administration Center for Devices & Radiological Health Digital Health Program, at 1 (July 2017), *available at* https://www.fda.gov/downloads/MedicalDevices/DigitalHealth/UCM568735.pdf.

changes under the Cures Act and to reduce regulatory burden in bringing health IoT (and other innovative products) to market:

1. **FDA's authority to regulate certain software is eliminated.** Section 3060 of the Cures Act amended the Food, Drug, and Cosmetic Act (FD&C Act) to exclude certain software functions from the definition of a medical device, and thus from FDA's regulatory oversight.[54] FDA has published two draft guidances to explain the applicability of these Cures Act provisions.[55] Under the statute, there are five categories of software functions that are *not* medical devices, and therefore not subject to FDA regulation. Health IoT can fall within any of these categories:
   - **Administrative support of a health care facility.** Software functions that are "for administrative support of a health care facility, including the processing and maintenance of financial records, claims or billing information, appointment schedules, business analytics, information about patient populations, admissions, practice and inventory management, analysis of historical claims data to predict future utilization or cost-effectiveness, determination of health benefit eligibility,

---

54. 130 STAT. 1131. *See* 21st Century Cures Act, https://www.congress.gov/114/plaws/publ255/PLAW-114publ255.pdf.

55. Clinical and Patient Decision Support Guidance: https://www.fda.gov/downloads/MedicalDevices/DeviceRegulationandGuidance/GuidanceDocuments/UCM587819.pdf; and Changes to Existing Medical Software Policies Resulting from Section 3060 Guidance: https://www.fda.gov/downloads/MedicalDevices/DeviceRegulationandGuidance/GuidanceDocuments/UCM587820.pdf.

population health management, and laboratory workflow,"[56] are not classified as a medical device.

- **Maintaining or encouraging a healthy lifestyle.** Software functions "for maintaining or encouraging a healthy lifestyle and . . . unrelated to the diagnosis, cure, mitigation, prevention, or treatment of a disease or condition," are not medical devices. FDA defines this type of software as that which "encourages or maintains a 'general state of health or healthy activity.'"[57] Any general wellness device could still be considered a medical device if the intended use is related to the diagnosis, cure, mitigation, prevention, or treatment of a disease or condition. Thus, a general sleep management mobile application and sensor intended for use by the average individual would not be considered a medical device; but a sleep management app and sensor intended for use in managing sleep apnea could be, and FDA could enforce its regulatory requirements if it determines that the app poses a high safety risk.
- **Electronic patient records.** Electronic patient records for use by health care professionals, which are certified under the ONC program and are "the equivalent of a paper chart," are not a medical device if the software is not intended for interpretation or analysis for the purpose of the diagnosis, cure, mitigation, prevention, or treatment of a disease or condition. For some types

56. 21 U.S.C. § 360j (o)(1)(A) and *Changes to Existing Medical Software Policies Resulting from Section 3060 Guidance*, https://www.fda.gov/downloads/MedicalDevices/DeviceRegulationandGuidance/GuidanceDocuments/UCM587820.pdf.

57. *General Wellness: Policy for Low Risk Devices, available at* https://www.fda.gov/downloads/medicaldevices/deviceregulationandguidance/guidancedocuments/ucm429674.pdf.

of EHR software that are not ONC-certified, FDA will exercise enforcement discretion.

- **Medical device data systems.** Software functions that meet the definitions of medical device data systems (MDDS),[58] medical image storage devices, or medical image communications devices, are not medical devices. This includes products that are *solely intended* to transfer, store, convert formats, and display medical device data and results. However, software functions that also *analyze or interpret* medical device data remain subject to FDA's regulatory oversight.
- **Certain clinical decision support (CDS).** CDS software that allows a clinician to independently review the basis for the software's recommendation will not be subject to FDA regulation as a medical device. FDA will take the same approach with patient decision support (PDS) software, which is decision-facilitating software intended for use by patients or caregivers (not health professionals).[59]

2. **Multifunction device guidance.** On April 28, 2018, FDA released a draft guidance outlining its regulatory approach to multifunction digital health devices[60] (devices where some functionalities fall under FDA's definition of a medical device, and other functionalities do not). The agency

58. *Medical Device Data Systems, Medical Image Storage Devices, and Medical Image Communications Devices: Guidance for Industry, available at* https://www.fda.gov/downloads/medicaldevices/deviceregulationandguidance/guidancedocuments/ucm401996.pdf.

59. *Draft Guidance for Industry: Clinical and Patient Decision Support Software, available at* https://www.fda.gov/downloads/MedicalDevices/DeviceRegulationandGuidance/GuidanceDocuments/UCM587819.pdf.

60. *Multiple Function Device Products: Draft Guidance for Industry and Food and Drug Administration Staff*, U.S. Food & Drug Administration (Apr. 27, 2018), *available at* https://www.fda.gov/downloads/MedicalDevices/DeviceRegulationandGuidance/GuidanceDocuments/UCM605683.pdf.

clarified that its enforcement focus will be on medical device functions that diagnose and treat patients.

3. **Pre-certification programs to streamline medical device approvals.** In keeping with its action plan, FDA has been explicit in its intent to streamline the approval of innovative medical devices. The Pre-Cert Program provides a "more streamlined and efficient regulatory oversight of software-based medical devices developed by manufacturers who have [1] demonstrated a robust culture of quality and organizational excellence, and [2] who are committed to monitoring real-world performance of their products once they reach the U.S. market."[61] Overall, FDA is clear that it is loosening its enforcement grip on medical device regulation in order to encourage innovation in the health IoT space and beyond.

These dramatic policy changes are designed to promote innovation by enabling new and modified products to come to market sooner. However, these changes can also lead to uncertainty for technology companies that are awaiting final FDA guidance, and the reduced regulatory oversight can raise new questions about liability risk.

VI. Legal Uncertainty: Managing Risk and Compliance in a Changing Environment

A. Liability and Risk Mitigation

What happens when something goes wrong—when data is inaccurate, when the analytic algorithm morphed on its own or included bias, or when the information wasn't properly integrated or was interoperable at a key decision point—and someone dies? There

61. *Digital Health Software Precertification (Pre-Cert) Program*, https://www.fda.gov/MedicalDevices/DigitalHealth/DigitalHealthPreCertProgram/default.htm (last visited Aug. 23, 2018).

are potential liability and compliance risks, as well as questions about who is responsible (e.g., the technology developer or the clinician using the tool?). How can organizations protect themselves in a landscape of uncertainty?

1. **Integrate best practices into products, software, and operational infrastructures.** In many regulatory regimes (including HIPAA), reasonableness remains the standard. As such, it is critical for companies developing or using health IoT products to develop internal policies and procedures to systematically reduce liability and risk to the best of their ability and to implement those policies and procedures through training and other means. Following best practices for quality management, designing with security and safety in mind, and using standards are all strategies to consider.
2. **Assign liability through contract.** Mitigating risk requires that all entities independently stay abreast of the overlapping regulatory oversight regimes, including health care, product liability, and torts, among others. However, because technology is developing faster than the law, the best strategy to apportion risk in an uncertain regulatory landscape is to set clear contractual expectations, warranties, limitations, and indemnities and obtain insurance coverage to cover potential liability.
3. **Collaborate for security risk mitigation.** Entities operating within the health IoT landscape may consider participation in Information Sharing and Analysis Organizations (ISAOs) as a security risk mitigation strategy. ISAOs are groups of private companies, nonprofit organizations, executive departments and agencies, and other entities that come together to share information related to cybersecurity risks and incidents, and to collaborate to respond in as close to real time as possible. ISAOs receive legal protections for sharing threat-related information.

B. Compliance and Enforcement

While the federal government's goal is to drive innovation for health IoT devices, maintaining awareness of the regulatory enforcement landscape is necessary in order to "see around the corner" in advance of potential liabilities and hefty penalties. Moreover, enforcement collaboration across various federal agencies means that health care organizations employing connected health technologies—providers, payers, and developers alike—must be vigilant about the crosscutting and interwoven regulatory regimes impacting connected health care.

1. **HIPAA enforcement (HHS OCR).** HHS OCR is responsible for enforcing the HIPAA Privacy and Security Rules by (1) investigating complaints filed with OCR, (2) conducting compliance reviews of covered entities and business associates, and (3) performing education and outreach to foster compliance with the Privacy and Security Rule requirements. In 2017, OCR settled with CardioNet for improper disclosure of health information, due to a failure to implement mobile device security.[62] OCR stated that "[t]his disregard for security can result in a serious breach, which affects each individual whose information is left unprotected."[63] OCR also works in conjunction with the Department of Justice (DOJ) to refer possible criminal violations of HIPAA and in close coordination with FTC in areas of concurrent jurisdiction.

62. *CardioNet Resolution Agreement*, https://www.hhs.gov/sites/default/files/cardionet-ra-cap.pdf; *see* Press Release, Office of the National Coordinator for Health IT, $2.5 Million Settlement Shows That Not Understanding HIPAA Requirements Creates Risk (Apr. 24, 2017), https://www.hhs.gov/about/news/2017/04/24/2-5-million-settlement-shows-not-understanding-hipaa-requirements-creates-risk.html.

63. *Id.*

2. **Information blocking enforcement (HHS OIG).** Given the focus on interoperability, HHS OIG will likely begin investigating allegations of information blocking once final regulations are published. Given the potential for significant penalties—up to $1 million per violation—the information-blocking rule will likely impact business practices that are deemed to interfere with, prevent, or materially discourage the access, exchange, or use of electronic health information.[64]
3. **Unfair and deceptive trade practices (FTC).** The FTC Act[65] allows enforcement against companies that engage in unfair or deceptive practices (including inaccurate security claims), fail to take reasonable security measures, or act inconsistently with their privacy policies. In June 2016, the agency settled[66] to resolve allegations[67] that Practice Fusion (a cloud-based EHR company) misled its consumers and failed to adequately inform them that the company's physician reviews would be posted publicly on the Internet, resulting in disclosure of the patients' sensitive personal and medical information.
4. **False Claims Act enforcement (DOJ).** DOJ—in conjunction with state attorneys general—are responsible for enforcement against organizations that submit false claims for government payments. For example, in May 2017, the

64. *See* 42 U.S.C. § 300jj-52(a).

65. 15 U.S.C. § 45(a).

66. *In re* Practice Fusion, Agreement Containing Consent Order, File No. 1423039, https://www.ftc.gov/system/files/documents/cases/160608practicefusionagree.pdf; *see* Press Release, Federal Trade Commission, Electronic Health Records Company Settles with FTC Charges It Deceived Consumers About Privacy of Doctor Reviews (June 8, 2016), https://www.ftc.gov/news-events/press-releases/2016/06/electronic-health-records-company-settles-ftc-charges-it-deceived.

67. *In re* Practice Fusion, Complaint, No. C-142-3039, https://www.ftc.gov/system/files/documents/cases/160608practicefusioncmpt.pdf.

DOJ settled with eClinicalWorks (eCW)[68] to resolve allegations that eCW misrepresented the capabilities of its EHR software, and therefore falsely obtained certification (as well as accompanying government payments) for its software under the EHR Incentive Program. In addition, the settlement resolved allegations that eCW paid kickbacks to certain customers in exchange for promoting its product.

VII. Making Sense of It All: Recommendations for Navigating the Future of the Health Care IoT Landscape

What opportunities are available for industry players to capitalize on the mushrooming wave of health IoT? What areas are ripe for leadership by private industry? And what does the future of connected health care look like?

1. **"Consumerized" medicine.** In a world of increasingly connected, informed, and engaged consumers, it is inevitable that the demand for a personalized, on-demand, streamlined, and cost-efficient customer experience (common outside of the health care marketplace) will spill over into and put pressure on the health care industry to follow suit. Health IoT will provide the data necessary for clinicians to step into this whirlwind of a marketplace. Ultimately, however, success in this new marketplace will depend on how well clinicians are able to translate, filter, synthesize, and ultimately utilize the insights gleaned from that data

68. U.S. *ex rel.* Brendan Delany v. eClinicalWorks, Complaint-In-Intervention, https://www.justice.gov/opa/press-release/file/970346/download; *see* Press Release, Department of Justice, Electronic Health Records Vendor to Pay $155 Million to Settle False Claims Act Allegations (May 31, 2017), https://www.justice.gov/opa/pr/electronic-health-records-vendor-pay-155-million-settle-false-claims-act-allegations.

to tailor the patient experience and optimize patient care outcomes.

2. **Optimizing big data analytics.** At first blush, health IoT is about creating real-time data—the invaluable currency necessary to inform change and drive action by both the clinician and the patient-consumer. However, while foundationally necessary, data on its own is insufficient to effectively maximize the power of connected care. In order for clinicians to effectively use the data at their disposal to make better-informed decisions, massive amounts of raw data from connected health devices must be turned into actionable information. As individuals continue to generate more data, the need for faster and more reliable data processing and analytical capabilities will only increase. The transition from cloud computing to edge computing[69] is one example, with edge computing created as a new data processing methodology to reduce the latency and lag times caused by

69. A replacement for cloud computing, "edge computing" or "edge analytics" is a technology that enables connected devices to process data created at the "edge," which is either within or much closer to the connected device itself (where the data is created), rather than in the separate cloud computing repository. "What Is Edge Computing?," CB INSIGHTS (Aug. 8, 2018), *available at* https://www.cbinsights.com/research/what-is-edge-computing/; *see* Deepak Dutt, "The AI And ML Arms Race: Can Edge Analytics Help?," FORBES (Aug. 20, 2018, 9:00 AM), https://www.forbes.com/sites/forbestechcouncil/2018/08/20/the-ai-and-ml-arms-race-can-edge-analytics-help/?source=bloomberg#20cb352fbb29 ("Edge analytics is the *collection, processing and analysis of data at the edge of a network either at or close to a sensor, a network switch or some other connected device. . . .* Edge analytics greatly reduces the latency of data analytics and critical decision making and lowers bandwidth, which is particularly beneficial in remote locations and real-time applications. Edge analytics also scales an organization's processing and analytics capabilities by decentralizing to the sites where the data is actually collected."). At a technical level, it has been described as a "mesh network of micro data centers that process or store critical data locally and push all received data to a central data center or cloud storage repository, in a footprint of less than 100 square feet." *Id.* The global edge computing market is estimated to reach $6.72 billion by 2022. *Id.*

the need to transfer data back and forth between the cloud. The industry will also continue to see more sophisticated data processing (perhaps in the form of AI and advanced machine learning) that can filter and differentiate the relevant from the irrelevant data, and provide clinical decision support that can sometimes mean the difference between life and death.

3. **Combining emerging technologies in health care.** The Fourth (Digital) Industrial Revolution and the demands of the marketplace will continue to drive the creation of innovative new technologies, as well as the combination of emerging technologies in health care, to optimize patient care and outcomes. These "stackable blocks" will permeate the health care industry, from leveraging blockchain to address privacy, security, and data integrity concerns; to integrating AI, cloud, and edge computing for data processing and analysis; to incorporating 3-D printing to streamline the manufacture of medical devices (and perhaps even 3-D printing of human tissue) to deliver precision medicine-based capabilities at the point of care.
4. **Balancing population health versus precision medicine.** With the increased proliferation of connected health data, the dual (and sometimes competing) goals of harnessing the power of individualized precision medicine while also managing population health will continue to play out in the health care industry. With the advent of increasingly sophisticated data processing mechanisms (like AI and edge computing), increases in the sheer volume of data analysis will allow clinicians, researchers, and even policy makers to glean pattern-based insights and make treatment, research, and overarching policy decisions accordingly. Making seismic—or even smaller-scale—shifts in treatment practice and health care policy will, however, require

repeated verification of the sources and reliability of the data underpinning such decisions, as well as any potential biases inherent in algorithmic-based processing.

5. **Partnerships and payment reform.** The seismic shift in health care delivery will not only impact the flow of data but also the fluidity between traditional and nontraditional industry players as well. As the industry breaks down the walls around data siloes, it must also reexamine the traditional (and previously more rigid) dividing lines between *who* delivers what aspect of the health care experience and *how* that care is delivered. Catalyzed by the transition to value-based care, payment incentives now exist that focus on the clinician's ability to render the most effective health care experience possible to patients—measured in health outcomes, not just office visits. These realigned incentives have spawned new partnerships and new entrants in the health care marketplace: Providers are becoming health plans; accountable care organizations (ACOs) have brought together doctors, hospitals, and other health care providers as coordinated care "teams" to deliver the most effective care possible to patients; and traditionally consumer-driven enterprises like technology companies are diving head first into the deep end of the health care pool. However, payment reform is still slow to reimburse for newer connected health technologies like PGHD—or the accompanying cost of big data analytics to make that data actionable. The federal government is slowly but surely creating reimbursement incentives for remote patient monitoring, virtual care, chronic care management, and behavioral health integration. The changes in payment will impact the value of health IoT to support population health and individual health care services.

Chapter 3

Drones

Taking the IoT into the Air

Matthew Henshon

I. Introduction

Drones, or UAVs (Unmanned Aerial Vehicles), have—and will continue to play—a unique role in the Internet of Things (IoT) ecosystem. While other devices (such as, for example, connected home thermostats) are now being retrofitted to become part of the IoT, the modern drone has been developed in an IoT environment; there are no *un*-connected drones, at least for all practical purposes. To paraphrase Chris Anderson, president of drone-maker 3D Robotics, the modern consumer drone is a smartphone with propellers.[1]

This chapter explores the role of drones as part of the IoT environment. The chapter begins with a brief overview of the history of drones, which originally were developed for military purposes, and then discusses the modern consumer era with the explosion of drone technology. The chapter then reviews the current state of UAV regulation in the United States, which is primarily under the purview of the Federal Aviation Administration (FAA). Finally, the chapter explores the unique elements of privacy involving airborne

1. Chris Anderson, Interdrone 2016 Keynote Address (Sept. 8, 2016), https://www.youtube.com/watch?v=t7qskPaX6Fc, beginning at 0:50.

technology, and how these privacy issues relate to the future of drones and the IoT.

II. Development of Drones

A. Early Military "Drones"

Drones have been contemplated since the earliest days of aviation. Over the century of manned flight, advances in unmanned aircraft have mirrored those of the more conventional manned type, but, over the past decade, UAVs have come into the popular consciousness. But drones—and their connectedness to the Internet—have their roots in the military.[2]

Military uses of unmanned aircraft presaged the use of manned flight. In the third century, Chinese general Zhuge Liang had "paper balloons fitted with oil-burning lamps to lift the balloons up in the air and fly over the enemy at night to frighten them."[3] In 1849, Austria attempted to bombard the city of Venice by "launch[ing] over 200 pilotless balloons carrying bombs controlled by timing fuses."[4] A hundred years later, Nazi Germany developed the V-1 rocket—the world's first cruise missile—as a way of attempting to bomb the Allies (and particularly, England) to the negotiating table. While an improvement from the Austrian balloons, which were subject to the vagaries of the wind, the V-1s were also "dumb" in the sense that there was no ability to control the flight once the rocket was launched. Nevertheless, the V-1s were murderously effective: From June 1944 to March 1945, the Germans launched over 9,000 V-1s, of which 5,208 landed, killing a total of 5,476 people.[5]

---

2. Dave Sloggett, Drone Warfare: The Development of Unmanned Aerial Conflict vi–vii (2014).

3. Jonathan B. Rupprecht & Donna A. Dulo, *A Brief History of Unmanned Aircraft*, *in* Unmanned Aircraft in the National Airspace 12 (Donna A. Dulo ed., 2015).

4. Sloggett, *supra* note 2, at 8.

5. *Id.* at 25.

B. Modern Military Drones

Drone technology made huge leaps in the late 1970s and early 1980s, thanks to the Israeli military looking to maintain aerial superiority over its (often unfriendly) neighbors. By the 1980s, the US began seriously investing in UAV design, thanks to an Israeli immigrant, in part because of the "War on Drugs" in South America, which often utilized airborne surveillance and interdiction.

But it was the Predator drone—which came of age technologically at the same time the United States suffered the 9/11 attacks and began the "War on Terror"—that changed public perception of drones. The Predator, the production of which had begun in the 1990s, became part of a new capability for the U.S. military—not just replacing manned aircraft, but with its ability to stay aloft for up to 40 hours consecutively, performing functions that manned aircraft simply couldn't do.[6] And as important—and revolutionary in the history of warfare—the drone operator did not have to be "in theater," risking his or her own life to perform the functions of surveillance or attack.

After the attacks of 9/11, drones—especially the Predator—became a mainstay of the U.S. response in the Af-Pak region. Dependable, durable, and (with an Internet connection) able to be piloted half-a-world away,[7] military drones like the Predator[8]

---

6. Daniel Terdiman, *The History of the Predator, the Drone That Changed the World*, CNET.COM (Sept. 20, 2014), https://www.cnet.com/news/the-history-of-the-predator-the-drone-that-changed-the-world-q-a/.

7. The fact that UAV military pilots can take part in a mission without ever having been in the geographic area (the "theater of war") raises unprecedented questions about the nature of military training, cohesiveness, and professionalism. *See, e.g.*, P.W. SINGER, WIRED FOR WAR: THE ROBOTICS REVOLUTION AND CONFLICT IN THE 21ST CENTURY 362–72 (2009). For a take on how filmmakers have viewed these questions, see Susan L. Carruthers, *Detached Retina: The New Cinema of Drone Warfare*, 41(4) CINÉASTE 21 (Fall 2016), https://www.jstor.org/stable/26356350 ("New technologies that facilitate long-range communication, surveillance, and lethal destruction seem to collapse physical distance while exaggerating psychological detachment. Boundaries between here and there, home and front, civilian and soldier have become blurred.").

8. Now generally supplanted by the superior MQ-9 Reaper.

became a breakthrough technology, beginning with the first flight that fired missiles on October 7, 2001.[9] Indeed, it was an unarmed Lockheed Martin RQ 170 drone that enabled the Obama Situation Room to watch the raid on Osama bin Laden's compound in Abbottabad in May 2011.[10] And although the United States is currently a leader in military drone technology, the proliferation of UAVs (while beyond the scope of this chapter) will undoubtedly bring challenges to U.S. policy makers;[11] currently, more than "30 nations have or are developing armed drones, and at least 90 nations, as well as some non-state actors, possess unarmed drones."[12]

C. Expansion of the Civilian Market

As the military use of drones expanded, interest was piqued by civilians as well. Foreign manufacturers were early adopters of drone technology, and drone use overseas has led that in the United States over the past decade. However, U.S. drone builders had one advantage: The investment in drone technology coincided with the rise of smartphones. Speaking at an industry conference in 2016,

---

9. Richard Whittle, *The Man Who Invented the Predator*, Air & Space (April 2013), https://www.airspacemag.com/flight-today/the-man-who-invented-the-predator-3970502/?page=1.

10. Nicholas Schmidle, *Getting Bin Laden*, The New Yorker (Aug. 8, 2011), https://www.newyorker.com/magazine/2011/08/08/getting-bin-laden.

11. *See* James Igoe Walsh & Marcus Schulzke, *The Ethics Of Drone Strikes: Does Reducing the Cost of Conflict Encourage War?* Strategic Studies Institute, US Army War College (Sept. 1, 2015); but UAV and related technologies may also enhance the peacekeeping abilities of organizations such as the United Nations. *See* A. Walter Dorn, *Smart Peacekeeping: Toward Tech-Enabled UN Operations*, International Peace Institute (July 1, 2016), https://www.jstor.org/stable/resrep09634.

12. Elisa Catalano Ewers et al., *Drone Proliferation: Policy Choices for the Trump Administration*, Center for a New American Security 4 (June 1, 2017), http://www.jstor.org/stable/resrep06354.3. Questions about enhanced export controls over UAV/UAS technology are also relevant here. *See* Export Controls Working Group, *UAV Export Controls and Regulatory Challenges*, Stimson (Sept. 1, 2015), https://www.jstor.org/stable/resrep10873.

Chris Anderson talked about leaving the editorship of *Wired* magazine to start 3D Robotics:

> Our drones, are—yes, they are flying robots—but they are also sensors in the sky. . . . This is the eyes and the ears of the Internet. And increasingly, we are going to be using the Internet as a brain, as well. This notion of a connected device is unique to what we do here. I had the fortune of getting into this business in 2007, the year the iPhone was released, and so as a result everything we did was oriented around smart phone architectures, and inherited everything smart phones have—connectivity, sensors, an incredible, Moores-Law-pace of processing. But by doing that, we inherited the architecture of the cloud as well—smart phones are a connected device. The old world—the aerospace world—thought of [airborne] vehicles as being a stand-alone category, with their own intelligence. But we thought of drones as being smart phones with propellers. And as a result, we found ourselves aligned with a generation long movement to start to combine the core and the edge—the sensors and the cloud—to extend the internet into the physical world and do something that no single device could do on its own.[13]

Currently, all drones and UAS (Unmanned Aerial Systems)[14]—military and civilian—require human control. However, as individual drones become "smart" and can pilot themselves with less-and-less human oversight, pervasive UAVs will give rise to an always-connected aerial presence—or the world of IoT. Likewise, as drones become more connected to the cloud—through better

13. Anderson, *supra* note 1, beginning at 0:50.

14. UAS includes both the aircraft (drone) and the information technology that connects it to the ground.

data connections and more robust capabilities, the flying drone will become a true IoT device.

An important factor to understanding drones is to understand the difference between piloted aircraft and UAVs. As Donna Dulo wrote in 2014, "[T]here is a spectrum of autonomy that lies between total pilot command and total autonomous control. . . . Pilot control . . . means that the operator is in full control of all three axes of the aircraft: the roll axis, the pitch axis, and the yaw axis."[15] But for drones, the pilot does not have total control of the three axes. The pilot may direct the drone in a general sense, but the machine is making its own decisions about aeronautics and keeping itself level. Likewise, from a safety standpoint, the UAV needs to have a plan in case communication with the pilot is lost[16]—whether by means of terrain, weather, or other similar technological glitches. In these instances of "involuntary autonomy," different drones[17] will respond differently, including hovering or attempting to return to base.[18]

The ability of drones to monitor and inspect (or to help humans monitor and inspect) far-flung geographic locales is one of their great selling points. In fields like medicine (delivery of medical

15. Donna A. Dulo & Cameron R. Cloar, *Considerations of a Legal Framework, in* UNMANNED AIRCRAFT IN THE NATIONAL AIRSPACE 126–27 (Donna A. Dulo ed., 2015).

16. A so-called "lost link . . . when the communications of the ground station are lost with the UAV, and the aircraft is forced to fly fully autonomously."

Id. at 130. Presumably, advances in communication technology, such as the coming upgrade to 5G (i.e., 5th Generation) in mobile networks, will make the lost-link problem less pervasive over time.

17. This known-risk—namely that the drone can drop its link to its pilot—has implications for where data that the drone is gathering is stored; currently, drones can store data in one of three places: on-board, with the pilot, or directly uploaded to the cloud. Choices can be made between data at the pilot and data in the cloud, but the subroutines or algorithms that dictate what the drone does in case of lost-link *must* be stored on-board the UAV.

18. Dulo & Cloar, *supra* note 15, at 130.

tests and/or vaccines to remote areas),[19] agriculture (delivery of pesticides[20] with much more accuracy than a plane),[21] or climate change and related wildlife research ("[l]ight-aircraft crashes are a major killer of wildlife biologists and a danger to pilots flying in remote areas, such as the Arctic"[22]), UAS use will be easier, cheaper, and safer than the current solutions. And, as Amazon has

---

19. Oriol Lopez, Eric Boivin & Eric Pujo, *UAV Network for Tb Diagnostics Delivery in Gulf Province, Papua New Guinea, in* HUMANITARIAN TECHNOLOGY SURVEY (Alistair D. B. Cook & Ennio V. Picucci eds., May 1, 2017), https://www.jstor.org/stable/resrep05932.6.

20. Alison Gillespie, *FAA Gives Approval to Pesticide-Spraying Drone*, 13(5) FRONTIERS IN ECOLOGY & ENV'T 236 (June 2015), https://www.jstor.org/stable/24891174.

21. Indeed, delivery of pesticides will just be scratching the surface of an IoT-enabled drone. *See Wendy Levy, Precision Agriculture: A Smart Farming Approach*, 185 SPORE 5–6 (June–Aug. 2017), https://www.jstor.org/stable/44242663:

> Ideally, agronomists and researchers want drones to collect data several times in a season to ensure they make well-informed decisions. Reliable data will comprise a wide range of indicators, including biomass, chlorophyll rate, leaf area index, emergence rate, water stress, missing plants, height or flowering. Drones also look at normalised difference vegetation index, which is a mapping method that identifies whether or not an area contains live green vegetation. Drone surveillance can also provide early warning of crop stress and crop health issues, providing images that enable precise and reliable statistics, a boon for evaluating field trials.

Agriculture is expected to be an early adopter of smart connected UAVs because almost "half the inputs in farming (fluids, pesticides, fungicides, and herbicides) [are] wasted since more was applied than needed or they [are] applied to the wrong places." Toby Stuart & Chris Anderson, *3D Robotics: Disrupting the Drone Market*, 57(2) CALIFORNIA MANAGEMENT REVIEW 107 (Winter 2015).

22. Victor V. Klemas, *Coastal and Environmental Remote Sensing from Unmanned Aerial Vehicles: An Overview*, 31(5) J. COASTAL RESEARCH 1262 (Sept. 2015), https://www.jstor.org/stable/43556484. Likewise, UAVs were used in Japan to assess damage at the Fukushima Daiichi nuclear power plant after the major earthquake in 2011. Naser Hossein Motlagh, Miloud Bagaa & Tarik Taleb, *UAV-Based IoT Platform: A Crowd Surveillance Use Case*, IEEE COMMUNICATIONS MANAGER 128 (Feb. 2017).

promised, delivery of consumer goods could also be a likely point-of-entry for UAS.[23]

The field that has most quickly embraced drone use, however, may be entertainment. With the cost of drones dropping, Hollywood has used them in increasing numbers to get unique shots that previously were unattainable—or prohibitively expensive.[24] Typically, drone-filmed scenes are aerial shots that track action, such as the opening scene in *Skyfall* (James Bond riding a motorcycle across the rooftop of the Grand Bazaar in Istanbul)[25] or Martin Scorsese's *The Wolf of Wall Street* (beach-house pool-party scene).[26] Indeed, when the FAA began issuing so-called Section-333-Exemptions after the passage of the FAA Modernization and Reform Act of 2012, six of the first exemptions issued were to film companies for use of drones on closed sets.[27]

23. Although some have posited that Amazon (and others) will add additional sensing capabilities to its drones for additional sources of revenue. See Motlagh, Bagaa & Taleb, *supra* note 22, at 129 ("While UAVs are used for their original tasks (e.g., parcel delivery by Amazon, power line monitoring by SharperShape), they can be simultaneously applied for offering numerous value added services (VASs), particularly in the Internet of Things (IoT) when they are equipped with remotely controllable IoT devices. . . . Through this platform, IoT data can be collected via remotely controllable IoT devices mounted on UAVs whenever triggered.").

24. Steven Flynn, "Drones in Movies: 7 Hollywood Movies Filmed with Drones," Feb. 18, 2016, https://skytango.com/drones-in-movies-7-hollywood-movies-filmed-with-drones/.

25. *Skyfall* (Eon Productions 2012). See video located at https://youtu.be/tHRLX8jRjq8 at 1:09 to 1:35. *See also* Susan L. Carruthers, *Detached Retina: The New Cinema of Drone Warfare*, 41(4) CINÉASTE 20 (Fall 2016).

26. *The Wolf of Wall Street* (Red Granite Pictures 2013). See video located at https://youtu.be/gLKsU0NxHDs at 0:01-0:04.

27. Reuters, *FAA Grants Six Movie, TV Companies Permission to Use Drones for Filming*, N.Y. DAILY NEWS (Sept. 25, 2014, 8:41 PM), http://www.nydailynews.com/news/politics/faa-grants-movie-tv-companies-permission-drones-article-1.1953272.

As drones become more and more sophisticated, the technology may likely merge with other pieces of the IoT.[28] For instance, 3D Robotics CEO Anderson said:

> [I]t's not about the drone anymore. It's about the data. How do we analyze it? How do we analyze it faster? . . . We are in the world of Big Data, and we have one of the biggest data sets around, and some of the biggest unsolved problems. . . . Drones are kind of a solved problem, by and large. What's not a solved problem is making them useful, going from toy to tool. . . . This is where we are starting to see the merger with cars . . . we are in the same business—we are solving the same problems, and often with the same companies [e.g., Google, Amazon, Microsoft]. . . . What's this really about is this "map"—there's going to be a collective map of the world, and it's going to be like the maps the old car companies had, with like streets, and latitude and longitude. It's 'N'-dimensional.[29] . . . [And] [t]his map will allow our drones go out into the world without having to rely entirely on its senses.[30]

One key moment will come when drones become fully autonomous. (Currently, as we shall see in Section III, all drones must be piloted by a human.) While humans may resist the desire to give up control of flying machines to the machines themselves, there is no question which will ultimately win out. As one author imagined in a military setting, "suppose two drones fight each other in the air. One drone cannot open fire without first receiving the go-ahead

28. For more on this concept, see Colin Snow, *Why Drones Are the Future of the Internet of Things*, sUAS News (Dec. 1, 2014), https://www.suasnews.com/2014/12/why-drones-are-the-future-of-the-internet-of-things/.

29. Anderson, *supra* note 1, beginning at 10:40.

30. *Id.*, beginning at 18:25.

from a human operator in some distant bunker. The other is fully autonomous. Which drone do you think will prevail?"[31]

Finally, while this chapter has discussed the role(s) that drones can play in warfare, other observers have noted that drones—mounted with cameras and other IoT sensors—can have important impacts on civil society, including popular and peaceful protests against repressive governments. Focusing just on cameras, an observer wrote:

> The third technological innovation, and arguably the most disruptive, is the fundamental break between the camera and the street level. Photography has had a symbiotic connection with the street for more than a century, as far back as Eugène Atget's street photography in Paris in the 1890s and Jacob Riis's documentary photography in New York at the same time. . . . The journalist's camera is positioned at eye level. . . . UAVs relocate the boundary between what is public and what is private. . . . [Likewise], [w]ork on the Internet of Things and Internet privacy suggests that much of what happens in seemingly private spaces is not actually private.[32]

The sensors on a drone can be used for other purposes, like tracking the movements of a herd of wild elephants that have been electronically tagged to help with conservation; in Kenya, the government has been expanding the UAV program at its national parks

31. Yuval Noah Harari, Homo Deus: A Brief History of Tomorrow 312 (2017).

32. Austin Choi-Fitzpatrick, *Drones for Good: Technological Innovations, Social Movements, and the State*, 68(1) J. Int'l Affairs 20–21 (2014), http://www.jstor.org/stable/24461704. Expansive use of drones will also need to be interpreted with regard to the First Amendment. *See* Joseph J. Vacek, *Citizen Use of Small Drones for Media Purposes under the FAA's Current and Forthcoming Regulations*, 5(2) J. Int'l Media & Entm't L., 255–56 (2014–2015).

"after a pilot program found that their presence reduced poaching by up to 96 percent."[33]

III. The Current State of UAV Regulation

A. FAA Modernization and Reform Act of 2012

While the future of autonomous drones is undoubtedly exciting, in the here-and-now, a large body of rules governs current drone flight. The "modern" era of civil UAVs (as opposed to public (i.e., governmental) UAV operators[34]) commenced with the passage of the FAA Modernization and Reform Act of 2012, signed into law on February 14, 2012 (the 2012 FAA Act).[35] In passing the bill, Congress put the FAA on a timetable to find a way introduce UAVs into the "National Airspace."[36] The FAA has been tasked with effecting this integration while maintaining its fundamental task of keeping the national airspace (NAS) safe.[37]

Within 270 days after enactment of the 2012 FAA Act, a "comprehensive plan" was to be finalized among all the key players in the airspace industry "to safely accelerate the integration of civil unmanned aircraft systems into the national airspace system."[38]

33. *Id.*

34. Civil aircraft are "aircraft other than public aircraft." (49 U.S.C. § 40102(a)(16)) Public aircraft are those owned and operated by the federal government or any state government (including the District of Columbia and US territories) (49 U.S.C. § 40102).

35. FAA Modernization and Reform Act of 2012, §§ 331–336, codified at 49 U.S.C. § 40101, *et seq.*

36. While states have some co-current jurisdiction, generally the airspace above 400 feet is under federal—and hence FAA—control on preemption grounds.

37. 14 C.F.R. § 91.13(a) ("No person may operate an aircraft in a careless or reckless manner so as to endanger the life or property of another.").

38. FAA Modernization and Reform Act of 2012, § 332(a)(1). The key players charged by Congress with development of the plan were "the Secretary of Transportation, in consultation with representatives of the aviation industry, Federal agencies that employ unmanned aircraft systems technology in the national airspace system, and the unmanned aircraft systems industry." *Id.*

The plan itself had a deadline to allow UAVs into the NAS no later than September 30, 2015.[39] Likewise, Congress instilled other short-term deadlines within the various provisions of the bill, including the creation of test ranges for UAVs,[40] expanding the use of UAVs in remote Arctic locations,[41] and safety assessments of then-existing UAS.[42] Finally, recognizing that the FAA had previously established rules in the early 1980s[43] to enable model aircraft hobbyists to navigate radio frequency (RF)-controlled planes in the NAS, Congress added a specific provision (section 336) to limit the FAA rule-making authority with respect to model aircraft—which would include many UAVs then being sold to hobbyists.[44] Taken as a whole, however, the 2012 FAA Act pushed the FAA to rapidly allow UAVs—which were gaining acceptance and market-share worldwide—into the NAS of the United States.

While not adhering strictly to all of the deadlines contained within the 2012 FAA Act, the FAA did, however, engage in an expedited rule-writing and finalizing process. The FAA essentially worked from the previously published rules for model aircraft and essentially updated them for drone flyers, provided that they were for recreational use only.

As the FAA began developing regulations for UAVs in the wake of the passage of the 2012 FAA Act, a distinction developed that had its historical roots in the model aircraft hobby; the FAA made a huge distinction between "commercial" and "recreational"

39. *Id.* § 332(a)(3).

40. *Id.* § 332(c).

41. *Id.* § 332(d).

42. *Id.* § 333.

43. FAA, Advisory Circular (AC 91-57, June 9, 1981), www.faa.gov/documentlibrary/media/advisory_circular/91-57.pdf.

44. FAA Modernization and Reform Act of 2012, § 336.

usages of drones, banning commercial usage of drones in 2007.[45] "Commercial" usage meant that the drone was operated by a "commercial operator":

> a person who, for compensation or hire, engages in the carriage by aircraft in air commerce of persons or property. . . . Where it is doubtful that an operation is for "compensation or hire," the test applied is whether the carriage by air is merely incidental to the person's other business or is, in itself, a major enterprise for profit.[46]

Prior to the passage of the 2012 FAA Act, commercial use of drones was essentially prohibited by the FAA in 2007.

During the period after the passage of the 2012 FAA Act until 2016, the FAA operated on a dual course. Behind the scenes, the FAA was writing draft and ultimately final regulations that would eventually permit commercial flights of drones.[47] But, publicly, the FAA took incremental steps to speed up the integration of UAVs into the NAS. The FAA originally relied on model aircraft rules from the 1980s for guidance to recreational UAV operators.[48] Building on the small aircraft exception in the 2012 FAA Act (section

---

45. Whether the FAA had the authority (at the time) to prohibit such commercial use became the focus of a highly publicized case, Huerta v. Pirker. Although Pirker initially prevailed at the administrative law judge level, the full National Transportation Safety Board (NTSB) ultimately ruled unanimously that the FAA had the proper authority for the 2007 ban. Huerta v. Pirker, NTSB Order No. EA-5730 (Nov. 18, 2014). As a practical matter, the issue was made moot by the 2012 FAA Act and the subsequent issuance of the Part 107 regulations.

46. 14 C.F.R. § 1.1. (1962).

47. "The Federal Aviation Regulations (FARs) are set forth in parts 1 through 199 of title 14 of the Code of Federal Regulations (CFR). The regulations provide the requirements for registration [14 C.F.R. §§ 45.1–49.63], airworthiness certification [14 C.F.R. §§ 21.1–43.17], licensing and certification of pilots and personnel [14 C.F.R. §§ 61.1–67.415]. . . among many others." Cameron R. Cloar, *Unmanned Aircraft in the National Airspace*, *in* UNMANNED AIRCRAFT IN THE NATIONAL AIRSPACE 92 (Donna A. Dulo, ed., 2015).

48. FAA, Advisory Circular, *supra* note 43.

336), the FAA published a revision to the 1981 document covering both model aircraft and UAVs.[49]

B. Section 333 and COAs

Also during the 2012–2016 period, the FAA accepted applications for test ranges to be used for the five-year period after enactment of the 2012 FAA Act.[50] Although the act required that the FAA establish these test ranges "[n]ot later than 180 days after the date of enactment," the FAA did not publish its Screening Information Request (SIR)[51] until more than a year after the 2012 FAA Act was signed, and the sites—located in Alaska, New York, North Dakota, Nevada, New Mexico, Texas,[52] and Virginia[53]—were announced in late 2013. More important, the sites offer a chance to test UAS, and

49. FAA, Advisory Circular (AC No. 91-57A, Jan. 11, 2016), https://www.faa.gov/documentLibrary/media/Advisory_Circular/AC_91-57A_Ch_1.pdf. Perhaps indicating the speed with which the bureaucracy was attempting to promulgate rules and regulations, the FAA apparently inadvertently cancelled the 1981 Circular (AC 91-57) before issuing the revision (AC 91-57A). See https://www.faa.gov/regulations_policies/advisory_circulars/index.cfm/go/document.information/documentid/22425.

50. FAA Modernization and Reform Act of 2012, § 332(c).

51. Many other federal agencies would consider a SIR to be a Request for Proposal (RFP). FAA, *Special Notice: Unmanned Aircraft Systems Test Site Selection (UASTSS)*, Solicitation/Contract #DTFACT-13-R-00002 (Feb. 14, 2013), https://faaco.faa.gov/index.cfm/announcement/view/13143.

52. For a detailed look at the Texas site (located at the Texas A&M campus in Corpus Christi) and some of the people working there, see Lango Deen, Freedom to Drone: Why Unmanned Aircraft Systems Are the Future, 30(2) Hispanic Engineer & Information Technology, 12–16 (Fall 2015), https://www.jstor.org/stable/43755448.

53. FAA, *Contact FAA Test Sites*, https://www.faa.gov/uas/research/test_sites/contacts/. While § 332(c) authorized six sites, the seventh (apparently New Mexico) was eventually added. See https://www.faa.gov/uas/research/reports/media/UAS-Test-Site-Data-Collection-and-Analysis.pdf. Section 332(c)(1) also required the FAA to "establish a program to integrate unmanned aircraft systems into the national airspace system at 6 test ranges." This program was supposed to be terminated five years after the date of enactment of the act, or 2017, but it appears to be ongoing.

the FAA[54] was to submit a report summarizing, among other items, "an assessment of the progress being made in establishing special use airspace to fill the need of the [DOD] . . . to develop detection techniques . . . [and] to validate the sense and avoid capability and operation of unmanned aircraft systems."[55]

In 2013, the FAA issued the NAS Roadmap First Edition, which included the FAA's goals for an important element of the application of IoT to drones: the development of Airborne Sense and Avoid (ABSAA) systems for individual airborne vehicles.[56] The Roadmap laid on a plan for certification of ABSAA without the requirement of visual observer in incremental steps over the period beginning in 2014 and continuing through 2020. But like many of the other timelines delineated in the 2012 FAA Act, it is not clear whether the FAA will meet its goals by the (self-imposed) target of 2020.

Section 333 of the 2012 FAA Act allowed certain UAV commercial operators to fly before the issuance of the regulations.[57] As previously mentioned, the first Section 333 exemptions were issued in September 2014 to film and video production companies.[58] While many of these Section 333 exemptions have expired (they are usually issued for two-year periods), it is likely that some remain operational.[59]

In the immediate wake of the 2012 FAA Act, commercial drone operations were permitted by the FAA under a "certificate of authorization" (COA) process, which was also authorized by the

54. Working with the Department of Defense.

55. FAA Modernization and Reform Act of 2012, § 332(c)(5).

56. FAA, *Integration of Civil Unmanned Aircraft Systems (UAS) in the National Airspace System (NAS) Roadmap* (First Edition—2013), at 54–56, https://www.faa.gov/uas/media/uas_roadmap_2013.pdf.

57. Now known as part 107 (see subsection C in this chapter).

58. Timothy M. Ravich, Commercial Drone Law 126, 128 (2017).

59. FAA, *Section 333 vs. Part 107: What Works for You?* (Aug. 29, 2016), https://www.faa.gov/news/updates/?newsId=86285.

act.[60] "A COA, according to the FAA, 'is an authorization issued by the Air Traffic Organization to a public operator for a specific UA activity.' Obtaining a COA follows an application process . . . [and if issued] authorizes an operator to use defined airspace and includes special provisions unique to the proposed operation."[61] COAs are one-off authorizations for specific flight plans; as no commercial flights were authorized as of the time of the 2012 FAA Act, essentially each individual commercial drone flight had to be authorized in the 2013–2016 period.

C. Part 107 Regulations

The environment for commercial drone operators changed significantly with the FAA's release of the Small UAS Rule (Part 107)[62] in June 2016, which became effective on August 29, 2016. Part 107 established rules for commercial UAV flights to occur without FAA approval in each case.[63] The rule created a process for obtaining a Remote Pilot Certificate, which would allow qualified operators to fly small UAVs (under 55 lbs/25 kg).[64] COAs would subsequently be required for flights that involved waivers from the standard operating procedures, including:

Flying at night	14 C.F.R. § 107.29
Flying directly over a person or people	14 C.F.R. § 107.39
Flying from a moving vehicle or aircraft, not in a sparsely populated area	14 C.F.R. § 107.25
Flying multiple aircraft with only one pilot	14 C.F.R. § 107.35

60. FAA Modernization and Reform Act of 2012, § 334(a).

61. Ravich, *supra* note 58, at 111–12.

62. Small UAS Rule, 14 C.F.R. pt. 107 (2016).

63. Prior to enactment of part 107 as mentioned previously, civil operators needed to obtain a COA (experimental airworthiness certificate) for their individual UAV to fly in the NAS; the COA system remains in place (post-Part 107) for drones weighing more than 55 pounds. Ravich, *supra* note 58, at 121.

64. Small UAS Rule, 14 C.F.R. § 107.53–.79 (2016).

Flying beyond the pilot's visual line-of-sight	14 C.F.R. § 107.31
Flying above 400 feet	14 C.F.R. § 107.51B
Flying near airports/in controlled airspace	14 C.F.R. § 107.41

In addition, the FAA may from time to time issue Temporary Flight Restrictions (TFRs) for instances such as presidential visits,[65] disaster areas,[66] or sports events such as the Super Bowl, Major League Baseball All-Star Game, or even the Sandia Classic Hang Gliding Competition.[67]

Issuance of the Part 107 regulations have gone a long way toward "normalizing" small drone flights for commercial purposes. Start-up drone flight companies now have a set of rules and regulations that allows them to operate without having to obtain one-off COAs. But the enabling of the 2012 FAA Act has not been without some hiccups. For instance, anticipating a large number of "toy" drones being bought for the 2015 holiday season, the FAA rolled out a drone registration program. The program, although inexpensive (three-year registration for $5) was ultimately challenged and the FAA's authority to demand such registration was ultimately rescinded by the D.C. Circuit.[68] However, shortly after the decision, Congress passed an overriding provision as part of a Defense Re-authorization bill, and the registration requirement is currently valid law.[69] The FAA recently reported that registration of unmanned aircraft has recently exceeded that of manned aircraft (325,000 vs. 320,000).[70]

65. *Id.* § 91.141.

66. *Id.* § 91.137.

67. Ravich, *supra* note 58, at 65.

68. Taylor v. Huerta, No. 15-1495 (D.C. Cir. May 19, 2017).

69. National Defense Authorization Act for Fiscal Year 2018, Pub L. No. 115-91, § 1092(d) (2017).

70. Thomas K. Grose, *Flight Risk*, 25(8) ASEE Prism 31 (Summer 2016), https://www.jstor.org/stable/43774661.

There is also a period of integration that will occur over the next few years with regard to pilots operating in the immediate wake of passage of the 2012 FAA Act; when previously issued, "Section 333 exemptions come up for renewal, the FAA will consider whether renewal is necessary for those exemptions whose operations are within the operational scope of Part 107. . . . If a Section 333 exemption is within [the scope of 107] . . . there may be no need for the FAA to renew an exemption under Section 333."[71] However, section 333 "only applies to the UAV operator itself (which, in some cases, could be the manufacturer itself). Additionally, Section 333 does not replace the COA process, and the Section 333 petitioners must also apply for and obtain a COA for any civil operations allowed under Section 333."[72]

In July of 2016, Congress passed the FAA Extension, Safety, and Security Act of 2016 (2016 FAA Act), which further encouraged unmanned aircraft to be integrated into the NAS. The 2016 FAA Act includes an entire section dealing with UAS safety, including authorizing the FAA administrator to create safety standards for operation of UAS,[73] creating a plan to manage unmanned systems traffic (together with NASA),[74] and research the effects of collisions between UAS and conventional airplanes,[75] among other items. With the 2016 FAA Act, Congress continues to press the

71. RAVICH, *supra* note 58, at 130.

72. Timothy M. Ravich, *Grounded in the Law*, *in* UNMANNED AIRCRAFT IN THE NATIONAL AIRSPACE 115 (Donna A. Dulo ed., 2015).

73. FAA Extension, Safety, and Security Act of 2016, Pub. L. No. 114-190, § 2203 (2016).

74. FAA Extension, Safety, and Security Act of 2016, Pub. L. No. 114-190, § 2208 (2016).

75. FAA Extension, Safety, and Security Act of 2016, Pub. L. No. 114-190, § 2212 (2016).

FAA into the rapid integration of drones into the airspace, despite the obvious safety[76] concerns and mission of the FAA.

D. Possible Future Regulation and the "IoT Drone"

As of this writing, the FAA regulations currently in place do not address the IoT element of drone usage specifically. But it is anticipated that forthcoming regulations will expand this regulatory framework, in part because of the expansion of both the drone and the IoT markets. Gartner Group calculates that three million drones were purchased by consumers and businesses in 2017, and the drone market will reach $11.2 billion by 2020.[77] The IoT market in general is currently expanding at a 20 percent annual rate, and will reach $267 billion by 2020, according to the Boston Consulting Group.[78]

UAVs will undoubtedly take a larger and larger piece of this expansion because of the unique capability of drones, as one observer noted:

> The marriage of IoT and drones eliminates the dependency on specific locations or specific devices for placing IoT sensors, as well as monitoring, managing, and collecting data from those sensors. This combination will deliver unprecedented levels of flexibility to capture and analyse data that

---

76. One interesting confluence of emerging technologies that the FAA will have to grapple with is the use of 3-D printing to build or modify a UAV. At the 2015 Dubai Airshow, Stratasys (3-D print company) teamed up with Aurora Flight Systems to unveil a UAV that had 80 percent of its parts fabricated by a 3-D printer. Thomas K. Grose, *Additive Manufacturing: PRINTED PLANE*, 25(4) ASEE PRISM 13 (Dec. 2015), https://www.jstor.org/stable/43827844.

77. Nick Ismail, *Ignore the Delivery Hype, IoT Will Fuel Explosive Drone Growth for Business Use*, INFORMATION AGE (Feb 20, 2018), https://www.information-age.com/iot-drone-growth-business-123470852/.

78. Louis Columbus, *Internet of Things Market To Reach $267B by 2020*, FORBES (Jan. 29, 2017), https://www.forbes.com/sites/louiscolumbus/2017/01/29/internet-of-things-market-to-reach-267b-by-2020/#2a0339eb609b.

otherwise would have been too expensive, too dangerous, or just too impractical to otherwise collect.[79]

The growth in these capabilities should allow expansion of data analytics in these areas—and likely uncover areas for additional measurement and data collection, creating a "virtuous circle" that should continue to drive the "IoT drone" market.[80] As an example, the small nation of South Korea has been at the forefront of using UAV technology as part of its reclamation of tidal areas for agricultural and other commercial purposes; as one study concluded, "the UAV provides superior functionality to survey large, difficult to access areas."[81] Sometimes, the data collection itself will create a market; prior to the drone era, Climate Corporation collected weather data via satellite and tried to sell the data with no luck. But when Climate analyzed the data and helped enhance a weather insurance product for farmers, it became a valuable company, eventually acquired by Monsanto for $1.1 billion in 2013.[82] Finally, like any other disruptive technology, the IoT drone will create winners and losers; speaking at an industry conference, the CEO of technology developer GEN5 Group noted that deploying "connected

79. Ismail, *supra* note 77. Upgrade in communications, such as the forthcoming 5G (i.e., 5th generation) mobile network, should accelerate this trend.

80. One unique problem that will need to be solved for true "IoT drones" is the continuous operation one. Because drones have no power supply (i.e., they are not tethered to a power source), there needs to be time for the drone to "rest" and essentially refuel. While longer battery lives will undoubtedly extend the operation period, they most likely require improvements in drone flight and landing to more effectively limit the drone's "downtime." *See, e.g.*, Hesseo Chae et al., *The IoT Based Automate [sic] Landing System of a Drone for Round-the-clock Surveillance Solution*, 2015 IEEE International Conference on Advanced Intelligent Mechatronics (AIM) (July 7–11, 2015; Busan, Korea), at 1575–80.

81. Jung Ok Kim & Jang Kang Lee, *UAV Application for Process Control of the Reclamation Project*, J. Coastal Research 313, Special Issue No. 79: The 2nd International Water Safety Symposium (Spring 2017), https://www.jstor.org/stable/44289529.

82. Stuart & Anderson, *supra* note 21.

smart drone[s]" in agricultural uses may result in "fields for growing crops . . . chang[ing] size and that today's supply chain of equipment could no longer be needed."[83]

An important milestone in the future regulation of drones will be the development of a fully robust "sense and avoid capability"[84] for unmanned aircraft systems, which—as was noted previously—is currently being studied by the FAA. Development of sense-and-avoid could also allow the FAA to move away from the current human-pilot-based system to a more autonomous drone, but the challenges are extensive:

> The limitation of payloads, especially in small UAVs, has hindered current collision avoidance technology to be integrated as the employed sensors must be lightweight, small in size and consume low power. The driving algorithm also needs to be computationally efficient and less complex as the size of main board memory is small and the processor has less speed with limited power supply.[85]

For manned aircraft, there are already communications systems like the Traffic Collision Avoidance System (TCAS) and Automatic Dependent Surveillance–Broadcast (ADS-B) technology; the latter is especially relevant because it allows ADS-B-equipped aircraft to exchange information such as altitude and velocity, but the system needs to be miniaturized to be installed on small UAVs.[86] But even if ADS-B were to be scaled down tomorrow, the system only works between cooperating aircraft—leaving out flying objects

83. Lawrence Garrett, *Internet of Things Could Enable Drones to Change the World*, American Institute of Aeronautics and Astronautics (June 9, 2017, 9:05 AM), https://aviation.aiaa.org/InternetOfThings/.

84. FAA Modernization and Reform Act of 2012, § 332(c)(5).

85. A. Zhahir et al., IOP Conference Series: Materials Science & Engineering 152 012035 (2016), http://iopscience.iop.org/article/10.1088/1757-899X/152/1/012035/pdf

86. *Id.*

such as birds as well as potentially malevolent objects such as a hypothetical drone flown by a terrorist.[87]

This last point highlights another large area of concern for "IoT drones"—namely, security.[88] While IoT security is covered elsewhere in this book, there are problems unique to drones that make them particularly vulnerable to hacking. First, most drones run on relatively unsophisticated wireless networks, which can be easily penetrated. This could mean seizing control of the drone itself, or using the drone as a backdoor into the (parent) company network.[89] Second, most of the data collected by the drone itself is unencrypted, which means it could be hacked as well.[90] Both of these vulnerabilities are perhaps a function of the recent emergence of the drone market; engineers have spent their time figuring out how to get the drone flying, rather than protecting it from hackers.[91] But like the sense-and-avoid systems, there is also a marginal cost—in weight or computing power or both—to adding robust security to

87. In a similar vein, at least one paper has attempted to calculate—in the context of police monitoring of a crowd for possible security threats—"how much impact the offloading of face recognition computation has on the energy consumption of UAVs and the overall processing time." Motlagh, Bagaa & Taleb, *supra* note 22, at 131. Needless to say, the "obtained results demonstrate clearly the benefits of computation offloading in saving energy and significantly improving system responsiveness in quickly detecting and recognizing suspicious persons in a crowd. Improvement in the performance becomes more noticeable for longer videos and also when the number of profiled persons is high." *Id.* at 133.

88. *See generally* Simon, Tobby & Global Commission on Internet Governance, *Cyber Security in a Volatile World*, at 93–104 (2017), http://www.jstor.org/stable/resrep05239.12.

89. Chad Mercer, *Drone Security Risks and How to Protect Against Them*, Security (Oct. 31, 2017), https://www.securitymagazine.com/articles/88462-drone-security-risks-and-how-to-protect-against-them.

90. *Id.*

91. "Hardening" a drone against hackers has been studied by the Defense Advanced Research Projects Agency (DARPA) through Its High Assurance Cyber Military Systems (HACMS). *See* Grose, *supra* note 70, at 33.

an object that is attempting to fight gravity for as long as its battery will allow it to.[92]

Finally, while the FAA has primary responsibility for airspace safety, other agencies are becoming involved. For instance, NASA has apparently "embarked on a wide-ranging research project, enlisting a large team of industrial and academic investigators to design a mostly autonomous, cloud-based UAS Traffic Management (UTM) system."[93] NASA anticipates finishing this project by 2019 and shortly thereafter presenting it to the FAA.

E. Underwater Drones

There is another whole family of drones that should be mentioned: underwater drones. As most[94] of these drones do not fly, they are generally outside the FAA's regulatory purview, yet as of this writing they appear ready to appear on the consumer and business markets. The technology for a submersible drone is obviously different than that of a flying drone, and while water is heavier than air, the advantages of water's buoyancy is somewhat mitigated by the problems of ensuring that water does not penetrate into the sophisticated electronics. And while the submersible drones will be undoubtedly popular among scuba divers,[95] fishermen, and boaters, the commercial and military IoT applications will also be extensive.

---

92. *See, e.g.*, Munch Chang & Tao Zhang, *Fog and IoT: An Overview of Research Opportunities*, 3(6) IEEE Internet of Things Journal 854, at 857 (Dec. 2016).

93. Grose, *supra* note 70, at 31.

94. With a few exceptions, like the prototype Loon Copter (www.looncopter.com), built by the Embedded Systems Research Laboratory at Oakland University (Michigan).

95. For example, the iBubble is intended to be a completely autonomous underwater drone, following (and videotaping, like a mobile GoPro camera) a scuba diver who wears a special wristband. The manufacturer is currently taking pre-orders at USD $3,299, which is significantly more expensive than typical consumer-orientated flying drones. *See* https://ibubble.camera/shop/.

IV. Privacy's Future Up in the Air: UAVs and Aerial Surveillance

Privacy is an underlying issue with many aspects of IoT, as is discussed in detail in Chapter 8. However, airborne observation or surveillance creates unique and unsettling problems, in part because of the unfamiliar "4th" dimension—in other words, the ability of UAVs to observe from afar, in ways that traditional barriers (fences, trees, walls, etc.) do not hide, creates a novel privacy issue. This heightened loss of privacy will be even more so as UAVs become integrated with IoT.

To think about privacy in general, review of Fourth Amendment jurisprudence can be informative. The Fourth Amendment reads in its entirety:

> The right of the people to be secure in their persons, houses, papers, and effects, against unreasonable searches and seizures, shall not be violated, and no warrants shall issue, but upon probable cause, supported by oath or affirmation, and particularly describing the place to be searched, and the persons or things to be seized.[96]

The relevant language is the first phrase. While technically delineating a restriction on the government (and the prosecutorial power), the Fourth Amendment also describes an aspiration—the right is not just a prohibition, but an actual legal claim.

In its jurisprudence, the Supreme Court has struggled with the limits on the right to privacy. In *Olmstead v. U.S.* (1928), the Court permitted literally wire-tapping—the physical interception of a telephone wire that connected an individual's home to the street line, but outside the property line. The *Olmstead* Court was focusing on the physicality of the interception—where it took place. Hence, because there was no trespass on the grounds of the

96. U.S. Const. art. IV amendment (1791).

homeowner, there was no privacy invasion. But as technologies advanced, that distinction became harder to defend.

By 1967, in *Katz v. U.S.*,[97] that physical distinction disappeared, as the Court found a right of privacy in a public telephone booth. The enduring phrase from *Katz*, however, is in Justice Harlan's concurrence, where he describes a "reasonable expectation of privacy" as the touchstone. However, Justice Harlan's formulation of a "twofold requirement, first that a person have exhibited an actual (subjective) expectation of privacy and, second, that the expectation be one that society is prepared to recognize as 'reasonable'"[98] is itself problematic because it is circular.

> An actual, subjective expectation of privacy obviously has no place in a statement of what Katz held or in a theory of what the fourth amendment protects. It can neither add to, nor can its absence detract from, an individual's claim to fourth amendment protection. If it could, the government could diminish each person's subjective expectation of privacy merely by announcing half-hourly on television that *1984* was being advanced by a decade and that we were all forthwith being placed under comprehensive electronic surveillance.[99]

Nonetheless, *Katz* remains the law, and the Harlan conception remains the test.

At least two U.S. Supreme Court cases involved airborne surveillance of private homes[100]—*California v. Ciraolo*[101] decided in

97. Katz v. U.S., 389 U.S. 347 (1967).

98. *Id.* at 361.

99. Anthony Amsterdam, *Perspectives on the Fourth Amendment*, 59 MINN. L. REV. 349, 384–85 (1974).

100. Another aerial surveillance case is *Dow Chemical*, but there the EPA flew over a corporate plant—not a private home—and the Court found no Fourth Amendment violation. Dow Chemical v. U.S., 476 U.S. 227 (1986).

101. California v. Ciraolo, 476 U.S. 207 (1986).

1986, and, three years later, *Florida v. Riley*.[102] In *Ciraolo*, police flying an airplane at 1,000 feet observed the defendant growing marijuana; the Court found—using the *Katz* formulation—no reasonable expectation "in order to observe what is visible to the naked eye."[103] Likewise, aerial observation of marijuana growing was sanctioned in *Riley*, but this time from 400 feet. Writing for the Court's plurality, Justice White wrote that "Any member of the public could legally have been flying over Riley's property in a helicopter at the altitude of 400 feet and could have observed Riley's greenhouse."[104] One of the dissents in *Riley*, however, raised the question of whether it was realistic for another member of the public to have observed the plants. Justice Brennan wrote that the policeman's "ability to see over Riley's fence depended on his use of a very expensive and sophisticated piece of machinery to which few ordinary citizens have access."[105]

Although Justice Brennan had left the bench by 2001, that concept of ubiquity of the technology was revisited by the Court and carried the day in *Kyllo v. United States*.[106] Like *Ciraolo* and *Riley*, *Kyllo* involved police searching for marijuana, but unlike the other two cases, the Court determined that the technology being used—a thermal imaging device—was an unlawful search. And part of the Court's analysis was the fact that the devices were not widely available. Indeed, Justice Scalia in writing for the *Kyllo* Court, described the thermal imaging technology in question as "not [being] in general public use."[107]

102. Florida v. Riley, 488 U.S. 445 (1989).

103. 476 U.S. at 215.

104. 488 U.S. at 451.

105. *Id.* at 460.

106. Kyllo v. United States, 533 U.S. 27 (2001).

107. *Id.* at 34. The Supreme Court's unfamiliarity with technologies has become a point of observation, even for those who are not formally part of the legal community. *See* Amelia Thomson-DeVeaux, *The Supreme Court Is Stubbornly Analog—By Design* (May 29, 2018, 9:00 AM), https://fivethirtyeight.com/features/the-supreme-court-is-stubbornly-analog-by-design/.

While privacy will be discussed more fully in Chapter 8, it is clear that the explosion of UAS technologies will collide with this line of Fourth Amendment cases. First, the question of observation from above—whether from 400 or 1,000 feet—will be in question. Indeed, a number of states have begun passing laws to limit or even prohibit aerial observation of private land.[108] And with highly functional drones being available for a few hundred dollars, it will not be long before they are considered (in Justice Scalia's words from *Kyllo*) "in general public use"—if we have not reached that point already. And the Court will have to try and define these limits.[109]

What is most remarkable is that the future of privacy in a world of ubiquitous drones will likely be defined by an article written before the Wright Brothers went to Kitty Hawk. In 1890, Samuel Warren and Louis Brandeis co-wrote "The Right to Privacy."[110] Citing then-modern advances like "[i]nstantaneous photographs" and "numerous mechanical devices," the two men predicted a new century where "'what is whispered in the closet shall be proclaimed from the house-tops.'"[111] But more basically, the two men described a fundamental element of the common law, and one that still animates us today: the limits and shape on the right to be "'let alone.'"[112] Future courts—and future lawmakers—will likely be struggling with that definition into the 22nd century.[113]

---

108. *See, e.g.*, California: AB 856 (amending the "anti-paparazzi statute") or Florida Sec. 934.50- "Freedom from Unwarranted Surveillance Act."

109. See the recent cell phone tracking case, where a 5–4 Court required a warrant to obtain records of which cell phone towers had been used by a particular phone. Carpenter v. U.S., 585 U.S. ___ (2018).

110. Samuel Warren & Louis Brandeis, *The Right to Privacy*, 4 Harv. L. Rev. 193 (1890).

111. *Id.* at 195.

112. *Id.*

113. For a discussion of the problems inherent in the FAA's ability to protect privacy, see, e.g., Melissa Barbee, *Uncharted Territory: The FAA and the Regulation of Privacy Via Rulemaking for Domestic Drones*, 66(2) Admin. L. Rev. 463–87 (Spring 2014), https://www.jstor.org/stable/24475503.

V. Conclusion

This chapter has traced the history of unmanned flying machines from the third century through the explosion of drone technology that occurred shortly after the year 2000. With both UAS and sensory technology now ubiquitous and getting cheaper, "IoT drones" will become more and more prevalent for many agricultural, energy, and other business tasks. The U.S. Congress has in the past decade taken aggressive steps to empower and accelerate the FAA's integration of drones into the national airspace, and those efforts will continue as we move forward. And as "IoT drones" will continue to be armed with new and better sensors, future regulation will probably include sense-and-avoid technology and security risks. Finally, with the growth of the UAS industry, law enforcement will undoubtedly also increase its use of drone technology, and the limits of privacy—both in terms of the Fourth Amendment and more generally—will be subject to review and revision.

Chapter 4

5G Wireless Communications

Enabling a New Internet of Things

Thomas L. Jarvis
J.C. Masullo

The Internet of Things (IoT) is a network of electronic devices linked by a communications system to a control center. As of 2018, there were an estimated 17 billion IoT connections, ranging from mobile phones to smart power meters, using communication networks as basic as Bluetooth or as sophisticated as 4G LTE cellular networks.[1] However, the soon-to-arrive fifth-generation (5G) communication technology is predicted to fuel exponential growth in the number of IoT systems, devices, and rate of deployment—perhaps as many as 30 billion devices by the year 2023. While the technical details of 5G cellular networks and the IoT are the obvious next wave of patent disputes, the basic architecture and capabilities of the IoT will inform a broad range of legal issues for the foreseeable future.

1. Ericsson, *Mobility Report* (June 2018), https://www.ericsson.com/assets/local/mobility-report/documents/2018/ericsson-mobility-report-june-2018.pdf.

I. Architecture of the IoT

Most IoT systems contain four architectural elements: sensors, a control center, actuators, and a communications network linking those elements. Sensors typically collect information, the communications network delivers the information to the control center, the control center evaluates the information and issues commands, the communications network delivers the commands to the actuators, and the actuators perform some action (Figure 4.1).[2] Each of those elements has a unique identifier (such as an IP address or a URI) that acts as an address for sending and receiving packets of data across shared communication networks.

II. Communications Networks

Telecommunications is a "general purpose technology" that, like the printing press, the telegraph, the telephone, and the Internet, enables multiple services for both public and private use. Wireless networks enabled mobile communications and first-generation IoT systems that are now an integral part of modern life.

Currently, "[d]ata transfer requirements for IoT vary from small, intermittent payloads like utility meters to large amounts of continuous data such as real-time video surveillance. Range requirements can span from very short distances for wearables to several kilometers for weather and agriculture applications."[3] Those needs are now served by a variety of short-range, relatively low-capacity wireless networks (e.g., Bluetooth and Wi-Fi) that can be used in conjunction with wired networks or in conjunction with long-range, higher-capacity wireless cellular systems.

---

2. *See, e.g.*, *IoT System | Sensors and Actuators*, BRIDGERA, https://bridgera.com/iot-system-sensors-actuators/ (last viewed on Sept. 1, 2018).

3. Jatin Parekh, *WiFi's Evolving Role in IoT*, NETWORK WORLD (May 11, 2017, 8:05 AM), https://www.networkworld.com/article/3196191/lan-wan/wifi-s-evolving-role-in-iot.html.

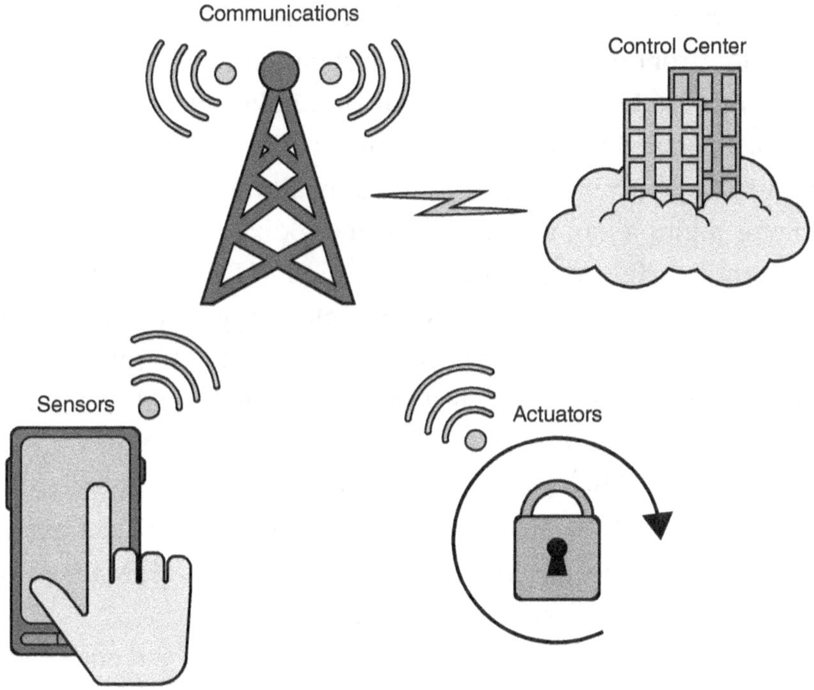

Figure 4.1 Architectural Elements of IoT

A. History of Wireless Cellular Networks

Over the past 40 years, four generations of mobile communications have gained wide-spread adoption. The evolutionary process for wireless networks is to layer new systems on top of legacy systems. First-generation (1G) and second-generation (2G) wireless networks did not provide modern data communications. Third-generation (3G) networks first provided limited data services that were sufficient for basic e-mail and web browsing, but not until the introduction of fourth generations (4G) networks were large-scale mobile IoT applications practical.

Early wireless mobile communications were based on proprietary radio interfaces that did not support roaming: Mobility was limited to the geographic area of the subscriber's carrier and roaming to other networks using the same or different technology was not generally available. The wireless communication industry was at the forefront of using voluntary standards setting organizations (SSOs) to establish and make available radio interface technologies that enabled roaming, and enabled multiple infrastructure and mobile phone providers to ensure compatibility of their products. Among multiple competing SSOs, the global organization is the International Telecommunications Union (ITU), a body of the United Nations that sets high-level technology goals and a more detailed role in wireless spectrum issues. The European Telecommunications Standards Institute (ETSI) technical committees and specification groups develop standards for a broad range of telecommunications industries. ETSI's 3rd Generation Partnership Project (3GPP) is focused on engineering specifications for the Global System for Mobile Communications (GSM), and the follow-on specifications for LTE and 5G.

4G networks were first deployed in about 2010 and enabled the first practical large-scale IoT systems. Technical specifications for 4G networks require high data transmission speeds, high aggregate data capacity for all users within a cell, and low latency (initial transmission delays).[4] In particular, networks with minimum speeds of 1 Gbit/s for stationary users and 100 Mbit/s users in fast-moving cars and trains, both with latency of less than 10 ms.[5] The performance expectation was to support mobile IP telephony, gaming services, high-definition mobile TV, video conferencing, and 3D television.[6]

---

4. ITU-R Report M.2134, *Requirements Related to Technical Performance for IMT-Advanced Radio Interface(s)* (2008), https://www.itu.int/dms_pub/itu-r/opb/rep/R-REP-M.2134-2008-PDF-E.pdf; Grace Petrin, *Radiocommunication Sector ITU-R FAQ on International Mobile Telecommunications (IMT)* (May 9, 2018), *available at* https://www.itu.int/en/ITU-R/Documents/ITU-R-FAQ-IMT.pdf.

5. Petrin, *supra* note 4.

6. Rakesh Sigh & Ranan Sigh, *4G LTE Cellular Technology: Network Architecture and Mobile Standards, Emerging Research in Management & Technology*, 5(12) INT'L J. EMERGING RESEARCH IN MGMT. & TECH. (Dec. 2016),

Long-Term Evolution (LTE) is the predominate 4G wireless network technology. While LTE is a convergence of complex radio communications and computer technologies,[7] the conceptual building blocks are understandable. LTE can be combined with 3G networks on a single frequency band;[8] thus network operators can continue to service voice and low-demand data services with 3G technology while providing high-speed data services with an additional layer of LTE technology.[9] LTE systems are also designed to emphasize software upgrades and minimize hardware upgrades as new versions are released, in particular upgrades to the software-defined and configurable radio systems.[10] These cost-saving technologies encouraged wide-spread adoption of LTE and its rapidly growing geographic coverage around the world.

Since the introduction of 3G cellular data services in 2000, there has been an estimated 400 million-fold increase in cellular data traffic.[11] One estimate is for a compound annual growth rate

---

available at https://pdfs.semanticscholar.org/b2ab/1c503c76a4b3870feaec5c3a6a157972a555.pdf.

7. A leading textbook summary of LTE is Erik Dahlman et al., 4G: LTE /LTE-Advanced for Mobile Broadband (2d ed. 2014).

8. Juan Irola, *New Same-Band Combining Technology Improves LTE Deployment,* Commscope White Paper (2015), https://www.commscope.com/Docs/Same-band_Combining_Technology_Improves_LTE_WP-109368-EN.pdf; Bohagen Frode & Jorgen Binningsbo, *HSPA and LTE—Future-Proof Mobile Broadband Solutions*, ISSN 0085 (2010), https://www.researchgate.net/profile/Bohagen_Frode/publication/239597233_HSPA_and_LTE_-_Future-proof_Mobile_Broadband_Solutions/links/56b0f88708aed7ba3fead7dd/HSPA-and-LTE-Future-proof-Mobile-Broadband-Solutions.pdf.

9. Irola, *supra* note 8.

10. Markus Mueck et al., *ETSI Reconfigurable Radio Systems: Status and Future Directions on Software Defined Radio and Cognitive Radio Standards*, IEEE Communications Magazine (Sept. 2010), *available at* https://hal-supelec.archives-ouvertes.fr/file/index/docid/556123/filename/342_P_11867_87.pdf.

11. *Cisco VNI Forecast and Methodology, 2015–2020 White Paper*, http://www.cisco.com/c/en/us/solutions/collateral/service-provider/visual-networking-index-vni/complete-white-paper-c11-481360.html (last updated Nov. 26, 2018).

(CAGR) of 45 percent, a rate that would result in doubling of data traffic every 1.87 years between 2016 and 2022, with smartphone traffic increasing by ten times and total mobile traffic for all devices by eight times.[12] This projected growth rate, which IoT deployments could further accelerate, is rapidly exhausting existing wireless capacity and necessitates a new generation of higher-capacity cellular data services. As in the past, rather than replacing earlier systems, 5G will provide an additional layer of connectivity for high-demand applications:[13] 3G and 4G networks will continue to provide current levels of broadband data communications, and SMS texting will continue to operate over the control channels of voice networks.

B. Primary Components of Wireless Cellular Networks

Architecturally, cellular networks have three main components: the Radio Access Network (RAN) that communicates over the air, the Core Network (CN) that connects the RAN to the network control services and external services, and the User's Equipment (UE, e.g., a mobile phone). More specifically, cellular RANs have a base station that encodes and formats data, and an antenna that transmits the data. The CN links the RAN to the cellular operator's internal control systems, such as access authorization, accounting, and security, and also to external systems like landline telephones, Internet, SMS texting, and other cellular systems (roaming). The UE can be as common as the mobile phone in your pocket or as specialized as a dedicated communications module installed in an industrial manufacturing machine.

---

12. Paul Schmitt & Elizabeth Belding, *Low on Air: Inherent Wireless Channel Capacity Limitations*, LIMITS (June 22–24, 2017), *available at* https://www.cs.princeton.edu/~pschmitt/docs/limits02-schmittA.pdf.

13. Fredric Kronestedt et al., *The Advantages of Combining 5G NR with LTE*, 9 Ericsson Tech. Rev. (Oct. 30, 2018), *available at* https://www.ericsson.com/assets/local/publications/ericsson-technology-review/docs/2018/etr-2018-09-5g-radiodeployment.pdf.

III. 5G Networks: The Specification Timeline

Planning and specifications for 5G wireless networks began in 2012 with the ITU's targets for 5G wireless networks specifications that would be finalized for implementation by 2020, a specification that became known as International Mobile Telecommunications 2020 (IMT 2020).[14] In 2015, 3GPP began engineering work on 5G technology with a "Feasibility Study on New Services and Markets Technology Enablers," that identified 74 future wireless network use cases that determined the capabilities required of 5G networks.[15] By December 2017, 3GPP approved Release 15 5G New Radio (NR) technical specifications, a non-stand-alone version of 5G NR that uses an LTE core network to provide broadband Internet service for non-mobile users.[16] On June 4, 2018, 3GPP released the specifications for 5G NR for mobile users and 5G Core Network (5GC)—the two essential components of the 5G mobile communications specification. While other feature specifications remain in development, the 5G NR and CN specifications provide the high speed, low latency, and spectral efficiency that will enable the next generation IoT.

Like prior generations, the term "5G" has a marketing function of referring to faster, higher-capacity, lower-latency wireless networks. As carriers face commercial pressures to meet those performance benchmarks without the significant capital expenses and

14. *See, e.g., ITU towards "IMT for 2020 and Beyond,"* ITU, https://www.itu.int/en/ITU-R/study-groups/rsg5/rwp5d/imt-2020/Pages/default.aspx (last accessed Dec. 14, 2018).

15. *TR 22.891: Technical Specification Group Services and System Aspects; Feasibility Study on New Services and Markets Technology Enablers; Stage 1 (Release 14)*, 3GPP (Sept. 10, 2015), https://portal.3gpp.org/desktopmodules/Specifications/SpecificationDetails.aspx?specificationId=2897.

16. The non-stand-alone mode revolves around enabling the enhanced Mobile Broadband (eMBB) use-case and anchors the connection in LTE while 5G NR carriers are used to increase data rates and take advantage of the reduced latency.

corresponding price increases necessary for actual 5G NR/CN systems, incremental improvements in existing wireless networks will be branded as "5G."[17] For example, some U.S. carriers plan to offer "5G Evolution Technology," which is in fact "LTE-Advanced," not 5G NR.[18] And while other carriers have announced a 2018 rollout of 5G broadband Internet service in selected cities, those Internet services are between fixed positions, not mobile 5G users.[19]

Best estimates are that initial deployments of mobile 5G networks will begin in late 2019, large-scale coverage will begin in 2020, and that full implementation may require five or more years.

IV. 5G Applications and Performance Objectives

The ITU's IMT 2020 specification classified 5G mobile network services into three groups: Enhanced Mobile Broadband (eMBB), Ultra-Reliable and Low-Latency Communications (URLLC), and Massive Machine-Type Communications (mMTC),[20] targeted at the following use cases:[21]

---

17. Ferry Grijpink et al., *The Road to 5G: The Inevitable Growth of Infrastructure Cost*, McKinsey (Feb. 2018), https://www.mckinsey.com/industries/telecommunications/our-insights/the-road-to-5g-the-inevitable-growth-of-infrastructure-cost.

18. Frank Rayal, *The Cost of 5G* (Apr. 23, 2018), https://frankrayal.com/2018/04/23/the-cost-of-5g/; *see*, Bernie Arnason, *The Path to 5G Can Get Confusing as AT&T Announces 99 5G Evolution Markets*, Telecompetitor (Oct. 4, 2018, 1:04 AM), https://www.telecompetitor.com/the-path-to-5g-can-get-confusing-as-att-announces-99-5g-evolution-markets/.

19. *See, e.g.*, Nick Statt, *Verizon Will Launch 5G Home Internet Service Starting October 1st*, The Verge (Sept. 11, 2018, 5:00 PM), https://www.theverge.com/2018/9/11/17847640/verizon-5g-first-home-broadband-internet-service-installations-october-1.

20. Heejung Yu, et al., *What Is 5G? Emerging 5G Mobile Services and Network Requirements*, 9 Sustainability 1848 (Oct. 15, 2017), available at https://www.mdpi.com/2071-1050/9/10/1848/pdf.

21. *5G Systems: Enabling the Transformation of Industry and Society*, Ericsson White Paper (2017), *available at* https://www.ericsson.com/assets/local/publications/white-papers/wp-5g-systems.pdf; *5G Network Architecture:*

- eMBB is analogous to "bigger pipes" that will provide high data bandwidth/throughput (>10 Gbit/s peak rates) for an increasingly digital lifestyle, and focuses on services that have high requirements for bandwidth, such as high-definition videos, virtual reality, and augmented reality.
- URLLC is analogous to "higher pressure" data flows for near-instantaneous (<1 ms) reactions, enabling latency-sensitive services, such as remote surgery, assisted and automated driving, and manufacturing robotics.
- mMTC is analogous to "high-density pipeline connections" (>1 M/km^2 connections) for services such as smart city and smart agriculture, which are envisioned to include tens of billions of connected devices.

Graphically, those 5G services will interact to support new IoT services such as those shown in Figure 4.2.[22]

In the abstract, 5G performance objectives are difficult to appreciate, but a comparison to 4G LTE performance is illuminating. Compared to 4G LTE, fully implemented 5G should deliver the following benefits:[23]

- 1,000 times the system capacity
- 10 times the spectral efficiency and energy efficiency
- 25 times the average cell throughput

A High Level Perspective, HUAWEI TECHNOLOGIES CO. LTD. (2016), *available at* https://www.huawei.com/minisite/hwmbbf16/insights/5G-Nework-Architecture-Whitepaper-en.pdf.

22. *Setting the Scene for 5G: Opportunities & Challenges*, ITU, (2018), *available at* https://www.itu.int/en/ITU-D/Documents/ITU_5G_REPORT-2018.pdf.

23. Rony K. Saha & Chaodit Aswakul, *Fundamentals of 5G Mobile Network: Architecture, Requirement, Densification, Cooperation, and Resource Management* (July 2016), Sec. 2.2, https://www.researchgate.net/publication/305536508_FUNDAMENTALS_OF_5G_MOBILE_NETWORK_Architecture_Requirement_Densification_Cooperation_and_Resource_Management.

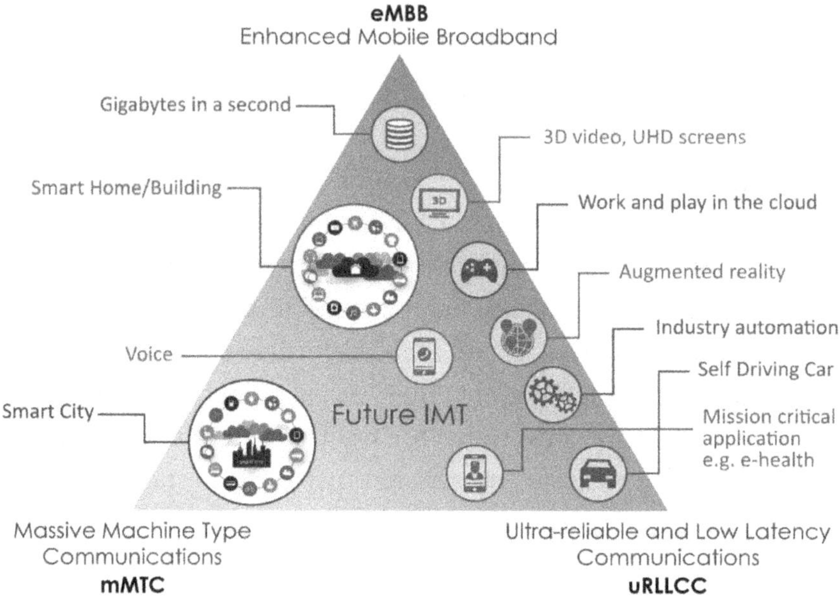

Figure 4.2 New IoT Services

- 10 times longer battery lifetime
- 5 times reduced latency
- 10 to 100 times higher user data rate
- 10 to 100 times higher number of connecting devices
- 10 Gbit/s for low mobility and 1 Gbit/s for high mobility peak data rate
- 100 times reduction energy per bit and cost per bit
- 10 to 100 times cheaper mm Wave spectrum (as compared to below 3GHz spectrum)
- 10 to 100 times cheaper small cells than macro-cells
- 350 km/hr to 500 km/hr mobility support (as compared to 250 km/hr for 4G networks)
- Ubiquitous communications between anybody, anything, anywhere, at anytime

V. The Technology Behind the Performance

A. 5G New Radio

5G New Radio (5G NR) is the next-generation RAN that will provide a quantum leap forward in terms of features, bandwidth, speed, reliability, and efficiency. Multiple LTE technologies are carried forward into 5G systems, but at higher capacity and capabilities. Some examples are IPv6 addresses (prior-generation IPv4 addresses are nearly exhausted), pure packet switching (no circuit switched voice communications), OFDMA and SC-FDMA multicarrier transmission, and Multiple Input Multiple Output (MIMO) antenna systems.[24] Some leading features of 5G NR are summarized in the following subsections.

1. Additional Spectrum

The 40 licensed frequency bands used for 3G and 4G cellular communications are quickly nearing their capacity constraints. The 5G NR specification covers 600 and 700 MHz bands and the 50 GHz millimeter-wave end of the spectrum in order to solve the rapidly approaching saturation of previously licensed spectrum. Those new spectrum bands are likely to be used for different purposes and in different environments, as described here:[25]

- Sub-1GHz bands are suitable to support IoT services and extend mobile broadband coverage from urban to suburban and rural areas. Cellular signals at these frequencies enable

24. *See id.;* Rakesh Singh, *4G LTE Cellular Technology: Network Architecture and Mobile Standards*, 5(12) INT'L J. EMERGING RESEARCH IN MGMT, & TECH. (Dec. 2016), *available at* https://pdfs.semanticscholar.org/b2ab/1c503c76a4b3870feaec5c3a6a157972a555.pdf.

25. *Road to 5G: Introduction and Migration*, GSMA (Apr. 2018), *available at* https://www.gsma.com/futurenetworks/wp-content/uploads/2018/04/Road-to-5G-Introduction-and-Migration_FINAL.pdf; GSMA, *5G Spectrum: GSMA Public Policy Position*, GSMA (Nov. 2018), *available at* https://www.gsma.com/spectrum/wp-content/uploads/2018/11/5G-Spectrum-Positions.pdf.

5G to create very large coverage areas and deep penetration into buildings.

- The 1–6 GHz bands provide a mixture of coverage and capacity for 5G services. There is a reasonable amount of existing mobile broadband spectrum identified within this range, which could be used for initial 5G deployments.
- Spectrum above 6 GHz can provide significant capacity due to the very large bandwidth that can enable massive channel sizes that can deliver multi-gigabit connectivity.[26] However, these millimeter bands reach much shorter distances and have limited ability to penetrate barriers such as building walls.

2. *Massive MIMO*

"MIMO" is the acronym for Multiple Input, Multiple Output communication technology that greatly increases the capacity of a communications link by simultaneously transmitting a signal over multiple paths. Early MIMO systems used multiple transmit and receive antennas to provide multiple simultaneous communication paths, resulting in greater bandwidth. While multiple antennas are still used in basic networks like home Wi-Fi, modern cellular MIMO networks now use additional techniques for simultaneously sending and receiving multiple data signals. Limited MIMO has been used in some 3G and LTE systems to support a relatively small number of simultaneous communication paths.

5G networks use Massive Multiple-Input Multiple-Output (Massive MIMO) to enable tens or even hundreds of multiple simultaneous streams of data communications between devices. Like the revolutionary impact of packet switched networks,

---

26. Theodore S. Rappaport et al., *Overview of Millimeter Wave Communications for Fifth-Generation (5G) Wireless Networks—with a Focus on Propagation Models*, IEEE Transactions on Antennas and Propagation, Special Issue on 5G (Nov. 2017), *available at* https://arxiv.org/pdf/1708.02557.pdf.

Massive MIMO enables very stable connections and high data rate communications. Massive MIMO is a key to the high data rates of 5G networks.

3. Beamforming

Conventional base stations transmit signals in all directions. 5G base stations use beamforming to detect the location of a mobile device and use an array of antennas to focus transmission of signals intended for that device to the direction of a device.[27] This directional division of the cellular space is known as spatial multiplexing and can significantly increase the total capacity of an individual cell.

Beamforming also enables greater range and building penetration for millimeter bandwidths. Millimeter power amplifiers have lower output power and greater multipath signal losses than longer wavelength portions of the spectrum. However, millimeter spectrum antennas are also much smaller and therefore more can be packed into the same device, enabling better beamforming performance.[28]

4. Full Duplex

Simultaneous transmission of overlapping signals in a single bandwidth is so challenging that earlier generation cellular systems used pairs of bands to enable real-time bi-directional overlapping voice communications (known as "half-duplex" systems). 5G systems will incorporate self-interference cancellation modulation technology and high-speed switching systems to enable "full duplex" simultaneous signal transmission and reception. While this move from half- to full-duplex suggests a theoretical 100 percent increase

---

27. Fredrick Vook et al., *MIMO and Beamforming Solutions for 5G Technology*, IEEE Int'l Microwave Symposium (IMS) (2014), *available at* http://www.academia.edu/24406180/MIMO_and_Beamforming_Solutions_for_5G_Technology.

28. *Id.*

in communications capacity, actual testing has confirmed at least a 30 to 40 percent improvement in mean throughput.[29]

5. *HetNets*

Heterogeneous wireless networks (HetNets) are a combination of different types of cellular nodes and overlapping cells that can provide different services and/or provide more capacity in high density user areas such as sports arenas. Prior-generation HetNets were limited by interference between the different overlapping bandwidths, resulting in degradation of overall system capacity, reduced quality of service, and higher frequency system outages.[30] 5G networks will use several interference solutions to enable large and small cells to operate in close, overlapping proximity without disruption.[31]

5G HetNets will integrate long-range eNodeB macro-cells (commonly referred to as cell towers) that cover large geographical areas with shorter-range micro-cells with a range of several hundred meters that can service shopping center-sized areas, pico-cells that can cover smaller areas such as a hotel, and/or femtocells with a range of about 10 meters that could cover a single home.[32]

HetNets enable combinations of long-range coverage but relatively slow data transmission rates of 5G eNodeBs with short-range

---

29. Nurul H. Mahmood et al., *On the Potential of Full Duplex Communication in 5G Small Cell Networks*, IEEE 81st Vehicular Technology Conference, IEEE Vol. 81 (2015), *available at* http://vbn.aau.dk/files/208396029/mahmood_fullDuplexPotential_vtcSp15.pdf.

30. O.F. Afolalu et al., *A Survey of Interference Challenges and Mitigation Techniques in 5G Heterogeneous Cellular Networks*, Int'l Conference of Sciences, Eng'g & Envtl. Tech. 1(2): 8-14 (2016), *available at* https://pdfs.semanticscholar.org/6665/1b46c97075740436707ed466609f4884f667.pdf.

31. Danqing Zhang & Xinji Tian, *Overview on Interference Management Technology for Ultra-Dense Network*, Open Access Library J., 5:e4675 (June 20, 2018), *available at* https://doi.org/10.4236/oalib.1104675.

32. *Small Cell Network White Paper*, GSA (Nov. 2016), *available at* https://www.huawei.com/minisite/hwmbbf16/insights/small_cell_solution.pdf.

but high-speed millimeter wavelength micro-, pico-, or femtocells. HetNet small cells can also support low-powered, "occasionally on" sensors and actuators in IoT applications such as agricultural soil moisture and temperature sensors and irrigation controls.[33]

B. 5G Core Network

The 5G Core Network (5GC) links the 5G NR to external interfaces (e.g., landlines, the Internet, etc.) and network control systems (e.g., accounting, network access, roaming, etc.).[34] While the prior generation LTE Evolved Packet Core (EPC) was an evolutionary advancement of prior packet cores, the 5GC is a revolutionary design that is based on cloud computing concepts and architecture.[35] Some leading features of 5GC are summarized in the following subsections.

1. Separation of Control and User Functions

The 5GC Control/User Plane Separation (CUPS) is the complete separation between control plane functions (controlling the user's connection, accounting, authentication, etc.) and user plane functions (delivering services such as data traffic).[36] By separating control and user functions, cellular operators can independently scale those functions to meet various demands such as

33. Tamoghna Ojha et al., *Wireless Sensor Networks for Agriculture: The State-of-the-Art in Practice and Future Challenges*, Computers & Elecs in Agriculture (Sept. 5, 2015), *available at* https://itra.medialabasia.in/data/Documents/M2M/publications/Wireless%20Sensor%20Networks%20for%20Agriculture%20-%20The%20State-of-the-Art%20in%20Practice%20and%20Future%20Challenges%20%5BCompAG%5D%20%5B2015%5D.pdf.

34. The 5G NR non-stand-alone radio interface is backwards compatible with the LTE Evolved Packet Core, enabling cost-saving mix and match deployment strategies.

35. GSMA, *Road to 5G*, *supra* note 25.

36. Erik Guttman & Irfan Ali, *Path to 5G: A Control Plane Perspective*, 6/1&2 J. ICT Standardization (May 3, 2018), *available at* https://www.riverpublishers.com/journal_read_html_article.php?j=JICTS/6/2/6.

high-volume versus low-volume data traffic, voice communications versus machine-to-machine communications, high-priority versus low-power applications, and low-versus high-mobility users, all of which can vary by location.

2. *Service-Based Architecture*

Prior CNs defined all interactions between different network functions as a series of procedures communicated indirectly through multi-hop pathways; for example, UE location changes were communicated through a four-hop path across multiple functional units.[37] In contrast, the 5GC is a service-based architecture where services can directly offer and consume services of other network functions; for example, UE location changes can be directly communicated to and managed by the control function that implements the carrier's roaming policies.[38]

The 5GC design implements in software many core network functions that 4G CNs implemented in hardware. These 5GC software functions can be remotely configured, dynamically modified, and managed in real time. While 5GC's required functions and interfaces can be implemented in a variety of software solutions, the architecture and functions are designed for simpler and architecturally flatter networks than the preceding LTE core networks.

3. *Network Slicing*

Network slices are independent end-to-end logical networks that run on shared physical devices, delivering an agreed-upon level of service.[39] In effect, users can obtain virtual private networks across a path of services necessary to accomplish their objectives. Net-

37. *Id.*
38. *Id.*
39. GSMA, *Network Slicing: Use Case Requirements* (Apr. 2018), *available at* https://www.gsma.com/futurenetworks/wp-content/uploads/2018/04/NS-Final.pdf.

work slices can include the entire range of services available on the physical network or a subset of those services that are necessary for the particular application. Moreover, network slices can span networks of multiple operators. Most importantly, network slicing can manage the competing demands for 5G NR resources—the most restricted and most expensive part of the mobile network.[40]

The ultimate objective and benefit of network slicing is to provide a specific solution for specific user needs. For example, a network slice could command the services necessary for a bundle of specific business functions, such as (1) an ultra-reliable data transmission network slice for the navigation and control of an autonomous vehicle plus (2) a separate high-bandwidth network slice for a video entertainment system of that vehicle.[41] Those two slices could each have different requirements for data speed, quality, latency, reliability, security, and transmission range. And that bundle of slices could span the networks of multiple operators that are necessary to provide coverage for the geographic range of the vehicle.

VI. Next Generation IoT Application Powered by 5G

5G will bring forth a paradigm shift in connectivity. A generation ago, few people would have predicted the many capabilities of a smartphone. While 5G will enable several foreseeable improvements in existing IoT services, we can't foresee the full array of new IoT services that are likely to evolve. "The technology promises to change our lives by connecting everything around us to a

40. R. Ferrus et al., *Management of Network Slicing in 5G Radio Access Networks: Functional Framework and Information Models* (Mar. 2018), *available at* https://www.researchgate.net/publication/323571197_Management_of_Network_Slicing_in_5G_Radio_Access_Networks_Functional_Framework_and_Information_Models.

41. GSMA, *supra* note 39.

network that is 100 times faster than our cellular connection and 10 times faster than our speediest home broadband service."[42] But this improvement is "not just about speed for speed's sake. While the move from 3G to 4G LTE was about faster connections, the evolution to 5G is so much more. The combination of speed, responsiveness, range, and 'always on' connectivity could unlock the full capabilities of other ground swells in technology, offering a boost to self-driving cars, drones, virtual reality and the internet of things."[43] Indeed, "[b]eyond speed, the biggest benefit of 5G is its low latency, or the short lag time between a device pinging the network and getting a response. While not necessarily noticeable, there is a lag with 4G LTE. A 5G network virtually eliminates it."[44]

While it is impossible to foresee all the new IoT services that will be built on the foundation of 5G, some broad categories are predictable.

Smart cities. Urban environments with advanced lighting, security, energy, transportation, and environmental monitoring systems to attract and retain the most desirable residents.[45]

Agriculture. Commercial farms and ranches with planting and harvesting at locally optimal times, minimal necessary use of irrigation and fertilizer, herd management, commodity market leverage, and global supply chain management are on the rise.[46]

---

42. *See, e.g.*, Roger Cheng, *Not Just Speed: 7 Incredible Things You Can Do with 5G*, CNET (Mar. 2, 2017, 5:00 AM), https://www.cnet.com/news/5g-not-just-speed-fifth-generation-wireless-tech-lets-you-do-vr-self-driving-cars-drones-remote/.

43. *See id.*

44. *See id.*

45. Mahashreveta Choudhary, *Technology—The Backbone of a Smart City*, GEOSPATIAL WORLD (May 22, 2018), https://www.geospatialworld.net/article/technology-the-backbone-of-a-smart-city/; *The 5G Economy: How 5G Technology Will Contribute to the Global Economy*, IHS ECONOMICS & IHS TECHNOLOGY 23 (Jan. 2017).

46. Walter Stiers, *IoT-Agriculture, The Iota in the Alphabet Soup?,* IBM BELGIUM, *available at* https://iot.ieee.org/images/files/pdf/summit/201705

Medicine. On-demand access to medical records and medical knowledge systems, logistics for patients, health care providers, and support services; supply chain management; and even remote diagnostics and robotic surgery are becoming cost-effective.[47]

Commerce. Globalization of Amazon and Alibaba, localized privacy and digital rights standards enforced at the individual and individual product level, blockchain transparency and security, and secure payment systems are rapidly advancing.[48]

Transportation/Hospitality. Autonomous vehicles; scheduling, maintenance, and bag tracing in civil aviation; and the business and leisure hospital industries are at the forefront of IoT.[49]

-stiers-summit.pdf; Krijn Poppe, *Big Opportunities for Big Data in Food and Agriculture*, WAGENINGEN UF 22 (Feb. 2016), https://www.oecd.org/tad/events/Session%202_Krijn%20Poppe%20OECD%20Big%20Data.pdf; Choudhary, *supra* note 45.

47. S.M. Riazul Islam et al., *The Internet of Things for Health Care: A Comprehensive Survey*, IEEE ACCESS (June 1, 2015), *available at* https://ieeexplore.ieee.org/stamp/stamp.jsp?tp=&arnumber=7113786; Ericsson, "*Advancing Remote Diagnosis and Robotic Assisted Surgery*," Ericsson, https://www.ericsson.com/en/cases/2016/5gtuscany/transforming-healthcare-with-5g (last visited Dec. 10, 2018).

48. JOHN ROSSMAN, THE AMAZON WAY ON IOT: 10 PRINCIPLES FOR EVERY LEADER FROM THE WORLD'S LEADING INTERNET OF THINGS STRATEGIES (2016); Yunusa A. Bena et al., *IoT on E-Commerce, Present and Future: A Review of Alibaba Case Study*, 11(1) J. INFO. SYSTEMS RESEARCH & INNOVATION 41–46 (Feb. 2017), *available at* https://seminar.utmspace.edu.my/jisri/download/Vol11-1/Paper7-Yunusa.pdf; Amina Badzar, Blockchain for Securing Sustainable Transport Contracts and Supply Chain Transparency: An Explorative Study of Blockchain Technology in Logistics, Master's Thesis, Lund University (May 24, 2016), *available at* http://lup.lub.lu.se/luur/download?func=downloadFile&recordOId=8880383&fileOId=8880390; Joan Feigenbaum et al., *Privacy Engineering for Digital Rights Management*, ACM Workshop on Digital Rights Management, 76–105 (Nov. 5, 2001), *available at* http://cs-www.cs.yale.edu/homes/jf/FFSS.pdf.

49. Mario Gerla et al., *Internet of Vehicles: From Intelligent Grid to Autonomous Cars and Vehicular Clouds*, IEEE World Forum on Internet of Things (2014), *available at* http://www.kresttechnology.com/krest-academic-projects/krest-mtech-projects/IOT/Mech%20IOT-2016-17/ABSTRACT%20AND%20BASE%20PAPERS/25.Internet%20of%20Vehicles%20From%20Intelli/25

Virtually all large-scale industries are turning to IoT to provide improved products and services at reduced costs.

The United States, China, and South Korea lead the global race for widespread 5G deployment, but China is poised to take the lead by clearing the regulatory red tape that will impede deployment in the United States. According to the Brookings Institute, China's likely first mover advantages will have long-lasting consequences: "As part of a five-year plan to deploy 5G by 2020, China's advanced wireless networks are projected to reach 428 million people by 2025, add more than RMB 6.3 trillion [about $900 billion] into their economy, and create more than eight million jobs. A 5G-ready China will not only be a global leader in product delivery, but also in technical patents, usability testing, and industry certifications."[50]

VII. Convergence of Technology, Divergence of Ownership Claims, Legal Solutions

The anticipated growth in IoT presents a convergence of technology that is reminiscent of the smartphones that integrated telecommunications and computer technology, which resulted in profound changes in business and personal lives, and in 2009 kicked off the smartphone patent wars. While the past can be prologue for the future, lessons learned from those smartphone patent battles provide some insight into how ownership interests in IoT systems will be allocated and compensated.

.pdf; Robert Moorman, *The Aircraft's Place in the IoT Revolution*, AVONICS INTERNATIONAL (June/July 2016), available at http://interactive.aviationtoday.com/avionicsmagazine/june-july-2016/the-aircrafts-place-in-the-iot-revolution/; Prasanna Kansakar et al., *Technology in Hospitality Industry: Prospects and Challenges*, arXiv preprint arXiv:1709.00105v2, *available at* http://people.cs.ksu.edu/~amunir/documents/publications/journal/Munir_Technology_Hospitality_av_CE_2018.pdf.

50. Nicol Turner Lee, *Will the US Be 5G Ready?*, BROOKINGS (July 13, 2018), https://www.brookings.edu/blog/techtank/2018/07/13/will-the-us-be-5g-ready/, citing *The Global Race to 5G*, CITA (Apr. 2018), *available at* https://api.ctia.org/wp-content/uploads/2018/04/Race-to-5G-Report.pdf.

A. Wireless Standards and Licensing Obligations

Mobile wireless communications are dependent on interoperability, meaning the ability of network and user equipment from multiple manufacturers to operate without interruption as users move across cellular systems or national borders. To achieve interoperability, suppliers form Standards Setting Organizations (SSOs) that negotiate agreed-upon technical interface standards. As part of those negotiations, SSOs require that their members (1) disclose their patents that cover proposed or adopted aspects of the standard (Standards Essential Patents or SEPs) and (2) agree to license those SEPs on Fair, Reasonable, and Non-Discriminatory (FRAND) terms. Volumes have been written about the objectives and risks of SSOs, SEPs, and FRAND obligations,[51] and the first generation of decisional law from the smartphone patent wars provides some guidance on how to operate SSOs and license SEPs without violating FRAND obligations. The challenge now is to recognize how that body of law and the existing economics of mobile communications will apply to the new realities of 5G IoT systems.

Focusing on global users, smartphones account for about 84 percent of all mobile phones sold,[52] the average selling price for smartphones is about $363,[53] and the average cost per user for

---

51. Exemplary discussions include Kirti Gupta, *Technology Standards and Competition in the Wireless Mobile Industry*, 22:4 Geo. Mason L. Rev. (2015), *available at* http://www.georgemasonlawreview.org/wp-content/uploads/2015/06/GuptaTechStandards.pdf; Thomas Cotter, *Comparative Law and Economics of Standard Essential Patents and FRAND Royalties*, 22 Tex. Intell. Prop. L.J. 311 (2014), *available at* http://scholarship.law.umn.edu/faculty_articles/237.

52. Press Release, Gartner, Gartner Says Worldwide Sales of Smartphones Returned to Growth in First Quarter of 2018, (May 29, 2018), https://www.gartner.com/newsroom/id/3876865.

53. Press Release, GfK, Global Smartphone Average Sales Price Sees Record Year-on-Year Growth in 4Q17 (Jan. 24, 2018), https://www.gfk.com/insights/press-release/global-smartphone-average-sales-price-sees-record-year-on-year-growth-in-4q17/.

mobile network services is less than $10/month.[54] Of course, users in developed countries spend more: North American consumers purchase higher-end phones with an average price tag of $452 and subscribe to more expensive mobile service plans with larger data allocations with an average cost in the United States of about $50/month.[55] In the aggregate, annual sales of smartphones total about 1.4 billion units with a total revenue of almost $500 billion,[56] and network operator 2G-4G revenues are about $1 trillion.[57]

Some studies have estimated that about 5 percent of the retail price of smartphones are attributable to the cost of 2G-4G and Wi-Fi SEP licensing fees.[58] Since there is no obvious demand for a smartphone without those SEP wireless communication capabilities, and since consumers continue to clamor for faster, higher bandwidth and lower latency wireless services, the patent royalty cost of that technology is apparently acceptable to consumers.

Prior 2G-4G SEP/FRAND licensing achieved interoperability, but those licensing regimens were largely managed by less than a dozen network equipment providers, about fifteen baseband chipset suppliers, and about 200 smartphone manufacturers,[59] most

54. GSMA Intelligence, Global Data, https://www.gsmaintelligence.com (last visited Dec. 17, 2018).

55. Press Release, *supra* note 53; *Global Mobile Trends*, GSMA (Oct. 2016), *available at* https://www.gsmaintelligence.com/research/?file=357f1541c77358e61787fac35259dc92&download.

56. GfK, *supra* note 53.

57. *The Mobile Economy 2018*, GSMA, *available at* https://www.gsma.com/mobileeconomy/wp-content/uploads/2018/05/The-Mobile-Economy-2018.pdf.

58. Jason Dedrick & Kenneth L. Kraemer, *Intangible Assets and Value Capture in Global Value Chains: The Smartphone Industry*, WIPO Economic Research Working Paper No. 41 (Nov. 2017), *available at* https://www.wipo.int/edocs/pubdocs/en/wipo_pub_econstat_wp_41.pdf.

59. Since 2007, at any one time there have been two dominant firms in the smartphone industry. However, the initial leaders, Nokia and Blackberry, have almost disappeared from the market, while Apple and Samsung have taken their

of which have dedicated licensing teams of business, technical, and legal professionals.

5G SEP/FRAND licensing will be different. The innovators of 2G-4G technology are also the primary innovators of 5G technology and will remain the primary licensors of that technology to implementers such as smartphone manufacturers. However, the legacy implementers of 2G-4G technology (primarily smartphone manufacturers) will be joined by very large numbers of new implementers of 5G technology in a broad range of industries and products, implementers who have no experience or existing resources for licensing telecommunications technology.

Consider the range of products that will be equipped with 5G technology. Some previously installed equipment with long-remaining productive lifespans will be retrofitted with 5G IoT technology in order to add remote monitoring, predictive maintenance, and integration with new equipment.[60] A tsunami of traditional products that will soon be equipped with 5G IoT capabilities based on the addition of turn-key communication and local processing[61]—think of a "smart refrigerator" that not only tracks bar codes of goods stored inside, each item's expiration date, reorders when supplies are low or projected demand will increase, and a grocery delivery service that fulfills those orders and replenishes

places with a combined 35.8 percent of shipments and 65 percent of revenues in 2015. Dedrick & Kraemer, *supra* note 58.

60. Thomas Lennvall et al., *Challenges When Bringing IoT into Industrial Automation*, IEEE AFRICON (2017), *available at* http://www.diva-portal.org/smash/get/diva2:1145146/FULLTEXT01.pdf; Dell, *Factory Optimization Solution Brief: Retrofitting Legacy Assets for IoT Enablement* (2017), *available at* https://www.emc.com/collateral/solution-overview/retrofitting-legacy-assets-iot-enablement.pdf.

61. A variety of IoT modules are already available or in development. *See* GSMA, Mobile IoT Modules https://www.gsma.com/iot/mobile-iot-modules/ (last visited Dec. 7, 2018).

its own inventory.[62] Turn-key IoT communication and processing modules are already available for 4G systems,[63] some are upgradable to 5G, and there is rapid development of a new generation of 5G communication and processing modules for integration into an extremely broad range of products.

This unprecedented volume of licensing activity will likely be negotiated and enforced by different mechanisms in different vertical industries. For example, smartphones could be licensed with the current negotiation and enforcement regimes. The anticipated small number of remote surgical system providers who will make the most use of advanced 5G capabilities could seek site licenses to reflect local economics and different systems of medical care payment systems. Low-cost commodity sensors like thermostats could benefit from standardized licenses and payment systems available over the Internet, and other creative systems can develop to reflect the value of 5G technology to the product as a whole.

B. Ownership Claims

The convergence of telecommunications and computer technology to form the IoT means that many owners of legacy and emerging technology will have IP ownership interests that are essential or optional to the success of 5G IoT. In 2011, patent-licensing industry experts estimated that smartphones embodied the technology of about 250,000 patents.[64] And as of 2017, even if narrowed to the top 20 GSM, UMTS, and LTE patent owners, those 20 companies own

62. Folasade Osisanwo et al., *Internet Refrigerator—A Typical Internet of Things (IoT)*, 3rd International Conference on Advances in Engineering Sciences & Applied Mathematics (ICAESAM 2015) (Mar. 23–24, 2015), *available at* http://iieng.org/images/proceedings_pdf/2602E0315051.pdf.

63. GSMA, *supra* note 61.

64. RPX Corp., Registration Statement (Form S-1) (Sept. 2, 2011), *available at* https://www.sec.gov/Archives/edgar/data/1509432/000119312511012087/ds1.htm.

an estimated 9,060 families of SEP that may need to be licensed in order to sell smartphones.[65]

5G IoT will enlarge the number of patents that may need to be licensed. Many of the technologies embodied by GSM, UMTS, and LTE standards are carried forward into 5G standards. In addition, those 5G technologies will be coupled with sensor and application devices that embody new fields of technology that are protected by additional families of patents. Private negotiations often achieve the patent licenses necessary for many companies, but otherwise litigation solutions may become necessary.

C. Legal Solutions

5G innovators will primarily enforce their patent rights through three dispute resolution bodies: (1) national courts such as the U.S District Courts, Germany's Landgerichte Courts, or China's Intellectual Property Courts and Tribunals; (2) customs authorities such as the U.S. International Trade Commission and Customs Border Protection, Germany's Zentralstelle Gewerblicher Rechtsschutz in Munich, or China's General Administration of Customs; or (3) through private arbitration and mediation proceedings. Disputes involving globally distributed telecommunications products are often first submitted to the U.S. International Trade Commission (ITC) due to the large size and high profitability of U.S. markets.

1. U.S. International Trade Commission Enforcement

The ITC exercises the authority of the executive and legislative branches to exclude from importation into the United States articles that infringe a U.S. patent that protects a domestic industry (19 U.S.C. § 337). Although sometimes criticized as a tool of

65. Joseph Siino, *Why Solving the Dilemma Is the Key to a Successful Future for IP Deal Making*, ViaGroup (July/Aug. 2017), http://www.via-corp.com/newsdetail.aspx?id=2344.

protectionist trade policies, in fact about one-third of all section 337 complaints are filed by non-U.S.-based companies.[66]

The ITC has jurisdiction over parties that sell for importation into the United States, import or sell after importation into the United States (collectively, "importers"). Like U.S. district courts, the ITC can exercise personal jurisdiction over persons and companies that have at least some minimal level of contact with the United States, or that appear and defend in a section 337 investigation. However, in addition, the ITC also has in rem jurisdiction over all products imported into the United States. The relocation of semiconductor and electronics manufacturing industries into Asia means that most telecommunications and IoT products are now imported into the United States and fall within the jurisdiction of the ITC.

To establish a violation of section 337, a patent owner must establish by a preponderance of the evidence that (1) a valid and enforceable U.S. patent is infringed, (2) by products imported into the United States, and (3) that there are significant investments in a U.S. domestic industry that exploits the patent.[67]

The procedures in section 337 investigations are similar to those in district court patent infringement cases in several ways: Section 337 provides the full gamut of discovery tools;[68] motions are available to resolve discovery disputes;[69] motions for summary disposition are available[70] (although less frequently granted than in district court); and formal trials are held.[71] However, there are important procedural differences. Section 337 patent infringe-

66. Keith E. Maskus, Private Rights and Public Problems: The Global Economics of Intellectual Property in the 21st Century (2012).

67. *See* 19 C.F.R. §§ 210.27–.32.

68. *See id.* §§ 210.27–.32.

69. *See id.* §§ 210.33–.34.

70. *See id.* § 210.18.

71. *See id.* §§ 210.35–.39.

ment investigations are typically completed in about 16 months,[72] whereas comparable cases in the district courts average about 30 months.[73] The ITC's expedited proceedings can provide within 16 months injunctive-type relief that is rarely stayed during appeal, a significant advantage in the electronics and telecommunications industries where products with short commercial lifespans can become obsolete before a district court action might reach trial. In fact, during the period from 2015 to 2018, about 45 percent of the ITC cases involved telecommunications and electronics products that will be involved in the 5G IoT.[74]

Section 337 investigations often involve extensive foreign discovery, complex technology (over various periods, about 40 to 70 percent of the cases involve the telecommunications, electronics, and semiconductor industries), voluminous briefs and written testimony, and high-demand trials that are compressed into very short time periods. While only about 3 percent of district court patent infringement cases proceed to trial, about 40 percent of section 337 investigations proceed to trial. The ITC's dedicated administrative law judges preside over discovery and a trial, and they issue an initial determination (ID) on all issues that bear on whether the importers have violated section 337—all within about 12 months. The ITC commissioners then take over the case for the final four months during which they can review and modify the findings in the ID, and then rule on remedy, bonding, and public interest issues.

---

72. *Section 337 Statistics: Average Length of Investigations,* U.S. Int'l Trade Comm'n, https://usitc.gov/intellectual_property/337_statistics_average_length_investigations.htm (last updated Oct. 23, 2018).

73. *2017 Patent Litigation Study: Change on the Horizon?*, PwC 7 (May 2017), https://www.pwc.com/us/en/forensic-services/publications/assets/2017-patent-litigation-study.pdf.

74. *Section 337 Statistics: Technology Areas of Accused Products*, U.S. Int'l Trade Comm'n, https://www.usitc.gov/intellectual_property/337_statistics_types_accused_products_new_filings.htm (last visited Dec. 19, 2018).

When a complainant wins, unless contrary to the public interest, the ITC must issue an exclusion order that directs the U.S. Customs and Border Protection (CBP) to stop further importations of infringing products.[75] If the importers who were found in violation have commercially significant inventories of infringing products, the ITC has the discretion to also issue a cease-and-desist order prohibiting certain enumerated commercial activities involving that inventory.[76] In practice, most telecommunications cases settle upon mutually agreed terms rather than proceeding to the actual issuance and enforcement of remedial orders.

2. U.S. District Court Enforcement

5G innovators can also assert their patent rights in the U.S. District Courts, sometimes in conjunction with asserting those same patents at the ITC.[77] The district courts hold original and exclusive jurisdiction over actions arising under the Patent Act and thus are not bound by the decisions of the ITC.[78]

With a few notable exceptions, district court patent actions are much slower than ITC proceedings—often requiring two to three years to proceed to trial, and in cases with overlapping invalidation proceedings at the U.S. Patent Office, as many as five years may pass before trial. Although about 4,600 patent infringement complaints were filed in 2017, typically only about 3 percent of those complaints culminated in a trial.[79] Many cases are settled, some are

75. 19 U.S.C. § 1337(d).

76. *Id.* § 1337(f).

77. ITC respondents have the unilateral right to stay any U.S. district court proceedings on the same patents until conclusion of the ITC proceedings and any appeals therefrom. 19 U.S.C. § 1659.

78. 28 U.S.C. § 1331. Except for ancillary issues such as breach of contract claims arising from the sale of a patent, as a general matter state courts do not have jurisdiction to enforce patents.

79. Docket Navigator Analytics, *New Patent Cases and Trials (2008–2018)*. For example, in 2017, 4,548 cases were initiated, but there were just 122 trials during the same time frame (2.7 percent).

resolved by summary judgment, and others are withdrawn due to lack of interest or litigation resources.

Plaintiffs and defendants have a constitutionally guaranteed right to a jury trial, but upon agreement of both, a judge can decide in lieu of a jury. While a well-educated and experienced judge might more easily comprehend the complex technology at issue in many patent cases, about 80 percent of patent infringement cases that go to trial are tried to a jury, probably because plaintiffs have generally obtained higher success rates and larger monetary damages before juries instead of judges.[80] While some wireless cellular technologies can be conceptualized for lay juries, many 5G technologies turn on esoteric engineering issues that are best described by Fourier transforms, matrix algebra, and other mathematical models that are beyond the working knowledge and interest of the typical jury pool—in those cases, many patent holders will opt for an ITC investigation where there are no juries and the judges focus on patent issues.

U.S. district courts can issue injunctive relief to stop further infringement of patent rights and can additionally award monetary damages for patent infringement. The Patent Act provides for the award of damages "adequate to compensate for the infringement, but in no event less than a reasonable royalty for the use of the invention made by the infringer."[81] The courts have recognized multiple grounds for calculating the appropriate compensation, but lost profits and reasonable royalties are the two most common means of determining appropriate damage awards.

3. Private Mediation and Arbitration Proceedings

Some 5G IoT patent disputes will be resolved by mediation or arbitration. While mediation and arbitration typically arise upon

80. *2017 Patent Litigation Study*, *supra* note 73.
81. 35 U.S.C. § 284.

agreement of the parties, such agreements exist in many license agreements that cover 3G and 4G technologies that will be carried forward into 5G NR and 5GC systems. Mediation and arbitration offer several advantages, including confidentiality and selection of arbitrators with applicable technical or legal expertise. But mediation and arbitration are also limited by difficulty in obtaining third-party discovery and the absence of direct appeals. Perhaps the most frequently discussed potential use of mediation and arbitration in telecommunications is to determine FRAND-compliant licensing terms.

InterDigital's and Huawei's 2014 decision to voluntarily submit their 3G and 4G patent infringement claims to arbitration initially consolidated multiple actions in multiple jurisdictions into a single arbitral proceeding and suggested a new willingness of major telecommunication companies to privately resolve their IP disputes.[82] This initially promising solution later ran aground when the arbitration award was later attached and enforced in multiple proceedings concerning the applicable law for determining the patent license terms that would comply with the applicable FRAND obligations.[83] Future mobile cellular licensing agreements are well advised to agree in advance on such fundamental issues as choice of law so that the potential advantages of arbitration are not lost to ambiguity in the agreement to arbitrate.

VIII. Conclusion

5G mobile communications will enable the IoT to deliver vast improvement in current services and a range of new services that exceed our current imagination. The underlying technology is evolutionary—it incorporates improved versions of earlier-generation

82. Eli Greenbaum, *Arbitration Without Law: Choice of Law in FRAND Disputes*, Res Gestae. 26 (2016), *available at* http://ir.lawnet.fordham.edu/res_gestae/26

83. *Id.*

solutions—and it is revolutionary in the introduction of fundamentally new features that depart from prior generations of wireless communications. The technical complexity of these 5G technologies, combined with the technical complexity of cloud-based real-time processing of very large volumes of data, and the development of artificial intelligence to manage these processes, will generate interesting and complex legal issues for years to come.

Chapter 5

Blockchain and the Internet of Things

Jay Johnson
Mark Rasmussen
Kerianne Tobitsch

I. Introduction to Blockchain Applications in the IoT

Blockchain is a significant technological innovation celebrated for its potential to disrupt traditional ways of business with more efficient and collaborative business models. It is a form of distributed ledger technology[1] that allows parties to transact without the need for a central authority. Most ledger systems in use today rely on some form of centralized control. Entities that participate in a centralized system must send transactions to the trusted central authority, which validates the transaction and keeps the ledger updated. Figure 5.1 depicts such a system.

In contrast to these centralized systems, a blockchain allows users to transact directly with one another without first having a central authority validate a transaction or keep the ledger updated.

1. In this chapter, we use "blockchain" to generically refer to all distributed ledger technology (DLT). There are many non-blockchain DLTs that are being developed, such as hashgraph and directed acrylic graphs, that possess different attributes but offer similar benefits.

Instead, blockchain transactions are recorded in a digital ledger, and identical copies of the ledger are maintained by the participants, or "nodes," of a distributed peer-to-peer network. This type of peer-to-peer system is depicted in Figure 5.2.

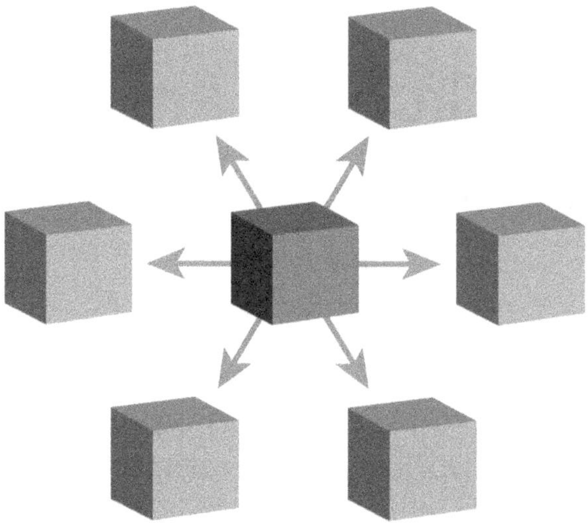

Figure 5.1 Centralized System

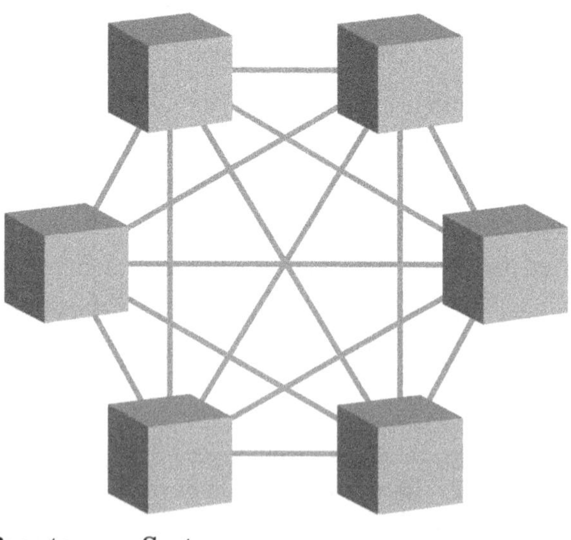

Figure 5.2 Peer-to-peer System

Figure 5.3 A Chain of Blocks

Each new transaction is broadcast to all of the nodes on the network and collected into a "block" of transactions, which is added to the ledger once it is validated and accepted by users controlling a majority of the computing power on the network. Each new block that is added is intertwined with the preceding block, creating an unbreakable chain of blocks that is rendered secure and immutable through cryptographic computations. Figure 5.3 depicts how new valid blocks are linked together with older blocks.

While bitcoin is the first and still most widely known blockchain application, the technology has various other potential applications, including to the IoT. In the IoT, for example, blockchain can be leveraged for inventory or supply chain management, among other things. Using blockchains to manage supply chains may enable companies to increase efficiencies by eliminating the central authority and allowing each participant in a supply chain to identify and record assets that are transferred and to better manage the flow of paperwork. Companies will be able to eliminate the errors and inefficiencies that come from maintaining their own databases and reconciling them against those maintained by other companies to track events on the supply chain. In addition, because of the immutable chain of events that is recorded on a blockchain, companies also will be able to keep a permanent record that provides one version of the truth that is determined by consensus.

The potential blockchain IoT applications are as varied as IoT products themselves. But to understand them requires an introduction to the concept of "smart code." Smart code is computer programming logic that can run on a blockchain or other distributed ledger technologies to automatically perform certain functions once predetermined conditions or requirements are met. For example, smart code could enable one person to automatically transfer an asset to another once a future event occurs. Smart code relies on inputs from external sources, or "oracles," to initiate the programming logic that performs the function. Legal agreements that include smart code are often referred to as smart contracts.

Given that an IoT ecosystem may consist of millions of Internet-connected devices, each capable of acting as an oracle to provide real-time data inputs, supply chain management is one particularly compelling application of the blockchain. Blockchain and smart contract technologies applied to the IoT offer a way to record and track events occurring throughout a supply chain. IoT sensors with GPS technology are capable of detecting a precise event or condition within a supply chain and sending a signal to initiate an operation through smart code that runs on a blockchain. For example, a furniture retailer could use an IoT device to detect the departure of a sofa from the retailer's warehouse and to automatically initiate a smart contract transaction with the manufacturer to replace the sofa. Combining IoT, smart contracts, and blockchain technologies can enable businesses to make better decisions about shipments, product availability, and vendor management.

Another area where blockchain and smart contract technologies could be deployed within the IoT is production management. Blockchain technologies deployed in IoT devices across a factory floor could record information gathered from IoT sensors about the status of each phase of manufacturing—for example, what parts need to be ordered or when maintenance might be required—and then execute smart code to automatically signal to other devices the appropriate actions to take in response.

Blockchain technologies also may be particularly useful for monitoring equipment in asset-heavy industries such as oil and gas, mining, agriculture, and utilities that have implemented the IoT through an extensive deployment of equipment sensors throughout the industrial setting.[2] A blockchain could maintain, for example, a list of key indicators in the industrial setting (such as yield, throughput, capacity utilization, and others), enabling IoT devices to monitor the performance of industrial equipment, signal the need for maintenance and repairs, and use smart code to order part replacements without human intervention. Using blockchain technologies in this manner also allows businesses to create a permanent and auditable record of transactions that have occurred.

Once theoretical, these and other blockchain applications are now close to reality, as companies develop IoT platforms capable of incorporating blockchain and smart code technologies.[3] This chapter will address the benefits of applying blockchain technologies to the IoT and the question of whether it is feasible for this application to become a reality on a meaningful scale with real world implications. The chapter will then assess the legal implications and challenges of combining blockchain technologies with the IoT. These include jurisdictional challenges, privacy concerns, and contractual implications. Finally, this chapter will examine potential legal claims and regulatory enforcement actions that could be brought against blockchain-based IoT platforms.

II. Consequences of Blockchain-Based IoT Platforms

IoT could benefit from improvements in processing power, storage capacity, security, interoperability and device communication

2. *The Industrial IoT: 125+ Startups Transforming Factory Floors, Oil Fields, and Supply Chains*, CB Insights: Research (May 5, 2017), https://www.cbinsights.com/research/top-startups-iiot/.

3. *See, e.g.*, Stan Higgins, *IBM Reveals Proof of Concept for Blockchain-Powered Internet of Things*, CoinDesk (Mar. 6, 2015), https://www.coindesk.com/ibm-reveals-proof-concept-blockchain-powered-internet-things/.

efficiencies, and standardization of IoT devices. Technical obstacles to widespread implementation of blockchain technologies at the scale needed to address certain of these challenges remain. For example, a blockchain would need to scale to accommodate the millions of connected devices serviced in an IoT ecosystem, and to process and compute information from an increasingly diverse array of transactions conducted by IoT devices. Nevertheless, blockchain technologies may be inherently capable of addressing certain of IoT's challenges. Consider two challenges in particular: cybersecurity and IoT device communications.

A. Cybersecurity

One of the greatest technical and legal challenges presently facing the IoT is cybersecurity. The massive distributed denial of service (DDoS) attacks in 2016 against popular Internet websites using the Mirai malware demonstrate the destructive capability of compromised IoT devices. There, IoT devices infected with Mirai were used as part of a botnet to conduct large-scale network attacks by flooding Internet servers with millions of requests, ultimately shutting down websites for a period of time. Many IoT devices, particularly everyday consumer products, do not incorporate security by design, potentially compounding the issue of vulnerable access points when a large number of unsecure, identical devices are distributed within an industrial environment or among consumers in widespread locations. Furthermore, it may be difficult to detect an attack that does not affect the performance of the IoT device, and it is difficult to monitor so many IoT devices deployed in different locations.

Blockchain technologies may be capable of improving the cybersecurity of IoT devices in some ways. For example, blockchain creates immutable transactional records secured through cryptography. Each block of transactions is converted into a unique hash, or digital fingerprint. Any changes in the data in a block will cause a change in the corresponding hash, and all network participants will know that data has been compromised. In addition, the hash of each block is incorporated into the hash of the next valid block, thus creating an ongoing chain. As a result, none of the information in a block can be changed without causing changes to subsequent blocks. Furthermore, with blockchain technology, there is not a central copy of the ledger stored in a single location. Rather, copies of the ledger are provided to each participant in the peer-to-peer blockchain network. This can improve cybersecurity in at least two ways: one, by eliminating the possibility of a single point of failure for a hacker to target, and two, by preventing an unauthorized participant or attacker from unilaterally modifying a piece of the chain. Large storage and processing power is needed to run some blockchains, however, and not all IoT devices are sufficiently capable of doing so.[4] Nor do all devices within an IoT network have the same computing capabilities, which means that not all IoT devices may be able to run the same computational algorithms at high speeds.[5]

B. IoT Device Communications

IoT networks currently rely on a centralized communication model known as the server/client paradigm, whereby IoT devices are identified and connected through central cloud servers with large processing and storage capabilities.[6] But centralized communication can suffer from speed, efficiency, and cost constraints. Blockchain technologies may allow devices to communicate with each other locally and in a more distributed fashion, improving

---

4. Ahmed Banafa, *IoT and Blockchain Convergence: Benefits and Challenges*, IEEE (Jan. 10, 2017), https://iot.ieee.org/newsletter/january-2017/iot-and-blockchain-convergence-benefits-and-challenges.html.

5. *Id.*

6. *Id.*; Ben Dickson, *Decentralizing IoT Networks through Blockchain*, TECHCRUNCH (Apr. 15, 2013), https://techcrunch.com/2016/06/28/decentralizing-iot-networks-through-blockchain/.

communication speed and reducing centralized data storage costs by shifting storage back to IoT devices themselves (a blockchain stores its ledger on nodes rather than a central server). This may be an obstacle for IoT devices that do not have sufficient storage capabilities for the ledger, especially as more transactions are recorded in a blockchain.

Technical solutions are needed before the IoT can make full use of blockchain technologies to overcome these and other challenges, and it may be premature and beyond the scope of this chapter to speculate on whether or how these technical challenges of incorporating blockchain technologies into the IoT will be overcome. Still, companies are presently exploring creative solutions to the aforementioned and other issues, such as storing only small blockchain segments on any given IoT device that involve transaction information pertaining to that device.[7] When technical challenges are resolved, blockchain-based IoT platforms could unleash new methods of business that will raise legal challenges.

III. Potential Legal Issues Raised by Applying Blockchain Technologies to the IoT

Blockchain technologies already have created legal issues that are not so easily addressed by existing standards and frameworks. This may prompt the development of new laws to address the unique issues raised by these technologies, or changes to the technologies themselves may be necessary to alleviate privacy, security, and other legal concerns. Consider the following:

A. Jurisdiction and Dispute Resolution

Disputes arising from the use of disruptive technologies like IoT and blockchain are inevitable. Both IoT and blockchain technologies challenge traditional approaches to jurisdiction and dispute

7. Higgins, *supra* note 3.

resolution because they are designed to interact seamlessly across both domestic and international borders with numerous devices and participants. This makes it difficult to apply existing legal standards and jurisdictional notions to disputes arising out of the use of blockchain-based IoT platforms.

A threshold issue in any dispute is identifying which parties can be sued. There are many participants in a blockchain that potentially could be held liable, including manufacturers of IoT products, creators of blockchain protocols, developers of applications that run on IoT platforms, and end users of blockchain technologies or IoT products. As emerging technologies, both blockchain and the IoT raise novel issues about which parties should bear liability and how to allocate liability among them. For example, should creators of blockchain platforms and protocols themselves be sued for activities conducted on the platform by the end users? How should liability be allocated among the various blockchain participants?

Existing frameworks can help assess how to allocate liability, but only to a point. For example, terms of service or end user license agreements are a common mechanism to establish the rights and obligations of parties and to address allocation and scope of potential liability. But incorporating blockchain into IoT products raises the additional question of which terms of service apply. Should there be a separate terms of service agreement for blockchain platforms, or should the terms of use for the IoT product govern the technology as a whole?

Another issue central to dispute resolution is the selection of an appropriate forum for the dispute. In the United States, jurisdiction is based on physical connections or interactions with a judicial forum. But this focus on "location" is difficult to reconcile with the virtual realm where blockchain exists. As a distributed ledger, blockchain by nature is designed to be decentralized with no central node. Nodes could be located anywhere and blockchain transactions could affect nodes in multiple locations. Courts in the

United States are just beginning to grapple with how to address these issues. For example, a federal court in Northern California recently considered the question of where a sales transaction recorded on the Ethereum blockchain took place for purposes of federal securities laws. The court first analyzed standard issues such as where the server hosting the website was hosted, where the operator of the website was located, and at which location was marketing directed. The court then reached a novel conclusion. Holding that the purchase occurred in the United States, the court reasoned that the "contribution of Ethereum . . . became irrevocable only after it was validated by a network of global 'nodes' clustered more densely in the United States than in any other country."[8] Does this mean that any company that transacts on the Ethereum platform subjects itself to the laws of the United States? It is not clear yet how competing assertions of jurisdiction by forums in more than one location will be resolved by other courts. Furthermore, blockchain users and their respective locations may be pseudonymous, making it difficult to identify and serve process on potential litigants.

B. Privacy Concerns

There are, of course, different types of blockchains that each present different privacy concerns. One that is accessible by anyone is typically referred to as a public, or permissionless, blockchain. *Permissionless* blockchains raise privacy concerns about the publishing and sharing of personal information by permitting any member of the public to access, download, or contribute to a blockchain. Blockchain developers may even make the complete transactional

8. *In re* Tezos Securities Litig., No. 17-cv-06779, Order on Defendants' Motion to Dismiss at 14 (N.D. Cal. Aug. 7, 2018).

record available for anyone to read.[9] While blockchain participants can choose to be pseudonymous by linking their transactions only to an electronic address, researchers have found ways to identify individuals by using cookies and other online tracking technologies.[10] Also, people often reveal their identity by transacting on centralized exchanges, many of which require customers to identify themselves before setting up an account. One way to alleviate privacy concerns is to use private, or *permissioned*, blockchains for transactions that involve personal information or sensitive commercial information. These are accessible only to participants who are invited to join. Another solution may be to store personal information away from the chain but publish a reference to the data on a blockchain.

Furthermore, it may be difficult for blockchain operators to comply with privacy-related regulatory obligations. Most notable at present is the European Union's General Data Protection Regulation (GDPR), which imposes certain obligations on a data controller, meaning those who control the purposes and means of processing personal data of EU residents.[11] It is not clear who the data controller is in a given blockchain. Indeed, some might argue that each blockchain node is a separate data controller with compliance obligations under the GDPR. The GDPR imposes obligations on data controllers that are not easy to implement on a blockchain. For example, individuals have the right to request deletion of their personal data, but blockchains are designed to be immutable and decentralized with each participant having a copy of the given blockchain ledger. Furthermore, the term "personal data," broadly

---

9. Nolan Bauerle, *What Is the Difference between Public and Permissioned Blockchains?*, CoinDesk, https://www.coindesk.com/information/what-is-the-difference-between-open-and-permissioned-blockchains/.

10. *Bitcoin Transactions Aren't as Anonymous as Everyone Hoped,* MIT Technology Review (Aug. 23, 2013), https://www.technologyreview.com/s/608716/bitcoin-transactions-arent-as-anonymous-as-everyone-hoped/.

11. Council Regulation 2016/679, art. 4, 2016 O.J. (L 119) 1, 65 (EU).

defined under the GDPR as any information relating to an identified or identifiable natural person,[12] potentially applies to a vast amount of data stored on a blockchain. To address these issues, companies are developing solutions to break the link between data stored on a blockchain and the corresponding individual in a way that may satisfy GDPR and other privacy laws.

In addition, the platform will need a mechanism to identify certain categories of information stored on a blockchain that are subject to sector-specific privacy rules. For example, protected health information (PHI) is subject to privacy requirements under the U.S. Health Insurance Portability and Accountability Act (HIPAA), which applies to certain "covered entities" and "business associates" in the health care sector. HIPAA's requirements include minimizing the amount of PHI shared with others to that which is necessary to accomplish an objective, as well as giving individuals the opportunity to obtain copies of their PHI. The IoT platform needs the capability to identify and apply appropriate treatment to these regulated types of data to comply with sector-specific laws.

Despite these privacy challenges, in some circumstances blockchain technologies can better enable compliance with privacy obligations. For example, the Federal Trade Commission (FTC) requires certain financial institutions to notify consumers about the sharing of their "nonpublic personal information" with third parties and to provide them with the option to opt out. Similarly, the GDPR requires data controllers to notify individuals about the collection and processing of their personal data and to provide the opportunity to withdraw consent in certain circumstances. Blockchain technologies may help entities subject to these laws better record when they provide these notices to consumers and to track consumer consents.

12. *Id.*

C. Contract Issues

Smart contracts that use IoT devices as inputs and run on blockchain platforms present other legal issues. As discussed previously, a smart contract incorporates smart code to recognize that certain conditions have been met and to impose consequences as a result. For example, applying smart contracts to the IoT is useful in the context of supply chain management by allowing automatic execution of payment or progression to the next phase of production once the smart code detects that certain supplies have been shipped. Though smart contract platforms are still in the development stage, companies are exploring ways to incorporate them. For example, a large container-shipping company is developing a blockchain system to manage its supply chain and obtain real-time access to shipping data, including information about temperature and container weight gathered through IoT and sensor data.[13]

General principles of contract law govern smart contract agreement and performance. In the United States, there must be an offer and acceptance of the essential terms of the contract, and the terms must be sufficiently definite to be enforceable.[14] Therefore, parties to a smart contract must determine how to express the terms of the contract. One option is to express all terms through provisions written into smart code. There are limitations to this approach because not all of the terms of a contract can be embedded into code. Terms that require the exercise of judgment, such as "reasonable" efforts or materiality, cannot be converted easily into code and may still require human intervention. Smart provisions lend themselves better to operational clauses that address a specific action to be taken under a contract, such as sensing when supply is running low and issuing a command to a supplier to ship more products.

---

13. *Maersk and IBM Introduce TradeLens Blockchain Shipping Solution*, IBM (Aug. 9, 2018), https://newsroom.ibm.com/2018-08-09-Maersk-and-IBM-Introduce-TradeLens-Blockchain-Shipping-Solution.

14. John Edward Murray, Jr., Murray on Contracts (5th ed. 2011).

Another option is to express terms through natural language in the form of a written agreement on paper or in a text file stored in the blockchain ledger. In this way, the smart code is merely a mechanism to implement the contract, but the smart code itself does not legally bind the parties. Alternatively, the parties could use a combination of smart code provisions and natural language provisions, but the contract will need to address circumstances in which either type of provision controls.

Smart contracts using code present an additional risk of mistake in performance due to flaws or bugs in the code. Given that smart contracts execute commands automatically, these flaws could result in business consequences before there is an opportunity to prevent or correct the error. In a supply chain context, this could result in the delivery of too many products, late shipment of products, or deliveries to the wrong location, all of which may trigger non-performance or material breach provisions in the contract or result in legal disputes between the parties. Parties should negotiate how to allocate liability between themselves in anticipation of potential flaws in the performance of the code. The parties may want to incorporate audit or testing requirements into the contract to agree on an acceptable level of performance of the code prior to implementing it under the contract.

Further complicating disputes involving smart contracts is the presence of the platform as an intermediary in the performance of a contract. The platform operates and maintains the blockchain ledger on which the smart code is deployed, but a flawed platform or one otherwise vulnerable to compromise could interfere with performance of the smart contract and give rise to two types of disputes: those between the parties to the contract themselves and those between the parties to the contract and the platform operator.

In anticipation of potential disputes, given the jurisdictional challenges explained earlier, parties to a contract should consider incorporating choice of law and choice of jurisdiction provisions into smart contracts. Parties may consider selecting jurisdictions that already embrace blockchain innovations. For example, Delaware amended its General Corporation Law to allow companies to maintain corporate records on a blockchain,[15] and Delaware extends statutory protections for written communications to electronic transmissions.[16] Arizona has authorized the use of smart contracts in corporate transactions and incorporates blockchain records under its state electronic recordkeeping laws.[17] Vermont recognizes the admissibility of a digital record registered in a blockchain[18] and provides authentication procedures for these records under its state rules of evidence.[19]

D. Liability

Developers of blockchain and IoT technologies may face exposure to civil claims or regulatory actions for privacy, cybersecurity, or other legal violations. Regarding the former, the range of potential civil claims may include negligence, negligent misrepresentation, breach of contract, invasion of privacy, unjust enrichment, conversion, and trespass to chattels. Plaintiffs will likely rely on a limited subset of these potential claims, such as negligence, that are more commonly asserted in the context of new technologies. A blockchain participant or user may assert a negligence claim if the blockchain code did not perform as intended or if there was a breach of security, or a negligent misrepresentation claim if the owner of a blockchain-based platform made a material misrepresentation as to the security of its technology. Such claims have already been asserted against operators of IoT products for failure to provide

15. S. 69, 149th Gen. Assem., 1st Reg. Sess. (Del. 2017).
16. *See* Del. Code Ann. tit. 8 §§ 151(f), 202(a), 232(c), 364.
17. Ariz. Rev. Sat. Ann. § 44-7061(E)(1)–(2).
18. *See* Vt. Stat. Ann. tit. 12 § 1913(b)–(c).
19. *See id.*; Vt. R. Evid. 902.

reasonable security consistent with industry standards.[20] The economic loss rule, which prohibits recovery in the absence of injury to person or property, presents an obstacle to plaintiffs here,[21] and it is notably very difficult to determine appropriate industry standards at this early stage in the development of blockchain technologies.

Tort claims for invasion of privacy may also be likely in light of the privacy concerns raised by blockchain-based IoT platforms. A plaintiff would have to demonstrate that the defendant captured information about the individual's private or familial activity, and did so in a way that was offensive to a reasonable person.[22] This claim could be asserted in the blockchain context if sensitive information about a person were published on the chain for all participants to view. Invasion of privacy claims have been asserted already in matters involving the IoT,[23] though the privacy concern may be greater in the blockchain context where it is difficult to erase information that becomes part of the ledger and once copies of the ledger are distributed to all blockchain participants.

Regulatory enforcement actions present another risk of liability. Blockchain-based IoT platforms may be subject to the requirements of the GDPR, for example, with potential fines for certain violations reaching up to EUR 20 million. The potential exposure under the GDPR is considerable, given that the GDPR contains broad terms that sweep over a range of data content and activities recorded in a blockchain, and the stringent privacy-related requirements in the GDPR are difficult to implement on a blockchain platform, as previously discussed.

---

20. *In re* Sony Gaming Networks & Customer Data Sec. Breach Litig., 996 F. Supp. 2d 942, 966–73 (S.D. Cal. 2014), *order corrected*, No. 11MD2258 AJB (MDD), 2014 WL 12603117 (S.D. Cal. Feb. 10, 2014).

21. *Id.* at 967–73.

22. *See, e.g.*, CAL. CIV. CODE § 1708.8(a).

23. *See, e.g.*, Hayes v. ToyTalk, Inc., et al., 2:16-cv-02111-JAK-PLA (ECF No. 1).

The FTC also has broad authority under Section 5 of the Federal Trade Commission Act to enforce consumer privacy and security by regulating unfair or deceptive practices. The FTC has exercised its authority to regulate unfair practices in the IoT context that are likely to cause substantial injury to consumers that cannot reasonably be avoided, such as where a technology captures images or records keystrokes without consumer knowledge or consent.[24] The FTC also may exercise its authority to regulate deceptive acts in the context of the IoT where companies fail to follow their own privacy and security policies.[25]

IV. Conclusion

Incorporating blockchain technologies into the IoT offers the opportunity to improve IoT capabilities and to develop new forms of communicating and transacting business, often in ways that are not yet fully understood. At the same time, these technologies present unique legal concerns that are still emerging at this early phase in blockchain development. Liability in the context of the IoT has already begun to take shape, but it is almost certain to evolve further once IoT platforms more fully implement blockchain. New laws or regulatory guidance may be needed to address the unique issues raised by the combination of blockchain and IoT technologies.

---

24. *See FTC Approves Final Order Settling Charges against Software and Rent-to-Own Companies Accused of Computer Spying*, Fed. Trade Comm'n (Apr. 15, 2013), https://www.ftc.gov/news-events/press-releases/2013/04/ftc-approves-final-order-settling-charges-against-software-and; *see, e.g.*, Decision and Order, DesignerWare, LLC, No. C-4390 (F.T.C. Apr. 11, 2013) (the FTC found that installing and turning on webcams on people's home computers without their knowledge or consent was an unfair practice).

25. *See Mobile Phone Maker BLU Reaches Settlement with FTC over Deceptive Privacy and Data Security Claims*, Fed. Trade Comm'n (Apr. 30, 2018), https://www.ftc.gov/news-events/press-releases/2018/04/mobile-phone-maker-blu-reaches-settlement-ftc-over-deceptive.

PART II

THE STATE (OR LACK THEREOF) OF IOT LAWS AND REGULATIONS

Chapter 6

U.S. Regulatory Framework for IoT

Laura Kim
Jennifer Johnson[1]

U.S. regulators are grappling with a variety of policy issues as businesses and consumers increasingly rely on Internet-connected products and services. While Internet of Things (IoT)-specific regulation in the United States is fairly limited at this time, federal and state regulators are considering a variety of regulatory approaches to oversight of IoT products and services. In some cases, regulators are exploring new regulation targeted to the IoT.

This chapter provides a brief overview of U.S. regulatory developments and trends in the IoT space, with emphasis on the following substantive areas of IoT: product safety regulation; privacy and cybersecurity regulations; IoT connectivity and spectrum regulation; banking, energy, and drones; and state law trends regarding autonomous vehicles and privacy. This discussion touches on

1. This chapter includes contributions from Sarah Wilson (product safety); Wade Ackerman, Elizabeth Guo, Christopher Hanson, and Christina Kuhn (medical device regulation); Laura Kim and Lindsay Brewer (privacy and cybersecurity); Susan Cassidy (procurement); Matthew DelNero and Thom Parisi (connectivity and spectrum); Michael Nonaka (financial services regulation); Jack Schenendorf (drones); Mark Perlis (energy); and Jake Levine (state regulatory trends).

regulatory initiatives, enforcement actions, and policy guidance from the Consumer Product Safety Commission (CPSC), Department of Transportation (DOT) and National Highway Traffic Safety Administration (NHTSA), Food and Drug Administration (FDA), Federal Trade Commission (FTC), Federal Communications Commission (FCC), Federal Aviation Administration (FAA), National Institute of Standards and Technology (NIST), Federal Energy Regulatory Commission (FERC), the federal banking agencies, and the State of California.

I. Product Safety Regulations

A. CPSC

The rise of connected devices over the past several years has yielded and will continue to yield numerous benefits to industry and the public alike. IoT-enabled devices make daily tasks easier and more convenient for consumers, reduce energy waste through remote operation of equipment and other physical apparatuses, facilitate wireless updates to software and firmware that improve product efficiency, and enhance manufacturers' ability to keep track of their products as they move through the supply chain.[2] However, the technology and data-dependent nature of IoT devices and the interconnectedness of products and components in the IoT ecosystem can pose potential risks to life and safety, risks that did not exist in the pre-digital era and that were not contemplated when most product safety laws and regulations were adopted, decades ago.[3]

2. *See* Organisation for Economic Co-Operation and Development, *Consumer Product Safety in the Internet of Things*, 267 OECD Digital Economy Papers 6, 17–18 (2018), https://read.oecd-ilibrary.org/science-and-technology/consumer-product-safety-in-the-internet-of-things_7c45fa66-en [hereinafter OECD Report].

3. *See id.* at 18–20; The Internet of Things and Consumer Product Hazards, 83 Fed. Reg. 13122, 13123 (Mar. 27, 2018) [hereinafter CPSC Request for Comments].

This is a topic to which the CPSC, America's chief product safety regulator, has paid growing attention in recent years.[4] In January 2017, the CPSC published a staff report identifying trends in the increasingly "smart" consumer product marketplace and potential hazards associated with emerging and future technologies, including IoT.[5] The report, which aligned with the CPSC's 2016–2020 Strategic Plan to advance the agency's understanding of consumer product hazards linked to new technology, contemplated that future efforts by the CPSC to eliminate or reduce the risks posed by such technology would likely be accomplished "through active participation in voluntary standards committees"

4. The United States is not alone in considering the impact Internet connectivity may have on the safety of consumer products. In March 2018, the Organisation for Economic Co-operation and Development, comprised of 35 member countries (including the United States), published a report discussing concepts and trends in the IoT space, consumer product safety benefits and risks posed by IoT, and policy challenges raised by IoT devices (including those involved in making distinctions between and among hardware, software, products, and services, and in allocating liability for IoT harms). *See* OECD Report, *supra* note 1. Two months later, the European Commission published a report recommending a reconsideration of key liability concepts in its Product Liability Directive, such as what constitutes a "product" in the context of IoT and what the appropriate burden of proof should be in the IoT environment. *See* European Comm'n, Report from the Commission to the European Parliament, the Council and the European Economic and Social Committee on the Application of the Council Directive on the Approximation of the Laws, Regulations, and Administrative Provisions of the Member States Concerning Liability for Defective Products (85/374/EEC) (May 7, 2018), https://eur-lex.europa.eu/legal-content/EN/TXT/PDF/?uri=CELEX:52018DC0246&from=EN. Further consideration of IoT is likely on the horizon in Europe and elsewhere in the world.

5. *See* U.S. Consumer Product Safety Comm'n, Staff Report—Potential Hazards Associated with Emerging and Future Technologies (Jan. 18, 2017), https://www.cpsc.gov/s3fs-public/Report%20on%20Emerging%20Consumer%20Products%20and%20Technologies_FINAL.pdf.

and "by collaborating with consumer and industry stakeholders and [its] federal partners."[6]

The CPSC has since further waded into the discussion of IoT safety issues. In March 2018, the agency commenced a proceeding aimed at exploring the safety issues and hazards related to connected consumer products.[7] Among other topics, the CPSC invited comment on the following:

- The potential benefits and harms associated with the use and misuse of IoT products.
- Whether new safety standards and certifications should be developed to address IoT safety, and whether any such standards or certification requirements should be mandatory or voluntary.
- What role (if any) the CPSC should play in regulating the IoT environment, and to what extent the CPSC should coordinate any regulatory efforts with those of other federal agencies and international bodies.
- How best to assign liability for IoT-related harms between and among various participants in the product supply chain.[8]

In May 2018, the CPSC held a public hearing at which advocates from industry associations, representatives from standard-setting organizations, cybersecurity professionals, members of the academy, and others presented testimony on the aforementioned topics, and the agency accepted written comments on these topics through June 2018. Insofar as the CPSC ultimately decides to take further regulatory action, however, the agency has made clear that

6. *Id.* at ii; *see also* U.S. CONSUMER PRODUCT SAFETY COMM'N, STRATEGIC PLAN 2016-2020: EXECUTIVE SUMMARY, https://www.cpsc.gov/s3fs-public/CPSC_2016-2020_Strategic_Plan_Executive_Summary.pdf.

7. *See* CPSC Request for Comments, *supra* note 3.

8. *See id.* at 13123–24.

any such steps likely would exclude consideration of data privacy and data security issues that may be implicated by IoT devices.[9]

B. DOT and NHTSA

Although the CPSC has recently take an interest in IoT safety issues, much of the activity in the IoT and related artificial intelligence (AI) spaces thus far has been directed toward autonomous vehicles, which fall under the jurisdiction of the DOT and its constituent agency, NHTSA. In September 2016, DOT and NHTSA released the first ever "Federal Automated Vehicles Policy," which provided the agencies' initial thoughts on the core frameworks on which manufacturers could rely in developing safe driverless vehicles.[10] A year later, DOT and NHTSA replaced this policy with a more streamlined version that provides voluntary guidance concerning safety design elements that should be incorporated into the design of autonomous vehicles and sets forth best practices for state legislators and highway safety officials to consider regarding potential autonomous vehicle regulation.[11]

To date, DOT and NHTSA have not adopted any mandatory standards with respect to autonomous vehicles. Notwithstanding this point, however, rulemaking activity in the space remains active: In January 2018, NHTSA commenced a rulemaking soliciting comments to identify unnecessary regulatory barriers in existing motor vehicle safety standards to the testing, compliance

9. *See id.*

10. *See* U.S. Dep't of Transp. & Nat'l Highway Transp. Safety Admin., Federal Automated Vehicles Policy: Accelerating the Next Revolution in Roadway Safety (Sept. 2016), http://www.safetyresearch.net/Library/Federal_Automated_Vehicles_Policy.pdf.

11. *See* U.S. Dep't of Transp. & Nat'l Highway Transp. Safety Admin., Automated Driving Systems 2.0: A Vision for Safety (Sept. 2017), https://www.nhtsa.gov/sites/nhtsa.dot.gov/files/documents/13069a-ads2.0_090617_v9a_tag.pdf.

certification, and compliance verification of vehicles with automated driving systems.[12]

C. FDA

The FDA plays a key role in regulating medical products, including medical devices that connect to the IoT. If a product is regulated by the FDA as a medical device, a myriad of federal requirements, including ones focused on cybersecurity, attach to the development and marketing of that product. This section addresses when devices are subject to FDA regulation, as well as the associated premarket and postmarket requirements, with discussion of FDA's evolving approach to digital health and the IoT.[13]

1. FDA's Jurisdiction over Medical Devices

FDA's primary regulatory authority stems from the Federal Food, Drug, and Cosmetic Act (FDCA), which defines a "device" as an instrument, apparatus, implement, machine, contrivance, or other similar or related article, including any component, part, or accessory, which is intended for use either (1) in the diagnosis of disease or other conditions, or in the cure, mitigation, treatment, or prevention of disease or (2) to affect the structure or any function of the body.[14] "Device" excludes a product that achieves its primary intended purposes through chemical action within or on the body or is dependent upon being metabolized for the achievement of its primary intended purposes; such a product is regulated under the FDCA as a "drug."[15]

---

12. *See* Removing Regulatory Barriers for Vehicles with Automated Driving Systems, 83 Fed. Reg. 2607 (Jan. 18, 2018).

13. Section II.B. in this chapter addresses FDA's increased focus on the cybersecurity of devices.

14. FDCA § 201(h), 21 U.S.C. § 321(h).

15. *Id.*

The FDA has long taken the position that software, including stand-alone software, is a device if it meets the aforementioned definition. However, the agency also has recognized that certain software as a medical device (SaMD) may warrant a more nuanced regulatory approach than other medical devices, such as an implantable pacemaker or a pregnancy test.[16] In addition, Congress recently clarified the types of SaMD under FDA's purview. The 21st Century Cures Act of 2016 amended the FDCA to explicitly state that FDA does not have "device" jurisdiction over a software "function" that is intended to perform one or more of the following:

- Provide administrative support of a health care facility (e.g., processing and maintaining financial records, claims or billing information, analyzing historical claims data to predict future utilization, laboratory workflow).
- Maintain or encourage a healthy lifestyle and is unrelated to the diagnosis, cure, mitigation, prevention, or treatment of a disease or condition.
- Serve as electronic patient records intended to transfer, store, convert formats, or display patient information, so long as the records are part of health information technology that is certified under section 3001(c)(5) of the Public Health Service Act (PHSA) and meet certain other requirements.[17]

16. The FDA also has issued guidance regarding certain mobile medical applications (MMA's). *See* Food & Drug Admin., Mobile Medical Applications: Guidance for Industry and FDA Staff (Feb. 9, 2015), *available at* https://www.fda.gov/downloads/MedicalDevices/.../UCM263366.pdf.

17. For example, technology that does not interpret or analyze patient records, including medical image data, for the purposes of diagnosis or other functions does not fall within the definition of a "device."

- Transfer, store, convert formats, or display clinical laboratory test or other device data (but not interpret or analyze the test data).
- For the purpose of providing patient-specific information to support or provide clinical recommendations to health care professionals, enabling the health care professional to independently review software recommendations so that the professional does not primarily rely on the recommendations to make a decision about an individual patient (this last category is commonly referred to as "clinical decision support," or "CDS," software).[18]

Whether and how these exclusions from FDA's jurisdiction apply to connected medical devices is not always clear. Congress directed FDA to take a function-by-function approach to regulating software—some of the software's functions may be excluded from FDA's jurisdiction, while others remain in the "device" definition. And for software that has multiple functions, FDA still may assess non-device functions to ascertain any impact on the "device" functions within FDA's jurisdiction.[19] FDA has issued draft guidance implementing the changes made by the 21st Century Cures Act,

18. The exclusion from FDA's jurisdiction will not apply if the software function "is intended to acquire, process, or analyze a medical image or a signal from an in vitro diagnostic device or a pattern or signal from a signal acquisition system." FDCA § 520(o)(1)(E), 21 U.S.C. § 360j(o)(1)(E).

19. *See* FDCA § 520(o)(2), 21 U.S.C. § 360j(o)(2); *see also* Food & Drug Admin., Multiple Function Device Products—Policy & Considerations: Draft Guidance for Industry & Food & Drug Admin. (Apr. 27, 2018), https://www.fda.gov/downloads/MedicalDevices/DeviceRegulationandGuidance/GuidanceDocuments/UCM605683.pdf.

which health and medical software innovators also use to help assess whether a digital health solution falls within FDA's purview.[20]

2. FDA Premarket Process for Devices

A medical device needs to undergo FDA premarket review before a manufacturer can introduce a device into the market, unless the device is exempt from the requirement.[21] For nonexempt devices, FDA has traditionally provided three pathways for a manufacturer to introduce a device onto the market: 510(k) notification, de novo review, and premarket approval (PMA). The vast majority of devices subject to premarket review are marketed under the 510(k) pathway. Under 510(k) notification, FDA reviews the information to determine whether the proposed device is "substantially equivalent" to a predicate device. If FDA determines that a device is not "substantially equivalent" to a predicate, the device would need an approved PMA to be marketed.[22] A PMA usually contains a complete description of the device as well as clinical study data

20. *See* Food & Drug Admin., Changes to Existing Medical Software Policies Resulting from Section 3060 of the 21st Century Cures Act: Draft Guidance for Industry and Food and Drug Administration Staff (Dec. 8, 2017), https://www.fda.gov/downloads/MedicalDevices/DeviceRegulationandGuidance/GuidanceDocuments/UCM587820.pdf; Food & Drug Admin., Clinical and Patient Decision Support Software: Guidance for Industry and Food and Drug Administration Staff (Dec. 8, 2017), https://www.fda.gov/downloads/MedicalDevices/DeviceRegulationandGuidance/GuidanceDocuments/UCM587819.pdf.

21. A Class I device is exempt from the section 510(k) notification requirement unless it is intended for a use of substantial importance in preventing impairment of human health, or it presents a potential unreasonable risk of illness or injury. *See* FDCA § 510(l), 21 U.S.C. § 360(l). FDA has also exempted certain Class II devices from section 510(k) notification, in accordance with section 510(m) of the act. *See, e.g.*, 21 C.F.R. § 890.5720 (water circulating hot or cold pack).

22. 21 C.F.R. § 807.100(a).

allowing FDA to determine whether the device is safe and effective.[23] Alternatively, the submitter can request "de novo" classification of low-risk devices to determine whether the device can be marketed without PMA approval.

In April 2018, the FDA announced a draft working model for a pre-certification program (Pre-Cert Program), a potential new pathway envisioned by the agency for sponsors to bring SaMD to market.[24] The new Pre-Cert Program working model is based on FDA's recognition that, unlike manufacturers of hardware devices that are modified every few months to years, developers of SaMDs modify their products every few weeks or months in response to real-world performance and user feedback.

If finalized, the Pre-Cert Program would consist of four basic components: (1) excellence appraisal and pre-certification; (2) review pathway determination; (3) streamlined premarket review; and (4) real-world performance. Under the proposed program, SaMD developers would be assessed by the FDA or an accredited third party and pre-certified if the developer demonstrates a culture of quality and organizational excellence. FDA would adopt a risk-based, streamlined regulatory approach to SaMD review for pre-certified developers that would either replace the need for a premarket submission to the agency or, for higher risk products, allow for streamlined premarket review. FDA will continue to accept public feedback on the working model of the

---

23. *See* Food & Drug Admin., PMA Application Contents, http://www.fda.gov/MedicalDevices/DeviceRegulationandGuidance/HowtoMarketYourDevice/PremarketSubmissions/PremarketApprovalPMA/ucm050289.htm.

24. Food & Drug Admin., Developing a Software Precertification Program: A Working Model (Apr. 2018), https://www.fda.gov/downloads/MedicalDevices/DigitalHealth/DigitalHealthPreCertProgram/UCM605685.pdf.

Pre-Cert Program and anticipates implementing the program in 2019; that said, some concerns have been raised about FDA's proposed approach.[25]

As discussed further in Section II.B, the FDA has identified key considerations for manufacturers to address during the premarket process for medical devices connected to the IoT. For example, FDA recommends that manufacturers establish design inputs for their devices related to cybersecurity and establish a cybersecurity vulnerability and management approach, as part of the software validation and risk analysis under 21 C.F.R. § 820.30(g).[26] In any premarket submission, a manufacturer of a medical device connected to the IoT should provide key information related to the cybersecurity of their medical device, including a summary outlining the plan for providing needed validated software updates and patches throughout the medical device life cycle to assure safety and effectiveness of the product.[27]

3. FDA Postmarket Considerations for Devices

All FDA-regulated devices are subject to "general controls," which impose a number of postmarket obligations on device manufacturers, including requirements and limitations on postmarket changes to a device. Device manufacturers must register their manufacturing establishment(s) and list the devices manufactured at the establishment(s).[28] Unless exempt, device manufacturers must comply

---

25. Letter from Sens. Patty Murray, Tina Smith, Elizabeth Warren, U.S. Senate, to Dr. Scott Gottlieb, Commissioner, FDA, and Dr. Jeffrey Shuren, Director, Center for Devices and Radiological Health, FDA (Oct. 10, 2018).

26. Food & Drug Admin., Content of Premarket Submissions for Management of Cybersecurity in Medical Devices: Guidance for Industry and Food and Drug Administration Staff at 4 (Oct. 2, 2014), https://www.fda.gov/downloads/medicaldevices/deviceregulationandguidance/guidancedocuments/ucm356190.pdf.

27. *Id.* at 6.

28. 21 C.F.R. pt. 807.

with the Quality System Regulation (QSR), which includes design control requirements and good manufacturing practice (GMP) requirements.[29]

Under the Medical Device Reporting (MDR) regulation, device manufacturers also must review all customer complaints and feedback and report to FDA certain adverse events or malfunctions. Specifically, a device manufacturer must submit a report to FDA whenever they become aware that (1) a device may have caused or contributed to a death or serious injury, or (2) a device has malfunctioned and would be likely to cause or contribute to a death or serious injury if the malfunction were to recur.[30]

Any correction or removal of a device (i.e., any action taken with respect to products already in the field, including a software update) that is taken to reduce a risk to health must be reported to FDA.[31] As discussed in Section II.B, the FDA has issued specific guidance concerning how manufacturers of devices connected to the IoT should address cybersecurity vulnerabilities in this postmarket context. Finally, for devices that are subject to premarket review, certain device modifications (including enhancements) also must undergo premarket review before implementation.[32] These requirements may limit the ability of certain software developers to iterate or push software updates to users, which is one reason why the FDA has been exploring the Pre-Cert Program noted previously.

II. Privacy and Cybersecurity Regulation

Several federal agencies regulate privacy and cybersecurity issues as they relate to IoT. The FTC has a general mandate to protect consumers from "unfair or deceptive acts or practices" as well as implement

29. *Id.* at pt. 820.
30. *Id.* at pt. 803.
31. *Id.* at pt. 806.
32. *Id.* §§ 807.81(a)(3), 814.39.

and enforce sector-specific laws in areas that often intersect with the IoT, such as children's privacy. Other agencies play a more particularized role in cybersecurity regulation, such as the FDA for medical device security. More broadly, the U.S. government also has begun to consider the development of cybersecurity standards for procurement, which affects a wide swath of companies operating in the IoT sphere.

A. The Federal Trade Commission

The FTC's oversight in the IoT space has primarily consisted of identifying and discussing areas in which its already-established authorities can be used to regulate relevant IoT-related conduct, and, in some instances, bringing enforcement actions pursuant to those authorities. The FTC enforces the Federal Trade Commission Act (FTC Act), which generally prohibits unfair or deceptive acts or practices across most industries and products.[33] The FTC also enforces other statutes that are relevant to IoT, such as the Children's Online Privacy Protection Act (COPPA), which requires certain operators of commercial websites or online services to obtain parental consent before collecting personal information from children.[34] These enforcement responsibilities directly involve privacy and data security concerns commonly associated with IoT, so the commission naturally has taken a keen interest in the growing prevalence of Internet-connected products and services and has monitored their impact on consumers, while also recognizing their benefits and innovative potential. The commission has recognized that IoT companies include entities that produce and market both

33. 15 U.S.C § 45(a)(1) (2012). The FTC Act does not apply to common carriers. *Id.* § 45(a)(2).

34. *Id.* § 6502.

consumer-facing and business-to-business technologies that connect physical objects to the Internet or each other.[35]

So far, the FTC's enforcement approach has been not to promulgate new IoT-specific regulations but rather to engage in public exchanges about how its existing regulatory tools apply in these new contexts, and then to bring enforcement actions using those tools when warranted. FTC's current response to IoT products builds upon its past work in the electronic marketplace, including the agency's fair information practice principles (FIPPs), guidelines for ensuring that the collection, use, and dissemination of personal information is fair and secure.[36] The commission's four underlying principles for online consumer protection include notice, choice, access, and security.[37]

1. Comments and Policy Statements

One component of the FTC's regulatory approach has been to use comments and policy statements to provide its views on IoT issues within its enforcement purview. In June 2018, the FTC filed a comment in response to a Consumer Product Safety Commission request, in which the FTC (1) outlined best practices for predicting and mitigating against security, safety, and privacy hazards; (2) recommended a process for encouraging consumers to register for safety alerts and recall information; and (3) opined on the

35. FED. TRADE COMM'N, INTERNET OF THINGS: PRIVACY & SECURITY IN A CONNECTED WORLD 5 (Jan. 2015), https://www.ftc.gov/system/files/documents/reports/federal-trade-commission-staff-report-november-2013-workshop-entitled-internet-things-privacy/150127iotrpt.pdf.

36. FED. TRADE COMM'N, PRIVACY ONLINE: FAIR INFORMATION PRACTICES IN THE ELECTRONIC MARKETPLACE, A REPORT TO CONGRESS 3 (May 2000), https://www.ftc.gov/sites/default/files/documents/reports/privacy-online-fair-information-practices-electronic-marketplace-federal-trade-commission-report/privacy2000.pdf.

37. *Id.* at 12.

role of government in IoT security.[38] The FTC staff recommended that IoT companies conduct risk assessments of their own security programs, evaluate the security of components and software from service providers, and continue to update and patch issues as they arise over time.[39] On the government side, the staff recommended that the CPSC leverage existing safety notification schemes to develop an online registration process for IoT security, and that it make any IoT-related regulations technology-neutral and flexible enough to adapt to technology changes.[40] The FTC also proposed a collaborative approach in the event that CPSC considered safety certification requirements for IoT devices: the CPSC could require IoT device manufacturers to publish standards to which they must adhere, and the FTC could take actions against companies that misrepresent their security practices in those certifications.[41]

In December 2017, the FTC issued an Enforcement Policy Statement regarding COPPA and children's voice recordings, an important and rapidly evolving issue in the IoT space for children.[42] This policy statement arose from the rise of IoT products, such as

---

38. *See* Comments of the Staff of the Federal Trade Commission's Bureau of Consumer Protection at 3, In the Matter of The Internet of Things and Consumer Product Hazards, Docket No. CPSC-2018-007 (June 15, 2018), https://www.ftc.gov/system/files/documents/advocacy_documents/comment-staff-federal-trade-commissions-bureau-consumer-protection-consumer-product-safety/p185404_ftc_staff_comment_to_the_consumer_product_safety_commission.pdf.

39. *See id.* at 6–9.

40. *See id.* at 9–10.

41. *See id.* at 10.

42. Fed. Trade Comm'n, Enforcement Policy Statement Regarding the Applicability of the COPPA Rule to the Collection and Use of Voice Recordings, 82 Fed. Reg. 235 (Dec. 8, 2017) (to be codified at 16 C.F.R pt. 312). An operator must still comply with other provisions of COPPA, including providing in its privacy policy clear notice of the collection and use of audio files and its deletion policy. The non-enforcement policy does not apply to situations when an operator requests information via voice that is otherwise considered personal information (e.g., a child's name) and does not extend to operators that use the audio file for a purpose other than conversion to text before its destruction (e.g., identification through voice recognition, or behavioral targeting). *Id.*

voice-controlled speakers where children's voices are used only to perform searches or similar functions.[43] The FTC stated that it would not take enforcement action against operators that did not obtain verifiable parental consent when they collected audio files containing a child's voice so long as they immediately converted the recording to text before promptly deleting the file.[44] This policy statement is just one example of how the FTC has attempted to address privacy concerns without hindering the development and adoption of new products in the IoT sphere.

2. *Workshops and Reports*

The FTC also has conducted numerous workshops and issued reports relevant to IoT consumer protection concerns. In November 2013, for example, the FTC hosted a workshop on the privacy and security implications of IoT products.[45] The workshop included

---

43. This policy statement was a part of the FTC's focus on privacy issues impacting children. In 2017 and 2018, FTC brought action against D-Link for inadequate security in its line of products, including baby monitors, and VTech for allegedly inappropriately collecting children's personal information in written form, among other alleged violations. *See* Complaint for Permanent Injunction and Other Equitable Relief, FTC v. D-Link Corporation, Case No. 3:17-cv-00039-JD (Jan. 5, 2017); Complaint, U.S. v. VTech Electronics Ltd., No. 1:18-cv-00114 (N.D. Ill. Jan. 8, 2018).

44. Fed. Trade Comm'n, Enforcement Policy Statement Regarding the Applicability of the COPPA Rule to the Collection and Use of Voice Recordings, 82 Fed. Reg. 235 (Dec. 8, 2017).

45. In addition to the workshops described in this section, FTC has studied and hosted workshops on mobile security, drones, connected TVs, and ransomware. *See* Fed. Trade Comm'n, Mobile Security Updates: Understanding the Issues (Feb. 2018), https://www.ftc.gov/system/files/documents/reports/mobile-security-updates-understanding-issues/mobile_security_updates_understanding_the_issues_publication_final.pdf; Fed. Trade Comm'n, Fall Technology Series: Drones (Oct. 13, 2016) (workshop), https://www.ftc.gov/news-events/events-calendar/2016/10/fall-technology-series-drones; Fed. Trade Comm'n, Fall Technology Series: Smart TV (workshop) (Dec. 7, 2016), https://www.ftc.gov/news-evensevents-calendar/2016/12/fall-technology-series-smart-tv; Fed. Trade Comm'n, Fall Technology Series: Ransomware (workshop) (Sept. 7, 2016), https://www.ftc.gov/news-events/events-calendar/2016/09/fall-technology-series-ransomware.

panel discussions on the smart home, connected health and fitness, connected cars, and privacy and security in a connected world.[46] Workshop participants discussed the benefits that IoT devices can provide across many industries and examined associated risks, such as unauthorized access to and misuse of personal information; facilitating attacks on other systems; and unfairly using collected data to make credit, insurance, and employment decisions. Workshop participants debated how the commission's Fair Information Practice Principles would apply to IoT companies and devices, with particular interest in the principles of notice, choice, data minimization, and security.[47] The commission published a report that summarized insights from the workshop and cataloged the commission staff's recommendations for best practices, encouraging self-regulatory programs rather than calling for new IoT-specific legislation or regulations.[48]

In January 2017, FTC released a Cross-Device Tracking Report following a workshop on the same topic. Companies use cross-device tracking to associate multiple devices to a single person for many purposes, including targeted advertising.[49] Opportunities for cross-device tracking are especially rich in the IoT space, where companies are increasingly seeking to create value by developing networks of smart devices that share information. The report explored the implications of cross-device tracking on consumers and how FTC Act principles would apply in this context. In addition to recognizing the benefits of the practice (e.g., improvements

---

46. FED. TRADE COMM'N, INTERNET OF THINGS: PRIVACY & SECURITY IN A CONNECTED WORLD 3–4 (Jan. 2015), https://www.ftc.gov/system/files/documents/reports/federal-trade-commission-staff-report-november-2013-workshop-entitled-internet-things-privacy/150127iotrpt.pdf.

47. *Id.* at ii.

48. *See generally id.*

49. *See* FED. TRADE COMM'N, CROSS-DEVICE TRACKING, 2–3 (Jan. 2017), https://www.ftc.gov/system/files/documents/reports/cross-device-tracking-federal-trade-commission-staff-report-january-2017/ftc_cross-device_tracking_report_1-23-17.pdf.

to customers' experiences across devices, fraud detection, and marketing efforts), the report also acknowledged attendant privacy challenges (e.g., lack of transparency, lack of consumer awareness about the potential scope of cross-device tracking, and limited consumer choice to opt out of data tracking).[50] Consistent with the FTC's approach on other IoT issues, the cross-device tracking report highlighted the role of self-regulatory organizations' efforts in this space, and also made recommendations to industry regarding data and security best practices.[51]

Along with the National Highway Traffic Safety Administration, the FTC hosted a workshop on June 28, 2017, to analyze the consumer privacy and security issues presented by automated and connected motor vehicles that collect significant user data from IoT sensors. The workshop and follow up report included discussion of the benefits and challenges of data collection by connected vehicles, appropriate privacy and security practices, the role of government agencies, and self-regulatory standards.[52]

3. *Enforcement Actions*

The FTC also has brought several enforcement actions in recent years that involve IoT devices, using authorities that preexisted

50. *Id.* at 5–10.

51. *Id.*

52. Fed. Trade Comm'n, Connected Cars: Privacy, Security Issues Related to Connected, Automated Vehicles (workshop) (June 28, 2017), https://www.ftc.gov/news-events/events-calendar/2017/06/connected-cars-privacy-security-issues-related-connected. Fed. Trade Comm'n, Connected Cars Workshop: Staff Perspective (Jan. 2018), https://www.ftc.gov/system/files/documents/reports/connected-cars-workshop-federal-trade-commission-staff-perspective/staff_perspective_connected_cars_0.pdf.

the technological developments.[53] In early 2018, toy manufacturer VTech Electronics Limited (VTech) settled with the FTC for $650,000 in response to allegations that the company violated COPPA.[54] The FTC alleged that VTech directed its app to children and had actual knowledge that children used the service, but collected children's personal information in violation of COPPA rules. In addition, the FTC alleged FTC Act violations for misrepresenting that identifying information submitted by customers would be transmitted in encrypted form.[55]

In February 2017, VIZIO, Inc., a smart TV manufacturer, settled with the FTC for $2.2 million based on charges that it collected viewing data on 11 million TVs without consumers' knowledge or consent. The complaint alleged that VIZIO also shared this viewing data with third parties for tracking and targeted advertising purposes.[56] The FTC alleged that these practices were unfair and deceptive in violation of the FTC Act and New Jersey consumer protection laws.[57] These recent cases illustrate that the FTC may take direct enforcement action to protect consumers from

53. *See, e.g.*, Decision and Order, *In the Matter of TRENDnet, Inc.*, No. C-4426 (FTC settled with electronics company TRENDnet for allegedly misrepresenting the security of its products by exposing security camera footage to online viewing without adequate protections); Joint Stipulation and Order Dismissing D-Link Corporation without Prejudice, FTC v. D-Link Corporation, et al., No. 3:17-cv-00039-JD (May 15, 2017) (FTC reached a settlement with D-Link after the commission alleged that the company failed to take reasonable steps to secure its routers and Internet Protocol (IP cameras); Agreement Containing Consent Order, *In the matter of ASUSTeK Computer, Inc.*, No. 1423156 (hardware maker ASUS settled FTC charges that insecure cloud services in its routers resulted in the compromise of consumers' connected storage devices and security flaws exposed home security networks to possible security threats).

54. Complaint, U.S. v. VTech Electronics, Ltd., No. 1:18-cv-00114 (N.D. Ill. Jan. 8, 2018).

55. *Id.* at 46. The settlement permanently prohibited VTech from violating COPPA or misrepresenting its security practices. *Id.* at 45–48.

56. Complaint for Permanent Injunction and Other Equitable and Monetary Relief, Federal Trade Commission v. VIZIO, Inc., No. 2:17-cv-00758 (D.N.J. Feb. 6, 2017).

57. *Id.* at 10–11.

IoT-related products and services when issuing guidance and self-regulation was insufficient.

B. FDA's Approach to Cybersecurity of Medical Devices

FDA is increasingly focused on cybersecurity issues for medical devices, since "compromised" devices may pose a risk to patient health (e.g., remotely turning off a patient's pace maker), as well as the confidentiality of personal medical information (e.g., theft of confidential patient data).[58] FDA has issued two final guidance documents for device manufacturers that highlight key premarket and postmarket cybersecurity considerations.[59]

In October 2014, FDA published its guidance on the content of premarket submissions for the management of cybersecurity in medical devices. This document sets forth recommendations for the design and development of devices, as well as the preparation of premarket submissions, that are intended to reduce the likelihood that medical devices will be compromised as a result of inadequate cybersecurity. The guidance supplements other standards generally applicable to software included in medical devices, as well as specific standards addressing cybersecurity risks in devices containing off-the-shelf software. The final guidance also adopts

58. Although, the FDA has not yet received any reports of an unauthorized user exploiting a cybersecurity vulnerability in a medical device in use by a patient. *See* Food & Drug Admin., Statement from FDA Commissioner Scott Gottlieb, M.D. on FDA's Efforts to Strengthen the Agency's Medical Device Cybersecurity Program as Part of Its Mission to Protect Patients (Oct. 1, 2018), https://www.fda.gov/NewsEvents/Newsroom/PressAnnouncements/ucm622074.htm?utm_campaign=CDRH%20New%202018-10-02&utm_medium=email&utm_source=Eloqua&elqTrackId=53B2CC014669AFBDEDB78521573755E0&elq=2b84f6f60c3b488a9d4205f80deadc4f&elqaid=5353&elqat=1&elqCampaignId=4277.

59. *See* Food & Drug Admin., Postmarket Management of Cybersecurity in Medical Devices: Guidance for Industry and Food and Drug Administration Staff (Dec. 28, 2016), https://www.fda.gov/downloads/medicaldevices/deviceregulationandguidance/guidancedocuments/ucm482022.pdf; Food & Drug Admin., Content of Premarket Submissions, *supra* note 25.

the National Institute of Standards and Technology's core cybersecurity framework.

In December 2016, FDA issued "Postmarket Management of Cybersecurity in Medical Devices." This second guidance document provides FDA's recommendations on a risk-based framework for medical device manufacturers to assess and remediate cybersecurity vulnerabilities. The guidance also outlines circumstances in which FDA intends to exercise enforcement discretion with respect to the requirements to report actions related to cybersecurity vulnerabilities as device corrections and removals under 21 C.F.R. part 806.

FDA recognizes that cybersecurity is an "evolving space."[60] In the near future, the agency plans to significantly update the guidances to reflect the FDA's most current understandings of and recommendations regarding cybersecurity.[61] As such, stakeholders generally should expect increased attention by the agency on the cybersecurity of medical devices. For example, on April 17, 2018, FDA issued a Medical Device Safety Action Plan, which outlined the desire for new postmarket authority to require that sponsors adopt policies and procedures for coordinated disclosure of cybersecurity vulnerabilities as they are identified.[62] Additionally, on October 1, 2018, the FDA announced two memoranda of understanding with multiple stakeholder groups to create information sharing analysis organizations (ISAOs), where medical device manufacturers will be able to share information about possible vulnerabilities and threats.[63] Manufacturers of connected devices should closely follow developments at the FDA on this front, as

60. *See* Food & Drug Admin., Statement from Gottlieb, *supra* note 57.
61. *Id.*
62. Food & Drug Admin., Medical Device Safety Action Plan: Protecting Patients, Promoting Public Health (Apr. 2018), https://www.fda.gov/downloads/AboutFDA/CentersOffices/OfficeofMedicalProductsandTobacco/CDRH/CDRHReports/UCM604690.pdf.
63. *See* Food & Drug Admin., Statement from Gottlieb, *supra* note 57.

the agency's regulatory approach to the cybersecurity of medical devices connected to the IoT will continue to evolve.

C. Cybersecurity and Government Procurement

As the single largest purchaser of goods and services in the world, the U.S. government has significant concerns about IoT with regard to critical infrastructure and its supply chain. Because an increasingly connected world heightens risks to security, privacy and physical safety, a standardized set of cybersecurity standards is critical to protecting IoT devices and systems from attack. The government has recognized these risks for IoT devices it procures, but is still early in formulating a comprehensive response that imposes obligations on individual contractors. Much of the technical analysis of the risks and the development of cybersecurity controls that are and will be imposed on government agencies and contractors doing business with the government are developed by a unit of the Department of Commerce known the National Institute of Standards and Technology (NIST).

NIST is charged with the developing and publishing the necessary information security standards and guidelines that are used to protect both government systems and government information on contractor systems.[64] Among those publications is NIST SP 800-171, which the Department of Defense (DoD) imposes on contractors whose internal systems process, store, or transmit covered defense information (CDI).[65] In general, CDI is controlled

64. *See* 44 U.S.C. § 3551–59. Recognizing the need to create a framework of security controls for federal information networks, Congress in 2002 passed the Federal Information Security Management Act (FISMA). FISMA sought to ensure the development and maintenance of minimum security controls required to protect Government information and information systems. NIST is charged with developing these standards pursuant to FISMA.

65. *See* DFARS 252.204-7012 (DFARS Cyber Rule); *Cybersecurity Update: DoD Releases Long-Awaited Final Rule*, Inside Government Contracts, https://www.insidegovernmentcontracts.com/2016/10/cybersecurity-update-dod-releases-long-awaited-final-rule/.

unclassified information (CUI)[66] that relates to the performance of a contract with DoD.

From an agency standpoint, DoD has been forward leaning in an attempt to protect unclassified government data. Since August 2015, most companies that contract with DoD have been required, among other things, to provide "adequate security" to protect CDI.[67] Adequate security means that a contractor had to "implement" the more than 100 security controls in NIST Special Publication (SP) 800-171 no later than December 31, 2017.[68] In December 2016, NIST issued Revision 1 to NIST SP 800-171. Among the revisions was a clarification that the systems covered by the publication were broad and included "for example: general purpose information systems; industrial and process control systems; cyber-physical systems; and individual devices that are part of the *Internet of Things*."[69] NIST further noted that "[a]s computing platforms and technologies are increasingly deployed ubiquitously worldwide and systems and components are connected through wired and wireless networks, the susceptibility of Controlled Unclassified Information to loss or compromise grows—as does the potential for adverse consequences resulting from such occurrences." Despite this recognition, only one security control

66. CUI is unclassified information of executive branch agencies that requires safeguarding or dissemination controls pursuant to and consistent with applicable law, regulations, and government-wide policies. For a detailed explanation of CUI, see https://www.archives.gov/cui/registry/category-list.

67. DFARS 252.204-7012(b). In November 2013, DoD issued its first version of the DFARS Cyber Rule, which imposed 51 security controls on contractor information systems. These 51 controls were a subset of the controls in NIST SP 800-53, which governs government systems. Eventually, NIST tailored these controls to address contractor systems when it issued NIST SP 800-171 in June 2015.

68. DFARS 252.204-7012(b)(ii).

69. *Protecting Controlled Unclassified Information in Nonfederal Systems and Organizations*, Rev. 1 at https://www.nist.gov/publications/protecting-controlled-unclassified-information-nonfederal-systems-and-organizations.

in 800-171 explicitly mentions IoT.[70] Nonetheless, NIST is clearly focused on the IoT and is working to develop appropriate security requirements that can be used by the government and industry to better secure IoT devices that contain or process CUI.

Congress also has become increasingly concerned about hardening the government's supply chain, especially from nation states that it believes represent a threat to the cybersecurity of devices and systems procured by the government. One approach that Congress has imposed to improve cybersecurity is to simply ban certain products from those procured by and for the government. For example, the Fiscal Year (FY) 2018 National Defense Authorization Act (NDAA) prohibits every U.S. government entity from using any "hardware, software, or services developed or provided, in whole or in part" by a Russian manufacturer, Kaspersky Labs, or its affiliates.[71] Similarly, in the FY 2019 NDAA, Congress directed that no executive agency may procure or obtain certain telecommunications equipment or services produced by certain entities controlled by or connected to the government of the People's Republic of China.[72]

In addition to Congress's attempts to harden the supply chain, DoD's regulatory work and NIST's development of SP 800-711, the Commission on Enhancing National Cybersecurity released its Report on Securing and Growing the Digital Economy (Report)

70. Security control 3.1.17 requires contractors to "protect wireless access using authentication and encryption." NIST further notes that "special attention" to devices that are part of the IoT and have access to contractor systems where CDI is processed, stored or transmitted must be taken. These same security controls are expected to apply to contracts with all agencies in the Executive Branch by the first quarter of 2019. *See* Semiannual Regulatory Agenda, 83 Fed. Reg. 1950 at 1955 (Jan. 12, 2018); NIST SP 800-171 Rev. 1 at v (indicating that a single FAR clause will apply the requirements of Special Publication 800-171 to all federal contractors not just those that contract with DoD).

71. *See* section 1634 of the FY 2018 NDAA; *see also* FAR 52.204-23 ("Prohibition on Contracting for Hardware, Software, and Services Developed or Provided by Kaspersky Lab and Other Covered Entities").

72. *See* FY 2019 NDAA at section 889.

in December 2016.[73] The commission was tasked with assessing the state of the nation's cybersecurity standards and developing actionable recommendations for securing and growing the digital economy.[74] Among the Report's recommendations was the need for the government to identify clear roles of responsibility, authorities, and rules of engagement for both private and government stakeholders to address the convergence of critical infrastructure with the IoT to "ensure security and continuity of government."[75] The Report further noted that collaborative public/private defensive efforts should include "coordinated protection and detection approaches to ensure resilience; fully integrated response, recovery, and plans; a series of annual cooperative training programs and exercises coordinated with key agencies and industry; and the development of interoperable systems."[76] Similarly, specific to the IoT, the Report recognized the need to increase research and development in both the private and government sector and to "improve standards, guidelines, and best practices available to secure these connected devices and systems."[77] Some of these recommendations required additional studies and reports by various government agencies.[78] To date, the cybersecurity requirements imposed on contractors have been unique to each agency. It is too early to tell, but perhaps the commission may assist with harmonizing at least some of the requirements across agencies, but that has not been the experience to date.

---

73. *See* Comm'n on Enhancing Nat'l Cybersecurity, Report on Securing and Growing the Digital Economy (Dec. 1, 2016), https://www.nist.gov/sites/default/files/documents/2016/12/02/cybersecurity-commission-report-final-post.pdf [hereinafter Report].

74. The commission was established by Executive Order 13718 in February 2016. *See* Exec. Order 13718, 81 Fed. Reg. 7441 (Feb. 9, 2016), https://obamawhitehouse.archives.gov/the-press-office/2016/02/09/executive-order-commission-enhancing-national-cybersecurity.

75. Report at 15.

76. *Id.*

77. *Id.* at 23–24.

78. *Id.* at 24–26.

Consistent with one of the Report's recommendations, in February 2018, NIST released a draft report, "NISTIR 8200 Interagency Report on Status of International Cybersecurity Standardization for the Internet of Things (IoT)," assessing the current status of worldwide regulation of IoT.[79] The purpose of the draft 8200 Report was to assist both federal agencies and private companies in planning and developing cybersecurity standards in their use and production of IoT components, products, systems, and services. NIST recognized the inconsistencies in the maturity of cybersecurity standards across industries, including areas where standards are currently nonexistent.[80] These inconsistencies appear to be a function of the prioritization of cybersecurity needs in networks. Traditionally, cybersecurity focuses on confidentiality, integrity, and availability (in that order), but prioritizing cybersecurity for an IoT device may be ordered differently depending on the use case. For example, Hardware Assurance is likely the most important issue for a medical device such as a pacemaker, whereas Identity and Access Management may be paramount for Smart Buildings. NIST is seeking comments from industry and government before finalizing the 8200 Report.

NIST continues to seek input from industry on these issues, including holding multiple events to gather stakeholder insights on cybersecurity and other risks for connected devices. For example, in October 2017, NIST hosted the IoT Cybersecurity Colloquium to bring together stakeholders across "government, industry, international bodies, and academia" and assess the risks imposed by

---

79. *See* Michael D. Hogan & Benjamin M. Piccarreta, NIST Interagency Int'l Cybersecurity Standardization Working Group, Interagency Report on the Status of International Cybersecurity Standardization for the Internet of Things (IoT): NISTIR 8200 (Nov. 29, 2018), https://csrc.nist.gov/CSRC/media/Publications/nistir/8200/draft/documents/nistir8200-draft.pdf.

80. *See* 8200 Report at Annex C.

the IoT.[81] Similarly, on July 11, 2018, NIST held a workshop with stakeholders to "help NIST with the development of the Cybersecurity for IoT Program and Privacy Engineering Program's publication," which will provide an "introduction to managing IoT cybersecurity and privacy risk for federal agencies."[82] Once these standards are set for government systems, contractors should expect to see similar standards developed for devices containing or connecting to contractor systems with CUI.

III. IoT Connectivity and Spectrum Regulations

The Federal Communications Commission (FCC) manages and enforces regulations that impact IoT devices in a number of ways, depending on the functionality of the device and the methods by which they connect to the Internet. Principally, these regulations fall into three main categories: (1) wireless and spectrum regulation; (2) equipment authorization procedures; and (3) VoIP and Internet-related regulation. IoT device makers may be surprised to see that various FCC regulations can apply to them, even if they would not necessarily think of their product as a communications device.

The wireless networks that help power so many different types of devices in the IoT depend on a variety of spectrum resources to operate, including both licensed and unlicensed options.[83] Depending on the IoT device's location and functionality, it may depend on various networks, including for example, home Wi-Fi

81. *See* NIST Cybersecurity for IoT Program, "Security and Privacy Considerations for IoT" Pre-Read Essay (2017), https://www.nist.gov/sites/default/files/documents/2017/10/10/iot_colloquium_pre-read_1.pdf.

82. Information on the NIST Cybersecurity for IoT Program can be found at https://www.nist.gov/programs-projects/nist-cybersecurity-iot-program.

83. The FCC regulates licensed and unlicensed spectrum. Licensed spectrum gives licensees access to dedicated airwaves, free from many forms of interference that might exist on unlicensed spectrum. However, utilizing unlicensed spectrum does not mean that it is unregulated. Part 15 of the FCC's rules sets forth requirements for the use of different types of unlicensed spectrum. *See* 47 C.F.R. pt. 15. The rules applicable to licensed spectrum vary depending on the characteristics of the spectrum subject to the licensing requirements.

and mobile Internet offerings, such as 4G-LTE, in order to achieve necessary connectivity. The FCC regulates the spectrum and runs auctions to make licensed spectrum available, including spectrum suitable for 5G use, which is critical for technological advances important to the IoT. For example, as of 2018, the FCC is planning auctions in the 28GHz and 24GHz bands, which are seen as good resources to facilitate 5G expansion.[84] The reason 5G is so important to IoT is because it enables additional capacity, increased download speeds, and reduced latency as compared to the current 4G LTE technology. Such features will enable more connected devices on the network and improve the quality of service to existing ones. These specific spectrum bands will be subject to license requirements, which many different network operators will vie to obtain, so they can create and expand some of the networks that will enable IoT devices to connect to the Internet.

Depending on the spectrum at issue, wireless networks are subjected to different network limitations, including interference and geographic restrictions. For example, with regard to the auctions for 28 GHz and 24 GHz mentioned previously, the FCC has decided to license these resources subject to the requirements found in part 30 of the FCC's rules.[85] Part 15, on the other hand, sets forth the rules and expectations for devices making use of unlicensed spectrum, such as may be used for Wi-Fi.[86] However, from a practical perspective, unless a given IoT device necessitates its own network or guaranteed minimum capacity and quality standards, many of these details may not be relevant. Licensed spectrum may be better

84. Public Notice, *Auctions of Upper Microwave Flexible Use Licenses for Next-Generation Wireless Services*, AU Docket No. 18-85, FCC 18-43, 2018 WL 1872353 (Apr. 17, 2018).

85. Second Report and Order, Second Further Notice of Proposed Rulemaking, Order on Reconsideration, and Memorandum Opinion and Order ¶¶ 23–27, *In re Use of Spectrum Bands above 24 GHz for Mobile Radio Services*, 32 FCC Rcd 10988, 10997–98 (2017) (GN Docket No. 14-177 et al.), 2017 WL 5654766.

86. *See generally* 47 C.F.R. pt. 15.

suited for devices that require such specifications, but for many other devices, unlicensed spectrum provides more than adequate connectivity. And as more licensed and unlicensed spectrum both become available, more IoT devices will continue to be able to connect, with decreased latency and increased speed.

Another aspect of the FCC's jurisdiction that implicates connected devices of different kinds relates to the FCC's requirements regarding equipment authorizations. Creators of IoT devices may be surprised to find out, in most cases, their products must receive such authorizations from the FCC before they may market and sell their devices. The functions of an IoT device, and the types of radio transmitters involved, could even require a single device to receive several different equipment authorizations from the FCC. And, importantly, it is not just the parts of the device that allow it to connect to the Internet that may require authorization; most individual electrical functions within a given device each must pass muster with the FCC. If it is a device that generates radio frequency (RF) energy, at least one subset of the FCC's rules will likely apply.[87] Once an IoT maker has determined what type(s) of RF devices a given IoT product contains, and the corresponding technical requirements, the FCC's Part 2 rules regarding Equipment Authorization Procedures lay out the administrative procedures that must be followed.[88] Without the proper authorization(s) in place, a company will not be able to market and sell its product.

87. RF devices subject to FCC equipment authorization requirements are primarily set forth in part 15 of the FCC's rules, and include incidental radiators (subpart A), unintentional radiators (subparts B and G), and intentional radiators (subparts C–F, and H). *See* 47 C.F.R. pt 15. These different classifications reflect whether the device's primary purpose is to emit RF signals. Notably, even intentional radiators may be operated without a license, but other devices, such as cell phones and smart phones, which operate in licensed spectrum, must also obtain equipment authorizations from the FCC. The technical requirements for devices using licensed spectrum can be found throughout title 47, depending on the exact spectrum at issue.

88. *See generally* 47 C.F.R. pt. 2, subpt. J.

Depending on an IoT device's capabilities, any other number of additional FCC regulations could also apply. This is particularly the case when an IoT device offers or facilitates functionality that is similar to traditional telecommunications services or Internet access services. For example, if an IoT device allows a person to place a VoIP call, accessibility requirements and the ability to place a call to 911 might apply.[89] These requirements do not apply in all circumstances, but depending on how the products are designed, and how they function, these more traditional telecommunications-style regulations may be relevant. Similarly, if a device is used to access advanced communications services, such as access to Internet browsers in wireless phones, the device must be accessible for people who are blind and visually impaired.[90] The applicability here is also quite broad, so device manufacturers need to be aware and analyze their products to determine whether they need to alter their designs to be in compliance.

FCC regulation will impact, and in many cases, enable the IoT. The FCC may create the networks on which devices will run, or, in many cases, issue rules that device manufacturers must bear in mind as they design and offer IoT products and services.

---

89. *See, e.g.*, 47 C.F.R. § 6.5 (a) (requiring "[a] manufacturer of telecommunications equipment or customer premises equipment [to] ensure that the equipment is designed, developed and fabricated so that the telecommunications functions of the equipment are accessible to and usable by individuals with disabilities, if readily achievable"); 47 C.F.R. § 9.5(b)(1) (requiring interconnected VoIP providers to "as a condition of providing service to a consumer, provide that consumer with E911 service. . . .").

90. *See, e.g.*, 47 C.F.R. § 14.1 (a) (stating that the rules regarding access to advanced communications services and equipment by people with disabilities apply to "[a]ny manufacturer of equipment used for advanced communications services, including end user equipment, network equipment, and software, that such manufacturer offers for sale or otherwise distributes in interstate commerce").

IV. Banking

The Office of the Comptroller of the Currency, Board of Governors of the Federal Reserve System, Federal Deposit Insurance Corporation, and Bureau of Consumer Financial Protection (the "federal banking agencies") recently have been conducting outreach to regulated institutions on technology and innovation issues, and many institutions, technology companies, and other service providers have identified IoT devices as both an opportunity and potential source of risk.[91] Banks increasingly are exploring the use of IoT devices, including connected home and car technologies, in order to deliver financial products or services. For example, consumers may use an in-home IoT device to check the balance of financial accounts or to seamlessly transfer funds to a family member or friend, receiving notification when the funds have been deposited. Given these uses, IoT devices present cybersecurity risks to financial information. Indeed, hackers have attempted to gain access to the financial information of customers of a Brazilian bank through IoT devices.[92] The federal banking agencies, however, have not taken action through rulemaking, guidance, or enforcement with respect to the safety and soundness of a bank's delivery of financial services through an IoT device or an IoT device's compliance with applicable banking laws and regulations.

---

91. *See, e.g.*, Peter Van Valkenburgh, Coin Center, Comments to the Office of the Comptroller of the Currency on Exploring Special Purpose National Bank Charters for Fintech Companies (Jan. 13, 2016), https://www.occ.gov/topics/responsible-innovation/comments/comment-coin-center-special-purpose-national-bank-charters.pdf; Edward J. DeMarco, Jr., The Risk Management Association Comments to the Federal Reserve, Office of the Comptroller of the Currency, and Federal Deposit Insurance Corporation on Enhanced Cyber Risk Management Standards (Jan. 13, 2017), *available at* https://www.fdic.gov/regulations/laws/federal/2016/2016_enhanced_cyberrisk_3064-ae45_c-006.pdf.

92. *See Hackers Target Bank Customers in Brazil with DNS Redirects*, PYMNTS (Aug. 10, 2018), https://www.pymnts.com/news/security-and-risk/2018/banco-de-brasil-malware-iot-cybersecurity/.

Banks' models for delivering deposit, credit, and other services to customers have evolved over time along with innovations in technology. Brick-and-mortar branches traditionally have been the central means for a bank to interact with customers, solicit applications for banking services, and make decisions to approve or deny customers' applications. The surge in smartphone use has led to a corresponding increase in mobile banking.[93] Moreover, banks increasingly are turning to alternative models to market products and services and to deliver those services to customers, including social networking platforms and IoT devices.

Numerous federal and state banking laws and regulations impose compliance requirements on the bank and/or its product or service regardless of whether the bank uses an in-person representative or an IoT device to market or deliver such product or service. Laws such as the Truth in Lending Act may require the bank to provide disclosures to customers regarding the terms and conditions that apply to a credit card product, including a credit card that is marketed through an IoT device.[94] Laws such as the U.S. Bank Secrecy Act require a bank to have systems in place to detect and report suspicious activity, including any activity identified through an IoT device.[95] The Electronic Fund Transfer Act requires a bank to limit the liability of a customer in connection with an unauthorized transaction that is initiated through an electronic fund transfer device such as a debit card, including if such debit card is used to purchase a good or service through an IoT device.[96]

---

93. *See* Ellen A. Merry, Federal Reserve, Mobile Banking: A Closer Look at Survey Measures (Mar. 27, 2018), https://www.federalreserve.gov/econres/notes/feds-notes/mobile-banking-a-closer-look-at-survey-measures-20180327.htm#fig4 ("The uses for smartphone technology have expanded, including the use of mobile phones for banking. In 2017, about half of U.S. adults with bank accounts had used a mobile phone to access a bank account in the past year.").

94. *See* 15 U.S.C. § 1601 *et seq.*

95. *See* 31 U.S.C. § 5311 *et seq.*

96. *See* 15 U.S.C. § 1693 *et seq.*

There are many other laws and regulations that regulate financial services. Banks and other financial institutions that intend to use an IoT device in their marketing or delivery of products and services should proceed carefully to ensure the device complies with these laws and regulations.

V. The Electricity Grid

The regulatory framework governing the U.S. electricity grid is evolving rapidly to keep pace with technological developments and economic opportunities associated with the IoT. Historically, the electricity grid consisted chiefly of interconnected, large, centralized power plants owned by vertically integrated electric utilities that served the on-demand needs of their local customers. Electricity flowed one way (from power plants to consumers), electricity prices were largely set through regulated cost-of-service ratemaking, demand and supply were not price responsive, and there were few opportunities for competitive electricity service providers to offer innovative services.

Today, and increasingly so in the future, the electricity system is being reimagined and restructured. Competitive wholesale electricity markets have burgeoned. Retail competition is being introduced and whole new classes of independent generators, renewables and storage resources, and "demand-side resources" that aggregate and externally control electricity use and sell the commodity value of usage reductions in the competitive electricity markets. The electricity grid of the future will feature two-way flows of electricity and critical digital information allowing consumers access to competitive electricity markets. Knitting this two-way electricity grid together will be a raft of IoT devices and communications capabilities, referred to collectively as the "smart grid," enabling real-time, price-responsive changes in both electricity demand and supply, which will reduce overall costs, while maintaining reliability of the physically interconnected electricity grid. For example, rooftop solar panels will be controllable by the grid operator and third-party aggregators of electricity supply, enabling output to be maximized. Within homes, electronically controlled thermostats, electric appliances, and lighting fixtures will also be remotely and increasingly automatically controllable, allowing residents opportunities to reduce peak-period electricity consumption, when prices are highest. Within office buildings, the entire suite of utilities, including HVAC and lighting, will be remotely and automatically controlled. Within factories, the grid operator and third-party "demand-side managers" will be able to reduce electricity consumption on-site, to better manage peak loads on the system as a whole, thereby earning utility credits against their electric bills.

Regulation of the "smart grid" involves both federal and state agencies. The Federal Energy Regulatory Commission (FERC) has jurisdiction over wholesale electricity markets and over transactions on, and the reliability of, the interstate electric grid. States have jurisdiction over retail electricity matters, which generally encompass end-user devices, distributed generation resources, such as rooftop solar, and local "micro grids," and demand-side resources. Novel jurisdictional and regulatory policy issues are arising as electricity consumers gain two-way access and exposure to competitive wholesale markets.

Under the Federal Power Act (FPA) FERC generally regulates transactions involving the bulk power grid, but not end users and their devices. Under FPA section 215, FERC approves and oversees enforcement of mandatory reliability standards developed by the North American Electric Reliability Corporation (NERC). NERC presently enforces 15 cybersecurity reliability standards, aimed at protecting the two-way flow of secure electronic communications that grid operators rely upon to keep generation on and transmission wires open so that the nation has a reliable, on-demand electricity system. These cybersecurity standards include:

- Technical operational, and procedural requirements for protecting bulk power grid cyber systems.

- Requiring certain levels of risk assessment and security awareness skills for personnel.
- Managing electronic and physical access to cyber systems.
- Setting incident response and recovery plan requirements.
- Preventing and detecting unauthorized changes to grid cyber systems.

DOE is also beginning to oversee electric grid cyber security.[97] If, in the future, end-user electricity devices in industrial and commercial facilities and in homes, become physically interconnected to the bulk power grid and communicable with grid operators, IoT devices may become subject to mandatory NERC or DOE cybersecurity regulations.

VI. Federal Aviation Administration Regulation of Drones

While historically associated with military operations, the civilian operation of unmanned aircraft systems (UAS), or more commonly, drones, has increased dramatically in the past few decades.[98] In addition to being used by hobbyists for recreational purposes, the multitude of potential commercial applications for UAS promises to transform business practices in countless industries.[99] The recent rise in popularity of UAS, and their increasingly complex operations, prompted an ongoing effort by the FAA to integrate UAS into the National Airspace System (NAS) through the development of a regulatory framework that ensures safety without unduly stifling the potential benefits

97. *See* Dep't of Energy, Office of Electricity Delivery & Energy Reliability, Multiyear Plan for Energy Sector Cybersecurity (March 2018), https://www.energy.gov/sites/prod/files/2018/05/f51/DOE%20Multiyear%20Plan%20for%20Energy%20Sector%20Cybersecurity%20_0.pdf.

98. Fed. Aviation Admin., *Integration of Civil Unmanned Aircraft Systems (UAS) in the National Airspace System (NAS) Roadmap* 4 (2nd ed., July 2018), https://www.faa.gov/uas/resources/policy_library/media/Second_Edition_Integration_of_Civil_UAS_NAS_Roadmap_July%202018.pdf.

99. *Id.*

of this technology.[100] The current regulations governing drones (discussed in the following paragraphs) are primarily concerned with safety and proper certification of drone pilots. There are currently no regulations governing privacy and cybersecurity, but it is likely that privacy and cybersecurity may be addressed in the future.

The FAA, the federal authority for all manned and unmanned aircraft systems, divides its UAS safety regulations into the following categories: (1) public aircraft, (2) model aircraft, and (3) civil aircraft.[101] The agency regulates each category differently but there is some overlap for operating rules, including, a registration requirement for all UAS weighing between 0.55 and 55 pounds[102] and an operator visual line-of-sight requirement for all UAS.[103]

Public aircraft. This category refers to UAS used by federal, state, or local government.[104] To operate legally in the NAS, the FAA requires the operator of public aircraft UAS to obtain a blanket Certificate of Waiver or Authorization (COA) from the agency.[105]

---

100. Fed. Aviation Admin., *FAA Aerospace Forecast Fiscal Years 2013–2033,* 65–66 (2013), https://www.faa.gov/data_research/aviation/aerospace_forecasts/media/2013_Forecast.pdf; Michael Herta, Adm'r, Fed. Aviation Admin., Address at AUVSI Xponential (May 10, 2017), https://www.faa.gov/news/speeches/news_story.cfm?newsId=21654.

101. Unmanned Aircraft Operations in the National Airspace System, 72 Fed. Reg. 29, 6689, 29, 6689–90 (2007).

102. The National Defense Authorization Act for Fiscal Year 2018 restored the FAA registration requirement for all UAS in the United States. H.R. 2810, 115th Cong. § 1092(d) (2017).

103. FAA Modernization and Reform Act of 2012, Pub. L. No. 112-95 § 336(c), § 336(c)(2) (2012) ("In this section, the term 'model aircraft' means an unmanned aircraft that is . . . flown within visual line of sight of the person operating the aircraft. . . ."); Operation and Certification of Small Unmanned Aircraft Systems, 81 Fed. Reg. 124, 42064, 124, 42066 (2016) ("visual line-of-sight (VLOS) only; the unmanned aircraft must remain within VLOS of the remote pilot in command and the person manipulating the flight controls of the small UAS. . . . [a]lternatively the unmanned aircraft must remain within VLOS of the visual observer").

104. Unmanned Aircraft Operations in the National Airspace System, 72 Fed. Reg. 29, 6689 (2007).

105. *Id.*

Model aircraft. UAS operated as model aircraft enjoy a lower level of agency oversight and exemption from future FAA rulemaking because their operation generally poses lower risks to the NAS.[106] To fly under "The Special Rule for Model Aircraft," the UAS must be flown strictly for hobby or recreational use; operated in accordance with aero-modeling safety guidelines;[107] weigh less than or equal to 55 pounds; operated in a manner that does not interfere with any manned aircraft; and its operator must give airports prior notice when flying within five miles.[108]

Civil aircraft. In 2016, the FAA amended its regulations to allow for the operation of civil aircraft UAS, or any drone operated for commercial purpose, under specific operating and certification requirements.[109] Aiming to mitigate risk and maintain the safety of the NAS, the FAA included a number of provisions in its final rule, such as requiring operators to obtain a remote pilot certification and for the aircraft to fly at or below 400 feet, at or under 100 mph, only during daylight hours, not directly over people, and to weigh less than 55 pounds, including payload.[110] The agency did include a waiver mechanism to allow individual operations to deviate from

---

106. FAA Modernization and Reform Act of 2012, Pub. L. No. 112-95, §336 (2012); FAA Interpretation of the Special Rule for Model Aircraft, 79 Fed. Reg. 122, 36172 (2014) ("consistent with FAA's enforcement philosophy, FAA's oversight of model aircraft has been guided by the risk that these operations present").

107. FAA, Definitions of terms in the Special Rule for Model Aircraft (Feb. 1, 2018) (explaining that model aircraft operators must operate their UAS in accordance with a "membership-based group that represents the aero-modeling community and provides a comprehensive set of safety guidelines emphasizing safe operations" and that they must "also follow modeling club rules for activities such as flying over people and flying at night").

108. FAA Modernization and Reform Act of 2012, Pub. L. No. 112-95, § 336(a) (2012).

109. Operation and Certification of Small Unmanned Aircraft Systems, 81 Fed. Reg. 124, 42064, 42066–67 (2016).

110. *Id.*

many of the operational restrictions if the applicant proved the proposed operation could be safely conducted.[111]

To enforce its UAS regulations, the FAA may assess civil and criminal penalties to violators as well as revoke or suspend a civil aircraft operator's remote pilot certificate.[112] As of 2018, the agency has pursued 70 enforcement cases.[113] The FAA also relies heavily on local law enforcement, and state tort law, to help combat unsafe or unauthorized UAS.[114]

The FAA faces new legal and regulatory challenges as it continues to apply its risk-based approach to integrating UAS into the NAS.[115] Commenters have raised privacy concerns over widespread UAS use and argue that the FAA, as the UAS regulatory body, should impose federal privacy standards on the industry.[116] To date, the agency has indicated that privacy regulation is beyond the scope of its authority.[117] Finally, while the agency sees its progress toward UAS integration as significant, the pace of that process, and the sweep of the regulation, has drawn criticism from commer-

111. *Id.* at 124, 42070–73.

112. *See* Fed. Aviation Admin. & Ass'n Unmanned Vehicle Sys. Int'l, *Unsafe Unauthorized UAS What Can You Do*, Workshop, Unmanned Aircraft System Symposium (2018) (detailing UAS regulation enforcement mechanisms).

113. *Id.*

114. *See* Fed. Aviation Admin. & Ass'n Unmanned Vehicle Sys. Int'l, *Local and State UAS Enforcement Authorities,* Unmanned Aircraft System Symposium (2017).

115. Operation and Certification of Small Unmanned Aircraft Systems, 81 Fed. Reg. 124, 42064, 42071 (2016) ("the FAA will continue working on integrating UAS operations that pose greater amounts of risk, and will issue notices of proposed rulemaking for those operations once the pertinent issues have been addressed").

116. "The FAA received about 180 comments on the NPRM raising concerns about the potential impacts of small UAS operations on privacy. Most commenters expressed support for UAS integration and recognized the many benefits of this technology across diverse industries but commenters discussed concerns regarding personal privacy, data privacy, private property rights, and intellectual property rights." *Id.* at 124, 42190.

117. *Id.* at 124, 42190–92.

cial UAS operators.[118] The agency plans to enable more complex UAS operations, which will greatly enhance commercial potential, including operations over people, operations beyond visual line-of-sight, and transportation of persons and property; however, these developments will likely not occur soon enough for UAS industry participants.[119]

VII. State Level Regulatory Trends

In a number of technology verticals, states, including most prominently California, have taken a leading role in developing the early-stage regulatory guidelines for a number of IoT issues. While these regulations span multiple areas, we focus next on autonomous vehicles and privacy.

A. Connected and Automated Vehicles

Connected and automated vehicles (CAVs) are in their infancy of technological development, as are the attendant policy and regulatory frameworks that will grow alongside them. As a general matter, the technology of autonomous driving has been defined along a spectrum, for which the Society of Automotive Engineers (SAE International) has defined six levels of automation: Levels 0–5.[120]

---

118. *Id.* at 124, 42084 ("approximately 40 commenters . . . expressed concern that the current framework is having an adverse effect on UAS development in the United States").

119. News Update, Fed. Aviation Admin., FAA Small Drone Rule Lets Unmanned Aircraft Soar (Sept. 6, 2017), https://www.faa.gov/news/updates/?newsId=88748.

120. *Path to Autonomy: Self-Driving Car Levels 0 to 5 Explained*, Car and Driver (Oct. 3, 2017), https://www.caranddriver.com/features/a15079828/autonomous-self-driving-car-levels-car-levels/. Note that various definitions are in use for self-driving vehicles (*see, e.g.*, Texas Senate Bill 2205 (2017), defining "Automated motor vehicle" as a motor vehicle on which "hardware and software that, when installed on a motor vehicle and engaged, are collectively capable of performing, without any intervention or supervision by a human operator" are installed.).

Level 0 technology refers to no automation and requires a human driver; Level 5 technology refers to full automation, requiring no human intervention (except, for example, the selection of a destination). Levels 1–4 represent some type of partial automation, requiring progressively less human interaction. For example, while automated cruise control qualifies as Level 1 automation, and driver assistance technology such as lane-crossing alerts are considered to be Level 2 technology, a driverless vehicle operating completely on its own but only in select conditions would be considered to be Level 4 technology.

CAVs have been the subject of bipartisan collaboration on Capitol Hill, where Congress has proposed legislation (the SELF-DRIVE Act in the House (passed in the House on September 6, 2017) and the AV START Act in the Senate) that would allow innovators to seek exemptions from state regulations that might ordinarily hamper the acceleration of new car design and technology deployments. Similarly, the federal Department of Transportation (DOT) has continued to provide an opportunity for comment on its guidance for autonomous vehicle technology, in anticipation of future regulatory action, including the recent announcement of an Advance Notice of Proposed Rulemaking for a national pilot program for CAV testing.[121]

While the federal government considers CAV policy, however, the states have forged ahead promulgating rules for permitting and testing, and in some states, legislation enabling permitting and testing of driverless mobility. This has, in turn, encouraged a nascent market of self-driving and connected vehicles developers, ranging from software developers and component manufacturers to entire CAV original equipment manufacturers (OEMs). In California, for example, the Department of Motor Vehicles (DMV) and the Public

121. *See* 83 Fed. Reg. 50872 (2018) ("Pilot Program for Collaborative Research on Motor Vehicles With High or Full Driving Automation").

Utilities Commission (CPUC) have recently issued permitting rules and authorization guidelines to autonomous vehicle (AV) makers and operators. These guidelines paved the way for OEMs and operators to begin driverless vehicle testing. The CPUC's recent Proposed Decision in R. 12-12-001 (April 6, 2018) contains a number of requirements for test AVs: for example, test AVs must have been in DMV-permitted drivered or driverless operation on California public roads for a minimum period of 90 days, and companies must include in their 90-day attestation reporting on data such as disengagements, collisions, hours of operation, and operating environment; operators are not permitted to split fares (e.g., no ridesharing); and operators must report a host of data, such as all communications between the passenger and the remote operator, vehicle miles traveled, and wait time. And the CPUC has suggested that it would consider creating an entirely new category—so-called Autonomous Vehicle Carriers (AVCs)—to facilitate further regulation and stakeholder engagement. (AV companies commenting in that proceeding have observed that the state's existing regulatory categories for Transportation Network Companies (TNCs) or Charter-Party Carriers (TCPs) would provide an adequate framework for the technology developments anticipated with autonomous vehicles.)

Elsewhere, 22 states have enacted legislation related to connected and automated vehicles. States have focused on specific issues, such as definition-setting,[122] preemption of local law,[123] data

122. *See, e.g.*, Colorado Senate Bill 17-213 Automated Driving Systems (2017), Connecticut Senate Bill 260 (2017), Texas Senate Bill 2205 (2017), Michigan Senate Bill 997 (2016).

123. Texas Senate Bill 2205 (2017).

generation and cybersecurity rules,[124] and exceptions from safety laws, such as the following of motor vehicles too closely, to allow for truck platooning technology commercialization.[125] Other states, such as Arizona for example, have fostered a regulatory environment in which autonomous vehicle operators remain free to test without a driver.[126] And in Pennsylvania, as a piece of autonomous vehicles legislation there stalls, SB 427, the Pennsylvania Department of Transportation (PennDOT) has asked companies to agree to adhere to a set of interim voluntary regulations, which would ultimately inform the regulation the legislature asks PennDOT to take up in the future.

B. Privacy

California has similarly led efforts to address consumer privacy in the Internet of Things. California enacted a new law, SB 327 (2018), which would require IoT manufacturers to equip their devices with "reasonable security features." The legislation reads, in relevant part:

> A manufacturer of a connected device shall equip the device with a reasonable security feature or features that are all of the following:
>
> (1) Appropriate to the nature and function of the device.

---

124. *See, e.g.*, The District of Columbia B22-0901 (2018) Fiscal Year 2019 Budget Support Emergency Act (requiring a study as to the "need for and use of autonomous vehicles data, including data from autonomous vehicle manufacturers and public and private vehicle-for-hire companies"), Oregon House Bill 4063 (2018) (establishing a task force that may study the State's "responsibilities relating to cybersecurity and privacy"), and North Dakota House Bill 1202 (2017) (requiring the study of "data or information stored or gathered by the use of [autonomous] vehicles").

125. Alabama Senate Bill 125 (2018).

126. *See, e.g.*, Arizona Executive Order 2015-09 (requiring state agencies to "undertake any necessary steps to support the testing and operation of self-driving vehicles on public roads in Arizona.").

(2) Appropriate to the information it may collect, contain, or transmit.

(3) Designed to protect the device and any information contained therein from unauthorized access, destruction, use, modification, or disclosure.[127]

This legislation would define "connected device" broadly as "any device, or other physical object that is capable of connecting to the Internet, directly or indirectly, and that is assigned an Internet Protocol address or Bluetooth address."[128]

In addition to what the State Legislature produced on its own, the threat of a voter-led initiative on the November ballot, the "California Right to Privacy Act" became law when its supporters struck a deal with state legislators to codify the key components of the initiative into a statute, SB 375, the California Consumer Privacy Act. It was also supplemented by a "cleanup" bill, SB 1121, designed to correct technical drafting errors inadvertently made during the negotiation process. Together, these statutes establish three new rights for consumers, which Californians may exercise regarding the collection and use of their personal information: first, to learn what categories of "personal information" a commercial business collected about the consumer (e.g., browsing history, employment data, unique identifiers, etc.); second, to learn the identity and contact information of each third party to whom a consumer's personal information has been sold or provided for commercial purposes; and third, to "opt out" of any sale or sharing of such information for commercial purposes.[129] This statute provides broad enforcement authorities by the attorney general and for a private right of action and civil penalties in connection with certain

127. California Senate Bill 327 (2018).

128. *Id.*

129. *See* Cal. Civ. Code § 1798.100 *et seq.*

violations.[130] The broad sweep of the California Consumer Privacy Act, and the speed with which it was enacted by the legislature, in lieu of a ballot initiative, almost certainly promises further revision and debate as to its specific components during subsequent legislative sessions.

California's recent privacy policy debates remain active. As such, they provide a perspective on trends in privacy policy, and in particular with respect to the way in which state governments approach consumer protection in IoT.[131]

130. *Id.*

131. While California remains the pioneering state in data privacy protection outside of perhaps any other jurisdiction not including Europe (General Data Protection Regulation), states (including California) have enacted more narrowly tailored technology privacy statues: for example, states have addressed children's online privacy (e.g., CAL. BUS. & PROF. CODE §§ 22580–22582; DEL. CODE § 1204C); e-reader privacy (e.g., ARIZ. REV. STAT. § 41-151.22; CAL. CIVIL CODE § 1798.90); and privacy policies for websites (e.g., CONN. GEN. STAT. § 42-471).

Chapter 7

IoT International Regulatory Challenges

The European Approach

Aida Joaquin Acosta

I. IoT Is a Complex Technology

In the global context, the Internet of Things (IoT) refers to a complex ecosystem of interconnected objects that typically gather information from the environment or from other data sources, analyze it, and actuate, with some degree of autonomy, upon the physical world.

The Organization for Economic Cooperation and Development (OECD) defines the IoT as an "ecosystem" of apps and services "driven by data collected from devices" about the environment.[1] IoT then uses cloud technology and big data analytics that facilitate aggregating data, allowing new apps and services and optimizing the services.[2]

The European Union Agency for Network and Information Security (ENISA) defines IoT as "a cyber-physical ecosystem

1. *The Internet of Things: Seizing the Benefits and Addressing the Challenges*, OECD 9 (2016), http://www.oecd.org/officialdocuments/publicdisplaydocumentpdf/?cote=DSTI/ICCP/CISP(2015)3/FINAL&docLanguage=En.
2. *Id.*

of interconnected sensors and actuators, which enable decision making."[3]

For the European Commission (EC), "the IoT represents the next step towards digitization where all objects and people can be interconnected through communication networks, in and across private, public and industrial spaces, and report about their status and/or about the status of the surrounding environment."[4]

II. The Importance of a Clear and Flexible Regulatory Framework for IoT

The OECD has chosen the European regulation for electronic communications as an example of a clear regulatory framework that "promotes investment when imposing proportionate and appropriate regulatory measures."[5]

The European Union believes that "[w]hile regulation can restrict some aspects of innovation, a lack of regulation would lead to a lack of clarity and unified vision, resulting in worse consequences over time."[6] The regulation of IoT, though, should be "flexible and proportionate,"[7] to adapt to technology advances,

---

3. *Baseline Security Recommendations for IoT in the Context of Critical Information Infrastructures*, ENISA 12 (2017), https://www.enisa.europa.eu/publications/baseline-security-recommendations-for-iot/at_download/fullReport.

4. *Commission Staff Working Document Advancing the Internet of Things in Europe, accompanying the Communication from the Commission to the European Parliament, the Council, the European Economic and Social Committee and the Committee of the Regions, Digitising European Industry—Reaping the Full Benefits of a Digital Single Market*, European Comm'n 5 (Apr. 19, 2016), https://eur-lex.europa.eu/legal-content/EN/TXT/PDF/?uri=CELEX:52016SC0110&from=EN.

5. *Supra* note 1, at 26.

6. Communication from the Commission to the European Parliament, the Council, the European Economic and Social Committee and the Committee of the Regions, *Digitising European Industry—Reaping the Full Benefits of a Digital Single Market*, European Comm'n 242 (Apr. 19, 2016); https://eur-lex.europa.eu/legal-content/EN/TXT/PDF/?uri=CELEX:52016DC0180&from=EN.

7. *Id.*

and to "balance considerations on potential benefits and harms."[8] The IoT needs a clear regulatory framework that establishes the requirements but remains technologically neutral, that is, guiding the solutions but not mandating to follow a specific option.[9]

III. The Shared Challenges of Building an Adequate Regulatory Framework for IoT

Notwithstanding the agreed-upon need for a global regulatory framework, it will be difficult to build a fine-tuned regulatory framework for the IoT: IoT devices have certain features that differentiate them from traditional IT (such as computers), and which create new legal challenges and add additional complexity to those of traditional IT systems.[10]

Certain features of IoT systems add complexity to the security and privacy challenges of traditional IT. For example, there are design constraints: IoT devices tend to be of "low complexity (low cost), have constrained power supplies (battery, solar),"[11] and sensors in IoT tend to be very small, hampering the addition of security and encryption functions that would need bigger chip surfaces to support them.[12]

Also, and related to their core functions, IoT devices are objects whose main function is usually not connecting to the

8. *Id.*

9. *Id.*

10. *See generally* https://eur-lex.europa.eu/legal-content/EN/TXT/PDF/?uri=CELEX:52018SC0137&from=en (pp. 9–11), which explains the characteristics of IoT that make them more complex than other technologies; Woodrow Hartzog & Evan Selinger, *The Internet of Heirlooms and Disposable Things*, 17 N.C. J.L. & Tech. 581 (June 1, 2016), https://papers.ssrn.com/sol3/papers.cfm?abstract_id=2787511.

11. Security & the IoT GSMA Industry Position, GSMA 2 (2017), https://www.gsma.com/iot/wp-content/uploads/2017/11/IoTSecurityposition.pdf.

12. Scott R. Peppet, *Regulating the Internet of Things: First Steps Toward Managing Discrimination, Privacy, Security, and Consent*, Tex. L. Rev. 135 (2014), https://texaslawreview.org/wp-content/uploads/2015/08/Peppet-93-1.pdf.

Internet itself—"refrigerators can cool all without WiFi,"[13] —whereas "[c]omputers that cannot connect to the Internet are of limited value"[14] today. Thus, IoT devices "are likely to be used long after the vendor stops servicing them with critical security updates."[15]

In addition, IoT devices are generally produced by "traditional consumer-goods makers rather than computer hardware or software firms"[16] who would have the relevant experience in securing systems.

These features of low cost, small-sized chips, power constraints, limited security systems, and updates make security and privacy issues of IT more complex in IoT devices.

Certain features of IoT can also create new legal challenges from those of traditional IT systems. For example, IoT devices, such as smart thermostats or smart door locks or smart medicine dispensers, have the ability to actuate upon the physical world, with a certain degree of autonomy, potentially creating new legal issues such as allocating liability of autonomous (or semi-autonomous) systems.[17]

IoT devices are also designed to fade into the background, facilitating involuntary privacy disclosures,[18] and are becoming pervasive, facilitating potential challenges related to surveillance.[19]

---

13. Hartzog & Selinger, *supra* note 10, at 586.

14. *Id.*

15. *Id.*

16. Peppet, *supra* note 12, at 134.

17. Commission Staff Working Document Liability for Emerging Digital Technologies Accompanying the Document Communication from the Commission to the European Parliament, the European Council, the Council, the European Economic and Social Committee and the Committee of the Regions, *Artificial Intelligence for Europe*, European Comm'n 22–23 (Apr. 25, 2018), https://eur-lex.europa.eu/legal-content/EN/TXT/PDF/?uri=CELEX:52018SC0137&from=en.

18. Clearly Opaque Privacy Risks of the Internet of Things, The Internet of Things Privacy Forum 3, 60–63 (May 2018), https://www.iotprivacyforum.org/wp-content/uploads/2018/06/Clearly-Opaque-Privacy-Risks-of-the-Internet-of-Things.pdf?d8bd54&d8bd54.

19. *Id.* at 150.

In addition, IoT devices are "data driven"[20] and the information they collect can be used with big data[21] to make inferences for relevant decisions that affect the user, and that could raise discriminatory issues.[22] IoT can also raise other ethical concerns in relation to human-machine interaction and autonomous decision making when IoT is coupled with AI, showing autonomous behavior.[23]

These regulatory challenges are shared by governments across the globe. To help address these challenges, the OECD recommends governments to understand "best practices and policy approaches in the emerging IoT environment."[24]

The EU has been very active in working on these legal challenges of the IoT in the past few years. This chapter introduces some of the main aspects of the IoT policy and regulatory approach of the EU: privacy, security, safety, and liability. The more technical issues and accompanying regulations are beyond the scope of this chapter. Nevertheless, the EU has important work in progress on a technical level on spectrum availability and network coverage; numbering, addressing, identification, and discovery of IoT devices; standardization and interoperability; and data flow and access to data.[25] The end of the chapter introduces recommendations for the regulation of IoT based on the EU experience.

IV. The EU Approach to the Legal Challenges of IoT: Privacy, Security, Safety, and Liability

A. The EU IoT Policy Objectives

Since 2009, the EU has been working on developing a clear regulatory framework for IoT to facilitate the uptake of the technology.

20. *Supra* note 17.
21. "Big data refers to large amounts of data produced very quickly by a high number of diverse sources," https://ec.europa.eu/digital-single-market/en/big-data.
22. Peppet, *supra* note 12, at 117.
23. *Supra* note 17.
24. *Supra* note 1, at 8.
25. *See generally supra* note 4.

EU regulators are aware of the potential of IoT for "well-being and economic growth"[26] and of the importance of facilitating the deployment of the technology to spread its benefits.[27] At the same time, the EU is concerned about the legal and social challenges and knows the importance of developing an appropriate regulatory framework to address those challenges and help with the rollout of IoT.[28]

The EU strategy on IoT began in 2009, when the European Commission (EC)[29] published the "Internet of Things: An Action Plan for Europe,"[30] which included several action lines to eliminate obstacles to the uptake of the technology.[31] Immediately after, from 2010 to 2012, the EC created a group of experts on IoT to advise on the challenges of IoT and help to deploy IoT throughout the EU.[32] More recently, since 2015, the EC has developed a series of measures to speed up the rollout of IoT.[33] For example, within

26. *The Internet of Things Opportunities and Challenges*, EUROPEAN PARLIAMENTARY RESEARCH SERVICE 7 (2015), http://www.europarl.europa.eu/RegData/etudes/BRIE/2015/557012/EPRS_BRI(2015)557012_EN.pdf.

27. *Supra* note 17, at 2–3.

28. *Id.*; *Communication from the Commission to the European Parliament, the Council, the European Economic and Social Committee and the Committee of the Regions on the Mid-Term Review on the Implementation of the Digital Single Market Strategy a Connected Digital Single Market for All*, EUROPEAN COMM'N 2 (May 10, 2017), https://eur-lex.europa.eu/resource.html?uri=cellar:a4215207-362b-11e7-a08e-01aa75ed71a1.0001.02/DOC_1&format=PDF.

29. The EC is the executive branch of the EU, proposing new legislation and monitoring its implementation.

30. *Communication from the Commission to the European Parliament, the Council, the European Economic and Social Committee and the Committee of the Regions, Internet of Things—An Action Plan for Europe* (2009); https://eur-lex.europa.eu/LexUriServ/LexUriServ.do?uri=COM:2009:0278:FIN:EN:PDF.

31. *Id.* at 5–11.

32. *Register of Commission Expert Groups, Internet of Things Expert Group*, EUROPEAN COMM'N, http://ec.europa.eu/transparency/regexpert/index.cfm?do=groupDetail.groupDetail&groupID=2514.

33. European Commission official website, The Internet of Things, https://ec.europa.eu/digital-single-market/en/policies/internet-things.

the Digital Single Market (DSM),[34] the EC highlights again the importance "to ensure legal certainty for the rollout and uptake of emerging digital technologies and to fully exploit their potential,"[35] and focuses on developing IoT as a key element for EU competitiveness.[36] In addition, the EC created in 2015 the Alliance for IoT Innovation,[37] an industry stakeholder group that "offers an opportunity to discuss regulatory and legal obstacles to further IoT take up."[38] The EC has also put in place different funding opportunities for research and testing IoT "to support the development and take-up of the technology"[39] under the H2020 Fund.

In this EU strategy to gain uptake of IoT, the key element is trust. The EC believes that "the main challenge for the acceptance of the IoT remains therefore users' trust in a broad sense."[40]

To build public trust in IoT, it is crucial to protect the fundamental rights of the European Charter affected by IoT,[41] working on issues such as privacy, security, liability, consumer and data protection, and safety. For example, the OECD identified privacy, security, liability, consumer protection, safety, as key issues to work on for increasing public trust in IoT;[42] and the EC recognized

34. The DSM is "the strategy of the EC to ensure access to online activities for individuals and businesses under conditions of fair competition, consumer and data protection," https://ec.europa.eu/digital-single-market/en/policies/shaping-digital-single-market.

35. *Supra* note 33; *supra* note 17.

36. *Supra* note 26, at 7.

37. European Commission official website, The Alliance for Internet of Things Innovation (AIOTI), https://ec.europa.eu/digital-single-market/en/alliance-internet-things-innovation-aioti.

38. *Supra* note 4, at 9.

39. European Commission official website, Research & Innovation in Internet of Things; https://ec.europa.eu/digital-single-market/en/research-innovation-iot.

40. *Supra* note 4, at 29.

41. *Id.* at 10. The fundamental rights of the European Chapter affected by IoT are mainly privacy, protection of personal data, and freedom to conduct a business.

42. *Supra* note 1, at 7.

that "[s]ecurity, liability, privacy and data protection are critical challenges for the IoT"[43] and that "[s]trengthening trust, security and end-to-end personal data protection and privacy . . . [in] IoT is a priority for the European Commission."[44]

B. The EU Regulatory Efforts on Privacy, Security, Safety, and Liability

The EU policy and regulatory efforts to build trust in IoT are focusing on two main groups of issues: (1) privacy and security and (2) safety and liability.

Several recent incidents of hackings and privacy breaches, and safety and liability issues of IoT, have raised concerns among policy makers and impacted the economy and public's trust in the technology. On the privacy and security front, media has reported security vulnerabilities of IoT devices, including an IoT vacuum cleaner allowing access to its camera;[45] a home assistant recording journalists' conversations;[46] and an IoT doll with security flaws risking children's privacy.[47] Related to safety, hackers took over control of an automated vehicle;[48] and hackers threaten to shut down IoT pacemakers.[49]

---

43. *Supra* note 4, at 30.

44. *Id* at 27.

45. John Leyden, *Doctor, Doctor, I Feel Like My IoT-Enabled Vacuum Cleaner Is Spying on Me*, The Register (2018), https://www.theregister.co.uk/2018/07/20/iot_insecurity_robo_vacuum_cleaners.

46. Rand Hindi, *Google Home Mini's Bug Shows Why Cloud-Based Voice Assistants Are a Idea*, Medium (2017), https://medium.com/snips-ai/google-home-minis-bug-shows-why-cloud-based-voice-assistants-are-a-bad-idea-6f1b4c569591.

47. Whitney Meers, *Hello Barbie, Goodbye Privacy? Hacker Raises Security Concerns*, The Huffington Post (2015), https://www.huffingtonpost.com/entry/hello-barbie-security-concerns_us_565c4921e4b072e9d1c24d22.

48. Andy Greenberg, *Hackers Remotely Kill a Jeep on the Highway—With Me In It,* Wired (2015), https://www.wired.com/2015/07/hackers-remotely-kill-jeep-highway/.

49. Nat Garun, *Almost Half a Million Pacemakers Need a Firmware Update to Avoid Getting Hacked*, The Verge (2017), https://www.theverge.com/2017/8/30/16230048/fda-abbott-pacemakers-firmware-update-cybersecurity-hack.

Other issues the EU has considered include distributed denial of governmental or company services attacks (DDoS) and allocation of liability from those attacks. Additionally, productivity loss and business disruption of these DDoS attacks has been considered. In one example, hackers took control over irrigators, disabling certain parts of cities' water systems.[50]

Given the preceding risks, privacy, security, safety, and clear liability rules are clear priorities for the EC as it facilitates the deployment of IoT and spreads their benefits to society. [51]

C. Privacy and Security

As the EC has stated, "[s]ecurity and the protection of personal data issues are a key concern for a successful take up of the IoT."[52]

1. Privacy

The IoT will have a significant impact on privacy. For example, a recent report highlighted that IoT will collect data about users' off-line behavior,[53] which could be combined with users' online data to generate precise users' profiles. The IoT will reduce private spaces[54] and change the "reasonable expectation of privacy" standard[55] as the IoT becomes more ubiquitous. Eventually, people may assume that recording is happening everywhere; and they will know that ubiquitous IoT devices exist and are collecting information from them.[56]

---

50. Martin Giles, *Hackers Could Turn Your Sprinklers into a Weapon*, MIT TECH. REV. (2018), https://www.technologyreview.com/the-download/611849/hackers-could-turn-your-garden-sprinklers-into-a-cyber-weapon/?utm_source=newsletters&utm_medium=email&utm_content=2018_08_13&utm_campaign=the_download.

51. *Supra* note 4, at 27.

52. *Id.* at 30.

53. *Supra* note 18, at 123.

54. *Id.* at 21.

55. *Id.* at 15–16.

56. See the executive summary as an example; *id.* at 5–6.

Given this reality, addressing privacy issues is an essential element of the EU strategy on IoT. "The Digital Single Market (DSM) Strategy has the objective to increase trust and security in digital services,"[57] and the EU key action to increase trust and security is to update its privacy regulatory framework, adopting the General Data Protection Regulation (GDPR) and reviewing the ePrivacy Directive.[58]

The EU has an underlying principle in the reform of its privacy framework: it seeks to avoid sectorial regulation and to develop a base privacy norm of direct application by EU Member States (MS) to prevent different interpretations across countries. This reform tries also to update privacy regulation to developments of technology.[59]

a. The General Data Protection Regulation

The General Data Protection Regulation (GDPR)[60] is the first pillar of the EU privacy reform. It entered into force on May 25, 2018, replacing the Data Protection Directive 95/46/EC.

The GDPR, as an EU regulation, is a binding legislative act of direct application to all MS, while the previous norm, the Data Protection Directive, as an EU directive, was not directly applicable: it established a goal but needed a national legislative act to implement it. By choosing a regulation for its privacy framework, the EU has strengthened privacy rights and harmonized data privacy laws across Europe.

57. *Id.* at 2.
58. *Id.*
59. *Id.* at 2, 4.
60. Regulation (Eu) 2016/679 of the European Parliament and of the Council of 27 April 2016 on the *Protection of Natural Persons with Regard to the Processing of Personal Data and on the Free Movement of Such Data, and Repealing Directive 95/46/EC* (General Data Protection Regulation), https://eur-lex.europa.eu/legal-content/EN/TXT/PDF/?uri=CELEX:32016R0679&from=EN.

The GDPR implements several critical changes to the Data Protection Directive that would affect IoT. For example, the GDPR:

1. Expands the territorial scope to controllers or processors of personal data[61] of any subjects residing in the Union, regardless of the controllers' or processors' location or primary place of business.[62]
2. Includes privacy by design and privacy by default paradigms. These paradigms add data protection measures—such as data minimization—from the design phase of data processing instruments; and they include measures to ensure that, by default, only the necessary data "for each specific purpose of the processing is processed".[63]
3. Mandates that consent to collect data should be presented in a clear and distinguishable manner, using an intelligible and plain language, and that it should be easy to withdraw consent.[64]
4. Establishes that the national supervisory authority should be notified of data breaches within 72 hours after a processor of personal data becomes aware of the breach, when the data breach is likely to "result in a risk for the rights and freedoms of the natural persons".[65]
5. Creates the right to know whether the subject's personal data is being processed, its purpose, and the right to access the subject's personal data, among other related rights.[66]

61. Personal data is "any information relating to an identified or identifiable natural person." *Id.* at 33.

62. *Id.* at art. 3, pp. 32–33.

63. *Id.* at art. 25, p. 48.

64. *Id.* at art. 7, p. 37.

65. *Id.* at art. 33.1, p. 52.

66. *Id.* at art. 15, p. 43.

6. Defines the right of subjects to be forgotten and the grounds for the subjects to have their data erased, except for a number of circumstances when processing is necessary.[67]
7. Creates the right of the subjects to receive their personal data in a portable format and to be able to transmit it to another controller.[68]

b. Proposal of ePrivacy Regulation

The second pillar of the EU privacy reform is the ePrivacy Regulation.[69] This regulation was proposed by the EC and is still under negotiation in the European Parliament (EP) and the Council of the EU.

The ePrivacy Regulation updates the Directive 2002/58/EC (ePrivacy Directive)[70] to "provide a high level of protection for users of electronic communications services."[71] The regulation aims to safeguard the confidentiality of communications of personal information.

The EC proposal widens the scope of the previous directive to include voice-over IP, messaging services, and web-mail e-mail services, expanding the previous protection that was given to telephony, SMS, and electronic mail services, and adapting the privacy regulation of electronic communications to technological change.[72]

---

67. *Id.* at art. 17, pp. 43–44.
68. *Id.* at art. 20, p. 45.
69. *Id.*
70. Directive 2002/58/EC of the European Parliament and of the Council of 12 July 2002 Concerning the *Processing of Personal Data and the Protection of Privacy in the Electronic Communications Sector* (Directive on Privacy and Electronic Communications) 37, https://eur-lex.europa.eu/legal-content/EN/TXT/PDF/?uri=CELEX:32002L0058&from=EN.
71. Proposal for a Regulation of the European Parliament and of the Council Concerning the *Respect for Private Life and the Protection of Personal Data in Electronic Communications and Repealing Directive 2002/58/EC* (Regulation on Privacy and Electronic Communications) 2, http://ec.europa.eu/newsroom/dae/document.cfm?doc_id=41241.
72. *Id.* at 13.

The ePrivacy Regulation is a lex specialis of the GDPR for electronic communications, which means that the regulation particularizes the GDPR to the case of electronic communications, adding specific provisions to protect electronic communications that include personal data. The ePrivacy Regulation proposal explicitly includes the IoT under its scope, as well: the proposal considers the machine-to machine (M2M) communication between IoT devices (transmissions of signals between machines over a network) to be an electronic communication service.[73] Therefore, as an electronic communication service, M2M communications will be within the scope of the ePrivacy Regulation proposal.

2. *Security*

Security of IoT is also critical and will be reinforced by new regulations on cybersecurity. A recent study foresees that investment in IoT security "will reach $1.5 billion in 2018, . . . [and] $3.1 billion in 2021"[74] and the study points to regulation as being the main cause of this increase, as industry will have to take actions to comply with future regulations.[75]

The EU has acknowledged the importance of a strong cybersecurity framework to increase consumer trust in emerging technologies,[76] and the EU has developed a specific cybersecurity strategy.

a. The Cybersecurity Package

The cybersecurity strategy of the EU is condensed in the new EU cybersecurity package adopted by the EC on September 13, 2017,

73. *Id.* at 13–14.

74. *Gartner Says Worldwide IoT Security Spending Will Reach $1.5 Billion in 2018*, Gartner Newsroom (2018), https://www.gartner.com/newsroom/id/3869181.

75. *Id.*

76. *Joint Communication to the European Parliament and the Council, Resilience, Deterrence and Defence: Building Strong Cybersecurity for the EU*, European Comm'n 2 (2017), https://eur-lex.europa.eu/legal-content/EN/TXT/PDF/?uri=JOIN:2017:450:FIN&from=EN.

but it is still being negotiated.[77] This package updates the first EU strategy on cybersecurity, released in 2013, to adapt it to the proliferation of connected devices.[78] The main elements of the new cybersecurity package include a proposal for regulation of the EU Agency for Network and Information Security (ENISA) and on a cybersecurity certification framework; guidance on interpretation on the Directive of Network and Information Security; and recommendations on coordinated response on large-scale cybersecurity crises.

b. The Cybersecurity Act

The Cybersecurity Act[79] is a proposal for a regulation that establishes a permanent mandate for ENISA[80] to allow the agency to provide support on cybersecurity to MS; and a cybersecurity certification scheme for Information and Communication Technologies products and services:[81] this certification scheme would be recognized across the EU, would be established by ENISA, and would not be compulsory, but there would be incentives to certify. This initiative tries to help with the current patchwork of cybersecurity certification schemes in Europe, where national certification initiatives exist that are not recognized by other MS.[82]

This certification scheme is connected to promoting open cybersecurity standards and the concept of "trust IoT label," which

77. *Id.*

78. *Proposal for a Regulation of the European Parliament and of the Council on ENISA, the "EU Cybersecurity Agency," and repealing Regulation (EU) 526/2013, and on Information and Communication Technology cybersecurity certification ("Cybersecurity Act")*, European Comm'n 2 (2017), https://eur-lex.europa.eu/resource.html?uri=cellar:1985b4b4-985e-11e7-b92d-01aa75ed71a1.0001.02/DOC_4&format=PDF.

79. *Id.*

80. *Id.* at 38–59.

81. *Id.* at 60–66.

82. ENISA Factsheet, *Cybersecurity EU Agency and Certification Framework* (2017), http://ec.europa.eu/newsroom/document.cfm?doc_id=46999.

will provide IoT consumers with information about a product level of security and privacy, similar to the labelling system used today to indicate energy efficiency of various appliances across the EU.[83]

In line with the certification initiative of the cybersecurity package, ENISA has developed baseline security recommendations for IoT, which include issues such as harmonization, awareness, interoperability, security, and liability.[84] ENISA's recommendations are meant to facilitate harmonization and serve as criteria for the certification initiative.[85] The objective is "to provide insight into the security requirements of IoT, . . . identifying potential good practices and security measures to apply in order to protect IoT systems."[86]

c. Guidance on the Directive on Security of Network and Information Systems

The cybersecurity package also includes guidance and additional interpretation of specific provisions of the Directive on Security of Network and Information Systems (NIS Directive)[87] to accelerate application of the package.

The NIS Directive entered into force in August 2016, and the deadline for MS to transpose it was on May 9, 2018. The directive provides legal measures to increase the level of cybersecurity in the EU and build MS's capabilities in cybersecurity. It has three main

---

83. *Communication from the Commission to the European Parliament, the Council, the European Economic and Social Committee and the Committee of the Regions ICT, Standardisation Priorities for the Digital Single Market*, European Comm'n 7 (2016), http://ec.europa.eu/newsroom/dae/document.cfm?doc_id=15265.

84. *Supra* note 3.

85. *Id.* at 2.

86. *Id.* at 1.

87. *Directive (EU) 2016/1148 of the European Parliament and of the Council of 6 July 2016 concerning Measures for a High Common Level of Security of Network and Information Systems across the Union*, https://eur-lex.europa.eu/legal-content/EN/TXT/PDF/?uri=CELEX:32016L1148&from=EN.

objectives: ensuring MS's preparedness via a response team[88] and national NIS authority,[89] cooperation among MS,[90] and promoting a culture of risk management and security across vital sectors and actors.[91]

The guidance contained in the cybersecurity package regarding the NIS Directive, in particular, in the EC Communication "Making the Most of NIS,"[92] includes best practices from MS and provides explanation of provisions of the directive to support MS in the implementation on the NIS Directive effectively.

d. Recommendations for Coordinated Crisis Response

In addition, the cybersecurity package includes a recommendation on coordinated responses to large-scale cybersecurity incidents and crises,[93] setting the cooperation procedures among MS in case of such incidents. This recommendation emerged right after November 2016, when the EC suffered a DDoS attack on its Internet service and web page, making those Internet services unavailable for several hours.[94]

88. *Id.* at art. 9, p. 17.
89. *Id.* at art. 8, p. 16.
90. *Id.* at art. 11, pp. 17–19.
91. *Id.* at arts. 14 & 16, pp. 20–22.
92. *Communication from the Commission to the European Parliament and the Council, Making the Most of NIS—Towards the Effective Implementation of Directive (EU) 2016/1148 Concerning Measures for a High Common Level of Security of Network and Information Systems across the Union* (2017), http://eur-lex.europa.eu/legal-content/EN/TXT/?qid=1505297631636&uri=COM:2017:476:FIN.
93. *Commission Recommendation on Coordinated Response to Large Scale Cybersecurity Incidents and Crises* (2017), http://ec.europa.eu/transparency/regdoc/rep/3/2017/EN/C-2017-6100-F1-EN-MAIN-PART-1.PDF.
94. Florian Eder, *Hackers Attack European Commission: Staff Warned of Cyberattack, but No Data Breach*, Politico (2016), https://www.politico.eu/article/hackers-attack-european-commission/.

D. Safety and Liability

Safety and liability are key aspects to build consumers' trust and uptake of IoT technologies. A clear and effective regulatory framework on safety and liability will allow technology innovation in the IoT to thrive. The EC stated that "[c]onsumers' trust and the uptake of these technologies will depend on whether they are perceived to be safe and on whether the legal framework is considered clear and effective to provide remedies to victims." In addition, companies and innovators need an effective regulatory framework, offering "legal certainty,"[95] which "is a key element for good business development."[96]

Both product safety and product liability regulations are related to each other and complement each other: safety regulations prevent cases of liability. "Product safety and liability are complementary legal frameworks aiming to provide trust and safety to consumers."[97]

In the EU, work on regulatory adaptation of these regimes started in 2015 and this work is still ongoing. In 2015, "the DSM Strategy emphasized the importance of legal certainty for the roll out of IoT."[98]

In 2017, the EC Communication on Building European Data Economy[99] "committed to assess whether the current EU legal rules for product liability are fit for purpose, when damages occur in the context of the use of IoT and autonomous systems."[100] Also,

95. *Supra* note 17, at 2.

96. *Id.*

97. *Id.* at 4.

98. *Supra* note 17, at 2.

99. *Communication from the Commission to the European Parliament, the Council, the European Economic and Social Committee and the Committee of the Regions, Building A European Data Economy* (2017), https://eur-lex.europa.eu/legal-content/EN/TXT/PDF/?uri=CELEX:52017DC0009&from=EN.

100. *Supra* note 17.

in 2017, the EP published a report, asking for liability rules for autonomous systems that would consider their safety aspects.[101]

And, in 2018, the EC published the Communication on "Liability for Emerging Digital Technologies" accompanying AI for Europe,[102] with the objective of providing a list of liability challenges related to emerging technologies,[103] which also considered the possibility of defining a liability framework for cybersecurity attacks.[104]

1. Product Safety Norms

Regarding product safety norms, IoT devices have to comply with the safety obligations provided in specific EU legislation.[105] A wide range of product safety requirements are harmonized through different pieces of legislation, for example, the Machinery Directive,[106] which establishes the EU legal safety rules for robots; the Low Voltage Directive,[107] applicable to household appliances such as vacuum cleaners; the Directive of Active Implantable

---

101. EP Resolution with Recommendations to the Commission on Civil Law Rules on Robotics, EUROPEAN PARLIAMENT 14–16, http://www.europarl.europa.eu/sides/getDoc.do?pubRef=-//EP//NONSGML+TA+P8-TA-2017-0051+0+DOC+PDF+V0//EN.

102. *Supra* note 17.

103. *Id.* at 3.

104. *Id.* at 20.

105. *Directive 2001/95/EC of the European Parliament and of the Council of 3 December 2001 on General Product Safety,* art. 1.2, p. 7 (2002), https://eur-lex.europa.eu/LexUriServ/LexUriServ.do?uri=OJ:L:2002:011:0004:0017:en:PDF.

106. *Directive 2006/42/EC of the European Parliament and of the Council on Machinery, and Amending Directive 95/16/EC* (recast) (2006), https://eur-lex.europa.eu/legal-content/EN/TXT/PDF/?uri=CELEX:32006L0042&from=EN.

107. *Directive 2014/35/EU of the European Parliament and of the Council on the Harmonisation of the Laws of the Member States Relating to the Making Available on the Market of Electrical Equipment Designed for Use within Certain Voltage Limits* (recast) (2014), https://eur-lex.europa.eu/legal-content/EN/TXT/PDF/?uri=CELEX:32014L0035&from=EN.

Medical Devices,[108] applicable to devices such as cardiac pacemakers and glucose monitors, and the Directive for Medical Devices,[109] for devices used for medical treatment or diagnosis; and the Radio Equipment Directive,[110] which would affect automated vehicles that incorporate GPS.

The rest of the products or safety aspects that are not included in specific harmonized legislation, such as the examples just mentioned, are covered by Directive 2001/95/EC on General Product Safety,[111] so that all products placed on the market are under an EU safety regulation.

While it undertakes the process of evaluating and adapting the EU product safety regulation to IoT, the EC has already evaluated the suitability of the Machinery Directive in light of emerging digital technologies such as IoT and AI;[112] a directive that is "the core European legislation regulating products of the mechanical engineering industries."[113] The evaluation concluded that the directive is fit for purpose,[114] although some provisions do not explicitly cover certain aspects of emerging digital technologies such as human–

---

108. *Council Directive on the Approximation of the Laws of the Member States Relating to Active Implantable Medical Devices* (1990), https://eur-lex.europa.eu/legal-content/EN/TXT/PDF/?uri=CELEX:31990L0385&from=EN.

109. *Council Directive 93/42/EEC of 14 June 1993 concerning Medical Devices* (2007), https://eur-lex.europa.eu/LexUriServ/LexUriServ.do?uri=CONSLEG:1993L0042:20071011:en:PDF.

110. *Directive 2014/53/EU of the European Parliament and of the Council on the Harmonisation of the Relating to the Making Available on the Market of Equipment and Repealing Directive 1999/5/EC* (2014); https://eur-lex.europa.eu/legal-content/EN/TXT/PDF/?uri=CELEX:32014L0053&from=en.

111. *Supra* note 105, at art. 2, p. 7.

112. See full evaluation report: *Commission Staff Working Document, Evaluation of the Machinery Directive* (2018), https://ec.europa.eu/docsroom/documents/29232/attachments/1/translations/en/renditions/native.

113. *Id.* at 4.

114. *Id.* at 37; European Commission Official Website, *Commission Publishes Evaluation Reports on EU Rules on Machinery Safety and Product Liability* (2018), https://ec.europa.eu/growth/content/commission-publishes-evaluation-reports-eu-rules-machinery-safety-and-product-liability_en.

machine collaboration.[115] In this respect, the EC is now going to study whether these issues would require a legislative change.[116]

In addition, European Standardization Organizations (ESOs) are developing harmonized standards for IoT, AI advanced robots, and autonomous systems.[117] The idea is that, if the IoT device follows the standard, the device would have "presumption of conformity with the European safety legislation, under which they are developed, in particular under the Machinery Directive . . . and Radio Equipment Directive."[118] Also, the ESOs are working on standards of products that combine different products and where different pieces of safety legislation apply.[119]

2. *Product Liability Norms*

At the EU level, product liability rules are defined in the directive concerning Liability for Defective Products or Product Liability Directive (PLD).[120] The PLD has been the EU product liability framework for defective products since 1985, and "it covers all types of products . . . including emerging digital technology products,"[121] such as IoT devices.

The PLD assigns liability to producers when defective products cause damages to victims or their property.[122] It defines a strict lia-

115. *Supra* note 112, at 29.

116. European Commission Official Website, *Commission Publishes Evaluation Reports on EU Rules on Machinery Safety and Product Liability* (2018), https://ec.europa.eu/growth/content/commission-publishes-evaluation-reports-eu-rules-machinery-safety-and-product-liability_en.

117. *Supra* note 17, at 5.

118. *Id.*

119. *Id.*

120. *Council Directive on the Approximation of the Laws, Regulations and Administrative Provisions of the Member States Concerning Liability For Defective Products* (1985), https://eur-lex.europa.eu/legal-content/EN/TXT/PDF/?uri=CELEX:31985L0374&from=EN.

121. *Supra* note 17, at 7.

122. *Supra* note 120, at art. 1, p. 30.

bility regime, so that the victim has to prove the damage, the defect on the product, and that the damage was caused by that defect.[123]

At a national level, the laws that implement the PLD generally coexist with other national product liability rules, which offer, to the victims, remedies based on different grounds from those of the PLD. [124] In that way, injured parties have a more comprehensive protection, and may be able to choose among different actions.

Currently, in the process of evaluating if the EU product liability regulation is fit to purpose in the light of emerging technologies and IoT, the EC has already evaluated the PLD.[125]

In the evaluation, the EC highlighted that PLD has generally been working well since 1985, adapting to new technologies, but it may need to be updated and clarify concepts to be more relevant and useful to the IoT.[126] Some of the concepts mentioned that would need clarification were about the definitions of product, producer, defect, and damage.[127] For example, the EC may need to clarify the concept of producer in the case of IoT devices, as devices can be refurbished or their features changed beyond producers' control; or update the concept of damages, to extend them not only to physical and material issues but also to privacy and cybersecurity damages.[128] As a result, the EC will issue a guidance document clarifying these concepts and the interpretation of PLD

---

123. *Id.* at art. 4, p. 31.

124. *Id.* at 30.

125. See full evaluation report: Commission Staff Working Document; *Evaluation of Council Directive 85/374/EEC of 25 July 1985 on the Approximation of the Laws, Regulations and Administrative Provisions of the Member States Concerning Liability for Defective Products* (2018), https://eur-lex.europa.eu/legal-content/EN/TXT/PDF/?uri=CELEX:52018SC0157&from=EN.

126. *Supra* note 112, at 8–9.

127. *Id.* at 9.

128. *Supra* note 117, at 17–19; *supra* note 112, at 9.

by mid-2019, and, if necessary, the EC will update the concepts that may need clarification.[129]

In addition, the EC will issue a report on the broader implications, and loopholes for the liability and safety frameworks for IoT, AI, and robotics by mid-2019.[130]

The EC will also create an expert group to help develop the PLD guide and to report on the orientations for the safety and liability frameworks for IoT.[131] The expert group will have two formations, one for each purpose: the PLD formation and the new technologies formation.[132]

E. Other Issues: Ethics

As IoT devices are rapidly incorporating AI into their systems, which empowers IoT devices with more autonomy, the EU is becoming more aware of the ethical impact of IoT.

The autonomy of IoT devices in decision making can raise ethical issues. Apart from making it difficult to assign responsibility of actions and allocate liability in autonomous systems, there are other concerns related more broadly to the ethical development of IoT and AI technologies, for example, the ethics of human machine interaction (HMI), ad targeting, and AI's effect on the working environment. For instance, related to HMI, home assistants can raise educational and social behavioral issues: how kids and adults

---

129. *Report from the Commission to the European Parliament, the Council and the European Economic and Social Committee on the Application of the Council Directive on the Approximation of the Laws, Regulations, and Administrative Provisions of the Member States Concerning Liability for Defective Products* 10 (85/374/EEC), https://eur-lex.europa.eu/legal-content/EN/TXT/PDF/?uri=CELEX:52018DC0246&from=EN.

130. *Id.*

131. *Id.* at 9–10.

132. *Supra* note 17, at 21.

interact with these devices, and the values these new interactions teach children.[133]

Related to ad targeting, consumers can be more easily manipulated with IoT AI-powered devices, as IoT devices connect with consumers in real time, for example, offering cheaper rides if the consumer agrees to modify the route to pass through advertised stores or restaurants.[134]

And in the working environment, some companies are encouraging employees to use wearable devices to facilitate their work and increase productivity,[135] raising concerns related to the potential abuse of this policy on privacy invasion and surveillance practices, or dehumanization of relationships.[136]

The EP has expressed the need to update the EU legal framework to incorporate ethical guidelines in relation to emerging technologies: the EP "[c]onsiders that the existing Union legal framework should be updated and complemented, where appropriate, by guiding ethical principles in line with the complexity of robotics and its many social, medical, and bioethical implications."[137]

---

133. Rachel Metz, *Growing Up with Alexa*, MIT Tech. Rev. (2017), https://www.technologyreview.com/s/608430/growing-up-with-alexa/.

134. Judith Donath, *Driverless Cars Could Make Transportation Free for Everyone—With a Catch*, The Atlantic (2017), https://www.theatlantic.com/technology/archive/2017/12/self-driving-cars-free-future/548945/.

135. Ceylan Yeginsu, *If Workers Slack Off, the Wristband Will Know. (And Amazon Has a Patent for It.)*, N.Y. Times (2018), https://www.nytimes.com/2018/02/01/technology/amazon-wristband-tracking-privacy.html.

136. *Id.*

137. *European Parliament Resolution of 16 February 2017 with Recommendations to the Commission on Civil Law Rules on Robotics (2015/2103(INL))*, European Parliament 7–8, http://www.europarl.europa.eu/sides/getDoc.do?pubRef=-//EP//NONSGML+TA+P8-TA-2017-0051+0+DOC+PDF+V0//EN.

As a result, the EC is now working on developing AI Ethical Guidelines.[138] The first draft was developed by the end of 2018 and built upon the Chapter of Fundamental Rights of the EU.[139] The AI Ethical Guidelines will consider issues such as "the future of work, fairness, safety, security, social inclusion and algorithmic transparency . . . and privacy."[140] In the process of developing these guidelines, different stakeholders will be involved, from the European AI Alliance,[141] industry, academia, to other civil society groups.[142] And the EC will review and adapt, if necessary, the regulatory framework for developing AI to ensure coherence with the EU's basic fundamental rights.[143]

V. Recommendations and Concluding Remarks

The EU has been working on a wide variety of regulations and public policies to address the challenges and leverage the opportunities of IoT. As a result, our analysis of the European regulatory framework is relevant not only to those considering implementations of IoT devices and systems in Europe but also presents more general lessons and principles to governments and industry in other regions.

Regulators and policy makers should take the following into account:

---

138. *Communication from the Commission to the European Parliament, the European Council, the Council, the European Economic and Social Committee and the Committee of the Regions, Artificial Intelligence for Europe* European Parliament 15–16 (2018), http://ec.europa.eu/newsroom/dae/document.cfm?doc_id=51625.

139. Charter of Fundamental Rights of the European Union (2000), http://www.europarl.europa.eu/charter/pdf/text_en.pdf.

140. *Supra* note 138, at 16.

141. European Commission Official Website, *Digital Single Market, The European AI Alliance*, https://ec.europa.eu/digital-single-market/en/european-ai-alliance.

142. *Supra* note 138, at 16.

143. *Id.*

- **Communication.** Maintain a fluent communication with all stakeholders to learn about IoT technology and generate more effective regulations.
- **Innovation.** Avoid overregulating IoT that could hamper innovation and adapt existing norms to the challenges presented by emerging technologies.
- **Certification.** Promote mutual recognition systems and certification schemes that are built upon international standards and, when possible, driven by markets, to facilitate international harmonization on privacy and security.
- **Institutional organization.** Consider creating a permanent body to engage with stakeholders and raise public awareness on cybersecurity measures.

Industry stakeholders, for their part, can consider the following:

- Acknowledge the security, safety, and privacy risks of adding Internet connection to things, and hire engineering experts to develop appropriate protective measures.
- Incorporate best practices and ethical considerations as early as possible in manufacturing and designing processes.
- Continue providing security updates for their IoT products and, at the moment of purchase, inform consumers until when they will provide security updates.
- Engage in public policy debates and regulatory processes to help governments understand the technology and produce more suitable public policies.

IoT challenges such as safety, security, privacy, and ethical issues are shared among governments and industry. Exchanging experiences and best practices across countries can help to address these challenges proactively. The EU experience highlights how proactive collaboration between stakeholders could help develop public trust in IoT technologies, enabling society to seize the benefits of IoT.

PART III

IOT RISKS AND POTENTIAL SOLUTIONS

Chapter 8

Privacy and the IoT

Consumer Rights and Emerging Legal Issues

Mauricio Paez
Cynthia Cwik
Kerianne Tobitsch[1]

I. Introduction

The ubiquitous and ever-expanding nature of the Internet of Things (IoT) amplifies the privacy and security concerns inherent to Internet-based technology. The IoT is capable of increasing both the volume and variety of personal information collected from individuals in ways unthinkable to the average person. Internet-connected fitness trackers or medical devices may gather information about an individual's medical condition, location, and daily routine. Smart televisions have the capability to compile information about an individual's viewing history, preferences, habits, and political affiliations. The increasing digitization of the industrial sector—such as the transportation, manufacturing, agricultural, and utilities sectors—through the IoT also means an exponential growth in data collection and processing. For example, connected

1. The authors thank Colleen E. O'Connor and Christina L. O'Tousa for assisting with the research for this work.

vehicles may generate information about an individual's driving habits, movements, personal associations, and locations, including information about whether an individual is visiting a doctor, the type of medical issue, and the frequency of those visits. Together, the highly personal information in data flows generated from consumer and industrial use of the IoT may reveal the habits, preferences, locations, affiliations, health conditions, medical history, and other information about individuals over time.

The IoT is even raising privacy concerns in places where few such concerns previously existed, resulting in renewed concerns of data misuse, particularly with pervasive monitoring that individuals may not expect or notice. For example, people may not realize that voice-activation technology embedded in a variety of smart devices in their own living rooms, such as smart televisions or speakers, could be monitoring or recording private conversations. The combination of IoT with other emerging technologies, such as artificial intelligence, augmented reality, and mobile computing is redefining what is considered personal information and forcing a reexamination of how to address data privacy concerns.

Privacy concerns surrounding the monitoring of private activities could have a potential economic impact for those individuals. The collection of large volumes of sensitive information is valuable to companies looking to develop new products and services, but also could result in profiling and economic decisions on the basis of that data, which some fear could have discriminatory effects. For example, companies could potentially analyze and use this data to make credit decisions, decide where to market certain goods or services, or decide whether to promote certain job or educational opportunities to a particular market segment.[2]

2. *Big Data: A Tool for Inclusion or Exclusion?*, FED. TRADE COMM'N (Jan. 2016), https://www.ftc.gov/system/files/documents/reports/big-data-tool-inclusion-or-exclusion-understanding-issues/160106big-data-rpt.pdf.

When compared to other major economies, privacy laws in the United States have not kept pace with the new privacy concerns raised by rapid technological changes in the IoT space. For example, the United States lacks a single, comprehensive federal scheme regulating privacy, and instead has a patchwork of federal and state constitutional, legal, regulatory, and common law principles. Congress has debated the adoption of comprehensive consumer data privacy laws in the wake of significant data breaches seemingly perpetrated by nation states, with various bills introduced in the House and Senate.[3] Pending the adoption of a comprehensive federal data privacy law, we should expect states to continue their regulation in this area.

This chapter first examines an individual's constitutional right to privacy in circumstances where IoT technologies are used to monitor or surveil the individual's movements and conduct. Next, this chapter provides an overview of the scope of federal regulatory enforcement authority in the IoT space and examines the application of this enforcement authority to special issues involving children, connected transportation, and medical devices. Finally, this chapter explains the various state statutory and common law claims that have been or could be applied to IoT technologies, and the litigation issues that arise in the IoT context.

II. Constitutional Right to Privacy under the Fourth Amendment

The Fourth Amendment serves to "to safeguard the privacy and security of individuals" against intrusions by the government.[4] The

3. *See, e.g.*, S. 2179 Data Security and Breach Notification Act of 2017, https://www.congress.gov/bill/115th-congress/senate-bill/2179/text; H.R. 4081, Consumer Privacy Protection Act of 2017, https://www.congress.gov/bill/115th-congress/house-bill/4081.

4. Camara v. Mun. Ct. of City & Cnty. of San Francisco, 387 U.S. 523, 528 (1967).

Fourth Amendment protects the privacy interests of individuals who "seek[] to preserve something as private" when that expectation of privacy is recognized as reasonable by society.[5] Recent decisions by the Supreme Court demonstrate that the privacy expectations protected by the Fourth Amendment apply to "innovations in surveillance tools."[6] This implicates the IoT, which incorporates novel technologies capable of monitoring movements, conduct, and geolocation, and may even identify associations that could draw other individuals into the net of surveillance.

In certain circumstances, an individual has an expectation of privacy in his physical location and movements.[7] Though it is generally understood that an individual does not have an expectation of privacy in movements he or she voluntarily conveys to the public, such as the movement of his or her car on a highway,[8] the Supreme Court has recognized that there may be a privacy interest when a technology conducts "more sweeping modes of surveillance."[9] For example, an individual has a reasonable expectation of privacy when every movement is being monitored by GPS over a long period of time.[10] In the IoT context, technologies capable of sweeping surveillance such as GPS are clearly incorporated into IoT products and services; yet, the extent of an individual's constitutional claim still would be a fact-dependent inquiry that depends on a variety of factors: whether the individual had knowledge that

5. Smith v. Maryland, 442 U.S. 735, 740 (1979).

6. Carpenter v. U.S., 138 S. Ct. 2206, 2214 (2018).

7. *Id.*

8. United States v. Knotts, 460 U.S. 276, 281 (1983) (finding no expectation of privacy in the movements of an individual's vehicle that the government tracked by planting a beeper in the vehicle to augment the view of law enforcement who were trying to follow the vehicle on public roads).

9. *Carpenter*, 138 S. Ct. at 2215.

10. United States v. Jones, 565 U.S. 400, 426–28 (2012) (finding that a suspect had a reasonable expectation of privacy in his movements tracked by a GPS device that law enforcement placed on his vehicle to remotely monitor his movements for 28 days).

the IoT products contained tracking capabilities; whether the individual had a choice in using the technologies; the individual's location in a private versus public place at the time of data collection; whether the products collected a continuous stream information; and whether there was a built-in capability to turn off this collection in certain circumstances.

An individual also has a reasonable expectation of privacy in certain historical records of his physical location data.[11] The Supreme Court recently held in *Carpenter v. United States* that an individual's location data captured by cell sites and maintained by a third-party wireless cell phone provider was protected by the Fourth Amendment.[12] Central to the Court's reasoning was that the location records were quantitatively different because of the sheer volume of data collected from 12,898 location points over a four-month period of time,[13] as well as qualitatively different because the records provided a detailed and comprehensive log of the individual's movements.[14] The location records were "time-stamped data" and provided "an intimate window into a person's life, revealing not only his particular movements, but through them his 'familial, political, professional, religious, and sexual associations.'"[15]

Many IoT devices generate and store similar quantities of highly personal data as in the cases considered by the Supreme Court. The IoT, through various sensor-based devices, has the ability to track activity in one's home and/or monitor an individual's movements, habits, and routines on a continuous basis, and records of this data are most often stored with third-party providers. Therefore, Supreme Court precedent recognizing the privacy interests inherent in certain

11. *Carpenter*, 138 S. Ct. at 2217.
12. *Id.* at 2212, 2217.
13. *Id.* at 2212.
14. *Id.* at 2216–17. The Supreme Court referred to cell phone location information as "detailed" and "encyclopedic." *Id.* at 2216.
15. *Id.* at 2217 (internal citation omitted).

technological innovations sets a foundation for possible constitutional claims involving records of IoT-generated data in the future.

Some IoT cases are beginning to raise constitutional issues under the Fourth Amendment. In *Arkansas v. Bates*, police investigated the death of a man that occurred in the suspect's home in Bentonville, Arkansas, where the suspect used a voice-activated speaker in his kitchen.[16] Local police issued a search warrant to the manufacturer of the smart speaker seeking all audio recordings and transcribed records related to communications between the speaker and the company's servers during a 48-hour period.[17] The company provided subscriber and purchase history information for the device, but initially refused to produce any recordings or transcripts from the device.[18] The company filed a motion to quash the search warrant, initially seeking to quash the subpoena on constitutional grounds.[19] The motion ultimately became moot when the suspect agreed to permit the company to produce the recordings and records.[20] However, it is expected that the Fourth Amendment will be tested in the IoT context in the future post-*Carpenter*. The key issue will be the scope of a "reasonable expectation" of privacy in an IoT-era, which will continue to be litigated.

III. Statutory Privacy Rights

A. Consumer Privacy

The IoT spans across industries including medicine, health, and transportation, leading to oversight and regulation of IoT devices

16. Compl., Arkansas v. Bates, No. CR-2016-370 (Cir. Ct. Benton Cnty., Ark.) (Aug. 26, 2016).

17. *Id.*

18. *Id.*

19. *Id.*

20. Elliott C. McLaughlin, *Suspect OKs Amazon to Hand Over Echo Recordings in Murder Case*, CNN Business (Apr. 26, 2017, 2:52 PM), https://www.cnn.com/2017/03/07/tech/amazon-echo-alexa-bentonville-arkansas-murder-case/index.html.

by various government administrative agencies. The Federal Trade Commission (FTC) has been the primary regulator of IoT devices under its broad authority to regulate consumer protection, though other agencies have a role in regulating the IoT when a particular technology falls within its jurisdiction. For example, the Food and Drug Administration (FDA) regulates connected medical devices and the National Highway Traffic Safety Administration (NHTSA) monitors connected vehicles.

The FTC has used its authority under the Federal Trade Commission Act (FTC Act) to enforce consumer privacy in IoT devices. Section 5 of the FTC Act grants the FTC the authority to regulate unfair or deceptive practices, which the FTC applies to regulate data privacy and security concerns. Under its authority to regulate deceptive privacy practices, the FTC brings enforcement actions against companies when they do not follow their own privacy policies posted on their websites. In one action, a mobile phone manufacturer claimed to transfer only the amount of data needed to perform services to third parties, but in practice it provided more information than needed to a third-party service provider engaged only to implement operating system updates, including the full content of consumers' text messages, real-time location data, call and text message logs, contact lists, and lists of applications used and installed on the mobile devices.[21] The FTC also applies its deceptive practices enforcement authority against companies that use consumers' data in contravention of the individuals' choices, such as when the company continues to use individuals' data after the individual opted out of a particular use or chose to terminate services.[22]

21. *Mobile Phone Maker BLU Reaches Settlement with FTC over Deceptive Privacy and Data Security Claims*, Fed. Trade Comm'n (Apr. 30, 2018), https://www.ftc.gov/news-events/press-releases/2018/04/mobile-phone-maker-blu-reaches-settlement-ftc-over-deceptive.

22. *See, e.g.*, Decision and Order, Google Inc., No. C-4336 (F.T.C. Oct. 13, 2011).

The FTC uses its broad authority under the FTC Act to prohibit companies from using data that causes or is likely to cause a substantial injury to consumers where consumers cannot reasonably avoid these injuries—such as where a technology can turn on webcams or record keystrokes without the knowledge or consent of the consumer—without substantial benefits to consumers.[23] For instance, a manufacturer and seller of Internet-connected smart televisions agreed to settle charges by the FTC and the Office of the New Jersey Attorney General for $2.2 million after the manufacturer collected viewer data without the consumers' knowledge or consent through software it installed in Internet-connected televisions.[24] The Stipulated Order required the company to obtain affirmative consent for collecting data and prohibited the company from making misrepresentations about the privacy and security of consumer information that the company collects.[25]

The FTC has advocated that companies developing IoT products provide reasonable security, limit the data they collect and retain, and provide notice and choice by seeking well-informed consent from consumers.[26] Adapting these traditional consumer protection measures to the IoT context can be a challenge. For instance, providing

---

23. *See FTC Approves Final Order Settling Charges against Software and Rent-to-Own Companies Accused of Computer Spying*, Fed. Trade Comm'n (Apr. 15, 2013), https://www.ftc.gov/news-events/press-releases/2013/04/ftc-approves-final-order-settling-charges-against-software-and; *see, e.g.*, Decision and Order, DesignerWare, LLC, No. C-4390 (F.T.C. Apr. 11, 2013) (the FTC found that installing and turning on webcams on people's home computers without their knowledge or consent was an unfair practice).

24. *VIZIO to Pay $2.2 Million to FTC, State of New Jersey to Settle Charges It Collected Viewing Histories on 11 Million Smart Televisions without Users' Consent*, Fed. Trade Comm'n (Feb. 6, 2017), https://www.ftc.gov/news-events/press-releases/2017/02/vizio-pay-22-million-ftc-state-new-jersey-settle-charges-it.

25. Stipulated Order for Permanent Injunction and Monetary Judgment, Fed. Trade Comm'n v. Vizio, Inc., No. 2:17-cv-00758 (D.N.J. Feb. 6, 2017).

26. FTC Staff Report, Internet of Things: Privacy & Security in a Connected World 53, at iii–v (2015).

consumer notice and choice can be difficult in IoT devices with no consumer interface to opt-in to data gathering activities. Companies will have to develop creative solutions, which may include developing video tutorials, providing choices during set-up, or having a website where individuals can set choices.[27] Recognizing these challenges, the FTC has incorporated elements of a use-based model into its regulatory approach. This means that the FTC takes into account how data will be used when determining whether a company needs to offer choices to consumers. If a use is consistent with the context of the consumer's interaction with the IoT device, for example when there is only pairing of an IoT device with another mobile device, then the company does not need to offer a choice to the consumer. But where the use is not expected, then the company needs to offer clear and conspicuous choices to the consumer.

States also have broad authority to regulate consumer privacy. Almost all states have data privacy laws covering consumer data, employee records, and certain data processing practices, with California, Illinois, Massachusetts, and New York adopting some of the most stringent consumer privacy protection laws and regulations. These state laws create statutory rights and provide remedies regarding data privacy and data security, and cover everything from data breach notification, implementation of reasonable data security, publication of data privacy practices, notice of data sharing, use of personal data for direct marketing, implementation of comprehensive written information security plans, and protection of discrete data elements, such as social security numbers, biometric data, employee records, and credit cards.[28] Most of these laws are enforced by state attorneys general, but some provide for a private right of action. These laws need to be taken into consideration where IoT devices capture, store, or transmit personal information as defined in these laws.

---

27. *Id.* at v.

28. For a more detailed discussion of these laws, *see* Section IV.A in this chapter.

Most recently, California has passed a comprehensive data privacy law, the Consumer Privacy Protection Act (CPPA) effective January 1, 2020,[29] aimed at regulating the protection and sale of consumer personal data, and providing for statutory damages for security breaches. This law contains similar consumer rights incorporated in Europe under its General Data Protection Regulation, including providing California residents with the right to request deletion of their personal information (the so-called right to be forgotten).[30] Personal information is defined in the CCPPA to include geo-location and IP addresses, data typically collected and used in some consumer IoT devices. California also recently amended its Civil Code[31] by requiring manufacturers of IoT devices to equip the device with a "reasonable security feature or features" to protect data being collected, transmitted, or maintained in the device. These new requirements now impose data security obligations to guard the IoT device and data from unauthorized access, destruction, use, modification, or disclosure.

B. Special Privacy Issues

1. Children

The FTC has focused its enforcement action on protecting the privacy of children. The FTC has authority under the Children's Online Privacy Protection Act (COPPA) to protect children's privacy.[32] To keep up with IoT technology, the Commission updated its guidance on COPPA to clarify that COPPA applies not only to websites and online service providers, but also to IoT devices such

29. *See* Section IV.A.3 in this chapter for more information on the CCPA.

30. Council Regulation 2016/679, art. 51, 2016 O.J. (L 119) 1, 65 (EU).

31. 2018 Cal. Legis. Serv. Ch. 886 (S.B. 327) (to be codified at Cal. Civ. Code § 1798.91.04(a)).

32. 15 U.S.C. 6501 *et seq.* (Pub. L. No. 105-277, 112 stat. 2681-728, enacted Oct. 21, 1998).

as connected toys.[33] For example, the FTC brought an enforcement action against a company for marketing "secure" Internet-connected cameras for home security and baby monitoring,[34] but the cameras' defective software exposed consumers to online viewing by anyone with the Internet address for the cameras, including the "unauthorized surveillance of infants sleeping in their cribs, young children playing, and adults engaging in typical daily activities."[35] The settlement prohibited the company from misrepresenting the cameras' security or the information they transmit, required the company to establish a comprehensive security program to protect the privacy of information stored and transmitted by its devices, and required the company to undergo third-party review of its security programs every two years for the next 20 years.[36] The FTC also settled an enforcement action for COPPA violations against an electronic toymaker for collecting the "personal information of hundreds of thousands of children" through its mobile application without providing direct notice or obtaining parental consent.[37]

Despite successes in enforcing COPPA, the FTC still faces traditional litigation obstacles, such as demonstrating injury or

---

33. *Children's Online Privacy Protection Rule: A Six-Step Compliance Plan for Your Business*, FED. TRADE COMM'N (June 2017), https://www.ftc.gov/tips-advice/business-center/guidance/childrens-online-privacy-protection-rule-six-step-compliance.

34. *Marketer of Internet-Connected Home Security Video Cameras Settles FTC Charges It Failed to Protect Consumers' Privacy*, FED. TRADE COMM'N, (Sept. 4, 2013), https://www.ftc.gov/news-events/press-releases/2013/09/marketer-internet-connected-home-security-video-cameras-settles.

35. TRENDnet, Inc., No. C-4426, 2014 WL 556262, at *3 (F.T.C. Jan. 16, 2014).

36. *Id.* at *7–*9.

37. Stipulated Order for Permanent Injunction and Civil Penalty Judgment, United States v. VTech Electronics Ltd., No. 1:18-cv-00114 (N.D. Ill. Jan. 8, 2018); *Electronic Toy Maker VTech Settles FTC Allegations That It Violated Children's Privacy Law and the FTC Act*, FED. TRADE COMM'N (Jan. 8, 2018), https://www.ftc.gov/news-events/press-releases/2018/01/electronic-toy-maker-vtech-settles-ftc-allegations-it-violated.

consumer harm. In a COPPA case against the manufacturer of smart baby monitors, the FTC alleged that the product's cameras were not secured properly and were vulnerable to hackers, in contravention of the company's claims on its website that its products contained advanced security features designed to protect the private images of consumers.[38] However, the district court granted a motion to dismiss in part, on the grounds that the FTC failed to allege an actual privacy harm to any consumers.[39]

The FTC has shown interest in IoT devices that collect children's geolocation data. In 2016, the FTC settled an enforcement action against a mobile advertising network for deceptively tracking the locations of hundreds of millions of consumers, including children, to serve them geographically targeted advertising without the consumers' knowledge or consent.[40] In April 2018, the FTC issued warning letters against two companies that collect children's geolocation data, alerting the companies that they may be in violation

38. Complaint for Permanent Injunction and Other Equitable Relief, Fed. Trade Comm'n v. D-Link Corp., No. 3:17-cv-00039 (N.D. Cal. Jan. 5, 2017).

39. Joint Stipulation and Order Dismissing D-Link Corporation Without Prejudice, Fed. Trade Comm'n v. D-Link Corp., No. 3:17-cv-00039-JD (N.D. Cal. May 15, 2017). Furthermore, the Supreme Court's decision in Spokeo, Inc. v. Robins makes it more difficult to establish standing based on an imminent privacy harm because harm must be "concrete and particularized." For more information regarding standing issues in privacy litigation, *see* Section IV in this chapter.

40. Complaint for Permanent Injunction, Civil Penalties and Other Relief, United States v. InMobi Pte Ltd., No. 3:16-cv-3474-EDL (N.D. Cal. June 22, 2016); *Mobile Advertising Network InMobi Settles FTC Charges It Tracked Hundreds of Millions of Consumers' Locations Without Permission*, Fed. Trade Comm'n (June 22, 2016), https://www.ftc.gov/news-events/press-releases/2016/06mobile-advertising-network-inmobi-settles-ftc-charges-it-tracked.

of COPPA.[41] The FTC issued one of these warnings to a company that manufactured a smart watch capable of recording a child's precise geolocation information, but did not provide notice to parents or obtain parental consent before collecting and using this data.[42]

The FTC has declined to pursue enforcement actions in certain circumstances involving children. For instance, the Commission has declined to apply COPPA to smart speakers that collect children's voice data without parental consent, convert the voice data into a text file for tasks that do not involve personal information, use the text file only for that purpose, and delete it after a brief period of time.[43] Nevertheless, manufacturers of smart speakers have started developing parental consent features to ease the compliance

---

41. *FTC Warns Gator Group, Tinitell that Online Services Might Violate COPPA*, Fed. Trade Comm'n (Apr. 27, 2018), https://www.ftc.gov/news-events/press-releases/2018/04/ftc-warns-gator-group-tinitell-online-services-might-violate; Husain Sumra, *Kids Smartwatch Makers Are in Trouble for Collecting Data Without Permission*, Wareable (Apr. 30, 2018), https://www.wareable.com/smartwatches/gator-tinitell-ftc-warning-kids-data-2018; Letter from Maneesha Mithal, Assoc. Director, Div. of Privacy and Identity Prot., Fed. Trade Comm'n, to Tinitell, Inc. (Apr. 26, 2018), https://www.ftc.gov/system/files/attachments/press-releases/ftc-warns-gator-group-tinitell-online-services-might-violate-coppa/coppa_tinitell_inc_letter_4-26-18.pdf. The company no longer sells devices.

42. Letter from Maneesha Mithal, Assoc. Director, Div. of Privacy and Identity Prot., Fed. Trade Comm'n, to Gator Group Co., Ltd. (Apr. 26, 2018), https://www.ftc.gov/system/files/attachments/press-releases/ftc-warns-gator-group-tinitell-online-services-might-violate-coppa/coppa_gator_group_co_ltd_letter_4-26-18.pdf.

43. *Enforcement Policy Statement Regarding the Applicability of the COPPA Rule to the Collection and Use of Voice Recordings*, Fed. Trade Comm'n, https://www.ftc.gov/system/files/documents/public_statements/1266473/coppa_policy_statement_audiorecordings.pdf; *see also* Devin Coldewey, *FTC Relaxes COPPA Rule So Kids Can Issue Voice Searches and Commands*, TechCrunch (Oct. 24, 2017), https://techcrunch.com/2017/10/24/ftc-relaxes-coppa-rule-so-kids-can-issue-voice-searches-and-commands/; John Patrick Pullen, *It's Finally (Sort of) Legal for Kids to Use an Amazon Echo, Says FTC*, Fortune (Oct. 24, 2017), http://fortune.com/2017/10/24/amazon-echo-alexa-children-kids-privacy/.

concerns of application developers that want to develop children's media applications.[44]

2. Connected Vehicles and Privacy Issues

The National Highway Traffic Safety Administration (NHTSA) has authority to regulate IoT technologies incorporated into Internet-connected vehicles.[45] Though NHTSA has not yet exercised its enforcement authority, it has issued guidance on connected cars. On September 12, 2017, NHTSA provided voluntary guidance for connected cars to promote safety and to provide best practices for vehicle cybersecurity.[46] Additionally, pending in the U.S. Senate is the Safely Ensuring Lives Future Development and Research in Vehicle Development (SELF DRIVE) Act to encourage the testing and development of highly automated vehicles (HAVs).[47] The bill would require each HAV manufacturer to develop a cybersecurity and privacy plan and provide consumers notice regarding how it uses vehicle occupant and driver information.[48] The bill also mandates the U.S. Department of Transportation (USDOT) to require safety assessment certifications for the development of a HAV or an automated driving system.

---

44. Sarah Perez, *Amazon Adds Parental Consent to Alexa Skills Aimed at Children, Launches First Legal Kids' Skills*, TechCrunch (Aug. 31, 2017), https://techcrunch.com/2017/08/31/amazon-adds-parental-consent-to-alexa-skills-aimed-at-children-launches-first-legal-kids-skills/.

45. Chapter 1 in this book discusses connected cars in detail.

46. *Automated Driving Systems 2.0: A Vision for Safety*, NHTSA, https://www.nhtsa.gov/sites/nhtsa.dot.gov/files/documents/13069a-ads2.0_090617_v9a_tag.pdf.

47. SELF DRIVE Act, H.R. 3388, 115th Cong. (2017); *H.R. 3388—SELF DRIVE Act*, Congress.gov, https://www.congress.gov/bill/115th-congress/house-bill/3388; *see also* Cecilia Kang, *Self-Driving Cars' Prospects Rise with Vote by House*, N.Y. Times (Sept. 6, 2017), https://www.nytimes.com/2017/09/06/technology/self-driving-cars-prospects-rise-with-vote-by-congress.html.

48. SELF DRIVE Act, H.R. 3388, 115th Cong. (2017); *H.R. 3388—SELF DRIVE Act*, Congress.gov, https://www.congress.gov/bill/115th-congress/house-bill/3388.

3. Medical Devices and Privacy Issues[49]

Smart medical devices can monitor chronic conditions, such as cholesterol levels or heart disease, and the information generated by these devices when aggregated and combined with artificial intelligence can be used to study health conditions across a population. This information, which can include protected health information (PHI), can trigger responsibilities for certain covered entities—typically, health care providers, health plans, and health care clearinghouses and their business associates—under the Health Insurance Portability and Accountability Act (HIPAA) to protect the privacy of patients when storing, handling, or transferring their PHI. For example, HIPAA may protect consumers of common health and fitness applications if these applications interact with covered entities such as health insurance companies or doctors, as in the circumstance where a patient gives a doctor direct access to patient healthcare information generated by a Fitbit.[50]

Though certain IoT companies handling health data may not be covered entities subject to HIPAA, including manufacturers of the smart medical devices, they may still be subject to guidance from the Food and Drug Administration (FDA).[51] The FDA is responsible for regulating mobile health applications and connected medical devices,[52] and has issued guidance to manufacturers of medical

49. Medical devices are addressed more extensively in Chapter 2 of this book.

50. Fitbit has announced that it supports HIPAA compliance and seeks to integrate with HIPAA-covered entities, including corporate wellness partners, health plans, and self-insured employers. *Fitbit Extends Corporate Wellness Offering with HIPAA Compliant Capabilities*, FITBIT (Sept. 16, 2015), https://investor.fitbit.com/press/press-releases/press-release-details/2015/Fitbit-Extends-Corporate-Wellness-Offering-with-HIPAA-Compliant-Capabilities/default.aspx.

51. Health information and medical devices are addressed more extensively in Chapter 2 of this book.

52. Connected medical devices allow individuals with medical conditions to manage and mitigate their diseases.

devices regarding the need to ensure the privacy and confidentiality of patients' medical data by implementing appropriate security measures.[53] The FDA also has issued several product-specific safety communications to inform patients and health care providers of cybersecurity vulnerabilities that could impact the privacy of medical data.[54] Nevertheless, the FDA has indicated that consumer wearables and general wellness products, such as fitness trackers, likely do not fall under the category of "medical devices" because they are not used to treat medical conditions,[55] and the FDA has stated that it would not "vigorously regulate wearable devices as long as they're not harmful and generally encourage healthy habits."[56]

---

53. *Cybersecurity*, U.S. Food & Drug Admin. (July 9, 2018), https://www.fda.gov/MedicalDevices/DigitalHealth/ucm373213; U.S. Food & Drug Admin., Postmarket Management of Cybersecurity in Medical Devices: Guidance for Industry and Food and Drug Administration Staff (2016).

54. According to the FDA, these vulnerabilities could allow for remote access and control to compromised devices and could ultimately lead to patient harm. *E.g., Firmware Update to Address Cybersecurity Vulnerabilities in Abbott's (Formerly St. Jude Medical's) Implantable Cardiac Pacemakers: FDA Safety Communication*, U.S. Food & Drug Admin. (Aug. 29, 2017), https://www.fda.gov/MedicalDevices/Safety/AlertsandNotices/ucm573669.htm (informing patients and health care providers about the release of a firmware update to mitigate vulnerabilities in implantable cardiac pacemakers); *Cybersecurity Vulnerabilities Identified in St. Jude Medical's Implantable Cardiac Devices and Merlin@home Transmitter: FDA Safety Communication*, U.S. Food & Drug Admin. (Jan. 9, 2017), https://www.fda.gov/MedicalDevices/Safety/AlertsandNotices/ucm535843.htm (confirming vulnerabilities in implantable cardiac devices and Merlin@home Transmitter); Jim Finkle, *FDA Warns of Security Flaw in Hospira Infusion Pumps*, Reuters (July 31, 2015), https://www.reuters.com/article/us-hospira-fda-cybersecurity-idUSKCN0Q52GJ20150731 (confirming potential remote access to the Symbiq Infusion System).

55. U.S. Food & Drug Admin., General Wellness: Policy for Low Risk Devices—Guidance for Industry and Food and Drug Administration Staff 2 & n.3 (2016).

56. Colin Lecher, *The FDA Doesn't Want to Regulate Wearables, and Device Makers Want to Keep It That Way*, The Verge (June 24, 2015, 2:07 PM), https://www.theverge.com/2015/6/24/8836049/fda-regulation-health-trackers-wearables-fitbit.

IV. IoT Privacy Litigation

The digitization and interconnectedness of the IoT is increasingly raising privacy concerns and exposing companies to enforcement action and consumer litigation risks. Litigation in the IoT area is still at an early stage, though litigation trends are beginning to develop from recent IoT cases or Internet cases more generally. This section discusses the statutory and common law claims potentially applicable to address consumers' IoT privacy concerns.

A recurring issue in these cases is the obstacle of establishing Article III standing for federal claims related to data breach and data privacy violations. To establish standing in claiming damages for data privacy or security breaches, a plaintiff must show that he or she (1) suffered an injury in fact, (2) that is fairly traceable to the challenged conduct of a defendant, and (3) that is likely to be redressed by a favorable judicial decision.[57] The injury-in-fact element requires a plaintiff to show an injury that is "concrete and particularized" and "actual or imminent," but not hypothetical.[58] Certain types of injuries are common in IoT cases—including loss of privacy and other intangible harms, mitigation expenses, and economic injuries—but these injuries may not be sufficient to establish standing. Intangible harms to privacy expectations typically are not sufficiently "concrete" to be cognizable injuries for purposes of Article III standing.[59] Intangible harms may only constitute a concrete injury in certain circumstances where "(1) an alleged intangible harm has a close relationship to a harm that has traditionally been regarded as providing a basis for a lawsuit, and

---

57. Spokeo, Inc. v. Robins, 136 S. Ct. 1540, 1545 (2016).

58. *Id.*

59. *See* Khan v. Children's Nat'l Health Sys., 188 F. Supp. 3d 524, 533 (D. Md. 2016) (concluding that the claim of injury from loss of privacy was not a concrete and particularized injury).

(2) Congress's judgment that a given harm should be elevated to the status of a legally cognizable injury."[60]

Alleged economic injuries must also be concrete to confer standing. Recently, some courts have been willing to recognize mitigation expenses—such as time spent reviewing one's credit accounts and expenses for replacing credit cards or purchasing credit monitoring services—as cognizable injuries.[61] Economic injuries stemming from inadequate security practices or design defects that render products vulnerable to hacking may be cognizable injuries. These economic injuries include overpayment where inadequate security makes a product worth less than the plaintiff paid for, as well as diminution in value where inadequate security caused an appreciable drop in value of the products on the market.[62]

Many federal and state law claims applicable to the IoT incorporate a standard of care, most often a "reasonableness" standard, so another issue in IoT cases is how to demonstrate compliance with these standards to maintain the privacy of personal information. These flexible standard-based laws are more adaptable than prescriptive rules and may evolve with new technologies and privacy needs. Standards are incorporated into both common law claims, such as negligence, or statutory claims, such as the Illinois

---

60. Dixon v. Washington & Jane Smith Cmty.-Beverly, No. 17-cv-8033, 2018 WL 2445292, at *8 (N.D. Ill. May 31, 2018) (internal citation and quotation marks omitted).

61. Attias v. Carefirst, Inc., 865 F.3d 620, 624 (D.C. Cir. 2017), *cert. denied*, 138 S. Ct. 981 (2018); Galaria v. Nationwide Mut. Ins. Co., 663 F. App'x 384, 388 (6th Cir. 2016) (ruling that plaintiffs' allegations of increased risk of fraud and identity theft, coupled with reasonably incurred mitigation costs, are sufficient to establish a cognizable Article III injury at the pleading stage of the litigation); Lewert v. P.F. Chang's China Bistro, Inc., 819 F.3d 963, 967 (7th Cir. 2016); Remijas v. Neiman Marcus Grp., LLC, 794 F.3d 688, 690 (7th Cir. 2015).

62. *See, e.g.*, *In re* VTech Data Breach Litig., No. 15 CV 10889, 2017 WL 2880102, at *5 (N.D. Ill. July 5, 2017) (overpayment argument); Carlsen v. GameStop, Inc., 833 F.3d 903, 908–10 (8th Cir. 2016); Flynn v. FCA US LLC, No. 15-cv-0855-MJR-DGW, 2016 WL 5341749, at *3 (S.D. Ill. Sept. 23, 2016).

Biometric Information Privacy Act.[63] "Reasonableness" requires a showing that the defendant implemented "reasonable" privacy and security measures, which may be evidenced by compliance with industry customs, practices, or standards. The National Institute of Standards and Technology (NIST) adopted the Framework for Improving Critical Infrastructure (NIST Framework),[64] and is considered the most widely accepted set of cross-industry standards for addressing information security and data protection.[65] Some regulators recommend that companies follow the NIST Framework in the development of IoT products to at least address security of personal information.[66] Alternatively, some sectors may develop

---

63. *See, e.g.*, Illinois BIPA, 740 ILCS 14/15(e) ("A private entity in possession of a biometric identifier or biometric information shall . . . us[e] *the reasonable standard of care within the private entity's industry*; and . . . protect from disclosure all biometric identifiers and biometric information in a manner that is *the same as or more protective than the manner in which the private entity stores, transmits, and protects other confidential and sensitive information.*" (emphases added)).

64. The NIST Framework is a set of standards and best practices developed through a collaboration between the government and the private sector to help organizations manage cybersecurity risks. NAT'L INST. OF STANDARDS & TECH., FRAMEWORK FOR IMPROVING CRITICAL INFRASTRUCTURE TECHNOLOGY 1 (2014), https://www.nist.gov/sites/default/files/documents/cyberframework/cybersecurity-framework-021214.pdf.

65. It is too early to determine how reasonableness standards will develop specifically in the IoT context, though NIST has begun developing recommendations to mitigate or reduce the concerns that could impact the adoption of IoT products and services. For example, NIST released a draft internal report in September 2018 to address technical trust-related issues in the IoT. *See* NAT'L INST. OF STANDARDS & TECH., NIST RELEASES DRAFT NIST INTERNAL REPORT (NISTIR) 8222, INTERNET OF THINGS (IOT) TRUST CONCERNS (Sept. 17, 2018), https://www.nist.gov/news-events/news/2018/09/nist-releases-draft-nist-internal-report-nistir-8222-internet-things-iot.

66. For example, the FDA recommends that manufacturers seeking approval of medical devices apply the NIST Framework in developing and implementing a cybersecurity program. U.S. FOOD & DRUG ADMIN., POSTMARKET MANAGEMENT OF CYBERSECURITY IN MEDICAL DEVICES 14 (2016), https://www.fda.gov/downloads/medicaldevices/deviceregulationandguidance/guidancedocuments/ucm482022.pdf.

industry-specific best practices, which are often developed as voluntary consensus standards by nongovernmental organizations.[67]

A. Potential Statutory Claims Related to the IoT

In light of the wide-ranging issues posed by Internet-connected technologies—including issues related to biometric privacy, video recording, and consumer protection—various state or federal statutes may apply to the IoT context. Most of these are pre-IoT statutes, which governed now-outdated technology, and litigants may face obstacles applying the terms of those statutes to modern technologies and services.

1. Biometric Privacy

Biometric data privacy statutes are an emerging area. Personal information like fingerprints, retina or iris scans, face scans, and voiceprints is increasingly collected and used in consumer and commercial devices, ranging from smart phone locks to timekeeping devices for employees to clock in and out of work. Authenticating a person based on his or her unique identifying attributes has become central to many new technologies because each person's biometric data is a unique "key" that is readily available for use.

A small number of states have enacted biometric data privacy laws to regulate the collection, use, and sale of biometric data, though only Illinois' Biometric Information Privacy Act (BIPA)[68]

67. In Cybersecurity Best Practices for Modern Vehicles, the NHTSA recognizes and supports industry stakeholder's efforts to create sets of voluntary standards, principles, and best practices for vehicle cybersecurity, and simply provides its own guidance as a resource to supplement, not replace, them. U.S. Dep't of Transp., Nat'l Highway Traffic Safety Admin., Cybersecurity Best Practices for Modern Vehicles 7–8 (2016), https://www.nhtsa.gov/staticfiles/nvs/pdf/812333_CybersecurityForModernVehicles.pdf.

68. *E.g.*, Illinois Biometric Information Privacy Act (BIPA), 740 Ill. Comp. Stat. Ann. 14/1–14/25.

has provided a private right of action.[69] BIPA requires private entities to inform individuals that they collect their biometric data, obtain a written release from individuals, develop a written policy governing the retention of the data, and use a reasonable standard of care to protect the data. Class action suits filed under BIPA have flooded the courts in recent years.[70] Many of the cases involve companies' use of biometric timekeeping technology for tracking employee work hours,[71] though some cases cover a range of other technologies, such as lockers that use renters' fingerprints as the "key."[72]

An important issue in BIPA cases is whether a certain type of information collected by an IoT product is a "biometric identifier" or "biometric information" as defined in the statute.[73] In particular, courts have concluded that data generated from facial recognition technology is a biometric identifier within the meaning of BIPA, even though technology companies have contested this classification. For example, a court denied a motion to dismiss a suit alleging that a company violated BIPA by failing to provide notice to individuals that it created facial geometry templates of their faces by using a facial scanning feature on photographs stored in the cloud.[74] The defendant argued that the templates were not biometric identifiers because they were developed indirectly from photographs,

---

69. *See* BIPA, 740 ILCS 14/20. Other state biometrics data privacy laws may be enforced by the state attorneys general. *See, e.g.*, Tex. Bus. & Comm. Code § 503.001; Wash. Rev. Code Ann. §§ 19.001.001–.004.

70. Over 50 class action suits have been filed under BIPA since 2014, and 25 are from 2018 alone.

71. *See* Dixon v. Washington & Jane Smith Cmty.-Beverly, No. 17 C 8033, 2018 WL 2445292 (N.D. Ill. May 31, 2018); Goings v. UGN, Inc., No. 17-CV-9340, 2018 WL 2966970 (N.D. Ill. June 13, 2018); Howe v. Speedway LLC, No. 17 C 7303, 2018 WL 2445541 (N.D. Ill. May 31, 2018).

72. *See* McCollough v. Smarte Carte, Inc., No. 16 C 03777, 2016 WL 4077108, at *1 (N.D. Ill. Aug. 1, 2016).

73. Rivera v. Google Inc., 238 F. Supp. 3d 1088 (N.D. Ill. 2017).

74. *Id.*

rather than by directly measuring a person's face, but the court rejected this argument by concluding that a biometric identifier is a set of measurements of a physical component used to identify a person, rather than a reference to the underlying medium.[75]

Another key issue in BIPA cases is whether the plaintiff has standing as a "person aggrieved" under BIPA. Courts have dismissed some cases for lack of standing where courts determined that there was no material risk of harm. For example, in one case against a video game developer, players alleged that the company failed to provide notice of biometric data collection as required by BIPA for a video game that collected players' facial scans to create personalized game avatars.[76] The court dismissed the action because there was no plausible allegation that the plaintiffs' biometric data would be used in a way not contemplated by the parties; there was no allegation that the defendant disseminated or sold the biometric data or used it for any purpose other than to create avatars.[77] However, another court found standing where plaintiffs alleged that their employer violated BIPA by using a timekeeping device that scanned and stored employees' fingerprints, and transferred that data to a third-party vendor of the devices, without providing adequate notice to employees.[78] The court reasoned that BIPA creates a legal right to privacy in personal biometric data and the right to control one's biometric identifiers, and therefore the plaintiffs sufficiently alleged harm of this privacy right when their employer disclosed their biometric data to the third-party service provider without their knowledge.[79]

---

75. *Id.*

76. Vigil v. Take-Two Interactive Software, Inc., 235 F. Supp. 499, 511 (S.D.N.Y. 2017).

77. *Id.*

78. Dixon v. Washington & Jane Smith Cmty.-Beverly, No. 17 C 8033, 2018 WL 2445292, at *1 (N.D. Ill. May 31, 2018).

79. *Id.* at *9.

2. Video Privacy

Companies may provide audiovisual materials or recording or video streaming services through IoT technologies, which raise potential liability risks under the federal Video Privacy Protection Act (VPPA).[80] The VPPA prohibits any "video tape service provider"—a term that has been interpreted as including online streaming service providers[81]—from knowingly disclosing personally identifiable information (PII) concerning its consumers to a third party.[82]

Whether the VPPA applies to a given IoT technology requires interpretation of vague terms under a statute enacted in a pre-IoT era. Users of certain IoT technologies may not be protected by the VPPA because they do not meet the definition of a "consumer" or "subscriber" under some interpretations of the statute. The VPPA defines a "consumer" as "any renter, purchaser, or subscriber of goods or services from a video tape service provider."[83] The term "subscriber" is not defined in the statute, and courts have taken different approaches when interpreting the term. Some courts have determined that users of free services are not subscribers. For example, the Eleventh Circuit determined that a person who downloads a free application to view content at no cost may not be a "subscriber" under the VPPA.[84] The Eleventh Circuit stated that while making a payment is not necessary to be a subscriber, the court should consider additional factors such as whether the individual registered an account, created a profile, obtained a user ID, signed up for services or transmissions, accessed restricted content, or

80. 18 U.S.C. § 2710.

81. *See In re* Hulu Privacy Litig., No. C 11-03764 LB, 2012 WL 3282960, at *6 (N.D. Cal. 2012).

82. 18 U.S.C. § 2710(b).

83. *Id.* § 2710(a)(1).

84. Ellis v. Cartoon Network, Inc., 803 F.3d 1251, 1257 (11th Cir. 2015).

otherwise established a relationship.[85] In another circumstance, the First Circuit determined that an individual streaming free content could still be a subscriber by virtue of providing his device ID and GPS location while streaming, even without taking steps to create an account or profile with the company.[86]

Another obstacle in applying the VPPA to the IoT context is whether the type of data collected by IoT technologies and disclosed to third parties constitutes PII under the VPPA. The statute defines PII as "information which identifies a person as having requested or obtained specific video materials or services from a video tape service provider."[87] IoT technologies often rely on unique identifiers, such as user IDs and cookies, but it is not clear whether this would be PII under the VPPA. Some courts have determined that a unique identifier, without more, is not PII.[88] However, a unique, anonymized identifier may be PII if steps are taken to link content viewed to a specific person, and whether this linkage occurred may be an issue of fact for a fact-finder.[89]

3. Data Security and Privacy Laws

A growing number of state laws impose a duty on entities to take reasonable steps to safeguard the privacy of personal information of state residents from disclosure to unauthorized persons. Many of these statutes apply to any company that owns, licenses, or maintains the personal information of state residents, regardless of where the company itself is located. Some states, such as California, require that businesses implement and maintain "reasonable"

---

85. *Id.*

86. Yershov v. Gannett Satelline Info. Network, Inc., 820 F.3d 482, 489 (1st Cir. 2016).

87. 18 U.S.C. § 2710(a)(3).

88. *In re* Hulu Privacy Litig., No. C 11-03764 LB, 2014 WL 1724344, at *11–12 (N.D. Cal. Apr. 28, 2014)

89. *See, e.g.*, *id.* at *11.

security practices to safeguard that data,[90] whereas other states, such as Massachusetts, detail specific mandatory security measures and require a written information security program.[91] Additionally, to the extent an entity provides state residents' personal information to a third party, it would be a best practice for that entity to impose contractual obligations on those third parties to implement and adhere to the same statutorily-mandated security standards or measures, and some states even require such a written agreement.[92]

Of particular note, the California Consumer Privacy Act of 2018 (AB-375) was signed into law on June 28, 2018, and is scheduled to go into effect on January 1, 2020. This law has been reported to be the nation's most wide-ranging consumer data privacy law, and it will impose new requirements regarding how businesses collect and store consumer personal information.[93] AB-375 will apply to for-profit businesses that collect and control California residents' personal information and conduct business in the State of California and (1) have annual gross revenues in excess of $25 million; or (2) receive or disclose the personal information of 50,000 or more California residents, households, or devices on an annual basis; or (3) derive 50 percent or more of their annual revenues from selling California residents' personal information.

AB-375 expands the definition of personal information to include IP addresses, employment-related information, and Internet search history, as well as "[i]nferences drawn from any of the [personal information] to create a profile about a consumer," and it does include a private right of action for any consumer whose "nonencrypted or nonredacted personal information . . . is subject

---

90. *See, e.g.*, CAL. CIV. CODE § 1798.81.5(b); ARK. CODE §§ 4-110-104(b); FLA. STAT. § 501.171(2).

91. *See, e.g.*, 201 MASS. CODE REGS. 17.03(1), 17.04.

92. *See, e.g.*, CAL. CIV. CODE § 1798.81.5(c); 201 MASS. CODE REGS. 17.03(2)(f).

93. *See, e.g.*, "California Adopts Sweeping Consumer Privacy Law," Jones Day Publication (July 2018).

to an unauthorized access and exfiltration, theft, or disclosure as a result of the business' violation of the duty to implement and maintain reasonable security procedures and practices appropriate to the nature of the information to protect the personal information."[94] AB 375 also provides consumers with the right to "opt out" of permitting a business to sell their personal information to third parties and the right to request that a business delete personal information that it has collected about the consumer.[95]

California recently passed a new law regulating the security of IoT devices and the privacy of information contained on the devices.[96] This law will go into effect on January 1, 2020. Manufacturers of IoT devices must equip the devices with reasonable security features[97] that are appropriate to the nature and function of the device, as well as the type of information it collects, contains, or transmits. Manufacturers must also design the device to protect the privacy and security of the information contained within the device from unauthorized access, destruction, use, modification, or disclosure. The state attorney general has enforcement authority, but there is no private right of action.

4. Consumer Protection and Unfair Competition Laws

State consumer protection and unfair competition laws govern unfair, deceptive, or unlawful acts or practices. These laws may serve as a catchall remedy for consumers to recover when few other options exist. The laws protect consumers against unfair or deceptive business practices, as well as prohibit affirmative

94. *See id.*

95. *See id.*

96. 2018 Cal. Legis. Serv. Ch. 886 (S.B. 327) (to be codified at CAL. CIV. CODE § 1798.91.04(a)).

97. These security features may include a "preprogrammed password [ ] unique to each device manufactured" and a "security feature that requires a user to generate a new means of authentication before access is granted to the device for the first time." *Id.*

misstatements or omissions of material facts in connection with the sale or advertisement of goods or services. Given that the term "unfair" is standard-based and judgment-laden, the prohibition on "unfair" business practices enables courts to apply the statute in a way that is consistent with evolving societal values and needs.[98] In interpreting these state consumer protection statutes, courts often consider interpretations from the FTC and the federal courts relating to section 5(a) of the FTC Act.[99] Some technology-related cases filed under these state statutes demonstrate how these statutes could be applied in the IoT context. For example, one court found that a plaintiff sufficiently pleaded that a company using an Internet-connected payment pad engaged in an unfair practice under state consumer protection law by allegedly failing to follow industry standards for payment card PIN security requirements.[100]

B. Potential Common Law Claims Related to IoT Privacy

Given that statutes may be rigid, contain outdated terms, or be under-inclusive in addressing new privacy threats from emerging technologies, litigants may turn to common law to try to remedy harms and deter harmful practices in the future.

1. *Negligence*

A common claim is that companies were negligent with respect to the privacy and security aspects of their IoT devices. A basic principle of negligence law is that everyone has a duty to refrain from

98. *See In re* Michaels Stores Pin Pad Litig., 830 F. Supp. 2d 518, 525 (N.D. Ill. 2011) ("To determine whether a practice is unfair under the [Illinois Consumer Fraud Act], the court considers whether the practice offends public policy, whether it is immoral, unethical, oppressive, or unscrupulous, and whether it causes substantial injury to consumers. A plaintiff does not need to satisfy all three criteria to support a finding of unfairness." (citations omitted)).

99. *See id.* at 525–26.

100. *See id.* at 525–27.

acts that would unreasonably expose others to a risk of harm. The standard of care for ordinary negligence is that of the reasonable person of ordinary prudence. Manufacturers and providers of IoT technologies who want to limit potential liability risk should consider implementing accepted industry standards and best practices governing the IoT, which can help a defendant establish that it took reasonable care to protect the privacy and security of users of IoT devices.

Plaintiffs face obstacles from the economic loss rule when pursuing negligence claims in the IoT context.[101] The economic loss rule in many states bars plaintiffs from recovering for purely economic losses that do not involve injury to person or other property under a negligence claim.[102] Given that negligence claims in the IoT context typically involve purely economic losses, such as losses stemming from inadequate security or breaches of personal information, this rule has prevented some plaintiffs from proving damages and thwarted their negligence claims.[103]

2. *Privacy Torts*

IoT technologies are constantly present, even in the private lives of consumers, and they have the capability to capture or record images, sounds, or information that an ordinary person would never expect to be disclosed to others. Many states have a tort for privacy violations that would apply in an IoT context, and some states, such as California, have even incorporated the right to privacy into their state constitutions. Privacy torts are meant to protect

101. *In re* Sony Gaming Networks & Customer Data Sec. Breach Litig., 996 F. Supp. 2d 942, 966–73 (S.D. Cal. 2014), *order corrected*, No. 11MD2258 AJB (MDD), 2014 WL 12603117 (S.D. Cal. Feb. 10, 2014).

102. *See In re* Experian Data Breach Litig., No. SACV151592AGDFMX, 2016 WL 7973595, at *8 (C.D. Cal. Dec. 29, 2016).

103. *See, e.g.*, *In re* Michaels Stores Pin Pad Litig., 830 F. Supp. 2d at 528–31.

an individual's reasonable expectation that their personal information will not be captured or disclosed in an offensive manner.

One of the most common types of privacy torts is an invasion of privacy. Although these will vary by state, one of the strongest formulations is in California where an invasion of privacy occurs when someone knowingly captures images or recordings of another individual engaging in private, personal, or familial activity and carries out the invasion in a manner that is offensive to a reasonable person.[104] Invasion of privacy torts have the potential to apply to countless circumstances involving IoT devices, though one area of emerging concern is the capability of smart speakers to listen constantly, even without the knowledge of individuals in the room, and send those recordings to a cloud server. For example, parents brought a putative class action against a toy manufacturer for invasion of privacy under California law because an Internet-enabled "talking" doll allegedly recorded, collected, stored, and shared audio recordings of children without parental consent.[105]

Another potential privacy tort claim applicable to the IoT context is intrusion upon seclusion or disclosure of private facts. A company may unlawfully intrude upon an individual's seclusion when its technology exceeds the scope of an individual's consent (if any) in intruding upon an individual's private affairs, and the intrusion would be highly offensive to a reasonable person.[106] Litigants have relied on this tort to allege deceitful use of tracking technologies, particularly when the claim involved vulnerable parties like children.[107] For example, in 2015, the Third Circuit vacated a district court's dismissal of a plaintiff's privacy claims

104. *See* Cal. Civ. Code § 1708.8(a).

105. *See, e.g.*, Hayes v. ToyTalk, Inc., et al., 2:16-cv-02111-JAK-PLA (C.D. Cal.) (ECF No. 1). The parties agreed to voluntarily dismiss the case in 2016. *Id.* (ECF No. 424).

106. Hoskins v. Howard, 971 P.2d 1135, 1142 (Id. 1998); *In re* Nickelodeon Consumer Privacy Litig., 827 F.3d 262, 293 (3d Cir. 2016).

107. *See In re* Google Inc., 806 F.3d 125, 153 (3d Cir. 2015).

against a technology company under the California Constitution and California tort law because "[a] reasonable factfinder could conclude that the means by which defendants allegedly accomplished their tracking, i.e., by way of a deceitful override of the plaintiffs' cookie blockers, marks the serious invasion of privacy contemplated by California law."[108]

3. *Trespass to Chattels*

To the extent that companies try to capture or monetize the massive amount of data that could be collected through IoT devices, users of the devices may be able to bring a trespass to chattels claim. Though not yet applied in the IoT context, litigants have pursued a claim of trespass to chattels (i.e., personal property) in other contexts where defendants sought to monetize the technology, data, or related property of others, but overstepped the limits of what is a permissible use in order to make a profit. A defendant could be liable for harm to the plaintiff's technology that is caused by or occurs in the course of using the technology for unauthorized purposes or in ways that exceed the scope of the plaintiff's consent.[109] Notable cases have involved the unauthorized practices of collection or use of data,[110] installation of software,[111] alteration of

---

108. *Id.*

109. Restatement (Second) of Torts § 256 (2d 1979).

110. Ebay, Inc. v. Bidder's Edge, Inc., 100 F. Supp. 2d 1058 (N.D. Cal. 2000); Register.com, Inc. v. Verio, Inc., 126 F. Supp. 2d 238, 249 (S.D.N.Y. 2000). For example, in Register.com, Inc. v. Verio, Inc., where a company's use of an automated robot to conduct searches and access data from the database of Register.com, a registrar of Internet domain names, exceeded the scope of Register.com's consent to access the database, the court issued an injunction making the company liable for any harm to Register.com's computer systems caused by that unauthorized access. Register.com, Inc. v. Verio, Inc., 126 F. Supp. 2d 238, 249 (S.D.N.Y. 2000).

111. Sotelo v. DirectRevenue, LLC, 384 F. Supp. 2d 1219, 1230 (N.D. Ill. 2005) (ruling that allegations of Spyware bombarding users' computers with pop-up advertisements stated a claim for trespass to chattels).

privacy and security controls,[112] delivery of spam e-mails,[113] and use of tracking technologies.[114]

There are limitations to this cause of action. Only actual damages can be recovered so, as with the other cases, a concrete harm must be established.[115] Moreover, because the interference with the plaintiff's possessory interference must be unauthorized, plaintiffs may need to point to a policy prohibiting the undesirable uses of the technology[116] or other actions giving notice that the uses were unwelcome.[117]

112. Mortensen v. Bresnan Commun., No. CV 10-13-BLG-RFC, 2010 WL 5140454 (D. Mont. Dec. 13, 2010) (ruling that plaintiffs sufficiently alleged that the defendant intentionally interfered with the possession of their personal property to state a claim for trespass to chattels, based on allegations that defendant altered the privacy and security controls on plaintiffs' computers activity).

113. Compuserve Inc. v. Cyber Promotions, 962 F. Supp. 1015, 1020 (S.D. Ohio 1997).

114. Bose v. Interclick, Inc., 2011 U.S. Dist. LEXIS 93663, at *27 (S.D.N.Y. Aug. 17, 2011) (surviving a motion to dismiss) ("Plaintiff's trespass to chattels claim regarding Interclick's placement of unauthorized Flash LSOs and history-sniffing code, considering there is no allegation that the devices materially affected the condition, quality, or value of the computer, is arguably sufficient to survive a motion to dismiss.").

115. *See* Am. Online, Inc. v. Nat'l Health Care Disc., Inc., 121 F. Supp. 2d 1255, 1277 (N.D. Iowa 2000) ("[O]ne who commits a trespass to a chattel is liable to its rightful possessor for actual damages suffered by reason of loss of its use." (quoting Vines v. Branch, 418 S.E.2d 890, 894 (Va. 1992)).

116. Am. Online, Inc. v. Nat'l Health Care Disc., Inc., 121 F. Supp. 2d 1255, 1260–61 (N.D. Iowa 2000) (explaining that AOL had policies that prohibited the posting or transmission of unsolicited advertising or promotional materials).

117. Register.com, Inc. v. Verio, Inc., 126 F. Supp. 2d 238, 249 (S.D.N.Y. 2000) (explaining that, because the defendant was on notice that its search robot was unwelcome since at least the date the lawsuit was filed, the plaintiff did not consent to the defendant's use of a search robot, meaning that the defendant's use of the robot to access the database exceeded the scope of the plaintiff's consent).

4. Breach of Contract and Breach of Express Warranty

Providers of IoT products typically craft terms of use or service (collectively, "use agreements") incorporating privacy terms and expectations that consumers must review and consent to before using the products or services. Breach of contract claims based on these use agreements, especially those involving promises not to access, sell, or transfer personal information, are fairly common in litigation involving IoT products.

Breach of contract claims may be difficult if a use agreement includes provisions that disclaim liability or disclose practices regarding collection, use, and sharing of personal information. If the plaintiff had a full and fair opportunity to review these terms before agreeing to them, it would be difficult to sustain a breach of express contract claim.[118] Furthermore, courts are likely to reject plaintiffs' challenges to these use agreements as unconscionable or unenforceable contracts on the grounds that users could just as easily select another similar product or service, or for "nonessential recreational activit[ies]" the user could simply forgo the activity.[119] Plaintiffs cannot get around the terms of a use statement by pleading a breach of implied contract claim because where an express contract exists on a subject matter, the terms of that agreement will control.[120]

V. Conclusion

Consumers and regulators alike are paying increasing attention to the unprecedented privacy concerns raised by the IoT, and the

118. *See, e.g.*, *In re* VTech Data Breach Litig., No. 15 CV 10889, 2018 WL 1863953, at *2–3 (N.D. Ill. Apr. 18, 2018) (involving terms of use for the purchase of Internet-connected toys).

119. *See, e.g.*, *In Re* Iphone Application Litig., 2011 WL 4403963, *8 (N.D. Cal. Sept. 20, 2011).

120. *E.g.*, *In re* VTech Data Breach Litig., No. 15 CV 10889, 2018 WL 1863953, at *2–3 (N.D. Ill. Apr. 18, 2018).

privacy concerns addressed in this chapter will only grow as IoT products and services continue to become more widespread and ubiquitous. Litigants largely have been applying existing statutory claims to address their IoT privacy concerns, and the FTC as the primary regulator of consumer IoT products and services has been applying its existing enforcement authorities. Yet, a new privacy landscape is emerging as states step in to address the privacy concerns of their residents, including the new California Consumer Privacy Act, and as companies adjust to rigorous privacy principles in other regions, most notably the EU's General Data Protection Regulation.[121] Providers of IoT products and services should incorporate protections for consumer privacy into the design of their products to keep pace with these changes and build products acceptable to consumers across borders.

121. The General Data Protection Regulation is addressed in Chapter 7 of this book.

Chapter 9

(In)security of the Internet of Things (IoT)

A Roadmap for Assessing the Risks

Lucy L. Thomson

> The potential for surprise in the cyber realm will increase in the next year and beyond as billions more digital devices are connected—with relatively little built-in security – and both nation states and malign actors become more emboldened and better equipped in the use of increasingly widespread cyber toolkits. . . . Ransomware and malware attacks have spread globally. . . . The availability of criminal and commercial malware is creating opportunities for new actors to launch cyber operations.[1]

---

1. The Honorable Daniel R. Coats, Director of National Intelligence (DNI), *Statement for the Record to the Senate Select Committee on Intelligence, Worldwide Threat Assessment of the U.S. Intelligence Community* (Feb. 13, 2018), *available at* https://www.dni.gov/index.php/newsroom/congressional-testimonies/item/1845-statement-for-the-record-worldwide-threat-assessment-of-the-us-intelligence-community [hereinafter *2018 Worldwide Threat Assessment*].

In 2016 the DNI said this about IoT: "Devices designed and fielded with minimal security requirements and testing, and an ever-increasing complexity of networks could lead to widespread vulnerabilities in civilian infrastructure and U.S. Government systems. Broader adoption of IoT devices and AI [artificial intelligence]—in settings such as public utilities and health care—will only exacerbate these potential effects." The Honorable James R. Clapper, Director

I. Widespread IoT Cybersecurity Risks Create Daunting Challenges

It is predicted that by 2020 there will be 20.4 billion devices connected to the Internet, impacting all aspects of personal life, and business and industry. These innovations promise better business management and greater efficiencies, but the IoT ecosystem that is now being created presents complex challenges. Gartner's latest Internet of Things Backbone Survey of Chief Information Officers (CIOs) and Chief Technology Officers (CTOs) showed that security was cited as the top barrier to IoT success (35 percent of respondents), as "the explosion of varying types of IoT endpoints creates an attack surface that has never before [been] seen." Privacy concerns (25 percent of respondents) and potential risks and liabilities (25 percent of respondents) were in the top five barriers cited, along with regulatory concerns (23 percent of respondents) as seventh highest concern.[2]

Total spending on endpoints and services reached almost $2 trillion in 2017.[3] Consumers are the largest group of users of connected things with 5.2 billion devices in 2017, 63 percent of the total. Spending for business-to-business (b2b) IoT systems (e.g.,

---

of National Intelligence, *Statement for the Record to the Senate Select Committee on Intelligence, Worldwide Threat Assessment of the U.S. Intelligence Community* (Feb. 9, 2016), *available at* http://www.dni.gov/files/documents/SASC_Unclassified_2016_ATA_SFR_FINAL.pdf.

2. Sanjit Ganguli & Ted Friedman, *IoT Technology Disruptions: A Gartner Trend Insight Report*, Gartner 6 (June 15, 2017), https://emtemp.gcom.cloud/ngw/eventassets/en/conferences/content/research-assets/IoT%20Technology%20Disruptions_%20A%20Gartner%20Trend%20Insight%20Report.pdf [hereinafter *Gartner IoT Technology Disrupters*].

3. Press Release, Gartner, Inc. Gartner Says 8.4 Billion Connected "Things" Will Be in Use in 2017, Up 31 Percent from 2016 (Feb. 7, 2017), https://www.gartner.com/en/newsroom/press-releases/2017-02-07-gartner-says-8-billion-connected-things-will-be-in-use-in-2017-up-31-percent-from-2016.

manufacturing, health care, agriculture, transportation, utilities, etc.) is expected to reach $267 billion by 2020.[4]

IoT in the workplace. As companies are modernized, they will expand the use of IoT devices such as security cameras, wireless locks, motion sensors, automated lighting and window shades, and climate control. Technologists are creating the "infrastructure of the smart office." Consisting of smartphones, wearables, and applications, their goal is to create an "intelligent workplace" to provide solutions to problems, facilitate decision making, measure performance, and take care of most routine tasks.[5]

Industrial Internet of Things (IIoT). IIoT includes smart electrical grids, connected health care devices and hospitals, intelligent transportation, smart factories, and other cyber-physical systems.[6] This infrastructure provides essential services, such as energy, water, telecommunications, transportation, and financial services, and is increasingly subject to sophisticated cyber intrusions.

According to the International Data Corporation (IDC), the three industries that are expected to spend the most on IoT in 2018 are manufacturing ($189 billion), transportation ($85 billion), and utilities ($73 billion).[7] Manufacturers will largely focus

---

4. *Id.*

5. Jason Corsello, *What the Internet of Things Will Bring to the Workplace*, WIRED, https://www.wired.com/insights/2013/11/what-the-internet-of-things-will-bring-to-the-workplace/; Nancy Pardo, *IoT at Work: Is Your Firm Wired for Success?* PTC, https://www.ptc.com/en/product-lifecycle-report/iot-at-work-is-your-office-wired-for-success.

6. *See, e.g.*, Industrial Internet Consortium, https://www.iiconsortium.org/index.htm. "An Industrial Internet of Things (IIoT) system connects and integrates industrial control systems with enterprise systems, business processes and analytics. It enables significant advances in optimizing decision-making, operations and collaborations among a large number of increasingly autonomous control systems."

7. *IoT and the Data Gold Rush: Findings from a Commissioned Study Conducted by Forrester Consulting on Behalf of Arm*, white paper, FORRESTER (Aug. 2018), https://pages.arm.com/rs/312-SAX-488/images/iot-and-the-data-gold-rush-forrester-arm.pdf.

on improving the efficiency of their processes and asset tracking, while two-thirds of IoT spending by transport will go toward freight monitoring and fleet management. IoT spending in the utilities industry will be dominated by smart grids for electricity, gas, and water. IDC puts spending on cross-industry IoT areas like connected vehicles and smart buildings at nearly $92 billion in 2018.

Torrents of data at risk. Internet-connected devices generally sense, collect, process, and transmit a wide array of data, ranging from consumer personally identifiable information (PII) to proprietary company information and infrastructure data used to make critical real-time decisions or to effect a change in the physical world. IDC predicts that 163 zettabytes (ZB), or one trillion gigabytes, of data will be created or copied each year by 2025, ten times more than in 2016. By 2035, the IoT will be composed of a trillion connected devices producing ten trillion data streams.[8] Cisco estimates that by the end of 2019, the IoT will generate more than 500 zettabytes per year in data—and in the years beyond, that number is expected to grow exponentially, not linearly. The amount of data stored on devices will be four and a half times higher than data stored in data centers, at 5.9 ZB by 2021.[9]

The convergence of information technology and physical infrastructure operations in which computers control a broad array of consumer and industrial devices and systems present significant security concerns. Many IoT devices that have little or no computer security and contain documented vulnerabilities are being connected to the Internet and to each other, creating widespread risks. Cyberattacks involving IoT can compromise the security, privacy, and safety of individuals and their homes, businesses,

8. *Id.*

9. *Cisco Global Cloud Index: Forecast and Methodology, 2016–2021*, white paper, Cisco, https://www.cisco.com/c/en/us/solutions/collateral/service-provider/global-cloud-index-gci/white-paper-c11-738085.html#_Toc503317517.

transportation systems, industrial control systems (ICS), and even entire cities[10] or industry sectors.[11]

There is increased risk for wide-scale or high-consequence events that could cause harm or disrupt services upon which our economy and the daily lives of millions of Americans depend.[12] High penetration of IIoT technology in critical infrastructure industries has resulted in increased risks. The damage that could be caused by IoT devices with inadequate security is far-reaching. IoT security breaches may pose life-and-death risks, the inappropriate use of personal data, or theft and fraud. A hacker attack on a smart grid system could potentially turn off power to millions of households and businesses, creating massive economic harm and threats to health and safety. Other potential consequences of an IoT/ICS incident can range from disruption of operations and services (damaging equipment, reduction or loss of production at one site or multiple sites

10. Steve Ranger, *What Is the IoT? Everything You Need to Know about the Internet of Things Right Now*, ZDNet (Aug. 21, 2018), https://www.zdnet.com/article/what-is-the-internet-of-things-everything-you-need-to-know-about-the-iot-right-now/.

Tod Newcombe, *Santander: The Smartest City*, Governing (May 2014), http://www.governing.com/topics/urban/gov-santander-spain-smart-city.html; Corinne Reichert, *Las Vegas Announces Smart City Plans with Cisco*, ZDNet (June 29, 2017), https://www.zdnet.com/article/las-vegas-announces-smart-city-plans-with-cisco/.

11. Sixteen government and private industry sectors have been designated as critical infrastructure (CI): Chemical; Commercial Facilities; Communications; Critical Manufacturing; Dams; Defense Industrial Base; Emergency Services; Energy; Financial Services; Food and Agriculture; Government Facilities; Health Care and Public Health; Information Technology; Nuclear Reactors; Materials and Waste; Transportation Systems; and Water and Wastewater Systems. Election systems are a CI "subsystem." *See* https://www.dhs.gov/critical-infrastructure-sectors; National Infrastructure Protection Plan (NIPP), *NIPP 2013 Partnering for Critical Infrastructure Security and Resilience,* https://www.dhs.gov/national-infrastructure-protection-plan.

12. *2014 Quadrennial Homeland Security Review (QHSR)* 40, Dep't of Homeland Security, *available at* http://www.dhs.gov/quadrennial-homeland-security-review-qhsr.

simultaneously) to catastrophic—jeopardizing national security or public safety (terrorist attack; release, diversion, or theft of hazardous materials; product contamination; or environmental damage).[13]

II. The Need for Risk-Based Assessment

In the short term, executives, policy makers, system owners, security experts, and their counsel must understand the IoT cyber risks and take appropriate action to protect their information systems in order to avoid the serious and even catastrophic consequences that could ensue. Most hacker attacks are opportunistic and target not only the largest businesses but all those that are unprepared. Taking the steps necessary to *prevent*, *detect*, and *respond* to security breaches and incidents should be everyone's primary goal. Conducting a risk assessment is an essential first step to determine how much risk is being introduced by implementing IoT devices in the environment and what can be done to mitigate it. In this high-risk IoT environment, mitigation of risk is paramount and requires a thorough understanding of the IoT ecosystem. In the longer term, industry and government officials must reach consensus on how to secure the IoT infrastructure.[14]

This chapter provides a risk assessment approach consistent with the National Institute of Standards and Technology (NIST) *Framework for Improving Critical Infrastructure Cybersecurity*, an important guide for organizations to use in assessing security

13. *Guide to Industrial Control Systems Security*, NIST Spec. Pub. 800-82 rev. 2, section 4.1.2, Potential Consequences, pp. 4–2, *available at* https://nvlpubs.nist.gov/nistpubs/SpecialPublications/NIST.SP.800-82r2.pdf. Chapter 10 discusses the tools the federal government could use to incentivize secure-by-design in IoT technologies.

14. The NIST Internet of Things (IoT) Trust Concerns report identifies 17 technical trust-related issues that may negatively impact the adoption of IoT products and services and must be addressed. *Internet of Things (IoT) Trust Concerns*, NIST (Oct. 17, 2018) page 2, *available at* https://csrc.nist.gov/CSRC/media/Publications/white-paper/2018/10/17/iot-trust-concerns/draft/documents/iot-trust-concerns-draft.pdf [hereinafter *NIST IoT Trust Concerns*].

risks and determining the maturity of their cybersecurity programs.[15] Recognizing the need to address the complexity of the environment in which IoT devices are implemented and used, the risk analysis is presented in the context of the potential "attack surfaces" of IoT devices—attack vector analysis of common attacks or other failures of well-known good security policy that is well accepted among technical security engineers and experts.

A roadmap through the types of information necessary for assessing the risks of IoT wherever they arise is presented in the IoT Risk Assessment—A Brief Overview, in Section VI.B, *infra*. Every information system is different, and risk assessments must be tailored to the data, design and architecture, hardware and software, and technology implementations of the system or network. Specific threats to and vulnerabilities in the system must be identified, as well as the likelihood that adverse events will actually occur. Organizations can then select appropriate security controls and develop remediation plans so that the risks will be reduced to a reasonable and appropriate level.

III. Changing Nature of the Global Threat

Previously, criminals launched cyberattacks primarily for financial gain; now, nation-states and organized criminal groups are attempting to damage, disrupt, or modify infected IoT and industrial control systems (ICS) and networks. Cyberattacks on organizations generally, and on critical infrastructure in particular, can have catastrophic effects on safety and public health, disrupting or cutting off essential services (e.g., health care and emergency services, food, transportation, energy and power, and water supply and waste management, to highlight just a few). Many of these threat actors have significant resources, funded by nation-states or through sophisticated money laundering operations.

15. NIST Framework for Improving Critical Infrastructure Cybersecurity v. 1.1 (April 2018), *available at* https://www.nist.gov/cyberframework [hereinafter *NIST Cybersecurity Framework*].

The Intelligence Community's 2017 Worldwide Threat Assessment[16] and the Foreign Cyber Threats report[17] identify prominent cyber adversaries—nation-states (Russia, China, North Korea, and Iran), terrorist groups, and cyber criminals. In addition, "hacktivists" launch cyberattacks that are politically or ideologically motivated. The 2018 Verizon Data Breach Investigations Report (DBIR)[18] found that almost three-quarters (73 percent) of cyberattacks were perpetrated by outsiders. Members of organized criminal groups were behind half of all breaches, with nation-state or state-affiliated actors involved in 12 percent. Over a quarter (28 percent) of attacks involved insiders.[19]

The Cyber Threats report concludes that "[d]espite ever-improving cyber defenses, nearly all information, communication networks, and systems will be at risk for years to come from remote hacking to establish persistent covert access, supply chain

16. The Honorable Daniel R. Coats, Director of National Intelligence, *Statement for the Record to the Senate Select Committee on Intelligence, Worldwide Threat Assessment of the U.S. Intelligence Community* (May 11, 2017), *available at* https://www.dni.gov/files/documents/Newsroom/Testimonies/SSCI%20Unclassified%20SFR%20-%20Final.pdf [hereinafter *2017 Worldwide Threat Assessment*].

17. The Honorable James R. Clapper, Director of National Intelligence, The Honorable Marcel Lettre, Undersecretary of Defense for Intelligence, Admiral Michael S. Rogers, USN Commander, U.S. Cyber Command, Director, National Security Agency, *Joint Statement for the Record to the Senate Armed Services Committee on Foreign Cyber Threats to the United States* (Jan. 5, 2017), *available at* https://www.dni.gov/files/documents/Newsroom/Testimonies/OKSASC_SFR_UNCLASSIFIED_3JAN2016-FINAL.pdf [hereinafter *2017 Foreign Cyber Threats report*].

18. *2018 Verizon Data Breach Investigations Report* (DBIR), 11th Ed., Executive Summary, at 1, https://enterprise.verizon.com/resources/reports/DBIR_2018_Report_execsummary.pdf [hereinafter *2018 Verizon DBIR*].

19. *Combating the Insider Threat, DHS National Cybersecurity and Communications Integration Center,* (May 2, 2014), *available at* https://www.us-cert.gov/sites/default/files/publications/Combating%20the%20Insider%20Threat_0.pdf.

operations that insert compromised hardware or software, malicious actions by trusted insiders, and mistakes by system users."[20]

The U.S. Departments of Commerce and Homeland Security released a report that offers a guide to government, civil society, and industry on actions that would dramatically reduce the threat of botnets[21] and similar cyberattacks. The Commerce/DHS Report concluded:

> To address the range of threats, all stakeholders, domestic and international, must more fully address automated, distributed attacks. At its core, that involves reducing the number of unsecured devices with access to the Internet to keep botnets to a manageable size, and developing mechanisms to share information about compromised systems and emerging attack trends up and down the network stack to the party (or parties) in the best position to respond to the threat.[22]

IV. Risks to Confidentiality, Integrity, and Availability

Protecting *confidentiality*, *integrity*, and *availability* are the three cornerstones of every security program.[23] In light of the massive

---

20. *2017 Cyber Threats report, supra* note 17.

21. Bots/botnets are everywhere in technology; they are automated programs/applications designed to perform a specific task, ranging from malicious bots that come with a virus to search engine spiders that crawl the Internet looking for new web pages, as well as, for example, Siri and Cortana. 2018 Verizon DBIR, *supra* note 18.

22. *Enhancing the Resilience of the Internet and Communications Ecosystem Against Botnets and Other Automated, Distributed Threats*, U.S. Dep't of Commerce & U.S. Dep't of Homeland Security, at 23 (May 30, 2018), *available at* https://www.commerce.gov/sites/default/files/media/files/2018/eo_13800_botnet_report_-_finalv2.pdf [hereinafter *Commerce/DHS Botnets Report*].

23. *Confidentiality*—protection of information against unauthorized disclosure, whether intentional or accidental. *Integrity*—protection of information against corruption, tampering, or other alteration; this capability includes

data breaches in recent years,[24] much attention has been given to protecting the *confidentiality* of personal data and sensitive and confidential information. The largest data breaches—spanning the financial, health care, retail, and government sectors—illustrate the heightened risk to millions of individuals when large datasets of sensitive personal information are compromised: Marriott/Starwood, 5 billion personal records compromised (2018); Yahoo, 1.5 billion user accounts compromised (2013 and 2014); Equifax, 145.5 million records breached (2017); e-Bay, 145 million records breached (2014); Target Stores, 110 million (2013); Sony Online Entertainment, 102 million (2011); JP Morgan Chase, 76 million (2014); Anthem BlueCross BlueShield, 69 to 80 million (2015); Home Depot, 56 million (2014); TJX, 46 million (2006–07); and Office of Personnel Management (OPM), 22.5 million security clearance records breached, 5 million fingerprints stolen (2015).

One of the most important observations of the 2015 Worldwide Threat Assessment is that future cyberattacks will be conducted to compromise the *integrity* of information, with a potentially devastating impact on key information systems that constitute the underpinnings of the economy:

> In the future [ ] we might also see more cyber operations that will change or manipulate electronic information in order to compromise its integrity (i.e. accuracy and

safeguarding the accuracy and completeness of information. *Availability*—ensuring that information and systems can be reliably and promptly accessed and used when they are needed.

24. In total, 11,239,084,942 records have been compromised in 8,908 breaches reported since 2005. *Chronology of Data Breaches*, Privacy Rights Clearinghouse, https://www.privacyrights.org/data-breaches. A website that goes by the name "information is beautiful" provides a visualization of thousands of the major data breaches over the past decade and serves as a useful resource to identify and learn about the massive data breaches that have affected the private sector and government. http://www.informationisbeautiful.net/visualizations/worlds-biggest-data-breaches-hacks/.

reliability) instead of deleting it or disrupting access to it. Decision-making by senior government officials (civilian and military), corporate executives, investors, or others will be impaired if they cannot trust the information they are receiving.[25]

Cyberattacks that successfully change or manipulate business records or decision-making systems could paralyze companies, bring operations to a halt, and undermine the trust in entire industry sectors. Databases are vulnerable to attacks and can be accessed through insecure IoT devices. The database vulnerabilities are well documented and include the use of default and weak passwords, failure to patch known vulnerabilities, misconfigurations, and excessive privileges granted to users. Specific security measures must be taken to protect personal data in the databases of organizations around the world. Having appropriate security controls such as encryption, audit logs, and backup is essential to mitigate the risks of these types of attacks.

In recent years, cyberattacks designed to restrict the *availability* of websites and services have been launched, primarily with distributed denial of device (DDoS) attacks in which multiple compromised computers, often infected with a Trojan virus,[26] are used to overwhelm a single targeted system, computer viruses that delete user data, or ransomware that encrypts data and demands payment for the encryption key to restore access to the data. According to

25. The Honorable James R. Clapper, Director of National Intelligence, Statement for the Record to the Senate Armed Services Committee, *Worldwide Threat Assessment of the U.S. Intelligence Community,* at 3–4 (Feb. 26, 2015), *available at* https://www.dni.gov/files/documents/Unclassified_2015_ATA_SFR_-_SASC_FINAL.pdf.

26. Malware disguised as legitimate software that will enable a cybercriminal to gain access to a user's system and spy on him/her, steal sensitive data, and gain backdoor access.

the Verizon Data DBIR, DDoS attacks accounted for 56 percent of the incidents reported in 2017.[27]

V. The Current State of IoT Security—The Complex Technology Infrastructure

Security is only as strong as its weakest link, and this is particularly true of the IoT. Its distributed architecture presents a plethora of vulnerable points in processing and storage where sensitive and proprietary data can be stolen and critical infrastructure can be compromised.

Experts agree that many low-power IoT devices are inherently insecure. Because low cost and speed to market are often priorities, security is often not built into the IoT design, or it may be minimal. Vulnerabilities are not eliminated and software is not updated regularly. When these devices hit the market, they do not have the ability to respond to the complex evolving threat landscape. Home security systems and household appliances, for example, whose device life cycle is much longer (more than ten years) than the software on the devices (about two years) may introduce risk for years to come when vendors fail to provide patching or support for the software in the future. IoT devices are also being used in ways they were not designed for, particularly medical devices that were originally intended to be stand-alone.

A. What Makes IoT Devices Vulnerable to Cyber Attacks? Common IoT Attack Vectors

The IoT heightens existing concerns about cybersecurity and introduces new risks.

Many IoT devices and systems are the result of the convergence of cloud computing, mobile computing,[28] embedded systems, big

27. *2018 Verizon DBIR*, *supra* note 18.

28. *See* Dr. Robert Thibadeau & Lucy L. Thomson, *Mobile Device Security*, ABA The SciTech Lawyer, Going Too Fast? Privacy and Security Challenges in a Mobile World, 9(1) SciTech Lawyer 24 (special, Summer 2013).

data,[29] low-price hardware, and other technological advances. From a security perspective, experts have identified "attack surfaces" associated with IoT devices.[30] Vulnerabilities in IoT devices create new attack vectors (i.e., entry points) for hackers. To fully appreciate how so much can go wrong with IoT security, it is important to understand the fundamental classes of security defects in the context of "attack surfaces" and what security measures exist to mitigate them.

Attack surfaces in the IoT infrastructure fall into three categories, all of which are further explained in the following sections: (1) IoT devices (a "thing"), including the operating system (OS) and software on the device; (2) a network of "things," devices, and sensors; and (3) the IoT ecosystem and the context in which the IoT network will operate.[31] With this taxonomy we can

29. *See* Lucy L. Thomson & Dr. Robert Thibadeau, *Security Challenges of the Big Data Ecosystem Require a Laser-Like Focus on Risk*, ABA The SciTech Lawyer, Big Data, Big Deal, 12(2) SciTech Lawyer 6–11, 19 (Winter 2016).

30. The Commerce/DHS Botnet Report describes in more detail the current status of the technical and policy domains of the Internet and worldwide communications ecosystem. *Supra* note 22, at 9–21. NIST analyzes three categories in terms of "trust concerns" with IoT. *NIST IoT Trust Concerns, supra* note 14.

31. Network communication is usually described in terms of "layers." Gartner, Inc. has created an IoT Reference Model that explains the IoT architecture with respect to communication within the IoT ecosystem. *See Gartner IoT Technology Disrupters, supra* note 2, at 4–5. The potential vulnerabilities in the IoT ecosystem fall into different layers of the IoT Reference Model. In the model, the layers define what capabilities an IoT component, function, or process must possess, while the tiers define where a component, function, or process operates in the IoT architecture. The interfaces define how data and control flow into, out of, and through the system. Endpoint technology inhabits the Device Layer; communications technology comprises the Communication Layer; data and analytics reside in the Information Layer; and Artificial Intelligence exists on the Function Layer. Security technology, as it is pervasive in its nature, touches each of these layers. Understanding the interaction and interdependence of each technology area with the IoT system as a whole will enable a better understanding of their impact.

classify attack surfaces and potential vulnerabilities in the IoT ecosystem.[32]

1. Security of the "Thing"

Most IoT systems contain four architectural elements: sensors, a control center, actuators, and a communications network linking those elements. Sensors typically collect information, the communications network delivers the information to the control center, the control center evaluates the information and issues commands, the communications network delivers the commands to the actuators, and the actuators perform some action.[33] In the most simple terms, a "thing" is an object equipped with sensors that gather data that will be transferred over a network and actuators that allow things to act (for example, to switch a light on or off, open or close a door, increase or decrease engine rotation speed, and more). Connected things produce huge volumes of data which need to be securely transmitted and protected from cybercriminals.

NIST has observed that due to the nature of various IoT devices, such as the need to be portable, IoT designs can pose barriers to cybersecurity. An overview of key device constraints and security concerns are described in Table 9.1:

---

32. For an analysis that focuses on the *Edge, Gateway, Cloud Platform,* and *Mobile Applications* components of an IoT ecosystem, *see* OWASP Framework Security Considerations, *available at* https://www.owasp.org/index.php/IoT_Framework_Assessment.

The *edge* code runs on actual IoT devices. Edge components may be resource constrained or operate in isolated environments. A *gateway* device is often used to aggregate and bridge communications from edge devices. The edge, or gateway, will communicate with a *cloud* component, often a web service, deployed in a company data center or a public cloud computing environment. The cloud component supports complex user interfaces, analytics capabilities, and provides access to data aggregation back ends. Finally, many IoT ecosystems consist of *mobile application* components that allow users to interact with the ecosystem via smartphones or tablets.

33. *See* Chapter 4, Figure 4.1 on page 97.

Table 9.1 NIST IoT Cybersecurity Considerations

Consideration	Device Constraint	Security Concern
Power Consumption	Many IoT devices require a long battery life, without access to a permanent power supply.	Power-efficient hardware may lack additional capabilities like ability to support encryption or hardware security mechanisms.
Low Cost	The consumer's perceived value of a device greatly depends on the cost to purchase and implement the device. Market drivers often require that companies produce devices at a very low cost.	In meeting these price pressures, devices may have low processing power and constrained hardware space, offering limited support for security mechanisms.
Life Cycle	The lifespan of devices vary greatly, some devices (like simple sensors) are short-lived, while others are meant to last for decades.	Over time, devices may become hardware-constrained and cannot be updated. Built in security mechanisms may be found vulnerable or deprecated, like old encryption suites.

Source: NIST MANAGING IOT CYBER AND PRIVACY RISKS, https://www.nist.gov/itl/applied-cybersecurity/iot-cybersecurity-considerations

Configuration. Vulnerabilities in the design and configuration of IoT devices lead to security breaches. Many IoT devices come with fixed or hardcoded credentials, utilities, and services that cannot be disabled, updated, or patched. Even if software is securely developed, improper configuration when deploying systems can expose them to compromise. Many of the vulnerabilities discovered are years or decades old and firmware packages may use old and/or unsupported versions of third-party components.

Weak passwords. Manufacturers have default, easy-to-guess user ID/password combinations to log in to IoT devices, and users may leave the device's log-in credentials unchanged. Because the default passwords are published online, they are among the known attack vectors for the devices. Passwords may be hardcoded into the IoT firmware, and the tools necessary to disable them are not present; thus, a user cannot feasibly change the password.

Lack of encryption. Many IoT devices do not support encryption. Hackers can intercept unencrypted data as it is transmitted to and from IoT devices.

Insecure wireless connections. These can be hijacked and used by hackers to install malware, gain control of the device or system, and steal personal data or corporate information or cause widespread damage to physical systems.

Backdoors. IoT devices may have a backdoor built in, ostensibly to make it easier to provide support for them. These "hidden" access mechanisms that consist of the user ID and password to an open port can also provide an entry point for hackers.

Subversion of the software development process. Not only is software development difficult to manage from a vulnerability perspective, but efforts to actively subvert software are increasing. For example, developers are in some cases specifically targeted for attack.[34] Malware has been detected in certain open source software libraries.[35]

Patches and software updates. Unlike traditional personal computers, there are few security upgrade processes for "things," such as patches or updates. When vulnerabilities are identified

34. *See* Brandon Levene et al., *Dimnie: Hiding in Plain Sight*, Palo Alto Networks Unit 42 (Mar. 28, 2017), https://researchcenter.paloaltonetworks.com/2017/03/unit42-dimnie-hiding-plain-sight/.

35. A National Counterintelligence and Security Center report identified adversarial software supply chain operations as a top emerging threat. *2018 Foreign Economic Espionage in Cyberspace* (July 2018), *available at* https://www.dni.gov/index.php/ncsc-newsroom/item/1889-2018-foreign-economic-espionage-in-cyberspace.

after IT devices are deployed, these devices may be difficult or impossible to patch.[36]

Sensor data. Sensor data may be tampered with, stolen, deleted, dropped, or transmitted insecurely, allowing it to be accessed by unauthorized parties. Various sensors, such as cameras and microphones, may be surreptitiously turned on.

Applications. Hackers can insert malware (malicious code) into applications (apps) to gain access to the device and to sensitive information. Some malware can cause users' personal information to be publicly disclosed without their knowledge.

2. A Network of "Things"

The distributed architecture of IoT presents a plethora of vulnerable points in processing and storage where sensitive and proprietary data can be stolen and critical infrastructure can be compromised. Things connected to the Internet are entry points for criminals. IoT multiplies the normal risks associated with any data communication. Each device increases the "surface area" available for breaches, and interoperability expands the potential scope of breaches. Every node is a potential entry point, and interconnection can spread the damage. What is more, cybercriminals can get the access to the "brain" of the whole IoT system and take control of it.

IoT devices have been compromised to create botnet armies used for distributed denial of service (DDoS) attacks or to attack underlying systems. The limited capability of client devices or sensors and the high frequency of communication between sensors and hubs makes security critical in an IoT solution. Ensuring protection of device identity, user identity, and data must be among the primary checkpoints while architecting the solution.[37]

36. *See Commerce/DHS Botnets Report*, *supra* note 22, at 16.

37. Namit Tanasseri, *Before the IoT Leap—Architectural Principles, Devices and Data*, ZDNet, (Apr. 11, 2018), https://www.zdnet.com/article/before-the-iot-leap-architectural-principles-devices-and-data/.

3. The IoT Ecosystem and the Context in Which IoT Devices Operate

Many vulnerabilities are the result of the IoT ecosystem in which the IoT devices are implemented. IoT devices are being used in ways they were not designed for. NIST has emphasized that it is important to ask whether the IoT device will be *fit for the purpose* in that environment, context, and at a specific point in time.[38] NIST has identified three high-level considerations that may affect the management of cybersecurity and privacy risks for IoT devices: (1) many IoT devices interact with the physical world in ways conventional IT devices usually do not; (2) they cannot be accessed, managed, or monitored in the same ways conventional IT devices can; and (3) the availability, efficiency, and effectiveness of cybersecurity and privacy capabilities are often different for IoT devices than conventional IT devices.[39]

This is particularly an issue with the already large installed base of IoT devices. As the DHS/Commerce Botnets report noted: "The scale and diversity of deployed devices make easy fixes difficult and provide additional attack surfaces for malicious activity," continuing that "Systems may also be vulnerable because support is unavailable. This is often the case for old devices."[40]

A leading IoT security project has identified 18 attack surface areas on IoT devices.[41] These include (1) the device itself;

38. *NIST IoT Trust Concerns*, *supra* note 14.

39. NISTIR 8228 (draft), *Considerations for Managing Internet of Things (IoT) Cybersecurity and Privacy Risks*, NIST (Sept. 2018), page v, *available at* https://csrc.nist.gov/publications/detail/nistir/8228/draft [hereinafter NISTIR 8228 (draft) *Managing IoT Cyber and Privacy Risks*].

40. *See Commerce/DHS Botnets Report*, *supra* note 22, at 16.

41. Open Web Application Security Project (OWASP), *available at* https://www.owasp.org/index.php/OWASP_Internet_of_Things_Project.

(2) interfaces such as web, cloud, and physical; and (3) ecosystem issues. Each attack surface has multiple potential vulnerabilities.

Table 9.2 shows how security architects categorize defects in the IoT ecosystem. The list of attack surfaces was created to assist manufacturers, developers, security researchers, and those looking to deploy or implement IoT technologies within their organizations to strengthen the security of their IoT ecosystem.[42]

IoT devices and systems create huge amounts of data. Data may be stored locally on IoT devices or transmitted to a cloud platform for processing. Cybersecurity vulnerabilities can put torrents of data at risk. Table 9.3 shows for various attack surfaces the types of data that could be compromised or stolen in a hacker attack that exploits vulnerabilities on IoT devices. Addressing this problem is critically important for executives and system owners who must protect their sensitive and confidential data. For example, account data and credentials such as user names and passwords could be stolen, giving criminals access to the IoT device and potentially entry to the entire network. Breach of personally identifiable data (PII) could occur if data is stored on the device or in the IoT unencrypted. PII in a database could be stolen in a SQL injection attack[43] on a website.

42. *Id.*

43. Attacker inserts arbitrary structured query language (SQL) (code) into a web application database query. *See*, J.M. Porup, *SQL Injection Explained: How These Attacks Work and How to Prevent Them*, CSO (Oct. 2, 2018), https://www.csoonline.com/article/3257429/application-security/what-is-sql-injection-this-oldie-but-goodie-can-make-your-web-applications-hurt.html.

Table 9.2 IoT Attack Surface Areas and Vulnerabilities

IoT Device—A "Thing"

An object equipped with sensors that gather data which will be transferred over a network and actuators that allow things to act.

Device Memory Sensitive Data • Cleartext usernames • Cleartext passwords • Third-party credentials • Encryption keys	**Local Data Storage** • Unencrypted data • Data encrypted with discovered keys • Lack of data integrity checks • Use of static same enc/dec key	**Hardware (Sensors)** (Acquire and Control Data) • Sensing Environment Manipulation • Tampering (Physically) • Damage (Physical)

Device Firmware
(Software Controls IoT Hardware)
• Sensitive data exposure
  o Backdoor accounts
  o Hardcoded credentials
  o Encryption keys
  o Sensitive information
  o Sensitive URL disclosure
• Firmware version display and/or last update date
• Vulnerable services (web, SSH, TFTP)
• Firmware downgrade possibility
	Mobile Application
	• Implicitly trusted by device or cloud
	• Username enumeration
	• Account lockout
	• Known default credentials
	• Weak passwords
	• Insecure data storage
	• Transport encryption
	• Insecure password recovery mechanism
	• Two-factor authentication
		Privacy
		• User data disclosure
		• User/device location disclosure
		• Differential privacy

Authentication/Authorization
(Access Control)
• Authentication/Authorization related values disclosure (session key, token, cookie, etc.)
• Reusing of session key, token, etc.
• Device to device authentication
• Device to mobile application authentication
• Device to cloud system authentication
• Mobile application to cloud system authentication
• Web application to cloud system authentication
	Device Network Services
	• Information disclosure
	• User and Administrative CLI
	• Injection/Denial of Service/Replay Buffer Overflow attacks
	• Unencrypted Services
	• Poorly implemented encryption
	• Firmware loaded over insecure channel
	• Credential management vulnerabilities:
	  o Username enumeration
	  o Weak passwords
	  o Account lockout
	  o Known default credentials
	• Insecure password recovery mechanism
		Administrative Interface
		• Standard set of web application vulnerabilities
		• Credential management vulnerabilities:
		  o Username enumeration
		  o Weak passwords
		  o Account lockout
		  o Known default credentials
		  o Insecure password recovery mechanism
		• Security/encryption and logging options
		• Two-factor authentication
		• Inability to wipe device

IoT Device Interfaces Edge, Gateway, Cloud Platform, and Mobile Applications		
Device Web Interface • Standard set of web application vulnerabilities • Credential management vulnerabilities: o Username enumeration o Weak passwords o Account lockout o Known default credentials • Insecure password recovery mechanism	**Update Mechanism** (Software Updates) • Update sent without encryption • Updates not signed • Update location writable • Update verification • Update authentication • Malicious update • Missing update mechanism • No manual update mechanism	**Physical Device Interfaces** • Firmware extraction • User & Administrative CLI • Privilege escalation • Reset to insecure state • Removal of storage media • Tamper resistance • Debug ports (UART, JTAG/SWD) • Device ID/Serial number exposure
Cloud Web Interface • Standard set of web application vulnerabilities • Credential management vulnerabilities: o Username enumeration o Weak passwords o Account lockout o Known default credentials o Insecure password recovery mechanism • Transport encryption • Two-factor authentication	**Vendor Backend APIs** • Inherent trust of cloud or mobile application • Weak authentication • Weak access controls • Injection attacks • Hidden services **Third-Party Backend APIs** • Unencrypted/Encrypted PII sent • Device information leaked • Location leaked	**Network Traffic** • LAN • LAN to Internet • Short range • Non-standard • Wireless (WiFi, Z-wave, XBee, Zigbee, Bluetooth, LoRA) • Protocol fuzzing
IoT Ecosystem		
Ecosystem (General) • Interoperability standards • Data governance • System-wide failure • Individual stakeholder risks • Implicit trust between components • Enrollment security • Decommissioning system • Lost access procedures	**Ecosystem Communication** • Health checks • Heartbeats • Ecosystem commands • Deprovisioning • Pushing updates	Source: Excerpts from OWASP IoT Attack Surface Areas Project (Nov. 2018).

Table 9.3 IoT Attack Surfaces > Vulnerabilities > Data at Risk

Attack Surface	Vulnerability	Data Type
ADMINISTRATIVE INTERFACE	Weak password policy Lack of account lockout	Credentials
LOCAL DATA STORAGE	Data Stored Without Encryption	PII
DEVICE FIRMWARE	Sent Over HTTP Hardcoded passwords Hardcoded encryption keys	Credentials Application Data
DEVICE PHYSICAL INTERFACES	Unauthenticated root access	***
WEB CLOUD INTERFACE	SQLi	PII Account Data
VENDOR BACKEND APIS	Permissive API Data Extraction	PII Account Data

SOURCE: OWASP ATTACK SURFACE ANALYSIS CHEAT SHEET

B. Types of Attacks Involving IoT Devices

While everyone is familiar with the massive data breaches that have made headline news, compromising sensitive and confidential data and putting hundreds of millions of individuals at risk of identity theft and fraud, less attention has been focused on cyberattacks that caused physical damage or bodily injury. Numerous cyberattacks on IoT devices have been reported.

As the use of IoT devices continues to grow, the likelihood of IoT breaches becomes more likely. Information is becoming the primary means of production, and as institutions forge ahead to adopt sweeping changes based on IoT technologies, the risks are legion and not well understood.

The methods of attack used to both steal data and cause damage to ICS and IoT devices are remarkably similar. Thus, the indictments of a Russian national charged in one of the largest known data breach prosecutions and the Russians charged by Special Counsel Robert Mueller are instructive; these cases provide fascinating details about how an IoT and ICS attack may unfold.[44] The FBI-DHS Technical Alert on Russian Government Cyber Activity Targeting Energy and Other Critical Infrastructure Sectors illustrates the steps involved in hacker attacks in a readily understandable format.[45]

Criminals can use or control IoT devices in a wide variety of ways: to compromise an IoT device; use IoT devices to conduct denial of service attacks; use the IoT device to make money (crypto-mining); take control of IoT devices and the controls of critical infrastructure and cause physical damage; and damage or destroy the IoT devices themselves.

1. Compromise IoT Devices and Use Them as Proxies

In an FBI Alert about the risks associated with Internet-connected IoT devices, the FBI warned that cyber threat actors can use unsecured IoT devices as proxies to anonymously pursue malicious cyber activities.[46] Cyber has become a way for attacks to start, even when a cyber event is not the end result. It is an entry point

---

44. United States v. Drinkman et al., No. 09-626 (JBS) (S-2) (D.N.J.) *available at* http://www.justice.gov/sites/default/files/opa/press-releases/attachments/2015/02/18/drinkman_vladimir_et_al_indictment_comp.pdf (second superseding indictment); http://www.justice.gov/opa/pr/russian-national-charged-largest-known-data-breach-prosecution-extradited-united-states (Feb. 18, 2015). United States v. Viktor Borisovich Netyksho et al., U.S. D.C. D.C. (July 13, 2018), *available at* https://www.justice.gov/file/1080281/.

45. US-CERT Alert (TA18-074A) *Russian Government Cyber Activity Targeting Energy and Other Critical Infrastructure Sectors*, at 2–7 (Mar. 16, 2018), *available at* https://www.us-cert.gov/ncas/alerts/TA18-074A

46. *Cyber Actors Use Internet of Things Devices as Proxies for Anonymity and Pursuit of Malicious Cyber Activities*, FBI (Aug. 2, 2018), *available at* https://www.ic3.gov/media/2018/180802.aspx [hereinafter *FBI Alert IoT as Proxies*].

for other activity that is not always directed toward information or information systems.

This FBI Alert (Figure 9.1) warns that cyber actors are using compromised IoT devices as proxies[47] to:

- Send spam e-mails.
- Maintain anonymity.
- Obfuscate network traffic.
- Mask Internet browsing.
- Generate click-fraud activities.
- Buy, sell, and trade illegal images and goods.
- Conduct credential stuffing attacks, which occur when cyber actors use an automated script to test stolen passwords from other data breach incidents on unrelated websites.
- Sell or lease IoT botnets to other cyber actors for financial gain.

Cyber actors typically compromise devices that have weak authentication, unpatched firmware or other software vulnerabilities, or employ brute force attacks on devices with default usernames and passwords. Many IoT cyber incidents involve exploitation of devices with little or no security, known vulnerabilities, and violations of well-accepted security practices.

2. *Weaponizing IoT Devices to Launch Distributed Denial of Service (DDoS) Attacks*

Intruders have initiated DDoS attacks that flood the victim's computer with useless information and prevent legitimate users from accessing it. This type of attack will use up all of the available communications bandwidth on a corporate network, making it unavailable to employees.

47. Brian Krebs, *IoT Devices as Proxies for Cybercrime*, Krebs on Security (Oct. 13, 2016), https://krebsonsecurity.com/2016/10/iot-devices-as-proxies-for-cybercrime/.

UNCLASSIFIED

Public Service Announcement

FEDERAL BUREAU OF INVESTIGATION

02 August 2018

Alert Number

I-080218-PSA

Cyber Actors Use Internet of Things Devices as Proxies for Anonymity and Pursuit of Malicious Cyber Activities

Cyber actors actively search for and compromise vulnerable Internet of Things (IoT) devices for use as proxies or intermediaries for Internet requests to route malicious traffic for cyber-attacks and computer network exploitation. IoT devices, sometimes referred to as "smart" devices, are devices that communicate with the Internet to send or receive data. Examples of targeted IoT devices include: routers, wireless radios links, time clocks, audio/video streaming devices, Raspberry Pis, IP cameras, DVRs, satellite antenna equipment, smart garage door openers, and network attached storage devices.

IoT proxy servers are attractive to malicious cyber actors because they provide a layer of anonymity by transmitting all Internet requests through the victim device's IP address. Devices in developed nations are particularly attractive targets because they allow access to many business websites that block traffic from suspicious or foreign IP addresses. Cyber actors use the compromised device's IP address to engage in intrusion activities, making it difficult to filter regular traffic from malicious traffic.

Figure 9.1 FBI Alert

In an October 2016 DDoS attack, the Mirai botnet scoured the web for IoT devices protected only by factory-default usernames and passwords. It then enlisted those vulnerable IoT devices such as Internet-connected cameras and DVRs to send junk traffic and temporarily overwhelm popular Internet sites, including Twitter, Amazon, Tumblr, Reddit, Spotify, and Netflix; these websites could no longer accommodate legitimate visitors or users. The Mirai botnet compromised more than 100,000 CCTV cameras to support DDoS attacks.

When the botnet source code was later released, it revealed 68 username and password pairs used by dozens of IoT products, including Internet routers, security cameras, printers, and digital video recorder (DVRs). In other cases, Internet-connected cameras used as baby monitors were hacked by exploiting default administrative passwords, violating the owners' privacy.[48]

More sophisticated botnets have followed. Known as Reaper or IoT Troop, hackers built on portions of Mirai's code but with a key

48. *Commerce/DHS Botnets Report*, *supra* note 22, at 46.

difference—instead of merely guessing weak passwords, it used numerous known security flaws in the code of insecure IoT devices to exploit a long list of devices.[49] The Reaper malware has pulled together a "grab-bag" of IoT hacking techniques that include nine attacks affecting routers from D-Link, Netgear, and Linksys, as well as Internet-connected surveillance cameras.[50]

University DDoS attack. An IoT-based security breach on a university campus led to a DDoS attack that made Internet access slow or unavailable to students. It was reported that with a massive campus to monitor, everything from light bulbs to vending machines had been connected to the network for ease of management and improved efficiencies. The botnet spread from device to device by brute-forcing (guessing) default and weak passwords. Once the password was known, the malware had full control of the device and would check in with command infrastructure for updates and change the device's password—locking the university out of 5,000 systems that were affected.[51]

DDoS attacks can impact anyone and are often used as camouflage, often being started, stopped, and restarted to hide other breaches in progress. These examples clearly demonstrate the risks posed by botnets of this size and scope, as well as the expected innovation and increased scale and complexity of future attacks.[52]

DDoS reflection and amplification. The risks coming from enterprise networks goes beyond the danger of hijacked IoT devices. Some network-based services allow malicious actors to amplify an attack through "reflectors," or services that can send large amounts of traffic to a spoofed target.

49. Brian Krebs, *Fear the Reaper, or Reaper Madness*? Krebs on Security (Oct. 27, 2017), https://krebsonsecurity.com/2017/10/fear-the-reaper-or-reaper-madness/.

50. *Id.*

51. 2017 *Verizon Data Breach Investigations Report (DBIR)*, 10th ed. https://enterprise.verizon.com/resources/reports/2017_dbir.pdf.

52. *Commerce/DHS Botnets Report, supra* note 22, at 6–7.

> Using a technique called traffic amplification and reflection, an attacker can reflect his traffic from one or more third-party machines toward the intended target. In this type of assault, the attacker sends a message to a third party while spoofing the Internet address of the victim. When the third party replies to the message, the reply is sent to the victim—and the reply is much larger than the original message, thereby amplifying the size of the attack.[53]

In 2018, GitHub was the victim of an attack that exploited a newly discovered vulnerability in the relatively obscure MemCacheD software. This type of DDoS attack was considered at the time the most intense ever.[54] Thus, using various techniques, the attacker can turn a small DNS query into a much larger payload directed at the target network.

3. Destroy or "Brick" IoT Devices—Permanent Denial of Service (PDoS) Attacks

BrickerBot attacks. Bots have exploited hardcoded passwords in unsecured IoT devices and caused a permanent denial of service. This attack renders the devices useless, as in a "bricked" state. BrickerBot is unlike other malware in the IoT threat landscape that typically amasses the infected devices into botnets that can be leveraged in DDoS attacks. BrickerBot instead executes a chain of malicious Linux commands that result in permanent damage in the device. Some of these commands include corrupting or misconfiguring the device's storage capability and kernel parameters,

---

53. Brian Krebs, *The Democratization of Censorship,* Krebs on Security (Sept. 25, 2016), https://krebsonsecurity.com/2016/09/the-democratization-of-censorship/.

54. Juan C. Perez, *Cryptomining Is All the Rage Among Hackers, as DDoS Amplification Attacks Continue*, Qualsys Inc. (Mar. 9, 2018), https://blog.qualys.com/news/2018/03/09/cryptomining-is-all-the-rage-among-hackers-as-ddos-amplification-attacks-grow.

hindering Internet connection, tampering with device performance, and wiping all files on the compromised device.[55]

4. Take Control of an IoT Device to Cause Physical Damage

Health care. Security flaws are pervasive in the health care industry.[56] Medical devices (dialysis machines, insulin pumps, pacemakers, and ICU climate controls) that lack appropriate security can potentially impact their safety and effectiveness. Among the dangers, they can disrupt the accurate delivery of medicine to patients, alter medicine dispensary inventory to produce the incorrect medicine, or deliver the wrong dosage to patients.

With minimal or no security and now connected to hospital networks, they are creating insecurities throughout the entire health care computing environment. The FDA has documented the risks and issued security guidance to address these problems.[57]

Warnings: Connected cardiac devices and infusion pumps. In 2017, the FDA observed that the St. Jude Medical implantable cardiac devices (pacemakers and defibrillators) are hackable; specifically, the device transmitter, which is responsible for reading and sharing device data with the physician, is a vulnerable attack vector.[58] The FDA advised that hackers can deplete the device battery

---

55. *BrickerBot Malware Emerges, Permanently Bricks IoT Devices* (Apr. 19, 2017), TRENDMICRO, https://www.trendmicro.com/vinfo/us/security/news/internet-of-things/brickerbot-malware-permanently-bricks-iot-devices.

56. Securing Hospitals, Independent Security Evaluators (ISE) (2016), https://www.securityevaluators.com/wp-content/uploads/2017/07/securing_hospitals.pdf.

57. U.S. Food & Drug Admin. (FDA), *Cybersecurity*, *available* at https://www.fda.gov/medicaldevices/digitalhealth/ucm373213.htm. FDA is collaborating with the National Health Information Sharing and Analysis Center (NH-ISAC) to disseminate cybersecurity information and coordinate incident response [hereinafter *FDA Cybersecurity*].

58. *Cybersecurity Vulnerabilities Identified in St. Jude Medical's Implantable Cardiac Devices and Merlin@home Transmitter*, FDA Safety Communi-

or can cause incorrect pacing and even shock.[59] The FDA has also issued two safety communications documenting the vulnerabilities of Hospira Infusion Pump Systems.[60]

Critical infrastructure. The United States obtained indictments against seven Iranian hackers for launching a massive coordinated campaign of denial of service attacks (DDoS) against 46 of the nation's largest financial institutions from 2011 through mid-2013, disabling computer servers and making networks unavailable for business. One of the hackers gained unauthorized remote access in 2013 to the Supervisory Control and Data Acquisition (SCADA) systems of the Bowman Dam located in Rye, New York, allowing him to obtain information about water levels and temperature and the status of the sluice gate, which is responsible for controlling water levels and flow rates.[61] Justice Department officials assessed the situation by stating: "The infiltration of the Bowman Avenue dam represents a frightening new frontier in cybercrime.... We now live in a world where devastating attacks on our financial system, our infrastructure, and our way of life can be launched from anywhere in the world, with a click of a mouse."[62]

Wireless electronic devices—padlocks and sniper rifles. In 2015, SafeTech Products launched a smart electronic padlock.

---

cation (Jan. 9, 2017), *available at* https://www.fda.gov/MedicalDevices/Safety/AlertsandNotices/ucm535843.htm.

59. St. Jude announced that professionals developed and implemented a patch fix for the existing bug. *St. Jude Medical Announces Cybersecurity Updates* (Jan. 9, 2017), http://media.sjm.com/newsroom/news-releases/news-releases-details/2017/St-Jude-Medical-Announces-Cybersecurity-Updates/default.aspx.

60. *FDA Cybersecurity, supra* note 57.

61. United States v. Fathi, Firoozi, et al., No. 16 CRM 48 (S.D. N.Y. 2016).

62. Press Release, Manhattan U.S. Attorney Announces Charges against Seven Iranians for Conducting Coordinated Campaign of Cyber Attacks against U.S. Financial Sector on Behalf of Islamic Revolutionary Guard Corps-Sponsored Entities (Mar. 24, 2016), *available at* https://www.justice.gov/usao-sdny/pr/manhattan-us-attorney-announces-charges-against-seven-iranians-conducting-coordinated.

However, the padlock did not encrypt its users' passwords when transmitted from a smartphone to the locks. Moreover, it did not force users to reset default passwords, which could be discovered easily by brute-force attacks. According to a settlement with the New York State Attorney General, the alleged security deficiencies and security representations were found to be contrary to New York State laws that prohibit deceptive acts or practices and false advertising.[63]

An attacker could also exploit vulnerabilities in the software of rifles remotely over the network.[64] By logging into the gun's network, which has a default password, a hacker can access the API and change the key variables in its target application, and then change the parameters involved in the calculation of the scope of the target, making the rifle either change its target or permanently disable the rifle.

Connected cars and UAVs. A number of incidents have been reported in which hackers have disabled driving systems, including killing the engine or abruptly engaging the brakes, putting passengers, other cars, and pedestrians at risk of serious damage, injury, or death.[65] Similarly, hackers have taken control of unmanned aerial vehicles by inserting malware into the software controls, stopping their motors, killing the auto pilot, and taking over the video cam-

63. A.G. Schneiderman Announces Settlement with Tech Company Over Sale of Insecure Bluetooth Door and Padlocks, Attorney General Letitia James (May 22, 2017), *available at* https://ag.ny.gov/press-release/ag-schneiderman-announces-settlement-tech-company-over-sale-insecure-bluetooth-door.

64. At a 2015 Black Hat Hacker conference, security researchers demonstrated how a wirelessly connected sniper rifle of a company named TrackPoint can be hacked.

65. Jason Levine, *Advantages of Connected Cars Come with Cybersecurity Risks*, Axios (Aug. 16, 2018), https://www.axios.com/advantages-of-connected-cars-come-with-cybersecurity-risks-08d361f2-d4fe-4f01-9995-7b2f35128f8c.html. Andy Greenberg, *A Deep Flaw in Your Car Lets Hackers Shut Down Safety Features*, WIRED (Aug. 16, 2017), https://www.wired.com/story/car-hack-shut-down-safety-features/; *Vehicle Cybersecurity*, NHTSA, *available at* https://www.nhtsa.gov/technology-innovation/vehicle-cybersecurity

era. Vehicles are vulnerable because Internet-connected computers in the entertainment systems are not properly isolated from the dashboard functions and driving systems (steering, brakes, and transmission). The vehicles' onboard diagnostic port can be used to hack into a car, and an attacker can gain wireless control remotely via the Internet.

Casino's customer data stolen through attack on a connected fish tank. Hackers attempted to steal data from a North American casino through a fish tank connected to the Internet. The network connections on the high-tech fish tank were set up to automatically feed the fish and send data on the tank's temperature. Hackers used the connected "smart" thermostat to gain a foothold in the casino's network, and then to access the casino's "high-roller" database.[66] Despite extra security precautions, hackers still managed to compromise the tank and send data to a device in Finland before the threat was discovered and stopped.

Corporate espionage with video conferencing. Hackers compromised 50 video-conferencing devices throughout a company's building. This was as simple as putting the model number and the word "exploit" into Google and receiving the readily available hacker exploit tool. One of the devices had begun to receive inbound connections, meaning someone outside the organization was accessing the device, and it was leaking quite a bit of data—10 GB of audio files leaving the network and heading to an unknown device. Further investigation revealed that the offense occurred in the boardroom during a two-week period when the directors were discussing a major merger. "It was a textbook case of corporate espionage."[67]

---

66. Selena Larson, *A Smart Fish Tank Left a Casino Vulnerable to Hackers*, CNN Business (July 19, 2017), https://money.cnn.com/2017/07/19/technology/fish-tank-hack-darktrace/index.html.

67. Justin Fier, *6 Emerging Cyber-Threats You Didn't See in the News*, Darktrace (Oct. 24, 2016), https://www.darktrace.com/en/blog/6-emerging-cyber-threats-you-didnt-see-in-the-news/.

5. *Take Over IoT Devices for Crypto-mining*

A security firm demonstrated that vulnerable Internet-connected devices, such as security cameras, consumer hardware graphics processing units (GPUs), and users' mobile devices, can be hijacked and turned into tools to mine cryptocurrencies.[68] IoT devices can be attacked and the computing power of all the gadgets can be used to mine currencies, such as the digital coin Monero. Cybercriminals have been actively engaged in crypto-mining malware activities, creating cryptocurrency-mining malware to infect these devices.[69] Cryptocurrency mining was the most detected network event in devices connected to home routers in 2017.

VI. The Path Forward: The Security Strategy for Executives, Corporate Boards, and Government Officials Includes Risk-Based Assessment

In light of the number of massive data breaches and well-documented IoT vulnerabilities, the need for all private and public sector organizations to develop, implement, and maintain an appropriate cybersecurity program is immediate and compelling.[70] In many cases, data breaches or other types of cyber incidents could have been

---

68. Arjun Kharpal, *15,000 Internet-Connected Devices Could Be Hacked to Mine $1,000 of Cryptocurrency in 4 days*, CNBC (Mar. 1, 2018), https://www.cnbc.com/2018/03/01/thousands-of-iot-devices-can-be-hacked-to-mine-cryptocurrency-avast.html.

69. Fernando Merces, *Cryptocurrency-Mining Malware Targeting IoT, Being Offered in the Underground*, TrendMicro (May 2, 2018), https://blog.trendmicro.com/trendlabs-security-intelligence/cryptocurrency-mining-malware-targeting-iot-being-offered-in-the-underground/.

70. The American Bar Association (ABA) adopted the following Resolution in 2014:

> The American Bar Association encourages all private and public sector organizations to develop, implement, and maintain an appropriate cybersecurity program that complies with applicable ethical and legal obligations, and is tailored to the nature and scope of the organization, and the data and systems to be protected.

prevented or detected early and the risks of the incident mitigated if the organization had undertaken proper security planning and implemented appropriate security safeguards. While cybersecurity challenges may seem daunting, existing frameworks, standards, and best practices provide a roadmap that public officials and business executives can follow to reduce the risks substantially.

Failure to implement appropriate security can and will lead to significant losses for businesses and owners and operators of critical infrastructure. Business could be temporarily disrupted, or if a sustained attack or breach of security occurs, the continuity of business could be severely affected and, in the worst scenario, organizations could be forced out of business.

Ultimately, an organization could face substantial and hard-to-quantify liability if a data breach occurred. Instead of waiting for a breach to take place, proactive measures must be implemented that will significantly lessen the likelihood of a compromise. These actions can potentially lead to reduced likelihood of liability.

A. Comprehensive Information Security Program

A cybersecurity program is comprised of a series of activities. These activities include, for example, governance by boards of directors and/or senior management; development of security strategies, plans, policies and procedures, and privacy compliance requirements; creation of inventories of digital assets; selection of security controls; determination of technical configuration settings; performance of annual audits; and delivery of training.[71]

An effective cybersecurity program requires trained personnel to evaluate the security impact of actual and proposed changes to the system, assess security controls, correlate and analyze security-related information, and provide actionable communication of the

71. *See* Industrial Internet of Things, Volume G4: Security Framework, Industrial Internet Consortium, IIC:PUB:G4:V1.0:PB:20160926 (2016), https://www.iiconsortium.org/pdf/IIC_PUB_G4_V1.00_PB-3.pdf.

security status across all levels of the organization. Administrative, technical, organizational, and physical controls help ensure the confidentiality, availability, and integrity of digital assets. Such controls should be carefully determined, implemented, and enforced.

Cyber response plans. To minimize the effects of cyber intrusions, it is necessary to plan a response. Organizations must be prepared if a cyberattack or data breach occurs, or if an event interrupts their operations.

B. IoT Risk Assessment

The FBI has emphasized that "[a]s our reliance on IoT becomes an important part of everyday life, being aware of the associated risks is a key part of keeping information and devices secure."[72] NIST observed that "[m]any organizations are not necessarily aware of the large number of IoT devices they are already using and how IoT devices may affect cybersecurity and privacy risks differently than conventional information technology (IT) devices."[73] In the high-risk IoT environment, mitigation of risk is paramount and requires an understanding of the IoT ecosystem because the options may be significantly different for IoT devices than conventional IT devices.

Cybersecurity is based on a systematic assessment of risks that are present in a particular operating environment. Risk assessments are undertaken to identify gaps and deficiencies in a cybersecurity program due to operational changes, new compliance requirements, an altered threat environment, or changes in the system architecture and technologies deployed.

Assessing risk requires organizations to identify their threats and vulnerabilities, the harm they may cause the organization, and the likelihood that adverse events arising from those threats and vulnerabilities may actually occur. Threats and risks exist with

72. *FBI Alert, IoT as Proxies, supra* note 46.

73. NISTIR 8228 (Draft) *Managing IoT Cyber and Privacy Risks, supra* note 39.

both physical and virtual assets, and since the two are becoming increasingly interconnected, all aspects of the cybersecurity threat must be addressed. Once organizations are aware of their existing IoT usage and possible future usage, they need to understand how the characteristics of IoT affect managing cybersecurity and privacy risks, especially in terms of risk response—accepting, avoiding, mitigating, sharing, or transferring risk.

Every information system is different, including its design and architecture, hardware and software, and technical implementation. The risk assessment template that follows provides a starting point—company and government officials must tailor their risk assessments to the data, architecture, and technology of the big IT system they own, oversee, or manage.[74] An IoT risk assessment should focus on specific characteristics and vulnerabilities of the IoT devices being implemented, as well as the environment(s) where the system is deployed.

---

74. NIST Guides for Conducting a Risk Assessment—NIST published the *Framework for Improving Critical Infrastructure Cybersecurity*, a set of industry standards and best practices to help organizations manage cybersecurity risks as part of their risk management processes, https://www.nist.gov/cyberframework. NISTIR 8228 (draft) *Managing (IoT) Cybersecurity and Privacy Risks* will help organizations understand and manage cybersecurity and privacy risks associated with IoT devices throughout their life cycles. The NIST *Guide for Conducting Risk Assessments*, Spec Pub 800-30 Rev. 1 (Sept. 2012), provides a step-by-step process for organizations on how to (1) prepare for risk assessments; (2) conduct risk assessments; (3) communicate risk assessment results to key organizational personnel; and (4) maintain the risk assessments over time. NIST Spec Pub 800-39 *Managing Information Security Risk* (Mar. 2011) focuses on organizational risk management.

See IoT Security Maturity Model: Description and Intended Use, Industrial Internet Consortium, IIC:PUB:IN15:V1.0:PB:20180409, (Apr. 9, 2018), https://www.iiconsortium.org/pdf/SMM_Description_and_Intended_Use_2018-04-09.pdf. "As an informed understanding of the risks and threats an organization faces is the foundation of choosing and implementing appropriate security controls, the model provides a conceptual framework to organize the myriad considerations. The framework helps an organization decide what their security target state should be and what their current state is. Repeatedly comparing the target and current states identifies where further improvement can be made."

IoT Risk Assessment—A Brief Overview	
NIST Cyber Framework	***Risk Management Program***
	IDENTIFY, PROTECT, DETECT, RESPOND, RECOVER The NIST *Framework for Improving Critical Infrastructure Cybersecurity* provides practical guidance for assessing security risks and a framework for determining the maturity of an organization's cybersecurity program. It maps the Cybersecurity Framework to other accepted security frameworks and standards.
Basic Steps	***Key Questions and Resources***
1. Identify relevant THREATS to the organization or threats directed through third-party entities	**Is Your Organization a Target?** Determine who your most likely cyber adversaries are, and what their motives may be (*e.g.,* financial vs. espionage vs. ideology). **Potential Threat Actors:** Nation-states (foreign espionage), organized criminal groups, terrorists, botnet operators, hackers/hacktivists, malicious insiders, third-party outsource and business partners. ***Resources*** Details of attack methodology used by hackers in several of the major data breaches. • The indictment of a Russian national charged in the largest known data breach prosecution. *United States v. Drinkman*, et al., No. 09-626 (JBS) (S-2) (D. N.J.) • Special Counsel Indictment of Russians. *United States v. Viktor Borisovich Netyksho*, et al., U.S. D.C. D.C. (July 13, 2018) • DHS-FBI Technical Alert: Russian Government Cyber Activity Targeting Energy and Other Critical Infrastructure Sectors, US-CERT Alert (TA18-074A) (March 16, 2018), pages 2–7

2. ***List VULNERABILITIES both internal and external to the organization***	**What Are Your Vulnerabilities?** The distributed architecture of IoT presents a plethora of vulnerable points in processing and storage where sensitive and proprietary data can be compromised. **Know Your Data! What Data May Be at Risk?** • What personal records and confidential business data are used, processed, or stored in the organization's information systems? • Determine where sensitive and confidential data resides in the system. Be sure to focus on Internet-visible components, websites, social media, and mobile devices. • Understand the devices or sensors that generate the data, the semantics or structure of the data, the communication protocols and the data flow. **Technology—Inventory Your System Assets! Where are the most vulnerable components in your network?** Evaluate the security vulnerabilities in IoT • Every IoT device has a unique identifier, specific capabilities about the data it can capture and transmit, communication model (uni/bi-directional), and the structure of the data. These are "Device Metadata" and "Device Schema." • Review expert reports of potential vulnerabilities, current and planned security controls and test results—are any of the vulnerabilities they identified evident in your network? • What is connected and remotely connecting to my systems? Who can access the network and systems? **People and Process** • Does the organization have an information governance strategy (including third-party governance)? • Have appropriate security policies been issued and are they being enforced? **Resources—Expert Reports on Potential Vulnerabilities** • US-CERT Alert (TA15-119A) Top 30 Targeted High Risk Vulnerabilities—"as many as 85 percent of targeted attacks are preventable." • OWASP Top 10 IoT Vulnerabilities (2014) https://www.owasp.org/index.php/OWASP_Internet_of_Things_Project#tab=IoT_Top_10

3. ***Assess IMPACT (i.e., harm) to the organization and individuals that may occur given the potential for threats exploiting vulnerabilities***	**Assess Impact on Confidentiality, Integrity, and Availability** **Confidentiality:** Know Your Data! What Protection Is Required? • Determine the criticality and sensitivity level of each type of data and how it must be protected. What access restrictions must be applied? Financial and Reputational Harm to Individuals and Organizations—The most sensitive personal records of hundreds of millions of individuals have been compromised. Proprietary corporate data has been stolen. Every breach of personal records exposes individuals to identity theft and fraud. Business data stolen threatens the viability of important company initiatives. **Integrity:** May see more cyber operations that will change or manipulate electronic information to compromise its integrity (i.e., accuracy and reliability) instead of deleting it or disrupting access. **Availability:** Hackers may conduct distributed denial-of-service (DDoS) operations and data-deletion attacks that undermine availability.
4. ***Determine LIKELIHOOD that harm will occur***	**Key Questions** How Likely Is It That a Breach Will Occur and Harm Will Result? Since 2005 nearly 8,908 data breaches have resulted in the compromise of 11,239,084,942 personal records. Given the epidemic of data breaches companies and governments are experiencing, many involving huge datasets, the likelihood that an IoT breach will occur is extremely likely. Review Data from Intelligence Agencies, e.g., *Worldwide Threat Assessments; 2017 Foreign Cyber Threat report*.

5. ADDRESS THE RISKS Organizations must understand the effect of the known IoT vulnerabilities in their particular network, and then decide how to address and mitigate the risks. **Actions to Address Risks:** **MITIGATE, AVOID, TRANSFER, ACCEPT** Risk assessments are the basis for the selection of APPROPRIATE SECURITY CONTROLS to address the risks identified and the development of REMEDIATION PLANS so that risks and vulnerabilities are reduced to a reasonable and appropriate level.	**Questions to Consider:** • Will implementing each type of IoT technology help fulfill mission priorities? • Is it possible to implement this technology given the current infrastructure? • Will implementing the technology introduce an unacceptable level of risk? • What do I need to do to ensure ongoing risk management of this new technology? ***Resources*** NIST Cybersecurity Framework NISTIR 8228 (DRAFT) Considerations for Managing Internet of Things (IoT) Cybersecurity and Privacy Risks Council on CyberSecurity, 20 Critical Security Controls for Effective Cyber Defense—Recommended set of actions that provide specific and actionable ways to stop today's most pervasive and dangerous attacks. "Prioritizes a list of the controls that would have the greatest impact in improving risk posture against real-world threats."[75] NIST Spec Pub 800-53 v. 5—Security and Privacy Controls for Federal Information Systems and Organizations (Draft Aug. 2017). Catalog of security and privacy controls for organizations to protect operations and assets, individuals, other organizations, and the nation from a diverse set of threats, including hostile attacks, natural disasters, structural failures, human errors, and privacy risks. Industrial Internet Consortium, IoT Security Maturity Model: Description and Intended Use Online Trust Alliance—Internet of Things (IoT) Trust Framework v. 2.5 (Internet Society) "Strategic principles necessary to help secure IoT devices and their data when shipped and throughout their entire life-cycle."
6. BE PREPARED	

Lucy L. Thomson © 2018 All Rights Reserved

75. The Council on CyberSecurity was established in 2013 as an independent, expert, nonprofit organization with a global scope committed to the security of an open Internet. http://www.counciloncybersecurity.org.

C. Implementing Technology and IoT Devices with Known Vulnerabilities Is Not "Reasonable Security"

Many data breaches and IoT incidents involve exploitation of known vulnerabilities and violations of well-accepted security practices. Standards of care are beginning to emerge.

Federal law enforcement agencies have brought cases against organizations that failed to employ reasonable security and put sensitive personal data at risk. Businesses have faced regulatory fines and investigations, civil damage actions, administrative proceedings, and criminal indictments.

The Federal Trade Commission (FTC) enforces laws prohibiting unfair and deceptive practices. It has taken enforcement action against companies that suffered a data breach and failed to employ "reasonable security." In particular, four FTC enforcement actions have been directed to security problems with IoT devices. These cases focused on inadequate security of wireless computer routers and Internet cameras that violated consumers' privacy (D-Link),[76] insecure home routers and "cloud" services that put consumers' privacy at risk (ASUS),[77] video cameras designed to allow consumers to monitor their homes remotely exposed the private lives of hundreds of consumers to public viewing on the Internet (TRENDnet),[78] and Internet-connected toys that collected personal information about children without obtaining parental consent (VTech Electronics).[79]

The FTC guidance, *Start with Security, A Guide for Business*, analyzes lessons learned from the more than 50 law enforcement

76. https://www.ftc.gov/news-events/press-releases/2017/01/ftc-charges-d-link-put-consumers-privacy-risk-due-inadequate.

77. https://www.ftc.gov/news-events/press-releases/2016/02/asus-settles-ftc-charges-insecure-home-routers-cloud-services-put.

78. https://www.ftc.gov/news-events/press-releases/2013/09/marketer-internet-connected-home-security-video-cameras-settles.

79. https://www.ftc.gov/news-events/press-releases/2018/01/electronic-toy-maker-vtech-settles-ftc-allegations-it-violated.

actions the FTC has announced, and describes the security lapses that led to those cases. The penalties for failing to employ reasonable security to protect personal data are onerous, ranging from substantial fines to third-party audits spanning the next 20 years.

In the first state attorney general action against a wireless security company for failing to implement adequate security in its IoT devices, the New York State Attorney General recently settled with wireless lock company Safetech, manufacturer of a smart electronic padlock.[80] Safetech did not encrypt its users' passwords when transmitted from a smartphone to the locks. Moreover, it did not force users to reset default passwords, which could be discovered easily by brute-force attacks, leaving consumers susceptible to hacking and physical theft.

D. Strengthening Security

This chapter builds on the overview of U.S. and global laws and regulations pertaining to IoT that is provided in Chapters 6 and 7. Privacy laws are discussed in Chapter 8. A deeper analysis of legal developments in various industry sectors, including health care and transportation (connected cars, UAVs), is included in several other chapters.

Even as warnings about IoT cybersecurity risks continue to be issued by the defense and intelligence community, policy makers, and cybersecurity experts, development and implementation of the IoT continues to explode.

- There are no comprehensive laws or regulations of the security of IoT devices.
- There is no oversight on the licensing of IoT device manufacturers.
- There are no governing authorities evaluating the security of IoT devices.

80. A.G. Schneiderman, *supra* note 63.

One legislative proposal, The IoT Cybersecurity Improvement Act of 2017 S. 1691, is designed to address the market failure by establishing minimum security requirements for federal procurements of connected devices.[81]

The State of California enacted legislation (SB 327) that adds to the existing privacy law new requirements for the security of connected devices. This legislation would require a manufacturer of a connected device to equip the device with a reasonable security feature or features that are appropriate to the nature and function of the device, appropriate to the information it may collect, contain, or transmit, and designed to protect the device and any information contained therein from unauthorized access, destruction, use, modification, or disclosure, as specified.[82]

Security by Design. In light of the documented vulnerabilities in the IoT, companies and government agencies must take immediate action to strengthen their security posture. To properly support an organization's risk management program, security must be incorporated into the architecture and design of the organization's information systems and supporting information technology assets.[83]

This includes constant monitoring of systems, security status, and risks, often referred to as continuous monitoring. Continuous monitoring of systems and networks is essential to protect against the broad range of serious threats to information systems.[84] Robust

81. Introduced on Aug. 1, 2017, 115th Congress (2017–18). *See* "Reflections on the Internet of Things" in which Senator Mark Warner discusses this proposed legislation.

82. California Civil Code § 1798.91.04 (eff. Jan. 1, 2020).

83. *See* OSWAP Developer IoT Security Guidance, *available at* https://www.owasp.org/index.php/IoT_Security_Guidance.

84. The SANS CIS Critical Security Controls: Guidelines provide guidance to maximize the impact of government and private sector security efforts, and identify 20 critical priority controls, most of which can be continuously monitored. Twenty Critical Security Controls for Effective Cyber Defense: Consensus Audit Guidelines, v. 7.0, https://www.sans.org/critical-security-controls/guidelines (the website provides a wealth of valuable information about the leading information security methodologies and how they relate to each other).

continuous monitoring will provide executives and security professionals with the information necessary to make cost-effective, risk-based decisions. Artificial intelligence (AI) is providing the capability to detect anomalies and thwart hacker attacks before damage is done or quickly to enable an effective response. Potential threats must be investigated, and targeted attacks can be detected in advance or addressed as they occur, enabling a highly proactive security posture.

Addressing IoT risk through the procurement process. As part of a comprehensive security program, the procurement process can be used to strengthen the security posture of organizations and their third-party business partners. The ABA Vendor Contracting Cybersecurity Checklist frames the issues that contracting parties should consider consistent with common principles for managing cyber risk.[85]

When contracting for products and services, organizations can specify cybersecurity requirements that third-party vendors must meet. Including cybersecurity in the procurement process can ensure that those purchasing and supplying delivery systems consider cybersecurity beginning with the design phase of system development. This will further ensure that cybersecurity is implemented throughout the testing, manufacturing, delivery, installation, and support phases of the product life cycle, improving overall reliability and reducing cyber risks. Contract representations and warranties can ensure that important cybersecurity conditions are agreed to and will be followed by third-party vendors.

Hackers and foreign governments have demonstrated the will, the knowledge, the capacity, and the resources to successfully penetrate information systems and steal the most sensitive data held by private sector and government organizations. The threat is imminent, and immediate action is required to assess the risks and implement appropriate security controls to protect the confidentiality, integrity, and availability of data and systems.

---

85. ABA Vendor Contracting Cybersecurity Checklist, https://www.americanbar.org/news/abanews/aba-news-archives/2017/03/new_aba_checkliste/.

E. OWASP Principles of IoT Security

Developed as part of the OWASP Internet of Things Project, these Principles were designed to enable manufacturers, developers, and consumers in any context to make better security decisions when building, deploying, or assessing IoT technologies.

1. Assume a Hostile Edge
   Edge components are likely to fall into adversarial hands. Assume attackers will have physical access to edge components and can manipulate them, move them to hostile networks, and control resources such as DNS, DHCP, and Internet routing.
2. Test for Scale
   The volume of IoT means that every design and security consideration must also take into account scale. Simple bootstrapping into an ecosystem can create a self-denial of service condition at IoT scale. Security countermeasures must perform at volume.
3. Internet of Lies
   Automated systems are extremely capable of presenting misinformation in convincing formats. IoT systems should always verify data from the edge in order to prevent autonomous misinformation from tainting a system.
4. Exploit Autonomy
   Automated systems are capable of complex, monotonous, and tedious operations that human users would never tolerate. IoT systems should seek to exploit this advantage for security.
5. Expect Isolation
   The advantage of autonomy should also extend to situations where a component is isolated. Security countermeasures must never degrade in the absence of connectivity.

6. Protect Uniformly
   Data encryption only protects encrypted pathways. Data that is transmitted over an encrypted link is still exposed at any point it is unencrypted, such as prior to encryption, after decryption, and along any communications pathways that do not enforce encryption. Careful consideration must be given to full data life cycle to ensure that encryption is applied uniformly and appropriately to guarantee protections. Encryption is not total—be aware that metadata about encrypted data might also provide valuable information to attackers.
7. Encryption Is Tricky
   It is very easy for developers to make mistakes when applying encryption. Using encryption but failing to validate certificates, failing to validate intermediate certificates, failing to encrypt traffic with a strong key, using a uniform seed, or exposing private key material are all common pitfalls when deploying encryption. Ensure a thorough review of any encryption capability to avoid these mistakes.
8. System Hardening
   Be sure that IoT components are stripped down to the minimum viable feature set to reduce attack surface. Unused ports and protocols should be disabled, and unnecessary supporting software should be uninstalled or turned off. Be sure to track third-party components and update them where possible.
9. Limit What You Can
   To the extent possible, limit access based on acceptable use criteria. There's no advantage in exposing a sensor interface to the entire Internet if there's no good case for a remote user in a hostile country. Limit access to white lists of rules that make sense.

10. Life Cycle Support
    IoT systems should be able to quickly onboard new components, but should also be capable of re-credentialing existing components, and deprovisioning components for a full device life cycle. This capability should include all components in the ecosystem, from devices to users.
11. Data in Aggregate Is Unpredictable
    IoT systems are capable of collecting vast quantities of data that my seem innocuous at first, but complex data analysis may reveal very sensitive patterns or information hidden in data. IoT systems must prepare for the data stewardship responsibilities of unexpected information sensitivity that may only be revealed after an ecosystem is deployed.
12. Plan for the Worst
    IoT systems should have capabilities to respond to compromises, hostile participants, malware, or other adverse events. There should be features in place to re-issue credentials, exclude participants, distribute security patches and updates, and so on, before they are ever necessary.
13. The Long Haul
    IoT system designers must recognize the extended lifespan of devices will require forward compatible security features. IoT ecosystems must be capable of aging in place and still addressing evolving security concerns. New encryption, advances in protocols, new attack methods and techniques, and changing topology all necessitate that IoT systems be capable of addressing emerging security concerns for years after they are deployed.
14. Attackers Target Weakness
    Ensure that security controls are equivalent across interfaces in an ecosystem. Attackers will identify the weakest component and attempt to exploit it. Mobile interfaces, hidden

APIs, or resource-constrained environments must enforce security in the same way as more robust or feature-rich interfaces. Using multifactor authentication for a web interface is useless if a mobile application allows access to the same APIs with a four-digit PIN.

15. Transitive Ownership
    IoT components are often sold or transferred during their lifespan. Plan for this eventuality and be sure IoT systems can protect and isolate data to enable safe transfer of ownership, even if a component is sold or transferred to a competitor or attacker.
16. N:N Authentication
    Realize that IoT does not follow a traditional 1:1 model of users to applications. Each component may have more than one user and a user may interact with multiple components. Several users might access different data or capabilities on a single device, and one user might have varying rights to multiple devices. Multiple devices may need to broker permissions on behalf of a single user account, and so on. Be sure the IoT system can handle these complex trust and authentication schemes.

https://www.owasp.org/index.php/Principles_of_IoT_Security

Chapter 10

Incentives to Address Homeland Security Risks with IoT Technology

Adam Isles

IoT devices hold tremendous promise across a wide variety of sectors—including but not limited to transportation, agriculture, manufacturing, smart homes, and health care. Moreover, they entail a number of specific homeland security use cases, including enhanced screening (contraband detection), situational awareness (drones), actuation (vehicles, gates), and better management of homeland security facilities.

And yet, IoT devices also create numerous security risks when not effectively secured. For example, bad actors have leveraged hundreds of thousands of poorly configured IoT devices by turning them into bots to launch massive Distributed Denial of Service (DDoS) attacks. IoT manufacturers are often perceived to prioritize time to market and innovative functionality over security and resilience.

So how to address the question of incentives? First, industry-informed secure-by-design practices—for example, on risk-based secure development, configuration and patching—need to be more broadly promulgated. Likewise, the federal government has meaningful tools in place to incent secure-by-design in IoT technologies.

Liability protection through the Support Anti-Terrorism by Fostering Effective Technologies (SAFETY) Act can provide an immediate incentive to spur development of secure IoT capabilities, while R&D funding can drive longer-term efforts. The procurement process can also be used to nudge industry to more secure-by-design practices. As secure-by-design practices become more broadly available, grant-making and regulatory authorities can be used to drive adoption.

It is critical that each of these federal tools be proactively used to build effective, enduring security into IoT systems. These technologies can make us safer and more efficient, but they have to be secure to do so.

I. Security Risks

Significant attention has been focused on cooptation of technology suppliers (for example backdoors associated with vendors of IT infrastructure and tools—e.g., Huawei, ZTE, and Kaspersky[1]) including manufacturers of IoT devices, particularly Closed Circuit Television (CCTV) systems. Indeed, the recently enacted National Defense Authorization Act of 2018 bans the purchase of video surveillance and telecommunications equipment produced by Hytera Communications Corporation, Hangzhou Hikvision Digital Technology Company, or Dahua Technology Company in any use that involves public safety, security of government facilities, physical security surveillance of critical infrastructure, and other national security purposes.[2] And yet security risks associated with IoT devices run much deeper, potentially leaving such devices

1. *See* https://www.dhs.gov/news/2017/09/13/dhs-statement-issuance-binding-operational-directive-17-01.

2. Pub. L. No: 115-232, sec. 889, Prohibition on Certain Telecommunications and Video Surveillance Services or Equipment, John S. McCain National Defense Authorization Act for Fiscal Year 2019, *available at* https://www.congress.gov/bill/115th-congress/house-bill/5515/text.

exposed, even assuming an otherwise well-intended manufacturer. A May 2018 report jointly issued by DHS and the U.S. Department Commerce, "Enhancing the Resilience of the Internet and Communications Ecosystem Against Botnets and Other Automated, Distributed Threats" (hereinafter the "DHS/Commerce Botnet Report") made the following stark statement:

> Unfortunately, IoT devices are often sorely lacking in security-focused features. These systems now offer the most attractive target to malicious actors, and are an increasingly large percentage of the devices in the ecosystem. In fact, the November 2016 Ericsson Mobility Report predicted that IoT devices will surpass mobile phones as the largest category of connected devices in 2018. Given the level of security on IoT devices, that is a daunting prediction.[3]

A starting point for effective security is risk assessment—in other words, not all IoT devices entail the same level or type of risk, and security measures should be informed by risks specific to the device in question. That said, a number of cross-cutting gaps have been identified in the way IoT devices are developed and shipped, including but not limited to:

- **Secure software development.** A number of reports have identified chronic problems in the way software is

3. U.S. Dep't of Homeland Security and Dep't of Commerce joint report, *Enhancing the Resilience of the Internet and Communications Ecosystem Against Botnets and Other Automated, Distributed Threats* 16 (May 2018), *available at* https://www.commerce.gov/sites/default/files/media/files/2018/eo_13800_botnet_report_-_finalv2.pdf. The report also noted the following: "Rapidly increasing deployment of insecure IoT devices has had the pernicious side effect of enabling cost-effective development of extremely large and widely distributed botnets. For example, the Mirai botnets have compromised hundreds of thousands of devices as a result of hard-coded administrative passwords. More recently, the Reaper botnet has compromised devices by targeting well-known software vulnerabilities."

developed, maintained, and retired in today's rapidly evolving technology sector—not just for IoT but across information technology environments in general. For example, the DHS/Commerce Botnet Report noted: "Common software development techniques result in, optimistically, a flaw every 2,000 lines of code—or more by many other metrics. Many of these bugs create exploitable security vulnerabilities, such as buffer overflows."[4] Compounding this problem is growing complexity of modern software: The Ford F-150 features more than 150 million lines of code[5]—as compared with two million lines of code for the Lockheed F22 Raptor.[6] Moreover, with respect to the ingredients into that code, open source software libraries are now widely used across global industry[7]—by some estimates, there will be almost a half-billion open-source libraries available to developers within a decade—and in modern software development environments code may change hundreds of times a day.[8] Likewise, software libraries may become outdated or otherwise vulnerable and "are not always closely tracked by manufacturers in the rapid development cycle."[9]

---

4. *See id.*

5. *See* Press Release, Ford, Ford Invests in Pivotal to Accelerate Cloud-based Software Development (May 5, 2016), https://media.ford.com/content/fordmedia/fna/us/en/news/2016/05/05/ford-invests-in-pivotal.html.

6. *See* Roberto Saracco, *Guess What Requires 150 Million Lines of Code . . .*, IEEE BLOG (Jan. 13, 2016), http://sites.ieee.org/futuredirections/2016/01/13/guess-what-requires-150-million-lines-of-code/.

7. A recent survey by Synopsys Black Duck found open source components in 96 percent of applications scanned. *See* Synopsys, 2018 Open Source Security and Risk Analysis Report, *available at* https://www.synopsys.com/content/dam/synopsys/sig-assets/reports/2018-ossra.pdf.

8. *See* Veracode/SourceClear, *The Busy Manager's Guide to Open Source Security*, *available at* https://www.sourceclear.com/resources/TheBusyManagersGuideToOpenSourceSecurity.pdf.

9. *See* DHS/Commerce Botnet Report, *supra* note 3, at 30. In fact, the U.S. Department of Commerce's National Telecommunications and Information

- **Subversion of the software development process.** Not only is software development difficult to manage from a vulnerability perspective, but efforts to actively subvert software are increasing. For example, developers are in some cases specifically targeted for attack.[10] Malware has been detected in certain open source software libraries.[11] A July 2018 report from the National Counterintelligence and Security Center identified adversarial software supply chain operations as a top emerging threat, noting in particular how the software update process for a Ukrainian tax firm (M.E. Doc) was the intrusion vector for the June 2017 notPetya ransomware attack.[12]
- **Configuration.** Even if software is securely developed, improper configuration when deploying systems can

---

Administration recently launched a process to "to develop greater transparency of software components for better security across the digital ecosystem." A key aspect of this discussion is a "software bill of materials" (SBOM). *See* Press Release, NTIA, NTIA Launches Initiative to Improve Software Component Transparency (June 6, 2018), https://www.ntia.doc.gov/blog/2018/ntia-launches-initiative-improve-software-component-transparency. The initiative's focus is to "identify how software component data can be shared, what practices can be easily and voluntarily adopted, and what policy and market challenges should be addressed by the broad community."

Some sectors are already advancing in demanding suppliers provide an SBOM. For example, the Financial Services Sector Coordinating Council developed a model set of vendor procurement requirements in 2016 that includes SBOM refences. *See* FSSCC Purchasers' Guide to Cyber Insurance Products, Appendix B, April 14, 2016, *available at* https://www.fsscc.org/files/galleries/FSSCC_Cyber_Insurance_Purchasers_Guide_FINAL-TLP_White.pdf.

10. *See* Brandon Levene, Dominik Reichel, & Esmid Idrizovic, *Dimnie: Hiding in Plain Sight*, PALO ALTO NETWORKS UNIT 42 (Mar. 28, 2017, 5:00 AM) https://researchcenter.paloaltonetworks.com/2017/03/unit42-dimnie-hiding-plain-sight/.

11. *See* Veracode/SourceClear, *supra* note 8.

12. *See* News Release, National Counterintelligence and Security Center, 2018 Foreign Economic Espionage in Cyberspace 12 (July 2018), https://www.dni.gov/index.php/ncsc-newsroom/item/1889-2018-foreign-economic-espionage-in-cyberspace.

expose them to compromise. According to the DHS/Commerce Botnet Report: "Systems shipped with inappropriate default configuration settings, such as hard-coded passwords, are more vulnerable in operation." The report also noted that even where appropriate security controls are present, "usability and user interfaces result in less-secure configurations."[13] In other words, it is not only critical that devices are shipped with secure default configurations but also that intuitive guidance be provided to users on how to operate devices securely.

- **Software patching.** Technical debt created by poor development processes compound post-development vulnerability remediation. Likewise, when vulnerabilities are identified after IT devices are deployed, these devices may prove difficult or impossible to patch—put another way, such vulnerabilities "are often far easier to exploit than to correct."[14] A recent report by Synopsys Black Duck found 8 percent of audited codebases contained Apache Struts, and 33 percent of those contained the Struts vulnerability that cause d the Equifax breach.[15] The problem extends to IoT devices: that same Black Duck report indicated that, of IoT applications scanned, 77 percent of the codebase contained open source, with an average of 677 vulnerabilities per application.[16]

To what extent is the lack of awareness based on a lack of IoT security guidance? A number of high-level guidance documents have been published on how to implement IoT security.

13. *See* DHS/Commerce Botnet Report, *supra* note 3, at 30.

14. *See id.* at 16.

15. *See* 2018 Open Source Security and Risk Analysis Report, *supra* note 7.

16. *See id.* The report did not, however, indicate whether those vulnerabilities were used in vulnerabilities (i.e., in such a way as they could be actively exploited).

In November 2016, DHS first published high-level IoT Strategic Principles that articulated six broad concepts, including:

- Incorporate Security at the Design Stage
- Advance Security Updates and Vulnerability Management
- Build in Proven Security Practices
- Prioritize Security Measures According to Potential Impact
- Promote Transparency Across IoT
- Connect Carefully and Deliberately

Other agencies have also developed more detailed sector-specific guidance. In 2018, the U.S. Food & Drug Administration published draft updated guidance on premarket submissions for "Management of Cybersecurity in Medical Devices," supplementing other previously issued guidance on medical device security.[17] In 2016, the National Highway Traffic Safety Administration published "Cybersecurity Best Practices for Modern Vehicles."[18] On the related category of secure software development, NIST issued a report with high-level recommendations on Dramatically Reducing Software Vulnerabilities at roughly the same time as the DHS Strategic Principles.[19]

IoT guidance has also been promulgated outside of the United States: in November 2017, the European Union Agency for Network and Information Security (ENISA), issued a significantly more detailed set of Baseline Security Recommendations for IoT.[20]

17. *See* https://www.fda.gov/medicaldevices/digitalhealth/ucm373213.htm.

18. *See* https://www.nhtsa.gov/sites/nhtsa.dot.gov/files/documents/812333_cybersecurityformodernvehicles.pdf.

19. Paul Black et al., *NIST Internal Report 8151, Dramatically Reducing Software Vulnerabilities: Report to the White House Office of Science and Technology Policy* (Nov. 2016), https://csrc.nist.gov/publications/detail/nistir/8151/final.

20. *Baseline Security Recommendations for IoT*, ENISA (Nov. 2017), https://www.enisa.europa.eu/publications/baseline-security-recommendations-for-iot.

A. Lack of Incentives

That said, even if more detailed authoritative guidance is promulgated, a serious question remains on whether it would be broadly adopted (and over what time period). The DHS/Commerce Botnet Report asserted that "[m]arket incentives appear to exacerbate the problem. Product developers prioritize time to market and innovative functionality over security and resilience. Security features are not easily understood or communicated to the consumer, which makes it difficult to generate demand."[21] The report continued:

> Many IoT product vendors have articulated plans to enhance the security of their products, but observers have expressed

---

21. DHS/Commerce Botnet Report, *supra* note 3, at 17. The report went on to offer the following points (see page 18):

> Such advances will require significant steps forward in awareness and education for product developers. All product developers must be equipped with the knowledge and skills required to apply the available tools for secure product development. The tool kits and components used by these vendors must reflect security concerns to achieve scale and keep pace with a changing developer workforce, and the partnerships and consortia driving standardized technology must empower developers to make and communicate security decisions. Meanwhile, operational-technology product developers must add basic security requirements to their product-specific knowledge and skills. At the same time, customers must be equipped with sufficient knowledge and information to select products designed to be secure in their environments, and must be aware of the risks presented by all devices, including legacy devices.
>
> Lastly, market incentives will need to align with these security advances, so that product developers who prioritize security and resilience equally with time to market and innovative functionality are rewarded. Clear signals regarding product security and resilience that are accessible to customers will help improve these incentives. However, the value proposition for better security will likely start in the enterprise environment due to its economies of scale; once there is a generally accepted security posture in a given product class, few manufacturers would be likely to ignore it.
>
> The report also noted that "While mitigations exist, many affected devices are not patchable. Since the passwords cannot be changed and the vulnerabilities cannot be patched, these devices will remain vulnerable throughout their lifecycle." (p. 26)

concern that market incentives are heavily weighted toward cost and time to market. Without evidence that customers will absorb the additional cost to develop more secure products, the industry may be incentivized toward a race to the bottom.

So how to address the question of incentives? Five broad incentive categories are relevant: (1) leveraging the power of federal procurement to drive toward more secure current-state and near-future-state IoT technology; (2) leveraging federal grant funding to accomplish the same; (3) using federal authorities to assess and regulate critical infrastructure to do the same; (4) leveraging federal research and development (R&D) resources to advance innovation around IoT security; and (5) providing legal liability limitation to IoT manufacturers and security companies that can demonstrate IoT cybersecurity effectiveness for both current-state and future-state IoT technologies.

II. Leveraging Homeland Security Procurement Authorities

The DHS/Commerce Botnet Report recommended that the federal government "should leverage industry-developed capability baselines, where appropriate, in establishing capability baselines for IoT devices in U.S. government environments to meet federal security requirements, promote adoption of industry-led baselines, and accelerate international standardization."[22]

DHS spends billions of dollars each year on acquisition, operation, and maintenance of assets with potential IoT application. Examples include:

- **Screening and situational awareness.** Based on its broad mission sets of guarding critical infrastructure; screening people and cargo; and patrolling land, sea, and air domains, DHS maintains a massive situational awareness capability.

22. *Id.* at 27.

Sensing and communications devices are core aspects of these capabilities. DHS has requested more than a quarter billion dollars in annual spending for Fiscal year 2019 on sensors alone—examples include:

Agency	FY 19 Budget Request
U.S. Customs & Border Protection leverages unmanned aerial systems, mobile camera systems, and unattended ground sensors to provide situational awareness along the U.S. border. Examples include: • Remote video surveillance systems • Integrated Fixed Towers • Mobile Video Surveillance Systems • Unattended Ground Sensors Additional non-intrusive inspection technologies are used to screen cargo at ports of entry.	$166 million[23]
Transportation Security Administration (TSA) secures civilian air transportation in part through a distributed system of screening technology (checkpoint and hold-baggage x-ray systems, magnetometers, explosives trace detection systems, and whole body imaging systems)	$110 million[24]
U.S. Secret Service protects the president, vice president, and other dignitaries in part through use of threat detection sensors (e.g., explosive detection systems, chemical/biological agent detectors, enhanced camera systems, and portable screening systems)	$10 million

23. U.S. Customs & Border Protection, Fiscal Year 2019 Congressional Justification, *available at* https://www.dhs.gov/sites/default/files/publications/U.S.%20Customs%20and%20Border%20Protection.pdf.

24. U.S. Transportation Security Administration, Fiscal Year 2019 Congressional Justification, *available at* https://www.dhs.gov/sites/default/files/publications/Transportation%20Security%20Administration.pdf.

The use of IoT technology could enable more efficient operation of these sensing technologies, but DHS has also historically experienced cybersecurity challenges in maintaining them.[25]

- **Smart buildings.** DHS manages thousands of facilities across the United States—DHS proposes to spend more than $2.6 billion in FY 19 operating and maintaining these facilities[26] (CBP alone maintains 135 Border Patrol Stations and 328 Ports of Entry, the Secret Service provides security for the White House complex, and FEMA operates numerous emergency and continuity of government facilities).[27]
- **Fuel depots.** U.S. Customs & Border Protection and U.S. Coast Guard air and marine assets make extensive use of fuel depots to supply air, marine, and surface transportation assets.
- **Surface transportation vehicles.** DHS component agencies, when considered together, maintain more than 30,000 vehicles—20,000 for CBP alone, plus 3,500 for TSA, 6,000

25. *See, e.g.*, DHS Office of Inspector General (OIG) Report 16-87: "IT Management Challenges Continue in TSA's Security Technology Integrated Program" (May 9, 2016), *available at* https://www.oig.dhs.gov/assets/Mgmt/2016/OIG-16-87-May16.pdf. While a follow-on OIG Report found that TSA had addressed many of these challenges, it also noted that (a) full remediation was still dependent on "time, money and contract changes," and that a basic disagreement existed on responsibility (as between TSA and airports) for securing closed-circuit television cameras. *See* DHS OIG Report 17-14: "Summary of Report on Audits of Security Controls for TSA Information Technology Systems at Airports" (Dec. 30, 2016), *available at* https://www.oig.dhs.gov/sites/default/files/assets/2017/OIG-17-14-Dec16-redacted.pdf.

26. *An American Budget, Object Class Analysis*, FY 19, Office of Management & Budget, *available at* https://www.whitehouse.gov/wp-content/uploads/2018/02/objclass-fy2019.pdf.

27. Across the federal government, the U.S. General Services Administration owns and leases over 376.9 million square feet of space in 9,600 buildings in more than 2,200 communities nationwide. *See* https://www.gsa.gov/real-estate/gsa-properties.

for ICE, over 650 for the U.S. Secret Service (including the presidential limousine), and an indeterminate number for the other DHS components.

The use of IoT technology could enable more efficient operation of these systems,[28] but could also introduce new vulnerabilities without proper security design, configuration, and maintenance. For its part, the Department of Defense has also identified a number of actions related to how it could more effectively build security into the acquisition of IoT capabilities[29]—many of the concepts articulated by DoD would also apply to DHS.

---

28. *See, e.g.*, U.S. Dep't of Defense, DoD Policy Recommendations for the Internet of Things, December 2016, Appendix C (Use Cases), which offers up DoD IoT use cases that could just-as-well apply in a homeland security context.

29. U.S. Department of Defense, DoD Policy Recommendations for the Internet of Things, December 2016. These concepts include:

- Each IoT acquisition must be supported by a business case.
- Each IoT implementation and associated data streams must be supported by a security and privacy risk analysis.
- IoT data must be encrypted at every point, where costs are commensurate with risk and value.
- IoT networks must be monitored to identify anomalous traffic and emergent threats.
- IoT data will be fed to analytics capabilities and cross-correlated to get the maximum utility from the information.
- IoT devices and Logical Processing Area Networks (LPANS) must be connected to as small a controlled network segment as feasible, rather than having unfettered access to the full IP network.
- IoT devices must only be acquired through approved contract vehicles.
- IoT device supply chains from factory to installation must be actively managed.
- Network operations must be able to verify the network identity of IoT devices, and track the provenance of the information they provide.
- Network operations must be able to detect, isolate, and remove unauthorized IoT devices.
- USCYBERCOM must oversee the policy and processes related to acquiring, testing, and operating IoT networks, and for monitoring the implementation of these policies and processes to ensure a safe, security provision of the associated capabilities (whether connected to the

In theory, the federal procurement process's ability to have an impact (beyond blacklisting nefarious suppliers) presupposes an IoT standard or technology that can demonstrate security effectiveness. That said, federal procurement authorities have been successfully leveraged in the past to bridge a gap between current-state technology and the actual federal need.

For example, in the aftermath of the September 11 terrorist attacks, DHS determined that it required sensors that could capture all ten fingerprints of arriving foreign visitors within acceptable accuracy rates and response times, and yet the technology to do so did not exist. Relying on standard government R&D processes could have taken years to generate an acceptable result (which only then would trigger a lengthy acquisition process), so starting in 2005 DHS took a different approach. DHS held an "industry day" with interested vendors to articulate its desired capability. To demonstrate the priority this issue had, the then-DHS secretary personally spoke at the event. To enhance vendor interest, the event was actually characterized as a government-wide industry day, with representatives from DoD, the Department of State, and even authorities from the United Kingdom and the European Commission.[30] The effect of this characterization was to demonstrate to the vendor community that the addressable market for such technology extended well beyond DHS. And the approach worked: by

NIPRNet, SIPRNet, or another network—such as facility control or building security or medical).

These recommendations should incorporate the following guidances:

- Changes to DoD 5000 series and Defense Acquisition Guidebook
- Changes to DoD 8500 series Cybersecurity and Risk Management
- New DFARS contract clauses
- JIE Technical Guidance and Reference Architectures
- An IoT overlay for NIST guidance

30. *See* Wilson P. Dizard III, *DHS Lays Out Requirements for 10-Fingerprint System*, WASH. TECH. (Nov. 14, 2006), https://washingtontechnology.com/articles/2006/11/14/dhs-lays-out-requirements-for-10fingerprint-system.aspx.

2007, ten print capture devices were being procured and deployed at ports-of-entry around the United States.

The argument could be made that IoT uses cases are sufficiently different as between various federal agencies that alignment on security-related requirements is impracticable. While use cases certainly vary, it also turns out that agencies buy a lot of the same—or very similar—products, as demonstrated earlier (cameras and other sensors, building management systems, vehicles, etc.). So a targeted strategic sourcing industry day would be possible and should be actively considered.

III. Leveraging Homeland Security Grants and Related Guidance to State and Local Authorities and Critical Infrastructure Operators

In 2018, DHS will award more than $1.6 billion in preparedness grants to state and local authorities.[31] These grants help state and local authorities improve capabilities for preventing, protecting against, responding to, recovering from, and mitigating terrorist attacks, major disasters, and other emergencies. IoT capabilities play an increasingly critical role in advancing preparedness but, as noted previously, could also introduce new vulnerabilities without proper security design, configuration, and maintenance.

Moreover, Disaster Relief Funding, which supports the reconstitution of state and local government services after a major disaster, can dwarf steady-state grant funding. For example, Superstorm Sandy resulted in more than $16 billion in public assistance funding, and estimates for FY 2018 Hurricane Maria-related public assistance spending are around $6.6 billion.[32] This funding can also, by impli-

31. Press Release, DHS, DHS Announces Funding Opportunity for Fiscal Year (FY) 2018 Preparedness Grants (May 21, 2018), https://www.dhs.gov/news/2018/05/21/dhs-announces-funding-opportunity-fiscal-year-fy-2018-preparedness-grants-0.

32. *Disaster Relief Fund, Monthly Report as of June 30, 2018*, Fed. Emergency Mgmt. Agency, https://www.fema.gov/media-library-data/153140086

cation, support the acquisition of IoT-enabled capabilities—sensors, building management systems, cars, fuel depots, and so on.

More broadly, the federal government spends over $500 billion annually on grants-in-aid to state and local governments, making grants-in-aid the third largest item in the budget after Social Security and national defense. While much of this funding is targeted at individual assistance, a subset—for example, airport improvement programs, highway and public transportation grants—fund acquisition of capabilities that will increasingly be IoT-enabled.

At least with respect to DHS grants, the agency has the ability to condition grant-funded equipment purchases on compliance with applicable security standards. The FY 2018 Homeland Security Grant Program grant guidance provides that "equipment must meet all mandatory regulatory and/or DHS/FEMA-adopted standards to be eligible for purchase using these funds."[33] Thus, to the extent that IoT security standards did exist and were adopted by DHS, equipment purchased through grant programs could be required to conform to such standards.

IV. Leveraging Existing Federal Authorities to Assess and Regulate Critical Infrastructure

As much as federal agencies spend on technologies with IoT application, this spending is likely eclipsed by private sector technology spend.[34] That does not, however, mean the government is without

---

0821-c2685e3d011f964d289d1c79f485ed2b/July2018DisasterReliefFund Report.pdf.

33. *DHS Notice of Funding Opportunity, Fiscal Year 2018 Homeland Security Grant Program* 68, *available at* https://www.fema.gov/media-library-data/1526578809767-7f08f471f36d22b2c0d8afb848048c96/FY_2018_HSGP_NOFO_FINAL_508.pdf.

34. DHS/Commerce Botnet Report, *supra* note 3, at 26, which offered that "the value proposition for better security will likely start in the enterprise environment due to its economies of scale; once there is a generally accepted security posture in a given product class, few manufacturers would be likely to ignore it."

ability to influence such spending. In fact, the federal government already has a number of regulatory authorities that give it the ability to set expectations on security of IoT devices.

- **Protection of federal facilities.** Federal offices are housed in a variety of facilities, including government-owned, government-leased, and mixed-use commercial properties. The Federal Protective Service (FPS), a DHS agency, provides security for a number of these facilities, including by working with property owners to define expectations around building and security technology. FPS' Advanced Technology Security Program (ATSP) inspectors address facility-automation risks to federal facilities, thereby securing building and security technology against potential threat to unauthorized access to information or control devices.[35]
- **Coast Guard.** The Maritime Transportation Security Act (MTSA) of 2002, enacted after the September 11 terrorist attacks, required the establishment of Area Maritime Security Committees for over 360 ports as well as the conduct of risk assessments and the development of risk-based security plans. In turn, plans may include "passenger, vehicle and baggage screening procedures; security patrols; establishing restricted areas; personnel identification procedures; access control measures; and/or installation of surveillance equipment."[36] It would be irrational to require the installation of unsafe security equipment, thus implicit in MTSA is the ability for the Coast Guard to insist on any security equipment installed pursuant to MTSA to be secure. The same holds true for other regulatory authorities referenced as follows.

35. DHS NPPD Fiscal Year 2019 Budget Justification. ATSP is a risk-based partnership between FPS and DHS. FPS' inspectors are responsible for Tier 1 and 2 activities. The National Cybersecurity and Communications Integration Center (NCCIC) conducts Tier 3 activities.

36. DHS Fact Sheet: Maritime Transportation Security Act of 2002, *available at* http://www.aapa-ports.org/files/PDFs/mtsa_press_kit.pdf.

- **Transportation Security Administration.** The Aviation and Transportation Security Act (ATSA) of 2001, enacted after the September 11 terrorist attacks, established the Transportation Security Administration and required the establishment of Airport Security Programs for over 450 airports across the United States.[37] As with MTSA, it would be irrational to require the installation of unsafe security equipment, thus implicit in ATSA is the ability for TSA to insist on any security equipment installed pursuant to ATSA to be secure.
- **Customs and Border Protection—CBP.** CBP maintains an industry partnership program with companies involved in importing goods into the United States whereby CTPAT members are considered to be of low risk, and are therefore less likely to be examined at a U.S. port of entry. In return, CTPAT members are expected to work with CBP to protect the supply chain, identify security gaps, and implement specific security measures and best practices—for example alarm systems and video surveillance cameras to monitor premises and prevent unauthorized access to cargo handling and storage areas.[38]
- **Chemical Facility Anti-Terrorism Standards (CFATS).** Initially enacted in 2007, CFATS is a federal regulatory program focused expressly on security at chemical facilities. Facilities are required to adhere to a set of risk-based performance standards. These standards not only include capabilities such as measures to screen and control access and detect intrusions, but they also include requirements to address cyber and sabotage risks.[39]

---

37. 49 C.F.R. § 1542, Airport Security.

38. CTPAT Overview, Minimum Security Criteria and Guidelines, *available at* https://www.cbp.gov/border-security/ports-entry/cargo-security/c-tpat-customs-trade-partnership-against-terrorism/apply/security-criteria.

39. DHS CFATS Risk-B Performance Standards Guidance, *available at* https://www.dhs.gov/sites/default/files/publications/CFATS-Risk-Based-Performance-Standards-508.pdf.

A. Non-DHS Regulations

Beyond DHS, a number of other federal agencies are authorized to regulate the use of IoT-enabled security technology. Examples include:

- **Financial institutions.** Almost all banks are regulated by agencies that fall under the umbrella of the Federal Financial Institutions Examination Council (FFIEC). The FFIEC provides guidance to bank examiners on regulatory expectations, including in managing security risks. FFIEC guidance references security and business continuity expectations around numerous technologies that support sensitive bank functions.[40]
- **Nuclear facilities.** All nuclear power facilities are required to comply with safety and security standards promulgated by the U.S. Nuclear Regulatory Commission pursuant to sections 3(c) and (e) of the Atomic Energy Act of 1954, as revised, and section 204(b)(1) of the Energy Reorganization Act of 1974. These standards apply both to physical and cyber protection of facilities themselves as well as to the transportation of nuclear material in transit.[41]
- **Utilities.** Security standards for electric utilities in the United States are established and enforced through a hybrid system: the North American Electric Reliability Corporation (NERC)[42] defines the standards and Federal Energy

---

40. FFIEC Information Security Booklet, *available at* https://ithandbook.ffiec.gov/it-booklets/information-security/ii-information-security-program-management/iic-risk-mitigation/iic8-physical-security.aspx.

41. Nuclear Regulatory Commission website, https://www.nrc.gov/security.html.

42. The North American Electric Reliability Corporation (NERC) was founded in 1968 by representatives of the electric utility industry, for the purpose of developing and promoting voluntary compliance with rules and protocols for the reliable operation of the bulk power electric transmission systems of North America.

Regulatory Commission (FERC)[43] approves them. FERC can also direct NERC to develop new standards, and it has done so for example by directing NERC to develop standards to address risks due to physical security threats and vulnerabilities.[44] NERC Physical Security Standard NERC CIP-014-2 requires, among other items, the development and implementation of a physical security plan for specified transmission facilities.[45] Separate standards require physical safeguards to protect medium and high-impact cyber assets, including physical and electronic access control systems.[46]

- **Health care facilities.** The Health Insurance Portability and Accountability Act of 1996 (HIPAA) established a series of requirements to protect the privacy of personal health information (PHI) and enforced by the U.S. Department of Health & Human Services. Covered entities are expected to maintain physical safeguards to protect PHI, and camera systems are considered as a common control to prevent unauthorized physical access, tampering or theft of PHI.[47]
- **Educational facilities.** Universities receiving federal funding are required to implement a variety of campus safety

43. The Energy Policy Act of 2005 (Energy Policy Act) gave the Federal Energy Regulatory Commission (Commission or FERC) authority to oversee the reliability of the bulk power system, including through approving security standards. *See* https://www.ferc.gov/industries/electric/indus-act/reliability/cyber security.asp.

44. *See* https://www.ferc.gov/media/news-releases/2014/2014-1/03-07-14.asp and https://www.nerc.com/pa/CI/Pages/Physical-Security-Standard-Imple mentation.aspx.

45. *See* https://www.nerc.com/_layouts/15/PrintStandard.aspx?standard number=CIP-014-2&title=PhysicalSecurity&jurisdiction=null.

46. *See* https://www.nerc.com/_layouts/15/PrintStandard.aspx?standard number=CIP-006-6&title=Cyber%20Security%20-%20Physical%20Security %20of%20BES%20Cyber%20Systems&jurisdiction=null.

47. HIPAA Physical Safeguard Standard guidance, *available at* https://www .hhs.gov/sites/default/files/ocr/privacy/hipaa/administrative/securityrule/phys safeguards.pdf.

requirements pursuant to the Jeanne Clery Disclosure of Campus Security Policy and Campus Crime Statistics Act and other federal laws and regulations.[48] Universities are required both to maintain smoke detectors and issue a timely warning for fires and specified crimes that represent an ongoing threat to student or employee safety.

Moreover, federal agencies regulate a much broader range of IoT devices for non-security related purposes—for example, NHTSA has regulatory authority over autonomous vehicle safety, and the Federal Aviation Administration has regulatory authority over aircraft safety. Such authorities have been interpreted to apply to autonomous vehicle[49] and aircraft[50] cybersecurity but are beyond the scope of this chapter. That said, all of the previously described authorities could be leveraged to advance secure-by-design practices.

V. Leveraging R&D Funding to Promote Security Effectiveness of IoT Systems

Beyond procurement, grant, and regulatory authorities, DHS and other agencies have dedicated research and development funding, some of

48. *The Handbook for Campus Safety and Security Reporting*, U.S. DEP'T OF EDUC. (2016), *available at* https://clerycenter.org/wp-content/uploads/2017/01/handbook-2.pdf.

49. *See, e.g.*, 81 Fed. Reg. 185, NHTSA Enforcement Guidance Bulletin 2016–02: Safety-Related Defects and Automated Safety Technologies (Sept. 23, 2016), *available at* https://www.nhtsa.gov/sites/nhtsa.dot.gov/files/documents/final_enforcement_guidance_bulletin.pdf, and Automated Driving Systems: A Vision for Safety, *available at* https://www.nhtsa.gov/sites/nhtsa.dot.gov/files/documents/13069a-ads2.0_090617_v9a_tag.pdf.

50. 78 Fed. Reg. 68985, Special Conditions: Boeing Model 777-200, -300, and -300ER Series Airplanes; Aircraft Electronic System Security Protection From Unauthorized Internal Access, Federal Aviation Administration (Nov. 18, 2013), *available at* https://www.federalregister.gov/documents/2013/11/18/2013-27343/special-conditions-boeing-model-777-200--300-and--300er-series-airplanes-aircraft-electronic-system, and Andy Pasztor, *FAA Advisory Body Recommends Cybersecurity Measures*, WALL ST. J. (Sept. 22, 2016, 9:47 PM), https://www.wsj.com/articles/faa-advisory-body-recommends-cyber security-measures-1474587049.

which can be applied to advancing novel approaches to IoT security. The DHS/Commerce Report also called for the following action:

> The federal government should promote the further development of tools for secure coding practices by sponsoring or performing targeted research . . . and sponsoring competitions for secure toolchains (multi-tool processes for software development) to demonstrate their effectiveness and productivity. The federal government should also work with industry and civil society to develop strategies that make it easier and cheaper to adopt these approaches—including education and training discussed in detail below—keeping in mind the requirements of small businesses, and work with the full range of stakeholders to make such a process observable and verifiable to third parties.[51]

The administration's FY 19 DHS budget requests includes over $40 million in dedicated cybersecurity-related research and development funding,[52] plus almost $300 million in additional R&D-related spend across DHS mission areas.[53] That said, the most meaningful resources to drive generalized technology innovation lie elsewhere in the U.S. government: total development funding in the administration's FY 18 budget proposal amounted to between $118 and $151 billion; depending on how "development" is classified, with the largest shares proposed for DoD, HHS, the

51. DHS/Commerce Botnet Report, *supra* note 3, at 30.

52. DHS National Protection & Programs Division, Fiscal Year 2019 Congressional Justification (R&D), *available at* https://www.dhs.gov/sites/default/files/publications/National%20Protection%20and%20Programs%20Directorate.pdf.

53. DHS Science & Technology Directorate, Fiscal Year 2019 Congressional Justification (S&T R&D), *available at* https://www.dhs.gov/sites/default/files/publications/Science%20and%20Technology%20Directorate.pdf.

Department of Energy, the National Aeronautics & Space Administration, and the National Science Foundation.[54]

R&D funding can serve as a game changer by incentivizing development of more secure technologies, but the nature of R&D investments usually involve extended timeframes. R&D funding should be deployed in two tracks: (1) advancing security of existing IoT devices and (2) promoting security-by-design in all classes of new IoT devices.

- For existing IoT devices, R&D funding could be leveraged to incentivize development and implementation of security solutions whose express purpose is to add a layer of security on top of IoT devices. Solutions could have a role across the assess-mitigate-monitor security risk management lifecycle. For example, innovation could be leveraged to help better threat-model and assess IoT related code and configuration; tools could also help mitigate risk (e.g., through IoT-focused detection and alerting functionality); and they could help monitor risk (e.g., through IoT-specific security testing functionality).
- For new IoT devices, R&D funding could be conditioned on a showing that security is effectively built-in to the design and operation of such devices. In other words, part of the overall determination on the effectiveness of the technology would be its ability to defend itself against a cyberattack.

VI. Leveraging Liability Limitation Authorities to Promote Security Effectiveness of IoT Systems

DHS has unique authorities to grant certain forms of liability protection where security effectiveness can be demonstrated. These authorities can and should be leveraged to advance secure IoT

54. Congressional Research Service Report: *Federal Research & Development Funding: FY 2018*, https://fas.org/sgp/crs/misc/R44888.pdf.

technologies. Following the terrorist attacks of September 11, 2001, there was a concern that the private sector would be reluctant to deploy security technologies and services in civilian environments due to the enormous liability risks involved in their deployment and use. In response to this climate, Congress passed the Support Anti-Terrorism by Fostering Effective Technologies (SAFETY) Act as part of the Homeland Security Act of 2002. The SAFETY Act was designed to encourage the development of anti-terrorism "technologies" (this term has been interpreted to include products, services and programs) by limiting liability related to the development, commercialization and deployment of such technologies, where effectiveness can be proven.

It does this by creating certain limited liability protections for "claims arising out of, relating to, or resulting from an Act of Terrorism" where "Qualified Anti-Terrorism Technologies" (including services) have been deployed. DHS's Science and Technology Directorate is responsible for the evaluation of technologies seeking SAFETY Act designation and must approve all technologies that receive the designation. Moreover, its approval process is timebound: Within 30 days after receipt of an application, DHS is required to notify the applicant in writing whether the application is complete. DHS is then required to make actual approval determinations within another 90 days (although clarification questions from DHS to the applicant can toll the 90-day requirement).[55]

Legislation has recently been introduced to expand SAFETY Act liability limitation coverage beyond acts of terrorism to qualifying cyber incidents.[56] Were this legislation enacted, it would significantly expand the incentive to invest in secure IoT technologies.

55. 6 C.F.R. pt. 25, Regulations Implementing the Support Anti-terrorism by Fostering Effective Technologies Act of 2002 (the SAFETY Act), 71 Fed. Reg. 110, (June 8, 2006).

56. *See* https://www.daines.senate.gov/imo/media/doc/Cyber%20Safety.pdf.

SAFETY Act approval comes in several forms—in particular "designation" and "certification." Benefits of SAFETY Act approval are described in the following table, as are requirements.[57]

	Benefits	**Select Requirements**
Designation	• Liability is capped at insurance coverage limits (these limits are determined by the DHS). • Exclusive action lies in federal court. • No Joint and Several Liability for non-economic damages. • No punitive damages or prejudgment interest.	• Prior United States government use or demonstrated substantial utility and effectiveness. • Availability of the technology for immediate deployment in public and private settings. • Existence of extraordinarily large or unquantifiable potential third-party risk exposure to the selling company or other provider of the technology. • Effectiveness of the technology in facilitating defense against acts of terrorism.
Certification	Designation benefits plus: • Can assert Government Contractor Defense that immunizes Sellers from liability for claims brought under the SAFETY Act. • Placed on SAFETY Act's Approved Product List for Homeland Security.	Designation requirements plus: • Performs as intended. • Conforms to the seller's specifications. • Safe for use as intended. • Seller is required to provide safety and hazard analyses.

57. *See* SAFETY ACT 101 Briefing, U.S. Dep't of Homeland Security, *available at* https://www.safetyact.gov/externalRes/refDoc/refGroup/8/SAFETY%20Act%20101%20Briefing.pdf. This presentation also identifies the complete set of requirements for obtaining Designation and Certification.

Like R&D funding, SAFETY Act coverage should be deployed in two tracks: (1) advancing security of existing IoT devices and (2) promoting security-by-design in all classes of new IoT devices.

- For existing IoT devices, SAFETY Act coverage could be leveraged to incentivize development and implementation of security solutions whose express purpose is to add a layer of security on top of IoT devices. Indeed, the SAFETY Act not only covers sellers of security tools (technically referred to as QATTs) but also protects downstream users of such tools assuming the tool is properly utilized: per the statute, "a cause of action . . . may not be brought against the buyers, the buyers' contractors, downstream users of the Qualified Anti-Terrorism Technology."[58] Thus Designation or Certification could provide liability limitation not only for the developer of IoT security tools, but also downstream IoT users.
- For new IoT devices, liability protection could be conditioned on a showing that security is effectively built-in to the design and operation of such devices. In other words, part of the overall determination on the effectiveness of an IoT technology development, as well as if it is performs as intended and is safe for use, would be its ability to defend itself against a cyberattack.

Unlike R&D funding, legal liability limitation under the SAFETY Act can be a powerful incentive with relatively immediate impact: as noted previously, the SAFETY Act approval process must be completed within 120 days, requires demonstration of actual effectiveness, and protects not only the seller but downstream users. Approaches developed through the SAFETY Act process could then be scaled through federal procurement, grant requirements, and regulations.

58. *Id.*

VII. Conclusion

IoT technologies will play an increasingly important role in America's ability to defend the homeland and carry out a number of other important functions across critical infrastructure sectors. Technology complexity, market pressures, and malicious actors create a dynamic of rapidly increased risks associated with the development and operation of IoT devices. It is vital that the producers of such technologies be incented to implement secure-by-design practices in bringing these products to market and supporting them in the field. Key secure-by-design components will include (1) risk-based secure development practices, including the provision of a software bill of materials; (2) secure configuration practices (both in terms of as-shipped configuration and guidance to customers); and (3) mechanisms for secure updates, upgrades, and patching.

The federal government has meaningful tools in place to incent security-by-design in IoT technologies. So how to address the question of incentives? Federal procurement power can have significant impact, but the concept presupposes an IoT standard or technology that can demonstrate security effectiveness. The same point holds for grant funding and regulatory authorities. That said, the more coordinated that approaches across federal (and state and foreign) buyers can be, the more likely they are to see a meaningful industry effort to advance the state-of-the-art. R&D funding can serve as a game changer by incentivizing development of more secure technologies, but the nature of R&D investments usually involve extended timeframes. By contrast, legal liability limitation—delivered through the Support Anti-Terrorism by Fostering Effective Technologies (SAFETY) Act—can be a powerful incentive with relatively immediate impact: the SAFETY Act approval process must be completed within 120 days, requires demonstration of actual effectiveness, and protects not only the seller but downstream users. Moreover, approaches vetted through the SAFETY Act process could then be scaled through federal procurement, grant requirements, and regulations.

Chapter 11

State Attorneys General Protect Consumers in the IoT Era

Ellen Rosenblum
Cheryl Hiemstra
Katherine Campbell

State Attorneys General are often on the front lines and among the first to respond to emerging consumer protection issues related to data security, consumer privacy, big data, and others involving emerging new technologies. They also play a unique and crucial role in developing and enforcing regulations that prohibit unfair and deceptive acts and practices that harm consumers.

The Internet of Things (IoT) presents both a consumer protection and an infrastructure security issue as more devices are connected to the Internet. The IoT will bring unique challenges that Attorneys General are particularly qualified to address, as they wear both consumer protection and law enforcement hats. From the consumer protection perspective, Attorneys General can spot the trends and issues facing a broad array of consumers on a problematic product or marketplace behavior, ranging from deceptive advertising to market-wide antitrust concerns.

IoT devices bring threats to cybersecurity—with problems ranging from malicious code inserted at the early supply chain stages to multi-vector attacks from IOT-powered botnets. From the law enforcement side, Attorneys General are able to enforce criminal laws, to participate in tackling threats with Information Sharing and Analysis Centers (ISAC), and to coordinate with other statewide entities for a more secure cyber infrastructure.

I. Role of State Attorneys General

State Attorneys General have broad authority to act in the public interest, combined with a responsibility to enforce state laws that protect consumers from unfair and deceptive practices. The state Attorneys General frequently use their consumer protection authority—derived from states' traditional police powers—to investigate violations of law, enjoin harmful conduct, redress consumer harm through injunctive relief and restitution, and deter further violations through strong civil penalties.

As the primary enforcers of consumer protection laws, state Attorneys General are in a unique position to identify emerging marketplace trends and address unfair or deceptive conduct as it occurs. State consumer protection offices are often the first to hear from consumers who have been the target of emerging scams and frauds, and their broad authority allows them to respond quickly. Many states have long-established consumer complaint call centers and online complaint portals. These consumer outreach efforts allow Attorneys General a unique look from the eyes of the consumer at the arising pattern and practices. State Attorneys General also have particular knowledge of local economies and understand how regulation and enforcement affects local businesses.

In the first state Attorney General action against a wireless security company for failing to implement adequate security in its IoT devices, the New York Attorney General recently settled with wireless lock company Safetech.[1] In 2015, SafeTech Products launched a new product—a smart electronic padlock. While clearly observable characteristics of the lock such as appearance, battery life, and "convenience," caught people's attention, what didn't meet the eye proved to be critical security flaws. Safetech did not encrypt its users' passwords when transmitted from a smartphone to the locks. Moreover, it did not force users to reset default passwords, which could be discovered easily by brute force attacks, leaving consumers susceptible to hacking and physical theft.

According to the settlement, the alleged security shortcomings were found despite the fact that the company promised "Privacy When You Want It, Security When You Need It." The Attorney General alleged that the security deficiencies and representations that Safetech made were contrary to New York state laws that prohibit deceptive acts or practices and false advertising, and that give the Attorney General power to enjoin repeated fraudulent or illegal acts.

II. Collaboration with the Federal Trade Commission

Early action by state Attorneys General can prevent a small problem from getting worse, and a local problem from becoming a national one. However, when nationwide issues do arise, the states often join forces to address unfair and deceptive conduct and provide consumers relief. Similarly, the states have a long history of working with federal agencies, like the Federal Trade Commission (FTC), to achieve their shared mandate to protect consumers. The states have some parallel enforcement authority with the FTC,

1. *A.G. Schneiderman Announces Settlement with Tech Company Over Sale of Insecure Bluetooth Door and Padlocks* (May 22, 2017), https://ag.ny.gov/press-release/ag-schneiderman-announces-settlement-tech-company-over-sale-insecure-bluetooth-door.

which fosters a partnership that can maximize limited resources, deter potential violators, and redress consumer harm.

For example, the State of Nevada and FTC worked together to permanently shut down the revenge porn site MyEx. The operators were ordered to pay more than $2 million for violating federal and state law by posting intimate images of individuals and their personal information without their consent and charging takedown fees.[2]

In 2017, New Jersey and the FTC obtained a judgment against VIZIO, Inc., one of the world's largest manufacturers and sellers of Internet-connected "smart" televisions, for collecting viewing histories on 11 million smart TVs without users' knowledge or consent.[3]

Pennsylvania, Connecticut, and the FTC worked together in 2015 on a joint action against a tech support scam that bilked consumers out of more than $17 million by pretending to represent major tech companies. The defendants in the case used Internet advertisements and pop-ups that appeared to be from well-known companies like Microsoft, Google, and Apple to lure consumers into calling them. When consumers called the phone numbers, they were further misled into thinking their computers were infected with viruses, malware, or security breaches, and were given a high-pressure sales pitch to pay for unnecessary tech support and repair services often costing hundreds and sometimes thousands of dollars.[4]

2. FTC v. EMP Media, Inc., 2018 U.S. Dist. LEXIS 107606 (D. Nev. June 15, 2018).

3. FTC, et al. v. VIZIO, Inc., et al., No. 2:17-cv-00758 (D.N.J. Feb. 6, 2017).

4. FTC, et al., v. Click4Support, LLC, et al., No. 2:15-cv-05777-SD (E.D. Pa, Jan. 10, 2018).

III. Data Breaches

Any brief overview of data breaches will reveal a dizzying and skyrocketing trend of more and worse breaches. State legislatures awoke to this problem first, and now every state has a law concerning how entities should handle data breaches.[5] State Attorneys General are able to band together to enforce these laws.

For example, in 2018, all 50 Attorneys General took joint action to address Uber's failure to report a data breach in a timely manner. Uber concealed for more than a year the breach of personal information of more than 57 million people. The settlement negotiated both monetary and injunctive terms.[6]

IV. Privacy, Big Data, and Consumer Protection

The state Attorneys General have significant expertise in enforcing state and federal privacy laws and regulations. They began focusing on technology-related privacy issues in the 1990s. Early enforcement actions targeted intrusive telemarketing, spam, spyware, and the absence of privacy policies. Since then, states have been adapting, enacting, and enforcing privacy laws as technology has changed, consumers' use of technology has evolved, and new threats have emerged.

Attorneys General are witness to a disheartening issue: consumer privacy and data security is often an afterthought in product and service development. This is particularly problematic with IoT devices. Businesses often do not adequately invest in privacy and security protections. Consumer data has inherent value and the free market alone does not adequately protect sensitive data.

---

5. *Security Breach Notification Laws*, NAT'L CONFERENCE OF STATE LEGISLATURES (NCLS), (Sept. 29, 2018), http://www.ncsl.org/research/telecommunications-and-information-technology/security-breach-notification-laws.aspx.

6. *Attorney General Madigan Leads $148 Million Settlement with Uber over 2016 Data Breach* (Sept. 26, 2018), http://www.illinoisattorneygeneral.gov/pressroom/2018_09/20180926b.html.

Consumers have voiced concerns to Attorneys General about what personal information businesses collect, how businesses inform consumers about data collection, and how businesses use and share consumers' data. Businesses must place privacy and security front and center in research and development of products and services.

The state Attorneys General use well-established processes to coordinate regional or national investigations and enforcement efforts. This both increases efficiency and minimizes the burden of concurrent investigations. Through multistate privacy and data security enforcement actions, states work together to obtain injunctive relief and impose civil penalties essential to deterring certain conduct in the marketplace. They require persons who collect personal information to be transparent about privacy practices and to act consistently with representations they make. They also require persons to take reasonable steps to protect data they collect from consumers.

Also important are the independent state actions that the state Attorneys General take under their respective state privacy laws. Many privacy and data security incidents disproportionally affect residents of a particular state. The state Attorneys General are best suited to respond to such incidents involving local businesses and affecting local consumers. For example, a data breach at a small local body shop is only likely to affect area consumers, but can be just as devastating to those consumers in a nationwide breach.

V. Innovations in State Privacy Laws and Regulations

State Attorneys General are often heavily involved with the development and introduction of legislation that supports their role as the chief enforcer of consumer protections. Developments in state laws showcase the role of the Attorneys General in using legislation to address emerging privacy issues. States continue to innovate and update laws to benefit consumers as technology evolves.

As healthcare records became increasingly digitized, many states began to cover patient data as personal information under their privacy laws.[7] Some states have developed laws aimed at protecting biometric data such as fingerprints, and voice and facial recognition data.[8] For example, Illinois and Texas laws prohibit commercial entities from capturing an individual's biometric identifier without his or her consent. Both states also require businesses to protect biometrics using a reasonable standard of care that is the same as, or more protective than, that used for other confidential or sensitive information. They also prohibit selling or disclosing a biometric without consent, with certain exceptions, such as for law enforcement purposes. Further, biometric factors that are unique to an individual could be used to covertly track or monitor the individual's movements, and many consumers fear that this information can be wrongly accessed and misused.[9]

A number of states have enacted laws that require entities to take reasonable safeguards to protect consumer data.[10] In 2017, Oregon updated its consumer law to hold companies accountable for their online privacy policies. Under the law, Oregon's Unlawful Trade Practices Act now applies to the privacy terms consumers agree to prior to downloading an app or other online tools.[11]

---

7. These states include Alabama, Arizona, Arkansas, California, Colorado, Delaware, Florida, Illinois, Kentucky, Maryland, Missouri, Montana, Nevada, New Hampshire, North Carolina, North Dakota, Oregon, Rhode Island, South Dakota, Texas, Virginia, and Wyoming.

8. These states include Arizona, California, Colorado, Delaware, Illinois, Iowa, Louisiana, Maryland, Nebraska, New Mexico, North Carolina, Oregon, South Dakota, Wisconsin, and Wyoming.

9. Samantha Moodie, *Facial Recognition and Biometrics*, NCLS (Nov. 2015), http://www.ncsl.org/research/civil-and-criminal-justice/facial-recognition-and-biometrics.aspx.

10. States include Arkansas, California, Connecticut, Florida, Indiana, Kansas, Maryland, Massachusetts, Minnesota, Nebraska, Nevada, New Mexico, Oregon, Rhode Island, Texas, and Utah.

11. Or. Rev. Stat. 646.607(12)

In 2018, Vermont enacted the first law in the nation establishing a registry and security standards specific to the data broker industry, which collects and profits from the sale of consumer information. Data brokers in Vermont now must register with the Attorney General, take standard security measures, and notify authorities of security breaches. Using consumer data for fraudulent purposes is now its own actionable offense.[12] Also in 2018, California passed the California Consumer Privacy Act of 2018 that affords consumers greater control over their online data.[13]

VI. Consumer Protection in Communication, Information, and Media Technology Networks

State Attorneys General often are the first to learn about consumer protection issues associated with Internet and online commerce. Every year, Attorneys General receive numerous consumer complaints regarding Internet transactions and learn about trends involving new online scams. They also are often the first to hear from consumers about deceptive advertising or billing practices by broadband providers.

States have worked with the FTC to protect consumers against Internet fraud. For example, in "Operation Tech Trap," the commission and many states cooperated in an effort to stave off online tech support scams.[14] In parallel settlements with Lenovo, the commission and 32 states addressed security vulnerabilities in pre-installed

12. 9 Vt. Stat. Ann. §§ 2430, 2446, 2447.

13. Cal. Assem. Bill 375, 2017–2018 Reg. Sess. (Cal. 2018).

14. Participating states include Alabama, California, Colorado, Connecticut, Florida, Hawaii, Massachusetts, Ohio, Pennsylvania, and Texas. Press Release, Fed. Trade Comm'n, FTC and Federal, State and International Partners Announce Major Crackdown on Tech Support Scams (May 12, 2017), https://www.ftc.gov/news-events/press-releases/2017/05/ftc-federal-state-international-partners-announce-major-crackdown.

online shopping adware.[15] Also, in *FTC v. Triangle Media Corp.*, the commission and the Nevada Attorney General halted online marketers responsible for deceptive "free trial" offers.[16]

The state Attorneys General have also enforced consumer protection laws against broadband providers. For example, in *State v. Charter Comm'ns Inc., et al.*,[17] the New York Attorney General's office took legal action against a broadband provider that misrepresented the broadband speeds it offered to consumers.

VII. Consumer Welfare Implications Associated with Data Mining

State Attorneys General know that companies are deploying algorithmic decision tools, artificial intelligence, and predictive analytics and understand these technologies are redefining how companies advertise, market, and price their products and services to consumers. The development of these technologies to process and make sense of big data raises significant consumer protection issues. In light of those concerns, Attorneys General have been conducting thoughtful research and listening to consumer and industry concerns alike. For example, in 2014 the Oregon Attorney General hosted a Privacy Symposium, drawing on knowledge from industry, consumer advocates, academics, and policy makers. Similarly, the Vermont Attorney General conducted several months of hearings on data brokers, and proposed legislation for a data broker registry, among other provisions.[18]

15. Press Release, Fed. Trade Comm'n, Lenovo Settles FTC Charges it Harmed Consumers with Preinstalled Software on its Laptops that Compromised Online Security, (Sept. 5, 2017), https://www.ftc.gov/news-events/press-releases/2017/09/lenovo-settles-ftc-charges-it-harmed-consumers-preinstalled.

16. FTC v. Triangle Media Corp., et al., 2018 U.S. Dist. LEXIS 110465 (S.D. Cal. June 28, 2018).

17. 162 A.D.3d 553 (N.Y. App. Div. 2017).

18. http://ago.vermont.gov/blog/2018/05/24/a-g-new-data-broker-law-is-good-for-vermonters.

An example of consumer welfare and privacy implications associated with the use of these technologies is the health insurance business's use of big data. Data brokers are able to provide health insurers with personal details about consumers, including race, education level, television-watching habits, marital status, and net worth. This very personal information may be sourced from social media, online purchases, or bill payments. The information potentially allows insurers to make a prediction about how much a consumers' health care might cost.

Similarly, the increasing availability of direct-to-consumer genetic testing and genealogy products has allowed the increased gathering and pooling of genetic data. Analysis of this data could be used to determine consumers' premiums for life, disability, and long-term care insurance. Drawing conclusions about health risks from big data could lead to a bias against some consumers and affect consumers' health insurance prices.

The financial services sector might also use these technologies to measure consumer creditworthiness, rather than relying on traditional factors such as FICO scores or income. Although using algorithmic methods and big data may have the potential to expand access to credit, these techniques raise several important consumer protection concerns:

- Creditors may rely on alternative data, such as geolocation or social networking data, which could have the effect of serving as a proxy for race or other impermissible characteristics in violation of federal and state fair lending laws.
- Consumers may lack the protections they have under federal laws such as the Fair Credit Reporting Act to correct inaccuracies and understand how their data is being used.
- Creditors may use alternative data to engage in predatory practices such as extending credit on terms consumers cannot repay.

In both the insurance and consumer financial services sector examples, consumers may not be aware of what personal information these industries collect, how they collect that information, and how the industries use or share their information. Not only does this wide swath of data collection have the potential for financial issues, the more information collected has implications for cybersecurity.

As the state Attorneys General have historically done with previous technological developments, they will continue to monitor industries' use of these emerging technologies for unfair or deceptive conduct.

Chapter 12

ICT in the States

The Challenges of Public Policy Making in the IoT Era

Michael Aisenberg

I. Federalism: An Obstacle or Opportunity for IoT?

The advent of pervasive reliance on software and software-enabled information and communications technologies (ICT) over the past four decades, accelerated by the Internet since the availability of the World Wide Web in the 1990s, has resulted in a state and local government-centered investment in infrastructure and a level of state-controlled activity that rivals, and in some respects exceeds, the vaunted U.S. federal ICT infrastructure. Not only is one uniquely state-sponsored activity—public education—frequently the locus of individual citizens' first serious exposure and training on the use and capabilities of sophisticated ICT devices, but the myriad institutions of state government have become among our nation's most prevalent consumer of ICT equipment, software, and services. In the aggregate, these state and local government functions constitute a significant emerging center of gravity away from the policy chambers of Washington, D.C. and its federally ordained legal structures.[1]

1. As documented by diverse annual survey data, state-supported public and higher education, courts, law enforcement and criminal justice, corrections,

Examples of the public policy nexi and consequences of this emerging state and local ICT center of gravity abound. Among the most visible—if not effective—examples of state "squeaky wheel" technology public policy responses are the wide adoption of variants of UETA (the electronic signature model statute two decades ago), the proliferation of California's "data breach" statutes in over 40 states,[2] and the adoption in 2017 of a rigorous data security obligation on New York-present financial service and banking institutions, administered by the NY State Department of Financial Services.[3]

It should come as no surprise, therefore, that the advent and growth of the phenomenon of ubiquitous device connectivity and other attributes of the IOT "ecosystem" broadly described elsewhere in this volume should reverberate into state, county, tribal, municipal, and other local (SCTML) government environments, sometimes referred to as the "sub-federal" jurisdictions. It is not the authors' intention in this chapter to resolve—or even catalog the myriad policy issues mutually contending for attention by both

taxation, benefits systems, and health care are all also notoriously ICT intensive, dependent, and as we shall explore, vulnerable. Additional critical infrastructures, including surface transportation and public works, water, the ground portion of the national aviation system represented by airports, port facilities, and others recognized as "government services" or government-affiliated are all also increasingly substantially dependent on their embedded software and software-enabled systems.

2. California's Breach Notification bill, S.B. 1386, 2002, became Civil Code sections 1798.29, 1798.82, and 1798.84, and variants have been adopted in over 40 states. In the intervening period, 19 congressional subcommittee hearings on breach notification proposals have been held, with no passage in either House.

3. In March of 2017, the New York Superintendent of Financial Services promulgated 23 NYCRR pt. 500, a regulation establishing detailed cybersecurity requirements for financial services companies. As of August 28, 2017, banks, insurance companies, and other financial services institutions regulated by NYSDFS were required to have a cybersecurity program designed to protect consumers' private data. Penalties began being imposed for non-compliance in September of 2018. A summary of the comprehensive array of specific regulatory measures is provided at https://www.law.com/newyorklawjournal/2018/06/28/062918ny_temkin2.

the federal government and SCMTL entities. Rather, it is to arm the reader and practitioners with an understanding of some important areas where the phenomena of ubiquitous software and software-enabled systems, operating in an environment characterized by the Internet of Things (IoT) and its associated global connectivity, may have left unaddressed or inappropriately allocated significant policy interests, important to consumers, to stewards of critical infrastructures, and to other stakeholders.

These issues, framed and brought into sharp profile by the continuing systemic extensions of interests and impacts associated with the growth of IoT and IIoT, include:

1. ICT acquisition policy among SCTML jurisdictions.
2. Privacy policy and its implication for systems security and data breach in an era of IoT.
3. Regulation of financial services institutions and multijurisdictional transactions.
4. The emerging role of SCTML Inspectors General to address fraud, waste, and abuse in ICT purchasing and deployment.
5. Considerations regarding federal regulatory preemption of state civil suit jurisdiction for injuries due to ICT products.

II. The ICT Public Policy Context: Congressional Policy Gridlock

The emergence of state and other sub-federal regulation of technology activities is often attributed to a lack of progress at establishing federal consensus regulatory and response structures through legislation. The decades-long failure to achieve a uniform federal "data breach" statute is a case in point. This absence of decisive congressional policy action on many cyber issues has resulted in two demonstrable responses: one, in the form of a continuingly expanding body of executive orders and presidential directives addressing aspects of cybersecurity, crime, and information sharing across administrations from Clinton to Bush II, Obama, and

Trump.[4] The second is a growing body of state statutes addressing cybercrime, data breach notification, and other ICT niche topics.[5]

Rather than addressing ICT policy issues that could—and arguably, would—benefit from being addressed through comprehensive federal policy in the form of congressional legislative action, many have instead been addressed by orders of the executive branch, directing only agency behavior and practice.

Some federal ICT policy structures have worked well; the directives in the complex of Clinger-Cohen, FISMA, FISMA II, and FITARA[6] designed to provide cybersecurity protection in the acquisition and deployment of federal agency increasingly networked ICT capabilities, is well designed and reasonably well-adapted across DoD and national security agencies. But, repeated unsuccessful efforts have been made to extend aspects of the FISMA cybersecurity regime to systems under the stewardship of SCMTL governments, and to critical infrastructures and commercial users. The Comprehensive National Cyber Initiative (CNCI) of the Bush administration, the NIST-directed Cyber Security Framework of the Obama administration, and Executive Order 13800 of the Trump administration all represent half-way cybersecurity policy efforts undertaken in the face of congressional inertia; but, interestingly, each is also increasingly more explicit in recognizing the role of software and software-enabled connected

4. NARA Catalog of EOs 2000–2017. https://www.archives.gov/federal-register/executive-orders/disposition.

5. *See, e.g.*, *Cyber Security Legislation 2017*, Nat'l Conference State Legis. (NCSL) (Dec. 29, 2017), http://www.ncsl.org/research/telecommunications-and-information-technology/cybersecurity-legislation-2017.aspx; *Table of Computer Crime Statutes*, Nat'l Conference State Legis. (NCSL), http://www.ncsl.org/GoogleResults.aspx?q=computer%20crime%20statutes.

6. *See* the series of ICT statutes including Clinger-Cohen, FISMA, FISMA II, FITARA; and OMB Circular A-130 (rev. 2016) as implementing policy for federal agency cybersecurity.

technologies—“IoT”—as a predicate for the resort to executive action.[7]

The lack of any truly comprehensive scope of these cybersecurity hygiene measures beyond now-routine federal civilian agency security regimes and practices—such as systems risk management, identity management, and access control—is evidence that both the policy and technology reach of these alternative instruments remain limited, as does their meaningful impact on their intended policy objective—whether a risk source or other systemic objective.

They do not achieve the most fundamental public policy objectives essential to the “IoT” era of pervasive connection of software and software enabled technologies: they do not direct change of vendor behavior or even effectively reach necessary private sector partners.

Congress is only recently thoughtfully addressing the risks arising from the continuing abuses, such as counterfeiting and foreign origin product impersonation in the commercial ICT supply chain.[8] Nor do they address the contract processes by which the $75 to $100 billion in ICT hardware and software are added annually by the states and 16,000 local jurisdictional bodies to the already trillion-dollar ICT installed base in SCMTL infrastructure.

The corpus of executive orders and other presidential directives that has proliferated in parallel with the asserted diminishing capacity of the Congress to reach consensus and pass substantive legislation is well documented. It is neither, however, as dramatic nor pervasive as champions and critics claim. For example, during

7. *See also, e.g.*, the NIST (NIST SP-800-37, SP-800-39) and DoD (DoDI 8510-01 (2014)) implementations of the “risk management” element of the Cyber Framework, and even more explicitly, DoDI 5200.44 “Trusted Systems and Networks.”

8. *See, e.g.*, sec 809, NDAA for FY 2018, secs. 807, 1634, 1646, 1659 NDAA for FY 2019, and the DHS BOD pursuant to its Whole of Government FISMA cyber authority directed by EO 13800.

the years of the Obama administration, the following major ICT/ cyber statutes were passed by the Congress:

- National Cybersecurity Protection Act of 2014
- FISMA II
- FITARA

During the same eight-year period, the following cyber-focused executive orders and presidential directives were issued:

EO	Subject	Date
EO 13587	Improve the Security of Classified Networks	2011
EO 13636	Improving Critical Infrastructure Cyber Security	2013
EO 13691	Cybersecurity Information, Promotion of Private Sector Sharing	2015
EO 13694	Cyber-Related Sanctions Designations, Treasury Department	2015
EO 13702	National Strategic Computing Initiative	2015
EO 13718	Enhancing National Cybersecurity Commission; establishment	2016
EO 13757	Malicious Cyber-Enabled Activities	2017
PPD 21	Critical Infrastructure Resilience and Security	2/12/2013
Presidential Memorandum	Establishment of the Cyber Threat Intelligence Integration Center	2/25/2015
PPD 41	United States Cyber Incident Coordination	7/26/2016

In fairness, the intent and appetite of the last administration to engage in top-to-bottom ICT/cyber policy reinvigoration was substantial; in February of 2016, 11 months before leaving office, the Obama administration released a broad multipronged Cybersecurity National Action Plan, a comprehensive agenda for action that was drafted to be and *should* have been an omnibus cyber policy statute, but instead became a largely unfulfilled cyber shopping list incorporating, inter alia:

- **Establishment of the "Commission on Enhancing National Cybersecurity**." Emphasizing partnerships between federal, state, and local government and the private sector in the development, promotion, and use of cybersecurity technologies, policies, and best practices.
- Proposal of a **$3.1 billion Information Technology Modernization Fund**, which will enable the retirement, replacement, and modernization of legacy IT that is difficult to secure and expensive to maintain.
- Formation of a new position—the Federal Chief Information Security Officer.
- A new **National Cybersecurity Awareness Campaign** launched by the **National Cyber Security Alliance.**
- Partner with technology firms like **Google**, **Facebook**, and **Microsoft**, and financial services companies such as **MasterCard**, **Visa**, **PayPal**, to secure their online accounts and transactions.
- A **federal government agency identity proofing and authentication action.**
- Systematic review to reduce USG reliance on Social Security numbers as an identifier of citizens.
- **Investment of over $19 billion for cybersecurity as part of the President's Fiscal Year (FY) 2017 Budget**.

While some of these proposals were incorporated in EOs and agency initiatives, most of these recommendations failed to secure congressional action and remained aspirational at the end of the authoring administration, and some that were adopted in 2016 were summarily reversed on January 20, 2017, and by EO 13800 later in 2017.

III. What Is at Stake in ICT Policy in the IoT Era?

It is a well-recognized principal of policy under our federal régime that congressional action—adoption of legislation and its codification in federal public law—is preferable to presidential actions, whether through executive order or less formal policy memoranda. Any of these non-statutory measures are by their nature limited in effect to the conduct of federal agencies under Article II authority, and do not reach the conduct of states, localities, or individual citizens.

Given the present policy realities and technology imperatives, the issue is not one of "theoretical Federalism," but rather a practical question: *What must the states and other sub-federal jurisdictions do to get the ICT policy framework right?* The balance of this chapter offers some possible answers for consideration.

In Information and Communications Technologies, the scope and scale of local interest is large, and growing.[9] The scope of the sub-federal interest is thus large and growing. Yet the 'domains of interest' of state policy action, especially statutory action, to date have been limited to squeaky wheel responses, addressing notorious issues such as cybercrime and data breach notification.

In fact, the areas of concern, and of potentially harmful behavior resulting in injury to citizens and economic loss reach far beyond these "tip of the iceberg" issues. They include the entire scope of the increasing ICT reliance in personal and business activities of citizens, as well as the unchecked expansive reliance of state and local institutions on ICT to support their proper execution. Failures of technology, abuses, frauds, and un-remediated anomalous functioning all may contribute to economic *and* physical harm. And in many instances, these harms occur without remedy, as slow or absent federal policy fails to keep pace with exploding presence of

9. Studies by Gartner and others in 2010–2015 report SCMTL commercial ICT investments in the $70 to $75 billion range, expected to have reached at least $78 billion by 2017, and destined to pass $100 billion annually by 2020.

ICT in local critical infrastructures, local businesses, workplaces, highways, and homes.

There is thus a public policy backdrop for ICT in the IoT era that is fragmented and incomplete, both at the U.S. national level, and in the allocation and management of issues between national and SCMTL jurisdictions. Against this fragmented backdrop, the impact of exploding IoT/IIoT and the associated growth of touch points between users, their systems, and the global network is only beginning to be appreciated, both as to its opportunities and benefits, and as to its growth in risks and harm.

IV. Issues of SCMTL ICT Policy Interest in the IoT Era

Five areas of ICT policy with IoT/IIoT implications demonstrate significant SCMTL relevance and interest, and will likely be among those proposed for legislative and administrative structural revisions of current practice. Until there is clear allocation of jurisdiction between national and local policy interests, practitioners and stewards of ICT-intensive assets would do well to pay attention to transactions and disputes in which these issues are implicated, because ambiguity and evolving policy treatment may provide operational, negotiation, contractual/transactional, and even litigation leverage. These five areas are listed here and further elaborated on in the sections that follow:

- Modernize local government contracting for technology.
- *Privacy policy* revision for the IOT era.
- Establish *state and local Inspectors General* as expert investigative bodies (to address vendor "sharp practices" and insider fraud).
- Undo *federal preemption of civil liability suits* for regulated connected (IOT) devices.
- Utilize state *Fusion Centers for Information Sharing* regarding ICT/IOT threats and vulnerabilities.

A. Modernize Contracting for Information and Communications Technology Devices, Software, Services

A watershed area for state action is one that recognizes the economic reality of the information economy. Software and software-enabled devices and appliances that propel this traffic, and its associated trillions of dollars' worth of commerce and other economic activity itself constitutes an enormous economic force of most definite material presence and impact.

As a consequence, the system and rules by which agencies of government acquire these most significant assets are important because of the investment they represent as an expenditure of taxpayer-generated funds, and because of the roles these systems play in both the management and execution of missions and functions of government at all levels.

ICT procurement, along with real estate costs and vehicles, is one of the top three acquisition areas of virtually every jurisdiction in the nation; ICT thus constitutes a significant portion of what citizens' tax payments are being used to pay for. At the federal level, the statutory scheme outlined earlier has produced a model of controls and reviews intended to allow most federal agencies to buy commercial, off-the-shelf ICT products at favorable terms and pricing. But because over $100 billion a year is spent on ICT by the federal government, the recognized presence of costly mishaps, poor negotiation, faulty pricing, supply chain abuse, and counterfeiting, not to mention outright insider theft, fraud, and other misconduct has resulted in a concomitant growth in the ICT-related work of each agency's Inspector General, as well as the congressional spending watch-dog agency, the Government Accountability Office (GAO).

Broad acquisition policies set out in the Federal Acquisition Regulations (FAR), the Defense Acquisition Regulations (DFAR), and ICT-applicable statutes such as the Clinger-Cohen Act, FISMA, FISMA II, and the Federal Information Technology

Acquisition Reform Act of 2014 (FITARA) all provide direction to federal acquisition officers on how to negotiate and obtain desired ICT devices at the best value.

One of the invaluable tools that has evolved in the wake of various statutory directions has been the Program Protection Plan (PPP).[10] The PPP is a planning and tracking tool consolidating all protection efforts associated with the acquisition life cycle of sensitive ICT in the Defense Department, but over time it has evolved to be used across the breadth of the national security community, as well as federal agencies seeking to exercise close control over their ICT investments.

Management tools like the PPP would find important useful applicability in state courts, law enforcement, corrections, taxation, and other sensitive SCMTL environments. PPPs, in conjunction with other security practices, are designed to deny access to Critical Program Information (CPI) to anyone not authorized, not having a need-to-know and prevent inadvertent disclosure of leading edge technology to foreign interests, by tracking each engagement, document, and other transactional element during the planning, consummation, and deployment of an ICT procurement.[11]

---

10. *See* Department of Defense Instruction (DoDI) 5000.02, Operation of the Defense Acquisition System.

11. DoD departmental guidance describes the process used to prepare a PPP when one is required:

- Any program, product, technology demonstrator, or other item developed as part of a separate acquisition process, and used as a component, subsystem, or modification of another program, should publish a PPP.
- Effectiveness of the PPP is highly dependent upon the quality and currency of information available to the program office.
- Coordination between the Program Management Office (PMO) and supporting [law enforcement] and security activities is critical to ensure that any changes in the system CPI, threat, or environmental conditions are communicated to the proper organizations.
- [Law enforcement activities] supporting the program protection effort should provide timely notification to the PM of any information on adverse interests targeting their CPI without waiting for a periodic production request.

Adoption of watershed tools such as PPP to support sensitive and large-volume/high value ICT acquisitions is only one example of multiple tools and techniques in the evolving federal acquisition arsenal that might be usefully adapted to revise state acquisition models. Many of the life cycle controls and tools routinely practiced in federal ICT acquisition, under both the FAR and DFAR could bring the benefits of embedded technology expertise, security, and management best practices throughout the ICT life cycle of system requirement definition, procurement planning, acquisition, deployment, and operations.

B. Privacy

One of the most vexing aspects of Information Technology policy with a state nexus presented by the proliferation of IoT technologies (software and software enabled devices, systems, and services) is the explosion in the parallel proliferation of global, network-wide distribution and availability of sensitive personally identifiable information (PII) propelled by the limitless connectivity these technologies enable.[12]

This data proliferation is true whether the point of origin is a consumer device under control of the data subject and the placement of the PII is intended, and even controlled by the subject, or whether that PII is in a data base, already collected by a third-party entity, whether or not explicitly consented to by the subject, or derivative of some series of data sharing and distribution transactions. And, the concomitant well-documented inability to effectively assess or control this proliferation leads to a challenge for law and policy on which the very nature of the future uses and

12. For the purposes of this discussion, we shall accept as true the proposition that the number of connections potentially reached by any single device is very large, and well beyond the capacity of any individual user to even assess, let alone control.

acceptability of the most robust potentials of IoT technologies may well depend.

Since the earliest articulations of privacy policy, in the Fair Information Practice Principles, whether versions promulgated by government[13] or by non-governmental organizations, one of the essential features of the construct has been the requirement of informed consent from the subject to the collection and use of their PII by the collecting entity.[14]

It may fall to the states as a policy venue to address online privacy in an IoT era. This will include the method and scope of online consent ("informed" or otherwise) in a manner that provides a sufficient foundation for U.S. global entities to make the assertion with European partners and governments that their privacy practices and legal obligations are at least consistent with—if not overtly coordinated through some 21st-century equivalent of the Data Safe Harbor—those imposed by the GDPR.

Many state privacy statutes already go well beyond the agency-only scope of PII stewardship obligations of the Federal Privacy Act, and jurisdictionally sweep in the behaviors of their state chartered corporate persons, and provide protection and remedies for individual citizens.[15] Looking into the future, the challenges will be several:

First, to determine whether there are practices in the privacy arena, obligating either collectors or stewards of PII, that are enforceable under existing state regimes, but functionally consistent

---

13. See FTC's articulation of FIPPs in *Privacy Online: A Report to Congress*, FED. TRADE COMM'N (June 1998).

14. *See* Robert Gellman, *History of Fair Information Practices*, v. 2.18 (last revised Apr. 11, 2017), https://papers.ssrn.com/sol3/papers.cfm?abstract_id=2415020.

15. See *New York State Financial Regulator NY DFS Cybersecurity Regulation*, 23 NYCRR 500 (Apr. 2017), and generic state "Little FTC" regulations in, for example, California, Massachusetts, New York.

with the emerging global privacy framework being driven by the EU's GDPR.

Second, posing the issue, we might ask, "do these Privacy-focused or other native state statutory jurisdictional structures assure meaningful fora and remedies for arguably injured users of IOT devices, in both consumer and commercial environments?" This includes the issue of civil jurisdiction in the state courts and the impact of federal regulatory preemption, discussed in more detail in the following sections.

C. Institution of State/Local Inspector General (IG) Functions

Another tool to add to the SCMTL ICT policy arsenal is an expert body to investigate, prosecute, and recover ill-gotten gains in the course of ICT acquisition and use. Technology acquisition is complex: it goes wrong even when well-planned and managed. Along with the dramatic growth in total IT acquisition by local governments have come increased cost-draining complexities, vendor problems, and outright fraud and abuse in the acquisition and deployment of ICT systems to support local government operations. These reported problems threaten to obliterate the economic benefits of ICT systems and data automation and frequently result in distractions of governments' core mission of public service, all at the expense of the taxpayer. Local governments are challenged to adapt to the responsibility of this growing stewardship of complex IT infrastructure investments. One response to increasing ethical, financial, and criminal abuses in local government operations has been the establishment of local independent Inspectors General offices by a growing number of major urban municipalities and counties.[16]

16. IG offices have been established in Chicago, Philadelphia, Yonkers, Jacksonville, Broward, Miami-Dade and Palm Beach Counties in Florida, Albuquerque, New Mexico, New Orleans and Montgomery County, Maryland.

The dominant "competing" approach to the role of an Inspector General in local government is to do nothing. Other approaches in some jurisdictions include the use of local auditor's offices or financial crimes sections of local prosecutors. These, however, only focus on criminal behavior or statutory violations of procurement procedures, not the range of abuses typically within the broader authority and scope of IG investigations.

IG offices may be established by statute, local ordinance, by the local executive, by a public initiative, or even an NGO (for example, in Chicago, the IG effort has its roots in the independent "Better Government Association"). But, as suggested, the major competing approach remains inertia—the absence of any investment by local governments in rooting out fraud, waste, and abuse associated with the expanding ICT investment. The core capability of a successful IG function is the office's ability to investigate and report on unacceptable practices. The metric of success is a record of changed behavior by acquiring agencies of government; and ultimately, in the ICT context, among the community of technology vendors.

The establishment of the function will eliminate the limitation engendered by its absence; Inspectors General act to identify and investigate waste and inefficient expenditure of public funds, which while related to roles filled by ethics officers and prosecutors, are not their responsibility. In the absence of IG roles, the investigation, auditing and remediation of abuses of local government operations could continue undetected and unaddressed, resulting in continuing cost to taxpayers. Significant successes are being achieved by the jurisdictions that have established local IG offices.

D. Reverse Existing Federal Preemption of State Civil Jurisdiction for Cyber-Based IoT Injuries

A variety of connected ICT devices, software, and software-enabled systems operating on global networks as part of the IoT are subject to federal regulation; as a result, injured individuals who may wish to seek a remedy from the vendor of a failed device—a manufacturer of an unmanned vehicle, or of a connected medical device, or of an electrical appliance that malfunctions and causes harm—may find their path to a judgment is blocked by the federal regulatory scheme.

For example, under present federal law administered by HHS' Food and Drug Administration (FDA), connected medical devices—particularly Class III medical devices whose operation might directly impact patient safety, where any failure might result in serious injury or death—are regulated by the FDA under the Food, Drug and Cosmetics Act (FDCA) and its related Medical Device Amendments (MDA). Because of this regulatory role, if an individual injured by a device sues the manufacturer in state court, the defendant will typically move to dismiss, based on the fact that the federal regulatory scheme places primary jurisdiction over complaints about the product with the federal agency.[17]

Both the statutory framework and associated jurisprudence with regard to the issue of state tort liability of drug manufacturers, and, by extension, medical device manufacturers for claims of damage in state civil litigation are convoluted, evolving and nearly silent on the specific issue of "technology" injuries. These are potential sources of injury resulting not from a failure of an FDA-regulated device to conform to its traditional FDCA "safety and efficacy" requirements but from harm resulting from a software error, connectivity failure, or other "cyber" fault unique to the fact of the device's connection to a network by which its functioning can be controlled, monitored, and impaired. There is little dispute over federal preemption regarding the specific issues

17. This is clear as to pharmaceutical products, presumed as to FDA-reviewed medical devices, and extended by judicial precedent to other federal regulatory régimes, including vehicles whose safety features are regulated by NHTSA and unmanned aerial vehicles regulated by the FAA.

under the FDA's statutory authority over clinical efficacy and medical safety. The concerns arise with respect to the FDA's scope of review and expertise to examine such ICT-specific issues as security of embedded software, network connectivity, or ability to control device access.[18]

But importantly, FDA regulatory review of these thousands of different devices, deployed to millions of health providers and individual patients have historically *not* been structured to determine if the devices have reliable networking software, are secure from external attacks and malicious tampering because of effective firewalls and encryption, or possess access controls which prevent unauthorized individuals from interacting with the device and the patient.

The various state tort liability statutes indeed seem to permit an individual to commence a suit for injury against a device manufacturer; however, withstanding a defendant vendor's motion to dismiss based on federal statutory assertion of "regulatory preemption" is far less certain and has produced a line of cases across multiple jurisdictions, with multiple Supreme Court reviews, which in sum lead to the conventional wisdom that such suits are "preempted by federal law."

The resulting jurisdictional barrier to a civil remedy for these injured individuals (or their survivors) works an obvious unfairness,

---

18. For much of the FDA regulatory landscape, including branded and generic drugs and many medical devices, the statutory schemes and jurisprudence have identifiable focus areas, which can be summarized as three classes of federal jurisdictional preemption articulated in the Supreme Court's opinions in several cases since 2009: express, implied, and obstruction preemption. Particularly for the many existing and emerging devices that can provide life-sustaining functionality of essential physiological systems, largely falling under FDA Class III pre- and postmarket agency reviews, the issue of regulatory compliance is limited to the devices' medical functionality and safety: does the infusion pump deliver the proper volume of medication at the proper intervals, does the oxygen concentrator resist contamination, will the defibrillator continue to deliver accurate voltage during a power failure?

especially when the failure was related to an aspect of the device's performance *not subject to the federal regulatory agency review.* Even those agencies, including some FDA premarket device reviews, which are beginning to address technology flaws such as bad software, counterfeit chips, and failed network security, are doing so prospectively, meaning, for example in the case of connected medical devices, that millions of devices may be in use, connected to networks, but never having been subject to expert review to identify flaws and failures of these network functions.

The result is an environment where citizens injured by network-rooted failures of these devices may be left with no recourse other than a complaint to the regulatory agency, with unlikely prospects of being made whole, particularly where the harm was not simple economic loss, but physical injury or death.

The solution to this uncertain, unfair, and potentially catastrophic limitation of jurisdiction is to counter it with a statutory grant of specific jurisdiction at the state level with particular reference to the federal regulatory régimes and focused specifically on devices where the software and network connectivity capabilities of the devices were never reviewed by the federal regulatory agency.

E. Fusion Centers for IoT Flaw Information Sharing

An additional SCMTL capability in this suite of ICT enhancements is to repurpose—or more precisely—expand the jurisdiction of the 79 existing, largely state-hosted Fusion Centers that were established across the nation in the wake of the 9/11 attacks and have continued to operate since that time. While the principal purposes of these joint federal/state/local centers established by the interagency DoJ/DHS Fusion Center capability were counterterrorism intelligence and drug interdiction, their structure and capabilities, coupled with multi-agency state and local representation, make them an ideal additional "eyes and ears" function in support of improved state and local ICT environments.

Because they maintain both an intra-state and national cross-Fusion Centers communications capacity, these centers can provide relief for a chronic problem of the ICT environment: the failure to promptly share and communicate the details of systems and networks failures, attacks, and other anomalies. By sharing in real time the existence of flaws in IT systems, software, and services, these centers can become a backbone element of a nationwide sharing environment long contemplated by the ISAC community, the Sector Coordinating Councils, and the ISAOs developed under the DHS/NIST Cyber Framework.

V. Future Paths

There is nothing particularly magical or substantively unprecedented by any of these proposals. Civil jurisdiction debates around federal preemption have swirled for years. The importation of federal best practices for ICT procurements that are relevant to the concerns of states and localities is neither unduly complex nor itself unprecedented. (States have been free to utilize GSA schedule procurement vehicles in a number of product areas for two decades.) As discussed, the number of localities adopting local Inspectors General capabilities is now perhaps in the hundreds, and it is growing. And Fusion Centers are currently utilized to share information on a 24/7 basis; it simply would be novel for them to adapt their capabilities to the routine sharing of ICT/IOT flaw, error, anomaly, or attack information.

From the perspective of pure policy making, once a critical mass of consensus on any of these various approaches is reached in the SCMTL community, the framework of authorities and organizational structures to implement them could be formalized and harmonized through a comprehensive uniform state statute addressing all of the discussed issues, to be developed by the Uniform Law Commission (ULC). Individual tailoring in the state legislatures could readily be accomplished to respond to unique local environments or interests, such as the presence of significant industries (financial services in New York, media and technology in California). For some, such as the long-lingering federal data breach discussion, a national approach is widely viewed as desirable; as this discussion demonstrates, however, the states have both adequate means and equities in each area to act without further delay.

The author's affiliation with the MITRE Corporation is provided for identification purposes only and is not intended to convey or imply MITRE's concurrence with, or support for, the positions, opinions, or viewpoints expressed by the author.

Chapter 13

IoT Licensing Issues and Interoperability

Christopher A. Suarez[1]

I. Introduction

As the Internet of Things (IoT) proliferates, there will be an increasing need for interoperability across IoT devices and systems. Every integrated IoT system controls and receives data from a wide range of devices, such as sensors that monitor temperature and motion, or actuators that turn on lights or tweak the temperature. Right now, we are at a point where many IoT systems operate to some extent in their own "walled gardens"; devices such as Google's Assistant, Apple's Homekit, and Amazon's Echo are designed to interoperate primarily with those companies' own sensor and actuator products, but pressure is mounting on those companies and others to make their IoT platforms increasingly interoperable with their competitors' products.[2] According to a recent study, 75 percent of consumers who plan to purchase a smart home device view it as essential

1. The statements and opinions expressed in this chapter are the author's own and do not necessarily reflect the views of, and should not be attributed to, Williams & Connolly LLP or its clients.

2. Shane Hedmond & Dustin Chapman, *Amazon's Alexa, Interoperability, and What Construction Can Learn*, CONSTRUCTION JUNKIE (Jan. 19, 2017), https://www.constructionjunkie.com/blog/2017/1/12/amazons-alexa-interoperability-and-what-construction-can-learn.

that the device connects seamlessly to other devices in their home network, regardless of brand.[3]

Beyond smart home systems and technologies, moreover, other technologies like connected cars will need to interface with a wide range of technologies, including GPS satellites, road sensor technologies, and more. To drive autonomously, connected cars will need to be familiar with the positions of other vehicles and objects on or near the road, and there may be a need to communicate between and among different vehicles.[4] These requirements may require the use of common networks (such as 5G) or new open communication standards that will facilitate interoperability.

With these principles in mind, this chapter discusses the seemingly inevitable need for interoperability and standardization in the IoT. It considers several IoT industries where interoperability will be particularly important, including the health care industry and the smart home and connected car industries just referenced. It then provides an overview of some of the implications of an interoperable IoT on technology licensing, with a particular focus on patent licensing issues that are likely to arise as the IoT grows.

II. The Trend toward Standardization and Interoperability in the IoT

As just noted, there is a growing trend toward standardization and interoperability across several IoT industries. In this section, we consider some of those trends in three specific industries: the medical IoT, smart homes, and connected cars. These trends, of course, could apply to other industries as well.

---

3. Dan Alamo, *75% of Smart Home Device Purchasers Value Interoperability*, Retail Dive (June 14, 2018), https://www.retaildive.com/news/75-of-smart-home-device-purchasers-value-interoperability/525476/.

4. Brad Schechter, *The Equation for Interoperability in Today's Connected World*, OpenText (June 25, 2015), https://www.covisint.com/blog/the-equation-for-interoperability-in-todays-connected-world/.

A. The Medical IoT

There are more than 3.7 million medical devices in use today that connect to and monitor various parts of the body. In the medical IoT space, interoperability will likely become increasingly relevant over time. Interoperability is such a concern in the medical space that entire patents have been devoted to it. For example, U.S. Patent No. 9,820,658, granted in 2017, is entitled "Systems and Methods for Providing Interoperability among Healthcare Devices."

There are numerous medical IoT devices, including wearable fitness monitoring devices that collect health data, including sleeping patterns, heart rate information, and other data; wearable treatment devices, including insulin pumps and electrical nerve stimulation devices; and hospital grade monitors, ventilators, and pumps. All of these devices can be used to monitor the health information of patients, and could be connected to the Internet or other networks to monitor the overall health and well-being of patients. Patents are being filed on these technologies nearly every day. One relatively recent example, filed by DexCom, was an application for a medical delivery pump that could administer medicine to a patient and be connected to one's smartphone, as shown in Figure 13.1.[5]

The challenge in the medical IoT is that medical devices use numerous different communications protocols and standards, whether radio frequency identification (RFID) within a hospital or clinical setting, or Wi-Fi (802.11) or cellular communication (4G or 5G) in a home setting.[6] These devices also need to be able to furnish and provide medical data in a streamlined way; there are

5. U.S. Patent Pub. No. 2015/0120317.

6. Known medical interoperability standards include HL7 v. 2.X / V3CDA (for Clinical Document Architecture), the Fast Healthcare Interoperability Resources Standard (FHIR), Common Technology Standards for distributing and updating terminological resources (CTS2), Digital Imaging and Communications in Messaging (DICOM), the UN Standard for International Electronic Data Interchange (EDIFACT), and Electronic Business Using eXtensible Markup Language (EbXML), among others.

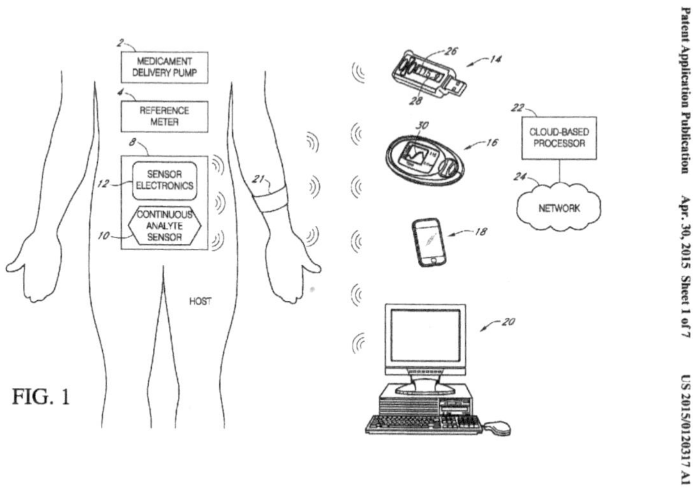

FIG. 1

Figure 13.1 A Framework for a Medical IoT Delivery Pump

unique standards for exchanging medical documentation, digital imaging, and international medical records, and these standards for data exchange are particularly important given the privacy concerns associated with medical data, and the need for consistency in treatment across borders and doctors' offices.[7] With so many standards potentially at play, medical devices will need to be compatible with and licensed for a wide range of technologies—each having numerous players.

B. Smart Home IoT Devices

Interoperability will also be critical in the context of smart home technology. As noted above, a recent study confirmed that nearly 75 percent of consumers want smart home devices to be able to connect seamlessly to their home electronic networks, and that the interoperability of devices matters far more than brand loyalty.[8] Consumers are going to want smart plugs, smart refrigerators, smart

7. For a discussion of IoT medical privacy issues, see the discussion in Chapter 2 of this volume.

8. Alamo, *supra* note 3.

floors, and other "smart" devices that can communicate with one another and monitor activities in the home seamlessly and without the need to cobble together numerous different configurations and applications. Right now, interoperability of smart home technologies remains quite low, which is limiting adoption.[9]

Unsurprisingly, numerous standards to promote interoperability among IoT devices have emerged over the years. One such standard is from the Open Service Gateway Initiative (OSGi), which is a specification that promotes interoperability among plug-and-play, modular Internet-enabled devices.[10] Standards like OSGi help facilitate communications and data collection across IoT devices in a streamlined way. OSGi is unique in that it is a relatively open standard; the OSGi Alliance and five major technology companies, including Nokia, IBM, Samsung, Makewave, and ProSyst Software agreed to license their patents to this standard on a royalty-free basis to encourage broad adoption.[11]

However, OSGi is simply a protocol that can be used to standardize IoT device installation, control, and monitoring. It does not itself furnish *connections* between devices; that has to be done via Wi-Fi, Bluetooth, cellular, or some other communications technology. IoT smart home devices employ numerous communications protocols, including Wi-Fi (802.11b, 802.11ah), Bluetooth, Zigbee, and Z-Wave.[12] There are pros and cons to each: Wi-Fi has

---

9. Tom Kevan, *The Smart Home's Pursuit of Interoperability*, DIGITAL ENGINEERING (July 1, 2018), https://www.digitalengineering247.com/article/smart-homes-pursuit-of-interoperability/.

10. Margaret Rouse & Jenifer Winter, *OSGi (Open Service Gateway Initiative*, SEARCHNETWORKING, https://searchnetworking.techtarget.com/definition/OSGi (last updated March 2011).

11. OSGi Alliance, *OSGi Non-Assert Patent Pledge*, https://www.osgi.org/osgi-non-assert-patent-pledge/.

12. These are the most commonly discussed IoT standards used in the Smart Home context, but there are many more, including IoTivity (Open Interconnect Consortium), AllJoyn (Allseen Alliance), Thread (Thread Group), OneM2M, WiFi HaLow (802.11ah), and ITU-T SG20. *See* Stephanie Lynn Sharron &

high data rates and good transmission ranges but consumes substantial amounts of power; Bluetooth has historically been a short-range technology but has low power consumption; and Zigbee and Z-Wave use mesh networking and low bandwidth communications. And some of these standards are proprietary while others are not—as an example, Z-Wave is a proprietary system while Zigbee is an open standard.[13]

Smart home systems often use some combination of the previously mentioned communication technologies to connect various sensor and actuator devices to a gateway or hub device, or to the Internet. Hub devices help solve the interoperability problem in the IoT context because they can be configured to be compatible with a wide range of communications protocols, and such hubs can be used to transmit data to the Internet cloud. For a hub to be useful, however, this also means that companies need to be licensed to a wide range of communications technologies. In sum, there is no escaping the need for interoperability in the smart home context, whether the interoperability is needed to standardize data collection and installation, or whether it is needed to streamline and harmonize communications between the numerous IoT devices in a smart home system.

C. Connected Cars

Another area where interoperability will be crucial will be in the realm of connected cars. Definitions of connected cars vary, but, in general, a "connected" car can refer to any car that communicates with the outside world, whether via GPS satellites, the Internet, or

---

Nikita A. Tuckett, *The Internet of Things: Interoperability, Industry Standards & Related IP Licensing Approaches*, Socially Aware (Feb. 2, 2016), https://www.sociallyawareblog.com/2016/02/02/the-internet-of-things-evaluating-the-interplay-of-interoperability-industry-standards-and-related-ip-licensing-approaches/.

13. Kevan, *supra* note 9.

near field communication. As connected cars become increasingly autonomous, interoperability will be crucial, because cars will need to know the location of other cars and objects on the road, and will need to be capable of communicating with GPS and Internet technologies in order to have a clear picture of other aspects of the environment, including weather and traffic patterns. Any connected car will need to be able to seamlessly communicate with the outside world to receive all of this needed data.

5G technologies will certainly facilitate increasingly seamless communications between connected cars and their surrounding environment. 5G technology, however, will not be widely deployed on cellular networks until at least 2020.[14] Therefore, recent operability testing for connected cars has focused on 4G LTE technology. For example, Rohde and Schwartz and Huawei recently (and successfully) tested the interoperability of LTE-V connected vehicles between connected cars in the wake of the World Internet of Things Conference in Wuxi, China—these tests demonstrated promise in establishing direct communications between vehicles using LTE technology.[15]

One interesting interoperability issue in the context of connected cars will be whether regulatory and state authorities will prioritize the use of Wi-Fi technology of 5G technology in connected cars in the near future. Wi-Fi has already been used for vehicle-to-vehicle (V2V) communications in Europe, which is based on short-range communications. However, vehicle-to-everything (C-V2X)

14. *See, e.g.*, David Nield, *Apple Tipped to Launch a 5G iPhone in 2020*, Techradar (Nov. 2, 2018), https://www.techradar.com/news/apple-tipped-to-launch-a-5g-iphone-in-2020.

15. *R&S and Huawei Conduct LTE-V Interoperability Tests for Connected Vehicles*, EverythingRF (Oct. 30, 2018), https://www.everythingrf.com/News/details/7101-R-S-and-Huawei-Conduct-LTE-V-Interoperability-Tests-for-Connected-Vehicles; *see also LTE-V: The Future Is Connected,* Audi MediaTV (Feb. 27, 2017), https://www.audi-mediacenter.com/en/audimediatv/video/lte-v-the-future-is-connected-3454.

technology would rely on 5G and be a more forward-looking solution.[16] Of course, a hybrid approach that includes both Wi-Fi and 5G may well emerge as the successful one, but industry groups that include BMW and Ford, among others, have wanted to ensure a focus on 5G, viewing Wi-Fi technology as a possible diversion.[17]

All of these issues will be important, because, as in the medical and smart home spaces, there has been an explosion of patents in the connected car space. There are thousands of patents in the connected car space—as but one example, Ford has at least 200 patents in the connected car area.[18]

III. Licensing in an Interoperable IoT

Assuming that the interoperability trend continues in the IoT space across these various technology areas, attorneys will need to understand the role relevant legal standards and licensing will play in an IoT era. Specifically, they will need to understand the importance of standards essential patents (SEPs), which became increasingly important with the rise of smartphone technology during the 2000s and 2010s. The smartphone patent wars generated a tremendous amount of litigation, primarily around the standardized 3G and 4G radio technology used by smartphones and their apps.[19] Smartphone manufacturers needed (and continue to need) licenses to 3G and 4G technology to compete in the marketplace. As the IoT

16. Diana Yordanova, *Industry Split on European Connected-Car Rules*, Wards Auto (Nov. 16, 2018), https://www.wardsauto.com/technology/industry-split-european-connected-car-rules.

17. *Id.*

18. *Which Companies Lead the Connected-Car Patent Race?*, NetScribes (Oct. 15, 2018), https://www.netscribes.com/companies-leading-connected-car-patents/.

19. The radio technology known as 3G and 4G was standardized as a result of a collaborative project known as 3GPP. A major participant in 3GPP is the European Standards Telecommunications Institute (ETSI). Many of the companies that participated in ETSI and 3GPP declared patents that are essential to the 3G and 4G telecommunications standards.

takes hold and even more standards (including 5G and the various standards just referenced) proliferate in the medical IoT, connected cars, smart homes, and other technology areas, the standards wars are likely to multiply, and device manufacturers in the IoT will need licenses to standardized technology applications.

A. Standards Essential Patents and Licensing

Typically, patents confer an unfettered right for the patentee to exclude competitors from practicing a technology. This means that, in most cases, patent owners can choose to grant (or refuse to grant) licenses to a particular technology as they please. But for patents that are "standards essential"—that is, necessary to implement a technological standard such as 4G, 5G, or Wi-Fi, for example—the obligations of licensors are typically different because standards bodies (such as the IEEE, 3GPP, or ETSI) usually place an obligation on the licensor to confer licenses on fair, reasonable, and nondiscriminatory (or FRAND) terms.

In the context of the IoT, several licensing principles will be relevant to whether a licensor has provided a possible licensee with a "fair" or "reasonable" license to patents or other protected intellectual property. In the United States, many of these principles are drawn from patent damages law. One principle, for example, is one of *proportionality* or *apportionment*. Under this principle, the royalty attributable to a patent "must reflect the value attributable to the infringing features [i.e., the technological contributions]" of the patent to the technology at issue, "and no more."[20] This principle "is 'the governing rule' 'where multi-component products are involved.'"[21] Indeed, expert evidence in American licensing cases must separate out the contribution of licensed patents to the

20. Ericsson, Inv. v. D-Link Sys., Inc., 773 F.3d 1201, 1226 (Fed. Cir. 2014).

21. Commonwealth Sci. & Indus. Res. Org. (CSIRO) v. Cisco Sys., Inc., 809 F.3d 1295, 1302 (Fed. Cir. 2015).

technology at issue from the technology that is unrelated to the patents in order to determine an appropriate FRAND rate.[22]

Generally speaking, the apportionment principle has been important in the context of the smartphone patent wars, as a particular patent may only relate to the technology incorporated into a portion of a single component of a smartphone (such as the phone's graphics processor), and not to numerous other components of the phone, such as the screen, radio interface, audio hardware, or whatever else. Clearly, a patent that bears on but one, relatively minor aspect of the standard should be worth far less than a patent that bears on several, crucial components of the device. And a high percentage royalty to obtain a license to a single patent (say, 5 percent), may make little sense in the context of a product—like smartphones—with thousands of components, particularly where there may be thousands more patents that will need to be licensed. This apportionment principle will likewise be important in the context of the IoT: Smart home platforms and connected cars have far more standards incorporated into their larger systems than smartphones do, and there may be greater challenges in apportioning the value of a particular patent to a given technological innovation in these contexts. Licensors and licensees will have to bear this challenge in mind when licensing patents in the IoT.

Apportionment is uniquely important in the context of SEPs, moreover, because patents should not be accorded disproportionate value simply because they are "essential" to an important standard, such as 4G or 5G. In some cases, an SEP may relate to a relatively minor aspect of a standard, or in other cases merely to "optional" portions of standards that are rarely, if ever, used. This is why, in *Ericsson v. D-Link*, the Federal Circuit pointed to unique considerations that apply to apportionment in the SEP context:

---

22. *See* VirnetX, Inc. v. Cisco Sys., Inc., 767 F.3d 1308, 1329 (Fed. Cir. 2014).

> When dealing with SEPs, there are two special apportionment issues that arise. First, the patented feature must be apportioned from all of the unpatented features reflected in the standard. Second, the patentee's royalty must be premised on the value of the patented feature, not any value added by the standard's adoption of the patented technology. These steps are necessary to ensure that the royalty award is based on the incremental value that the patented *invention* adds to the product, not any value added by the standardization of that technology.[23]

Again, when considering an appropriate license, the actual contribution of a licensed patent to the technology in a product is what it is crucial, not the mere fact that there is a patent that covers the technology or that a particular patent happens to be "standards essential." Additionally, even where a patent is "essential" to a standard that is important to a particular product, there may be hundreds or thousands of SEPs that cover a particular standard—some of those SEPs are more valuable than are others.[24]

Another, related principle to the apportionment principle is the *smallest saleable unit* principle. Under this principle, "where a damages model apportions from a royalty base, the model should use the smallest salable patent-practicing unit as the base."[25] For example, if a patent to be licensed relates only to the "infotainment" system of a connected car, the royalty base from which to calculate a percentage royalty should be the "infotainment" system

23. *Ericsson*, 773 F.3d at 1232.

24. In some instances, a standardized technology (such as 2G or 3G) may comprise thousands of standards essential patents. Often, litigators and damages experts will engage in patent counting exercises to determine the relative value of a company's SEPs, as well as technical and other analyses to understand the contribution of any given patent to the relevant standard. *Industry Report—How to Count and Valuate Standard-Essential Patents*, IAM (Nov. 15, 2017), https://www.iam-media.com/how-count-and-valuate-standard-essential-patents.

25. *CSIRO*, 809 F.3d at 1302.

(or perhaps even a separately sold chip within that infotainment system), rather than the car as a whole. This principle (1) prevents licensors from being unfairly compensated for technology that is not related to the licensed patent; and (2) avoids misleading fact finders, including juries or arbitrators, by placing undue emphasis on the value of an overall product.[26]

Additional factors can be used to determine reasonable patent-licensing royalties, including a list of several factors known as the *Georgia Pacific* factors.[27] These "factors" include numerous pieces of evidence that are relevant to a hypothetical negotiation that would have taken place between a potential licensor and licensee,[28] and frequently emphasize the use of comparable licenses that license similar patents or technologies, the nature of

---

26. *Id.* Note that an exception to the smallest saleable unit principle is known as the "entire market value" rule. Under this "narrow exception," "if a party can prove that the patented invention drives demand for the accused end product, it can rely on the end product's entire market value as the royalty base." *CSIRO*, 809 F.3d at 1302 (citing LaserDynamics, Inc. v. Quanta Computer, Inc. 694 F.3d 51, 67 (Fed. Cir. 2012)). This exception will rarely, if ever, be invoked in the IoT, where products will be so complex and have so many components that it will be exceedingly difficult to show that a particular patented technology is the singular driver of demand for a complete connected car or smart home automation system, for example.

27. *See* Georgia-Pacific Corp. v. U.S. Plywood Corp., 318 F. Supp. 1116, 1120 (S.D.N.Y. 1970).

28. The full list of *Georgia-Pacific* factors relevant to a reasonable royalty analysis includes:

1. The royalties received by the patentee for the licensing of the patent in suit, proving or tending to prove an established royalty.
2. The rates paid by the licensee for the use of other patents comparable to the patent in suit.
3. The nature and scope of the license, as exclusive or nonexclusive; or as restricted or nonrestricted in terms of territory or with respect to whom the manufactured product may be sold.
4. The licensor's established policy and marketing program to maintain his patent monopoly by not licensing others to use the invention or by granting licenses under special conditions designed to preserve that monopoly.

the relationship between the parties to those licenses, and the value of the patented technology at issue.[29] The "comparable license" methodology "begins with rates from comparable licenses and

---

5. The commercial relationship between the licensor and licensee, such as, whether they are competitors in the same territory in the same line of business; or whether they are inventor and promoter.
6. The effect of selling the patented specialty in promoting sales of other products of the licensee; that existing value of the invention to the licensor as a generator of sales of his non-patented items; and the extent of such derivative or convoyed sales.
7. The duration of the patent and the term of the license.
8. The established profitability of the product made under the patent; its commercial success; and its current popularity.
9. The utility and advantages of the patent property over the old modes or devices, if any, that had been used for working out similar results.
10. The nature of the patented invention; the character of the commercial embodiment of it as owned and produced by the licensor; and the benefits to those who have used the invention.
11. The extent to which the infringer has made use of the invention; and any evidence probative of the value of that use.
12. The portion of the profit or of the selling price that may be customary in the particular business or in comparable businesses to allow for the use of the invention or analogous inventions.
13. The portion of the realizable profit that should be credited to the invention as distinguished from non-patented elements, the manufacturing process, business risks, or significant features or improvements added by the infringer.
14. The opinion testimony of qualified experts.
15. The amount that a licensor (such as the patentee) and a licensee (such as the infringer) would have agreed upon (at the time the infringement began) if both had been reasonably and voluntarily trying to reach an agreement; that is, the amount which a prudent licensee—who desired, as a business proposition, to obtain a license to manufacture and sell a particular article embodying the patented invention—would have been willing to pay as a royalty and yet be able to make a reasonable profit and which amount would have been acceptable by a prudent patentee who was willing to grant a license. *Id.*

29. *Id.*

then 'account[s] for differences in the technologies and economic circumstances of the contracting parties.'"[30]

B. FRAND Obligations and Standard Setting Organizations

Familiarity with the preceding principles—including apportionment and comparable licenses—will be important to any practitioner who seeks to be involved in technology licensing in an IoT era. And a basic understanding of those tools will be useful to someone trying to license any technology, even if the technology is not "standards essential." For SEPs, however, it will be particularly important for practitioners to place the SEP licensing obligations in their proper context: in particular, they will need to understand both the particular standardized technology at issue and the standard setting organization (SSO) that developed the particular standard. As noted previously, ETSI/3GPP is the SSO that oversees the development of the 3G, 4G, and 5G standards. And the Institute of Electrical and Electronics Engineers (IEEE) is the SSO behind the development of Wi-Fi standards, including 802.11b and 802.11ah (HaLow).

Knowledge of both the technology and SSO relating to a particular SEP is very important for practitioners involved in the licensing of any standardized technology for several reasons. *First*, the technical specifications for each standardized technology (such as 4G) are developed according to processes developed by the particular SSO, and practitioners should be familiar with those processes. Typically, organizations like ETSI hold numerous meetings to develop the standards, and the minutes of these meetings provide insights into the companies and key players who developed and provided input into the standards. *Second*, and more importantly,

30. *CSIRO*, 809 F.3d at 1303 (quoting *Finjan, Inc. v. Secure Computing Corp.*, 626 F.3d 1197, 1211 (Fed. Cir. 2010)).

each SSO has its own policies around intellectual property rights, including policies relating to how standard-setting participants must (1) declare patents to a particular standard; and (2) license those patents to fellow participants in the standards-setting process, or to others.

The SSOs' intellectual property right policies provide valuable information about the treatment of SEPs by the relevant organization, and can constitute contractual obligations. As an example, the ETSI policy, as adopted on October 8, 2018, has a provision (section 6.1) that strongly encourages patent owners to license their essential IPR on FRAND terms.[31] And, if a member of ETSI who contributes to a standard refuses to provide such licenses, ETSI has intricate policies (section 8) that encourage the member to reconsider and, if not, procedures that would remove the member's technology as an "essential" component of the standard.[32] Thus, ETSI's policies virtually ensure that SEPs associated with 3G, 4G, and eventually 5G technologies will be subject to FRAND obligations. This happens in practice via an ETSI declaration form. On these forms, the relevant SEPs are declared by the patentee as being essential to a particular standard, and the patentee makes the FRAND commitment (pursuant to section 6.1 of the ETSI policy) on the very same form.[33] The IEEE has similar policies, including a policy (section 6.2) that encourages all SEP holders to license SEPs at "reasonable rates" and to declare their intent to provide such licenses using a letter of assurance that is similar to the ETSI declaration form.[34] The IEEE's IPR policy also

31. ETSI Rules of Procedure, Annex 6: ETSI Intellectual Property Rights Policy (Apr. 18, 2018), https://www.etsi.org/images/files/IPR/etsi-ipr-policy.pdf.

32. *Id.*

33. *Id.*

34. IEEE-SA Standards Board Bylaws—Policies and Procedures, IEEE (last visited Nov. 25, 2018) https://standards.ieee.org/about/policies/bylaws/sect6-7.html#loa; IEEE Letter of Assurance for Essential Patent Claims (last

promotes FRAND licensing. It encourages patentees to disclose sample licensing agreements, terms, and maximum licensing fee or rate commitments.[35] The IEEE policy is also noteworthy in that it expressly incorporates both the apportionment and smallest salable unit principles discussed earlier, along with the use of comparable licenses, in defining what may be "consider[ed]" in determining what a "reasonable rate" could be to license an SEP.[36]

IPR policies of other IoT-related SSOs are worth noting. For example, OSGi—an open specification—has IPR policies that ensure that any contributors to the OSGi specification furnish trade secret and copyright licenses to OSGi and its participants, along with royalty free licenses to essential patent claims that read on the standard.[37] The Zigbee Alliance's IPR policy provides members with the *option* to declare essential IPR, but when essential IPR—that is, "necessary patent claims"—are declared, each member agrees to furnish a FRAND license to the other members of the alliance (sections 2, 3).[38]

These IPR policies have been relied upon by courts to enforce FRAND obligations on patentees around the world. American courts have made clear that, through FRAND declarations and commitment letters through the IEEE, patentees, including Ericsson, Motorola, and Innovatio, have entered into certain "binding" commitments to license their essential patents on FRAND terms.[39]

visited Nov. 25, 2018), https://development.standards.ieee.org/myproject/Public//mytools/mob/loa.pdf

35. *Id.* (Policy).

36. *Id.* (Policy).

37. *See* OSGi Appliance, *OSGi Alliance Inc. Intellectual Property Rights Policy, Amended and Restated as of May 23, 2011*, https://www.osgi.org/wp-content/uploads/OSGi-Alliance-Intellectual-Property-Rights-Policy1.pdf *(sections 1.1–1.3)*

38. Zigbee Alliance Intellectual Property Rights Policy, https://www.zigbee.org/zigbeealliance/governing-documents/.

39. Ericsson v. D-Link, Sys, Inc., 773 F.3d 1201, 1209 (Fed. Cir. 2014); Microsoft Corp. v. Motorola, Inc., 696 F.3d 872, 878 & n.6 (9th Cir. 2012);

In another recent case in the American courts, a judge in the Central District of California addressed the ETSI IPR policy, holding that this policy constituted a binding commitment against Ericsson.[40] And most recently, the FTC prevailed over Qualcomm when Qualcomm tried to circumvent IPR policies from two additional SSOs—the Telecommunications Industry Association (TIA) and the Alliance for Telecommunications Industry Solutions (ATIS)—which likewise required SEP holders, including Qualcomm, to license SEPs on FRAND or "reasonable" terms, including to their direct competitors.[41] Thus, when patentees hold SEPs and fail to provide FRAND licenses or negotiate those licenses in good faith, they run the risk of being sued in court and compelled to furnish a license on reasonable terms as a result. As both the Ninth and Federal Circuits have held, an "SEP holder 'cannot refuse a license to a manufacturer who commits to paying the RAND rate.'"[42] And UK courts recently enforced the ETSI FRAND obligation on Unwired Planet so that it would be required to provide a license to Huawei to 2G, 3G, and 4G patents on FRAND terms.[43] Given this trend,

---

Microsoft Corp. v. Motorola, Inc., 854 F. Supp. 2d 993, 999 (W.D. Wash. 2012); *In re* Innovatio, 2013 WL 5593609, at *4 (N.D. Ill. Oct. 3, 2013) ("[T]he letters of Innovatio's predecessors in interest to the IEEE constitute binding contractual commitments to the IEEE and its members.").

40. TCL Commc'n Tech. Holdings, Ltd. v. Telefonaktiebolaget LM Ericsson, No. 14-CV-341-JVS, 2018 WL 4488286, at *5 (C.D. Cal. Sept. 14, 2018) ("*TCL Commc'n*") (holding that under French law, ETSI's acceptance of a standard that incorporates a SEP "forms a contract which includes the patent holder's obligation to license").

41. *See* Fed. Trade Comm'n v. Qualcomm Inc., 2018 WL 5848999 (N.D. Cal. Nov. 6, 2018); *accord Ericsson*, 773 F.3d at 1230.

42. *Id.* (quoting Microsoft Corp. v. Motorola Inc., 795 F.3d 1024, 1031 (9th Cir. 2015)).

43. *See* Jorge L. Contreras, *Unwired Planet v. Huawei: An English Perspective on FRAND Royalties*, PATENTLYO (Apr. 10, 2017), https://patentlyo.com/patent/2017/04/unwired-perspective-royalties.html; Unwired Planet Int'l Ltd. v. Huawei Techs. Co. Ltd., HP-2014-00004, [2017] EWHC 711 (Pat) (May 4, 2017), https://www.judiciary.uk/wp-content/uploads/2017/04/unwired-planet-v-huawei-20170405.pdf.

patentees should be increasingly wary of refusing to license SEPs or attempting to license those patents on unreasonable terms.

C. Royalty Stacking and Patent Hold-Up

One concern that may become increasingly relevant in the context of IoT licensing is the phenomenon of royalty stacking. Another related concern is patent hold-up.[44] As a technology area (such as the IoT) becomes flooded with standardized technology, the number of players involved in the standardization naturally increases, as previously discussed. Standards essential patents (or SEPs) will therefore become more prevalent as well. FRAND obligations, as noted earlier, help ensure that royalties are "reasonable" so that all technology manufacturers can implement the standards and do so at a reasonable cost. Although royalties may seem reasonable in isolation, they are sometimes revealed as being unreasonable when one accounts for all of the patents that are pertinent to a particular standard. The "stacking" of royalties for standardized technologies, therefore, is sometimes referenced as a concern in emerging technology areas. And, unsurprisingly, given the importance of standardized technology, the law seeks to deter a single licensor from "holding-up" use of a standardized technology—this is why IPR policies like ETSI's try to encourage all SEP holders to declare their patents to standards and agree to their licensing principles. All

44. *See* Ericsson, Inc. v. D-Link Systems, Inc., 773 F.3d 1201, 1209 (Fed. Cir. 2014) ("SEPs pose two potential problems that could inhibit widespread adoption of the standard: patent hold-up and royalty stacking. Patent hold-up exists when the holder of a SEP demands excessive royalties after companies are locked into using a standard. Royalty stacking can arise when a standard implicates numerous patents, perhaps hundreds, if not thousands. If companies are forced to pay royalties to all SEP holders, the royalties will "stack" on top of each other and may become excessive in the aggregate. To help alleviate these potential concerns, SDOs often seek assurances from patent owners before publishing the standard. IEEE, for example, asks SEP owners to pledge that they will grant licenses to an unrestricted number of applicants on "reasonable, and nondiscriminatory" ("RAND") terms. IEEE Br. at 16–18.").

adopters of IoT technologies will need to be aware of the possibility of stacked royalties and patent hold-up in the future.

The concerns about royalty stacking are legitimate in the IoT context. In 5G alone, numerous entities have already placed their IP stakes in the ground. Since 2012, more than 1,500 patent applications have been published for patents related to 5G, and these patents are distributed across dozens of assignees. Just six of those assignees—including Samsung, Nokia, Intel, Huawei, and Ericsson—represent more than half of those patents. For this reason, any major manufacturer of 5G technology will have to ensure they are licensed to 5G technology across all of the patentees who have declared "essential" patents to the 5G standard. This creates both logistical and financial challenges, and 5G is but one standard that may apply to IoT technologies.

Patent pools may be one way to address the royalty stacking challenge in the emerging IoT. These are organizations that consolidate patents from several companies in a particular technology area into a larger pool for the purposes of licensing. Patent pools can lower transaction costs for both licensors and licensees. For licensors, they can reduce overhead and promote economies of scale (such as avoiding the complexity of each company managing its own licensing); and for licensees, they can streamline licensing efforts by reducing the number of parties with which they would otherwise need to negotiate.

Unsurprisingly, patent pools have already begun to emerge in the context of the IoT. In the connected car and smart home sector, for example, a group of several companies came together to pool patents with a company called Avanci.[45] The members of the patent clearinghouse include around 20 well-known companies, including Blackberry, Ericsson, Interdigital, Nokia, Panasonic, Qualcomm, Sony, Sharp, and ZTE. These companies license their IoT patents

45. Avanci: Home, http://avanci.com/ (last visited December 7, 2018).

(relating mostly to 2G, 3G, and 4G communications), and claim to provide "one-stop access to the essential patented technology needed to fuel your wireless connected devices."[46] Avanci advertises its offerings as being FRAND, and Avanci claims to price its licensing offerings based on the value its patent pool contributes to the technology being licensed (rather than a model that simply licenses the patent pool on a percentage of a product's sales price, for example).[47] For connected cars, Avanci has already announced that it will charge between $3 to $15 per car to license its patent portfolio, and BMW has already entered into a licensing deal with the group.[48] Other companies, such as Sisvel and Via licensing, have also offered patent pools of various 3G, 4G, and Wi-Fi patents that may be used for IoT communications and similar applications.[49]

But patent pools will not be a panacea for IoT licensing. They will not necessarily be a "one-stop shop," as Avanci claims, because certain key stakeholders are not members of Avanci, and almost inevitably key patent holders will not be a member of every pool. Additionally, the scope of the IoT standardized technologies will likely extend well beyond the coverage of any particular patent pool—even if, for example, that patent pool happens to have control over all 5G—or Wi-Fi—patents. As one publication put it, "[i]f Avanci is focused narrowly on 3GPP-type licenses, while GE,

---

46. *Id.*

47. Avanci: Accelerating IoT Connectivity (White Paper), http://avanci.com/wp-content/uploads/2017/01/2016-Avanci-WP-Final-_-Jan-24.pdf.

48. Richard Lloyd, *Avanci Announces Pricing for Auto Sector–Range from $3 to $15 Per Car*, IAM MEDIA (Dec. 14, 2017), https://www.iam-media.com/frandseps/avanci-announces-pricing-auto-sector-range-3-15-car; Richard Lloyd, *Deal with BMW Is the First of Many with Auto-Makers, Says Avanci Boss*, IAM MEDIA (Dec. 4, 2017), https://www.iam-media.com/litigation/deal-bmw-first-many-auto-makers-says-avanci-boss.

49. Richard Lloyd, *Via and Sisvel Launch New Mobile Platforms as Patent Pools Continue to Respond to Rapidly Evolving Market*, LEXOLOGY (Feb. 27, 2018), https://www.lexology.com/library/detail.aspx?g=20d05ae8-a685-4922-88d3-ee9ed1654e62.

for instance, or Ford Motor, has a separate patent pool for their area of the IPR land-scape, chaos will ensue, or at least a royalty burden which is impossible for makers of tiny modules priced at a few dollars or less."[50] Thus, while patent pools may create some efficiencies, they will not solve all of the challenges of licensing in an interoperable IoT.

D. Licensing Principles and Strategies

In light of the foregoing, there are several principles and strategies that practitioners should consider in the context of the IoT when either providing or pursuing licenses to IoT technologies. The threat of litigation is real. In the past year, Broadcom has filed patent litigation against Toyota and BMW on connected car technologies relating to entertainment systems and receipt of satellite signals, and the flood of litigation will inevitably continue.[51]

This section considers the principles and strategies that may apply depending on whether the technology being licensed is a standardized one or a proprietary, non-standardized technology.

1. Standards Essential Patents in Communications and Other Standardized Technologies

In the context of SEPs, we have previously discussed many of the relevant principles. Recently, key 5G industry players in CEN and CENELEC, also known as the European Committee for Standardization, published patent-licensing guidance that could be used in the context of the IoT. These principles include:

---

50. *Ericsson's Patent Pool Is Far from the New Start the IoT Needs*, THE REGISTER (Oct. 3, 2016, 8:02 AM), https://www.theregister.co.uk/2016/10/03/ericssons_patent_pool_is_far_from_the_new_start_the_iot_needs/.

51. *Broadcom Makes $1 Billion Patent Claim Against Volkswagen: Der Spiegel*, REUTERS (Nov. 2, 2018, 11:10 AM), https://www.reuters.com/article/us-volkswagen-patents/broadcom-makes-1-billion-patent-claim-against-volkswagen-der-spiegel-idUSKCN1N71T2.

1. Owners of patent rights which are essential for using standardised technologies (SEPs) should allow access to that patented technology for implementing and using the standard.
2. Both the SEP owner and the potential licensee should act in good faith with respect to each other with the aim of concluding a FRAND licence agreement in a timely and efficient manner.
3. Each party should provide to the other party, consistent with the protection of confidentiality, information that is reasonably necessary to enable the timely conclusion of a FRAND licence.
4. "Fair and reasonable" compensation should be based upon the value of the patented standardised technology to its users.
5. A SEP owner should not discriminate between similarly situated competitors.
6. If the parties are unable to conclude a FRAND licence agreement within a reasonable timeframe they should seek to agree to third party determination of a FRAND licence either by a court or through binding arbitration.[52]

These principles represent but one possible perspective on possible licensing principles that may be relevant to the IoT, and other perspectives may well emerge. No matter what licensing principles one chooses to adopt, concepts of FRAND will be increasingly important and vital in an IoT era. As the IoT becomes more ubiquitous and standardized, and as the legal principles become more

52. Press Release, IP Europe, 5G Developers Publish Patent Licensing Guidance To Help More Companies Create Connected Products for the IOT (Oct. 11, 2018), https://www.iptalks.eu/5g-developers-publish-patent-licensing-guidance-to-help-more-companies-create-connected-products-for-the-iot/.

established, licensors will be under increased scrutiny to provide licenses on FRAND terms, particularly if patents are increasingly used (or sought to be used) to stifle innovation.

From a strategic standpoint, both licensors and licensees will also need to be strategic in seeking to understand the overall SEP landscape in the IoT. How many technology standards are necessary to promote useful interoperability amongst technologies in the IoT? If licenses are needed to all of those technologies, what sorts of licensing royalties are realistic in the aggregate, given the costs of manufacturing IoT devices? Given the appropriate aggregate amount of royalties, how should the royalties be divided across the various IoT standards, and within those standards? Should the licensing revenue primarily go toward 5G technologies or other technologies? And within a technology like 5G, how should licensing revenue be apportioned across the various licensors, assuming that all of the relevant licensors have not become members of a common pool? These are the sorts of strategic questions and analytical considerations that will be crucial in an IoT era.

2. Implementation Patents, Trade Secrets, and Other Technologies

While most of this chapter has focused on SEPs and standardized technologies, the interoperable IoT will also contain numerous innovations that are not related to standards. This will include "implementation" patents that are not essential to any particular standards, trade secrets that remain proprietary and under lock and key, and other technologies or "know how" that may be useful to a particular company that wishes to become involved in the IoT.

For these technologies, licensors will not be compelled to provide licenses on FRAND terms. Instead, they will be empowered to make the usual business decisions they would make when licensing most technologies. The decisions regarding whether and how to license will depend on whether the licensor wishes to foster competition in the marketplace. If the technologies are particularly unique and innovative (yet also not crucial to IoT interoperability), the technology holder may well decline to license the technology to possible competitors. But there may be advantages to providing licenses to and scaling a technology that could take off across the IoT. If companies choose to license these non-standardized technologies, they should just be mindful of the implications of entering into a license that could be deemed somewhat "comparable" to a license to an SEP that may otherwise be in the patentee's portfolio. Licensees will want to hold licensors accountable for their past licensing activity (if applicable) and also ensure they have an accurate understanding of the technology being licensed, whether through research or expert analysis.

When considering an overall licensing strategy (including both standardized and non-standardized technologies), it will be important to understand the context of IoT technologies. No matter what, companies that operate in the IoT will likely need to obtain licenses to communications and other standards-based technologies, as discussed in significant detail earlier in the chapter. But separate from the question of *taking* licenses, IoT companies in the health care, connected cars, smart home, and other technology sectors will need to decide the extent to which they will plan to *give* licenses their own patents, trade secrets, and other technologies. One question for any company emerging in the IoT space is whether to license its patents or take a more siloed or isolationist approach. Naturally, providing licenses to other companies could promote technology collaboration and more interoperability (at the possible risk of helping competitors), while taking a more isolationist approach could confer a competitive advantage but deter standardization.[53] The latter approach may not work in the context

53. Bijal Vakil, *Insight: Biggest Roadblocks to Getting Driverless Cars on the Road—The High Stakes of Patent Protection in the Era of Self-Driving Cars*, Bloomberg Law (Sept. 13, 2018), https://www.bna.com/insight-biggest-roadblocks-n73014482506/.

of the IoT, where "walled gardens" may go the way of AOL, Prodigy, and CompuServe in the days of the early Internet. Tesla is an example of a company that has taken the former approach; it has, to date, taken the view that anyone can use their patents in an effort to advance their technology, in what it terms an "open source" patent movement.[54] There may be pros and cons to both approaches, but whatever strategy is chosen by a company in the IoT should be informed by the overall legal context.

54. Elon Musk, *All Our Patent Are Belong To You,* Tesla (June 12, 2014), https://www.tesla.com/blog/all-our-patent-are-belong-you.

Chapter 14

Liability and Connected Products

Litigation and the IoT

Richard M. Martinez

I. Introduction

The Internet of Things (IoT) brings objects of all kinds onto the Internet; objects like doors, cars, lights, houses, tractors, and medical devices, to name a few. First, the sensors and devices, coupled with connectivity and ever-increasing data storage capacity, can capture a breathtakingly comprehensive, real-time history of events in the physical world. This isn't history book history. This is a log of anything that moves on the planet. Millions of peoples' heart rates are captured and stored, as is video footage from homes, the opening of garage doors, and the turning off of lights to name a few. People are developing (knowingly and unknowingly) a digital personal history of their every step, of opening the refrigerator, and even every beat of their heart.

Second, those sensors are increasingly coupled with actuators, also connected to the Internet. A good garage door opener used to be able to open the door from down the street. Now, through the wonders of the information superhighway, you can open the door of your home in Minneapolis from the beach in Cabo. But, unfortunately, so can a hacker in Indonesia or a burglar from a van in front of your house. Similarly, garage door openers were never the source of data nor possible avenues for privacy invasions. These garage IoT sensors and controls can now track movements within a home, the coming and going of children and owners, and can reveal the occupancy of the home. Sensors can trigger e-mail alerts and possibly provide unwanted insights into the activities of the homeowners. These same avenues of attack and possible sources of privacy risks can exist for countless other IoT devices.

The collection of new, personal forms of data and the remote control of the physical world enabled by the IoT brings with it new varieties of potential injury and an intricate liability regime. At the core, these injuries are the result of vulnerabilities in computer code, interdependencies between the various objects and sensors that make up the IoT, the networking landscape, and exploitation of these vulnerabilities by cyber criminals. The potential for new forms of injury are bringing new forms of regulation and liability. This chapter first examines what can go wrong when IoT vulnerabilities are exploited, identifying four general categories of injury an IoT plaintiff might allege. The chapter then examines four corresponding general theories of liability that are developing to litigate IoT cases.

A. When the Internet Meets Things: Potential Injuries and Damages from the IoT

1. Cyber Attacks: The IoT as a Gateway

Perhaps one of the most significant challenges posed by the IoT is the sheer number of products—not necessarily designed with cybersecurity or privacy in mind—that represent potential vulnerabilities on the global network. Some estimate that there will be 50 billion connected devices by 2020.[1] This is harrowing, considering

1. Leta E. Gorman, *The Era of the Internet of Things: Can Product Liability Keep Up*, 84(3) DEFENSE COUNS. J., https://www.iadclaw.org/publications-news/defensecounseljournal/the-era-of-the-internet-of-things-can-product-liability-laws-keep-up/.

even one vulnerable device may be all that is necessary for a hacker to gain access to entire networks.[2] Moreover, the FBI has warned that malicious cyber actors are actively searching for, and compromising, IoT devices for use as proxies to route malicious Internet traffic for cyberattacks and computer network exploitation.[3] IoT devices are attractive to malicious cyber actors because they can provide anonymity by transmitting all Internet requests through the IP address of the victim's device. Those devices residing in developed nations—for instance a connected TV or home camera in the United States—are particularly attractive targets because they allow access to many business websites that block traffic from suspicious or foreign IP addresses. Cyber actors use the compromised device's IP address to cloak their own home base and intentions, and thereby engage in intrusive activities, making it difficult to filter regular traffic from malicious traffic. This in turn allows these malicious actors to use IoT devices to send spam e-mails; maintain anonymity; disguise network traffic and Internet browsing; buy, sell, and trade illegal images and goods; and sell IoT botnets to other cyber actors for financial gain. Manufacturers racing to market "smart" products may incorporate connectivity—and security in turn[4] as an afterthought or an add-on—not realizing the ramifications that vulnerable devices can have on the global network. These ramifications can be potentially costly and catastrophic.

In September of 2016, a prominent cybersecurity website, KrebsOnSecurity, was the victim of a cyberattack carried out by over a million hacked "smart" devices that overwhelmed the site

---

2. Lily Hay Newman, *An Elaborate Hack Shows How Much Damage IoT Bugs Can Do*, Wired (Apr. 16, 2018, 1:00 PM), https://www.wired.com/story/elaborate-hack-shows-damage-iot-bugs-can-do/.

3. Public Service Announcement, FBI, Cyber Actors Use Internet of Things Devices as Proxies for Anonymity and Pursuit of Malicious Cyber Activities, https://www.ic3.gov/media/2018/180802.aspx.

4. Security can be compromised by weak password standards, default account credentials, lack of encryption, and user interface vulnerabilities.

with excess traffic.[5] After the attack, the site's owner warned that there are millions of "insecure or poorly secured IoT devices that are ripe for being enlisted in these attacks at any given time. And we're adding millions more each year."[6] Just a month later, hundreds of thousands of IoT devices were enlisted in the Dyn cyberattack, one of the largest Distributed Denial of Service (DDoS) attacks in history.[7] A DDoS attack floods a server or its network providers with Internet traffic, to overwhelm their capacity to handle incoming network packets, thereby preventing users to access connected systems, devices, or services such as e-mail or online accounts.[8] Hackable devices were commandeered and made to simultaneously bombard critical servers with excessive traffic, crippling Internet service for much of the eastern United States.[9]

B. The Harms from IoT Attacks Can Be Substantial

These denial of service attacks are not just inconvenient. They can result in massive losses. Early estimates conclude that on average, a denial of service attack can cost up to $1.5 million.[10] Cybercrime

5. Alan Butler, *Products Liability and the Internet of (Insecure) Things: Should Manufacturers be Liable for Damage Caused by Hacked Devices?*, 50 U. MICH. J. L. REFORM 913, 913 (2017).

6. Brian Krebs, *The Democratization of Censorship*, KREBSONSECURITY (Sept. 25, 2016), https://krebsonsecurity.com/2016/09/the-democratization-of-censorship/.

7. Tim Greene, *How the Dyn DDoS Attack Unfolded*, NETWORKWORLD (Oct. 21, 2016, 4:52 PM), https://www.networkworld.com/article/3134057/security/how-the-dyn-ddos-attack-unfolded.html.

8. *Understanding Denial-of-Service Attacks*, NAT'L CYBERSECURITY & COMMUNICATIONS INTEGRATION CENTER, https://www.us-cert.gov/ncas/tips/ST04-015 (last revised June 28, 2018).

9. *Id.*

10. Butler, *supra* note 5.

generally can cost a company $21 million per year.[11] Researchers are continuing to develop new means of calculating economic harm resulting from the exploitation of IoT devices, with more elaborate models seeming to substantiate considerable economic harm.[12] Once an IoT device is compromised, cyber criminals can mount attacks on other systems or networks, send spam e-mails, steal personal information, interfere with physical safety, and leverage compromised IoT devices for participation in DDoS attacks. This challenge is educating and gaining buy-in on cybersecurity from a diverse group of manufacturers making appliances, industrial equipment, and other traditionally "dumb" goods, as well as the individuals and organizations using these devices. The harm one vulnerable device can facilitate can be dramatic and far-reaching. And the rising costs associated with IoT vulnerabilities may inevitably fuel additional litigation as parties seek to recover for their losses.

C. The Growing Threat: From Stuxnet to Hackable Cars

In 2010, the Natanz uranium enrichment plant in Iran experienced multiple rapid centrifuge failures.[13] With facts developing like those in a spy movie plot, it became apparent that a sophisticated, complex, computer virus had infiltrated the secure systems at the

11. Ponemon Inst., Cost of Cyber Crime Study: Insights on the Security Investments that Make a Difference 13 (2017), https://www.accenture.com/t20171006T095146Z__w__/us-en/_acnmedia/PDF-62/Accenture-2017CostCybercrime-US-FINAL.pdf#zoom=50.

12. Kim Fong, Kurt Hepler, Rohit Raghavan, & Peter , *rIoT: Quantifying Consumer Costs of Insecure Internet of Things Devices*, University of California, Berkeley, School of Information, https://groups.ischool.berkeley.edu/riot/.

13. Kim Zetter, *An Unprecedented Look at Stuxnet, the World's First Digital Weapon*, Wired (Nov. 3, 2014, 6:30 AM), https://www.wired.com/2014/11/countdown-to-zero-day-stuxnet/. Kim Zetter provides a fascinating account of the Stuxnet attack in her book *Countdown to Zero Day: Stuxnet and the Launch of the World's First Digital Weapon* (Crown, Nov. 11, 2014).

plant and quietly accelerated the centrifuges to precipitate their failure.[14] Public and defense officials took notice of how software vulnerabilities can expose real systems and infrastructure to crippling damage.[15] The ability of hackers to cause damage in the real world emerged as a reality as early as 2007. A vulnerability in generator control systems allowed manipulation of circuit breakers, inducing an out-of-phase condition that can destroy the generator.[16] These stranger-than-fiction exploitations of the IoT were not about to be limited to battles between nation-states.

In 2015, *Wired* magazine journalist Andy Greenberg agreed to be a crash-test dummy for "white hat" (ethical) hackers Charlie Miller and Chris Valasek.[17] While Greenberg drove a Jeep Cherokee, Miller and Valasek accessed vehicle control processes, operated the radio and the windshield wipers, and then cut the transmission.[18] When Greenberg wrote about the test, the article not only sparked fear, it also spurred a class action lawsuit.

Journalist Andy Greenberg's demonstration with "white hat" hackers prompted Jeep consumers to pursue a class action lawsuit against Fiat Chrysler of America (FCA) in 2015.[19] Jeep recalled

14. *Id.*

15. Ron Rosenbaum, *Richard Clarke on Who Was Behind the Stuxnet Attack*, SMITHSONIAN.COM (Apr. 2012), https://www.smithsonianmag.com/history/richard-clarke-on-who-was-behind-the-stuxnet-attack-160630516/.

16. Michael Swearingen et al., *What You Need to Know (and Don't) about the AURORA Vulnerability*, POWER (Sept. 1, 2013), http://www.powermag.com/what-you-need-to-know-and-dont-about-the-aurora-vulnerability/?pagenum=2.

17. Andy Greenberg, *Hackers Remotely Kill a Jeep on the Highway—with Me in It*, WIRED (July 21, 2015, 6:00 AM), https://www.wired.com/2015/07/hackers-remotely-kill-jeep-highway/. In an interesting twist that reflects the role of white hat hackers in both identifying and safeguarding against vulnerabilities, the hackers covered in the WIRED Magazine article subsequently were employed in Uber's Advanced Technology Center. Greenberg, *The Jeep Hackers Are Back to Prove Car Hacking Can Get Much Worse*, WIRED (June 2, 2016), https://www.wired.com/2016/08/jeep-hackers-return-high-speed-steering-acceleration-hacks.

18. *Id.*

19. Greenberg, *Hackers Remotely Kill*, *supra* note 17.

over 1.4 million Dodge, Ram, and Jeep vehicles when the installed 3G "Infotainment" center was shown to be susceptible to remote hacking.[20] Plaintiffs claimed that FCA knew of the problem but failed to sufficiently notify owners and take steps to correct the issue.[21] Instead of a proposed nationwide class, a federal district judge in the Southern District of Illinois opted in July 2018 to certify a smaller class from Illinois, Michigan, and Missouri. The judge also dismissed claims of fraud and unjust enrichment in September 2017, leaving in place breach of warranty and damages claims.[22] The case is ongoing.

The Jeep case also illustrates the complexities of responding to IoT threats. FCA issued a recall of the affected vehicles. The recall didn't actually require Jeep owners to bring their cars, trucks and SUVs to a dealer—nor did it require a mechanic to replace any parts. Instead, consumers were provided with a USB drive containing a software update they could install through the port on their vehicle's dashboard. Many IoT devices—from light bulbs and connected coffee mugs to routers and cameras, may require software or firmware upgrades to remedy security vulnerabilities. Some changes may be beyond the attention span or capabilities of average consumers. These facts illustrate the challenges of maintaining the security of an IoT device. In some cases, security can come from a multilayered approach. For instance, FCA also responded to the Jeep security issue by making network changes designed to prevent remote access to connected vehicles, which apparently

20. Karina Basso, *Fiat Chrysler Sued in Hacking Class Action Lawsuit*, Top Class Actions (Aug. 6, 2015), https://topclassactions.com/lawsuit-settlements/lawsuit-news/89165-fiat-chrysler-sued-in-hacking-class-action-lawsuit.

21. Christina Davis, *Jeep Hacking Class Action Lawsuit Granted Partial Certification*, Top Class Actions (July 9, 2018), https://topclassactions.com/lawsuit-settlements/lawsuit-news/851554-jeep-hacking-class-action-lawsuit-granted-partial-certification.

22. *Id.*

satisfied the researchers who first reported the threat.[23] That change came in addition to the software upgrade consumers were intended to install on the vehicle itself.

For many, the Jeep incident hits closer to home than the cyber risks posed by DDoS and other cyberattacks that may appear to some as more remote or esoteric. Owners of devices that become part of a DDoS attack may not even realize it. But when cars drive off the road or garage doors start opening or toasters start spontaneously overheating, the Internet of Things and its potential risks become all too real. It is this kind of injury that draws the most attention and may largely drive the new developments in regulation and liability.

We have been living with data breaches and other cybercrimes for almost as long as we have been living with the Internet. The prospect of the objects in our daily lives turning against us has proven sufficiently alarming to seek new assignments of liability for vulnerabilities in networks, ecosystems, and the devices connected to them. Just as important, the rapid spread of connected devices has dramatically expanded the attack surface for cyber actors. Moreover, the complex ecosystems and network environments that an ever-increasing number of IoT devices exist within will also effect the ability to respond to and mitigate IoT risks.

D. Risks to Privacy: Harms without Data Breaches

Privacy was the first, and perhaps remains the foremost, issue in the information age.[24] Privacy for convenience is the "grand bargain of the internet."[25] We love our Netflix recommendations, but even as

23. Andy Greenberg, *After Jeep Hack Chrysler Recalls 1.4M Vehicles for Bug Fix*, Wired (July 24, 2015), https://www.wired.com/2015/07/jeep-hack-chrysler-recalls-1-4m-vehicles-bug-fix/.

24. Chapter 8 in this book discusses privacy issues with regard to the IoT.

25. Adam Satariano, *What the G.D.P.R., Europe's Tough New Data Law, Means for You*, NY Times, May 6, 2018, https://www.nytimes.com/2018/05/06/technology/gdpr-european-privacy-law.html.

far back as 2012, we were concerned when retailers could tell that a customer was pregnant based solely on tracking purchases.[26] In contrast to what can be gleamed from product purchases, imagine what can be inferred with the vital signs from your Fitbit or Apple Watch or conversations with Alexa, Siri, or Google Home. The inferential power of modern algorithms challenges what we think we want to keep to ourselves. Many of the same challenges exist in the IoT era, but there are new wrinkles.

First, the smart devices in the IoT collect a whole new set of very personal data and do so at exponentially increasing capacities. Names, addresses, and Social Security numbers are the PII of the past. In the age of the IoT, there are now databases that may contain your daily heart rate, health habits, conversations with Alexa, and the temperature of your house. The potential for artificial intelligence to connect seemingly random dots to draw further insights about individuals only compounds the risk. The IoT adds the problem of sheer volume and extrapolation to the issue of privacy. The more data a hacker has access to, the less important any one piece of data is. This makes creating a hierarchy of PII difficult.

Second, the IoT brings a new version of very personal privacy intrusions. Hackers can break into baby monitors and surveillance cameras and watch residents in their own homes. Nothing may break or burn, and nothing may get stolen, not even "data." But the idea that our homes are not our own is unnerving. Insecure IoT devices bring opportunity for troubling new privacy concerns.

IoT devices will also increasingly require new practices surrounding privacy, as consumers and corporate users of connected devices encounter new products and services that collect data in unanticipated ways or in seemingly unfamiliar settings. Take for

---

26. Kashmir Hill, *How Target Figured Out a Teen Girl Was Pregnant Before Her Father Did*, Forbes, (Feb. 16, 2012, 11:02 AM), https://www.forbes.com/sites/kashmirhill/2012/02/16/how-target-figured-out-a-teen-girl-was-pregnant-before-her-father-did/#2d3b73bd6668.

instance the sale of a car by a consumer, or fleet sales of company cars by corporate owners. If basic security steps are not routinely taken before selling the vehicles, the result could be the loss of a massive amount of corporate and personal data. Systems in modern cars track and store more information than users realize—data that could be accessible to the next person in the driver's seat. Potentially, that can include contact lists and other data downloaded when a phone is synced, log-ins for apps, location data, and even entry codes for office or home. Connections to home or corporate Wi-Fi can persist, as can subscription services. Further complicating this mix, the process of clearing data varies by make and model. If owner's manuals and manufacturers' websites properly warn and advise of such risks, courts may be willing to dismiss claims related to invasion of privacy or intrusion upon seclusion. Nonetheless, car manufacturers and those involved in the auto resale industry may also wish proactively to adopt technologies and practices that automatically reset data defaults in connection with the sale of a car.[27]

E. Consumers in a Market of Complex Goods

What the IoT means to the everyday consumer is that there is more to the goods they buy than what meets the eye. Complex goods leave the door open for marketplace damages when consumers do not know fully what they are getting. The ever-increasing array of IoT devices contain wide-ranging capabilities (e.g., from customized lighting to medical devices) and exist within a complex network environment with many interdependencies between products that weren't necessarily designed with each other in mind.

Industry groups are only beginning to map the complex IoT relationships of various devices, IoT systems, and IoT environments. For instance, the National Institute of Standards and

27. *See* Cahen v. Toyota Motor Corp., 147 F. Supp. 3d 955, 958 (N.D. Cal. 2015), *aff'd*, 717 F. App'x 720 (9th Cir. 2017).

Technology (NIST) has been conducting workshops on considerations for managing IoT cybersecurity and privacy.[28] Similarly, the Food and Drug Administration has co-authored a report focused on planning for cybersecurity incidents around connected medical devices.[29] While new standards may emerge quickly, the fact that the standards are still under development may further complicate the legal landscape as litigants seek to shift costs related to IoT security and privacy.

F. Liability and the IoT

This section starts where the first section left off. Marketplace liability relies on relatively well-established principles of contracts, warranties, and fair trade practice theories. Given the complexity and interdependencies of the IoT and the questions it presents for other areas of law, it is not surprising that plaintiffs have turned to known theories when pursuing liability in the IoT.

II. Claims of Deceptive and Unfair Trade Practices

The first wave of litigation addressing this question has already come ashore. It constitutes the first efforts of consumers and regulators to assign liability to IoT manufacturers for vulnerabilities in their products. The Federal Trade Commission (FTC) has brought

28. *Considerations for Managing IoT Cybersecurity and Privacy: Risks Workshop Summary What We Heard and Next Steps*, NIST (July 11, 2018), https://www.nist.gov/sites/default/files/documents/2018/08/10/considerations_for_managing_iot_cybersecurity_and_privacy_risks_workshop_summary.pdf.

29. *Medical Device Cybersecurity Regional Incident Preparedness and Response Playbook*, The MITRE Corporation, October 2018, *available at* https://www.mitre.org/publications/technical-papers/mitre-creates-playbook-on-medical-device-cybersecurity. The "Playbook" focuses on "threats or vulnerabilities that have the potential for largescale, multi-patient impact and raise patient safety concerns," that "are occurring with greater frequency," and concludes that "[s]ecuring critical infrastructure is a shared responsibility across many stakeholders." *Id.* at 1.

over 50 suits under theories of deceptive and unfair trade practices.[30] The basic consumer protection statute enforced by the FTC is section 5(a) of the FTC Act, which provides that "unfair or deceptive acts or practices in or affecting commerce . . . are . . . declared unlawful."[31] As a general proposition, these cases proceed under a theory that an IoT company made deceptive claims about the security of its products and engaged in unfair practices that put consumers' privacy at risk. Frequently, the claims begin by relying on a representation made about the product, perhaps relating to the product's security or privacy protections.

The following cases illustrate the range of allegations brought by the FTC and the financial toll exacted against IoT manufacturers for allegedly falling short on adequate security measures.

A. ASUSTek Computer Inc.

In February 2016, the FTC announced that it reached a settlement with Taiwan-based computer hardware maker ASUSTek Computer Inc. (ASUSTek) after the agency contended that security flaws in its routers put the home networks of hundreds of thousands of consumers at risk.[32] According to the FTC's complaint, ASUSTek introduced a feature known as AiCloud on its routers in August 2012 that had "multiple vulnerabilities that would allow attackers

30. U.S. Chamber Institute for Legal Reform, The Internet of Things *in* Torts of the Future 43 (2017), https://www.instituteforlegalreform.com/uploads/sites/1/_Torts_of_the_Future_Addressing_the_Liability_and_Regulatory_Implications_of_Emerging_Technologies_April_2017.pdf?pagename=uploads/sites/1/Torts_of_the_Future_Addressing_the_Liability_and_Regulatory_Implications_of_Emerging_Technologies_.pdf.

31. 15 U.S.C. § 45(a)(1).

32. Jane E. Kirtley & Scott Memmel, *Rewriting the "Book of the Machine": Regulatory and Liability Issues for the Internet of Things*, 19 Minn. J. L. Sci. & Tech. 455 (2018) *citing* Press Release, Fed. Trade Comm'n, ASUS Settles FTC Charges that Insecure Home Routers and "Cloud" Services Put Consumers' Privacy at Risk (Feb. 23, 2016), https://www.ftc.gov/news-events/press-releases/2016/02/asus-settles-ftc-charges-insecure-home-routers-cloud-services-put.

to gain unauthorized access to consumers' files and router login credentials."[33] The FTC further alleged that ASUSTek failed to provide notice to consumers that the vulnerabilities existed, nor did it advise consumers how to disable AiCloud features that would mitigate the vulnerabilities.[34] The settlement required ASUSTek to establish and maintain a comprehensive security program subject to independent audits for the next 20 years. Additionally, it required ASUSTek to notify consumers about software updates or other steps to protect themselves from security flaws.[35]

B. D-Link Systems, Inc.

In January 2017, the FTC filed a complaint in the Northern District of California against another Taiwan-based company, D-Link Systems, Inc. (D-Link), claiming their Internet cameras and routers contained inadequate security measures. Because D-Link targeted the U.S. market and failed "to take reasonable steps to secure the routers and Internet-protocol cameras they designed," the FTC claimed that thousands of routers and cameras were vulnerable to cyberattacks.[36] In September 2017, a federal judge dismissed three of the six claims the FTC alleged because they failed to provide concrete evidence that any actual consumer injury occurred where

33. Complaint, ASUSTeK Comput., Inc., No. C-4587, File No. 142-3156, at *2 (F.T.C. July 8, 2016).

34. *Id.*

35. Press Release, Fed. Trade Comm'n, FTC Approves Final Order in ASUS Privacy Case (July 28, 2016), https://www.ftc.gov/news-events/press-releases/2016/07/ftc-approves-final-order-asus-privacy-case/.

36. Complaint for Permanent Injunction and Other Equitable Relief, Fed. Trade Comm'n v. D-Link Corp., No. 17-CV-00039 (N.D. Cal. filed Jan. 5, 2017), https://www.ftc.gov/system/files/documents/cases/170105_d-link_complaint_and_exhibits.pdf.

personal data was accessed or exposed.[37] As of January 2018, the FTC had not refiled the dismissed claim and the case was ongoing.[38]

C. Lenovo Group Ltd.

On September 5, 2017, Lenovo Group Ltd. (Lenovo) agreed to no-fault settlements with the FTC and 32 states after allegations by the FTC claimed that the ad software it installed in their computers compromised users' web security and invaded their privacy.[39] The case stems from 2014 when Lenovo began selling laptops to U.S. consumers that came with software that transmitted the user's sensitive personal information such as "login credentials, financial information, Social Security numbers, and medical records" when accessing websites through a browser.[40] The settlement required Lenovo to obtain user consent before installing the software, to provide an opt-out mechanism before packing products with similar software, and to develop a comprehensive data security software program for any software it installs in future products.[41] A separate state agreement required Lenovo to pay $3.5 million to 32 different state Attorneys General.[42]

37. Paul Roberts, *Court Balks at FTC's D-Link Complaint, Wants Proof of Harm*, Security Ledger (Sept. 21, 2017, 6:21 PM), https://securityledger.com/2017/09/court-balks-ftcs-d-link-complaint-wants-proof-harm/.

38. Jimmy Koo, *FTC Reports on 2017 Privacy, Data Security Enforcement*, Bloomberg BNA Privacy & Data Sec. Blog (Jan. 24, 2018), https://www.bna.com/ftc-reports-2017-b73014474565/.

39. Daniel R. Stoller, *Lenovo Settles FTC, State Ad Software Security, Privacy Claims*, Bloomberg BNA: News (Sept. 5, 2017), https://www.bna.com/lenovo-settles-ftc-n73014464166/.

40. Press Release, Fed. Trade Comm'n, Lenovo Settles FTC Charges It Harmed Consumers with Preinstalled Software on Its Laptops that Compromised Online Security (Sept. 5, 2017), https://www.ftc.gov/news-events/press-releases/2017/09/lenovo-settles-ftc-charges-it-harmed-consumerspreinstalled.

41. *Id.*

42. *Id.*

D. Vizio Inc.

In February 2017, Vizio Inc. (Vizio) agreed to pay a $2.2 million settlement to the FTC and the New Jersey Attorney General's Office for failing to inform consumers of a TV feature—"Smart Interactivity"—that enabled the collection of their viewing data.[43] The complaint also alleged that Vizio used unfair and deceptive data tracking when it appended consumer demographic information to the collected data and sold it to third parties.[44] As part of the settlement, a judge in the Central District of California required Vizio to "prominently disclose and obtain affirmative express consent for its data collection and sharing practices."[45] The judge also ordered Vizio to delete data collected before March 1, 2016, and to implement a comprehensive data privacy program and perform biennial assessments.[46]

E. VTech Holdings Ltd.

The FTC reached a settlement with VTech Holdings Ltd. (VTech) in January 2018 concerning children's toys and alleged violations of the Children's Online Privacy Protection Act (COPPA), which requires companies to ensure that children's information is protected, and that they disclose to parents how their collected data is

---

43. Hayley Tsukayama, *Vizio Agrees to Pay $ 2.2 Million to Settle FTC's Television-Spying Case*, WASH. POST, Feb. 6, 2017, https://www.washingtonpost.com/business/economy/vizio-agrees-to-pay-22-million-to-settles-ftcs-television-spying-case/2017/02/06/3d4d4b16-ec8f-11e6-9662-6eedf1627882_story.html.

44. Complaint P 22, FTC v. Vizio Inc., NO. 17-CV-00758 (D.N.J. filed Feb. 6, 2017), https://www.ftc.gov/system/files/documents/cases/170206_vizio_2017.02.06_complaint.pdf; *see also FTC Takes Multiple Steps towards Privacy and Security for IoT Consumers*, *in* PRACTICING L. INST. COMMUNICATIONS LAW IN THE DIGITAL AGE 2017, at 393, 393–400 (2017).

45. Stipulated Order for Permanent Injunction and Monetary Judgment at § II.A., Fed. Trade Comm'n v. Vizio Inc., NO. 17-CV-00758 2017 WL 7000553, at 2 (D.N.J. filed Feb. 14, 2017).

46. *Id.* §§ III, IV.

used.[47] The action involved Kid Connect, a mobile application that allowed children to communicate with other children after parents or other adults downloaded and registered the app.[48] Among other allegations, the FTC argued that VTech failed to "develop, implement or maintain a comprehensive information security program" and "implement adequate safeguards and security measures."[49] Even further, the FTC claimed that VTech was not aware of a "reasonably foreseeable vulnerability[y]" until a journalist informed them they had been hacked by someone using remote access to the company's computer network.[50] As part of its settlement with the FTC, VTech was required to implement a comprehensive data security program subject to independent audits for 20 years and were "permanently prohibited from violating COPPA in the future."[51]

F. Standard Innovation Corp.

In March 2017, Standard Innovation Corp. (Standard) agreed to settle a proposed class action lawsuit by paying plaintiffs $3.75 million for a privacy violation associated with their We-Vibe line of connected adult toys. At issue was the secret collection of user information, including when their product was being used and on what setting. The purveyor of sex toys agreed to stop collecting user information and destroy the data it had collected. It also agreed to establish settlement funds to compensate both users of their app

47. Press Release, Fed. Trade Comm'n, Electronic Toy Maker VTech Settles FTC Allegations That It Violated Children's Privacy Law and the FTC Act (Jan. 8, 2018), https://www.ftc.gov/news-events/press-releases/2018/01/electronictoy-maker-vtech-settles-ftc-allegations-it-violated; Complaint at 17–21, U.S. v. Vtech, No. 1:18-cv-114 (N.D. Ill. filed Jan. 8, 2018).

48. *Id.* at 23–38.

49. *Id.* at 25.

50. *Id.* at 28.

51. Press Release, Fed. Trade Comm'n, Electronic Toy Maker VTech Settles FTC Allegations that It Violated Children's Privacy Law and the FTC Act (Jan. 8, 2018), https://www.ftc.gov/news-events/press-releases/2018/01/electronictoy-maker-vtech-settles-ftc-allegations-it-violated.

and purchasers of the device, which totaled approximately 400,000 people.[52]

G. ADT LLC

In a March 2016 complaint, plaintiffs Michael Edenborough and Patricia Wilson alleged that ADT LLC (ADT) was fully aware that its wireless system was vulnerable to disruption and hacking because of a lack of encryption dating back as far as 2012, an admission ADT disclosed in a 2016 Securities and Exchange Commission filing.[53] In October 2016, a federal court in California dismissed several of plaintiffs' claims but allowed them to proceed on a claim of fraudulent omission.[54] In March 2017, the same federal judge approved a $16 million settlement that would pay $15 or $45 to each class member who made a claim, depending on when they signed their ADT contract.[55] As of March 2018, the proceedings have been paused by the U.S. District Court pending a potential en banc Ninth Circuit review of a $200 million multi-district settlement involving automakers Hyundai and Kia.[56] Both sides in that dispute have urged the full Ninth Circuit to review the case, claiming the panel's ruling that the lower court should have considered state law variations before approving the settlement is out of step with precedent. Many of the cases to this point have stalled on standing issues. Courts have been reluctant to recognize an injury for the threat or apprehension of a hack that sends an SUV off

52. Diana Novak Jones, *Web-Enabled Vibrator Class Action Ends With $3.75M Deal*, LAW 360 (Aug. 15, 2017), https://www.law360.com/articles/954375.

53. Steven Trader, *ADT Alarm Hackability Suit Trimmed, Fraud Claim Remains*, LAW 360 (Oct. 24, 2016), https://www.law360.com/articles/854829.

54. *Id.*

55. Daniel Siegal, *ADT Agrees To Pay $16M to End Alarm Hackability Suits*, LAW 360 (Mar. 24, 2017), https://www.law360.com/articles/905893.

56. Ben Kochman, *ADT Settlement Paused Amid 9th Circ. Hyundai Class Row*, LAW 360 (Mar. 29, 2018), https://www.law360.com/articles/1027842/adt-settlement-paused-amid-9th-circ-hyundai-class-row.

the road. What happens when the hack of an IoT device actually occurs leads to other considerations of liability, starting with the issue of privacy.

III. Liability for Diminished Value

Civil suits have been brought under theories of breach of warranty and unfair and deceptive practices. But the search for new theories of liability continues, as litigants struggle to find a theory that best accommodates the complex legal and factual landscape. One emerging theory is recovery for diminution in value of the goods bought.[57] Essentially, plaintiffs are claiming they would have paid less if they had known about the data security and privacy vulnerabilities. This approach allows for the potential "battle of the experts," with experts for both sides arguing about a range of potential diminution in value.

The plaintiffs in *Cahen v. Toyota Motor Corp.* brought suit against automobile manufacturers, claiming that the cyber vulnerabilities of their cars represented violations of contract and theories of fair practice under the laws of three different states—Illinois, Michigan, and Missouri.[58] However, without an instance of actual hacking to point to, the suit was dismissed for lack of standing.[59] In a similar case, the plaintiffs in *Flynn v. FCA U.S. LLC,* brought suit largely based on the Andy Greenberg article posted on *Wired.*[60] These plaintiffs were only a little more successful, in part because, thanks to the publicity of the article, plaintiffs could allege a drop in market value of their cars. In *Ross v. St. Jude Medical*, plain-

57. Daniel Fisher, *The Internet of Things (You Can Sue About)*, FORBES (June 3, 2015, 8:28 AM), https://www.forbes.com/sites/danielfisher/2015/06/03/the-internet-of-things-you-can-sue-about/#2369b8661cb1.

58. Cahen v. Toyota Motor Corp., 147 F. Supp. 3d 955, 958 (N.D. Cal. 2015), *aff'd*, 717 F. App'x 720 (9th Cir. 2017).

59. *Id.*

60. Flynn v. FCA U.S. LLC, 2016 WL 2880102 No. 15-cv-0855-MJR-DGW (S.D. Ill. Sept. 23, 2016). Greenberg, *Hackers Remotely Kill*, *supra* note 17.

tiffs similarly brought an action based on a report that medical devices such as pacemakers could potentially be hacked.[61] The claims were dismissed voluntarily and defendant St. Jude Medical filed a separate defamation suit. Maker of children's educational toys VTech successfully defended against claims that its products were vulnerable to hacking and exploitation.[62] The claims were first dismissed for lack of standing.[63] The amended complaint was ultimately dismissed as plaintiffs did not sufficiently plead breach of contract, breach of implied warranty of merchantability, violation of consumer fraud and deceptive business practices statute, or unjust enrichment.[64] *Hello Barbie* was also the subject of a similar lawsuit. Plaintiffs alleged that the doll was vulnerable to hacking and brought suit for unfair practice, negligence, and invasion of privacy.[65] The suit settled.

IV. Possible New Statutory Bases of Liability

The issue of injury leads us to the issue of privacy. Privacy and data breaches were one of the first issues in the information age, and while the IoT adds new dimensions and complexities, as discussed previously, the issue of invasion of privacy persists. Just as injury has held up the unfair practice and marketplace lawsuits brought against IoT manufacturers, injury has always been a roadblock in privacy suits. Unlike the claims discussed earlier, which arguably are speculative in that in some cases a breach has not yet occurred, victims of privacy breaches have always been challenged by courts, even after hacks, to show a "concrete" and "particularized"

61. Ross v. St. Jude Medical, 2:16-cv-06465 (C.D. Cal. 2017).
62. *In re* Vtech Data Breach Litig., 2018 WL 1863953 (N.D. Ill. Apr. 18, 2018).
63. *Id.*
64. *Id.*
65. Archer Hayes v. ToyTalk, Inc., 2015 WL 8304161 (Cal. Super. Dec. 7, 2015).

injury.[66] Furthermore, statutory protections for IoT privacy have proven weak.[67] However, this may be changing with new privacy and cybersecurity statutes emerging, and a possible trend to adopt European-style privacy legislation in the United States.

V. The California Consumer Privacy Act of 2018

California recently passed sweeping data privacy reform.[68] California has adopted the most comprehensive consumer data privacy laws in the United States similar to other foreign jurisdictions. On June 28, 2018, Governor Jerry Brown signed the California Consumer Privacy Act of 2018 (AB-375) into law. Unanimously passed by the California state legislature, the statute will impose significant changes on how businesses collect, store, sell, and otherwise process consumer personal information, significantly changing the data privacy legal landscape for large businesses in the United States. When the law comes into effect in January 2020, consumers will have expanded control over their personal information, and businesses will have additional obligations related to notice, disclosure, and response to consumer requests. Most notably, the new law provides for statutory damages in the case of data breaches. The law permits a private action when a business fails to implement reasonable security procedures and practices, and this leads to unauthorized access and exfiltration of data.[69]

The statute authorizes a private right of action for "[a]ny consumer . . . whose nonencrypted or nonredacted personal information . . . is subject to an unauthorized access and exfiltration,

---

66. *See* Clapper v. Amnesty Int'l, 568 U.S. 398 (2013); Spokeo, Inc. v. Robins, 136 S. Ct. 1540 (2016).

67. Dan Massoglia, *The Webcam Hacking Epidemic*, Atlantic (Dec. 23, 2014), https://www.theatlantic.com/technology/archive/2014/12/the-webcam-hacking-epidemic/383998/.

68. *See* Daisuke Wakabayashi, *California Passes Sweeping Law to Protect Online Privacy*, NY Times, June 28, 2018, https://www.nytimes.com/2018/06/28/technology/california-online-privacy-law.html.

69. Cal. Civ. Code § 1798.150.

theft, or disclosure as a result of the business' violation of the duty to implement and maintain reasonable security procedures and practices appropriate to the nature of the information to protect the personal information."[70] Consumers can recover damages of between $100 and $750 per incident, or actual damages, as well as seek injunctive or declaratory relief. This will require a business to evaluate the reasonableness of data security measures employed to protect personal information, or elect to deploy encryption more widely.

A. California's First Step to Regulate Security of IoT Devices

In September of 2018, California enacted legislation making it the first state to expressly regulate the security of IoT devices. The new law takes effect on January 1, 2020. In contrast to existing California data privacy laws protecting only personal information, the new law aims to protect the security of both IoT devices and any information contained on IoT devices.

The law requires a manufacturer that sells or offers to sell a connected device in California to equip the device with a reasonable security feature or features that are all of the following: "(1) Appropriate to the nature and function of the device. (2) Appropriate to the information it may collect, contain, or transmit. (3) Designed to protect the device and any information contained therein from unauthorized access, destruction, use, modification, or disclosure."[71]

While the law only vaguely defines the term "security feature," it provides that, subject to the preceding requirements, a connected device equipped with a means for authentication outside a local area network will be deemed a reasonable security feature if either of the following requirements are met: "(1) The preprogrammed

70. *Id.* (emphasis added).

71. 2018 Cal. Legis. Serv. ch. 886 (S.B. 327) (to be codified at Cal. Civ. Code § 1798.91.04(a)).

password is unique to each device manufactured;" and "(2) The device contains a security feature that requires a user to generate a new means of authentication before access is granted to the device for the first time."[72]

The law also has a broad definition of "connected device," which is defined as "any device, or other physical object that is capable of connecting to the Internet, directly or indirectly, and that is assigned an Internet Protocol address or Bluetooth address."[73] As such, the law is not limited to mere consumer devices, but potentially includes, to the extent a device is not subject to other federal law or regulations, industrial IoT devices, retail point-of-sale devices, and health-related devices that connect to the Internet and that receive an IP address or Bluetooth address.

The new IoT law does not provide for any private right of action, and it can be enforced only by the attorney general, a city attorney, a county counsel, or a district attorney. Along with other limitations and exclusions to its applicability, the law specifically does not apply to connected devices subject to security requirements under federal law, it does not limit law enforcement from obtaining information from connected devices (as authorized by law or pursuant to court orders), and it does not apply to anyone subject to the federal Health Insurance Portability and Accountability Act of 1996 (known as HIPAA) (Public Law 104-191) or California's Confidentiality of Medical Information Act (part 2.6 (commencing with section 56) of division 1).

VI. The Big Question: Product Liability in the IoT

While marketplace liability is getting off the ground and privacy continues to be an issue, the looming question on the minds of

72. S.B. 327 (to be codified at CAL. CIV. CODE § 1798.91.04(b)).
73. S.B. 327 (to be codified at CAL. CIV. CODE § 1798.91.05(b)).

manufacturers and legal practitioners is product liability in the IoT. Returning to the commandeered SUVs, there is real concern that consumers can be fairly dealt with, their privacy can be protected, and yet now they can suffer real harm. When real harm flows from goods people buy, tort law generally is the route to recovery. Software has traditionally been sheltered from liability. But this could see change in the age of IoT.

First, tort law generally does not recognize suits for purely economic losses.[74] Outside the context of IoT, software generally operates in a world of economic and other intangible consequences. This puts software problems often under the reach of the economic loss rule.[75] But this is what the IoT is all about. Vulnerabilities in software in consumer products, appliances, and vehicles can lead to real, actual harm. When vulnerable software can be responsible for a house fire or an auto accident, the issue of purely economic losses is moot.

Second, traditionally, there is no duty to warn or protect another from the intentional torts or criminal acts of third parties.[76] This is significant because of the role hackers play in exploiting the defects of vulnerable IoT devices. Arguably, vulnerable software in an IoT device poses no inherent risk to consumers by itself. Tort law is rightfully wary of imposing liability on parties to know, anticipate, and prevent the willful actions of others. However, the law evolved to recognize a duty when there exists a "special relationship" between a plaintiff and defendant and whether the third-party action was reasonably foreseeable to the defendant.[77] This is where liability in the IoT will likely attach, despite the required

74. East River S.S. Corp. v. Transamerica Delaval, Inc., 476 U.S. 858 (1986).

75. *See* NMP Corp. v. Parametric Technology Corp., 958 F. Supp. 1536 (N.D. Okla. 1997).

76. U.S. Chamber Institute for Legal Reform, The Internet of Things, 42.

77. *Id.*

involvement of third-party hackers. Today, hacking is not only foreseeable, it is considered nearly inevitable. A recent study by Lillian Ablon of the RAND Corporation shows that such hacker markets are now dominated by "financially driven, highly organized, and sophisticated groups," complete with managers, quality control officials, technical support, warranties, and refund policies. The money to be made in finding and exploiting smart device vulnerabilities is a multiple of what could be made working for the manufacturer.[78] To think that hackers may not target or find vulnerable devices is naive. The foreseeability of exploitation of insecure devices makes a duty to prevent it likely.

Third, software developers have long been able to put off liability through end-user license agreements and terms of use, which have been upheld by courts.[79] However, the policy reasons for this position change in the IoT. Courts and the public alike are apprehensive about rogue vehicles, appliances, and medical devices. Furthermore, IoT devices are not software, they are devices with software. Arguably, it is more difficult to rationalize a blender or oven manufacturer successfully subjecting a consumer to an onerous end-user license agreement simply because some part of the product is software.

Even considering that traditional obstacles to tort liability for vulnerabilities in software exploitation on the IoT, tort theories for IoT devices still need to be developed. A negligence action must establish that (1) the plaintiff suffered an injury; (2) the manufacturer owed a duty to the plaintiff; (3) the manufacturer breached that duty; and (4) the breach was the actual and proximate cause

78. Paul Bond, *The Internet of Things (You Can Sue About)*, FORBES (June 3, 2015), https://www.forbes.com/sites/danielfisher/2015/06/03/the-internet-of-things-you-can-sue-about/#43c8b90e1cb1.

79. *See* ProCD Inc. v. Zeidenberg, 86 F.3d 1450 (7th Cir. 1996); Mortenson Co. v. Timberline Software Corp., 140 Wash. 2d 568 (Wash. 2000) *en banc*.

of the injury.[80] What exactly is the standard of care? Cyber threats constantly evolve. That may be the most pressing question to answer, as well as what are the duties of manufacturers of component parts. Many consider a products liability claim to be the most appropriate action for establishing liability with the IoT. To succeed in a products liability claim, the plaintiff must show that (1) the plaintiff suffered an injury; (2) the defendant sold a product; (3) the defendant is a commercial seller of such products; (4) at the time of sale, the product was in a defective condition; and (5) the defect functioned as the actual and proximate cause of the plaintiff's injury.[81] To show a defect under the fourth element, there are three categories: a manufacturing defect, a design defect, and a failure to warn. The IoT presents challenges to establishing these defects. For example, it is not clear if there is a post-sale duty to warn, as would be the case should a manufacturer learn of a potential vulnerability a hacker could exploit stemming from previously unknown methods.

In sum, tort liability for vulnerable IoT devices is not a foregone conclusion and is the subject of academic debate. Some propose new theories of liability that incorporate elements of older theories.[82] What is clear is that many are seeking to impose liability (and to shift costs) elsewhere, whether to manufacturers or to other users of the IoT. Arguably, they are the least cost avoider. The trickle-down effect of placing liability on software creators for vulnerable software may be unavoidable.

80. John C.P. Goldberg et al., Tort Law: Responsibilities and Redress 48 (4th ed. 2016).

81. *Id.* at 912.

82. *See* Michael Rustad & Thomas Koenig, *The Tort of Negligent Enablement of Cybercrime*, 20 Berkley Tech. L.J. 1553 (2005).

VII. Yet Unknown Question: Global and International Liability

The potential for global and worldwide attacks, precipitated through insecure or compromised devices, seems to be acute in the world of the IoT. Increasingly nation-states, hacktivists, and other global bands of cyber actors are taking aim at the IoT. Numerous global hacks have been the subject of criminal prosecution within the United States. These prosecutions detail elaborate, global schemes conducted by rogue governments and other actors. Their efforts have led to multinational harms that present unique litigation challenges beyond the range of the liability issues discussed earlier, and beyond the scope of this chapter. But the challenges to recovery for global cyber IoT incidents are huge. A botnet that cripples hospital systems across the globe will lead to real harms, including injury and possibly the death of patients, as well as incident response and remediation expenses for businesses and other economic harms and liability exposures. IoT device manufacturers and multinational entities that rely on IoT devices may increasingly face global litigation exposure in jurisdictions outside of the United States.

VIII. Conclusion

The Internet has frequently required a compromise of convenience for privacy, and security has seldom been mandated (by legislation or regulation) in any proscriptive way. The IoT is allowing us to realize the power of data and information flow for helping around the house, automating tasks, and improving health to name just a few uses. The physical and digital world—once relatively separate—are becoming inseparable. This opens the door for new types of technology that may offer additional conveniences and benefits, but also opens the door for new forms of risk and complex interdependencies. Vulnerable devices can be the jumping off point for a crippling attack on entire regions of the globe, or could provide access for hackers to turn smart devices into weapons. Who should be responsible for preventing these attacks? Software developers have traditionally been able to avoid liability for vulnerabilities in their products, but a confluence of new realities suggests this protection may not be sustainable. Others within this complex ecosystem may increasingly face scrutiny and responsibility. Whether or not imposing liability on IoT device manufacturers and users is the solution is hotly debated, but most agree that liability in some form is on its way. How that liability will attach will depend on the nature of the vulnerability, the extent of the injury, and how far courts push the law to address these harms.

Chapter 15

Challenges for Electronic Discovery in the IoT Era

Christopher A. Suarez[1]
Lucy L. Thomson

In the future, important evidence may be created on an Internet of Things (IoT) device. The International Data Corporation (IDC) predicts that 163 zettabytes (ZB), or one trillion gigabytes, of data will be created or copied each year by 2025. That's ten times the 16.1 ZB of data generated in 2016. By 2035, the IoT will be composed of a trillion connected devices producing 10 trillion data streams.[2] Cisco estimates that by the end of 2019, the IoT will generate more than 500 zettabytes per year in data—and in the years beyond, that number is expected to grow exponentially, not linearly. The amount of data stored on devices will be 4.5 times higher than data stored in data centers, at 5.9 ZB by 2021.[3]

1. The statements and opinions expressed in this chapter are the author's own and do not necessarily reflect the views of, and should not be attributed to, Williams & Connolly LLP or its clients.

2. IoT and the Data Gold Rush: Findings from a Commissioned Study Conducted by Forrester Consulting on Behalf of Arm, FORRESTER (Aug. 2018), *available at* https://pages.arm.com/rs/312-SAX-488/images/iot-and-the-data-gold-rush-forrester-arm.pdf.

3. Cisco Global Cloud Index: Forecast and Methodology, 2016–2021 White Paper, CISCO, https://www.cisco.com/c/en/us/solutions/collateral/service-provider/global-cloud-index-gci/white-paper-c11-738085.html#_Toc503317517 (last updated Nov. 19, 2018).

For IDC, the three industries that are expected to spend the most on IoT in 2018 are manufacturing ($189 billion), transportation ($85 billion), and utilities ($73 billion).[4] Manufacturers are adding sensors to the components of their products so they can transmit data back and better understand how they are performing. Manufacturers, for example, will focus largely on improving the efficiency of their processes, supply chains, and asset tracking, while two-thirds of IoT spending by transport will go toward freight monitoring, followed by fleet management. IoT spending in the utilities industry will be dominated by smart grids for electricity, gas, and water.

The IoT is expected to impact three main areas within the industrial space: building automation, manufacturing, and resources. Factories and industrial facilities will use the IoT to improve energy efficiency, remote monitoring and control of physical assets, and productivity.

Meanwhile, over the past several years, e-discovery has broadened in scope. Discovery that was once limited to PDF copies of documents now includes numerous file types, including e-mails, presentation files (e.g., PowerPoint), word processing files (e.g., Word), source code files, spreadsheet files (e.g., Excel), and audio and video files, among others. Discovery also can come from numerous types of storage media and devices, including traditional hard disk drives and computers, network storage on servers, USB and card-based memory on cameras and smartphones, and data stored by IoT devices such as virtual assistants (e.g., Amazon's Alexa), fitness wearables (e.g., Fitbit), and home automation technology (e.g., Nest thermostats and Ring doorbells).

4. FORRESTER, *supra* note 2.

I. e-Discovery of IoT Data Is Complex

Before the IoT era, electronic data and forensics were relatively simple. Traditional file types have metadata (such as author, date, and change history information) that makes e-discovery easier. For example, it was possible to identify an e-mail or a Word document's custodian because that information was in the metadata or text of the e-mail or document. Dates and other time information could also be determined with relative ease, as could change histories, version control data, and other similar information. For these reasons, document collection of traditional e-discovery documents was relatively straightforward as well.

In light of new file formats and IoT devices, however, e-discovery and forensics will become more complex. In an interview, U.S. Magistrate Judge Andrew Peck, author of leading e-discovery decisions,[5] identified a number of challenging issues that must be addressed with IoT e-discovery:[6]

- Is there relevant information in those devices?
- Is the information actually *in* the device or is it in the company headquarters' servers?
- How do you get it?
- What is kept?
- How long is it kept?
- How do you preserve it if you want to preserve it?

As he explained, "[a]ll the issues we've been going through with emails . . . are largely resolved by a judicial decision or industry practice even if there are some lawyers who still don't get it.

5. Da Silva Moore v. Publicis, No. 1:2011cv01279—Doc. 175 (S.D. N.Y. 2012); Rio Tinto v. Vale, No. 14 Civ. 3042 (RMB)(AJP) (S.D.N.Y. Mar. 3, 2015); and Hyles v. City of New York, 1:2010cv03119—Doc. 97 (S.D.N.Y. 2016).

6. Casey Sullivan, *Judge Peck on the IoT, TAR, and Avoiding 'Discovery About Discovery,'* Logikcull (June 5, 2017), https://blog.logikcull.com/judge-peck-on-the-iot-tar-and-avoiding-discovery-about-discovery.

We're in the infancy of the IoT and other technologies, [and] th[is] is going to still be a problem for years and years to come."[7]

With the IoT, metadata may need to expand to include contextual information about IoT sensors like their calibration, type, and locations. That additional metadata, along with sensor readings themselves, will be needed to understand the scope of IoT data needed for discovery. For example, a Nest thermostat could send useful metadata that reveals the times and dates when a home is unoccupied, as could a SmartTV, which could reveal when a TV is being watched or not.

A. Types of IoT Data

IoT devices produce a variety of types of data that may be important in litigation.[8]

- **Status data.** The most prevalent, and basic, type of IoT data. Virtually everything will generate data like this as a baseline. In many markets, status data will be mostly used as raw material for more complex analyses, but it will also have a significant value of its own.
- **Location data.** Where is my product? Did it make it to its destination? Location is a logical extension of GPS. Agriculture will make extensive use of location data because owners have to track equipment across huge geographical areas. Consumer products help people with many tasks, and larger markets exist for serving commercial and industrial customers, particularly where there are numerous assets to track, few employees, and the need to track things in real, and near-real, time.

---

7. *Id.*

8. David Friedman, *Get to Know the Four Types of Data in the Internet of Things*, Readwrite (Aug. 13, 2015), https://readwrite.com/2015/08/13/five-types-data-internet-of-things/.

- **Automation data.** Automation spans the spectrum from controlling heating systems, lighting, and more. The challenge will revolve around carving out applications and rules of conduct.
- **Actionable data.** Think of this as status data with a follow-up plan. Business owners want to fix problems but worry that the cost, time, and headaches will outweigh the benefits. There are two ways around this problem: automation (see preceding point) that can change the immediate state of a system, and persuasion that can urge people to change their behavior or make long-term investments.
- **Creating a feedback loop with IoT data.** Do you know what your customers think? In the near future, manufacturers will analyze data from their connected products to better understand how their products are used. IoT will create a feedback loop from consumer to manufacturer, where product builders will examine real-world behaviors to encourage continued product improvements and innovations.

The rich set of IoT data sources will include evidence from events taking place in the physical world. When used in conjunction with one another, the data can inform an historical situation that may have occurred with little or no reliable human witness evidence.

B. Collection and Preservation of IoT Data[9]

The multiple stage process by which data is created on IoT devices and stored or transferred may prove to be unwieldy for e-discovery. Detecting the presence of IoT systems and where relevant data is stored, as well as the identification of a particular user's data and where it is stored, poses major challenges.

9. *See* Chapter 4 for a description of IoT architecture.

Initial data creation takes place on IoT devices; data may be stored locally on the device, stored on a hub, or sent over the Internet to a cloud platform. Depending on the device, the network and power consumption restraints, data can be sent in real time, or in batches at any time. Data transfer (and the way the data is encoded or encrypted) may also vary depending on the communication protocol—such as Wi-Fi or 5G—that is used to transmit the data across the airwaves.

Data may also be transferred to and organized on a central system. Ongoing use of that data for the future may be done by multiple users and for many purposes, including analyzing time-series data and carrying our automated tasks based on specified conditions. Big data analytics of IoT data allows companies to create vast data sets and analyze them.

Generally, devices undergoing forensic investigation should not be turned off to preserve the modified, created, and accessed times of files. The situation is much more complex with the IoT, which involves extracting data from devices with limited storage. Leaving the devices running will use power, and, more importantly, data may be overwritten or compressed if the devices cannot interact with a central provider to store their data, because they collect more data than they can store.

Therefore, e-discovery requests and responses must take into consideration the data to be provided, and at what point in time. Capturing volatile evidence before it becomes unavailable will be an issue. A decision must be made whether to preserve the evidence on the devices by allowing data transfer from the scene to a cloud service or, alternatively, sever the connection between the devices and the cloud and attempt local extraction of evidence from devices that may be of a proprietary nature.

More challenges may arise because IoT service providers often store data on behalf of their users. This means that individuals may not have direct access to their own data, or it may be presented to them in a different format than that in which it is stored. This complicates the preservation process, as the e-discovery request may have to be served on both individuals and their service providers.

Analysts look at IoT data in various ways. One framework developed by SCDigest is instructive for understanding the complexity of the huge volumes of IoT data that may be the subject of e-discovery. The analysis focuses on five types or levels of IoT data.[10]

- **Level 1.** Data collected by IOT-connected devices, usually through sensors. This would include the identity/serial number of thing (machine, pallet, etc.) and other attributes such as location, temperature, humidity, operating data, and so on.
- **Level 2.** The subset of that data sent on to a data repository. Some but usually not all of the data collected will be sent on; often, but not always, in the cloud. The data may be sent in real time or in batches.
- **Level 3.** The collection of that data from millions or billions of individual IoT-generated date feeds into a data repository, cloud-based or not.
- **Level 4.** General reporting based on that consolidated database, for example, how many machines are in the field, how many are operating, what is their utilization, and hundreds of other reports.
- **Level 5.** Use of this database information for advanced analytics applications to provide even greater, generally non-obvious insight into what is happening. This will often involve predictive analytics. There will be hundreds of

10. *RFID and AIDC News: The Five Types of Data in the Internet of Things: Industrial Applications for IOT Leading the Way, though Information Logistics Will Be Key to Success*, SCDigest (Mar. 10, 2015), http://www.scdigest.com/ontarget/15-03-10-2.php?cid=9081.

these potential applications; some for a company deploying IoT systems for its own benefit, and others designed for customers to either add value to a product or wrap in a separate service.

C. Chain of Custody

The transfer and aggregation of data/evidence from IoT devices presents a challenge for documenting the chain of evidence. New techniques are required to track the transit of data across an IoT environment. Such techniques will facilitate the identification and extraction of data assumed to have been modified or deleted due to the constraints of IoT devices.

Even with the metadata, it may be difficult to gain useful information from IoT data without full information about when and how the data was transmitted. For example, an IoT device user's identity may be difficult to ascertain because IoT device users are more "fluid" than e-mail users, and IoT information may be transmitted or shared among a large number of devices. Such chain of custody challenges may make it more difficult to identify the custodian or speaker in audio files recorded by virtual assistants, just as it will be more challenging to know whose movements a particular fitness wearable is tracking at a particular moment, or whether input data from a smart thermostat was entered by a homeowner or a third-party hacker or intruder. In these and analogous circumstances, it may be difficult to know whether it is worthwhile to pursue e-discovery of IoT device data because that information may not be relevant to the person or subject being investigated.

D. Privacy Issues

Concerns regarding IoT data and privacy must be addressed in e-discovery. The data stored and processed in the IoT can be of a sensitive nature. On the other hand, IoT data may not in itself be personally identifiable, but its combination and correlation with other datasets, both virtual and real, can provide significant insight into personal activity and environmental conditions. Anonymization techniques may be inadequate and reveal personal information by joint analysis of many data sets. Legal frameworks may need to be updated to ensure that the data gathered in the IoT ecosystem is not misused.

E. IoT Forensics

The data stored and transmitted by IoT devices may need to be forensically analyzed in different ways before being produced in litigation.[11] The extraction and preservation of data from devices and services running in the IoT will present challenges because of the inconsistency of proprietary data formats, protocols, and physical interfaces. No universal standard for interoperable IoT data has emerged. The wide range of proprietary formats available means that more sophisticated software tools will be needed to analyze and produce the different types of data.

Further, for privacy and security reasons, IoT data is often encrypted, and may be interspersed with "dummy" data in the cloud or on the device to reduce the risk of unwanted eavesdropping. These protections may require additional forensic analysis on IoT data before it is produced for litigation.

F. Scope of IoT Data Collection and Proportionality

In an IoT era, the appropriate scope of "document" collection and data retention policies will be more complicated. Fitness tracking, personal assistants, and other IoT data has already been produced and deemed relevant in litigation, sometimes over objections based on First Amendment, privacy, or other grounds. Electronic discovery is already an immense proportion of litigation budgets. The

11. *See, Guide to Integrating Forensic Techniques into Incident Response*, Spec. Pub. 800-86, NIST (Aug. 2006), *available at* https://nvlpubs.nist.gov/nistpubs/Legacy/SP/nistspecialpublication800-86.pdf.

unrestrained collection and production of IoT data could be costly, wasteful, and much of the data could be of little value. Attorneys will need to consider (as with all discovery) whether requested IoT e-discovery is proportional to the needs of the case.

G. Analysis, Predictive Coding, and Artificial Intelligence

Though IoT will generate more data (and thus, more data to discover), emerging technology has already improved the efficiency and ease of document collection and review. Techniques like "predictive coding" use artificial intelligence to identify relevant documents, making it possible to review and collect documents with fewer search queries. As law firms and corporations take advantage of artificial intelligence, these technologies will improve not only document review and collection, but our broader understanding of the e-discovery issues facing IoT data.

H. Authentication of IoT Data

The widespread use of IoT devices has created unprecedented challenges in legal proceedings as the courts decide how to properly authenticate digital information under the current judicial rules and procedures. While the basic legal requirements for establishing a foundation for admissibility of evidence in U.S. courts are well-established, their applicability to digital data and devices from which electronic evidence is generated raises many difficult evidentiary issues and questions.

While U.S. courts have been admitting computer records into evidence since the 1970s when computer systems became available for business and some personal use, "traditional" foundations for electronic evidence have focused on the relationship between the information and the computer.[12] Documents were admitted based

---

12. IMWINKELRIED, EVIDENTIARY FOUNDATIONS, § 4.03[2] *et seq.*, *see also* GEORGE PAUL, FOUNDATIONS OF DIGITAL EVIDENCE (ABA 2008).

on the assumption that information produced from a computer is inherently reliable.

Now that the nature of digital evidence is significantly different from the early days of mainframe or stand-alone computers, traditional foundations for computer records may no longer be adequate to address the complexities of modern information systems from which electronic evidence is generated—because digital information may be created easily and without any verifiable record of who did so, and it can be changed, often without detection.

To authenticate digital evidence, 21st-century foundations must focus more broadly on the key components of an information system: People—Process—Technology.[13] Factors to be considered in evaluating the integrity of digital data include who created the evidence, what processes and technology were used, and what was the chain of custody throughout the entire digital evidence life cycle. Strategies for facilitating admissibility of digital evidence require advance planning to systematically document these key aspects of the electronic evidence.

Presenting the findings of IoT investigations poses a new challenge: Data will often have undergone aggregation and processing using analytic functions that can alter the structure and meaning of the data. At the device level, compression techniques may reduce the granularity of the data in order to preserve limited resources, such as memory, battery life, network bandwidth, and so on. Devices may adopt differing descriptor formats or may retain a proprietary format.

There are several challenges that can be made to the authenticity of digital records created on IoT devices:

---

13. *See*, Lucy L. Thomson, *Mobile Devices: New Challenges for Admissibility of Electronic Evidence*—As mobile devices, social media, and web archives change the nature of digital evidence, will the courts be able to address the increasing complexity? ABA The SciTech Lawyer, Mobile Transformation, 9(3/4) SciTech Law 32–36 (Winter/Spring 2013).

- **Identity management challenge—Who is the author of the records?** Courts look for ways to tie the author to the digital information offered into evidence. Whether a message, document, video, or photo was included in an e-mail or posted on a website, it is important for the proponent to provide testimony about who the author is.
- **Is the computer program that generated the records reliable?** Was the output of the computer what it is purported to be?
- **Were the records altered, manipulated, or damaged after they were created?** Changes to photographs and videos can be made using Photoshop or graphic design programs, while hackers can alter websites, change databases, and other electronic media. Often they cover their tracks by changing audit log records.
- **Incompleteness and integrity.** Is the evidence the entire record or conversation? In a challenge to the authenticity of e-mail transcripts, "instant messages," and "chats," a court held that "obvious omissions" in some of the communications go to the weight rather than the admissibility of the evidence.[14] However, a Nebraska federal court excluded entirely a "cut-and-paste" version of chat room conversations, finding that the omissions made the evidence "not authentic."[15]

In order to demonstrate that digital evidence is what the proponent claims it to be, the foundation must take into account not only the legal requirements of procedure and evidence, but must also include an evaluation of each of the key components of the information system from which the evidence was generated. Given the complex, and sometimes piecemeal, nature of data collected

14. U.S. v. Lebowitz, 647 F. Supp. 2d 133 (N.D. Ga. 2009).
15. U.S. v. Jackson, 2007 WL 1381772 (D. Neb. 2007).

and transmitted by IoT devices, there will be legitimate questions regarding how this data should be produced. On the one hand, it may be unduly burdensome to produce broad swaths of sensor data; but on the other hand, producing or collecting too little data may create misleading impressions in litigation. The rigor with which an evidentiary foundation must be established depends on the purpose for which the electronic information is being offered into evidence, whether there is any reason to believe the evidence is not authentic, and the extent to which the data and information can be corroborated.

II. Information Governance for Executives and Corporate Counsel

The IoT creates enormous challenges for companies and other organizations that must manage their IoT data and produce it if a discovery request is presented in litigation. The Electronic Discovery Reference Model (EDRM)[16] provides a useful framework for executives and corporate counsel to use in identifying key e-discovery issues with managing the huge volumes of IoT data in the organization. The EDRM features nine distinct e-discovery "stages" that include process-centric stages, which include information governance, identification, preservation, and collection, and data-centric phases, which include processing, review, analysis, production, and presentation.

- **Information governance.** Processes, policies, standards, and metrics that ensure the effective and efficient use of information in enabling an organization to achieve its goals.
  - *IoT issues*: Organizations must have an effective governance structure in place in order to mitigate e-discovery

16. Created in 2005 by e-discovery experts and consultants, George Socha and Tom Gelbmann, the EDRM provides a visual framework for the e-discovery process. https://www.edrm.net/frameworks-and-standards/.

risk and expense, from initial creation of ESI (electronically stored information) through its final disposition. This means having a complete picture of all IoT devices and the data they create, and how the data are stored, analyzed, transferred, shared, and secured. Commentators have suggested that a potential solution to identification of data and sources may be the integration of IoT device data into Building Information Modelling, a digital representation of the physical and functional characteristics of a facility.[17]

- **Identification.** Locating potential sources of ESI early and determining the nature of the data that will be collected.
  - *IoT issues*: To meet the Early Case Assessment requirement, company officials must be able to provide a prompt assessment of IoT data and analyses available to respond to a discovery request. Disparate computing centers with sensors are collecting and creating large amounts of data, not as part of the traditional enterprise model. Legacy systems present equally difficult issues. Older databases and devices may be in existence in remote facilities, online or off-line. Companies are losing knowledge of how they are connected, how they are secured, and who has access to them. Therefore, companies should be proactive in understanding the complete nature of the IoT data that they collect, monitor, analyze, and store.
- **Preservation.** Ensuring that ESI is protected against inappropriate alteration or destruction.
  - *IoT issues*: How does an organization place a *Litigation Hold* on IoT devices, and potentially the entire IoT device ecosystem? How does an organization place a

17. National Institute of Building Sciences, National-BIM-Standard—United States, ver. 3 (NBIMS-US), *available at* http://www.nationalbimstandard.org/.

Litigation Hold on office or consumer devices such as a wireless lock, microware, refrigerator, or thermostat? Many IoT devices have a limited ability to save the data they generate. Thus, data could be deleted or written over quickly. It will be important for companies to consider how to maintain the integrity of IoT data, particularly given the fluidity and complexity of the data.

- **Collection.** Gathering ESI for further use in the e-discovery process (processing, review).
    - *IoT issues*: Gathering data from IoT devices will require the collaborative efforts of company stakeholders, including IT and legal.
- **Processing.** Reducing the volume of ESI and converting it, if necessary, to forms more suitable for review and analysis.
- **Review.** Evaluating ESI for relevance and privilege.
- **Analysis.** Evaluating ESI for content and context, including key patterns, topics, people, and discussion.
    - *IoT issues*: Legal counsel will need to coordinate closely with entities in the company responsible for "big data" and analytics. Counsel will also need to consider how IoT data is collected or analyzed in any cloud-based application.
- **Production.** Delivering ESI to others in appropriate forms and using appropriate delivery mechanisms.
- **Presentation.** Displaying ESI before audiences (at depositions, hearings, trials, etc.), especially in native and near-native forms, to elicit further information, validate existing facts or positions, or persuade an audience.

III. ABA Ethics Rules: A Deeper Understanding of New Technologies Is Needed

In the digital age, there are many ways to cast doubt on the authenticity of electronic evidence. While the courts continue to grapple with the authenticity of digital evidence, including e-mail, websites, and social media, most courts—on whatever grounds—have found the information to be admissible. Indeed, notwithstanding the genuine risk of unreliability due to hacking or other malicious (or possibly even innocuous) changes to data collected by emerging IoT or similar devices, the courts continue to admit such information into evidence.

Attorneys should keep apprised of ongoing technology changes and their implications on e-discovery. Rule 1.1, comment 6, of the ABA Model Rules of Professional Responsibility makes clear that "a lawyer should keep abreast of changes in the law and its practice, including the benefits and risks associated with relevant technology." A lawyer should not throw up his or her hands and commit discovery violations for allegedly being "computer illiterate," and thus should be mindful of these emerging trends for that reason as well.[18] Many questions remain unanswered, but in an IoT era an attorney should consider emerging technology and the role it should play in e-discovery.

As the volume of digital evidence continues to grow exponentially, and its importance to the outcome of cases remains critical, a deeper understanding of the nature of IoT data and records will be required to make meaningful decisions about the data's authenticity and relevance in litigation. Sound and informed information governance practices must be adopted to determine whether the evidence fulfills the legal requirements for authenticity, reliability, and integrity. And all lawyers should be prepared to engage in discovery battles in the emerging IoT.

18. *See* Martin v. Northwestern Mutual Life Ins. Co., 2006 WL 148991 (M.D. Fla. Jan. 19, 2006).

Chapter 16

The IoT and Intellectual Property

Robert Maier[1]

I. Introduction

The Internet of Things (IoT) raises a number of interesting intellectual property (IP) questions. IoT devices themselves—sensors, communication devices, and the processors and software that drive them—run headlong into a thicket of IP issues, including patents, trade secrets, and copyrights. Additionally, some of the most interesting questions surrounding IoT and IP may concern the data collected by these devices and transmitted to larger servers for processing as part of larger big data systems. "Big data" generally refers to extremely large data sets that may be analyzed computationally to reveal patterns, trends, and associations—commonly referred to as "insights"—about the world around us. These derived insights can often lead to better informed and improved business decisions across all industries.

A number of issues arise at the intersection of IP and IoT/big data systems. For example, are the collected data or methods used to collect the data patentable? Is the collected data subject

1. With special thanks to Baker Botts associates Josh Sibble, Jonathan D. Cocks, and other of our colleagues who provided invaluable assistance in the research and drafting of this chapter.

to copyright protection? Can it be maintained as a trade secret? And perhaps the most pressing question for corporate counsel and negotiators of big data/IoT agreements: who owns the data collected by IoT devices?

Data ownership with respect to the IoT will become an increasingly significant legal issue as manufacturers, businesses, and individuals more regularly and systematically capture, store, process, and share more information. The capture and analysis of this data can raise data privacy and security concerns for IoT systems as more and more devices become connected "things." While the individual data collected by and the algorithms implemented by IoT devices have some legal protections, for example, in IP law, those protections may not extend so far as to thoroughly protect the proprietary transformation or use of IoT data increasingly collected and analyzed by companies across all industries. Solutions to these problems, however, may come in the form of appropriate contracts, including data usage agreements. This chapter addresses these and other questions about IoT data and IP.[2]

II. Patent Law

A host of patent law issues can arise in the context of IoT systems, including divided infringement,[3] patent exhaustion, and valuation

2. A reader interested in the topic of big data can find more detailed discussion in ROBERT MAIER & JOSHUA SIBBLE, BIG DATA HANDBOOK: A GUIDE FOR LAWYERS (2018).

3. "Divided infringement" can arise when a patent claim covers multiple steps of a method, with each step being performed by a different actor in the system—for example, a claim that covers the first step of a content provider's making software available for or download over the Internet, and then a second step of an end user's downloading and executing of that software. Given the distributed nature of IoT and big data systems, divided infringement is an issue to carefully consider in this context—both from the perspective of the patent holder, who should take care to draft patent applications in such a way as to avoid or minimize divided infringement problems, and from the perspective of accused infringers or those seeking to avoid infringement, who should carefully

and damages. The most significant patent law issue in this context, however, may come in connection with the question of whether inventions in the IoT and big data context are patent-eligible in the first place under 35 U.S.C. § 101—an issue that has plagued courts in the recent years since the Supreme Court's decision in *Alice Corp. v. CLS Bank International*.[4] This is particularly true for inventions that rely heavily on the collection and processing of data (which, after all, are the hallmarks of IoT and big data). Indeed, in the years since *Alice*, it has become increasingly difficult to obtain and assert patents in these fields.

The patent-eligibility of IoT systems can depend on a host of factors. For example, factors that weigh in favor of patent-eligibility include claiming a specific technological improvement, solving a problem in a technological area, or combining generic components in an unconventional manner.[5] On the other hand, merely collecting, storing, or manipulating data weigh against patentability.[6] By

---

consider these issues when designing business operations and analyzing risks associated with IoT patents held by others.

4. Alice Corp. v. CLS Bank Int'l, 134 S. Ct. 2347 (2014).

5. Additional recent decisions that provide guidance as to inventions that may be patent-eligible include, for example, Core Wireless Licensing v. LG Elecs., Inc., 880 F.3d 1356 (Fed. Cir. 2018) (improved display interfaces, particularly for electronic devices with small screens, that allow a user to more quickly access desired data and application functions in the electronic device are patent eligible); Finjan, Inc. v. Blue Coat Systems, Inc., 879 F.3d 1299 (Fed. Cir. 2018) (a computer security method that scans a downloadable and attaches results of the scan to the downloadable in the form of a security profile is patentable); and Visual Memory LLC v. Nvidia Corp., 867 F.3d 1253 (Fed. Cir. 2017) (a computer system that uses programmable operational characteristics configurable based on processor type is patentable).

6. On the other hand, a number of cases have also found inventions in this and related computing spaces to be unpatentable: *see, e.g.*, SAP Am., Inc. v. Investpic, LLC, 2018 WL 2207254 (Fed. Cir. May 15, 2018) (systems and methods for performing statistical analysis of investment information are not patentable); Voter Verified, Inc. v. Election Sys. & Software, LLC, 2018 WL 1882917 (Fed. Cir. 2018) (voting system that provides auto-verification of a ballot is not patentable); Intellectual Ventures I LLC v. Capital One Fin. Corp., 850

way of illustration, in *Fitbit Inc. v. AliphCom et al.* the court granted in part and denied in part defendants' motion for judgment on the pleadings that three U.S. patents are invalid under 35 U.S.C. § 101. First, in denying defendants' motion with regard to the plaintiff's biometric monitoring device, the court noted,

> [the] claims are directed to a particular variant of heart rate data collection: selective heart rate data collection through minimized user interaction. . . . [T]hese restrictions comprise a substantial portion of the collective substance of the claims and color their character as a whole. . . . By automating the point at which data collection stops and combining that with a single-gesture trigger, the claims focus on an improvement to heart rate monitors as a technological tool, which overcomes the problem of bulky user interfaces and provides a way to more easily and efficiently gather a selective heart rate reading.[7]

On the other hand, the court there granted defendants' motion with respect to the asserted claims of plaintiff's physical activity detection patent as the claims were directed toward an abstract idea. "[T]he wearable band with a motion detection component and LEDs 'merely provide a generic environment in which to carry out the [] idea of [collecting and reporting data on cumulative physical activity].' This adds little to the substance of the claim. Instead,

---

F.3d 1332 (Fed. Cir. 2017) (a system and method for retrieving, manipulating, updating, creating, and displaying extensible markup language documents for a mobile application is not patentable); and Electric Power Group, LLC v. Alstom S.A., 830 F.3d 1350 (Fed. Cir. 2016) (systems and methods for performing real-time performance monitoring of an electric power grid by collecting data from numerous sources and analyzing and displaying results are not patentable).

7. 2017 WL 819235 (N.D. Cal. 2017). *Cf.* TDE Petroleum Data Solutions, Inc. v. AKM Enterprise, Inc., 657 Fed. Appx. 991 (Fed. Cir. 2016) (claims directed to storing, gathering, and analyzing data—without anything more—are patent ineligible under 35 U.S.C. § 101).

the focus remains on the collecting and reporting functions themselves. So characterized, the 'character as a whole' of claim 20 is an abstract idea."[8] Likewise, the court granted defendants' motion with respect to the claims of plaintiff's physical activity monitoring notification patent. The court stated,

> these claims are directed to collecting and analyzing information to detect a particular condition, and notifying a user at a particular time when that condition is detected. They are not directed to anything more technically specific—the claims do not focus on (or even recite) specific algorithms or give technical details about structures that must be used to perform the claimed functions. Instead, they focus on the high-level functions of collecting, analyzing, and notifying themselves. This focus is an abstract idea.[9]

Moreover, the federal circuit has been increasingly reluctant to grant section 101 subject matter eligibility motions at the 12(b) motion to dismiss stage.[10]

In the wake of *Alice*, the patentability of IoT systems remains a continuously evolving and difficult question for courts.[11] However,

---

8. 2017 WL 819235, at 9.

9. *Id.* at 14.

10. *See* Berkheimer v. HP Inc., 881 F.3d 1360 (Fed. Cir. 2018) (finding patent-eligible claims directed to a system for digitally processing and archiving files in a digital asset management system, which improved efficiency of the computer system, but finding ineligible claims that did not provide such improvements); and Aatrix Software, Inc. v. Green Shades Software, Inc., 882 F.3d 1121 (Fed. Cir. 2018), *reh'g en banc denied*, 890 F.3d 1354 (Fed. Cir. 2018) (concluding that while the ultimate determination of eligibility under section 101 is a question of law, there can be subsidiary fact questions that must be resolved en route to the ultimate legal determination; a complaint may contain factual allegations regarding patent-eligible subject matter that, when accepted as true, prevents dismissal pursuant to rule 12(b)(6)).

11. *See, e.g.*, *Berkheimer*, 881 F.3d at 1360, and *Aatrix Software*, 882 F.3d at 1360 (each with concurring opinions pleading for guidance from the Supreme Court or Congress in the § 101 context).

those working in this space can use the guidance provided in the case law to draft patent applications and claims to strengthen their patent applications.

In terms of litigation and licensing, many believe the IoT space is becoming ripe for a patent war, given the large number of companies jockeying for position by stockpiling patents directed to IoT technologies.[12] In light of the growing competition in this area of IP, companies across industries have of late been focusing on specific areas of enforcement and legal and regulatory concerns for protecting, enforcing, and licensing rights relating to IoT devices.[13]

IP in the IoT era can be valuable, yet complicated, due to the collision of ideas that emerge as manufacturers from various sectors operate and compete for the same space.[14] In order to successfully interoperate, "IoT devices from different manufacturers will have to be able to work together—which means there's likely to be a great deal of overlapping utility patents."[15] For example, various market sectors compete in telecommunications, including car manufacturers, smart home device manufactures, and power companies.

Currently, there is no common framework for IoT communication across all IoT devices. But "[o]nce a communication infrastructure becomes ubiquitous, it stands a stronger chance of

---

12. *See generally* Steven Pepe, Kevin J. Post & Lance W. Shapiro, *Internet of Things: Next Patent War Zone*, Bloomberg Law, Big Law Business (Jan. 10, 2018), https://biglawbusiness.com/internet-of-things-next-patent-war-zone/. *See also Internet of Things: 2017 Litigation Update*, Unified Patents (Mar. 30, 2018), https://www.unifiedpatents.com/news/2018/3/28/internet-of-things-2017-litigation-update.

13. *Internet of Things: Patent Landscape Analysis*, LexInnova, http://www.wipo.int/edocs/plrdocs/en/internet_of_ things.pdf (last visited July 30, 2018).

14. Prigya Arora, *Internet of Things: Imminent IP Issues*, IIPRD (Sept. 27, 2017, 8:04 AM), http://www.iiprd.com/internet-of-things-imminent-ip-issues/.

15. Rob Bloom, *Protecting Your Intellectual Property in the Internet of Things*, IP Watchdog (Oct. 5, 2017), http://www.ipwatchdog.com/2017/10/05/protecting-intellectual-property-internet-of-things/id=88653/.

becoming the backbone of subsequent IoT systems."[16] Moreover, generic patents relating to telecommunication may be applicable to IoT telecommunications that span several different IoT device types. As such, any manufacturer, start-up, or competitor could be infringing another company's IP without knowledge, even if in an unrelated industry.[17] For these reasons, many players in the IoT and big data space consider both offensive and defensive strategies to enhance the strength of their patent portfolios. A broad, strong, and diverse patent portfolio allows for ownership of important offensive IP that can also be utilized defensively as a litigation deterrent.

Ultimately, with the IoT patent race in full force, companies would be well-served in the coming years to (1) build a comprehensive patent portfolio in this space, covering all aspects of patentable inventions that touch on IoT, and (2) carefully monitor and address the risks associated with IoT patent thickets owned by others—including both operating companies and well-funded patent assertion entities (PAEs) and non-practicing entities (NPEs).

PAEs are businesses that acquire patents from third parties and seek to generate revenue by asserting them against alleged infringers. Many PAEs are controlled by larger entities, or parents, and derive the majority of their total revenue from patent-licensing activities. NPEs are individuals or companies who hold a patent with no intentions of commercially developing it. Instead, most NPEs typically derive the majority of their total revenue from patent assertion and licensing activities. Given the prevalence of software patents in the big data and IoT space, the number of NPEs is expected to be significantly higher as compared to other technology spaces. For instance, from 2012 to 2017, NPE litigation activity for IoT technologies remained consistently high (between 85 percent and 98 percent of all IoT litigation).[18] Ultimately, the IoT and big

16. *Id.*
17. *Id.*
18. *Id.*

data arena is in its infancy and, as such, PAEs and NPEs all view it as fertile ground for stockpiling large patent portfolios to later assert against operating companies.

A. Software Patents Outside the United States

The patent race is also on outside the United States, and the patent-eligibility of software-related inventions varies by country. Generally, the European Patent Convention (EPC) does not permit patents for discoveries, scientific theories, mathematical equations, schemes, rules, methods for performing mental acts, playing games, doing business, and programs for computers, "as such."[19] Computer programs, however, may avoid this exclusion when the claim is combined with other technical subject matter. "In practice, features incorporating technical computer implementation of software, such as an AI-equipped surgical robot system" have passed this test.[20]

In order to fully consider the "as such" test in relation to claims directed towards computer programs, it is necessary to look to the case law of Technical Boards of Appeal of the European Patent Office. An exemplary case in this regard is T 1173/97 (IBM),[21] which held "[a] computer program product is not excluded from patentability under Article 52(2) and (3) EPC if, when it is run on a computer, it produces a further technical effect which goes beyond the 'normal' physical interactions between program (software) and computer (hardware)." "It follows that computer programs are not considered to be programs for computers 'as such' (and are therefore not excluded from patentability by Article 52 EPC) when

19. European Patent Convention (EPC), Article 52, paras. 2–3 (Eur).

20. Jeffrey J. Jones et al., *Legal Issues Related to the Development of Automated, Autonomous, and Connected Cars*, White Paper (Nov. 2017).

21. Case T 1173/97, Computer Program Prod./IBM, 1999 O.J. E.P.O. 609.

those programs have a technical character as a result of producing a further technical effect."[22]

Japan, on the other hand, has no software-specific subject matter eligibility exclusions. Therefore, a patent that claims a software application and generally defines tangible components of a computer qualifies for patent protection.[23] "A mathematical algorithm per se is not patent eligible in Japan, but should be eligible if defined with reference to implementation by computer hardware."[24]

China generally falls somewhere in between the European Union and Japan in these respects, as "computer programs are considered rules and methods for mental activities" and, therefore, not eligible for patent protection under article 25 of the Chinese patent law. Accordingly, an "invention relating to computer programs is eligible for patent protection only if it constitutes a technical solution. Defining a software invention in terms of computer implementation is typically sufficient to satisfy patent eligibility. Accordingly, computer-implemented AI inventions are likely to be patent eligible."[25]

B. Enforcement of IoT Patents

IoT technology is by its very nature interactive, and the applications available are seemingly limitless. Originally, the Internet was built to allow for communications between large, powerful computers. Today, however, new protocols are being developed for smaller mobile devices to support IoT goals.

Due to this interactivity, scenarios can arise in which more than one party is involved in the potential infringement of a

---

22. Rupert A. Knights et al., *Patent Eligibility of Software Patents in the U.S. and Europe: A Post-Alice Consideration*, 8 Landslide n.1, at 5 (2015).

23. Japan Patent Office, *JPO Guidelines: Eligibility for Patent and Industrial Applicability*. Part III, Ch. 1 (Japan).

24. *Id.*

25. Chinese State Intellectual Property Office, *Guidelines on Examination of Patents (promulgated by Order No. 74)* (Apr. 7, 2017) (China).

patent. Third-party liability is generally addressed under the patent statute's inducement and contributory infringement provisions, although joint infringement may also apply.[26] That said, historically, the Federal Circuit applies the "control or direction test," which may be difficult to meet.[27] IoT devices are, by their very nature, distributed—they collect information from end users, transmit that information across a network to a hub or multiple hubs, and ultimately that information is received and processed. The burgeoning popularity and importance of these networked IoT systems may well force the hands of lawmakers to reconsider liability for multiparty infringement.[28]

III. Trade Secret Law

While patents remain a strong form of IP protection, patenting is not always a viable option given the difficulty in patenting certain inventions in the IoT context, including, in particular, the software algorithms, vast amounts of data captured by IoT devices, and some of the methods for gathering that data. As an alternative, trade secret law may offer effective protection of commercially valuable proprietary information.[29] In the fields of IoT and big data systems, trade secret law has also been used to protect the algorithms and analytic techniques used to glean valuable information from data.[30]

Prior to the passage of the Defend Trade Secrets Act (DTSA) in 2016, state law provided the sole remedy for trade secret

26. W. Keith Robinson, *Patent Law Challenges for the Internet of Things*, 15 Wake Forest J. Bus. & Intell. Prop L. 668 (2013).

27. *Id.*

28. *Id.* at 669.

29. Office of Policy & External Affairs, USPTO, *Trade Secret Protection in the U.S.*, 2–3, https://www.nist.gov/sites/default/files/documents/mep/marinaslides.pdf (last visited July 30, 2018).

30. *See, e.g.*, Steve Lohr, *Google Schools Its Algorithm*, N.Y. Times (Mar. 5, 2011), http://www.nytimes.com/2011/03/06/weekinreview/06lohr.html ("[Google's] algorithm is a tightly guarded trade secret").

misappropriation. However, after the passage of the DTSA, trade secret holders now have a uniform federal cause of action for misappropriation and easier access to federal courts in addition to the rights provided by state trade secret laws.[31]

A. Uniform Trade Secrets Act (UTSA)

Although the UTSA does not expressly contemplate computer source code as protectable (as the DTSA does) for state causes of action, the definition of a trade secret under the UTSA is likely to protect big data systems.[32] Although state trade secret laws vary, every state that has passed trade secret legislation has adopted the UTSA in some form, except for New York and Massachusetts.[33]

Under the UTSA, a trade secret is,

> information, including a formula, pattern, compilation, program,[34] device, method, technique, or process, that: (i) derives independent economic value, actual or potential, from not being generally known to, and not being readily ascertainable by proper means by, other persons who can obtain economic value from its disclosure or use, and (ii) is the subject of efforts that are reasonable under the circumstances to maintain its secrecy.[35]

---

31. Bret A. Cohen et. al., *Explaining the Defend Trade Secrets Act*, ABA Bus. L. Today (Sept. 2016), https://www.americanbar.org/content/dam/aba/publications/blt/2016/09/trade-secrets-201609.pdf.

32. *See* Jon Neiditz, *A Recipe for New Info Governance and Data Asset Protection*, Law360 (Jan. 7, 2014), http://www.kilpatricktownsend.com/~/media/Files/articles/2014/NEIDITZLAW360.ashx.

33. Patrick J. Coyne, *What You Should Know About the Defend Trade Secrets Act*, Law 360 (June 28, 2016), http://www.finnegan.com/resources/articles/articlesdetail.aspx?news=1444a1c9-e0d0-4e07-afd4-3fd671d2fafc.

34. Under the UTSA a "compilation" and/or a "program" may include a computer program, as the definition of a trade secret was drafted broadly; *see, e.g.*, Josh Rich, *President Obama Signs Defend Trade Secret Act*, PatentDocs (May 11, 2016), http://www.patentdocs.org/trade-secrets/.

35. Uniform Trade Secrets Act § 1(4) (Unif. Law Comm'n 1985).

Misappropriation of a trade secret is defined as:

> (i) acquisition of a trade secret of another by a person who knows or has reason to know that the trade secret was acquired by improper means; or (ii) disclosure or use of a trade secret of another without express or implied consent by a person who (A) used improper means to acquire knowledge of the trade secret; or (B) at the time of disclosure or use knew or had reason to know that his knowledge of the trade secret was (I) derived from or through a person who has utilized improper means to acquire it; (II) acquired under circumstances giving rise to a duty to maintain its secrecy or limit its use; or (III) derived from or through a person who owed a duty to the person seeking relief to maintain its secrecy or limit its use; or (C) before a material change of his position, knew or had reason to know that it was a trade secret ad that knowledge of it had been acquired by accident or mistake.[36]

Injunctive relief is available under the UTSA. Specifically, "[a]ctual or threatened misappropriation may be enjoined."[37] Damages are also available under the UTSA.[38]

B. Defend Trade Secrets Act (DTSA)

The federal DTSA is particularly relevant to the IoT because it more expressly allows for the protection of computer source code as a trade secret. Trade secret holders may also find the nationwide applicability and access to federal courts afforded by the DTSA preferable to the misappropriation remedies and forums available under state trade secret law.

36. *Id.* § 1(2).
37. *Id.* § 2(a).
38. *Id.* § 3(a)–(b).

Under the DTSA, trade secrets are defined as:

> all forms and types of financial, business, scientific, technical, economic, or engineering information, including patterns, plans, compilations, program devices, formulas, designs, prototypes, methods, techniques, processes, procedures, *programs, or codes*,[39] whether tangible or intangible, and whether or how stored, compiled, or memorialized physically, electronically, graphically, photographically, or in writing if the owner thereof has taken reasonable measures to keep such information secret; and the information derives independent economic value, actual or potential, from not being generally known to, and not being readily ascertainable through proper means by, another person who can obtain economic value from the disclosure or use of the information.[40]

The DTSA defines misappropriation of a trade secret in substantially the same way as the UTSA. Injunctive relief is available under the DTSA.[41] Additionally, damages are also available.[42]

39. Like the UTSA, the definition of a trade secret is broadly drafted under the DTSA as it was based on the definition provided in the UTSA. As such, "compilation," "program," and "code" also may include a computer program. *See, e.g.*, Rich, *supra* note 33; *see also DTSA Definition of Trade Secret: Everything You Need to Know*, UPCOUNSEL, https://www.upcounsel.com/dtsa-definition-of-trade-secret (last accessed Nov. 21, 2018).

40. 18 U.S.C. § 1839(3) (2018) (emphasis added).

41. *Id.* § 1836(b)(3)(A)(i)(II) (a court is cautious in granting injunction when the injunction would "prevent a person from entering into an employment relationship, and that conditions placed on such employment shall be based on evidence of threatened misappropriation and not merely on the information the person knows; or (II) otherwise conflict with an applicable State law prohibiting restraints on the practice of a lawful profession, trade, or business").

42. *Id.* § 1836(b)(3)(B)(i)(I)–(II) ("[A]ctual loss caused by the misappropriation of the trade secret" and "for any unjust enrichment caused by the misappropriation of the trade secret that is not addressed in computing damages for actual loss.").

Exemplary damages may also be available when the trade secret is "willfully and maliciously misappropriated."[43]

Under the DTSA, a court may issue an ex parte civil seizure order under 35 U.S.C. § 1836 "providing for the seizure of property necessary to prevent the propagation or dissemination of the trade secret that is subject of the action."[44] The DTSA seeks to prevent trade secrets from being revealed in courts. Specifically, "[t]he court may not authorize or direct the disclosure of any information the owner asserts to be a trade secret unless the court allows the owner the opportunity to file a submission under seal that describes the interest of the owner in keeping the information confidential."[45]

C. Differences between Patent and Trade Secret Protection

As discussed previously, IoT technology broadly includes anything from the devices that capture data to software applications that analyze the captured data. In light of the Supreme Court's decision in *Alice*, which has made it more difficult to patent software and other data-analysis aspects of IoT, developers may be interested instead in pursuing trade secret protections. While trade secrets offer benefits when compared to patents, they are not without limitations and challenges.

For example, to prevail on a claim for trade secret misappropriation, the trade secret holder must show that the accused party "misappropriated" the trade secret through improper access or theft. This kind of evidence can in some instances be difficult to muster. Moreover, unlike patents, which typically expire 20 years from the date of the patent application, trade secret rights can exist in perpetuity, so long as the trade secret owner maintains

43. Cohen et al., *supra* note 31.

44. 18 U.S.C. § 1836(b)(2)(A)(i), but civil seizures will be ordered only in extraordinary circumstances, *see id.* § 1836(b)(2)(A)(ii).

45. *Id.* § 1835(b).

the secrecy of the trade secret and the other requirements of trade secret are observed.[46] Indeed, some have postulated that "[a]ll of a company's innovative IoT technology should start off as a trade secret. Whether portions of that technology remain protected only as a trade secret or be publicly disclosed to obtain patent protection is a strategic choice base on business goals and legal needs."[47]

Recent lawsuits demonstrate some of the difficulties in relying on trade secret law. As just one example, *Allied Portables, LLC v. Youmans* demonstrates how the IoT and its constant flow of data can undermine trade secret protection.[48] In that case, the district court found that information allegedly taken by the defendants—pricing information, customer lists, sales routes, and a business plan—constituted a trade secret; however, the court declined to issue a preliminary injunction, finding no irreparable harm because the alleged confidential information was over a year old and the nature of the plaintiff's business had changed over time. Given the real-time collection by IoT devices, it is easy to imagine a defendant arguing that the data it collected months ago is now stale and not entitled to heightened protection as a trade secret. Additionally, contractual restrictions alone may be insufficient to protect information a company considers a trade secret.[49] The best approach includes multiple layers of protections for trade secrets—including contractual obligations, data classification, and security controls.[50]

---

46. Kenie Ho, *Protecting the Revolution: Internet of Things Trade Secrets*, Inside Counsel (Oct. 6, 2016), https://www.finnegan.com/en/insights/protecting-the-revolution-internet-of-things-trade-secrets.html.

47. *Id.*

48. No. 2:15-CV-294-FTM-38CM, 2015 WL 6813669, at *6 (M.D. Fla. Nov. 6, 2015).

49. Stephen Reynolds, *How to Protect Your Company's Trade Secrets in the Industrial IoT*, Ice Miller, http://www.icemiller.com/proposals/2023/How%20to%20Protect%20Your%20Company%E2%80%99s%20Trade%20Secrets%20in%20the%20Industrial%20IoT.pdf (last accessed Sept. 10, 2018).

50. *Id.*

Ultimately, while trade secret protection offers certain advantages over and above patent law, there are limitations and challenges inherent in trade secret protection, in particular in the IoT context.

IV. Copyright Law

Unlike patents and trade secrets, copyright protection does not allow a rights holder to exclude others from using ideas or information, and thus raw data itself is not copyrightable.[51] However, copyright law may protect an original arrangement or compilation of raw data, including data collected and stored by IoT devices.[52] According to the U.S. Copyright Office, "[a]n application to register a database typically covers the selection, coordination and/or arrangement of data, information or files, but does *not* cover the data, information or files unless they are specifically claimed in the application."[53] Ultimately, copyright law is interesting and important to IoT systems because those systems are fundamentally designed to gather, collect, and transmit data, and copyright law affords protections for collections of data.

Moreover, copyright law offers an important means by which IoT device manufacturers can protect their intellectual property because most IoT products contain software—which is protectable under copyright law.

---

51. Feist Publ'ns, Inc. v. Rural Tel. Serv. Co., 499 U.S. 340, 344 (1991) ("Facts are not copyrightable.").

52. *Id.* at 348 ("[The compilation author's] choices as to selection and arrangement, as long as they are made independently by the compiler and entail a minimal degree of creativity, are sufficiently original that Congress may protect such compilations through the copyright laws."); Gemel Precision Tool, Co. v. Pharma Tool Corp., 1995 WL 71243, at *4 (E.D. Pa. Feb. 13, 1995) ("While it is true that factual information generally accessible to the public is not protected by copyright law, the compilation of those facts may be copyrightable.").

53. U.S. Copyright Office, Compendium of U.S. Copyright Office Practices § 1002.6 (3d ed. 2017) [hereinafter Compendium] (emphasis added).

By way of example, when a consumer purchases an IoT connected device, in addition to owning the physical product, they also require use of the underlying software. Sale of the physical product, however, includes a license for the software.[54] "Beyond the scope of the license, IoT products introduce a host of interrelated legal issues. For example, counterfeit of IoT products may be subject to criminal copyright liability. Because the software in IoT products is typically licensed even when the products in which the software is embedded are sold, corporate acquisitions, bankruptcies and other restructurings, and tax planning have become more complicated as to entities in the IoT product space."[55]

Under U.S. copyright law, a copyright owner has the exclusive right to create derivative works based on the owner's copyrighted work.[56] With respect to data gathered in an IoT system, the ownership of derivative works frequently comes into play when databases are shared between parties (e.g., a licensor and a licensee).[57] As discussed in the following section, the fair use doctrine can create uncertainty regarding the ownership of derivative works, highlighting the importance of a comprehensive data usage agreement addressing data ownership.

A. Derivative Works and Fair Use

A copyright exception for transformative derivative works exists under the fair use doctrine.[58] Under the fair use doctrine, a court

54. John A. Polito, Lucy Wang & Spencer H. Wan, *Copyright's Role in the Internet of Things*, LAW360 (Oct. 24, 2016, 12:21 PM), https://www.law360.com/articles/851301/copyright-s-role-in-the-internet-of-things.

55. *Id.*

56. COMPENDIUM § 507.2.

57. Aaron K. Tantleff, *Licensing Big Data*, *in* BIG DATA: A BUSINESS AND LEGAL GUIDE 91, 95 (James R. Kalyvas & Michael R. Overly eds., 2015) ("For example, a licensee may license a database and then spend hundreds of hours mining the database for information generating analysis and new sets of data based on the derivative works of such data mining and analysis.").

58. 17 U.S.C. § 107 (2018).

will look to four factors: "[1] the purpose and character of the use, [2] the nature of the copyrighted work, [3] the amount and substantiality of the portion used in relation to the copyrighted work as a whole, and [4] the effect of the use upon the potential market for or value of the copyrighted work."[59] Under the first factor, "the purpose and character of the use," a court will look to whether the use is transformative, that is, "altering the original with new expression, meaning, or message."[60] A key question, therefore, is whether IoT analysis transforms a data set. A data licensee may argue that its big data analysis alters the original data set with new meaning so as to transform the data set.[61] On the other hand, the licensor may argue that the analysis is not so great so as to transform the copyrighted database.[62] In this way, certain transformative IoT and big data activities may help to avoid infringement by way of the fair use doctrine.

B. First Sale Doctrine in Copyright

The first sale doctrine of copyright law (hereinafter FSD) is an old concept, originally described by the Supreme Court in 1908.[63] Now codified in 17 U.S.C. § 109, the FSD prevents a copyright owner from controlling the distribution or resale of a copyrighted work after the first sale of that work.[64] The Supreme Court in *Kirtsaeng v. John Wiley & Sons, Inc.*,[65] held that the FSD also applies to any copyrighted work that is lawfully made and sold abroad.

The FSD has historically protected resellers of copyrightable content, but its applicability is less certain in the digital space. In

59. *Id.*; *see More Information on Fair Use*, COPYRIGHT.GOV, https://www.copyright.gov/fair-use/more-info.html (last updated July 2018).

60. Campbell v. Acuff-Rose Music, Inc., 510 U.S. 569, 569 (1994).

61. *See id.*

62. *See id.*

63. *See generally* Bobbs-Merrill Co. v. Straus, 210 U.S. 339 (1908).

64. 17 U.S.C. § 109 (2018).

65. Kirtsaeng v. John Wiley & Sons, Inc., 568 U.S. 519 (2013).

2013, the U.S. District Court for the Southern District of New York held in *Capitol Records, LLC v. ReDigi Inc.* that "the first sale defense is limited to material items, like records, that the copyright owner put into the stream of commerce."[66] This decision cast uncertainty over the FSD's application in the digital space as it is the creation of the new file on a different physical storage drive that determines the outcome; however, the Second Circuit's anticipated appellate ruling may clarify the FSD's role.[67]

C. Sui Generis Right in the EU

In 1996, the EU adopted Directive 96/9/EC concerning the Legal Protection of Databases, which may provide a remedy for protecting IoT databases.[68] This directive vests a sui generis right in the maker of a database that shows "there has been qualitatively and/or quantitatively a substantial investment in either the obtaining, verification or presentation of the contents."[69] Specifically, there are three requirements to gain the IP right: (1) the maker of the database is a national of an EU member state or is a company located within the EU community with operations genuinely linked with the economy of an EU member state; (2) the maker made a "substantial investment" in obtaining, verifying, or presenting the data; and (3) the data was formed into a database.[70]

66. 934 F. Supp. 2d 640, 655 (S.D.N.Y. 2013).

67. Lee Burgunder, *Digital Resale & Copyrights: Why the Second Circuit Won't Buy It*, IP WATCHDOG (Oct. 11, 2017), http://www.ipwatchdog.com/2017/10/11/digital-resale-copyrights-second-circuit-wont-buy/id=88965/.

68. *Protection of Databases*, EUR. COMM'N, https://ec.europa.eu/digital-single-market/en/protection-databases (last updated June 1, 2018).

69. *Directive 96/9/EC of the European Parliament and of the Council of 11 March 1996 on the Legal Protection of Databases*, 2004 OFFICIAL J. EUR. COMMUNITIES 77/20, *available at* http://eur-lex.europa.eu/legal-content/EN/TXT/PDF/?uri=CELEX:31996L0009&from=EN.

70. Adam Rendle, *Who Owns the Data in the Internet of Things?*, TAYLORWESSING (Feb. 2014), https://united-kingdom.taylorwessing.com/download/article_data_lot.html.

In a typical IoT scenario, where multiple entities may collect and interact with the data, recognizing the maker will usually be the most difficult step.[71] "The maker will be the entity who:

- takes the initiative in obtaining, verifying or presenting the contents of the database; and
- assumes the risk of investing in that obtaining, verifying or presenting."[72]

It is important to note that although 96/9/EC vests data rights in an entity that meets these requirements, it does not necessarily exclude entities that fail them. In situations where 96/9/EC is not met, uncertainty remains.

D. Copyright in the EU

Generally, under EU law, applications developed to provide functionality, or related services, to connected devices may be protected by copyright if they are original. The program code and/or any preparatory design material may be protectable by design copyright, while the graphic interface may be protectable by traditional copyright as an intellectual work.[73]

V. IoT Data Ownership and Pitfalls

In addition to the obvious data privacy and data security concerns that arise in connection with IoT systems, another intellectual property-related issue—data ownership—will become an increasingly important and hotly contested legal issue as manufacturers, businesses, and individuals record, store, and use more and more data over time, and then vie over ownership of that data.

71. *Id.*
72. *Id.*
73. Audrey Lefevre, *Internet of Things: Intellectual Property Focus for the Protection of Connected Devices*, INTELL. PROP & ENT. L. (July 2017).

IoT data ownership is a complex issue and the IP rights associated with the data may not afford enough protections and certainty. Solutions to these problems may come in the form of appropriate contracts that clearly delineate rights and ownership in areas such as the gathering, anonymizing, notifying, and use of customer data in an IoT environment.[74] While different industries and companies may take varied approaches to regulating the transfer of data control and title, the common denominator is well-crafted contractual language that protects both the consumer's interests and feeds a growing data ecosystem.[75]

A. Data Usage Agreements (DUAs)

The proliferation of the IoT has enabled widespread collection of big data about nearly every aspect of the world around us. Once collected, this data can then be analyzed using big data and AI tools and techniques.[76] As discussed previously, there are various IP protections that may apply to the IoT data that is stored on devices and servers, along with the algorithms that aggregate and analyze that data. Beyond those protections, the ownership and usage of data is typically governed through, and mostly limited by, data usage agreements (DUAs).[77]

DUAs are contractual agreements between a user, who typically generates data in an IoT system, and a data holder, broker,

---

74. Prigya Arora, *Internet of Things: Imminent IP Issues*, IIPRD, (Sept. 27, 2017, 8:04 AM), http://www.iiprd.com/internet-of-things-imminent-ip-issues/.

75. David Knight, *Who Owns the Data from the IoT?*, Network World, (Jan. 30, 2017, 4:00 AM), https://www.networkworld.com/article/3152837/internet-of-things/who-owns-the-data-from-the-iot.html.

76. Philip Kushmaro, *The IoT and Big Data: Making the Connection*, Huffington Post (Sept. 23, 2016), http://www.huffingtonpost.com/philip-kushmaro/the-iot-and-big-data-maki_b_12116608.html.

77. Doug Geisler, *Driving Data with Unintentional New Uses: Internet of Things*, Avnet, https://www.avnet.com/wps/portal/apac/resources/technical-articles/article/iot/driving-data-with-unintentional-new-uses-internet-of-things/ (last visited Nov. 26, 2018).

or analyst who collects, analyzes, or otherwise makes use of the collected user data.[78] Potential users, or data subjects, include corporate clients and individual consumers. Analysts provide the technology that collects and analyzes users' data.[79]

1. Data Scope in DUAs

Typically, the owner of machine-generated IoT data is the entity who holds title to the device that collected the data.[80] Data ownership and control differ, however, as data may be owned by one party and controlled by another. "Possession of data does not necessarily equate to title."[81] Possession is control, and control follows the data. Accordingly, control is relinquished when a data set is copied and transmitted elsewhere. On the other hand, title is ownership.[82] Furthermore, agreements in the consumer space may be subject to government oversight, thus resulting in certain industries (e.g., health care) that must comply with a network of statutes and agency rules.

From square one, before any further terms of a DUA are drafted, the scope of the term "data" should be clearly defined.[83] Data can be defined broadly or narrowly. It is important that data be clearly defined in accordance with the expectations of the parties. The parties should also consider whether the agreement will

---

78. Peter Leonard, *Making the Most of Your Data: Getting Data Analytics Contracts Right*, IAPP (Mar. 21, 2016), https://iapp.org/news/a/making-the-most-of-your-data-getting-data-analytics-contracts-right.

79. *Big Data Analytics Services*, HITACHI, https://www.hds.com/en-us/services/big-data-analytics-services.html (last visited June 28, 2018). For purpose of the chapter, all recommendations are from the perspective of an analyst, and, except where otherwise noted, all users are assumed to be corporate users.

80. *See* Knight, *supra* note 75.

81. *Id.*

82. *Id.*

83. David W. Tollen, *The Big Data Licensing Issue-Spotter*, TECHCONTRACTS (Dec. 8, 2015), https://techcontracts.com/2015/12/08/the-big-data-licensing-issue-spotter/#_ftn4.

cover "derived data" (i.e., new data generated through analysis of the original data set using big data processing).[84] In addition to defining the scope of data covered, the parties should also agree on a format for data delivery.

2. Ownership of Data

DUAs should determine and clearly state which party in an IoT system will own any gathered or processed data.[85] Typically, the users, or data subjects, will retain ownership of the data and license it to the analyst; however, a DUA can alternatively provide for data ownership to transfer from the user to the analyst.[86] The DUA should also specify the ownership of derived data or other results of data analysis.[87] When ownership is retained by the user, a DUA can include a preservation clause to that effect.[88] When ownership is transferred, a DUA can include an assignment clause. Licensing data often results in the generation of new data. A DUA should clearly define the scope and ownership of derived data. Derived data may be defined broadly to include derivative works, or it may be defined more narrowly, to separate other derived data from derivative works.[89]

One way to facilitate agreement over data ownership is to include a license-back provision in a DUA. Under a license-back provision, whichever party grants ownership of the data under the

---

84. *Id.*

85. *Id.*; *see Cutting Edge Issues in IP Ownership: Big Data and New Technologies*, ASS'N CORP. COUNS. 1, 14–15 (June 1, 2016), https://www.acc.com/chapters/wash/upload/BakerHostetler-Cutting-edge-issues-in-IP-ownership.pdf [hereinafter *IP Ownership*].

86. Tollen, *supra* note 83; *see* Leslie T. Thornton & Edward R. McNicholas, *Governing Information with Vendors–Contracting with Service Providers*, 5 SUCCESSFUL PARTNERING BETWEEN INSIDE AND OUTSIDE COUNSEL § 82.17 (2015) [hereinafter Thornton].

87. Tollen, *supra* note 83.

88. *See id.*

89. *See id.*

agreement receives a license to use the data. Licensing back may allow the party that does not own the derived data to nevertheless use the results of the analyst's work.

3. Ownership of Derived Data

As noted previously, a key question in IoT systems is the question of who owns the data. A related question arises once the data is used in a big data system: once big data analytics are applied to a data set, such that the data set is transformed, who owns the transformed data set?[90] On one hand, analysts may argue that performing data analysis provides the original data set with new meaning and commercial value and as a result created new intellectual property by transforming the data set in important ways.[91] On the other hand, users may argue that the change is not so great that it meaningfully transforms the copyrighted database, and therefore no new rights should be created from the data.[92]

To avoid these types of conflicts over the original data set and the derived data, and related disputes about who owns the associated copyrights, a DUA should expressly allocate the ownership interest between parties so that ownership rights are clear regardless of any background IP rules.[93] Additionally, because ownership of the original data set (as opposed the transformed data set) will often remain with the user, analysts should ensure that they have licenses to the data set from end users.[94] Typically, on this end of the spectrum, there is a give-and-take approach where a vendor may collect in-depth data from a sensor platform in order to optimize the user's experience. "Here, the contract allows all data to be exchanged in return for incentives such as a curated service or

90. *See IP Ownership*, *supra* note 85, at 23.
91. *See* Tollen, *supra* note 83.
92. *See id.*
93. *See id.*
94. *See id.*

discount. This approach conveys all data usage rights and data title once the end user opts in."[95]

4. Other Considerations

Beyond the questions of ownership and IP, a DUA should define the scope of the analyst's license to the user's data by delineating data usage rights, data use restrictions, and data distribution restrictions.[96] Analysts (including corporations, data brokers and marketplaces, and those that transform big data) will typically seek expansive licenses to users' data, including broad usage rights, minimal use restrictions, and broad distribution rights, while users, or data subjects (those generating the data), may wish to only grant narrow licenses with specific usage rights, strict use restrictions, and limited distribution rights.[97] Depending on these restrictions, the IP rights associated with certain IoT data may be quite limited.

A strong data usage agreement also should define the contours of usage rights and restrictions. Data usage rights define the breadth of the analyst's rights to use the data set. It is typically important, from the perspective of a data analyst, to secure broad usage rights to maintain flexibility. Users may attempt to constrain usage rights through a narrow license.[98] Alternatively, usage rights can be crafted broadly, and usage restrictions can be imposed on this right. This approach provides the analyst unfettered access to the data but constrains the analyst's usage via restrictions.[99]

Usage restrictions, on the other hand, enable the user to limit the scope of a data license.[100] A wide variety of creative usage restrictions may be crafted. Customer restrictions limit the third

95. *See* Knight, *supra* note 75.
96. *See id.*
97. *See id.*
98. *See id.*
99. *See id.*
100. *See id.*; Thornton, *supra* note 86.

parties for whom the analyst may provide services based on analysis of the user's data set.[101] The user may want to impose narrow field of use restrictions. The analyst might not have a strong preference on field of use restrictions. Anonymity requirements may obligate the analyst to analyze only anonymized data and may set restrictions on the analyst's usage rights for the anonymized data. The analyst, in accordance with an agreement may be obligated to anonymize the data, or the user may provide the analyst with an anonymized data set.[102] In either case, a user may seek to impose restrictions on the analyst's ability to extract or discern identifying information from the anonymized data set.[103] Similarly, a license may also include distribution restrictions that can limit the analyst's ability to redistribute raw data or anonymized versions of the raw data sets.[104]

These and a host of other issues should be considered when negotiating new IoT and Big Data usage and collection agreements. As industry partnerships in this area continue to form, all parties can benefit from the business certainty provided by well-crafted agreements, and well-demarcated lines on ownership of collected data, derived data, and the IP associated with that data.

VI. Conclusion

As we stand at the brink of a golden age of the IoT, the information that is acquired and protected is becoming an increasingly valuable strategic asset that can hold the key to great benefits; but it can also leave open a number of questions related to intellectual property.

There is no denying that the IoT will continue to bring about innovations that transform the way we do business and the way we live. Companies across industries will be well served today by

101. *See* Tollen, *supra* note 83.
102. *See id.*
103. *See id.*
104. *See id.*

being mindful of how to protect the information and IP they generate related to IoT, and also to plan their business strategies mindful of the risks inherent in IoT and big data systems. Companies that do not keep up with these trends in collecting and harnessing information to improve their processes, or who do not prepare business strategies that capture and protect IP and avoid the IP of others, may be significantly disadvantaging themselves relative to their competition. While IP will provide some protections, other tools, such as well-crafted data usage agreements, will also be important in providing and protecting the rights needed to maximize flexibility in the way that they use data collected from IoT devices.

Chapter 17

When Things Get Hacked

Insurance Coverage for IoT-Related Risks[1]

John Buchanan
Dustin Cho[2]

I. Introduction

Hackers can do more than steal your data. When they access IoT-connected things—whether household appliances, medical devices, industrial control systems, smart grids, or smart cities—hackers and other bad actors can damage property and endanger lives.

Reports in recent years highlight some disturbing potential threat scenarios. Russian government cyber actors could gain remote access to networks capable of disrupting critical U.S. infrastructure, including the energy sector and the power grid.[3]

1. Earlier versions of this chapter were prepared for the 2016 and 2018 CLE Conferences of the ABA Litigation Section Insurance Coverage Litigation Committee.

2. The authors are lawyers in the Washington, D.C. office of Covington & Burling LLP, who represent policyholders exclusively in coverage litigation. The authors also gratefully acknowledge the contributions of Covington associate A.J. Carvalho and former Covington associate Patrick Rawsthorne. The opinions stated in this chapter are those of the authors and should not be attributed either to their law firm or to its clients.

3. *See, e.g.*, Dep't of Homeland Security & Fed. Bureau of Investigation, Technical Alert 18-074A, "Russian Government Cyber Activity

Cyber soldiers sitting behind computers in Tehran could open the floodgates on a nearby dam.[4] Or the threat could be as banal and close to home as bored teenagers down the street hijacking your "smart" home appliances,[5] or, more ominously, the city's trolley system.[6]

These novel threats arise from what the National Institute of Standards and Technology refers to as "cyber-physical" or "smart" systems, that is, the "co-engineered interacting networks of physical and computational components" that allow the real world and digital world to interact in unprecedented ways.[7] Unfortunately, as other chapters of this book discuss, the protections against unauthorized electronic access in many "smart" IoT-connected systems are often not so smart. Hence the reports of hacks on a wide variety of networked IoT devices ranging from smart toilets[8] to drones[9] to

---

Targeting Energy and Other Critical Infrastructure Sectors," https://www.us-cert.gov/ncas/alerts/TA18-074A (rev. Mar. 16, 2018) (hereinafter DHS-FBI Alert); Rebecca Smith, *Russia Hacks Its Way into U.S. Utilities,* WALL ST. J. (July 24, 2018); US WARNS PUBLIC ABOUT ATTACKS ON ENERGY, INDUSTRIAL FIRMS, BUS. INS. (Oct. 23, 2017, 12:30 PM), http://www.businessinsurance.com/article/20171023/NEWS06/912316709/US-warns-public-about-attacks-on-energy,-industrial-firms.

4. Joseph Berger, *A Dam, Small and Unsung, Is Caught Up in an Iranian Hacking Case,* N.Y. TIMES, (Mar. 23, 2016), https://www.nytimes.com/2016/03/26/nyregion/rye-brook-dam-caught-in-computer-hacking-case.html.

5. *See Kashmir Hill, Here's What It Looks Like When a 'Smart Toilet' Gets Hacked,* FORBES (Aug. 15, 2013), http://www.forbes.com/sites/kashmirhill/2013/08/15/heres-what-it-looks-like-when-a-smart-toilet-gets-hacked-video/.

6. *See Graeme Baker, Schoolboy Hacks into City's Tram System,* THE TELEGRAPH (Jan. 11, 2008), http://www.telegraph.co.uk/news/worldnews/1575293/Schoolboy-hacks-into-citys-tram-system.html.

7. Cyber-physical systems homepage, Nat'l Inst. of Standards & Tech., http://www.nist.gov/cps/ (last visited Jan. 7, 2018).

8. *See Hill, supra* note 5.

9. *See SkyJack: Hacker-Drone That Can Wirelessly Hijack & Control Other Drones,* RT NEWS (Dec. 6, 2013), https://www.rt.com/news/hacker-drone-aircraft-parrot-704/.

medical devices.[10] The federal government's alerts and subsequent security briefings in 2018[11] have raised the general level of awareness of potentially massive physical losses from hacking the IoT or industrial IoT, including attacks on power grids or other networked critical infrastructure.

These increased warnings of the risk of massive physical losses from cyberattacks naturally raise the question whether that risk can be mitigated by insurance. In fact, a 2015 report titled "Business Blackout," prepared by Lloyd's and Cambridge University, anticipated the types of IoT-related attacks on critical infrastructure that have been the subject of the 2018 federal government warnings and analyzed what insurance implications might flow from them.[12] Specifically, the report hypothesized a (now all too plausible) scenario, in which a cyberattack on a utility's industrial control systems disables or destroys multiple power generators in a "smart" grid, resulting in cascading losses throughout the blacked-out power grid and beyond.[13] Such losses could include first-party physical property damage and business-interruption loss for utilities and their customers, third-party property damage and bodily injuries arising from the grid shutdown, and even looting and other social unrest, with accompanying liabilities for the businesses affected.[14]

10. *See* Tarun Wadhwa, *Yes, You Can Hack a Pacemaker (and Other Medical Devices Too)*, Forbes (Dec. 6, 2012), http://www.forbes.com sites/singularity/2012/12/06/yes-you-can-hack-a-pacemaker-and-other-medical-devices-too/.

11. DHS-FBI Alert, *supra* note 3; Awareness Briefings: Russian Activity Against Critical Infrastructure, Nat'l Cybersecurity & Commc'ns Integration Ctr (NCCIC), https://share.dhs.gov/p344qjbhqu03/.

12. Lloyd's Emerging Risk Report, *Business Blackout: The Insurance Implications of a Cyber Attack on the US Power Grid* (May 2015), *available at* http://www.lloyds.com/~/media/files/news%20and%20insight/risk%20insight/2015/business%20blackout/business%20blackout20150708.pdf.

13. *Id.* at 11–13.

14. *Id.* at 16–19.

The cyber insurance market has exploded in recent years; dozens of insurers now offer some kind of cyber coverage.[15] Most cyber-related policies address the intangible losses that accompany network intrusions and data hacks—with a particular focus on privacy-related losses.[16] Thus, while coverage is subject, as always, to the specific (and widely variable) wordings of these nonstandard policy forms, if an attack on IoT-connected devices involves conventional data privacy losses, then most available cyber policies can be expected to provide some protection.

But insurance protection for so called cyber-physical risk—the physical losses that may result from the cyber peril of an IoT-related attack—presents a more complex question under many commonly available insurance policies. In fact, most off-the-shelf cyber forms expressly *exclude coverage for physical bodily injury and property damage.*[17] Originally, insurers drafted such exclusions to prevent cyber policies from duplicating the coverage traditionally afforded by standard-form commercial general liability (CGL) and first-party property policies.[18]

But do conventional liability and property policies still clearly cover bodily injury or property damage when it arises from a cyberattack involving IoT devices? This chapter analyzes coverage issues that may arise under traditional CGL and property policies where cyber-physical risks are involved, including the arguments that insurers may raise to escape coverage under such policies

15. *See, e.g.*, Julie Greenwald, *Cyber Insurance Comes of Age*, Bus. Ins. (Nov. 6, 2017), http://www.businessinsurance.com/article/20171106/NEWS06/912317022/Cyber-insurance-comes-of-age.

16. *See* Richard S. Betterley, *The Betterley Report: Cyber/Privacy Insurance Market Survey 2018*, 42–69 (June 2018) (charting availability of coverage for various data privacy-related losses under 32 different cyber insurance forms).

17. *See id.* at 72–75, 88–90 (charting the availability both of first-party coverage for direct damage to equipment and of third-party coverage for bodily injury and property damage).

18. *See infra* note 19.

and the arguments that policyholders may raise in rebuttal. It then discusses examples of the specialty insurance products that have started to emerge to provide coverage (at a price) for physical harms from cyber perils. It concludes with a few general observations and recommendations for insuring IoT-related risks.

II. Commercial General Liability Insurance Coverage for Bodily Injury or Property Damage Caused by Cyber Attacks through the IoT

Cyber insurance is now widely available; but as indicated earlier, most cyber policies currently exclude third-party liability coverage for bodily injury and property damage. The explanation commonly provided for this exclusion is that "such losses are covered under CGL . . . policies."[19] But in fact, most recent standard-form CGL policies now incorporate their own cyber-related exclusions—the scope of which is not always clear. This section discusses the evolution of those exclusions and the coverage issues they present in the context of IoT risks.

A. Cyber Exclusions in the CGL Form

Since the turn of this century, the Insurance Services Office (ISO) has repeatedly revised the standard CGL policy's bodily injury and property damage liability coverage part (titled "Coverage A") with respect to cyber-related risks. First, in 2001, the standard CGL policy was revised to state that damage to electronically stored data would not be considered damage to tangible property.[20] Next, in

---

19. Robert Bregman, *Cyber and Privacy Insurance Coverage,* 37(11) IRMI, The Risk Report 1 (July 2015), ("The [cyber] policies exclude claims alleging bodily injury and property damage because such losses are covered under CGL/property insurance policies.").

20. The 2001 Insurance Services Office CGL policy form added the following two sentences to the definition of "property damage":

> For the purposes of this insurance, electronic data is not tangible property. As used in this definition, electronic data means information, facts

2004, it was revised to exclude "[d]amages arising out of the loss of, loss of use of, damage to, corruption of, inability to access, or inability to manipulate electronic data." According to ISO, this new exclusion, "Exclusion p," removed coverage for damage to physical property caused by loss of electronic data.[21] In 2013, a sentence was added to Exclusion p that carved out from the exclusion any "liability for damages because of 'bodily injury.'"[22] That is to say, the new sentence expressly *preserved* coverage for bodily injury arising out of the loss of electronic data.

In May 2014, ISO published two versions of an endorsement that revises Exclusion p: one with a "limited bodily injury exception" and one without.[23] The latter endorsement, in part, reverts to the 2004 variant of Exclusion p—it excludes any damages arising out of the loss of electronic data, regardless of whether the damages are because of bodily injury or property damage.[24] The former

> or programs stored as or on, created or used on, or transmitted to or from computer software, including systems and applications software, hard or floppy disks, CD-ROMS, tapes, drives, cells, data processing devices or any other media which are used with electronically controlled equipment.

Note that property damage is defined as physical injury to tangible property (including resulting loss of use of that property) and loss of use of tangible property that is not physically injured. *See* ISO Properties, Inc., *Commercial General Liability Coverage Form, CG 00 01 10 01* § V.17, at 15 (2000).

21. *See* ISO Properties, Inc., *Commercial General Liability Coverage Form, CG 00 01 12 04* § I.A.2.p, at 5 (2003). The definition of "electronic data" used in this exclusion was the same as the definition of "electronic data" that the 2001 standard CGL policy had introduced in its definition of "property damage."

22. *See* Insurance Services Office, Inc., *Commercial General Liability Coverage Form, CG 00 01 04 13* § I.A.2.p, at 5 (2012).

23. ISO also published a third version that applies only to Coverage B, the coverage for "personal and advertising injury liability" (thus omitting the revisions to Exclusion p in Coverage A). *See* Insurance Services Office, Inc., *Exclusion—Access or Disclosure of Confidential or Personal Information (Coverage B Only), CG 21 08 05 14* (2013).

24. The "limited bodily injury exception not included" endorsement states in relevant part:

endorsement in part adheres to the 2013 edition of Exclusion p, which preserves coverage for damages because of bodily injury.[25]

B. Exclusion p, ¶ (1): "Access to . . . Nonpublic Information"

What was new and identical in both 2014 endorsements was the addition of paragraph (1) of Exclusion p—an exclusion for all damages (whether because of bodily injury or not) arising out of "[a]ny access to or disclosure of any person's or organization's confidential or personal information, including patents, trade secrets, processing methods, customer lists, financial information, credit

---

> This insurance does not apply to: . . . Damages arising out of: (1) Any access to or disclosure of any person's or organization's confidential or personal information, including patents, trade secrets, processing methods, customer lists, financial information, credit card information, health information or any other type of nonpublic information; or (2) The loss of, loss of use of, damage to, corruption of, inability to access, or inability to manipulate electronic data.

Insurance Services Office, Inc., *Exclusion—Access or Disclosure of Confidential or Personal Information and Data-Related Liability—Limited Bodily Injury Exception Not Included, CG 21 07 05 14* (2013).

25. The "limited bodily injury exception" endorsement states in relevant part:

> This insurance does not apply to: . . . Damages arising out of: (1) Any access to or disclosure of any person's or organization's confidential or personal information, including patents, trade secrets, processing methods, customer lists, financial information, credit card information, health information or any other type of nonpublic information; or (2) The loss of, loss of use of, damage to, corruption of, inability to access, or inability to manipulate electronic data. . . . However, unless paragraph (1) above applies, this exclusion does not apply to damages because of 'bodily injury.'

Insurance Services Office, Inc., *Exclusion—Access or Disclosure of Confidential or Personal Information and Data-Related Liability—with Limited Bodily Injury Exception, CG 21 06 05 14* (2013).

card information, health information or any other type of nonpublic information."[26]

In isolation, the undefined terms "access to" and "nonpublic information" are sufficiently vague that an aggressive insurer might argue, for example, that a hospital's or medical device manufacturer's liability for bodily injury caused by alteration of a patient's dialysis machine settings would constitute excluded damages because they arose out of "access to . . . any person's health information or any other type of nonpublic information"; or similarly, that liability for property damage or personal injuries resulting from a hacker's manipulation of the data regulating industrial control systems in a nuclear plant or power grid arose from "access to . . . nonpublic information" and thus is excluded.

In response, insureds would argue that this exclusion, read within its context, cannot reasonably encompass all traditional bodily injury and physical damage caused by hacking of industrial control systems, malicious or negligent alteration of medical device settings, or other types of access to nonpublic electronic data regulating networked "things" through the IoT, for at least the following reasons:

- **"Nonpublic Information."** The settings and controls of devices and machinery, though not necessarily accessible to the "public," are not reasonably construed as "any other type of nonpublic information" as contemplated by the exclusion. The interpretive canon of ejusdem generis[27] instructs us that when a series of items in a list share a certain core characteristic, a "catchall" term at the end of the list should not be read to stretch beyond what the specifi-

26. *See supra* notes 24 and 25.

27. "Under the principle of *ejusdem generis,* when a general term follows a specific one, the general term should be understood as a reference to subjects akin to the one with specific enumeration." Norfolk & W. Ry. Co. v. Am. Train Dispatchers Ass'n, 499 U.S. 117, 129 (1991).

cally listed items have in common. In these endorsements, the specifically listed types of "nonpublic information" preceding the catchall phrase are all traditionally confidential information whose confidentiality is recognized, and protected, by law.[28]

Networked device settings and machine instructions do not generally enjoy either legal or popular recognition as inherently private information. Such data are qualitatively different from the specific categories of protected information listed in paragraph (1) of Exclusion p: "trade secrets, processing methods, customer lists, financial information, credit card information, [and] health information." Under this interpretive principle, therefore, the catchall term "and any other nonpublic information" in the exclusion endorsements would be read to include other categories of information whose confidentiality is recognized under and protected by the law; but it would not be stretched to encompass a qualitatively different type of "information"—the data regulating electronic control systems.

Reinforcing this reading, both endorsements specifically list examples of the damages to which the exclusion applies—all of which are damages associated specifically with data privacy breaches:

> This exclusion applies even if damages are claimed for notification costs, credit monitoring expenses, forensic expenses, public relations expenses or any other loss, cost or expense incurred by you or others

28. The exclusion's list of various types of "confidential information" arguably starts after the first term, "patents." While patents are publicly disclosed once granted, they share legal protections similar to those enjoyed by other enumerated types of information such as "trade secrets."

arising out of that which is described in Paragraph (1) or (2) above.[29]

All of these types of expense relate to common responses to data breaches, and indeed it is difficult to conceive how the first two items in the list—notification costs and credit monitoring expenses—could arise in the event of traditional physical bodily injury or property damage. This clause's focus on privacy-breach damages reinforces the conclusion that the exclusion was intended only for privacy-related liabilities and not for physical harm that happens to have resulted from a malfunctioning electronic device.

- **"Access To."** Although manipulation of a machine's or device's settings may involve "access to" those settings, the scenarios of concern do not "aris[e] out of" the access to the data that comprises those settings (much less their "disclosure" to the public). Rather, they arise out of the overwriting or overriding of that data—whether intentionally (through hacking) or unintentionally (through user error or a programming bug). In context, damages "arising out of . . . [a]ny access to or disclosure of . . . nonpublic information" means damages arising out of *obtaining* nonpublic information—the damages that typically arise from privacy breaches. When the hacking of industrial control systems or networked devices results in physical harm, by contrast, the cause is not the obtaining of nonpublic information, that is, the prior, correct settings for the machinery or devices in question; rather it is the introduction of new instructions

29. Insurance Services Office, Inc., *Exclusion—Access or Disclosure of Confidential or Personal Information and Data-Related Liability—Limited Bodily Injury Exception Not Included, CG 21 07 05 14* (2013); Insurance Services Office, Inc., *Exclusion—Access or Disclosure of Confidential or Personal Information and Data-Related Liability—with Limited Bodily Injury Exception, CG 21 06 05 14* (2013).

that override the original settings. For example, a hacker could alter a dialysis machine's settings even if he could not read the "information" in those settings before he overwrote them. Likewise, a hacker could disrupt a digital signal that provides instructions to a networked device without necessarily receiving or decoding the original intended signal.

In other words, the types of hacking that affect the operations of networked devices do not typically arise out of accessing any *information*—what the exclusion requires. Instead, they arise from someone's access to the system or location where the information is stored. What causes the harm is the new, erroneous digital settings or instructions that replace the original settings or instructions. Whether or not those original, correct settings are considered "nonpublic information," the intruder's access to that information is beside the point: the harm arises from the newly introduced malicious information, not from access to the "nonpublic information" itself. Unless the insurer can provide compelling forensic evidence that the essential cause of physical loss was the release rather than the alteration of confidential information in device settings, the exclusion should not apply.

- **Extrinsic Evidence.** The insurance industry's contemporaneous explanations of Exclusion p are also at odds with a broad reading that precludes coverage for all sorts of traditional bodily injury and property damage merely because some link in the causal chain of events involved "access to . . . nonpublic information." The memorandum that ISO submitted to regulators in 2013 explaining its adoption of these endorsements states that "damages related to data breaches, and certain data-related liability, are not intended to be covered under the abovementioned coverage part.

These types of damages may be more appropriately covered under certain stand-alone policies including, for instance, an information security protection policy or a cyber liability policy."[30] Although the memorandum also notes that the endorsement without the "limited bodily injury exception" would "result in a reduction of coverage," the memorandum is clear that this statement applies only to the extent that that endorsement reverts from the 2013 amendment of Exclusion p with respect to the loss of electronic data.[31] ISO's stated intent not to reduce coverage, but rather to limit the new exclusion to the types of risks that are covered by common cyber liability policies, is consistent with an ISO executive's explanation of the endorsements shortly after they were introduced; he identified other "standalone" ISO insurance products that were available "to provide certain coverage with respect to data breach and access to or disclosure of confidential or personal information," thus suggesting that the new exclusions were intended to dovetail with cyber policies.[32] The insurer view is that neither the

30. Insurance Services Offices, Inc., *Access or Disclosure of Confidential or Personal Information Exclusions Introduced*, Commercial Lines Forms Filing CL-2013-ODBFR, at 7, 8 (2013) (on file with authors).

31. *See id.* at 8 ("However, when this endorsement is attached, it will result in a reduction of coverage *due to the deletion of an exception* with respect to damages because of bodily injury arising out of loss of, loss of use of, damage to, corruption of, inability to access, or inability to manipulate data.").

32. *See ISO Comments on CGL Endorsements for Data Breach Liability Exclusions*, Ins. J. (July 18, 2014), available at http://www.insurancejournal.com/news/east/2014/07/18/332655.htm (quoting Ron Biederman, assistant vice president, Commercial Casualty at ISO: "As the exposures to data breaches increased over time, standalone policies started to become available in the marketplace to provide certain coverage with respect to data breach and access to or disclosure of confidential or personal information. For instance, ISO Information Security Protection Policy EC 00 10 contains both first and third party coverage through eight separate insuring agreements which address data breach and other cyber-related exposures.").

freestanding ISO cyber policies he referenced nor any other commonly available cyber policy form provides coverage for traditional physical bodily injury and property damage caused by rogue electronic devices.

C. Exclusion p, ¶ (2): "Loss of . . . Electronic Data"

Paragraph (2) of Exclusion p uses the same language used in CGL policies since 2004 to exclude damages arising out of "[t]he loss of, loss of use of, damage to, corruption of, inability to access, or inability to manipulate electronic data."[33] As noted earlier, since 2014 this exclusion comes in two different versions. The "limited bodily injury exception" version, like the 2013 standard CGL policy, expressly preserves coverage for bodily injury. The other version, like the 2004 standard CGL policy, contains no express carve-out for bodily injury. In both formulations, as with paragraph (1), the applicability of this paragraph (2) exclusion to cyber-physical loss—physical harms arising from IoT hackers overwriting or overriding the controls of electronic device.

Some cyberattacks, however, may not depend upon the introduction of new data, but rather may involve destruction or disruption of network transmissions or device instructions. This raises the question whether the paragraph (2) exclusion applies to physical harms resulting from these types of attacks. Ultimately, the question of coverage for such attacks may entail questions about how the harm arose; that is, whether or not the significant cause of the damage was the "loss of," or "inability" to access or manipulate, data.

---

33. Insurance Services Office, Inc., *Exclusion—Access or Disclosure of Confidential or Personal Information and Data-Related Liability—Limited Bodily Injury Exception Not Included, CG 21 07 05 14* (2013); Insurance Services Office, Inc., *Exclusion—Access or Disclosure of Confidential or Personal Information and Data-Related Liability—with Limited Bodily Injury Exception, CG 21 06 05 14* (2013).

In sum, Exclusion p in the standard CGL form appears—both from its drafting history and in the context of the policy's wording—to be aimed at the privacy risks covered under separate cyber policies. But its uncertain application in the context of IoT-related cyber-physical harm may well give rise to highly technical—and no doubt costly—coverage disputes, with the insurer bearing the burden of proving that this exclusion precludes coverage for harm from an IoT attack.

III. First-Party Property Coverage

Many first-party property policies do not explicitly address coverage for physical harm from a cyberattack.[34] Some, like the ISO's standard "all risks" and "named perils" policies, may not mention cyber-related risks at all in their cause of loss forms.[35] Others may include cyber exclusions targeting only harm to intangible property.

If such a cyber-silent policy is an "all risks" policy, meaning it covers losses unless caused by a specifically excluded peril, then coverage for physical damage from a cyberattack should presumptively exist. As one commentator has observed, however, some in the insurance industry assert that standard all risks policies were not created with cyber perils in mind.[36] But an insurer's failure to anticipate a novel risk should not negate the core function of an "all risks" policy; it promises coverage unless an exclusion applies.[37] Without a cyber-specific exclusion to rely on, an insurer facing a claim for physical losses from a cyberattack would likely have to

34. *See* Lloyd's Emerging Risk Report, *supra* note 12, at 37.

35. ISO Properties, Inc., *Commercial Property, Causes of Loss—Special Form, CP 10 30 09 17 (2016); ISO Properties, Inc., Commercial Property, Causes of Loss—Broad Form, CP 10 20 10 12 (2011); ISO Properties, Inc., Commercial Property, Causes of Loss—Basic Form, CP 10 10 10 12* (2011).

36. *See* Alex Lathrop, *Does Traditional Coverage Apply When Cyber Attacks Cause Physical Damage?*, Property Casualty 360, at 3 (Dec. 29, 2016, 3:00 AM), http://www.propertycasualty360.com/2016/12/29/does-traditional-coverage-apply-when-cyber-attacks?slreturn=1515084401&page=3.

37. *See id.*

show that the attack fits within some non-cyber-specific exclusion to justify denying coverage.

If a cyber-silent policy is written on a "named perils" basis—meaning it covers only harms from expressly enumerated risks—coverage could still be found in many cases. Under the standard ISO policies, and most others, cyberattacks, as such, are not named perils. Still, they may sometimes fall within the scope of a named peril's definition. For example, the ISO policies name "vandalism" as a covered risk and define it as "willful and malicious damage to, or destruction of," insured property.[38] To be sure, some insurers may balk at coverage under such a provision because cyber-physical risks seem so far a cry from traditional forms of vandalism like a brick through a window. But the "vandalism" definition is silent on means and relates only to intent—and many IoT hackers "willfully" or "maliciously" destroy insured property. Even if a cyberattack does not fit within a named peril's definition, it may result in such a peril—for example, a fire or explosion. In cases where hacking either counts as a named peril or creates such a peril, an insurer would again need to point to a non-cyber exclusion to justify a denial of coverage. This potential exposure to the risk of cyber-physical damage under garden-variety property policies and other traditional policies has been characterized as the "silent cyber risk" that many insurers must evaluate more carefully.[39]

---

38. See Alex Lathrop & Janine Stanisz, *Hackers Are After More Just Data: Will Your Company's Property Policies Respond When Cyber Attacks Cause Physical Damage and Shut Down Operations?, 28* Envtl. Cl. J. 286 (2016) (raising the possibility that an attack might count as "vandalism" and analyzing coverage for physical damage from multiple, hypothetical cyberattacks under both all risks and named perils policies).

39. *See, e.g.,* Scott Stransky, *Uncovering Silent Cyber Risk,* Property Casualty 360 (July 27, 2017, 8:00 AM), http://www.propertycasualty360.com/2017/07/27/uncovering-silent-cyber-risk; Insurers Grapple with Cyber-Attacks That Spill over into Physical Damage, The Economist (Dec. 1, 2016), https://www.economist.com/news/finance-and-economics/21711086-only-cyber-calamity-will-reveal-how-ready-industry-insurers-grapple.

Although many property policies are still silent on cyber risks, some insurers are attempting to exclude them through endorsements or otherwise. For instance, one form common to energy, marine, and industrial property policies, the Institute Cyber Attack Exclusion (CL 380), excludes from coverage any damage "arising from the use or operation, as a means for inflicting harm, of any computer, computer system, computer software programme, malicious code, computer virus or process or any other electronic system."[40] Another London Market form, LMA 3030, excludes from property terrorism insurance "[l]oss or damage by electronic means including but not limited to computer hacking or the introduction of any form of computer virus or corrupting or unauthorised instructions or code or the use of any electromagnetic weapon."[41] These exclusions remain untested in the courts; whether one of them would preclude coverage for the particular circumstances of any given IoT hack may both raise subtle interpretive questions and require a fact-intensive technical analysis.

As new, nonstandard policy wordings proliferate to address the emerging risk of physical property damage from hacking of networked devices, first-party property insurance buyers will increasingly need sharp eyes, and perhaps sophisticated coverage advice, to evaluate what protection their policies provide.

IV. Emerging Coverage Solutions

Given the potential for coverage disputes under traditional CGL and property policies, as well as the growing potential for cyber-physical exposures from IoT-connected things, many policyholders may

40. The International Underwriting Association of London, *Institute Cyber Attack Exclusion Clause, CL 380 (Oct. 11, 2003), available at* http://www.iuaclauses.co.uk/site/cms/contentDocumentLibraryView.asp?chapter=8&category=57.

41. Lloyd's Market Association, *Terrorism Insurance Physical Loss or Physical Damage Wording,* LMA 3030 (Sept. 1, 2006), *available at* http://www.lmalloyds.com/LMA/Wordings/lma3030.aspx.

seek purpose-built coverage for risks of physical harm from cyber perils. The market for such products, like the threats they cover, is still evolving. A 2018 market survey of cyber insurance products indicates that such coverage options are still confined to a relative handful of insurers.[42]

Nonetheless, the number of insurance products that explicitly cover physical damage from cyber risks can be expected to grow steadily over the next several years. Some signs are already pointing in this direction. As reported in the insurance trade press, FM Global has reported increased inquiries about its products offering cyber-physical coverage;[43] AIG announced in 2017 that it would include cyber coverage in its commercial casualty policies—a move that would likely eliminate Exclusion p and the accompanying coverage issues discussed earlier;[44] and Chubb has introduced an endorsement to address, in part, uncertainty over what happens when a cyber incident creates damage traditionally covered under a property policy.[45] In the United Kingdom, meanwhile, the government-backed terrorism reinsurer, Pool Re, announced in 2017 that it would offer coverage for physical damage from cyberterrorism, following a report on the issue that it produced with the University

---

42. See Betterley, *supra note 16, at 88–90* ("Third-party Coverage: Bodily Injury and Property Damage" summary chart).

43. *See* Katie Dwyer, *Cyberattacks Reach the Physical Realm,* RISK & INSURANCE (July 27, 2017), http://riskandinsurance.com/cyberattacks-reach-physical-realm/.

44. *See, e.g.,* Suzanne Barlyn, *AIG to Include Cyber Coverage to Commercial Casualty Insurance,* REUTERS, (Oct. 26, 2017, 1:06 PM), https://www.reuters.com/article/us-aig-cyber/aig-to-include-cyber-coverage-to-commercial-casualty-insurance-idUSKBN1CV2XE.

45. Judy Greenwald, 2017 Innovation Awards: Chubb Global Cyber Facility and Property and Casualty Endorsements, BUS. INS. (Oct. 2, 2017), http://www.businessinsurance.com/article/00010101/NEWS06/912316218/2017-Innovation-Awards-Chubb-Global-Cyber-Facility-and-Property-and-Casualty-En (quoting a Chubb executive as saying, "There are questions, for instance, as to what happens if a cyber incident leads to damage covered by traditional property policies. . . . We don't want uncertainty for our clients.").

of Cambridge's Judge Business School.[46] This reinsurance protection may motivate commercial insurers to offer coverage for cyber-physical risks that they may currently attempt to exclude.

These market developments are too numerous, and too fluid, to warrant a comprehensive survey that could become obsolete within a matter of months. But one relatively recent insurance product offers a glimpse into where the market may be heading in response to these novel risks. Global insurance broker Marsh has developed a broad proprietary policy wording, known as Cyber CAT 3.0, crafted to maximize coverage across a range of insurance coverage lines for evolving cyber risks.[47] Cyber CAT 3.0 is specifically promoted as providing "Internet of Things coverage for negligence in the design or manufacture of an IoT product and/or service," as well as coverage for "[p]roperty damage to tangible property caused by a cyber event" and "[b]odily injury and property damage liability resulting from a cyber event."[48]

Policyholders desiring greater contract certainty around cyber-physical risks should consider carefully these new policies and endorsements. Some, like the Marsh form, show promise to prevent the gaps or coverage disputes identified in this chapter. Over the next decade, as the risk of cyber-physical harm grows more salient, more and more specialty insurance products can be expected to respond to rising market demand for more secure protection against such harms.

46. See T. Evan, et al., *Cyber Terrorism: Assessment of the Threat to Insurance; Cambridge Risk Framework Series, Centre for Risk Studies*, University of Cambridge (Nov. 2017).

47. *See Cyber Cat 3.0 Fact Sheet*, MARSH, *available at* https://www.marsh.com/content/dam/marsh/Documents/PDF/US-en/Cyber%20CAT%203.0%20Fact%20Sheet%20Final%20Spring%202018.pdf.

48. *Id.* at 2.

V. Conclusions and Recommendations for Entities with IoT Risk Exposures

Both insurers and insureds are confronting a relatively novel set of risks: old-fashioned physical harms arising from newfangled cyber perils. Many insureds confronted with these cyber-physical losses will argue that they should be covered under their conventional all-risk general liability and first-party property policies. Some insurer-side claims handlers may look for reasons why these risks should fall outside the policy terms.

To address these new issues, insurance purchasers would be well advised to take the following steps:

- **Understand the cyber-physical risks involved.** This means surveying the industrial control systems and other networked "smart" devices that the insured either manufactures or uses in its own operations; hardening the cybersecurity of those systems and devices; and thinking through the potential consequences of a cybersecurity failure.
- **Understand how all policy language will respond to those risks.** This means at a minimum analyzing the policy terms under cyber, technology errors and omissions, general liability, property and any other potentially applicable lines of coverage, such as kidnap and ransom policies and even directors and officers policies. Do the "dovetailing" exclusions actually dovetail? Or do they leave gaps—whether because they contemplate protection from another line of coverage that in fact has a reciprocal exclusion, or merely because the coverage grant in one line fails to align intelligently with the exclusion in another?
- **If possible, plug the gaps and clarify the coverage grants.** To clarify coverage specifically for cyber-physical risks, insurance buyers may request changes in their existing lines of coverage or explore the purchase of specialty coverage solutions.

- **Expect disputes.** They are virtually inevitable at the claims stage with any previously unrecognized or underestimated risk. But attention to both the big picture and the nitty-gritty details at the underwriting stage should reduce the chances that IoT-related risks and cyber-physical losses will generate the next big wave of coverage litigation.

Chapter 18

Corporate Counsel and the Internet of Things

Joe Whitley
Melissa Goldman

The rapid growth of the Internet of Things (IoT) has transformed businesses across sectors creating new markets and efficiencies. Nearly 73 percent of executives responding to a 2017 survey reported they were already investing in IoT, and 68 percent said they plan to invest in the next three years.[1] The IoT infrastructure consists of multiple networks of sensors and smart objects designed to connect consumer and industrial devices and systems, and exchange and act on data to allow for automation and performance improvement. The multitude of connections in an IoT ecosystem is exceedingly complex and can result in the generation of billions of data points. Much of the IoT focus has been on issues that impact businesses that incorporate IoT into their consumer product portfolios; however, industrial and commercial applications are becoming commonplace. In the industrial space, transportation companies are employing automated trucking, remote controlled cargo ships, and unmanned airplanes. Manufacturers

1. PwC Governance Insight Center, *The Essential Eight Technologies Board Byte: The Internet of Things*, (Oct. 2017), https://www.pwc.com/us/en/governance-insights-center/publications/assets/essential-emerging-technologies-internet-of-things.pdf.

are using embedded sensors to predict machinery failures. Oil and gas companies are implementing "smart" valves, which receive information to control the flow of materials. Commercially, almost every organization is or is considering automating their workflows and routine tasks. While we are just at the beginning of the IoT revolution, it is safe to say these advancements will impact all organizations and their in-house counsel regardless of what the entity produces or the services the entity delivers.

I. Impact of IoT on Corporate Governance

Just as innovations in IoT will force companies to rethink the basic mechanisms to conduct business, so too will general counsel and boards of directors need to rethink the corporate governance ecosystem. The integration of connected devices and information technology services poses major legal and operational challenges. As the adage goes, when everything is connected, everything is at risk. Companies will typically have an established group of individuals who function together to provide cohesive corporate governance. This group may generally consist of a board of directors, general counsel, and compliance officer. Depending on the size of the organization and the regulations with which it must comply, organizations may have or may consider adding a security officer. The variety and sophistication of threats IoT introduces, particularly with regard to cybersecurity, requires a reevaluation of the roles of these stakeholders to ensure a defensible, scalable, and effective governance program.

A. Role of General Counsel

As always, the general counsel must possess a deep understanding of the various legal frameworks, as well as geopolitical acumen, that impact his or her client. These characteristics, however, become crucial in the IoT environment as successful counsel must measure risk, not just identify it, and must weigh it so that the organization can pursue initiatives with confidence. Legal departments must develop systems to stay current on rapidly evolving laws that impact their clients' use of IoT and communicate regulatory developments to operational stakeholders to address changes proactively. The general counsel is in a unique position to manage the risks attendant with IoT. Acting increasingly as an advisor to the CEO and board of directors, the general counsel often has deep knowledge of the business and corporate strategies. The general counsel who can foresee risks and changes in the regulatory or enforcement climate can identify a line of business or operational process that needs to exited. Whereas the compliance and security officers deal with risk from an operations perspective, the general counsel looks at the same risk and sees potential lawsuits, regulatory actions, and the associated reputational and financial fallout. Lawyers are generally trained to ask probing questions and think several steps ahead, which is a skill set that can help organizations prepare for a range of potential outcomes. In this new IoT landscape, the general counsel's role is to use his or her legal knowledge and training to help the enterprise maximize value. Accordingly, the general counsel should act as the quarterback of the governance team, coordinating with all relevant departments, and have input on processes to identify and mitigate threats.

Aside from keeping pace with a multitude of rapidly evolving regulations impacting their clients' use of IoT, the proliferation of IoT devices raises new issues for corporate counsel requiring them to be forward thinking and act collaboratively. The biggest threat IoT poses is cybersecurity. By now, hopefully most corporate counsel are familiar with the importance of addressing security and compliance risks. IoT applications, however, have special challenges in this regard, given the vast amounts of data they collect, process, and transmit. Legal departments must prepare to address unique liability issues both in tort and contract. For example, interconnected technologies make it problematic to determine the perimeter of each supplier's liability when there is a malfunction. IoT that incorporates artificial intelligence compounds this problem as such systems rely on an enormous amount of collected data amassed from multiple sources, making it difficult to discern the reason a machine made a specific decision at a specific time. Contractually, counsel must pay special attention to liability clauses and service levels because the efficiency of IoT technology often depends on information coming from other systems. Such information may be inaccurate, corrupt, or introduce viruses into connected systems. Accordingly, service levels may not be as predictable due to the occurrence of external factors, which are not typically considered force majeure events. General counsel must equip their legal departments to steer their companies through a multitude of risks associated with rapidly developing technology in an ever-changing legal landscape.

To be effective, general counsel must have a comprehensive appreciation of how their clients and vendors use IoT. General counsel must cultivate a technical fluency to understand how the enterprise uses technology and the associated risks. Often, the general counsel must act as an interpreter of dense technical issues, such as when negotiating complex liability or service level provisions, explaining the gaps that could make the organization vulnerable to cyberattacks, or addressing misconduct. Explaining what those vulnerabilities are in laymen's terms and understanding the company's obligations are challenging. Counsel must understand the tools their companies and critical suppliers use to manage cyber risk to IoT connected devices or networks and how effectively those tools mitigate related legal risk. Legal departments must also recognize which systems in what locations collect what types of data and from whom. Among other things, counsel should carefully consider whether the collection of data increases the burden of responding to or the risk profile of discovery requests by regulators or private litigants. This allows for informed counsel to business units within the organization on practical strategies regarding how to prioritize and approach internal initiatives. It is also crucial for building security requirements, data ownership, use rights, and other protections into agreements, as well as ensuring any data transfers are performed in compliance with applicable law.

General counsel should work closely with the Information Security Officer (ISO) and be included in incident response planning and exercises to acquaint the ISO with legal issues likely to arise during a cyber incident. This will allow counsel to address legal issues in advance. If a cybersecurity event occurs, general counsel should be involved as early as possible and to the fullest extent possible. Any third-party forensic firms should ideally be engaged through the general counsel's office as opposed to through the ISO or compliance officer. All investigations regarding the incident should be conducted at the direction of counsel to the extent possible. This not only affords maximum protection to the company under the attorney-client privilege and work product doctrine, but allows counsel to address the many issues that arise separate and apart from the actual attack. Additionally, counsel should draft appropriate press releases and coordinate with internal or external public relations personnel to address media inquiries. Counsel should also determine the timing of any press releases to ensure any release does not conflict with governmental, shareholder, or client notifications. Furthermore, counsel should prepare the consumer notifications and disclosures to various agencies if disclosure requirements are triggered.

B. Role of Information Security Officer (ISO)

The ISO is responsible for the operational aspects of securing the organization from a technical standpoint. If an organization implements IoT solutions it should strongly consider adding an ISO in an executive position if it does not have one already. In fact, recently promulgated regulations, such as those issued by the New York

State Department of Financial Services, mandate the appointment of a chief information security officer who reports to the company's board of directors.[2] Traditionally, the ISO's primary responsibilities were to design systems, policies, and procedures so as to protect the enterprise's hardware, software, and data from attack or theft. Increasingly, the requirements surrounding the design of networks and technical infrastructure with respect to cybersecurity are impacted by considerations beyond that of the information technology department. For example, on October 16, 2018, the Security and Exchange Commission's (SEC) Division of Enforcement issued an investigative report advising public companies that internal accounting control systems that factor in such cyber-related threats, and related human vulnerabilities, may be vital to maintaining a sufficient accounting control environment and safeguarding assets.[3] The report specifically cautioned that failure to consider cyber-related threats of spoofed or manipulated electronic communications when devising and maintaining a system of internal accounting controls could be a violation of federal securities law.

Aside from the need for collaboration among the ISO and other departments to ensure compliance with law, the opportunities and risks inherent in an IoT environment further support that ISOs move beyond the role of compliance monitors and become strategic contributors in a leadership position. Many ISOs recognize they can benefit from greater executive interaction and a larger role in strategy, but they face challenges in expanding their role. General counsel should work closely with ISOs in overcoming these roadblocks. These positions should view each other as strategic allies.

2. 23 NY Compilation of Codes, Rules & Regulations 500.04.

3. SEC, Release No. 84429, *Report of Investigation Pursuant to Section 21(a) of the Securities Exchange Act of 1934 Regarding Certain Cyber-Related Frauds Perpetrated Against Public Companies and Related Internal Accounting Controls Requirements* (Oct. 16, 2018), https://www.sec.gov/litigation/investreport/34-84429.pdf.

ISOs can assist counsel in understanding the technical issues and security gaps that make the organization vulnerable to a cyberattack. Counsel can assist ISOs by exposing them to the entity's strategic objectives, so they can better align business and information security strategies.

The position of ISO should evolve into more of an advisory role that provides guidance to the organization regarding the implications of new or emerging threats and opportunities as the business advances new IoT initiatives. One way to accomplish this is involving the ISO in the contracting process. Agreements for IoT initiatives often rely on integrating systems to exchange proprietary and sensitive data. The ISO must have visibility into these contracts during negotiations and can prove instrumental in helping counsel identify potential risks and threats. Similarly, ISOs should involve counsel when conducting and acting on security risk assessments. Increasingly, regulations are mandating that organizations use specific risk assessment methodologies. Accordingly, assessments sometimes purport to go beyond findings of fact to conclusions of law; for example, that a given organization is or is not "HIPAA compliant." The general counsel and the ISO should view security assessments as a joint professional project. Whereas the ISO, or his designee, should make factual findings regarding the identification and categorization of risk, the general counsel should determine the legal implications of the ISO's findings. For example, as it is impossible to protect every piece of data in an organization, ISO must work with counsel to understand which data is critical to the enterprise, where it resides, and the impact if it becomes lost or compromised. Collaboration between the general counsel and the ISO is essential as they each manage different aspects of the same risk.

C. Role of Compliance Officer

Both the compliance officer and general counsel roles serve an organization's need to comply with the law, but they have different functions in that regard. In certain instances, the position of a compliance officer is mandated by statute, and the appointment of that individual is the direct responsibility of the board of directors. Even when not expressly required by law, organizations should typically separate the legal and compliance positions. While the general counsel provides legal advice on defining and establishing appropriate company standards in the context of attaining business objectives, the compliance officer serves a management function in implementing and overseeing organizational processes to meet those standards.

The compliance officer is charged with implementing a compliance program that proactively detects and corrects misconduct. In this way, the compliance officer can lend support to the general counsel and the ISO in ensuring the policies, procedures, and protections established by these individuals are followed. Generally, the compliance department has particular competencies in the areas of policy management, monitoring, auditing, and enforcement. These core competencies often overlap with security activities. To the extent possible, organizations should consider shifting these functions to the compliance department to ensure uniform processes. For instance, if a single department is charged with maintaining and managing policies across the organization, this ensures policies do not conflict among departments. This in turn reduces the liability risk or internal confusion among organization personnel regarding what is expected of them. It is imperative that the compliance officer, general counsel, and ISO work together to reinforce each other's efforts. For example, vendors represent one of the most significant cybersecurity vulnerabilities at any company. Prior to engaging a vendor, the ISO may conduct due diligence by running vulnerability scans, among other things, and then establish policies with respect to that vendor. The general counsel can also ensure such policies and other protections are incorporated into the vendor's contract provisions. The compliance officer can support these vendor management efforts by regularly monitoring and auditing the vendor to ensure the vendor complies with the policies and contract provisions established by these stakeholders and report back to legal if he or she finds the vendor in breach. The key to an effective IoT risk program is having the compliance officer work collaboratively with the general counsel and security officer to avoid silos.

D. Role of Board of Directors

In the United States, the primary responsibility of a corporate board of directors is to protect the shareholders' assets and maximize corporate value. To that end, boards of directors are charged with overseeing multiple aspects of executive management's activities and for the overall direction of the company. This includes oversight of the organizational risk. A critical component of a board's risk oversight is ensuring the adequacy of a company's cybersecurity measures. In the United States, the median loss per cyberattack event is $15 million.[4] The U.S. Council of Economic Advisors estimates that companies lose an average of 0.8 percent of their market value in the seven days following the news of an adverse cyber event.[5] Cybersecurity risks are particularly emphasized when an organization adopts IoT into its corporate strategy. When IoT is implemented the risks go beyond data breaches, which in and of themselves can be devastating if they result in stolen intellectual property. The connected nature of IoT systems and the automated workflows that result means cyberattacks can also interfere with a company's operations, causing a loss in sales during the period of disruption and potentially a loss in future revenues or business

4. The U.S. Council of Economic Advisors, *The Cost of Malicious Cyber Activity to the U.S. Economy*, 8 (Feb. 2018), https://www.whitehouse.gov/wp-content/uploads/2018/03/The-Cost-of-Malicious-Cyber-Activity-to-the-U.S.-Economy.pdf.

5. *Id.*

opportunities due to reputational harm. Directors who ignore the organization's cybersecurity weaknesses do so at their own peril. Shareholder suits against boards of directors alleging breaches of fiduciary duties and oversight failures for failing to guard against cyberattacks have become increasingly common.[6]

Although formalizing the board's risk oversight function is generally a best practice for boards of any entity to ensure adequate protection of corporate value, in some cases it may be required. The SEC has noted that "risk oversight is a key competence of the board" and requires publicly traded companies to disclose the board's role in risk oversight.[7] The SEC has not mandated a specific risk oversight role, but it has suggested that companies describe "how the board administers its risk oversight function, such as through the whole board, or through a separate risk committee or the audit committee."[8] While management is responsible for the day-to-day risk management, boards are generally responsible for overseeing that the corporation has established and implemented appropriate risk management. Boards should carefully consider the type and amount of risk that the organization is willing to accept in the pursuit of its business. Increasingly, shareholders, regulators, and other stakeholders are calling for organizations to articulate risk appetite statements, which will then be integrated into the strategy, culture, and business operations.[9] It is crucial for the board to understand the critical links among IoT strategy, business plans, and risk. The board should examine whether the risk management and cybersecurity programs designed and implemented by management are consistent with the company's strategy and risk

6. Commissioner Luis. A. Aguilar, SEC, *Boards of Directors, Corporate Governance and Cyber-Risks: Sharpening the Focus* (June 10, 2014).

7. Proxy Disclosure Enhancements, SEC Rel. No. 33-9089 (Dec. 16, 2009), 74 Fed. Reg. 68334, http://www.sec.gov/rules/final/2009/33-9089.pdf.

8. *Id.*

9. The Risk Management Association, *A Framework for Setting Risk Appetite* (2013), https://www.rmahq.org/WorkArea/DownloadAsset.aspx?id=6006.

tolerance, whether the programs function effectively, and whether the organization has mechanisms in place to escalate and address risk-taking beyond the company's determined tolerance.

There is no "one size fits all" approach to a board's risk oversight function, but the goal is to give proper attention to a company's perceived risks to ensure sufficient preparedness. Generally, the business judgment rule should apply to the decisions that directors make regarding oversight of cybersecurity issues, so long as they abide by the core standards of care, loyalty, and good faith that apply to board decisions generally as determined by the entity's state of incorporation. Oftentimes the technical nature of a cybersecurity issue leaves directors feeling ill equipped to tackle cyber risk decisions. Detailed technological understanding is not yet required by the board[10] and many directors choose to rely on management and outside experts on such issues. However, a board is well-advised to consider adding a member with cybersecurity expertise. Alternatively, as with other audit and risk issues, a board may assign cybersecurity oversight to its existing audit or risk committee. Some experts have suggested that boards establish a new committee to deal exclusively with cybersecurity issues to oversee a range of areas including, but not limited to, cyber insurance, cybersecurity budgeting, incident response plans, business continuity plans, insider threats, vendor management, cyberattack prevention and response, recruitment of information technology personnel, and cybersecurity training.[11] As the board determines

10. Recently, Congress has proposed the Cybersecurity Disclosure Act of 2017, which does not mandate public companies to have a cybersecurity expert on their boards, but does require them to explain in SEC filings whether such expertise exists, and, if not, why the expertise is unnecessary. S. 536, 115th Cong. (2017–2018).

11. David R. Fontaine & John Reed Stark, *Cybersecurity: The SEC's Wake-up call to Corporate Directors*, Harv. L. Forum on Corp. Governance & Fin. Reg. (Mar. 31, 2018), https://corpgov.law.harvard.edu/2018/03/31/cybersecurity-the-secs-wake-up-call-to-corporate-directors/.

the roles and responsibilities of different board committees in overseeing specific categories of risk, it is important to ensure that, taken as a whole, the board's oversight function is coordinated and comprehensive.

II. Strategies for General Counsel during a Security Incident

The best strategy for managing cyber risk is prevention; however, not all incidents can be stopped. Incidents can occur in countless ways. Guidelines issued by the National Institute of Standards and Technology recommend that organizations should generally prepare to handle any incident, but acknowledge that it is infeasible to develop step-by-step instructions for handling every incident.[12] The risk with most cyber events is the loss or theft of personal data, competitively sensitive data, and intellectual property. However, for companies operating in an environment that utilize IoT solutions as part of their operations or offer connected products, the risk profile raises significantly. Cyberattacks can disrupt corporate systems for weeks, bringing operations to a crippling halt. For industrial organizations that operate in the energy, utilities, or transportation sectors, the risk is even greater. For these companies, a cyberattack can result in serious injury or even death. Specifically, this could be the result of malicious actors hacking connected vehicles or gaining operational access to specialized control systems in power grids to manipulate physical infrastructure.

As the adage goes, there are only two kinds of companies, those who know they have been hacked and those who do not yet know they have been hacked. Companies generally learn about cybersecurity breaches in one of three ways. First, a company may "manually" discern the issue by recognizing an anomaly such as account lockouts, delayed system speeds, or the ability to access

12. Nat'l Inst. of Standards & Technology, Special Pub. 800-61 Revision 2.

files. Casual conversations among employees may also result in cyber incident identification. For example, a large number of employees discussing someone has used their information to file fraudulent tax returns could indicate that the company or a vendor was compromised. Second, an organization's security controls may automatically alert it to an event such as through intrusion detection software, anti-virus, firewalls, and other tools designed to detect security incidents. Third, law enforcement may inform an entity that the company has experienced a security event. While the facts and circumstances underlying the event itself will dictate the appropriate incident response, certain aspects of the response will depend on how the organization was alerted to the problem.

A. Internal Investigations

An important first step for general counsel is to consider how best to obtain protection under the attorney-client privilege and work product doctrine over the documents and discussion involved in an internal cybersecurity investigation. Failure to do so could lead to costly disclosures and exposure of information that should have received protection if privilege issues were properly considered. Maintenance of privilege and work product is particularly challenging when a cyber event involves customer breach notifications, media requests, and parallel government investigations. Recent case law in this area is instructive on possible approaches for structuring internal investigations, which counsel should consider in light of the facts surrounding the incident and potentially latent circuit splits.

One approach (GM approach) was considered in the case *In re General Motors LLC Ignition Switch Litigation*. In *General Motors*, an automobile manufacturer engaged outside counsel to conduct an internal investigation regarding ignition switch malfunctions and delays in recalling affected vehicles.[13] As part of the investigation,

13. 80 F. Supp. 3d 521, 524 (S.D. N.Y. 2015).

the law firm collected and reviewed over 41 million documents and conducted over 350 interviews of over 200 witnesses.[14] The firm prepared a 315-page investigation report, including citations to many witness interviews the firm conducted, that was presented to the manufacturer's board of directors and provided to Congress, the Department of Justice, and the National Highway Traffic Safety Administration (NHTSA) as part of their ongoing investigations into the defects and recalls.[15] Despite the fact that the cover and each page of the report was clearly marked "Privileged and Confidential: Protected by Attorney–Client Privilege and As Attorney Work Product," the NHTSA made the report publicly available on its website.[16] Later, the manufacturer provided the report to plaintiffs in a subsequent products liability case, who then sought to compel production of any notes or transcripts of the interviews underlying the report.[17] The manufacturer asserted protection over the interview notes, summaries, and formal memoranda prepared by investigative counsel.[18] The court held the privilege applied to the extent the materials reflected witness communications because the manufacturer's intent to make the report public did not mean it intended to make the underlying communications public.[19] The court reasoned that the manufacturer's intent to keep the witness communications confidential was evidenced by the factual content in the report and the warnings given at the start of each interview informing the witnesses that the purpose of the interview was to provide legal advice to the manufacturer and stressing the need for confidentiality.[20]

14. *Id.*
15. *Id.* at 524–25.
16. *Id.*
17. *Id.* at 525.
18. *Id.*
19. *Id.* at 527–28.
20. *Id.*

The limitations of the GM approach were demonstrated in *Wadler v. Bio-Rad Laboratories, Inc.*[21] In *Wadler*, a former employee sued an employer and board of directors claiming wrongful termination under whistleblower provisions of the Sarbanes-Oxley Act, among other federal and state laws.[22] The employer hired outside counsel to complete a worldwide investigation into the potential violations raised by the former employee, as well as a separate investigation specifically into the allegations of wrongful termination.[23] Outside counsel presented a 41-page PowerPoint presentation to the SEC that provided a timeline of the former employee's communications with the board's audit committee, addressed the concerns the employee raised in detail, described the involvement of the employer's legal department and the specific investigative efforts of outside counsel and the specific advice provided by counsel regarding the issues (Bio-Rad Presentation).[24] The former employer sought to exclude evidence on the grounds that it was protected by attorney-client privilege.[25] The court distinguished the Bio-Rad Presentation from the report in *General Motors* in that the Bio-Rad Presentation "[did] not just state conclusions; it also described the underlying investigation by outside counsel in great detail."[26] The court concluded the disclosure of the Bio-Rad Presentation to the SEC waived privilege not only as to the document itself but also any privileged communications about the specific matters disclosed in the presentation.[27]

Another approach (Target approach) was demonstrated in *In re Target Corporation Customer Data Security Breach Litigation*, which involved a class action against a retail store after computer

21. 212 F. Supp. 3d 829 (N.D. Cal. 2016).
22. *Id.* at 833.
23. *Id.*
24. *Id.* at 833–34.
25. *Id.* at 833.
26. *Id.* at 852.
27. *Id.* at 851.

hackers stole credit and debit card information as well as other personal information of customers.[28] The Target approach involved retaining outside counsel to obtain legal advice about the breach and possible legal ramifications shortly after discovering the possibility that a data breach had occurred.[29] Once the retail store publicly announced the breach, in-house counsel directed the store to establish a task force and had outside counsel engage a third-party vendor to assist with an internal investigation.[30] The retail store had the vendor provide two teams each to handle a two-track investigation. One team would act as part of the task force coordinating activities on behalf of the store's in-house and outside counsel and educating them on the breach to provide legal advice in anticipation of litigation and regulatory inquiries.[31] The other team conducted a separate, non-privileged investigation to learn how the breach happened and enable the store and credit card companies to respond quickly and appropriately to the technical aspects of the breach.[32]

The store and vendor put in place a screening mechanism that prevented the disclosure of information between the two teams about the substance of the attorney-directed investigation.[33] The retail store asserted protection under the attorney-client privilege and work product doctrine with respect to only one of the vendor's teams, which was involved in the attorney-directed investigation.[34] After an in camera review of the documents at issue, the court concluded that they were protected from disclosures.[35] The dual-track nature of the Target approach allowed store counsel to move quickly from the first report of breach to conduct an investi-

28. MDL No. 14–2522, 2015 WL 6777384, (D. Minn. Oct. 23, 2015).
29. *Id.* at *1.
30. *Id.*
31. *Id.*
32. *Id.*
33. *Id.*
34. *Id.*
35. *Id.* at 2.

gation under privilege without delaying the practical need for the security team to mitigate the technical threat and prevent further disclosures.

There are many approaches to successfully maintain the attorney-client privilege and work product doctrine in the context of a cybersecurity incident and subsequent internal investigation. General counsel should be involved as soon as possible and give significant thought as to how best to preserve privilege while not interfering with security concerns. Whether an organization implements a single investigation or a dual-track investigation, the case law discussed previously provides some important takeaways. Companies should ideally hire outside counsel to conduct the investigation and engage third-party experts as needed. Counsel should carefully document which engagements and activities are for the purpose of providing legal advice. If the organization anticipates having to disclose details regarding the incident to customers, government officials, or other third parties, such disclosures should be limited to the facts surrounding the incident. Counsel should be especially sensitive about revealing the contents of any communications, analyses, or conclusions.

B. Working with Law Enforcement and Other Governmental Entities

There are multiple ways an organization may find itself working with law enforcement or other governmental entities in responding to a cybersecurity incident. Depending on the impact of the attack, law enforcement may proactively contact the company as described earlier. Alternatively, the company may want to report criminal events involving cybersecurity to law enforcement, particularly if intellectual property theft is involved. Further, if the entity owns or operates control systems involved with critical infrastructure sectors, the entity may elect to request government technical assistance.

If the company learns of the breach through law enforcement, such as the Federal Bureau of Investigation (FBI), the best thing to do is to understand what information the agency has that can assist counsel and what information the agency is seeking to obtain from the company. Law enforcement cyber investigations can be criminal in nature or involve national security. Agencies will have greater latitude in sharing information with entities when the security incident does not involve a national security investigation. Another important item to establish is who is in charge of the investigation and obtain his or her contact information to the extent possible. For example, the FBI often runs investigations out of field offices around the United States. An FBI agent in one state could be the primary investigator but may call an agent in another state to execute aspects of the investigation, such as informing a company that it has been breached. Accordingly, the agent who initially interacts with an organization may only be carrying out a directive from the primary investigator and may not know details regarding the attack. It is important to recognize that government investigations of cybercrime can be lengthy and organizations have little control regarding when it will end.

Organizations that act as control system vendors for sectors deemed to be U.S. critical infrastructure may be eligible to receive free assistance regarding cybersecurity incidents from the Industrial Control Systems (ICS) Cyber Emergency Response Team (ICS-CERT). This program, offered through the Department of Homeland Security (DHS) National Cybersecurity and Communications Integration Center (NCCIC), assists control systems vendors and asset owners/operators to identify security vulnerabilities and develop sound mitigation strategies that strengthen their ICS cybersecurity posture and reduce risk. There are 16 critical infrastructure sectors that were established by Presidential Policy Directive 21 (PPD-21), National Infrastructure Protection

Plan.[36] NCCIC serves as the national hub for cyber and communications information, technical expertise, and operational integration to operate a 24/7 situational awareness, analysis, and incident response center. NCCIC offers a number of services to various stakeholders.[37] NCCIC offers private industry services free of charge in a number of areas, including network protection, information exchange, incident response, malware analysis and vulnerability coordination, cybersecurity assessments, and cybersecurity training.[38]

C. Special Considerations for Public Companies

Public companies that experience a cyber incident or identify certain cyber risks have additional considerations in responding to such issues. In 2011, the SEC, through the Division of Corporation Finance, first advised public companies that although no existing disclosure requirement explicitly refers to cybersecurity risks and incidents, public companies may still be obligated to disclose such risks and incidents.[39] In February 2018, the SEC issued updated cybersecurity guidance reiterating that publicly held companies must "timely" disclose material cybersecurity risks and incidents in registration statements, periodic reports, and current reports.[40]

---

36. The 16 sectors include (1) chemical; (2) commercial facilities; (3) communications; (4) critical manufacturing; (5) dams; (6) defense industrial base; (7) emergency services; (8) energy; (9) financial services; (10) food and agriculture; (11) government facilities; (12) health care and public health; (13) information technology; (14) nuclear reactors, materials, and waste; (15) transportation systems; and (16) water and wastewater system.

37. ICS-CERT, *Frequently Asked Questions*, https://ics-cert.us-cert.gov/Frequently-Asked-Questions.

38. Homeland Security, *NCCIC Services for Private Industry*, https://ics-cert.us-cert.gov/sites/default/files/documents/NCCIC%20Service%20Menu%20-%20Private%20Industry.pdf.

39. *See* CF Disclosure Guidance: Topic No. 2—Cybersecurity (Oct. 13, 2011), *available at* https://www.sec.gov/divisions/corpfin/guidance/cfguidance-topic2.htm.

40. Sec. & Exch. Comm'n, Commission Statement and Guidance on Public Company Cybersecurity Disclosures, Nos. 33-10459, 34-82746 (Feb. 26, 2018).

The guidance provided that the materiality of cybersecurity risks or incidents is fact-specific. To determine whether a cybersecurity issue is "material," organizations should look to the impact that the risk or incident has on the business and scope of operations, the nature of the potentially compromised information, and the range of harm that could ensue.[41]

While companies are not expected to publicly disclose specific, technical information or vulnerabilities regarding their cybersecurity systems in such a way that it provides a "roadmap" for penetration, the SEC cautioned against material omissions.[42] The SEC considers omitted information to be material if there is a substantial likelihood that a reasonable investor would consider the information important in making an investment decision or that disclosure of the omitted information would have been viewed by the reasonable investor as having significantly altered the total mix of information available.[43] Public companies also must consider any obligations that may be imposed by exchange listing requirements, which may be more or less stringent than those required by the SEC. For example, the New York Stock Exchange requires listed companies to "release quickly to the public any news or information which might reasonably be expected to materially affect the market for its securities."[44] Miscalculations in determining the materiality of cybersecurity risks or incidents can be dire. Directors, officers, and corporate insiders are prohibited from trading a public company's securities while in possession of material nonpublic information, which the SEC has advised can include knowledge of a cybersecurity incident experienced by the company.[45] Accordingly, if a pub-

41. *Id.*

42. *Id.*

43. *Id.*

44. NYSE Listed Company Manual Rule 202.05—Timely Disclosure of Material News Developments.

45. Sec. & Exch. Comm'n, Commission Statement and Guidance on Public Company Cybersecurity Disclosures, Nos. 33-10459, 34-82746 (Feb. 26, 2018).

lic company decides against disclosing a cybersecurity incident or even possible security gap, which later proves to be material, this decision can have significant ramifications on the company as well as the individual who effectuated the trade.

The disclosure requirements regarding cybersecurity incidents raise some practical issues for publicly traded companies that experience an event, particularly concerning the timing of the disclosure. The SEC advised that where a company becomes aware of a material cybersecurity incident or risk it must make "appropriate disclosure timely and sufficiently prior to the offer and sale of securities."[46] The SEC acknowledged that a company may require time to discern the implications of a cybersecurity incident or to cooperate with law enforcement, which may impact the scope of the disclosure.[47] Importantly though, the SEC cautioned that an ongoing internal or external investigation does not provide a basis for avoiding disclosures of a material cybersecurity incident.[48] This guidance presents unique challenges for publicly traded companies with respect to mitigation after a cyberattack. Going public with news of a security incident risks tipping off the malicious actors, which can not only impede the investigation but also may create further security risks as it may cause hackers to change tactics, allowing them to thwart countermeasures. Also, law enforcement often encourages, or even demands, that the incident not be disclosed, especially when an attack implicates national security concerns. The tension between disclosure and security may place public companies in an untenable position. Accordingly, for public companies it is especially important that ISOs and in-house counsel work together and engage outside counsel as quickly as possible after suspicion of a cyberattack or incident to collectively determine the best course of action.

46. *Id.*
47. *Id.*
48. *Id.*

III. Future Outlook

IoT is a disruptive force and its full impact will not be felt for some time. One cannot predict in absolute terms where these technologies will take us in the years to come. The only certainty is that the role of general counsel and the function of corporate legal departments will continue to evolve in response. Increased speed to market gives competitors an advantage when it comes to innovation. To be effective, general counsel must stay current with emerging technologies and anticipate their impact on compliance. With the increasing intensity of the regulatory environment and its effects on business outcomes, corporate counsel must ensure better and faster collaboration with corporate stakeholders. Developing this competency in the legal department is critical to protect the organization and support compliance efforts without inhibiting growth.

Chapter 19

What Employers Need to Know about the Internet of Things

Peter Gillespie

I. Employers Have a Significant Role to Play as the Internet of Things Expands

Internet of Things (IoT) devices offer both the promise of advancement in workplace productivity and safety, as well as a new set of compliance challenges from a privacy and data security perspective. As an example, the City of Chicago recently joined a number of other municipalities and governments in requiring hotels to provide panic buttons to workers who might face harassment or abuse from guests.[1] Providing workers with radio-frequency identification equipped bracelets or similar devices that can transmit real-time location information and a distress signal may be one way that affected employers could comply with these requirements

1. Chicago, Illinois Municipal Code § 4-6-180 (2018); similar requirements are being considered elsewhere and are in effect in New York City, Washington DC, and Seattle. *See* Dori Goldstein, *Hands Off, Pants On: Is It Time for Panic Buttons?*, BLOOMBERG BNA HR BLOG (Nov. 27, 2017), https://www.bna.com/hands-off-pants-b73014472456/.

and protect workers from possible harm.[2] Employers should understand that employees may not be as keen to wear these devices if they could also be used to monitor bathroom breaks, smoking habits, off-duty activities, or other personal activities.[3]

The introduction of IoT devices to the workplace presents potential risks to employers. Consider, for example, a situation in which a top executive of an organization meets with another executive of a competing organization. During this meeting, one executive presents the other with a soccer ball as a gift. However, the ball has been embedded with a chip that allows for the transmission of data under certain conditions.[4] As it turned out, while the security risks associated with that particular soccer ball were more likely speculative than real, as has been explored in greater detail throughout this book, no business can afford to ignore the possibility that security and design flaws in IoT-enabled devices could

2. For additional safety-related applications of wearable or IoT devices, *see* Ayliffe Brown, *A Smart Employee for a Productive Work Place*, WEARABLE-TECHNOLOGIES (July 23, 2015), available at https://www.wearable-technologies.com/2015/07/a-smart-employee-for-a-productive-work-place/; Bruce Brown, *Real-Time Wearable Hydration Sensor*, HEALTH TECH INSIDER (Feb. 2, 2017), http://healthtechinsider.com/2017/02/02/real-time-wearable-hydration-sensor/; Aviva Rutkin, *Wearable Tech Lets Boss Track Your Work, Rest and Play*, New Scientist (Oct. 15, 2014), https://www.newscientist.com/article/mg22429913-000-wearable-tech-lets-boss-track-your-work-restand-play/; John Boitnott, *Wearable Tech Is Improving Employee Productivity and Happiness*, ENTREPRENEUR (Apr. 28, 2015), https://www.entrepreneur.com/article/245458; Iestyn Armstrong-Smith, *You Wear It So Well*, THE ANALYTICAL SCIENTIST (Jan. 24, 2014), https://theanalyticalscientist.com/issues/0314/you-wear-it-so-well/.

3. Indeed, several states already have laws on the books prohibiting employers from requiring employees to implant RFID microchips into their bodies. These states include California, CAL. CIV. CODE § 52.7; Missouri, MO. REV. STAT. § 285-035-1; North Dakota, N.D. CENT. CODE § 12.1-15-06; Oklahoma, OKLA. STAT. § 63-1-1430; and Wisconsin, WIS. STAT. § 146.25.

4. Vernon Silver, *Putin's Soccer Ball for Trump Had Transmitter Chip, Logo Indicates*, BLOOMBERG (July 25, 2018, 11:06 AM), https://www.bloomberg.com/news/articles/2018-07-25/putin-soccer-ball-for-trump-had-transmitter-chip-logo-indicates.

be exploited to cause harm, jeopardize trade secrets or confidential information, or create embarrassment for an organization.

As the number of ways in which IoT evolves into an everyday part of both the business and consumer worlds grows, employers will be required to assess potential privacy and security risks, as well as the manner in which IoT devices may touch upon particular aspects of labor and employment laws. Analyzing these considerations requires a fairly sophisticated understanding of how the devices function, as well as the range of laws that might apply to the data generated by these devices. Unless employers keep a close eye on these details, the adoption of IoT technology in the workplace could create unanticipated landmines.

This chapter explores generally applicable legal requirements that might apply throughout the United States to non-medical or health-related data that employers may gather, whether deliberately or inadvertently, about employees through IoT-enabled devices or equipment, as well as recommendations for how employers can stay ahead of possible risks and potential liability.

II. Legal Requirements for Employers

A. IoT-Related Privacy Risks for Employers

Employers should be mindful of privacy considerations that are inherently associated with devices that have the potential to reveal detailed, highly personal information about their employees, including their activities outside of the work environment. From a high-level perspective, employers can take some measure of comfort from the fact that many courts have found that employees do not have a reasonable expectation of privacy when employer-owned equipment or technology is involved, the employer has a legitimate business interest, and when the information at issue relates to events that occurred during normal work hours.[5] On the

5. *See, e.g.*, Bingham v. BayCare Health Sys., No. 8:14-cv-73-T-23JSS, 2016 U.S. Dist. LEXIS 94590, at *11 (M.D. Fla. July 20, 2016) ("[A] policy reserving

other hand, employers should be wary of technologies that provide the ability to track or monitor an employee's off-duty activities or where the employee is located during non-working hours.[6] Indeed, employers should recognize that courts will likely have little sympathy for an employer that gathers employee data in a manner that "provides an intimate window into a person's life, revealing not only his particular movements, but through them his familial, political, professional, religious, and sexual associations."[7]

In the context of employment laws, many of the requirements applicable to employers have generally been created at the state or local level in reaction to specific events and have lagged advances in technology. For example, following several news reports that

---

the right to access and monitor employee accounts is sufficient to support a finding that an employee has no reasonable expectation of confidentiality in e-mails transmitted over an employer's e-mail system"); Thygeson v. U.S. Bancorp., No. CV-03-467-ST, 2004 U.S. Dist. LEXIS 18863 (D. Or. Sept. 15, 2004) (no reasonable expectation of privacy where employee used his employer's computer and network for personal use, saved personal information in a location that was accessible by his employer, and the employee handbook prohibited personal use of the employer's computer); TBG Ins. Servs. Corp. v. Superior Ct., 96 Cal. App. 4th 443 (Cal. Ct. App. 2002) (no reasonable expectation of privacy in an employer-owned computer located at employee's home); Garrity v. John Hancock Mut. Life Ins. Co., No. 00-12143-RWZ, 2002 U.S. Dist. LEXIS 8343 (D. Mass. May 7, 2002) (no reasonable expectation of privacy for e-mails sent on computer system owned by employer and where the employer has a legitimate business interest in protecting its employees from harassment); Smyth v. Pillsbury Co., 914 F. Supp. 97, 101 (E.D. Pa. 1996) ("Moreover, the company's interest in preventing inappropriate and unprofessional comments or even illegal activity over its e-mail system outweighs any privacy interest the employee may have in those comments.").

6. *See, e.g.*, Cunningham v. N.Y. State Dep't of Labor, 997 N.E.2d 468 (N.Y. 2013) (unlawful and unreasonable search found where the employer "conduct[ed] a GPS search without making a reasonable effort to avoid tracking an employee outside of business hours"). In addition, more than half the states in the U.S. restrict an employer's ability to make employment decisions based on at least some of an employee's lawful, off-duty activities.

7. Carpenter v. United States, 138 S. Ct. 2206, 2217 (2018) (internal quotation omitted).

raised concerns as to whether employers may require job applicants to disclose social media passwords or subject their non-public social media content to a background review, 26 states enacted restrictions on employer access to applicant or employee social media accounts.[8] Similarly, in response to concerns about the use of biometric identifiers as part of retail commercial transactions, Illinois enacted the Biometric Information Privacy Act (BIPA).[9] In addition, employers should understand that specific legal requirements applicable in the workplace are nearly always associated with sensitive or confidential information about a person, such as genetic and biometric data, medical information, a Social Security number or bank account number, credit history, arrest records, or background check reports, to name a few.

Further complicating the analysis, IoT devices may be subject to existing legal requirements that had little to do with electronic data privacy at the time that they were enacted. For example, many

8. Ark. Code § 11-2-124; Cal. Lab. Code § 980; Colo. Rev. Stat. § 8-2-127; Conn. Gen. Stat. § 31–40x; 19 Del. Code § 709A; 820 ILCS 55/10; La. Rev. Stat. § 51:1951 *et seq.*; 26 M.R.S. § 616 *et seq.*; Md. Lab. & Employment Code § 3-712; MCL §§ 37.271–37.278; Mont. Code Ann. § 39-2-307; Neb. Rev. Stat. § 48-3501 *et seq.*; NRS § 613.135; N.H. Rev. Stat. § 275:74; N.J. Stat. Ann. § 34:6B-6; N.M. Stat. § 50-4-34; 40 Okla. Stat. § 173.2; O.R.S. § 659A.330; R.I. Gen. Laws § 28-56-1 *et seq.*; Tenn. Code § 50-1-1001 *et seq.*; Utah Code § 34-48-201 *et seq.*; 21 V.S.A. § 4951; Va. Code Ann. § 40.1-28.7:5; RCW §§ 49.44.200 & 49.44.205; W.V. Code Ann. § 21-5H-1; Wis. Stat. § 995.55.

9. 740 ILCS 14/1. Since July 2017 more than 25 cases have been filed in the state and federal courts in Illinois by private parties to enforce BIPA requirements, many of which were directed at employers. Although BIPA was intended as a consumer protection statute, claims against employers generally involve biometric time clocks that were arguably introduced into the workplace without employers first having provided employees with notice and consent documentation required by the statute. A few other states, including Michigan, Texas, New York, and Washington, also have similar provisions or requirements applicable to biometric data, but BIPA is the only statute that includes a private right of action and provides for statutory civil penalties.

companies have introduced wearable devices that are intended to allow consumers to gather data about their health, physical activities, sleep patterns, or fitness. Employers that might want to consider encouraging employees to use these types of devices would be hard-pressed to find rules directly applicable to such a situation. Nevertheless, the use of these types of devices by employees could conceivably run afoul of statutes such as the Health Insurance Portability and Accountability Act of 1996 (HIPAA), the Americans With Disabilities Act (ADA), and the Genetic Information Nondiscrimination Act (GINA).[10] The gist of the concern as to each of these statutes is whether data collected by these wearable devices could violate existing obligations for employers not to misuse employee medical information.

When considering what privacy laws might apply to the use of IoT technology in the workplace, employers should have a clear understanding of the kinds of data these devices may generate or capture about an employee in order to determine whether existing laws may govern the information created or transmitted by these devices. Employers also need to account for the storage of and access to such data. After assessing the implications of IoT devices, an employer should incorporate IoT-specific considerations into their employee handbooks and privacy and record-keeping policies. Human resources professionals have an important role in identifying the legal nuances that may come into play, and should collaborate with information technology professionals in developing plans and policies that will reduce the risk of being blindsided by claims stemming from information that may be collected from employee IoT devices.

---

10. For an in-depth discussion of legal and privacy issues relating to wearable IoT devices that monitor health, see Elizabeth A. Brown, *Article: The Fitbit Fault Line: Two Proposals to Protect Health and Fitness Data at Work*, 16 Yale J. Health Pol'y L. & Ethics 1, 5–6 (2016).

B. State Data Protection Statutes

Currently, other than eavesdropping or wiretapping statutes, very few states in the United States have significant data privacy statutes governing employers. Connecticut and Delaware require employers to provide notice to employees prior to engaging in certain types of workplace electronic monitoring.[11] Other states prohibit employers from installing GPS devices on employee-owned vehicles without consent.[12] Only California has enacted a comprehensive data privacy protection statute, the California Consumer Privacy Act of 2018 (CCPA),[13] which is scheduled to become effective on January 1, 2020. This statute applies to (1) companies with annual gross revenues of $25 million; (2) businesses that collect for commercial purposes the personal information of 50,000 or more California residents, households, or devices annually; or (3) businesses that derive 50 percent or more of their annual revenue from selling California residents' personal information.[14] The CCPA extends certain

11. Conn. Gen. Stat. § 31-48d; 6 Del. Code § 19-7-705. Also, in the public sector, Colorado and Tennessee require public entities to adopt a policy related to employee e-mail monitoring. Colo. Rev. Stat. § 24-72-204.5; Tenn. Code § 10-7-512.

12. *See, e.g.*, Cal. Penal Code §635.7; Del. Code Ann. Tit. 11, §1335(a)(8); Tex. Penal Code Ann. § 1606.

13. Cal. Civ. Code § 1798.198(a) (2018).

14. The CCPA defines "Personal Information" (or PI) as "information that identifies, relates to, describes, is capable of being associated with, or could reasonably [be] linked, directly or indirectly, with a particular consumer or household." Cal. Civ. Code § 1798.140(o)(1). The definition of PI is very broad and includes 11 different categories of information, such as addresses; persistent or probabilistic identifiers that can be used to identify a particular consumer or device, records of personal property, products or services purchased, obtained or considered, or other purchasing or consuming histories or tendencies; Internet or other electronic network activity information, professional or employment-related information; or any consumer profile. *Id.*

protections to "any natural person who is a California resident," which necessarily includes employees. Therefore, employers that employ at least one individual who is living or domiciled in the state (even employers that are not based in California), may be subject to the CCPA, at least with respect to those employees who live or work in California.

Among the requirements contained in the CCPA, employers must inform employees at or before the point of collection about the categories of PI collected and the purposes for which they will be used. This information could be made available in a privacy policy notice provided to current employees or job applicants. Employers must also notify employees when their PI might be sold or disclosed to third parties, such as in a corporate merger or other similar business transaction. Importantly, covered employers cannot gather other categories of employee PI without providing an additional prior notice. Further, the CCPA provides that employees can ask their employers to disclose the categories and specific items of PI collected, and can even request that their employers delete their PI. Employers cannot ask employees to waive their rights under the CCPA or retaliate against employees who exercise their rights under the statute.

In order to stay ahead of the curve on CCPA-related compliance issues, employers should carefully assess whether IoT devices are generating, gathering, or storing employee PI, as well as whether the devices can be used in a manner such that they could trigger obligations under the CCPA. IoT devices or equipment both inside and outside the workplace should be included in data maps, inventories, or other records of all personal information pertaining to California employees, and should be included in required disclosures or privacy policies. To the extent that such IoT devices create or transmit PI, employers will also need to assess how to comply with requests to delete such information or to provide such information to a requesting employee.

C. National Labor Relations Act

Although the National Labor Relations Act (NLRA) substantially pre-dates the advent of IoT, employers (even non-union employers) should ensure that their policies and practices relating to IoT devices and data do not run afoul of the protections afforded by this statute. Section 7 of the NLRA provides that employees have "the right to self-organization, to form, join, or assist labor organizations, to bargain collectively through representatives of their own choosing, and to engage in other concerted activities for the purpose of collective bargaining or other mutual aid or protection," as well as the right "to refrain from any or all such activities."[15] Section 8(a)(1) of the NLRA makes it an unfair labor practice for an employer "to interfere with, restrain, or coerce employees in the exercise of the rights guaranteed in Section 7" of the act.[16] In recent years, the National Labor Relations Board (NLRB) has taken an active role in reviewing employer policies—even in non-union settings—to identify policies that may appear to unlawfully restrict an employee's protected rights. These policies have included, among others, restrictions on statements that employees may make on social media, electronic communications, and e-mail policies which employers may need to modify as part of a comprehensive assessment of IoT-related issues. In June 2018, the NLRB General Counsel issued a memorandum that provided guidance on the types of policies that would draw board scrutiny based on the board's balancing test of (1) the nature and extent of the rule's potential impact on protected rights, and (2) the employer's legitimate justifications for the rule.[17] Employer policies and practice relating IoT devices or data should be reviewed to confirm that these policies do not impair an employee's Section 7 rights. Arguably, an employer

15. 29 U.S.C. § 157.
16. *Id.* § 158(a)(1).
17. NLRB General Counsel Memorandum 18-04 (June 6, 2018).

that has the ability to listen in surreptitiously on employee "water-cooler discussions" through an IoT-enabled "smart watercooler" could eventually find itself in hot water with the board.

Among other considerations, employers should consider whether IoT devices could be used to track the location of employees. For unionized workforces, the NLRB has previously held that using GPS technology to track employees could be the subject of mandatory bargaining.[18] In addition, the NLRB has long held that an employer engages in unlawful surveillance "when it surveils employees engaged in Section 7 activity by observing them in a way that is 'out of the ordinary' and therefore coercive."[19] However, where an employer monitors protected activity but is able to show a legitimate business concern, the board has permitted such activity to occur and found no violation of the act.[20] It should not be difficult to imagine that an employer's near-constant ability to use IoT devices for the purpose of tracking each employee's precise location, listening in on private conversations, or keeping tabs on an employee's physiological activity could have a chilling effect on employees who are engaged in activities protected by the NLRA. For these reasons, when assessing the categories of data that employee IoT devices might track, capture, or record, employ-

---

18. *See, e.g.*, BP Exploration of Alaska, Inc., Case No. 19-CA-29566 (July 11, 2005).

19. Aladdin Gaming, LLC, 345 NLRB 585, 585–86 (2005), petition for review denied, 515 F.3d 942 (9th Cir. 2008); *see also* Allservice Plumbing & Maint., Inc., 2011 NLRB LEXIS 669, *41 (N.L.R.B. Dec. 1, 2011) (unlawful surveillance found where a supervisor went to a restaurant where a union meeting was being held, the supervisor stayed for 30 minutes, interrogated employees about their union activity, and had no other purpose beyond observing the union meeting).

20. *See* Smithfield Foods, Inc., 346 NLRB 1225 (2006) ("[I]n light of the physical proximity of the handbilling to the [Employer's] property and the temporal proximity of the previous trespassing incident, the [Employer's] concern about a recurrence was reasonable and, therefore, the security guard's redirection of the security camera was not unlawful.").

ers should be mindful of not obtaining data that might be construed as a means of discouraging union organizing or other protected activities. If an employer has the ability to track employee locations using IoT-generated data, employees should be provided with and be encouraged to use mechanisms that prevent the employer from monitoring their activities during non-working hours or when engaged in non-business-related activities.

D. Wage and Hour Laws

Arguably, location tracking and similar monitoring considerations inherent with the IoT technology could open up significant new ways of evaluating the merits of wage and hour disputes. For example, overtime claims in "off the clock" cases, which would otherwise rely on the credibility and accuracy of witness testimony to determine if and when employees had been engaged in uncompensated work, would likely settle quickly if both parties had access to reliable data that could establish when disputed work had been performed and when an employee could not credibly claim to have been engaged in work-related activities. For example, door swipe records and computer logins can, in some instances, provide a rough idea of when certain types of employees appeared for work or were engaged in compensable activities in situations where employees did not track their time directly. Data from IoT devices could play a similar role in future cases. Also, employers that subject employees to extensive monitoring during both working and non-working time may have a harder time overcoming an assumption that employees who are being monitored should be compensated for periods of time when their activities are being tracked.

Employers should become familiar with whether they create or maintain IoT data that could serve as a backstop against conventional timekeeping records. For purposes of complying with applicable time and recordkeeping requirements under state or federal law (or resolving wage and hour disputes), employers may want to consider storing relevant data for the same period of time in which payroll records are kept.[21] In that same vein, employers that require employees to use or update IoT devices for work-related purposes should assess these activities against their obligation to pay employees for all hours worked. Employees might claim, for example, that putting on certain IoT-enabled devices constitutes a work-related activity that technically commences their work days. In prior cases, employees have argued that updating software, receiving work instructions electronically, or maintaining equipment effectively extended their workdays and they should be compensated accordingly.[22] Employers who fail to provide employees with a means of recording or reporting these hours could face possible claims.[23]

E. Litigation: Data Retention Requirements

The use of IoT-enabled devices or equipment in the workplace may raise many litigation hold and e-discovery compliance concerns for employers. Companies may have an obligation to preserve and produce data that is created by IoT devices either located in the workplace or used by employees. Among other considerations, IoT devices may help establish where an employee was located during different parts of the day, or whether the employee was operating or interacting with equipment or devices during different periods

21. *See, e.g.*, 29 U.S.C. § 211 ("Every employer . . . shall make, keep, and preserve such records of the persons employed by him and of the wages, hours, and other conditions and practices of employment maintained by him . . . ").

22. *See, e.g.*, Gomley v. Crossmark, Inc., No. 1:13-cv-00420-BLW, 2015 U.S. Dist. LEXIS 54037, at *6 (D. Idaho Apr. 22, 2015) (Finding that employee should have been paid each day starting from the time when she needed to "check work e-mails, sync a [employer-provided] handheld device . . ., organize store folders, and load her car . . . .").

23. *See, e.g.*, Allen v. City of Chi., 865 F.3d 936, 942 (7th Cir. 2017) (affirming finding that off-duty workers could not claim additional pay for checking "Blackberry" devices where the employees "had a way to report that time, but they did not use it, through no fault of the employer . . . .").

of time. Employers and their counsel should account for possibly relevant information from IoT devices when preparing litigation holds or discovery plans in litigation. In addition, employers should anticipate what information would likely be relevant in the event of a dispute and investigate whether it is possible to obtain such information in a usable format in the event that it is needed. By taking these steps, employers may be better positioned to either review or disclose IoT data in the event of a lawsuit, or to make the case that such data is not reasonably accessible without creating an undue burden on the employer.

Moreover, once a party reasonably anticipates litigation, the duty to preserve evidence also applies to data generated or produced by IoT technology and devices.[24]

III. Steps Employers Should Take to Stay Ahead of IoT Risks

To reduce the risk of employee claims and the potential for problems associated with IoT data privacy and security, companies should keep a few best practices in mind:

- **Prepare and distribute appropriate notices.** Employees commonly receive privacy notices from their employers through handbooks and when logging into employer-owned computers. Similar notifications should be given, when possible, to employees who are interacting with IoT devices or equipment, or where data from employee-owned IoT devices may be collected by the employer. These notices should reflect a careful assessment of information that may be collected, which will reduce the chance of an employee

24. *See* Zubulake v. UBS Warburg LLC, 220 F.R.D. 212, 218 (S.D.N.Y. 2003) ("Once a party reasonably anticipates litigation, it must suspend its routine document retention/destruction policy and put in place a 'litigation hold' to ensure the preservation of relevant documents.").

claiming to have been misinformed about the scope of the employee's understanding, consent, or authorization relating to IoT data.

- **Collect only data that is needed.** Especially when an IoT device offers the promise of improved workplace efficiency and safety, employers may find it irresistible to want more data. In theory, the richer the data set, the better the conclusions that can be made about areas that may need improvement. But, as a general rule, employers that collect broader ranges of data and more information subject themselves to a wider range of legal rules, which can be ever-changing. Employers should expect that applicable legal requirements may change, depending on the type of information they obtain, especially to the extent that the particular data creates a risk of identity theft to their employees or may pertain to medical issues. Employers should also anticipate significant concerns over situations in which the employer could conceivably monitor an employee's activities outside of the workplace. Also, when employers maintain data that creates the risk of identity theft, employers may become subject to state beach notification laws if their data becomes compromised. To reduce possible compliance headaches, employers should identify a strong business case for collecting data about employees.
- **Do not overlook home offices and employee-owned IoT devices as data sources.** With the increase in IoT-enabled devices in the average home, employers now need to account for the possibility of a data breach arising from devices located in their employees' homes—particularly when employees telework and use Internet-connected devices in both their home network and the office. Employers should develop policies, akin to "Bring Your Own Device," or "BYOD," policies, providing employees with information

about requirements for devices located in employees' personal residences or vehicles. An IoT policy should define (1) who is authorized to introduce IoT devices to the company network; (2) which devices and applications are permitted and what security requirements apply; (3) which websites or cloud services employees can use for business purposes; and (4) what the consequences are for failing to comply with these rules.

- **Restrict public access.** While employees may have given at least some consideration to network security for a home office environment, they should also be aware of risks to employer data security when employees use public Wi-Fi networks, such as at an airport or a local coffee shop, or in transit. To protect sensitive data, employees need to be thoroughly trained on the ways in which IoT devices can compromise data security when connecting to internal systems from outside of the workplace.
- **Monitor the workplace environment.** The addition of IoT devices to an employer's network is nearly inevitable, so businesses should proactively monitor and track those increasing connections. Employers must know what devices are on their networks, and should actively monitor who is connecting to all key systems.
- **Be thoughtful about data retention.** It may be tempting for an employer to keep confidential and personal data for extended periods of time. However, employers that maintain larger data sets generally also face increased compliance costs when they are asked to respond to requests for information. Employers that need to maintain data for long periods of time should consider whether aggregating data is a workable solution, as maintaining data in a de-identified form may reduce the risks associated with data loss or data breaches.

- **Check agreements.** Whenever an employer introduces new IoT-enabled hardware, the company should thoroughly review and evaluate any associated data agreements. Confirm what information is being collected, where it is stored, transferred, or shared, and who has access to it. This information should be incorporated into employee privacy policies, handbook provisions, and consent forms, when required.
- **Training.** Employers need to educate employees on a routine basis about the risks of using personal devices and protecting company-owned information. Without a solid understanding of the importance of password management, data encryption requirements, and general cybersecurity practices, a lack of employee awareness will create opportunities for data breaches. Data security and privacy policies are not worth the paper they are printed on (or the additional marginal cost for maintaining them in cloud storage) if these policies are not routinely followed by everyone in the company.

IV. Conclusion

As the scope of IoT devices and applications continues to expand, employers should regularly review IoT-related issues with an eye toward how these issues could affect their compliance with their existing labor and employment requirements. As a rule of thumb, employers should remember that a clear privacy policy or privacy notice to employees will go a long way in reducing the risk of a claim that the employer has been using or collecting an employee's information improperly. In order to properly document these types of policies, employers will need to know what types of data they are able to collect about employees through IoT-enabled devices, whether at work, while in transit, or at home. An assessment of these points should also provide an employer with a foundation for evaluating potential data security risks, as well as possible data retention plans, that account for IoT devices and data.

Chapter 20

Get SMART on Training

Make Privacy and Security a Part of the Organization's Culture

Ruth Hill Bro
Jill D. Rhodes

I. Data Protection Training Basics and Core Principles

In a connected world, everything is "smart": devices, products, services, offices, factories, houses, and even entire cities. What is not so smart, however, is ignoring the corresponding privacy and security issues, which threaten the growth of the Internet of Things (IoT) and put all organizations at risk. Smart businesses (whether they make or use IoT devices and networks) are recognizing that they must make privacy and security a part of the organization's culture.

- **Making IoT devices/networks.** Research by Bain & Company indicated that security is the primary barrier to adoption of IoT and that customers would buy more (about 70 percent more) and pay more (about 22 percent more) for secure IoT devices.[1] Likewise, a recent study by the Economist

1. *See* Syed Ali, Ann Bosche, & Frank Ford, *Cybersecurity Is the Key to Unlocking Demand in the Internet of Things*, BAIN & COMPANY (June 13, 2018), https://www.bain.com/insights/cybersecurity-is-the-key-to-unlocking-demand-in-the-internet-of-things/.

Intelligence Unit indicated that consumers worldwide are deeply worried about collection and sharing of personal information by IoT.[2] Lack of privacy and security awareness in the employees and vendors who create IoT devices and networks can translate into deficiencies in product and service offerings (which could put a damper on potential profits) and open the business to liability (which could jeopardize profits and damage the organization's reputation).

- **Using IoT devices/networks.** The Internet, mobile devices, and ever more sophisticated computer technology (all connected to each other and always on) make it easy to collect, analyze, combine, reproduce, and disseminate data, thereby enhancing efficiency and cost-effectiveness but also escalating the risk of making catastrophic mistakes at the speed of light. Yet, employees often do not really understand that the latest smart technology at work or home (TVs, appliances, toys or gadgets, automated fish tanks, security cameras, digital assistants, voice-controlled smart home hubs, etc.) could be invisibly eavesdropping on confidential discussions using connected microphones, spying via built-in cameras, or providing a new attack vector for accessing the organization's digital assets.

In fact, any business (including law firms) that works with personal and sensitive data must develop a strategy for protecting that data. When assessing how to do so, organizations often mistakenly rely on technology as the solution. In fact, four factors are key to implementing a proper information security and data protection program in any setting:

2. *See* Fredric Paul, *People Are Really Worried about IoT Data Privacy and Security—and They Should Be*, Network World (Mar. 28, 2018, 7:10 AM), networkworld.com/article/3267065/internet-of-things/people-are-really-worried-about-iot-data-privacy-and-securityand-they-should-be.html.

- Establishing the appropriate *governance* for the data, such as policies and the oversight of an executive level committee tasked with reducing data protection risk;
- Ensuring that the *people* working with the data know how best to protect it;
- Assessing data protection and usage *processes*; and
- Employing appropriate *technology* to protect the network.

Note that only one of the four factors is focused on the technology. The other three factors revolve around people, with two of them (governance and processes) providing a structure for behavior. That said, unless a culture is developed that includes the protection of data, the value of strong governance and processes is marginalized. This chapter focuses on the culture—the people aspect of that equation. Most data missteps in an organization are directly linked to something an employee or contractor did, whether intentionally or unintentionally. The easiest way to address this risk is to create a culture of data protection by educating employees and others about the risk and their role in protecting personal and sensitive data.

Education and training can be provided by many facets of the organization, whether human resources (HR), the chief privacy officer (CPO), the chief information security officer (CISO), or others. Regardless of which groups do the training, it is critical that they work together to produce a common vision and message that are then disseminated across the organization.

A. Why Train on Data Protection?

All organizations are increasingly recognizing that data underpins virtually everything that they do and—like other valuable business assets—that data should be protected.

The trend is to adopt a reasoned and comprehensive strategy that makes data protection a part of the corporate culture and the responsibility of every individual working for the business, starting with the C-suite and continuing through every facet of the business.[3] Such an approach is designed to:

- Minimize missteps that can hit the bottom line (costly litigation; external audits; time and resources consumed in responding to government, press, or disciplinary commission inquiries or investigations; adverse media coverage; damage to client or customer relationships; and so on), and
- Help businesses achieve a competitive advantage, enhance their profile and image, and enrich their relationship with clients and customers.

Yet making data protection a part of the corporate culture is easier said than done:

- Properly addressing data protection issues can require a comprehensive understanding of rapidly changing applicable law in 50 states and territories, at the federal level, and globally (where client or customer data might originate, where third parties might be providing U.S.-based businesses with 24/7 services, etc.). Many laws (particularly for government entities and regulated industries) and lawyers' professional rules of responsibility expressly or by implication require appropriate data protection training for employees and sometimes contractors and third-party associates as well.[4]

---

3. This trend is in keeping with the "Privacy by Design" (PbD) and "Security by Design" (SbD) movements that are transforming the way that businesses protect data in an information-driven age. *See, e.g., Privacy by Design: The 7 Foundational Principles,* by Ann Cavoukian, Ph.D., Distinguished Expert-in-Residence, Privacy by Design Centre of Excellence, Ryerson University and former Ontario Privacy Commissioner, http://www.ryerson.ca/pbdce; see also *Start with Security: A Guide for Business,* FED. TRADE COMM'N, http://www.ftc.gov/startwithsecurity, for insights and guidance on SbD gleaned from over 50 FTC data security settlements.

4. For further discussion about the types of legal and professional responsibility requirements placed on lawyers and law firms, which often include

- Command of the law is not enough, as businesses are often tried in the court of public opinion or are challenged by third-party watchdog groups, regardless of the current legality of the entity's practices.
- Likewise, technological innovation is occurring at a startling and accelerating pace, and employees often fail to understand the risks of the latest "smart" technology at home or in the office.

Change is the watchword, and businesses and their cultures must be nimble in spotting trends and addressing issues that were not even on the radar screen months before.

Business leaders often breathe a sigh of relief once the state-of-the-art security system is installed and comprehensive data protection policies and procedures have been established. Yet notwithstanding adoption of the latest technology and sound data protection principles, businesses are only as strong as their weakest (human) link:

- The disgruntled or downsized "Gen X" employee who has it in for the organization and whose system access was not terminated on the last day of employment.
- The IT director who fails to install patches on a regular basis, thereby leaving networks vulnerable.
- The HR leader who uses company-issued equipment (smartphones, fitness trackers, vehicles, etc.) to track the location (and, in some cases, the physical condition) of employees on the job and after hours.

---

education and training, see Thomas J. Smedinghoff & Ruth Hill Bro, *Lawyers' Legal Obligations to Provide Data Security*, and Peter Geraghty & Lucian T. Pera, *Lawyers' Obligations to Provide Data Security Arising from Ethics Rules and Other Law*, *in* THE ABA CYBERSECURITY HANDBOOK: A RESOURCE FOR ATTORNEYS, LAW FIRMS, AND BUSINESS PROFESSIONALS, ABA Cybersecurity Legal Task Force (2d ed. 2018).

- The oblivious hardware developer who overlooks the need to build physical security (including tamper-proofing measures) into the device.
- The harried software developer, trying to deliver on time and on budget, who fails to use secure coding practices, configure the device properly so that upgrades are easy and manageable, and enable remote wiping in case of compromise.
- The super-connected, tech-savvy "Millennial" employee who overshares on social media and underestimates how that may sabotage the company's confidential data or IoT product development.
- The road-warrior employee who violates internal data security policies on mobile technology/"bring your own device" by his actions (losing a laptop, phone, or unencrypted flash drive on a plane or rideshare vehicle) or inaction (not implementing the latest software patches).
- The "Baby Boomer" CEO who unleashes ransomware by clicking on a link that looks like it came from a colleague or board member.
- The administrative assistant who provides confidential information after receiving a fraudulent e-mail that appears to be coming from her supervisor or a trusted business partner.
- The third-party vendor who fails to encrypt traffic between IoT devices and servers and then stores data overseas without appropriate security controls.
- The purchasing manager who buys Internet-connected Closed-Circuit TV cameras (CCTV) without realizing its administrative password will need to be changed to prevent it from being targeted by malicious third parties or used in a Botnet-type attack.[5]

---

5. The Mirai Botnet attack, which occurred on October 12, 2016, and brought down a significant portion of the major Internet services, leveraged IoT devices using 61 username/password combinations frequently used for defaults. *See* Josh Fruhlinger, *The Mirai Botnet Explained: How Teen Scammers and CCTV*

Countless studies, audit trails, and surveys over the years have repeatedly confirmed that the biggest data protection threats come from within one's own organization. Most missteps are unintentional. Many mistakes can be avoided and risks can be minimized with appropriate training and awareness-raising. Yet this is often an overlooked component of data protection initiatives—the missing link when it comes to security.

B. What Does SMART Training Look Like?

What does training actually mean, and what are businesses doing to address data protection's weakest link? Over the years, this question has been posed to CPOs drawn from various industries, locations, and corporate cultures,[6] and a consistent pattern of answers has emerged. In short, when conducting training, businesses need to be SMART:

Start training on hiring.

Measure what you do.

Annually provide training.

Raise awareness and provide updates continually.

Tailor training by role.

In considering these SMART training steps and what they mean for one's business, it is important to keep in mind that the particular data protection training that is right for one entity is not necessarily right for another, even if they are in the same industry

---

Cameras Almost Brought Down the Internet. CSO (Mar. 9, 2018, 3:00 AM), https://www.csoonline.com/article/3258748/security/the-mirai-botnet-explained-how-teen-scammers-and-cctv-cameras-almost-brought-down-the-internet.html.

6. Chapter co-author Ruth Hill Bro has posed such training questions since 2005 in her recurring column called *CPO Corner: Interviews with Leading Chief Privacy Officers,* which features 17 questions designed to identify trends and best practices, showcase the diverse range of CPOs, and capture key benchmarking and practical implementation information regarding data protection issues; *see* interviews posted at ABA, Section of Science & Technology Law: E-Privacy Law Committee, www.ambar.org/eprivacy.

or are organizations of similar size. Businesses differ in many ways—for example, the degree of centralization, their corporate cultures, the jurisdictions in which they operate, their objectives, their resources and budget, their existing data protection infrastructure, their buy-in from senior management, and so on.

1. S—Start Training on Hiring

Given the fundamental role of data in everything a business does, training on how to protect that data should start on day one. Data protection training should be provided to all new employees and, increasingly, to contractors as well. In cases where it is not feasible to do such training for all employees initially (due to bandwidth, budget, or other constraints), businesses might choose to focus training on selected employees (e.g., HR personnel and those in key business roles or units).

In the employee context, training is provided as a part of employee orientation. Such training can take different forms, using a variety of media:

- An initial in-person, instructor-led session (large group, small group, or one-on-one, as appropriate), which can encourage interaction (but may not always be scalable or practical for some organizations in all situations), and/or
- An intranet/computer-based training module.

Coverage can include a wide range of topics, including:

- High-level overviews applicable to all employees and contractors;
- Instruction on relevant data protection laws and regulations (and professional rules of responsibility, where applicable), internal policies and procedures, fundamentals of the relevant technology, and industry best practices;
- Protecting confidentiality and security of data; and
- Steps to take when addressing a suspected data breach.

Such training should be coordinated with other training (regarding records management, code of conduct, etc.) and should be reviewed to avoid contradictions and conflicts in approach and message. Consideration should be given to whether the time, format, and content are suitable across different parts of the organization. Issues of translation, local law, and local customs can come into play here as well.

2. *M—Measure What You Do*

Measurement and assessment are a core component of many of these initial training sessions as well as in follow-up training. Administering tests (e.g., a graded online quiz) can help to confirm understanding and gauge the overall effectiveness of the training; it can also help to ensure that the work has actually been done. For example, employees and contractors could be required to correctly answer four of five assessment questions at the end of each training section. Broader measurements—such as comparisons of incidents and types of missteps before and after training—can also help businesses to make training more effective while demonstrating return on investment (which can be important in making the case for budget).

3. *A—Annually Provide Training*

It is prudent (and in some cases required under applicable law, rules, or policies) to ensure that employees annually receive a data protection training update, along with corresponding assessments or tests. Where relevant, certification or continuing legal education (CLE) or professional responsibility credit could be provided, thereby offering an additional incentive to do the training. Such follow-up instruction is often computer-based, so it can be deployed to diverse geographic locations and in a time frame that is convenient for the person receiving the training. Sometimes these annual updates are a part of annual recertification regarding business conduct guidelines.

4. R—Raise Awareness and Provide Updates Continually

It is impossible to integrate appropriate data security practices into a culture by using just introductory training on hiring and mandatory annual training. To address this, businesses need to look for ways to raise data awareness and update employees on data protection on an ongoing basis. This is due to a number of factors, including the speed with which the issues change, the different ways in which people learn, the need for reinforcement, and so on. With ongoing awareness-raising, businesses can integrate information security practices in such a way that they become as commonplace as turning on a computer.

5. T—Tailor Training by Role

Going beyond high-level, one-size-fits-all training allows for training to be tailored to focus on specific roles of individuals, different generational challenges, and specific requirements for contractors and third parties. Tailoring of data protection training can take various forms, depending on the organization:

- Start with a Data Protection 101 online course that is available on demand (successfully completing it results in a certificate). The basic module can then be supplemented by training and awareness-raising specific to role (HR, those involved heavily in data handling, contractors, product design, engineering, sales, purchasing, senior executives, lawyers, paralegals, administrative assistants, etc.), business unit, geographic location, and the like.
- Determine who should receive direct training from, or at least meet in person with, the CPO, CISO, CIO or IT director, legal counsel, or other qualified trainers. It is helpful for those tasked with training to meet with selected employees to learn about their data practices

and then tailor training efforts accordingly. For example, some CPOs meet regularly with the company's engineering, product design, and sales teams to raise important issues in planning meetings and gain insights to develop appropriate training.

- Ask data protection officers (or other relevant individuals) associated with the business lines to develop training and tools to enable the application of data protection policies to their respective areas.
- Hire specialists, internally or externally, to refine and enhance training efforts.
- Not all training and awareness-raising comes from within. Small firms or solo practitioners, those who lack specialized staff, and others looking for cost-effective approaches should take advantage of online training modules, relevant CLE courses and conferences, resources offered by bar associations (the American Bar Association and the ABA's Sections, Divisions, Forums, and other entities; state and local bar associations; specialty bar associations; etc.), training publications, and the like.
- As noted previously, training for some roles (e.g., lawyers) may be accompanied by certification or CLE or professional responsibility credit.

Businesses that use SMART training can provide the missing link that will help make data protection a part of the culture and turn their employees into one of their strongest links when it comes to protecting one of the most valuable assets of any business.

II. SMART Training in Action

Implementing a SMART training program does not have to be complicated or require significant budget. The program pays for itself by reducing the risk of data loss and increasing awareness about data protection.

A. Understanding the Basics of Employees: Role and Generational Differences

First, any training program should assess and understand the recipients of the training. As just mentioned, the role of the employee in the organization will make a difference in the type of training received. An associate working with e-discovery matters and technology every day will have different considerations than a mail clerk or even sales staff or senior executives.

In addition, generational differences play a role in how training should be developed, the type of training and communication that a person prefers to receive, and how best to provide the training. Cam Marston, in his practical and often humorous book *Generational Insights: Practical Solutions for Understanding and Engaging a Generationally Disconnected Workforce*,[7] discusses how each generation differs in its approach to learning:

- **Baby Boomers** (born 1946–1964) tend to continue to hold key leadership positions (e.g., partners) in the organization. They focus on work ethic and often measure it in terms of hours spent rather than productivity. They value face time and relationships and seek loyalty. They look for those willing to put in whatever time is necessary to complete the task and support the team.[8] When training Baby Boomers, it is critical to include preevaluation of technology skills and training that is participatory but not intimidating.[9]

---

7. Cam Marston, Generational Insights: Practical Solutions for Understanding and Engaging a Generationally Disconnected Workforce (2010).

8. *Id.* at 33–34.

9. *Id.* at 39.

- **Gen Xers** (born 1965–1979) often have a more entrepreneurial spirit and are focused on challenging or reinventing the status quo. They tend to seek open communication, no matter their title or status. Unlike Baby Boomers, Gen Xers focus on productivity rather than time. They often seek a person, not a company, where their loyalty will lie.[10] Training programs should address the Gen X employee's career goals and be flexible, providing options and choices. For Gen Xers to see training as valuable, senior-level management must demonstrate its commitment to the training as valuable.[11]
- **Millennials** (born 1980–2000) tend to be the most idealistic of the three groups. Unlike Gen Xers, who prefer to work independently with few checkpoints, Millennials want constant communication and positive reinforcement and prefer regular checkpoints at each phase of their work.[12] Training programs for Millennials need to be group-oriented (where practical), interactive, and fun. They prefer that everyone be allowed to take a role in some part of the teaching as well as the learning.[13]

Given the diverse nature of the workforce and the different means by which people learn and absorb information, any training or education campaign must integrate a variety of employee perspectives and capabilities and incorporate a variety of approaches.

10. *Id.* at 35.
11. *Id.* at 41.
12. *Id.* at 35, 37.
13. *Id.* at 42.

B. Building an Effective and Diverse Program

Leveraging the SMART principles described previously, any organization can quickly and easily build an ongoing training and education campaign.

First, it is critical to make the campaign fun and creative. While the message of data protection is serious, the delivery does not need to be. People of all generations tend to learn more through consistent messaging that has a direct impact on their lives. Those working on the data protection training should develop easy, fun, and catchy slogans that employees will remember.

One example is the SAFE program,[14] an information security awareness program that was developed to help employees remember how best to protect and secure sensitive information:

Secure the organization's data: Where are you storing client data? How are you deleting it?

Asset protection: Do you know where your computer/iPad/ phone is?

Friend or **F**oe: Who is sending you an e-mail? Is it something you expected or phishing?

Encrypt: Are you encrypting sensitive e-mails before sending them out?

A program such as SAFE can be used throughout the year to educate staff; different themes within each of the four SAFE categories can be featured.

Next, identify something, such as a mascot, that represents the organization and symbolizes data protection to help lighten the delivery of a serious message. For example, Option Care, which

14. The SAFE program was developed by Jill Rhodes, who is a co-author of this chapter. For further information, contact Ms. Rhodes at jill.rhodes@optioncare.com.

provides infusion services to patients in their homes, uses a mascot named "The Infuser."

The Infuser's motto is "Infusing Security into Everything We Do." Every time employees see this mascot and message, they are reminded about protecting sensitive information. It is a fun, easy, and quick cue that costs very little to the organization to develop and implement.

Third, ensure that training is continuous, and use various methods to implement it. In addition to mandatory training at specific times (when employees join the organization and subsequent annual training), continuous education is key to any successful cultural transformation. The following are some ideas to keep the momentum going:

- Leverage current newsletters, and place brief articles within them that discuss data protection.
- Conduct e-mail campaigns (monthly or as needed) with data protection guidelines, relevant media coverage, and so on to remind everyone (or otherwise make them aware) of relevant policies and practices.
- Offer periodic "Data Protection Awareness Weeks" or "Security Awareness Drives" with guest speakers and other special events.
- Strategically place wall posters and other communications that promote data protection.
- Publish monthly articles on the company and line-of-business intranet home pages to raise data protection awareness.
- Send periodic e-mails to highlight ongoing opportunities for online training and in-person sessions conducted by members of the data protection team or outside speakers.
- Develop white papers and other material related to relevant data protection topics (aiming for greater frequency and detail over time).

- Remind employees that data protection training is an important part of their job by including it as a factor in their annual performance evaluation; celebrate successes and reward those who meet the objectives (and, if needed, identify opportunities for growth and improvement).

Fourth, involve employees directly. Hold data protection competitions between divisions, offices, or floors in a building with the goal of identifying an employee/group activity that protected the organization's information in a noteworthy way. Recognize the individual or group winners, name them in the monthly newsletter or blog, and provide a pizza lunch for the winner—the more recognition, the better.

Build an ambassador/liaison or similar program across the organization. Whether it is by office, region, subject matter expertise, or business unit, identify a way to have a data protection representative in each. Although senior leadership is important, the representative should be a mid-level employee who still has influence with peers, subordinates, and leadership. Meet with the data protection ambassadors/liaisons regularly to discuss data protection issues and (in line with the preceding discussion about Millennials) ensure that they are a part of the solution by having them serve as the leaders who will train and educate the employees they work with on a regular basis.

Educate employees about how to protect data at home as well as in the workplace. Data protection does not start when a person logs into the network, or end when she shuts down for the evening. Everyone's family members and friends are constantly touching sensitive and/or personal digital data. Whether it is through social media or new mobile apps, data is being collected. By educating employees to protect data in all facets of their lives, they will approach data protection more holistically in their daily work life.

All of these methods are easy, cheap, fun, and effective ways to communicate and educate employees about enhancing data protection in the organization. As noted earlier, it is critical to find ways to measure the success of these campaigns (the M in SMART training).

C. Measuring Success (through Phishing Campaigns and Other Means)

One of the easiest ways to measure the success of a campaign is to test employees by phishing them directly. Phishing normally occurs when a malicious e-mail is sent either directly to an individual (spear phishing) or to many in the hope that the target will click on a link within the e-mail and then spread a virus that could infect the individual's computer, at a minimum, or the entire enterprise network. Ransomware has often been caused by phishing.

As part of a SAFE campaign (Friend or Foe), organizations can implement their own company-wide phishing campaign, sending fake "malicious" e-mails to employees, as someone trying to harm the organization would do. When an employee clicks on the e-mail, instead of infecting the system, the employee receives an educational message about phishing (including the fact that had the e-mail been from a malicious source, harm could have come to the organization). This type of campaign measures the click rate and, when conducted regularly, can be used to monitor those who are clicking regularly. As a result, specific training can be developed for those individuals or groups. Phishing programs provide a quantitative measurement related to security awareness.

Reporting numbers also can provide both quantitative and qualitative opportunities for measuring success. As more training and education occurs, employees will report more incidents. As employees become more aware of the need to protect information, they also become more aware of ways in which the organization needs to improve. The reporting should be celebrated, and any issues should be addressed. As incidents are tracked, greater information becomes available about employee knowledge and understanding of data protection, which then contributes to future education.

In the end, a data breach or loss will most likely occur as a result of something an employee did or did not do. The best way to prevent such missteps is to build a culture within the organization that promotes the protection of information.

III. Ten Key Points

1. Make data protection a part of the corporate culture and the job of every individual.
2. Recognize that the biggest risks to data come from the people working for the organization and that training and raising awareness are essential to reducing those risks.
3. Be SMART in training: **S**tart training on hiring. **M**easure what you do. **A**nnually provide training. **R**aise awareness and provide updates continually. **T**ailor training by role.
4. Recognize that one size doesn't fit all; it is important to undertake training that fits a business's own needs.
5. Build a program that represents the organization's employees both from a role perspective and a generational one.
6. Make any training campaign fun and interesting—let the employees lead it through ambassador/liaison programs and in other ways.
7. Train employees on how to protect information in all facets of their lives, not just in the workplace. By helping them protect their family and friends at home, they will further integrate these practices at work.
8. Reward! Reward! Reward! Use competitions with prizes to further induce employees to become more aware and supportive of data protection across the organization.
9. Measure success through phishing programs and tracking of reporting of incidents and responses.
10. Know that training and awareness-raising is a never-ending journey (not a destination) that can require changes in direction in response to changes in the law, technology,

media coverage, and one's own experiences and new business initiatives. Adapt accordingly, while keeping message delivery mechanisms light and easy-to-understand for all of the people who work for the organization.

Chapter 21

Back to the Future

Anticipating Regulatory Hurdles within IoT Pelotons

Brian Subirana

I. IoT Is Funneling Increasing Policy Complexity

Uber offers a service centered around the Internet of Things (IoT): drivers, passengers, and real-time traffic information is coordinated using information collected from thousands of sensors—the service is challenging norms that have been established for decades, so much so that it is being bombarded by hundreds of lawsuits from governments, associations, competitors, drivers, and passengers. The courts have trouble developing criteria to assess whether the service is more like a regular cab service or instead a car-for-hire service. Should the same labor laws apply to cab and Uber drivers? Is the service even legal? What on-boarding practices should be employed? In case of an accident, how should liabilities be assigned? Can Uber drivers carry and/or sell merchandise? Courts around the world are using conflicting criteria to answer these questions while Uber is settling many lawsuits at great cost to the company. Additional legal hurdles will come from other value propositions it is embarking on, including Uber Eats, self-driving Ubers, new logistic services, and the many more services it is poised to develop as part of its leadership in the sharing economy.

This is not an isolated example, and the Uber story is a perfect one to illustrate why this book is so important at this juncture. What differentiates the IoT from most other technologies is that it has already changed (or will change) the nature of most industries. This expansion into a wide range of industries will create entirely new policy challenges. Many are outlined in the rest of this book, and there are many more to come.

As new IoT technologies are created, the number of combinations of technological possibilities will increase exponentially[1] into unregulated arenas. The intersection of robotics and vehicles yields self-driving cars. The intersection of the Internet and entertainment yields iTunes and Netflix. The intersection of photovoltaic power generation on rooftops and networking is driving the smart grid. The intersection of genetics and big data is driving pharmacogenetics. And low earth orbit satellites launched by the burgeoning commercial space industry may well lead to new universal Internet access. No sector is immune to the domino effect of creativity, and IoT is at the center of it all. Technological progress seems to be more rapid today than it was even a decade ago. The numbers—whether patents filed, businesses disrupted, venture investments, or the changing nature of jobs—show the pace of change has indeed accelerated tremendously in recent years. Basic research around MIT and other campuses across the world promise to funnel this acceleration for the foreseeable future.

What is missing is a way to develop and evolve regulatory environments that can adapt to future needs as IoT continues to change the world—something that is needed today but perhaps wasn't as dire even a decade ago. For this exact purpose, we developed a tool we call the Peloton.

---

1. Sanjay Sarma & Brian Subirana, *How to Build an Innovation Radar: Road-Mapping, News-Mapping and Innovation*, GS1 White Paper (2018).

II. IoT Peloton Road Mapping

In the mid-2000s, our Radio Frequency Identification Device (RFID) lab at MIT, the MIT Auto-ID Laboratory, developed the concept of the Peloton,[2] a term drawing inspiration from bicycle road races such as the Tour de France. In search of a similar goal, riders naturally tend to form competitive[3] clusters during the Tour because of the reduction in aerodynamic draft, which has been estimated to be up to 95 percent.[4] In some cases, teams will sacrifice the energy of one rider to pull a designated cyclist, running away in pairs to try to lead the race. Companies and technologies, in our view, naturally form similar clusters (i.e., Pelotons), and coordinating in a competitive way enables convergence on technology road map milestones, standards, and regulations. A business peloton may include players that don't directly compete, for example decreases in computer memory prices funnel increases in networking equipment. However it is not an entire ecosystem, because it only includes the players "drafting" each other in search of a similar business benefit. In fact several competitive business pelotons may exist within an ecosystem, for example, VHS versus Beta, PC versus MAC, Windows versus UNIX. One peloton may lobby against another to establish certain policies that benefit its interests. Often IoT-based pelotons enter into unchartered territories requiring aggressive policy making given that the business benefits developed challenge current regulatory options. It is in these cases that the Peloton Tool we developed can help.

---

2. Brian Subirana, Sanjay E. Sarma, Richard Lee & Jamshed Dubash, *Peloton Planning Tool: Applying the Peloton to the EPC Industry, GS1 EPC Global White Paper Collection (May 2005).*

3. The rides will cooperate to save energy but are still competitive, and may at some point "leave the pack" to establish dominance over the rest of the peloton.

4. B. Blocken et al., *Aerodynamic Drag in Cycling Pelotons: New Insights by CFD Simulation and Wind Tunnel Testing, 179* J. WIND ENG'G & INDUS. AERODYNAMICS 319–37 (2018).

One of the earliest examples of business-benefit-driven peloton policy making is that of the bar code. Even though the technology was invented in the 1940s, it was not until decades later and a proper policy-making consortium was created that the technology brought any tangible business benefits to society. It was only with an agreement involving technology providers, retailers, and CPG manufacturers that the use at scale of this primitive IoT technology made any business sense. To this date, GS1 is still a policy-making standard body that manages the bar code standard and many other derivative ones.

Perhaps GSM cellular radio technology represents the biggest and most impactful example to date of business-benefit-driven peloton policy making like the one IoT requires. Starting in 1983, GSM evolved from 2G to many other standards now reaching the biggest share of phones and networks in the world. The European Telecommunications Standards Institute (ETSI) was involved in defining protocols for the standard but also in establishing regulatory issues such as spectrum allocation. Another example of business-benefit-driven peloton road mapping is the SEMATECH research consortium, established in 1987 to conduct research in semiconductor fabrication in the United States.[5] It counted many of the key semiconductor companies of the day in its ranks, and in the 1990s pioneered the concept of pre-competitive collaborative road maps. Because it was a consortium, SEMATECH was externally focused and therefore served as an early and visible example of road mapping in general, and industry collaboration in particular.[6] Collaboration between companies has been studied from different

5. Karen H. Brown, *SEMATECH and the National Technology Roadmap: Needs and Challenges, in 2438* Advances in Resist Technology and Processing XII 33–38 (Int'l Society for Optics and Photonics, 1995).

6. Elias G. Carayannis & Jeffrey Alexander, *Strategy, Structure, and Performance Issues of Precompetitive R&D Consortia: Insights and Lessons Learned from SEMATECH, 51(2)* IEEE Transactions on Eng'g Mgmt 226–32 (2004).

perspectives, including a consideration of antitrust,[7] and is generally thought to "lift all boats."

Going forward, one of the hardest things will be to determine which actors should play a role in an IoT Peloton Tool Policy Exercise. In the case of IoT in Retail of Consumer Products Goods, for example, peloton players include Retailer, Industry, and Supplier companies. But a hard issue is to determine which players in particular need to be brought into policy-making exercises. In my laboratory, we lived this firsthand. During the development of RFID standards, Professor Sanjay Sarma and I, together with The Gillette Company and graduate student Vineet Thuvara, put a Peloton Tool into practice with vendors and end users to facilitate policy collaboration across industry players.[8] We used this process to drive RFID convergence pre-competitively for standards and milestones. For example, if consumer goods manufacturers decide to tag individual, at source products with RFID chips, then, to reap the full business benefits, forklift manufacturers will need to incorporate RFID readers, and processes will need to be adapted, which, in turn, means distribution centers will need to amend 3PL contracts.[9] Moreover, these tagged devices may make it all the way to consumer homes, and privacy concerns will need to be taken care of too. But manufacturers may choose a different route and only add tags at the pallet level (instead of the individual item level), which has entirely different IoT implications, including the elimination of most privacy issues. Thus, the exact choice of players in a peloton will be largely determined by the evolution of commercially available technological components and by the choice of how these are

---

7. David J. Teece, *Information Sharing, Innovation, and Antitrust, 62* ANTITRUST L. 465 (1993).

8. Vineet Thuvara, The Peloton Approach: Forecasting and Strategic Planning for Emerging Technologies: A Case for RFID. SM thesis, Massachusetts Institute of Technology, 2006.

9. Third Party Logistic Contract.

used in practice. In some cases, two pelotons may exist with conflicting priorities and the legal environment may have a significant impact in which of the two pelotons wins. In our example, privacy regulations have favored tagging options that tag pallets or, if they tag "units," also known as "eaches," that are removed before reaching the end consumer. Both the technical and legal implications of a new IoT technology will always hinge on its implementation choices.

From a policy-making point of view, perhaps the hardest thing to establish before peloton constituents can be identified are the business benefits around appropriate regulations in an emerging IoT area, since these regulations will guide the contractual relationships in the new regulatory environment. The business benefits of a given technology will also serve to identify the actors, the beneficiaries, and the associated legal conditions around which to regulate. For example, a business benefit may be the use of RFID for a more efficient and real-time way of tracking inventory, which can result in benefits at the warehouse and store level, including less shrinkage, better promotion management from the store's backroom to the shelves, electronic proof of delivery, and lower out-of-stocks. To estimate the benefits, one requires a flexible and robust financial model as an important ingredient of any Peloton Tool. The financial model can be used to prioritize which business benefits make more sense and when they should be introduced. It is only in the context of this information that policy efforts can kick in and be effective.

Thus, establishing business benefits should be one of the key driving guidelines of any IoT regulatory effort. There should thus be a balance between regulation in the IoT and their impact on those benefits.

Let's now turn back to our suggested first step in a "back to the future" peloton policy exercise: establishing business benefits that can justify IoT investments.

III. Anticipating IoT Long-term Peloton Business Benefits

To identify potential peloton business benefits of emerging IoT technologies, as a starting point, there are many excellent examples of technology or trend radars[10] available freely on the Internet. Most are "broad spectrum" and capture ideas, memes, and general fronts in industry, business, policy, society, and economics. Some are specific to particular sectors, such as logistics[11] or insurance.[12] Either way, depending on the diligence of the author, they can be effective windows into the future. Many of these trend radars are compiled by companies for thought leadership. And deservedly so.

For the remainder of this chapter, we present emerging IoT-related technology areas that call for further broad policy making beyond what has been covered earlier in the book and that naturally call for a peloton approach to define the regulatory environment. We present key business benefits, which have not been properly regulated and cannot be yet fully realized by current IoT technology developments. The focus is on three key areas: matter, life, and information. The technologies that are presented have been demonstrated in the laboratory to a certain extent and impose serious policy challenges. It is the result of preparing a course on IoT,[13] first developed at MIT and which then served as one of the key components of a Harvard class,[14] centered on explaining the

10. https://www.gs1-germany.de/innovation/trendforschung/trendradar; https://www.munichre.com/topics-online/en/2018/06/future-technologies-tech-trend-radar-2018.

11. https://www.logistics.dhl/content/dam/dhl/global/core/documents/pdf/glo-core-trend-radar-widescreen.pdf, (last visited Aug. 2018).

12. https://www.munichre.com/topics-online/en/2018/06/future-technologies-tech-trend-radar-2018, (last visited Aug. 2018).

13. Sanjay Sarma, IoT online MIT class led by Prof. Sarma involving several MIT faculty, 2016.

14. Brian Subirana, E-11, Harvard University class on the Frontiers of Artificial Intelligence led by Prof. Subirana and involving several MIT faculty,

frontier of AI technologies. The central assumption behind this exercise is that by looking at the IoT-related research being conducted by MIT researchers, one can gain a perspective of what is the frontier of the possible and the not-yet-possible. In other words, it is by thoroughly exploring this frontier that one can assess what may be the state of commercial IoT may be five to ten years down the road and be better equipped to adapt appropriate policy, laws, and regulations (Figure 21.1).

Figure 21.1 Illustration of an IoT Scenario That May Be Ten Years Away

The following scenario will be used to elaborate the full spectrum of technologies to come.

2017, https://www.extension.harvard.edu/course-catalog/courses/introduction-to-the-challenges-and-opportunities-of-big-data-the-internet-of-things-and-cybersecurity/15525.

Just as Dr. Brown passes the last bottle of orange juice to her robot assistant, from the shopping bag brought home by her chocolate Labrador, she receives an augmented reality notification that a neighbor's baby cot has noticed an arrhythmia in the baby's heart. Dr. Brown runs out of the front door looking over the vitals as her peripheral vision keeps track of the emergency alert lights flashing from the sidewalk guiding her to the address where the emergency is continuing to unfold. Several drones are dispatched from the hyper local clinic and arrive with the appropriate equipment for infant resuscitation, alongside appropriately diluted adrenaline and fluid preparations for just such an occasion. The drones automatically load supplies at a neighboring pharmacy. A local community self-driving car has repurposed itself to serve as an ambulance, tracks Dr. Brown, and picks her up to drive the last two miles to the address at speeds up to 100 mph with all other vehicular traffic paused for a couple of seconds to allow them to pass safely with ease. The minute in the car is of vital importance, as Dr. Brown uses it to establish a full diagnosis and an action plan based on a voice-based interaction with the AI agent that guards the cot-sensing intelligence. The concerned parents are just starting to grasp the gravity of the situation and as panic is about to set in, they are relieved as Dr. Brown and the equipment drones enter the room to save their baby's life.

A. Information: Security of IoT

Self-driving cars can do things that human-operated cars can't. For example, such cars can travel safely at higher speeds or work collectively to help a given vehicle arrive at a destination faster, like in the preceding scenario (assuming, of course, that pedestrians and everyone else are seamlessly integrated into the norms and policies around the IoT). The value of Dr. Brown arriving a minute earlier may be the difference between life and death for the neighbor's baby. However, as stated in the self-driving cars chapter (Chapter 1), the security risks are tremendous. Imagine what would happen if an attacker can control the actions taken by a vehicle or even control the traffic lights of a town.

After extensive research on the subject, Professor Sarma concluded that three peloton-based initiatives are required[15] to regulate security:

1. There needs to be a clearly agreed architecture with hourglass boundaries like the Internet. This simplifies the prevention and recovery from attacks.
2. There need to be standards that go beyond the current closed-garden approaches that do not allow for proper interoperability like in the preceding scenario. Interoperability is key.
3. The government needs to step in, very much like DARPA did for the Internet, to set clear test beds that companies can use to benchmark security.

Sarma argues that the best way to address security in the long run is by way of a cloud-based platform where every device has a unique connection to the cloud. The cloud would then manage security and distribute messages to and from the device, including software updates and deprecation instructions. This approach has the merit of benefiting from all the extensive research and practice on cloud security. It also makes sense in a context where 5G technologies will be increasingly relevant for the IoT.

Without a peloton of security, the issue is getting worse every year, in at least two dimensions: The number of security threat options increases together with the rise of the IoT, and the potential damage is skyrocketing. Imagine, for example, if all pacemakers stopped working at the same time, if all microwave ovens where set on fire simultaneously, all self-driving cars crashed with each other, or if thousands of drones dropped grenades on a full stadium. All these examples are only possible with an unsecure IoT, and

15. Sanjay Sarma, *I Helped Invent the Internet of Things. Here's Why I'm Worried about How Secure It Is,* POLITICO (2015).

there are many more to come. We really don't have any assurance that some of these examples will not happen. In fact, many of us in the industry believe it is the one technology where the value delivered is getting worse and the risks are getting bigger as time goes by. Perhaps security is the only technology in the history of mankind that is progressing backwards. There needs to be more collaboration in the security space, especially as the IoT evolves, and perhaps regulators need to step in more aggressively.

B. Life: Wake Neutrality of Artificial Intelligence IoT Devices

In the preceding vignette, Dr. Brown interfaces via voice with an AI agent in the closest self-driving car available. To ensure compatibility of interfaces requires a neutral way of communicating with IoT infrastructures. The issue faced here also impacts simpler benefit areas like the one illustrated in this example:[16] You want to order an ice cream cake from Joe's Gelateria for pickup in 30 minutes on your way home from work. You can dial the phone number with any phone or check their web page with any browser, but if you use your smart speaker things are a bit more cumbersome since each conversational commerce hardware manufacturer has its own way of getting you started and there is no central and standard repository of wake words (e.g., "Alexa" for Amazon's Echo device).

Just like the Internet has the Domain Name System[17] (DNS) and phone networks have the North American Numbering Plan (NANP), we feel the voice space would greatly benefit by a standard "Voice Name System" (VNS) that would initially focus on these wake words. Standard does not mean lack of competi-

16. Brian Subirana, Renwick Bivings & Sanjay Sarma, *"Wake Neutrality" of Artificial Intelligence Devices, in* ALGORITHMS AND LAW (M. EBERS & S. NAVAS EDS), CAMBRIDGE UNIVERSITY PRESS (FORTHCOMING 2019).

17. https://tools.ietf.org/html/rfc882.

tion. Quite the contrary, it may mean, instead, a more flourishing competitive landscape. The barcode, for example, helped simplify retail processes and fostered competition between store inventory management philosophies and even among technology suppliers. Using the current Internet DNS (Domain Name System) approach may be a starting point, but it's not sufficient because voice is ambiguous. Voice domain name registrars could manage the registration process for wake constructs, including name resolution clashes and IoT prompts, and be involved in addressing two other key issues surrounding conversational commerce and the voice AI space in general: security and privacy.

Joe loses big time without a standard.[18] Joe's Gelateria loses too, but also the big players, including large on-ground retailers like Target and Walmart and the dominant e-retailers including Amazon and Google. We next define "wake neutrality" of IoT devices:

> (Artificial Intelligence) "Wake Neutrality": Conversational Commerce service providers will make a configurable and explainable effort at directing a user's direct or agent-mediated indirect request to its intended AI software agent without altering the service, whether by throttling speeds, increasing complexity, or blocking access altogether based on the user, the agent being requested, or the owner of such agent.

In an open conversational commerce AI/IoT environment scenario, such as the one required in Dr. Brown and Joe's scenarios, anyone can direct any device to their desired AI handler by simply prompting the device with an appropriate and standard "wake word" (or another comparable action, including EEG recorded

18. Brian Subirana, Sanjay Sarma, Richard Cantwell, Mark Taylor, Kees Jacobs, Shannon Warner, Gwendolyn Graman, Chris Hunt, & Jon Stine, *Time to Talk: The Future for Brands Is Conversational (Jan. 2018).*

thoughts and hand gestures) so that associated software agents are then subsequently allowed to wander around on their own as if they were delegated human butlers. Without a peloton policy exercise, this vision will not be possible, as wake neutrality standards won't emerge unless some agreement is developed. There are more things that need to be regulated in this scenario.

Voice is complicated to regulate because it's ambiguous, neither race nor gender *neutral, and because it reveals significant amounts of information*[19] about the person through its tone, choice of words, and semantic constructs. Elsewhere[20] we establish six policy requirements for wake word architectures in "open conversational commerce" (OCC): explainability, auditability, quality, configurability, institutionalization, and nondiscrimination.

Beyond virtual assistants, one of the current frontiers in Artificial Intelligence is whether AI devices will be able to engage in conversations with humans and develop characteristic personalities. Recent research on AI and medicine suggests that these devices may soon be even able to predict certain medical conditions and even suicide attempts better than humans.[21] But, should they be allowed to do so? Under what conditions? The unexplainability of such algorithms prevents formal scrutiny by smart law enforcement agents and poses many yet unresolved security[22] and legal issues.[23]

---

19. Scott R. Peppet, Regulating the Internet of Things: First Steps toward Managing Discrimination, Privacy, Security and Consent, 93.1 TEX. L. REV. 85–178 (2014).

20. Subirana, Bivings & Sarma, *supra* note 16.

21. Erwin Loh, *Medicine and the Rise of the Robots: A Qualitative Review of Recent Advances of Artificial Intelligence in Health,* BMJ LEADER (2018): LEADER-20.

22. Miles Brundage et al., *The Malicious Use of Artificial Intelligence: Forecasting, Prevention, and Mitigation (2018),* arXiv preprint arXiv:1802.07228.

23. Simon Stern, Introduction, *Artificial Intelligence, Technology, and the Law, 68 supp. 1* U. TORONTO L.J. 1–11 (2018).

Voice is just one way in which an IoT infrastructure may be called into action. Wake neutrality may also mean establishing protocols so that an IoT device can get a response from another device such as in the scenario when the car talks directly to the cot. Basic policy research is required to expand wake neutrality to include non-voice-based forms of awaking IoT infrastructures—especially automated ways, such as when a self-driving car is traveling through a town full of IoT sensors.

C. Matter: Legal Programming with High-Resolution Management, Blockchain, and a Packetized IoT Supply Chain

One aspect of the preceding scenario is that drones automatically find drugs at a nearby pharmacy. To this end, one would require the ability to pick up and deliver goods using drones. In a way this is a simple example, because thanks to IoT, the exchange of goods may be done eventually automatically in such a way that goods flow naturally and seamlessly, very much like how information is packetized and distributed on the Internet.[24] Eventually, we believe that merchandise will be swapped so that delivery is automated. This will require developing legal programming[25] approaches that can execute contracts in some form of blockchain public ledger every time merchandise is automatically swapped using the IoT.

To make that vision possible, today we can track people's locations, vital signs, visual appearance in public spaces, digital transactions, page views, e-mails, and social media account activity. This

---

24. Brian Subirana, Sanjay Sarma, Dominic Endicott & Gitanjali Swamy, *"Packetizing" the Real World, IESE* ALUMNI MAGAZINE 22–25 (JULY–SEPT. 2004).

25. Brian Subirana & Malcolm Bain, Legal Programming. *Designing Legally Compliant RFID and Software Agent Architectures for Retail Processes and Beyond, Research monograph published by Ed. Springer, 2005.*

is just the beginning. Recent research conducted at MIT suggests we will soon be able to cheaply see through walls using Wi-Fi,[26] locate objects indoors within one square centimeter, extract sound from potato chip bags using high-speed cameras,[27] or even determine whether one has been diligent about car maintenance using a mobile phone's built-in microphone.[28] Some colleagues at MIT believe eventually we will be able to do high-resolution management[29] on our bodies and brains thanks to our ever-larger ability to track thousands of body parameters and advances in genetic engineering funneled by CRISPR.

IV. A Very Long-Term IoT Business Benefit Scenario

The scenario presented earlier is based on current research and most pieces of it have already been demonstrated independently. We will now create an even more futuristic scenario, perhaps possible in the next quarter century, combining several active IoT-related research efforts at MIT, most yet to be prototyped. If these efforts succeed, we may develop tools that can sense life (including brains), genetically modify living organisms, packetize the supply chain, and high-resolution manage business processes to an extent consistent with the following business benefit scenario (Figure 21.2):

---

26. Fadel Adib & Dina Katabi. *See Through Walls with WiFi!, 43(4) ACM (2013).*

27. A. Davis et al., *The Visual Microphone: Passive Recovery of Sound from Video, 33.4* ACM Trans. Graph (2014).

28. J.E. Siegel, R. Bhattacharyya, S. Kumar & S.E. Sarma, *Air Filter Particulate Loading Detection Using Smartphone Audio and Optimized Ensemble Classification*, 66 Eng'g Applications of Artificial Intelligence 104–12 (2017).

29. Brian Subirana, Sanjay Sarma & Elgar Fleisch, *High-Resolution Management*, IESE Alumni Magazine 8–13 (July–Sept. 2006).

As the sun rises, Dr. Brown's dog, Muddy, with language abilities genetically enhanced, has almost finished a morning self-geofenced walk and is heading back for breakfast at the family home. Muddy's sensors detect *Cacyreus Marshalli* in one of the neighbor's geraniums, which, as a result, is subsequently combated by a genetically modified butterfly freed just in the spot by a drone from the local garden store. As Dr. Brown puts the meal on the table, while laughing with the home personal assistant, finds out the orange juice is likely to run out so she places an order by her brain scanner. Muddy receives an alert through his feedback collar that there are some groceries to be picked up. Meanwhile, Dr. Brown is keeping a somewhat watchful eye on Muddy through the collar's 360 stereoscopic camera and location tracking displayed on the kitchen countertop. Inside the shop, Muddy receives further feedback through the collar directing him to where the collection dog flap is located. After picking up the shopping for Dr. Brown and a couple of other neighbors, Muddy looks outside and notices the driverless taxi that has its destination set to return Muddy home. As he approaches the car, the door opens and Muddy is securely fastened in as the taxi pulls away from the curbside.

Figure 21.2 Illustration of an IoT Scenario That May Be 25 Years Away

Technology research alone may not be enough to prepare us for the many policy choices yet to be made before key elements of such scenario are regulated. Some of the legal programming challenges associated with this scenario require further research before we can even make initial suggestions: How should we regulate AI-empowered IoT generic sensors that can see through walls, talk to animals, and even independently activate emergency response actions? How should we police cheap brain scanners that can read the "truth" in the mind? Will talking animals have labor rights, bank accounts, a say on how they are treated, and perhaps even a right to be part of the democratic apparatus? Just like humans can develop freely and arbitrarily their own personality, do we let AI agents have any personality and even build deep relationships among each other and with customers?

Eventually we may face a boundary where we need to review what being human means and what makes us more happy. We may find out some prefer using technological progress to enjoy a paleolithic hunter gathering style of life!

V. Establishing Policy Options for IoT Pelotons

Once long-term business benefits have been identified, one can take the necessary steps to address all regulatory hurdles in such a way that policy does not become a major showstopper for IoT initiatives. To do so, business benefits must be identified and quantified, and a clear sequence of events must be planned. This will enable the "peloton" riders, or vectors as we call it, to plan jointly a course of action. We believe the Peloton Planning Tool developed at MIT can help setting policies going forward because it:

- provides a big-picture, systematic viewpoint of the impact of IoT in an industry;
- ensures industry alignment on key policy events;
- facilitates sharing and collaboration within the industry;

- assists in planning, prioritizing, and directing critical resources, including regulatory efforts; and
- enhances understanding of interdependencies between critical milestones (and their legal impact).

Many of the legal rules that were taken for granted in the 20th century are up in the air in the 21st because of IoT. Why buy power from the grid if you can generate your own power? Why purchase a car when you can Uber or use a rideshare bicycle? Why go to grocery stores when you can shop online? Why get a regular job when you can earn a living on UpWork? Why rent an office when you can co-work at WeWork? Why rent a hotel room when you can AirBnB? Why take a train when you can Rdvouz? These trends are providing a fertile ground for IoT innovations to take off, making peloton regulatory efforts more necessary than ever before.

In addition to identifying policy issues for specific IoT pelotons, we have researched areas that may be common to multiple pelotons. We have been researching this topic since the 2017 Winter Davos meeting where Internet of Things was earmarked as one of the areas of highest unrealized impact potential for society. Led by Sanjay Sarma, founder of my laboratory, The World Economic Forum, MIT and GS1 subsequently partnered to identify what are some of these policy challenges that need to be addressed going forward. To do so, a series of meetings and two round tables where organized: one at the 2017 Summer Davos that I moderated and one in the 2018 Winter Davos that Sarma led. Table 21.1 summarizes, in our own words, one of the results of such efforts in the form of five challenges identified as hurdles for broad adoption that we feel are going to be present in most IoT peloton exercises—future efforts should be targeted at recommendations to address the identified issues by specific pelotons, or perhaps, even by broad international government agreements.

Table 21.1 Five Generic IoT Yet Unresolved Issues That Will Impact Most IoT Peloton Exercises

Mainly technical	Architecture: There are too many siloed initiatives that need to be connected. This is reflected in a myriad of noncompatible architectures.	Mapping of existing solutions
		Connecting initiatives and standards
		Integration protocols
	Security: There is too much uncertainty of the potential effects of accidental or malicious IoT infrastructure security breaches, which could have targeted or massive devastating effects.	Surveillance human organization
		Cognitive firewall
		Access control protocol update
		Depletion
Mainly nontechnical	Governance: How should the international IoT infrastructure be governed to ensure accountability and local compliance?	Role of public and private institutions
		Data policies worldwide
		Accountability
		Long-term maintenance
	Value Metrics: How should we measure the impact of IoT in sustainability, employability, economic growth, and human well-being?	Macroeconomic impact
		Impact on the labor market
		Sustainability
		Business models
	Lifelong Learning: IoT is evolving quickly and decentralized making it a challenge to stay up-to-date with relevant developments.	Scientific progress
		Technical expertise
		Policy

The five issues identified—architecture, security, governance, value metrics, and lifelong learning—in one way or another call for significant changes in the regulatory environment. Without such progress it will be hard to fully hurdle any of these issues. For example, without a broad agreement on a consumer facing product tagging architecture, the benefits of a CPG IoT peloton will not arrive to the consumer homes; securing a self-driving IoT peloton infrastructure requires developing a mechanism to recall or deplete devices, a mechanism that cannot be put in place unless standard SLAs are agreed upon. Indeed, today, regulations can have a very significant impact on the ability to operate, and not only in the IoT arena. For example, drone industry in the United States has been held back by regulations. Social perceptions can also have a significant impact, whether of vaccines or of genetically modified foods. Privacy and security are particularly important today, and understanding and creating strategies to address these concerns proactively is essential. In some cases, like in animal brain interface research, the regulation itself may be a hurdle to develop a research agenda.

International regulations, geopolitics, and economics are also essential in considering a business benefit to focus on. How will trade disputes affect the sector's ability to manufacture, export, and import? What about climate change and extreme weather, and their impact on supply chains? Piracy? The price of oil or the commodities? Rare earth minerals, for example, have buffeted the renewables space recently after China imposed export quotas, and the United States, recently, banned imports.[30] Questions about the availability of minerals such as neodymium have affected the motors used by companies such as Tesla. These questions and more will be raised as the IoT expands in the future.

30. https://investorintel.com/sectors/technology-metals/technology-metals-news/new-us-defence-law-bans-magnets-china-creates-new-demand-potential-alkane/ (last visited Sept. 2018).

Index

D

Q

R

V

W

Z

From the Section of Science & Technology Law

ABA SECTION OF SCIENCE & TECHNOLOGY LAW

Blockchain for Business Lawyers

By James A. Cox and Mark W. Rasmussen

To order visit **www.ShopABA.org**
or call **(800) 285-2221.**

AMERICAN BAR ASSOCIATION
ABA Publishing

From the Section of Science & Technology Law

ABA SECTION OF
SCIENCE & TECHNOLOGY LAW

Cybersecurity for the Home and Office

The Lawyer's Guide to Taking Charge of Your Own Information Security

By John T. Bandler

To order visit **www.ShopABA.org**
or call **(800) 285-2221.**

AMERICAN BAR ASSOCIATION
ABA Publishing

From the American Bar Association

AMERICAN BAR ASSOCIATION
ABA Publishing

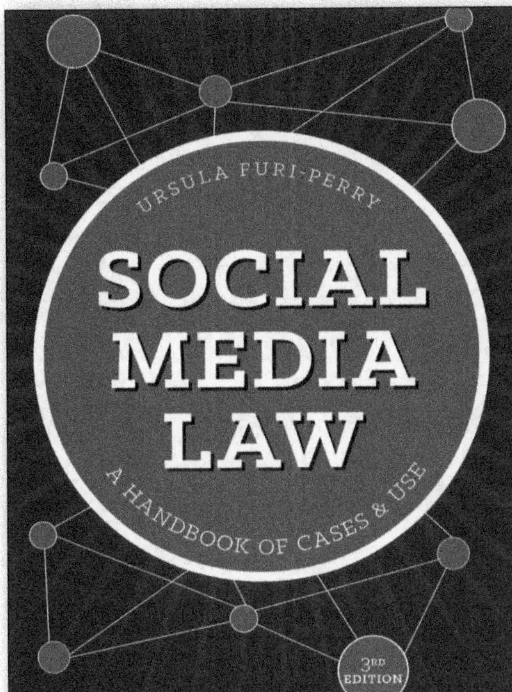

Social Media Law
A Handbook of Cases & Use, 3rd Edition
By Ursula Furi-Perry

To order visit www.ShopABA.org
or call (800) 285-2221.

From the American Bar Association

AMERICAN BAR ASSOCIATION
ABA Publishing

The Power of Licensing

Harnessing Brand Equity

By Michael Stone

To order visit **www.ShopABA.org**
or call **(800) 285-2221.**